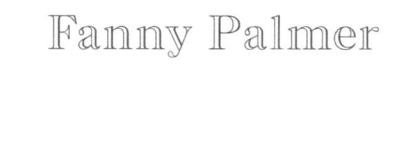

Fanny Palmer

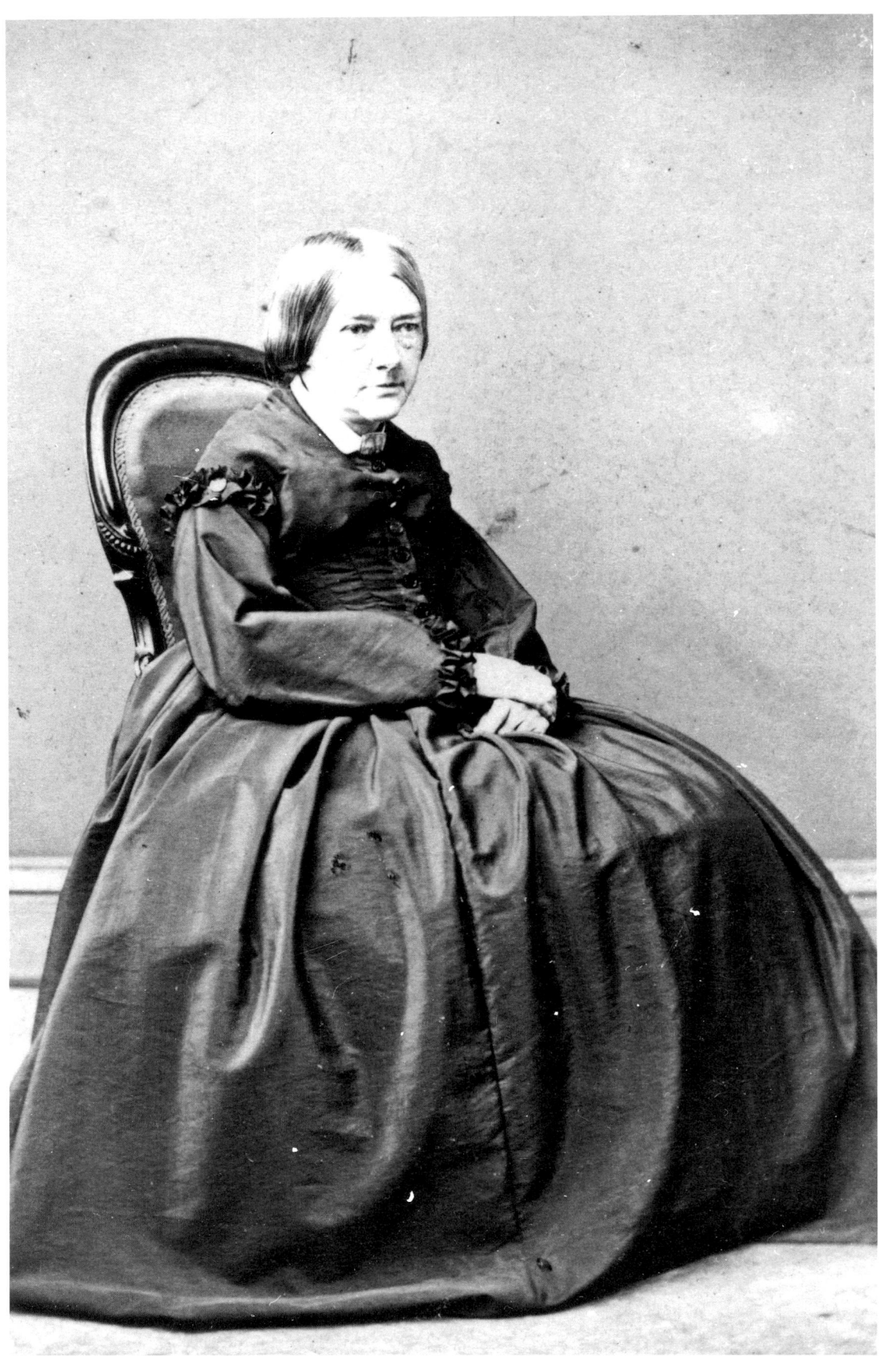

Frances ("Fanny") Flora Bond Palmer, ca. 1865. Courtesy of the Archives of American Art, Smithsonian Institution.

FANNY PALMER

The Life and Works
of a Currier & Ives Artist

Charlotte Streifer Rubinstein

Edited by Diann Benti

Syracuse University Press

The generous assistance of the following is gratefully acknowledged:

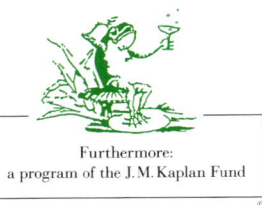

Furthermore:
a program of the J.M. Kaplan Fund

For a listing of books published and distributed by Syracuse University Press,
visit www.SyracuseUniversityPress.syr.edu.

ISBN: 978-0-8156-1095-3 (hardcover)

Library of Congress Cataloging-in-Publication Data

Names: Rubinstein, Charlotte Streifer, author. | Benti, Diann, editor.
Title: Fanny Palmer : the life and works of a Currier & Ives artist /
    Charlotte Streifer Rubinstein ; edited by Diann Benti.
Description: First edition. | Syracuse, New York : Syracuse University Press, 2018. |
    Includes bibliographical references and index.
Identifiers: LCCN 2017053217 | ISBN 9780815610953 (hardcover : alk. paper)
Subjects: LCSH: Palmer, F. (Fanny), 1812–1876. | Women lithographers—
    United States—Biography. | Lithographers—United States—Biography. |
    Currier & Ives—Biography. | Palmer, F. (Fanny), 1812–1876—Catalogs.
Classification: LCC NE2312.P36 R83 2018 | DDC 763.092 [B] —dc23
    LC record available at https://lccn.loc.gov/2017053217

Manufactured in the United States of America

This book is supported in part by funds from the American Historical Print Collectors Society, mostly through a generous bequest from society member Wendy Shadwell (1942–2007). The American Historical Print Collectors Society was founded in 1975 to foster the collection, preservation, study, and exhibition of original historical American prints. Over the past forty-plus years, the society has supported the publication of hundreds of articles, catalogs, and monographs on a wide variety of eighteenth- and nineteenth-century printmakers, printing methods, publishers, and artists. The American Historical Print Collectors Society is very pleased to be able to add *Fanny Palmer: The Life and Works of a Currier & Ives Artist* to that body of scholarship.

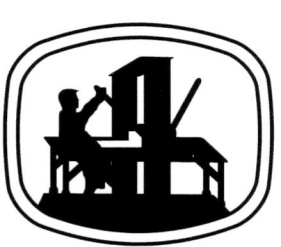

Contents

A Gallery of Prints by Fanny Palmer follows p. *56*.

Editor's Preface

IN 1863, a contemporary writer wrote of Frances Flora Bond Palmer (1812–76), "She is probably the only lady professionally engaged in this business [lithography] in the United States."[1] Almost forty years later, lithographer Charles Hart remembered Palmer in similar terms "as the only professional lady lithographic artist that I am aware of in America."[2]

In one sense, Palmer's trajectory from the daughter of an attorney in Leicester, England, to an artist and lithographer working in New York City could only have been accidental—it had such little precedent. But there is clear evidence that Palmer intended to be recognized as a professional in her own right. After she and her husband, Edmund Seymour Palmer, immigrated to the United States in the early 1840s, only their very earliest prints named Edmund Seymour as the lithographer: "Lith of E.S. Palmer." Very quickly, the imprint changed to "F. & S. Palmer." Later it would be "F. Palmer & Co."

Charlotte Rubinstein gained familiarity with Fanny Palmer in the 1970s while writing *American Women Artists: From Early Indian Times to the Present*.[3] When *American Women Artists* was published in 1982, Charlotte began planning a full-length biography of Palmer.

Charlotte's work continued the research begun by New York art dealer Harriet Endicott Waite in the late 1920s. Waite was among the first to compile a historical record of the powerhouse printmaking firm of Currier & Ives, which employed Palmer from the late 1840s through the 1860s. Beginning her research less than twenty years after the company closed, Waite was able to conduct in-person interviews with former Currier & Ives employees as well as with their family members and friends. But, as Waite remembered in 1957, information about Palmer had been "difficult to obtain."[4] She inventoried her research: an advertisement in the *Brooklyn Daily Eagle*; thirty telephone calls and multiple day trips tracking down surviving relatives and acquaintances; two half-days spent in the offices of the Brooklyn cemetery where Palmer and her family are buried; a few days at the Brooklyn Board of Health and the New York Public Library.[5] Waite's research formed the foundation of Harry T. Peters's seminal two-volume work on the company: *Currier & Ives: Printmakers to the American People* (1929–31).[6]

In the 1960s, art historian Mary Bartlett Cowdrey wrote the first article focused solely on Palmer. Where Waite had had the benefit of time, Cowdrey had the benefit of materials—in the 1940s she worked at the New-York Historical Society and at the Old Print Shop, both of which held strong collections of Palmer's work. In correspondence, Cowdrey indicated plans to create a comprehensive checklist of Palmer's work,[7] but the checklist remained unpublished at the time of her death in 1974.

Charlotte's research on Palmer expanded from the information collected by Waite and Cowdrey, and her article "The Early Career of Frances Flora Bond Palmer" appeared in the *American Art Journal* in 1985 with the optimistic note that she was "gathering material for a monograph on Fanny Palmer."[8] This pursuit would consume Charlotte's scholarly life for almost thirty years. Her task became nearly Herculean with her decision to include a complete checklist of all of the prints Palmer worked on—from her early days as a lithographer in Leicester through her time as an independent lithographer in New York City and into her many years as a staff artist for Currier & Ives.

Research into Currier & Ives is made difficult by the lack of any substantial archive of their business records. Even today Harry Peters's volumes and Harriet Endicott Waite's research materials from the 1920s remain the primary source for information on the company.

This lack of records for Currier & Ives is not unusual among American lithographers and printers. As Georgia Barnhill has commented, the business histories of lithographic firms are "difficult to reconstruct because so little primary material has survived fire and trash bins."[9] It is an ironic twist that for those individuals whose livelihoods revolved around printing, so few records remain documenting their own professions and lives.

Compounding the problem of such a scant documentary footprint is the limited time historically devoted to cataloging prints and ephemera in American research institutions. Charlotte scoured collections, mailing form letters to libraries across the country asking if they had any prints by Palmer. The current checklist of Palmer's work counts roughly five hundred different images, but that number will likely be inaccurate even before the ink dries on the pages of this book as more examples of Palmer's work will inevitably emerge through new cataloging.

We should have similar hopes for the archival record of lithographers and printers such as Currier & Ives. Although there may not be a complete lithographer's archive waiting to be discovered in an attic, increased access through digital libraries and improved cataloging offers new ways to find and link together documents that were previously hidden or scattered across many collections and libraries.

Indeed, during the editing of this book, additional information about Palmer emerged in an unpublished history of lithography written by lithographer Charles Hart in 1902. Hart shed further light on Palmer's influence:

> On her arrival in America, the lady commenced business for herself. Mr. Joseph Knapp, who was afterward so well known in Lithographic and Insurance circles, was an apprentice of hers. He was, when with Mrs. Palmer, a handsome and athletic young man, and frequently came in to the Endicott's place of business for Mrs. Palmer. It was from Mrs. Palmer that he learned to make the Rubbing Stuff, which has since played such an important part in the making of tint and color stones for lithographic printing. Mrs. Palmer is the only professional lady lithographic artist that I am aware of in America.[10]

Hart's description hints at the many different ways one might approach Palmer. Charlotte approached Palmer's work chiefly from the perspective of an art historian. But Palmer was an artist, a lithographer, a businesswoman, an employee, a wife and mother, and an immigrant from England to New York. Her story falls at the intersection of social, business, printing, and art history, and Charlotte's work is a jumping-off point for future scholarship related to Palmer's life, work, and influence.

The process of collecting and editing Charlotte's manuscript—of continuing not only her work but also that of Waite

and Cowdrey—reminds us of how quickly the research landscape has changed. Waite had proximity to living memories, Cowdrey had proximity to the physical materials, and Charlotte had the ever-growing strength of the Internet as a tool for research.

In our attempt to include in this volume as many images of Palmer's prints as possible, special thanks must be expressed to the libraries, archives, and museums that in recent years have so generously loosened their permission policies and reduced or eliminated reproduction fees in the interest of increased scholarly use of their collections. Among them are the American Antiquarian Society, the Huntington Library, the Library of Congress, the Metropolitan Museum of Art, the New York Public Library, the Sheridan Libraries of the Johns Hopkins University, the University of Leicester, the University of Pittsburgh, the Yale Center for British Art, and the Yale University Art Gallery.

This project also benefitted from the intellectual generosity and scholarship of a dedicated group of researchers, collectors, librarians, and scholars working to create a virtual archive and network of knowledge about the history of American printmaking. Many of these individuals are connected through the American Historical Print Collectors Society, whose support was integral to seeing this book published.

In 1986, Currier & Ives collector Dr. James Brust invited Charlotte Rubinstein to the American Historical Print Collectors Society annual meeting to speak on Fanny Palmer. There she discovered a group of kindred souls and became a regular at the society's meetings. From then on at each annual meeting, Charlotte updated the group on her book's progress. In late 2013, she telephoned Jim and told him that she had been diagnosed with acute leukemia. Knowing she would be unable to see the book finished, she asked him to take on the enormous task of bringing the project through to publication. This was the last time they spoke; Charlotte died only weeks later. Since then, Jim has been unwavering in his dedication to fulfilling his promise to Charlotte. From a jumble of research papers, electronic files, and clues, he pieced together the shape of this project. In early 2014, he asked for my help in turning her extensive set of files into a book worthy of her decades of research. During the process, Jim was instrumental in garnering support and funding and has remained enthusiastic and committed throughout. At points where progress might otherwise have stalled, he revived momentum. Without Jim as its champion, Charlotte's story of Fanny Palmer might never have been told.

A number of people shared their wisdom, insight, and kindness over the thirty-year process of completing this book. In particular,

Robert Newman of the Old Print Shop in New York City and collector John Zak contributed not only their knowledge and insight but also a lion's share of the Currier & Ives images used in this book. Sue Rainey, Gigi Barnhill, and Patty Ecker read the entire manuscript draft and provided valuable advice and comments.

Unfortunately, Charlotte did not leave a list of acknowledgments, but among the individuals she would surely have thanked as well as those to whom Jim and I are grateful are Lauren Hewes and Jackie Penny of the American Antiquarian Society; Clayton Lewis of the Clements Library at the University of Michigan; David Mihaly and Krystle Satrum of the Huntington Library; Robin Jenkins of the Leicestershire County Record Office and Alexandra Davy of the Leicestershire County Council; Constance McPhee of the Metropolitan Museum of Art; Sean Corcoran of the Museum of the City of New York; Marilyn Kushner of the New-York Historical Society; Keith Ovenden of the Record Office for Leicestershire, Leicester and Rutland; Helena Wright of the Smithsonian's National Museum of American History; David Reel of the West Point Museum; as well as Ruth Ann Appelhof, Roger Barry, John Bennett, Joseph Benti, Squire de Lisle, Roger Genser, Philip Jacobs, Susan Lasdun, Jay T. Last, Robin Paisey, G. C. Parkes, Phyllis Peet, Wendy Shadwell, Aubrey W. Stevenson, Hilda Stoddart, David Tatham, Michael Twyman, and Richard Samuel West. And, finally, our thanks go to Dr. Joan Rubinstein, Charlotte's daughter, for her willing cooperation; to copy editor Annie Barva, who expertly edited the manuscript; and to the staff of Syracuse University Press for helping with the logistics of publication.

Diann Benti

Author's Introduction

It is likely that during the latter half of the nineteenth century, more pictures by Mrs. Fanny Palmer
decorated the homes of ordinary Americans than those of any other artist, living or dead.
—Ewell Newman, "The History and Romance of Currier & Ives Prints"

THE NAME "CURRIER & IVES" has long been synonymous with classic American printmaking. Yet few make the same connection with the name "Frances Flora Bond Palmer." Palmer's relative anonymity is striking in light of the fact that she created roughly two hundred of the well-known lithography firm's most famous prints. Her images—of country scenes, steamboats and railroad trains, and the iconic covered wagons crossing the plains—have become woven into the tapestry of American culture and history.

Because of the great variety of subjects she tackled and the popular appeal of her work, Palmer can be seen as a kind of Norman Rockwell of her day, an important chronicler of mid-nineteenth-century America. An English artist, after immigrating to the United States she portrayed her adopted country romantically in all of its strengths and unwittingly revealed some of its weaknesses as well.

Arrayed chronologically, Palmer's lithographs present sweeping images of the times, from busy scenes of New York Harbor to the farmlands of Long Island; from American clipper ships outstripping the boats of every other nation to steamboats plowing up the Hudson; from the transcontinental railroad to the awe-inspiring mountains of the Far West. Palmer never hesitated to tackle epic themes. She even created battle scenes that include the Mexican War's Battle of Palo Alto and the attack on Fort Fisher during the Civil War.

Romantic "concoctions" Palmer's prints may sometimes be, as art historian Patricia Hills has pointed out,[1] but they reflect the dreams and aspirations of Americans of that period. Racism and sexism sometimes appear in her prints, as they did in the work of other artists of her day. Her scenes of Victorian family relationships among men, women, and children have a special irony in light of Palmer's own family situation—she was the main support of her husband and children. Yet here and there her prints show a more independent viewpoint, and many of them capture the poetry of the American landscape in a way that still moves us deeply.

Palmer's work is often dramatic and strong but until recently has not been perceived that way. Faintly deprecating remarks portrayed her as the little woman who somehow made use of a polite accomplishment to meet a family emergency. Listen, for example, to Harry T. Peters, prominent collector and author of the landmark book *Currier & Ives: Printmakers to the American People*, which greatly influenced all who subsequently wrote about the company: "Her work, while perhaps not the equal of that of some of the more distinguished Currier & Ives artists, had great charm, homeliness, and conscientious attention to detail. Her major contribution was to the backbone of the Currier & Ives list, the great mass of cheap prints that sold at ridiculously low prices to the great mass of the people, a simple, uncritical, but hugely appreciative audience."[2] Peters made this claim despite the fact that Palmer's assignments were not the "mass of cheap prints" but the large-folio prints sold by the company at much higher prices.

In 1937, Russel Crouse, listing the artists at Currier & Ives, put her last, with the following feeble (and inaccurate) praise: "One artist of considerable skill did little more than prepare the backgrounds against which others sketched their ideas. She was Fanny Palmer, an English woman who might have done even greater things but for her handicaps."[3] Yet in his book two full-page color images of dynamic railroad trains are inscribed "del. by F. F. Palmer."[4]

A number of errors appear in early accounts about Palmer's work. Peters believed that she designed the compositions but never drew them on the lithograph stones. We now know that she was a skilled lithographer with a canny understanding of her craft, one of the few on the Currier & Ives staff who both designed compositions and drew on the stones as well. Peters also believed that "F. Palmer & Co." at Nassau Street in New York City was the lithographic firm of some unknown (male) person.[5] There is now proof that F. Palmer & Co. was indeed the firm of Frances Flora Bond Palmer, who continued to run the company under her own name after her husband quit the business. Other errors arose from the hazy and biased recollections of friends and relatives in the interviews conducted by Harriet Endicott Waite in the 1920s, the source of much of the information we have about Palmer.

It was Mary Bartlett Cowdrey, however, who in 1962 wrote the first substantial appraisal of the artist's career, "Fanny Palmer, an American Lithographer."[6] Cowdrey corrected some but not all of the errors. She was also unaware of the sources of some of the prints. One of the tasks I have undertaken is to begin to sort out Palmer's totally original prints from those that she adapted from the drawings, paintings, and prints of others. Only in this way can we begin to recognize the artist's own viewpoint and handwriting. I have also located a number of works that have not previously been found by scholars.

Little has been known about Palmer's early career in her hometown of Leicester, England. In fact, she became a professional lithographer even before immigrating to New York City in her thirties. The mythology of the downtrodden artist who became hunchbacked from bending ceaselessly over the printing stone—forced to work because her husband was an alcoholic—begins to fade. It is replaced by a rather different image of an enterprising professional, one of the most versatile and prolific lithographers of her day. Her life is in fact a true American fable—the story of a struggling immigrant who came to the United States to start a new life for herself and her family and rose to the top of her profession, although the public generally never knew her name. The time has come to make a proper estimate of Palmer's place in American art.

Fanny Palmer

1

A Childhood in Leicester

FRANCES FLORA BOND was born in Leicester, England, on June 26, 1812, and baptized in St. Margaret's Anglican Church, a building that she later portrayed in an early print. Her parents could not have imagined that this child would become one of the premier artists at the leading lithographic publishing firm in the United States. In fact, there were very few lithographic presses in England in the year of her birth; the new medium had barely established a toehold in Great Britain. Besides, girls from upper-class families were not expected to enter such a profession; it was assumed that they would become the wives of well-to-do men and restrict themselves to the domestic sphere.

The family had some claims to social status. Fanny's father, Robert Bond, a childless widower when he married twenty-three-year-old Elizabeth Springthorpe, was a successful attorney who voted Tory and belonged to the Church of England. His new wife's distinguished family included a vicar, a physician, and the noted architect John Johnson, one of Leicester's most famous citizens. Elizabeth Bond inherited several properties from her uncle and father during the marriage.

The Bonds had five children: Felicia (1811), Frances Flora (1812), Maria (1815), Harriet Ann (1819), and Robert Jr. (1821).[1] Frances, known as "Fanny" from her early years, developed a particularly enduring and close relationship with her younger sister Maria and baby brother, Robert.[2] They remained a devoted trio throughout their lives, sharing artistic interests and immigrating together to the United States. All three eventually drew upon their involvement in the arts to make a living.

In later years, Palmer declared that she had learned to draw at the age of eight.[3] One can picture her, with her sister Maria and later with Robert, sketching the peaceful scenery around Leicestershire—especially the picturesque Charnwood Forest area, dotted with ancient castles, ruins, wooded paths, and rocky outcroppings, where the locals frequently picnicked and took pleasant outdoor excursions. These scenes became subjects of Palmer's

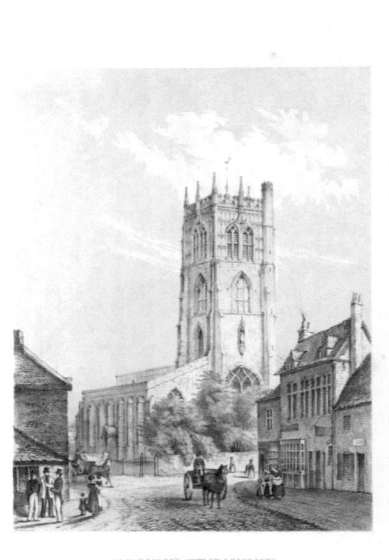

2. *St. Margaret's Church, Leicester.* July 1842. Illustration from J. F. Hollings, *Sketches in Leicestershire: From Original Drawings with Historical and Descriptive Notices* (Leicester, UK: John Sydney Crossley, 1846). Courtesy of the University of Leicester. (Checklist 1-47)

earliest prints and later found echoes in her lithographs of American rural life.

The city of Leicester, located one hundred miles northeast of London, was a farmers' market town surrounded by a rich agricultural region where sheep and cattle grazed and vegetable and seed production had been carried on for centuries. Although the family home on Market Street was in a middle-class neighborhood, the cattle market was close by, so that as a small child Fanny must have frequently seen animals being driven down the nearby lanes, a subject that appears in *Hallaton Church* (1842; p. 2), one of her early British prints. Indeed, the artist never missed an opportunity to include a cow or sheep in her many lithographs of farm and country.

But there was another side to Leicester. For centuries a center of the woolen industry noted for the manufacture of hosiery

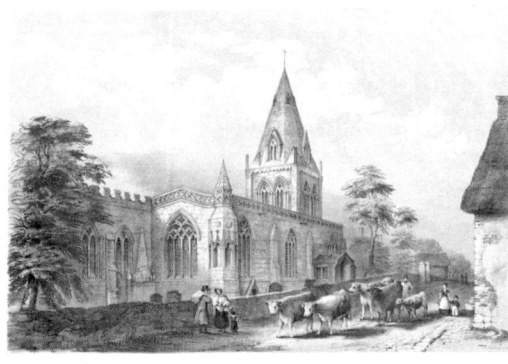

3. *Hallaton Church.* December 1842. Illustration from J. F. Hollings, *Sketches in Leicestershire: From Original Drawings with Historical and Descriptive Notices* (Leicester, UK: John Sydney Crossley, 1846). Courtesy of the University of Leicester. (Checklist 1-60)

and gloves, the town, like many others in England at that time, was beginning to feel the effects of the Industrial Revolution. The average life span of a working man was around twenty years. The polluted Soar River periodically flooded the low-income end of town, and economic depressions, unemployment, and difficult conditions among the frame knitters gave rise to sporadic demands for social reform.[4]

Fanny Bond and her siblings eventually felt the effects of these economic cycles when their father met business reverses, but as a child she was reportedly sheltered from this setback and was raised in luxury. In later years, her sister Maria claimed that up to the age of twenty-three (in 1838) she "hadn't known what it was to lace up her own shoe."[5] The cheerful gentility described by all who knew Fanny undoubtedly dates from these early years.

Of course, it may be that the Bond children were never quite as well off as they later claimed. After immigrating to New York City, Maria and Fanny may have exaggerated their economic position in England in order to move in the best society and thus to attract pupils, serve as chaperones to well-born young ladies, and find other sources of income. American friends had the impression that the artist's brother had graduated from Eton, but in fact there is no record of such attendance. Nevertheless, there were several good schools for boys in Leicester, and Robert Jr. did manage to acquire a background in music and art.

Although Robert did not study at Eton, Fanny and Maria did attend Miss Linwood's academy for girls. Friends in the United States later had the impression that this school was "in London," but it was actually located in Linwood's home (known as "the Old Priory") on Belgrave Gate (p. 3), a busy street not far from the Bond household. The Bond sisters, dressed in the bonnets and high-waisted empire shifts of that era, could walk from their home, past the shops and houses to the Old Priory, or be dropped off by the family carriage. It was probably at this school that Fanny received her first serious art instruction and was inspired to become a professional.

An important benefit of this early education was the character of its director, Mary Linwood (1755–1845). One of Leicester's most illustrious citizens, Linwood was also, amazingly for the time, place, and her gender, a nationally recognized artist. The large stitchery "paintings" for which she became renowned were executed in her workroom, where her students watched or assisted her. A rare example of a creative woman who moved freely in the world, Linwood presented young Fanny Bond with a model of strength and independence, someone to emulate later on when financial necessity forced her to seek ways of making a living.

"Genius, virtue, and unparalleled Industry" was a contemporary's description of Mary Linwood.[6] She was nine years old when her family moved from Birmingham to Leicester, where her enterprising mother, Hannah Linwood, founded the girls' seminary that Mary later took over and administered throughout a long life. Mary's mother, an expert needleworker, also taught her daughter to embroider so well that by the age of thirteen the precocious girl had completed her first needlework "picture," inspired, according to legend, by the gift of a set of engravings. She soon began to copy, in wool and silk yarn, paintings by Gainsborough, Reynolds, van Ruisdael, Rembrandt, Raphael, and others. At twenty-one, Linwood was already exhibiting needlework pictures at the Society of Artists, and by the age of thirty-two she had attracted the attention of the royal family. According to an article in the *London Morning Post* in April 1787, Linwood "was introduced to her Majesty at the Queen's House, where she had the honour of exhibiting several pieces of needle-work, wrought in a style superior to anything of the kind ever yet attempted. She received from her Majesty [Queen Charlotte] the highest of encomiums."[7]

No doubt encouraged by praise from royalty, the artist mounted a permanent exhibition in London at the Pantheon on Oxford Street, where members of the nobility visited "in numerous and respectable parties."[8] When that building burned down,

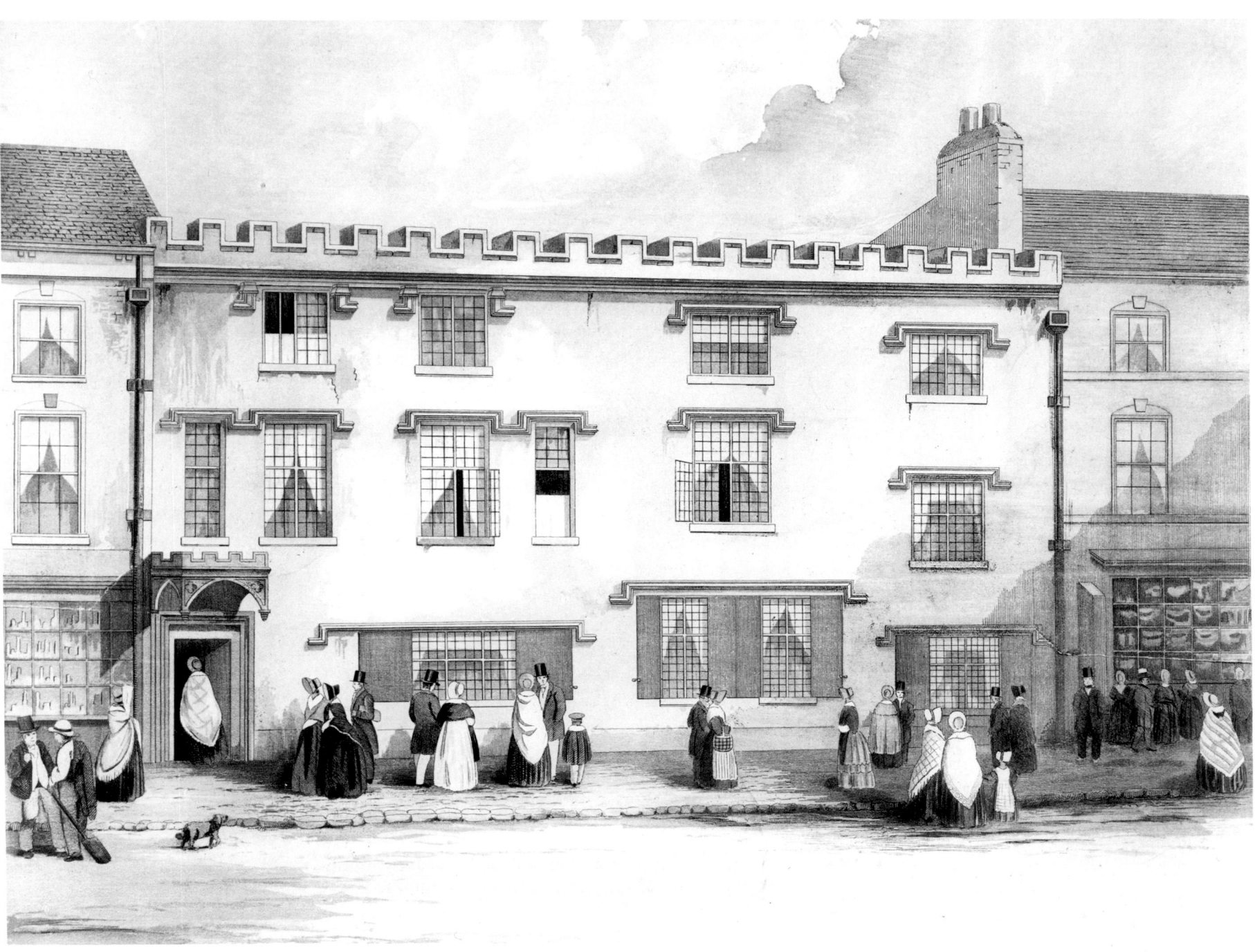

4. *Mary Linwood's House, Belgrave Gate, Leicester.* Lithograph by A. B. Pillans. Courtesy of the Leicester Arts and Museums Service.

she hired rooms in Hanover Square for several years, and—never shy about promoting herself—sent her collection on tour to Dublin, Edinburgh, and other cities between 1804 and 1808.

Linwood finally hit upon the idea of setting up a rather unusual permanent exhibition in London in her own gallery, rebuilt from the ruins of the Old Saville House on the north side of Leicester

Square. There it remained for more than thirty years, supported by admission fees until her death. According to a mid-nineteenth-century book on needlework, the exhibit was the "triumph of modern art in needlework . . . one of the Lions of London."[9] All of this activity took place while the artist continued to live in Leicester and to maintain a boarding school for girls.

A painstaking perfectionist, Linwood used a kind of tammy cloth (a coarse canvas) made especially for her, supervised the dyeing of her yarns, and sometimes dyed them herself if she wasn't satisfied with the colors. One of her students described the schoolmistress at work. Seated at a canvas stretched on a vertical frame and assisted by young girls who supplied her with threaded needles held in pincushions, Linwood worked rapidly, "knee deep amidst skeins, balls, tangles, and clouds of all imaginable shades."[10] Her stitches were unorthodox, varying in length and direction to imitate paint strokes.

Of course, this kind of work—copying paintings in stitchery and then framing them under glass to look like oil paintings—might offend purists today, but in Linwood's own day people found this verisimilitude impressive. "They looked so much like paintings it was hard to believe that they were done by a needle," wrote one viewer.[11] History painter Benjamin West described her "extraordinary industry," and landscape artist Joseph Farington noted in his diary, "It is calculated that she worked 15,000 ft. of Needlework" (this when she had only completed half her works).[12]

As generous as she was successful, Fanny's schoolmistress encouraged young talent. In 1802, early in his career, artist John Constable wrote in a letter, "I have done little in the painting art since I have been in town yet. A copy of a portrait and a background to an ox for Miss Linwood is all."[13] She helped the young Leicester artist John Flower secure an apprenticeship with a painter in London.[14] A letter recommending a Miss Bracebridge for a position demonstrates that she gave support to young women who needed to earn an income.[15]

In later years, Mary Kirby wrote in her memoir of the awe she felt in the presence of her aging schoolmistress: "After [lessons were over,] we were allowed to go into the workroom, and read aloud to Miss Linwood who was very dignified and of a great age and wore two pair of spectacles at a time."[16] Linwood continued to run her academy until the age of eighty-eight, when she took her last annual trip to check out her long-running exhibition in London. Two years later she caught the flu and died in 1845 at the age of ninety.

An artist who demanded technical excellence in her own work, Linwood must have set up a respectable drawing course at her school. A list of student expenses reveals that the girls bought drawing paper, pencils, and ink for their lessons.[17] Letters mention that they saved and cherished their student paintings and occasionally bought works from their schoolmistress.[18] It seems likely, therefore, that Fanny Bond received better-than-average instruction in drawing, perspective, and watercolor rendering. The least-adequate part of the young artist's training presumably was figure drawing. Nineteenth-century attitudes made it unthinkable for women to draw from the nude model; they could draw a "naked" face or a "naked" cow without loss of reputation, but not a "naked" body.[19] This may account for some weakness in Palmer's rendering of figures compared with her skill at portraying landscapes, architecture, and animals.

The headmistress borrowed old master works from private collections to copy, so the Bond sisters must have seen paintings at the school as well as steel and wood engravings, etchings, mezzotints, and perhaps some examples of lithography, the exciting new print medium that was beginning to arouse great interest at this time.

Lithography had been invented only two decades before Fanny Bond was born, when Alois Senefelder, a struggling Bavarian playwright looking for an inexpensive way to print his texts, discovered that if he drew with a greasy crayon on a smooth limestone slab and then wet the surface with water and rolled printer's ink over it, the ink would stick to the part where the crayon had made its mark but would be repelled by the wet surface where there was no grease drawing. The reason for this was simple: water and grease do not mix. After inking, the dampened stone could be placed on a press bed with a paper and cover over it and rolled through under pressure.

Far less expensive and time-consuming than the difficult techniques of engraving and etching, the new medium had opened up the possibility of a mass market, a truly democratic art, capable of rendering subtle tones and shadings printed directly from the lithographer's drawing. Lithography soon spread from Germany to France and England, so that by the time Fanny Bond was fourteen years old, she might have watched Mary Linwood's protégée John Flower drawing *Views of Ancient Buildings in the Town and County of Leicester* (1826) on stone with a lithograph crayon at his popular studio-gallery on Southgate Street.

Fanny's schoolmistress also undoubtedly expanded her young student's awareness of the distinguished tradition of women artists in England. Maria Cosway had painted Linwood's portrait, and Fanny and her family surely visited her teacher's exhibition in London as well as the Royal Academy, where Angelica Kauffman, recognized as one of Europe's leading neoclassical history painters, had been a founding member (she designed the oval paintings for the lecture hall ceiling in the academy building). There were also a few women lithographers in England by that time, mostly amateurs dabbling in the field. Perhaps while peering into the windows of London print dealers, Fanny came across Elizabeth Gould's splendid bird lithographs or the *Landscape Alphabet* album, an important example of early creative British lithography drawn by "L. E. M. Jones" (actually *Miss* L. E. M. Jones).[20]

In later years in New York City, Fanny and her sister Maria praised their education at Miss Linwood's school.[21] The history of art has typically been filled with examples of young male artists influenced by their male masters or women artists trained by their fathers. But today scholars are beginning to uncover the hidden history of women influencing one another. From Hannah Linwood to Mary Linwood to her pupil Fanny Bond, we see the influence of women on one another, passing through three generations.

2

F. & E. S. Palmer

Lithographers of Leicester

Although Fanny Bond may have regarded her training at Miss Linwood's school as a "polite accomplishment"—part of a woman's customary preparation for life as the wife of a squire or businessman—records suggest that soon after her marriage, financial pressures and personal inclination drove her to earn an income as an artist.

In July 1832, twenty-year-old Fanny Bond married Edmund Seymour Palmer, age twenty-two, at St. Mary's Church in Newington, Surrey, a suburb of London.[1] She might have met him during "the season," when well-to-do families spent time in London, enjoying the sights and attending festivities where their marriageable sons and daughters could meet and mingle.

Edmund seems to have been a young man with good prospects. At the time he met Fanny, he was living at the home of a London surgeon in Crutched Friar, a neighborhood located near the publishing and printing industry; it is even possible that he was training for work as a printer or lithographer. At age nineteen, three years before his marriage, he had inherited a trust fund of twenty-two hundred pounds set up "for his maintenance, education, cloathing [*sic*] and advancement" by the Reverend Thomas Clare,[2] a distant relative by marriage who was the vicar of the historic St. Bride's Church on Fleet Street (known then, as now, as the church of the press and publishing industry). In his will, the good reverend appointed three men, including the Reverend Josiah Forshall, keeper of manuscripts at the British Museum, to administer the trust that provided young Edmund with an annual income. Clearly, Fanny's young husband was connected to respectable, cultivated people who were interested in his welfare.

Eleven months after their marriage, the young couple returned to Fanny's hometown in time to be near her family for the birth of their first child, a daughter, Frances, who was christened at St. George's Church on June 19, 1833. Edmund signed the baptismal certificate with the description "Gentleman." Two years later, Fanny bore a son, Edmund Jr., in Wales, a favorite tourist destination for Leicester citizens—especially artists, who loved to paint the picturesque scenery.[3] (Fanny later showed a painting of Snowden, Wales, at the National Academy of Art when she first arrived in New York City.)

With a modest trust fund and the prospect of an inheritance from Fanny's father, the couple must have looked forward to a rosy future, but around this time the Bond family fortune seems to have gone into a decline. Fanny's mother died in 1837, and her father soon followed his wife to the grave, dying intestate on June 15, 1839. Probate records in the London Record Office reveal that the claims of creditors left a meager estate of three hundred pounds.[4]

Even before her father's death, Frances Palmer had begun to conduct drawing classes. An announcement in the *Leicester Journal* on July 12, 1839, reads: "Mrs. Palmer will *Re-open* her Drawing School for young Ladies and Gentlemen on Monday the 22nd of July. For terms apply to Messrs. Combe and Crossley [booksellers] or to Mrs. Palmer, Nelson street, London Road."[5]

On the same page, Fanny's older sister, Felicia Bond Gill, was advertising that she was once again providing childcare at her late father's address. Felicia had married a promising young Leicester architect, Abraham Gill, who died two years after their marriage, leaving her to raise their young daughter alone. Clearly, the Bond siblings were making multiple efforts to eke out a living.

At the same time, the general economic situation in Leicester was deteriorating. Conditions became so difficult during the Hungry Forties, a period of depression all over England, that groups of unemployed glove-and-hosiery knitters were begging from door to door. In the terrible winter of 1839–40, "people were actually dying of starvation and others were selling or bartering the last articles they possessed, even their shoes, in order to buy bread."[6]

Charles Dickens has described in his novels the terror experienced by members of the British middle class as they faced the possibility of being forced down into poverty. Indeed, Dickens himself never got over the nightmare of seeing his father thrown into debtor's prison and of having to work in a shoe-blacking factory as a small child. One can well imagine the fears experienced by the Palmers at that time.

In 1840, Edmund Palmer, perhaps shocked by his father-in-law's failure to leave a will, hastened to reassure Fanny that she had a modicum of security by drawing up "the last Will and Testament of me Edmund Seymour Palmer of Leicester, Gentleman," bequeathing to his "dear Wife" whatever might remain of his trust at the time of his death and any other real or personal estate that he might have acquired, "whether in Great Britain, America or elsewhere[,] . . . for her own absolute use and benefit without being subject to the debts, control or engagements of any after-taken husband."[7] In that era, a woman's property belonged to her husband, and he could squander it unless it was legally protected in her name. The reference to "America" suggests that the Palmers were already considering moving to the United States if that proved necessary.

Edmund showed sensitivity to his wife and her family in the way he wrote this will. If his wife died before him, their children would share the estate equally, and if they too were deceased, it would go to Fanny's unmarried sister, Maria Bond. Fanny's nineteen-year-old brother, Robert, a young man expected to support himself, was not included but was one of the witnesses to the will.

However, Fanny was not waiting for some ephemeral inheritance; that year, 1840, she had already begun her career as a commercial artist, F. F. Palmer. A new railroad line connecting London and Nottingham had just opened a station in Leicester, and she was busy sketching important landmarks in the surrounding area for illustrations in *The Midland Counties' Railway Companion* (1840). This handbook, issued by a local publisher, contained fares, schedules, and descriptions of noteworthy sights along the route. Her name is on the cover (she contributed the largest number of drawings), along with those of the wood-and-steel engravers who transferred her pencil sketches into prints.[8]

There were good reasons for producing such illustrated handbooks at that time. The incursion of the railroad on the countryside of England was arousing angry opposition. Not only were landed aristocrats opposed to train lines on or near their estates, but intellectual leaders such as John Ruskin and Charles Dickens objected to the encroachment of noise, steam, and pollution on pristine areas of Great Britain. Poet William Wordsworth wrote to the *London Morning Post*, deploring in mournful verse the proposals for a new train line through his beloved Lake District: "Is then no nook of English ground secure / From rash assault?"[9]

Directors of the railroad companies, hoping to convince the public that the new lines would bring great economic benefits without destroying the charm of local neighborhoods, encouraged the publication of prints and manuals illustrated with pictures of the new bridges and stations as well as of picturesque landmarks that could be seen by travelers as they rolled along. Palmer's pencil drawing of Ullesthorpe Station and the vignette woodcut adapted from it in *The Midland Counties' Railway Companion* show a local couple peering over a fence to admire the new track and platform (pp. 8–9). In *The Trent Bridge*, sheep graze peacefully in a meadow before a large cast-iron bridge described in the text as "a handsome structure and we believe the largest bridge of iron used for railway purposes." A woodcut of the town of Mountsorrel features a picturesque windmill, and Palmer's drawing of the imposing new neoclassical Leicester Station was transformed into a full-page steel engraving (p. 10). These and other images already demonstrate Palmer's solid knowledge of perspective, her feeling for picturesque composition, and her sturdy, assured method of rendering landscape and architecture.

Less-pleasant aspects of the era are also unwittingly revealed in the illustrations. Palmer's image of the viaduct at the Sileby line (p. 228) shows a new overpass cutting right between houses in a village inhabited by poor frame knitters. Additional noise and smoke must have intruded on this neighborhood, but Palmer's rendering is idyllic. She also drew Leicester's New Union Workhouse (a poorhouse for indigents) and the New County Lunatic Asylum (p. 11), both conveniently close to the train tracks and described in the handbook as examples of "the Age of Improvement." Although Palmer didn't know it at the time, she was getting excellent training for her future role as a creator of optimistic images of the young democracy across the Atlantic. Decades later, the artist would create a glowing Currier & Ives lithograph of Blackwell's Island (p. 100), the location of New York City's new insane asylum, workhouse, prison, and quarantine center for smallpox victims.

The publishers of *The Midland Counties' Railway Companion*, Richard Allen (a Nottingham bookbinder, engraver, and printer) and Edward Allen (a Leicester printer), employed several artists to sketch scenes in their districts for woodcuts and steel engravings. Palmer drew twelve out of twenty-five of these

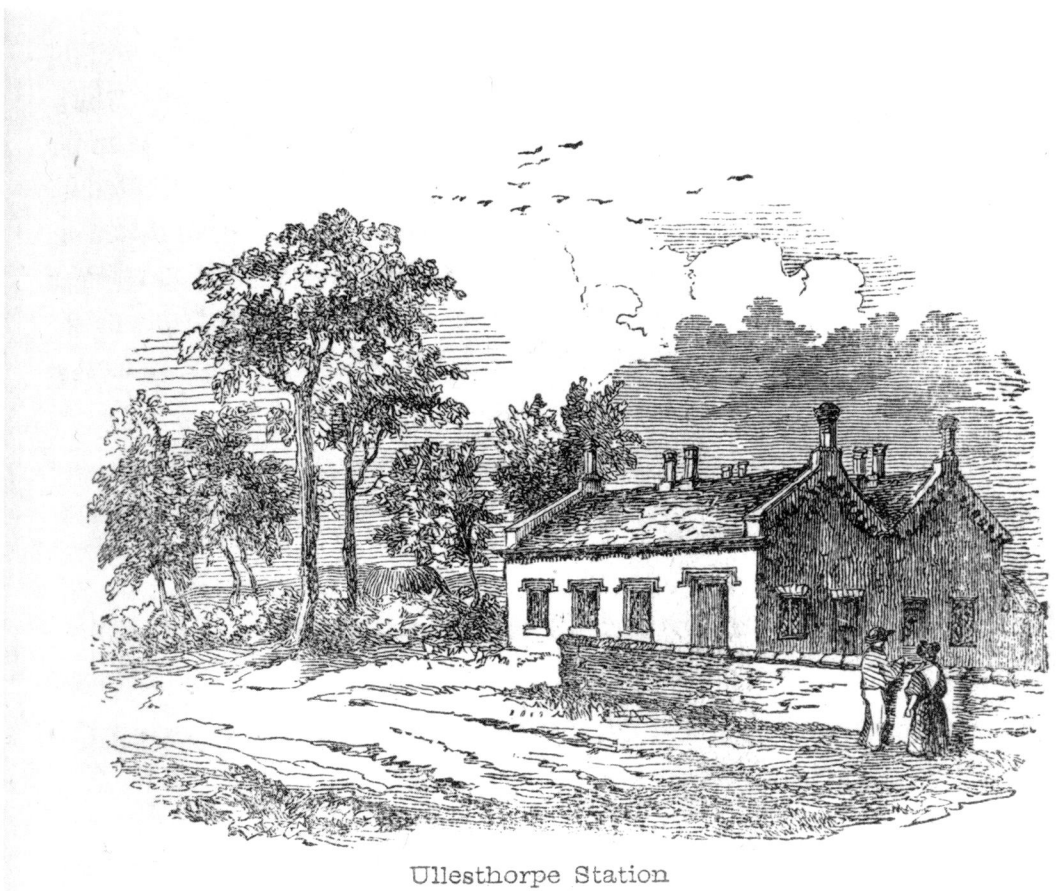

Ullesthorpe Station

5. *Ullesthorpe Station*. Illustration from *The Midland Counties' Railway Companion* (Nottingham, UK: R. Allen; Leicester, UK: E. Allen, 1840), 99. Courtesy of the Huntington Library, San Marino, CA, RB 4516. (Checklist 1-11)

drawings—more than any other artist who contributed to the project. Three of her drawings have been located, but we know that she also made nine others because she is named as the artist in the handbook's list of illustrations. The entire project must have been carried out in haste to take advantage of the new market. In the rush to publication, many white spaces on the pages, obviously allotted for illustrations, were left blank.

The British census reveals that by 1841 major changes had taken place in the Palmer household. Edmund, Fanny, and their two children were living next door to Fanny's siblings Robert and Maria Bond, who were perhaps pooling their resources in a house on Princes Street (today Princess Road), which was at that time an upper-middle-class residential address. In the census, Robert is listed as a "clerk," and the unmarried Maria describes herself as "independent."[10]

The most striking change, however, is that Edmund now lists himself as "printer" instead of "gentleman." The Palmers had in fact decided to open a lithography business together. According to

the terms of his trust, when he reached the age of twenty-five, one thousand pounds would become available "towards establishing him in some respectable business or profession."[11] He was now twenty-nine, so this sum would have enabled the couple to buy a press, paper, ink, rollers, lithograph crayons, chemicals, and the fine Bavarian limestone slabs from the quarries in Solnhofen that, after their serendipitous discovery by Senefelder, had turned out to be unsurpassed in the world of lithography. These slabs, which came in various thicknesses and sizes, were expensive but lasted indefinitely. When the image drawn on a stone was no longer needed, it could be ground off, leaving a fresh surface for a new drawing.

The couple probably anticipated making a decent living; they faced little local competition. The lithography business was still centered in London and had not yet spread much into the provinces; only one other lithographic printer was listed in the Leicester business directory, and local artists (such as John Flower) were still sending their drawings or completed stones to the capital to be printed.

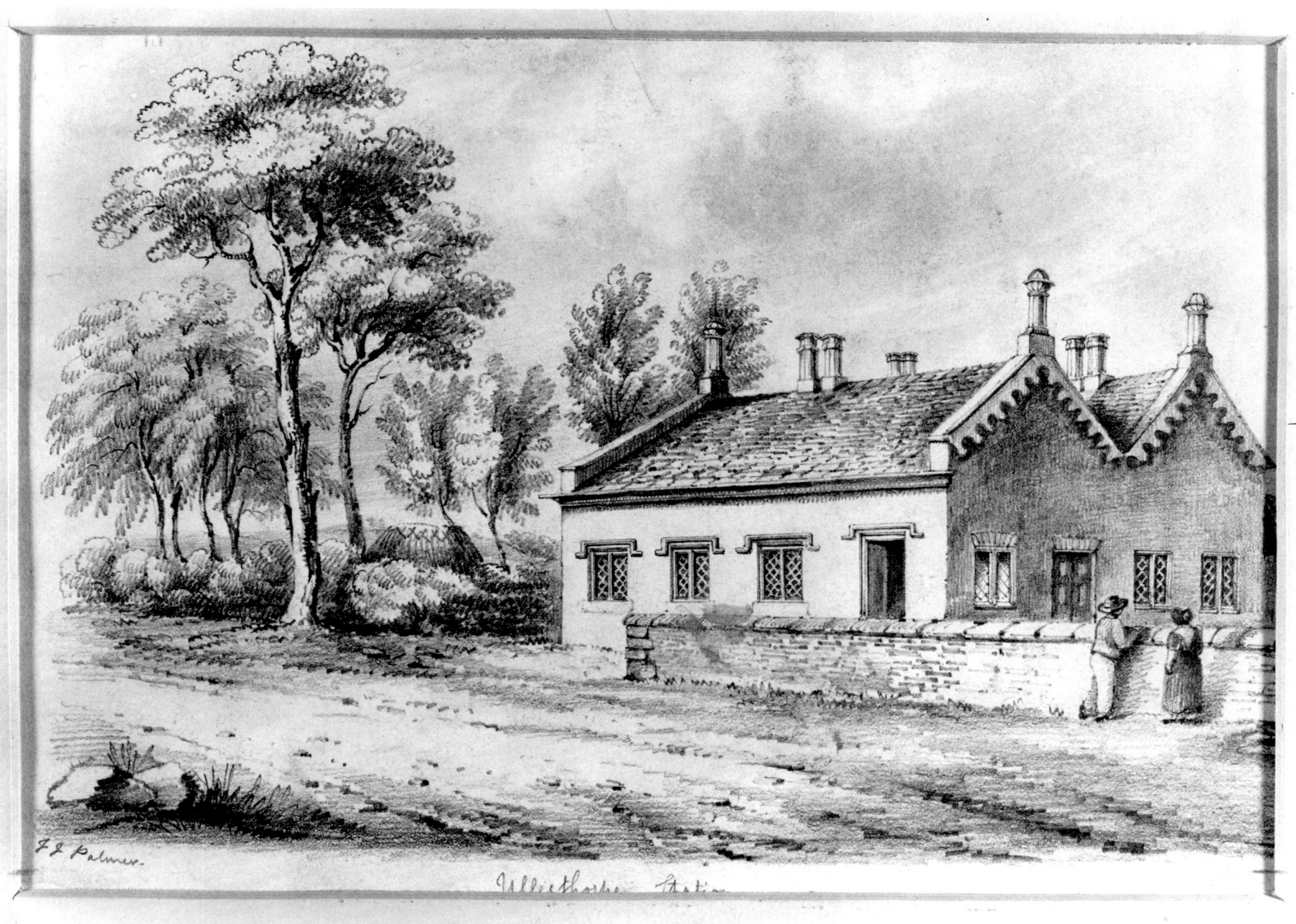

6. *Ullesthorpe Station*. Undated, ca. 1840. Pencil drawing. Courtesy of the Leicestershire County Council Museums Service. (Checklist 4-20)

It was around this time that Fanny Palmer seems to have traveled to London to take instruction from one of the most distinguished lithographers in Europe. Evidence for this trip can be found in a book entitled *The Employments of Women*, published in the United States during the Civil War by Virginia Penny, an early feminist who hoped to open up new opportunities for women by collecting information from those who had secured work in various fields. When Penny queried Palmer about how she

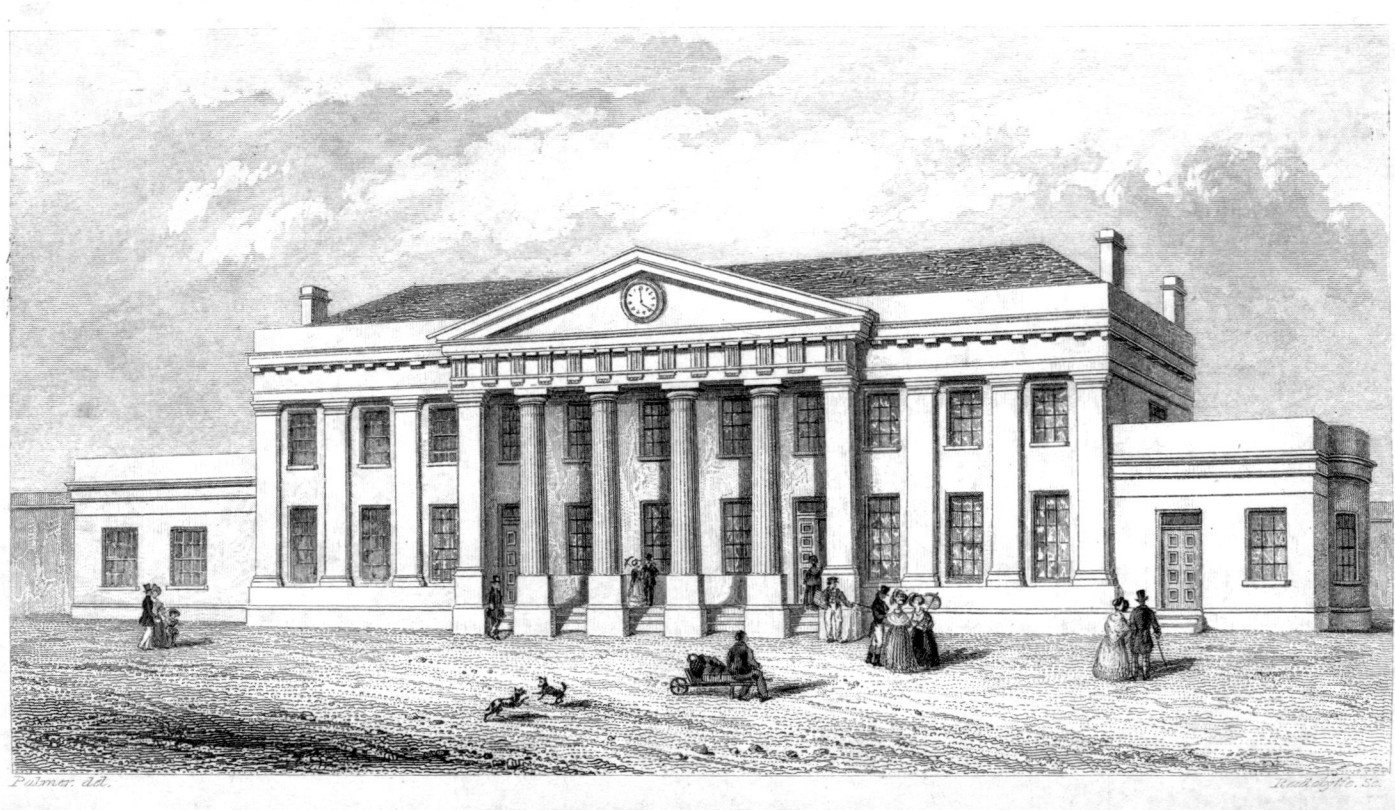

LEICESTER STATION.

Palmer. del. *Radclyffe. sc.*

Published by Rich.ᵈ Allen, Nottingham, & E. Allen, Leicester.

had managed to become one of the premier lithographers at the largest lithographic publishing company in the United States, the artist replied, somewhat bizarrely, that she had studied with "a distinguished artist of London who executed entirely with his left hand, having lost three fingers on his right when he was a child."[12]

Only one person fits this description of a seven-fingered mentor: the renowned lithographer Louis Haghe (1806–85).[13] Born into a family of architects in Tournai, Belgium, Haghe, despite his disability, had been "encouraged to draw in his father's office" at a very young age.[14] He became an early prodigy, already a skilled watercolorist and lithographer at seventeen, when he immigrated to London to pursue his career. By 1833, he was the leading artist for William Day, one of the few publishers who specialized in lithography as a medium for fine prints rather than for the usual pedestrian commercial work. The firm, renamed Day & Haghe at one point, became the most successful lithographic printing house

7. *Leicester Station*. Illustration from *The Midland Counties' Railway Companion* (Nottingham, UK: R. Allen; Leicester, UK: E. Allen, 1840), facing p. 73. Courtesy of the Huntington Library, San Marino, CA, RB 4516. (Checklist 1-8)

in London and was designated "lithographer to the king" and then to the queen. Not only was Haghe a lithographer, but he was also a noted watercolorist and one of the favored artists of Queen Victoria, who invited him to attend royal events and make sketches for use in her private records.[15]

That Fanny Palmer, a young matron from the Midlands with no reputation in the field, would apply for training from such a prominent figure seems remarkable.[16] She evidently had a firm belief in her own talent and, like her schoolmistress, Mary Linwood, saw herself among the elite in her field. Evidence also

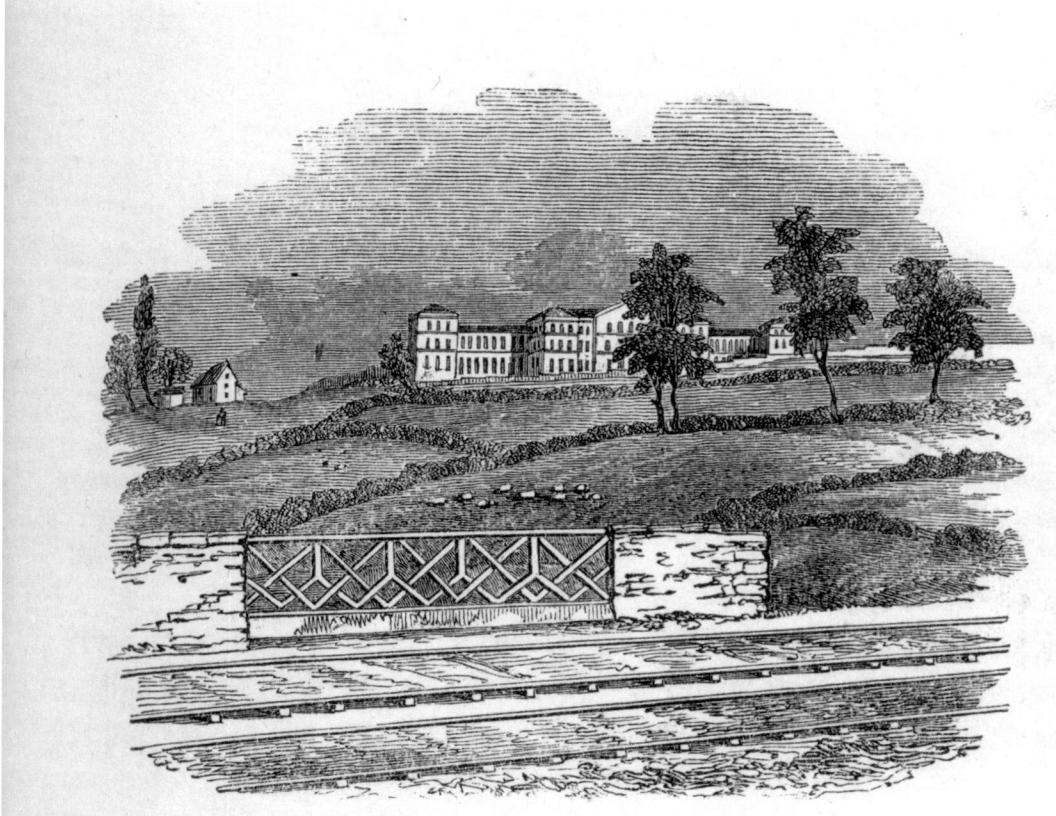

The New County Lunatic Asylum.

8. *The New County Lunatic Asylum*. Illustration from *The Midland Counties' Railway Companion* (Nottingham, UK: R. Allen; Leicester, UK: E. Allen, 1840), 93. Courtesy of the Huntington Library, San Marino, CA, RB 4516. (Checklist 1-10)

suggests that lithography teacher and student shared a sympathy of temperaments. A colleague in Haghe's firm described him as "one of the finest men I have had the luck to know—generous and good in every way. It has been my fortune to meet in life many worthy friends, but Louis Haghe had so many good qualities, that I cannot place him second to any."[17] Palmer was later similarly described as not only cultivated and hardworking but also generous and kind, "always assisting some poor artist. Always giving to those in need."[18] If, however, Palmer invented the entire story of studying with Haghe in order to impress people (which isn't likely), at the very least such a fabrication would show that she was influenced by and modeled her technique after one of the top graphic artists in the field.

In the busy workshop at 6 Gate Street, amid the thumping of presses and the trundling of heavy stones and in Haghe's pleasant upstairs studio overlooking Lincoln's Inn Fields, the Palmers would have witnessed superb draughtsmanship and printing skills as well as the division of labor and collaboration of several artists

that Mrs. Palmer later encountered at Currier & Ives. There were specialists in architecture, landscape, and portraiture. One lithographer was nicknamed "Admiral" because of his expertise at rendering boats ("new clippers to Australia, or the last great steamer for the American passage").[19] Many of the artists worked at home and sent completed drawings or stones to the company, as Mrs. Palmer did in later years for Currier & Ives.[20]

She also would have seen the skill, patience, and experience required to draw and print a lithograph successfully. First of all, there was the difficulty of drawing a complex subject backward on the stone so that it would look right after reversing itself in the printing process. Crayons and pencils, varying from hard to soft and from fine points to half-inch-wide points, had to be applied with the right pressure and technique in order to print well. Artists held their breath as they worked. Errors were difficult to correct—the slightest smudge of perspiration from the lithographer's hand or a drop of saliva could repel the ink and spoil the print. It was possible to make minor changes by scraping off parts of the drawing and redoing it, but for major corrections it was sometimes necessary to grind off the entire drawing and start over again.[21]

The completed image then had to be carefully treated with a weak solution of nitric acid and gum arabic in just the right strength and for just the right amount of time in order to bond the crayon grease permanently to the stone and make the wet empty spaces more resistant to ink. Intermediate tones could easily be lost because of poor etching, inking, or printing by an unskilled craftsman.

Haghe was noted for his extensive use of the tint stone—a second stone inked in transparent color and usually printed before the black-and-white key print was added (p. 13). The tint could be a background tone or laid on in areas. By using several tint stones in succession, more than one color could be printed. Skillful printing techniques were necessary to align one color precisely over the other without blurring the image. Palmer used the tint stone with her earliest lithographs in England and the United States and later at Nathaniel Currier's company.

Unlike such rivals as the pioneering London printer Charles Hullmandel and his associate James Duffield Harding, who were experimenting with freer techniques—attempting, for example, to capture the evanescent wash effects of watercolor in lithography—Haghe's approach was meticulous but conservative, "characterized by its carefully laid tones and its confident and stylish handling of the crayon in the foregrounds."[22] Like her teacher, Palmer used straightforward, conservative methods of drawing with crayon throughout her career, employing a confident, vigorous, and varied line. Haghe, who spent many hours drawing in his architect father's office while growing up, was expert at rendering architecture and landscapes—subjects at which Palmer would also excel.

By 1842, Edmund Palmer was advertising as a lithograph printer in Thomas Cook's *Trade Directory of Leicester*:

Works illustrated in chromolithography. Every description of fancy lithographic printing executed in the highest Parisian and London taste, and in the first Style of the Art. Views, architectural and botanical drawings, maps, plans of estates, railway sections, elevations, law forms, invoice heads, tickets, checks, fac similes [sic], circulars and writings, of every description, and in every character.[23]

Not mentioned in this high-flown blurb, so typical of the era, is the fact that Frances Palmer was his partner. Mr. Palmer listed himself in the Leicester directory as a "lithographic draughtsman and printer,"[24] but there is no mention of his wife, although she was the principal artist. This ambiguity may have simply reflected convention or been necessary in order to preserve the Palmers' dignity—because middle-class married women of that era were supposed to be supported by their husbands—or perhaps it was felt that they would not attract as much business if a woman were listed as the principal creative figure. Prior to this point, Mrs. Palmer had drawn sketches for woodcuts and engravings carried out by other craftsmen. When she and her husband opened a lithography business, she began not only creating many original compositions and lithographing them on stone but also converting the drawings of other artists into lithographs. Mr. Palmer acted as the printer and sometimes the publisher. The indefatigable Mrs. Palmer also continued to conduct drawing classes while turning out lithographs with her husband and raising two small children. On July 22, 1842, she once again advertised in the *Leicester Journal* that her "Drawing Academy would be held on Saturday, July 30, at the usual hour."[25]

At that time, there was a vogue for topographical prints—picturesque views of European countries and faraway exotic places for armchair travelers to enjoy and for tourists to bring back as mementos of their trips. Indeed, Louis Haghe had made his reputation with lithographs of scenes from France, Germany, and England and later of David Roberts's famous paintings of Egypt and the Holy Land.[26] Presumably inspired by all of this, the Palmers saw a place for themselves as creators of a series of prints that would publicize the charms of their own district, Leicestershire. One of their first assignments was to produce a number of illustrations for a book by a local scholar, Thomas Rossell Potter. *The History and Antiquities of Charnwood Forest* (1842; pp. 14–15, 229–33) was about Charnwood Forest, a picturesque and historic region north of Leicester. Potter's stated goal was to acquaint tourists, scholars, and the general public with the area's remarkable history, genealogy, picturesque ruins, splendid scenery, and natural history. In the introduction, he wrote, "There is no district of England, equally deserving of notice, of which so little has been written. . . . [It] has been passed over with as little mention as if it was [sic] a blemish instead of a beauty on the face of the County."[27] The illustrations are poignant because they show (albeit with some romanticizing) what the region looked like in 1842, before extensive coal mines, granite and slate quarries, railroad lines, agricultural enclosures, and new suburbs altered many areas.

These images of rocky outcroppings and picturesque manors, churches, and ruins, enlivened with either yellow- or green-tinted

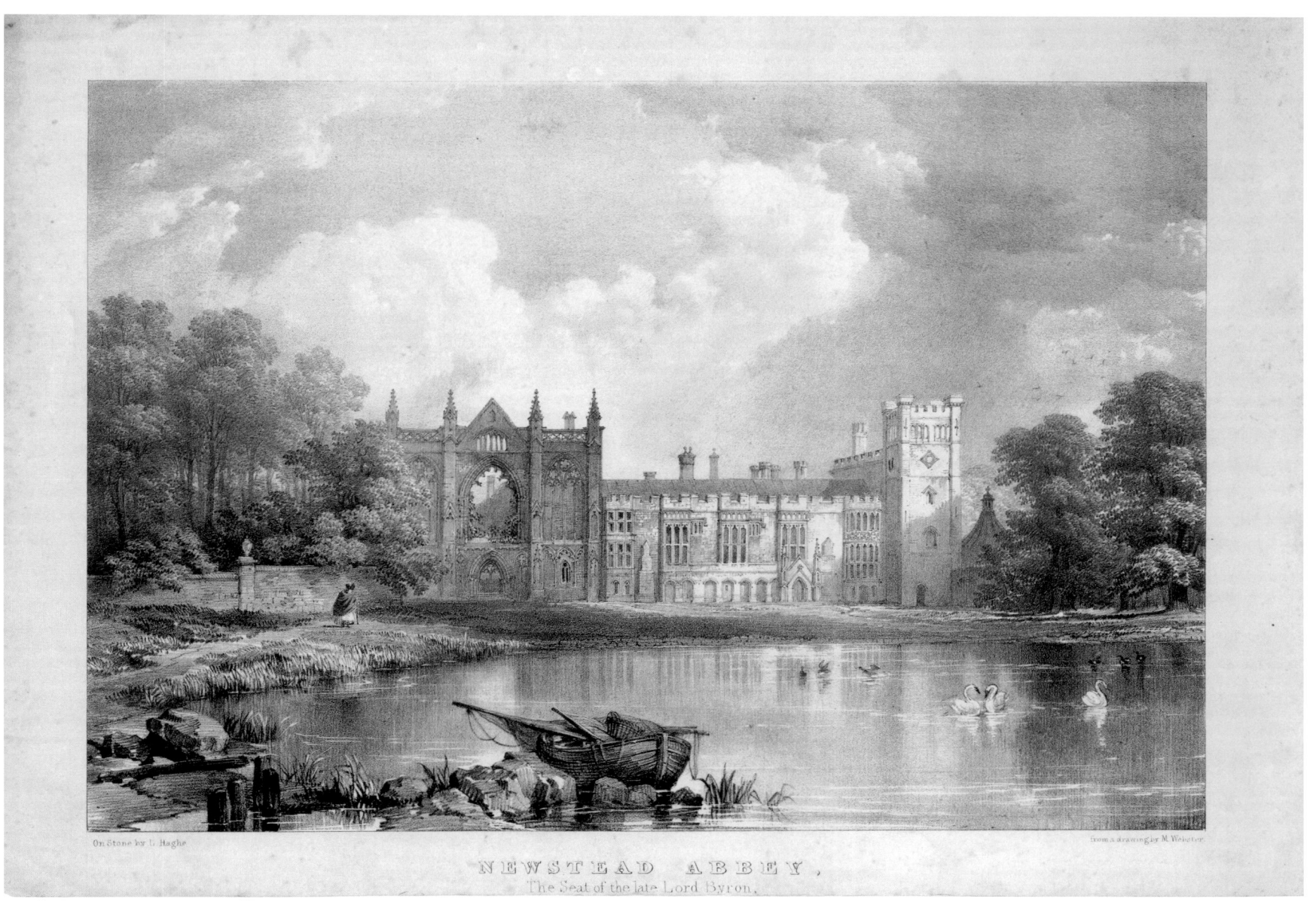

NEWSTEAD ABBEY,
The Seat of the late Lord Byron.

9. *Newstead Abbey, The Seat of the Late Lord Byron.* Undated. Lithograph by Louis Haghe on moderately thick, slightly textured, cream, wove paper. Courtesy of the Yale Center for British Art, Paul Mellon Collection.

areas, carry the imprint "F. F. Palmer, litho." below the image on the left and "Printed by E. S. Palmer, Leicester" on the right. A charming vignette of a bird in the section on ornithology is a very early example, perhaps the first, of an F. F. Palmer lithograph accented with areas of hand-painted watercolor (p. 233). In some cases, the illustrations are signed "F. F. Palmer, del." and "Allen, sc.," indicating that Mrs. Palmer had made the drawings, but Mr. Allen had carried them out as engravings rather than lithographs (with "sc." standing for *sculpsit*, "engraved by"). From the beginning, Fanny used the nongendered name "F. F. Palmer" or "F. Palmer" to sign her work.

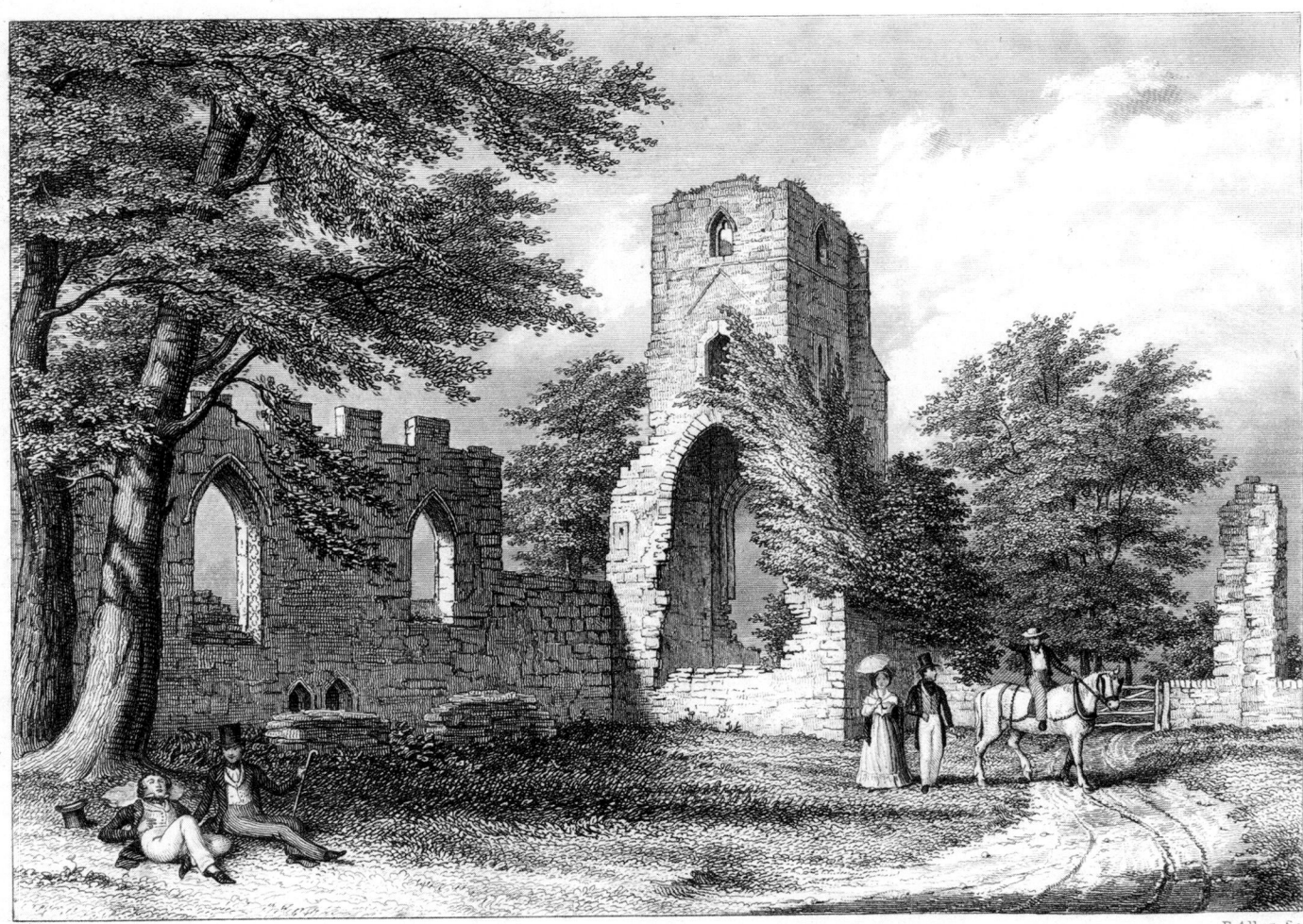

F.F. Palmer. del.

R. Allen. Sc.

ULVESCROFT PRIORY.

Published by R. Allen. Nottingham. and E. Allen. Leicester.

In order for lithographs to be used as book illustrations, the stones had to be printed on separate pages from the letterpress type and then "tipped in" (bound in) with a protective tissue over them. This was a more expensive process than using woodcuts, which could be printed on the same page with the type. Therefore, although color lithography soon became ubiquitous for producing colored prints, labels, and posters, the most inexpensive

10. *Ulvescroft Priory.* Illustration from T. R. Potter, *The History and Antiquities of Charnwood Forest* (London: Hamilton, Adams; Nottingham, UK: R. Allen; Leicester, UK: E. Allen, 1842), frontispiece. Courtesy of the Huntington Library, San Marino, CA, DA670.C44 P8. (Checklist 1-13)

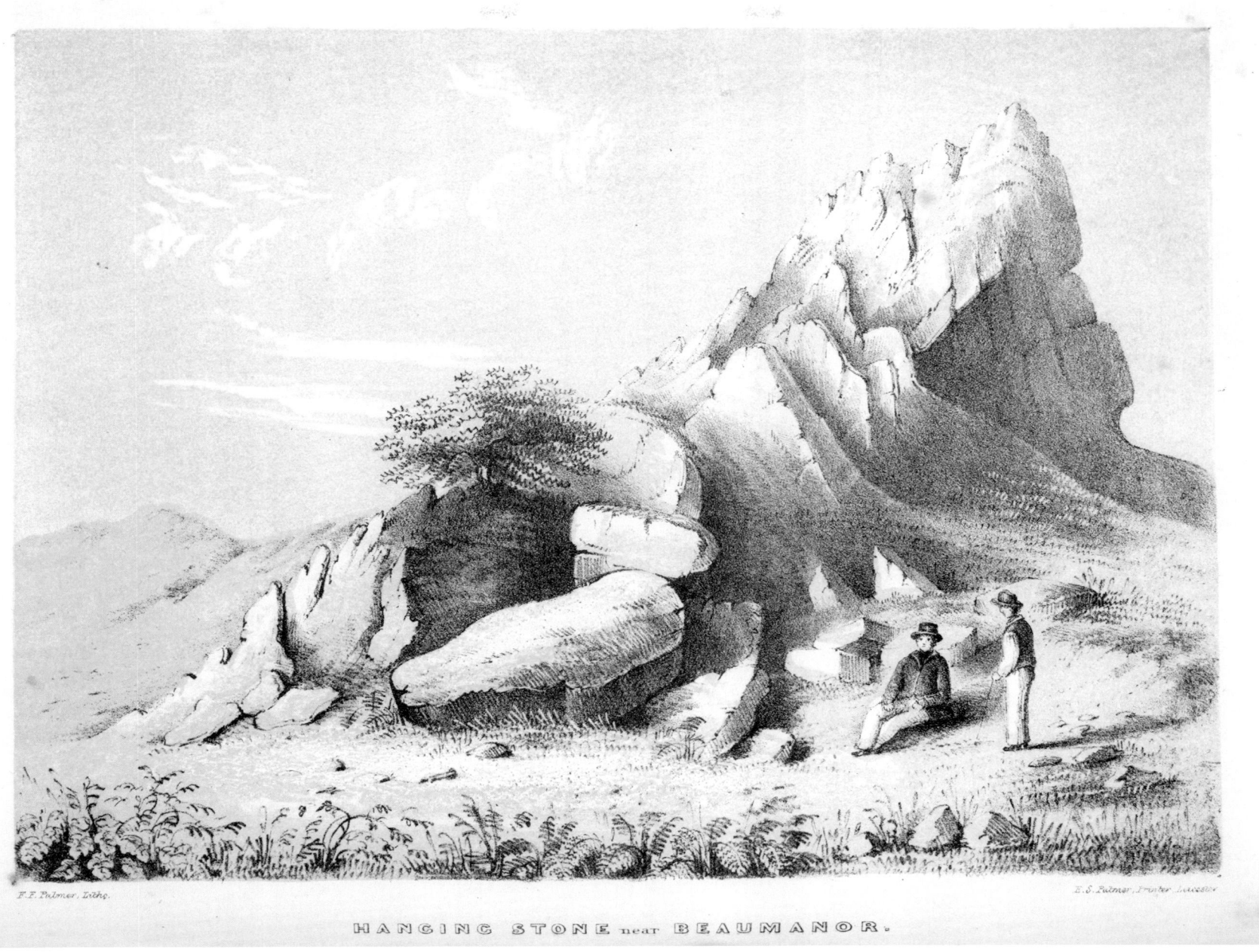

HANGING STONE near BEAUMANOR.

11. *Hanging Stone Near Beaumanor.* Illustration from T. R. Potter, *The History and Antiquities of Charnwood Forest* (London: Hamilton, Adams; Nottingham, UK: R. Allen; Leicester, UK: E. Allen, 1842), opposite p. 73. Courtesy of the Huntington Library, San Marino, CA, DA670.C44 P8. (Checklist 1-19)

and widely used method of book and magazine illustration continued to be woodcuts and, later, wood engravings until the advent of photographic reproduction. The use of tinted lithographs and black-and-white steel engravings rather than woodcuts in *The History and Antiquities of Charnwood Forest* indicates that it was a more ambitious and upscale project than the railway handbook.

In fact, the project associated the Palmers with many of the distinguished leaders and intellectuals of the region. The list of subscribers at the beginning of the book was headed by "Her

Most Gracious Majesty Adelaide, the Queen Dowager," followed by the names of a plethora of dukes, marquises, earls, barons, and lords, as well as "Sir Thomas Potter, Knt." A second list in smaller type includes "Mr. E. S. and Mrs. Palmer," along with Ambrose Lisle Phillipps and many other notables, some of whom are cited in the text.

The first art review of an F. F. Palmer lithograph appeared in the *Leicester Journal* on May 13, 1842. She had chosen a newsworthy subject: the new Leicester library, which was regarded as an architectural jewel and a community-gathering place and was causing great excitement in the city. This lithograph of the neoclassical News Room and Library (1838), designed by Leicester architect William Flint, made an excellent introduction of the Palmers' work to the community.[28] The new building was a source of civic pride and a social hub.

> Leicester General News Room and Library—A perspective view of this ornament to our town, drawn on stone, by Mrs. Palmer, executed in tinted Lithography, by Mr. E. J. [sic] Palmer, has just been published. . . . In this specimen before us, we have proof also that the difficult process of Lithography is skilfully conducted by a resident Lithographer. Of this view, although we pretend not that Mrs. Palmer's drawing on stone equals in the handling the productions of the long-practiced Barnard,[29] nor, that the finer specimens of [Charles Joseph] Hulmandel's [sic] Press do not surpass, in the more delicate effects, those of Mr. Palmer's; it is impossible to deny that the former is an accomplished Artist, and the latter a skilful director in this beautiful art; and we look forward with pleasure to the promised appearance of their joint efforts in the publication of a series of views, in numbers, of the most picturesque localities in our Town and Country.[30]

It is clear from this review that the Palmers were newcomers to the field and were regarded as a bit unsophisticated compared to the leading artists in London. It also reveals that Mrs. Palmer not only made drawings but also lithographed them on stone and that Mr. Palmer was the printer. The article also announced that they were about to issue a series of topographical lithographs, which did, in fact, begin to appear a month later under the general title Sketches in Leicestershire. On June 24, 1842, the *Leicester Journal* carried the following advertisement:

> Just published, imperial folio, price 5s. The first number of Sketches in Leicestershire containing 3 views.

The extensive patronage this work is receiving enables the Publisher to give an additional plate in each number. The work will be completed in twelve monthly parts, consisting of 36 Plates and upward of 30 Views. E. S. Palmer, Princes Street, Leicester.[31]

Twenty-seven of the proposed thirty views were ultimately published, of which thirteen were entirely designed and drawn on the stone by F. F. Palmer. Of the remaining fourteen prints, she adapted three from drawings by William Parsons, a prominent local architect and amateur artist;[32] three from T. F. Lee, a drawing master at the Proprietary School for boys; seven from B. F. Scott, a local artist (who also designed the vignettes on the cover); and one from a sketch by Ambrose Lisle Phillips, a wealthy landowner, philanthropist, and distinguished Catholic writer. This list of collaborators suggests that the Palmers were well connected socially in their community.

The first group of prints was reviewed enthusiastically in the *Leicester Journal* on July 1, 1842:

> SKETCHES IN LEICESTERSHIRE—We take the earliest opportunity of recommending this very promising work, the first number of which has just appeared to the notice of our readers. The views . . . *The Hanging Rock*; *St. Mary's Church, Leicester, from the S.W.*; and that most picturesque and interesting of all the heights included in this extensive range of the Charnwood, Beacon Hill. Each is managed with great artistic effect; and the manner in which the lithographer has fulfilled his [sic] task is deserving of every commendation. . . . The view of Beacon Hill is in Mrs. Palmer's most tasteful and successful style, and is distinguished by a boldness and freedom not often exhibited by a female pencil. . . . The tint delicately thrown upon the sky moreover, (apparently a soft and tranquil autumnal heaven,) is the very finish required as a contrast to the stern features of the rugged landscape which frowns beneath it. . . . We cordially recommend Mrs. Palmer's work to the notice, not only of all attached to our local scenery, but of all interested (as who in these days is not!) in the general progress and advancement of the graphic art.[33]

This review is revealing. It indicates that Mrs. Palmer was already recognized as an artist in the community even though Mr. Palmer did not include her name in his advertisement for their business. We also hear the tedious refrain, ever present in descriptions of women's work, "The view of Beacon Hill . . . *is*

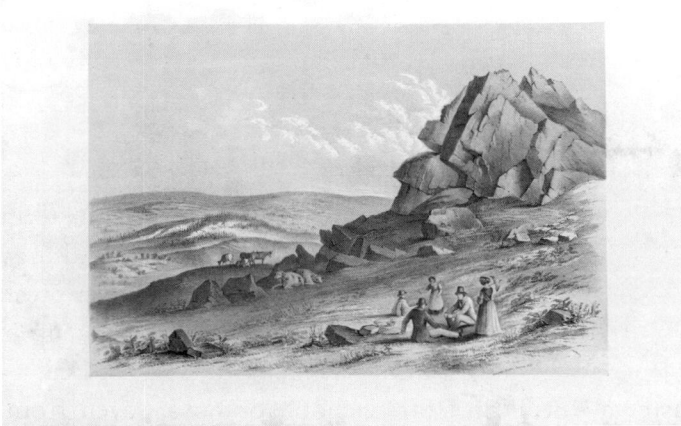

12. *Granite Rocks, Beacon Hill.* 1842. Illustration from J. F. Hollings, *Sketches in Leicestershire: From Original Drawings with Historical and Descriptive Notices* (Leicester, UK: John Sydney Crossley, 1846). Courtesy of the University of Leicester. (Checklist 1-46)

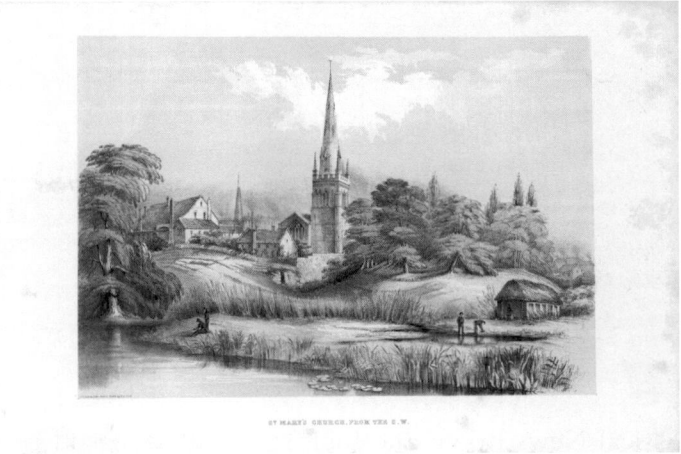

13. *St. Mary's Church. From the S.W.* 1842. Illustration from J. F. Hollings, *Sketches in Leicestershire: From Original Drawings with Historical and Descriptive Notices* (Leicester, UK: John Sydney Crossley, 1846). Courtesy of the University of Leicester. (Checklist 1-45)

distinguished by a boldness and freedom not often exhibited by a female pencil" (emphasis added). Even in the twentieth century, American painter Lee Krasner and sculptor Louise Nevelson were thought to have received high praise when teachers said their work was as good as a man's.[34]

Also interesting is the reference to the "tint delicately thrown upon the sky." F. F. Palmer was using a buff-colored tint to enrich the image and imitate the look of the drawing as it originally appeared on the warm tone of the lithograph stone. She used the method of scraping away or blocking out some parts of the grease that was rolled over a second stone in order, for example, to create lighter shapes in clouds.

Perhaps the finest of these early compositions is *St. Mary's Church. From the S.W.*, taken from a sketch by B. F. Scott. In this view from the River Soar, boys play amid rushes and water lilies, with the church in the distance surrounded by a medley of buildings, including smokestacks. A rolling movement of curves carries the eye across the composition. The forms of trees, branches, hills, and thatched roofs are defined in a pleasing embroidery of crayon strokes.

The prints also reveal an interest in architectural details. A print of the windows of St. Mary's Church and Ashby Folville Church (p. 18) and another of the doorways of Bagworth and Horninghold Churches (p. 18) are skillful renderings of gothic motifs. Above all, the views of cobbled streets, thatched-roof houses, and

people picnicking in the countryside or sauntering among historic ruins display a charming romanticism that later endeared Palmer to Americans when she began to depict Long Island, New York City, and the Hudson River valley.

The *Leicester Journal* also gave a favorable review to the second number of Sketches in Leicestershire on August 12, 1842:

> The premise of excellence, displayed in the first number of this highly meritorious work, is more than sustained by the series of plates . . . which has just been placed in our hands. . . . [T]he view of Loughborough from Cote's Hill . . . is characterized by a free and vigorous style of drawing, and unquestionably a considerable improvement in the figures introduced. The general arrangement and keeping of the landscape also, we consider a very creditable proof of Mrs. Palmer's skill and judgment in composition.[35]

A day later, on August 13, 1842, a review in the *Leicester Chronicle* noted enthusiastically that Palmer didn't hesitate to include such "modern" elements as factories with smokestacks and a "railway-train speeding along" in the print *Loughborough from Cotes Hill* (p. 19).[36] In the foreground of this entirely original composition, two hunters with guns are coming up over the curve of a hill, following their hunting dogs. The eye is led back by curving masses of tree branches to a distant view of Loughborough,

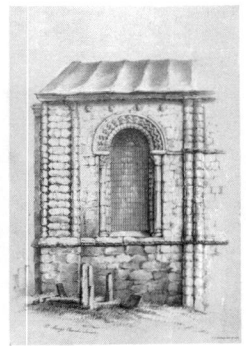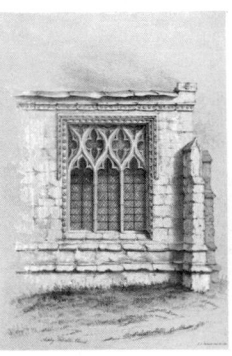

14. *St. Mary's Church, Leicester; Ashby Folville Church.* Undated, ca. 1842–43. Illustration from J. F. Hollings, *Sketches in Leicestershire: From Original Drawings with Historical and Descriptive Notices* (Leicester, UK: John Sydney Crossley, 1846). Courtesy of the University of Leicester. (Checklist 1-65)

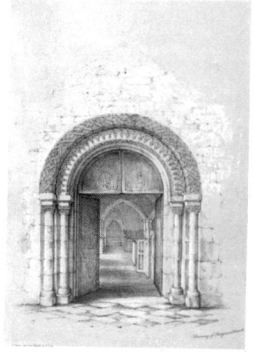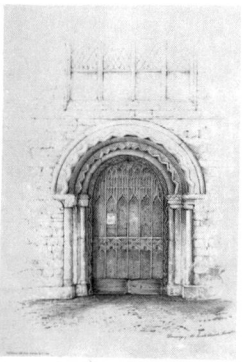

15. *Doorway of Belgrave Church; Doorway of All Saints Church, Leicester.* Undated [September 1842]. Illustration from J. F. Hollings, *Sketches in Leicestershire: From Original Drawings with Historical and Descriptive Notices* (Leicester, UK: John Sydney Crossley, 1846). Courtesy of the University of Leicester. (Checklist 1-55)

where, amid a peaceful country landscape, tiny smokestacks and factories can be seen competing in height with the gothic tower of the town church. On the left, through an opening in the trees, a tiny locomotive moves across the landscape, trailing a line of smoke.

As in so many paintings and prints of the era, both in England and the United States, the encroachment of industrialism on the pastoral scene appears to be felicitous. There is a curious melding of jolly old England and the new Dickensian industrial society, implying that the old and the new can live together in harmony. One would never guess that the peaceful scene in the distance was the site of Luddite riots so severe that they had forced a mechanized lace-making industry out of town.[37] The reviewer hints that Mrs. Palmer's figure drawing is not her strongest point ("a considerable improvement in the figures introduced"), the one weakness that continued to be noticed in her work.

By September, the couple was using a common sales pitch, suggesting that collectors had better buy immediately: "None of the early numbers can be supplied after the first of October as the Drawings will be destroyed."[38] The third number was reviewed in the *Leicester Journal* on September 9, 1842:

SKETCHES IN LEICESTERSHIRE . . . containing views of Ashby-de-la-Zouch Castle; the Monastery of Mount St. Bernard,

on the Forest; and the old West Bridge. . . . [T]he series continues to deserve unqualified praise. . . . [T]he artist-like treatment of most of the views, gives them value and interest beyond limits of our own immediate locality . . . but if we were to make a suggestion, it would be, that a manifest improvement to [Ashby Castle,] . . . as to some other of Mrs. Palmer's drawings, would accrue from a little more attention to the grouping of her lights and shadows—a little more Rembrandt treatment.[39]

The reviewer ended on a high note: "The work should have a place in every portfolio, and on every drawing-room table, in the country." A day later the rival *Leicester Chronicle* wrote, "These beautiful sketches most assuredly deserve a large and increasing sale; and if such be not the case . . . we can only lament that there should be so great want of taste and spirit in the country," and it commended *Ashby De La Zouch Castle from the S.* (p. 20) as "wholly the production of Mrs. Palmer; and both as regards the sketch and the lithography, she is entitled to the highest praise."[40]

When the fourth number of Sketches in Leicestershire was reviewed on October 28, *Ulvescroft Priory* (p. 21) was praised in the *Leicester Journal*, and the reviewer concluded, "Our opinion upon the general merit of Mrs. Palmer's work has been so often expressed before, that eulogy on the present occasion must, we fear, appear much like tedious iteration."[41]

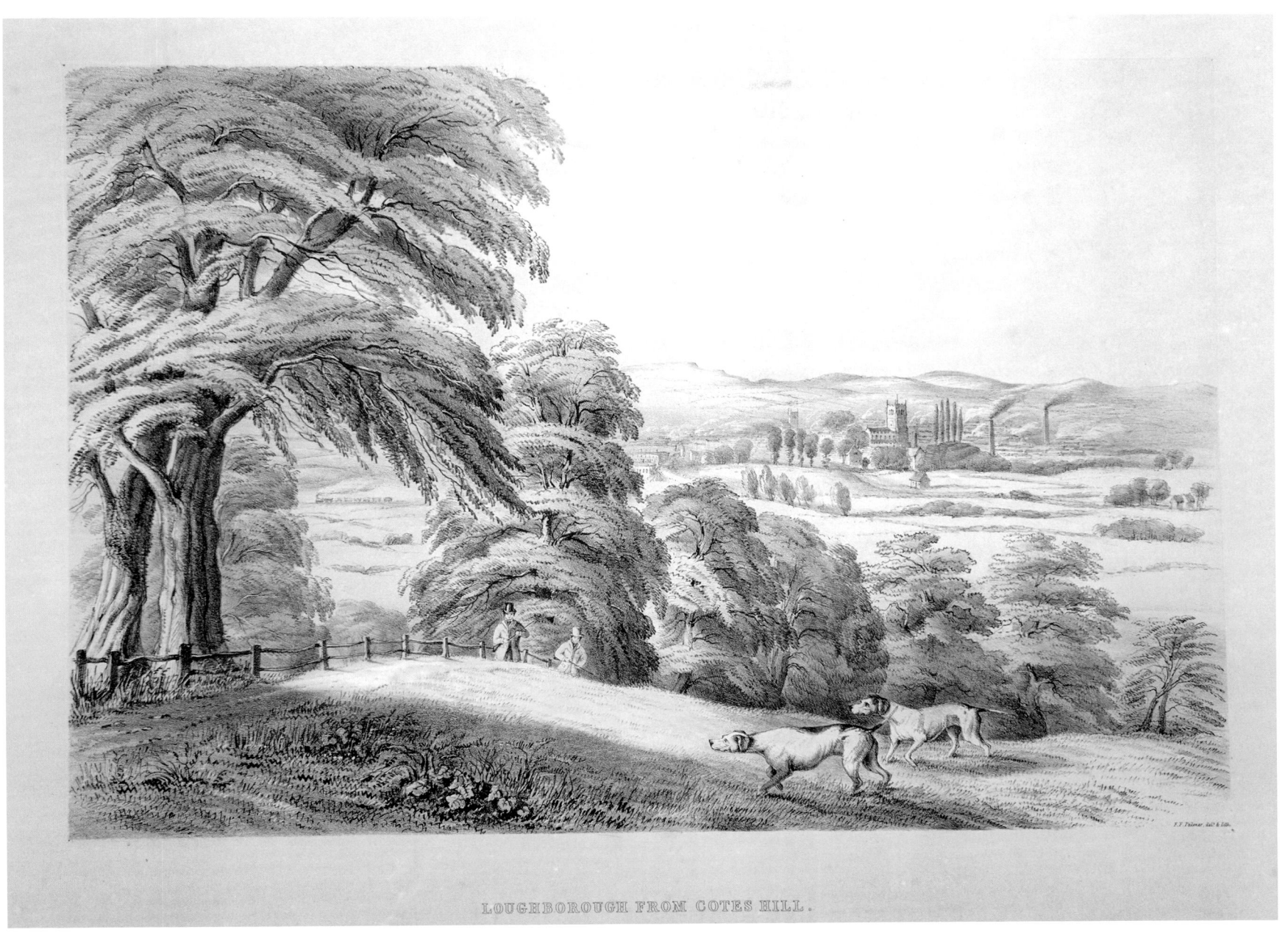

LOUGHBOROUGH FROM COTES HILL.

16. *Loughborough from Cotes Hill.* 1842. (Checklist 1-49)

On November 26, an advertisement in the *Leicester Chronicle* announced that the fifth number was being issued under the patronage of Her Majesty, the Dowager Queen Adelaide. A month later another notice stated that the sixth number was on hand, including *Hallaton Church* (p. 2), entirely by F. F. Palmer, and *The Old Blue Boar Inn, Leicester* (p. 21), taken from architect William Parsons's sketch of the recently destroyed historic inn where Richard III had stayed on the eve of the Battle of Bosworth. Like many subjects in the folios, these images were meant to evoke a rich sense of local British history.[42]

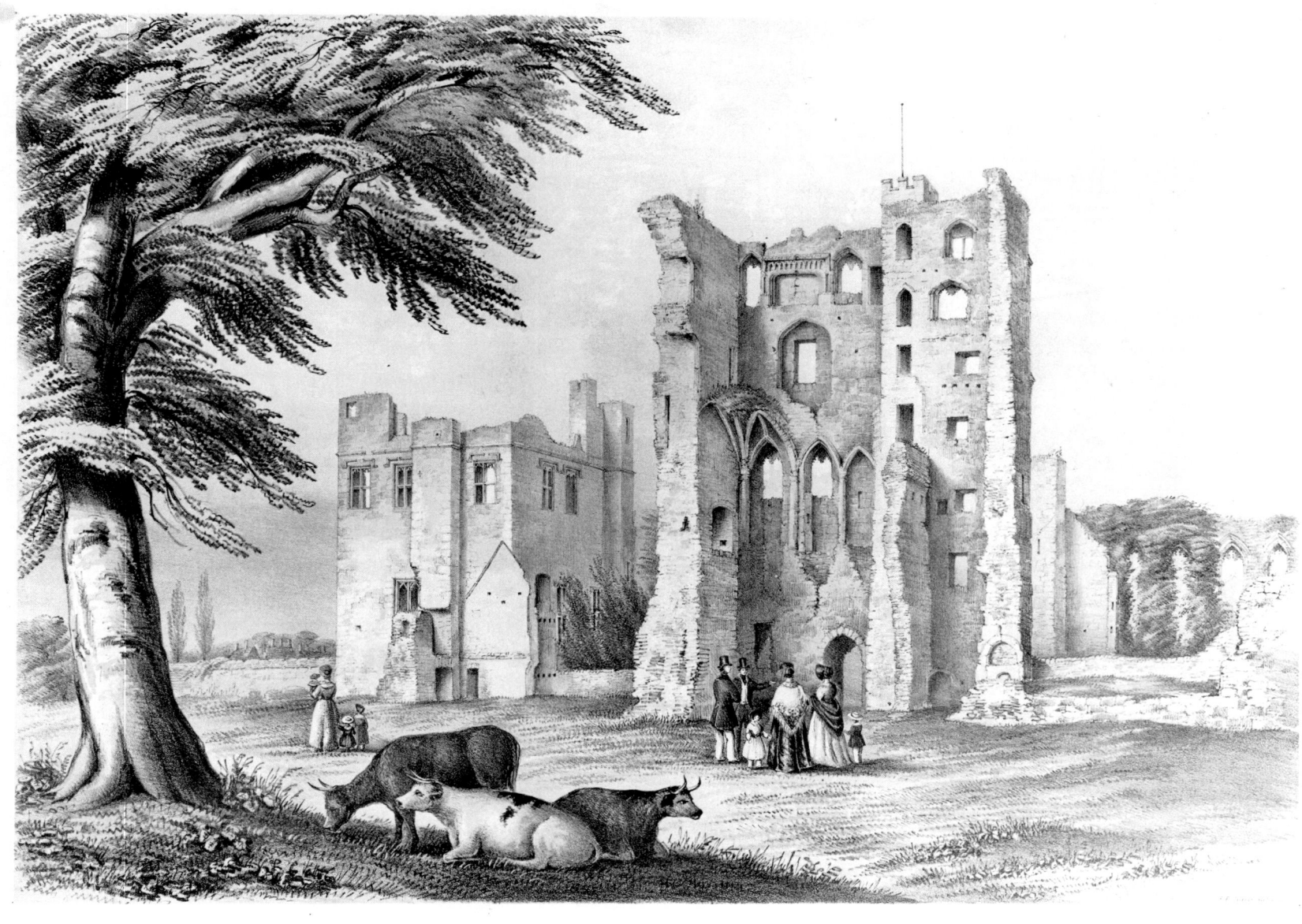

While newspapers were heaping praise on the Palmers for their work, the economy in Leicester was worsening. Workers were marching through the streets carrying signs calling for "bread or blood" and engaging in spontaneous strikes and riots. Mary Kirby, daughter of a wealthy Leicester hosier, described in her memoir "how the maids ran to close the shutters when they heard the marching mobs approaching, and how she and her sisters hoped that if the worst came to the worst they would be saved from molestation by the fact that one of these maids was a relative of Thomas Cooper" (a prominent labor leader).[43]

17. *Ashby De La Zouch Castle from the S.* 1842. Courtesy of the Leicestershire County Council Museums Service. (Checklist 1-50)

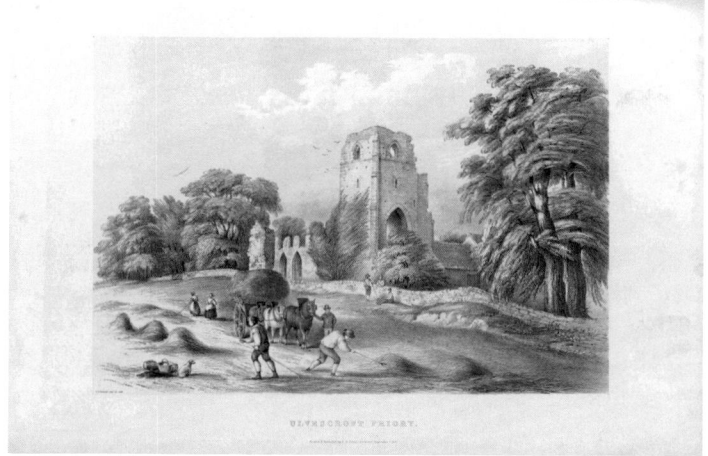

18. *Ulvescroft Priory.* 1842. Illustration from J. F. Hollings, *Sketches in Leicestershire: From Original Drawings with Historical and Descriptive Notices* (Leicester, UK: John Sydney Crossley, 1846). Courtesy of the University of Leicester. (Checklist 1-54)

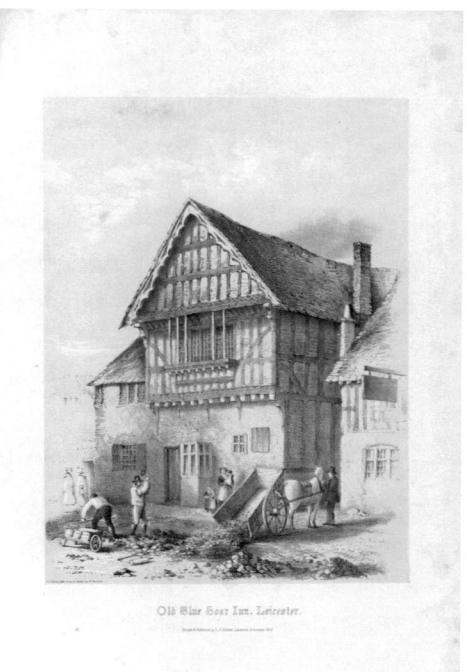

19. *The Old Blue Boar Inn, Leicester.* 1842. Illustration from J. F. Hollings, *Sketches in Leicestershire: From Original Drawings with Historical and Descriptive Notices* (Leicester, UK: John Sydney Crossley, 1846). Courtesy of the University of Leicester. (Checklist 1-62)

It was also becoming increasingly clear that despite all of Fanny and Edmund's efforts the Palmer business was not prospering. An ominous note was sounded in the *Leicester Chronicle* on December 17, 1842. After praising Mrs. Palmer's work and noting that the Sketches series had recently been honored with the patronage of the dowager queen, the reviewer continued: "And sincerely do we hope that the knowledge of this fact may induce many of that numerous class who are often decided as to whether they shall patronize any undertaking by the number of great personages who lend it the sanction of their names, to hasten to swell the ranks of Mrs. Palmer's subscribers, *who it is to be feared, are by no means so numerous as they should be.*"[44]

Up to December 30, when the sixth number was announced ready, the Sketches had appeared regularly every month, as promised. Now an awkward hiatus of six months ensued before a notice of the seventh and eighth numbers appeared in the *Leicester Journal* on June 16, 1843. This time there was a new petulant tone in the Palmers' advertisement as they heaped scorn on earlier efforts in the field:

This Work is intended to supply those interested in the County, as well as lovers of the fine Arts in general, with a series of Views . . . of those edifices within its limits, which, either from their antiquity or architectural merit, seem most worthy the attention of the public. In this view,

the work may be considered as supplying many palpable deficiencies in the histories of Throsby and Nichols,[45] in neither of which the pictorial illustrations can be considered as rising to mediocrity, while in selection of subjects for the engraver, some of the most marked and interesting scenes in the country have been neglected.[46]

A list of pictures "already printed" as well as some "intended for future Publication" followed in this notice, including some prints that appear not to have been created as part of the series, specifically those of Melton Church, Beaumanor Rocks, Jewry Wall, and Bottesford Church.

Although the Palmers had announced their intention of completing all twelve parts of the Sketches in Leicestershire, no further announcement of new prints appeared in the newspapers after the eighth part. It seems clear that the Palmers and Fanny's brother and sister, Robert and Maria, had lost hope about their prospects in England and had decided to immigrate to the United States.

In 1846, about two and a half years after their departure, a bound volume of twenty-four prints of the Sketches in Leicestershire series was published by John Sydney Crossley, a local bookseller who had evidently acquired the Palmers' unsold prints. Mr. J. F. Hollings, one of the masters at a boys' school and an expert in local history, wrote a full-page description for each plate. In his preface, he spoke of "Mrs. Palmer, a skilful and accomplished lithographer," and of how she had met a need in the community by documenting many of the important local points of interest around Leicester that John Flower had not included in his work.[47]

But the Palmers were not there to see the publication of this book. Like so many millions of aspiring immigrants before them, they had left for the New World.

3

Brave New World

EDMUND AND FRANCES PALMER, their eleven-year-old daughter and nine-year-old son, and perhaps Robert Bond Jr. arrived in New York City sometime between late June 1843 and the beginning of October 1843.[1] One can readily imagine the family's excitement as Edmund lifted up his children to see the lively waterfront scene dotted with a variety of sailing vessels, steamboats, and ferries, while Fanny sketched the crowded array of low buildings punctuated by occasional church spires. A pencil sketch of the New York waterfront in 1845 shows her response to this scene (p. 24).[2] Later, some of her earliest lithographs for Nathaniel Currier would be views of the lower New York City shoreline.

Fanny's sister Maria came separately on the packet ship *Liverpool*, entering New York harbor on October 11, 1843. Her name and description, "Miss M. Bond, age 25, unaccompanied," jump off the passenger list because of their gentility; almost all the other passengers are listed as "laborers" or "unemployed."[3] One conjures up an image of the neatly dressed young woman (who had described herself as "independent" on the Leicester census), standing alone at the rail, with squalling children and their families in the background. After arriving in New York City, Maria continued to live in her sister's household until the year of Fanny's death, but their young bachelor brother, Robert, set himself up at a separate address in Manhattan.

E. S. Palmer, "lithographer," is listed for the first time in Doggett's *New-York City Directory for 1844 & 1845*.[4] The address at 55 Ludlow Street was on a block of new two- and three-story wooden tenements on the Lower East Side, a district inhabited at that time by native-born white laborers, artisans, and shopkeepers as well as by a sprinkling of German immigrants, many of whom lived in apartments above the ground-floor businesses. The back alleys of the unpaved and cobble-stoned neighborhood were filled with workshops and small factories that accounted for 64 percent of the manufacturing establishments in the built-up portion of the city.[5] From a neighboring ward, Manhattan's largest

hog slaughterhouse perfumed the area, and they were not far from the docks and shipyards where some of the world's most splendid clipper ships were being built and where sailors and prostitutes roamed the waterfront.

One can guess at Mrs. Palmer's reaction to such an environment after living all her life among the genteel families of Leicester. Nevertheless, in the perennial spirit of American immigration, when the Palmers found that the streets were not paved with gold, they set about painting them gold. With astonishing speed and enterprise, the couple began to make contacts and issue prints. Many of their earliest New York lithographs are signed with the Ludlow Street address, but a few bear the legend "E. S. Palmer and E. Jones, lith." at 128 Fulton Street. (During his life, Edmund Seymour Palmer's name appeared in a variety of forms in print, including "E. S. Palmer," "S. Palmer," "E. Palmer," and "Seymour Palmer.") The Palmers had quickly formed some kind of working relationship with the established lithographer Edward Jones, and Edmund was listed as his partner in the 1844–45 directory.[6] Before long, however, Frances and Edmund had their own business address. The 1846–47 directory includes separate listings for both "Seymour" and "Francis [*sic*]" Palmer, lithographers, at 43 Ann Street as well as at a home address at 230 East Broadway.[7]

The gently reared Frances Palmer had landed in the heart of Walt Whitman's "Manahatta," with its "numberless crowded streets" bubbling with horse-drawn trolleys, wealthy citizens in carriages, strolling crowds, parades, masses of new immigrants, female street hawkers selling apples and hot corn, beggars, and rag pickers hunting through the trash. One observer compared the din of "iron wheels on granite pavements" to "the sound of Niagara . . . not so deep and thunderous however, but sharper and harsher—a great corroding roar."[8]

Fashionable East Broadway was the commercial street where one went to see "successful businessmen in suits of an appropriately conservative cut, the dandy with his beard and thin trouser

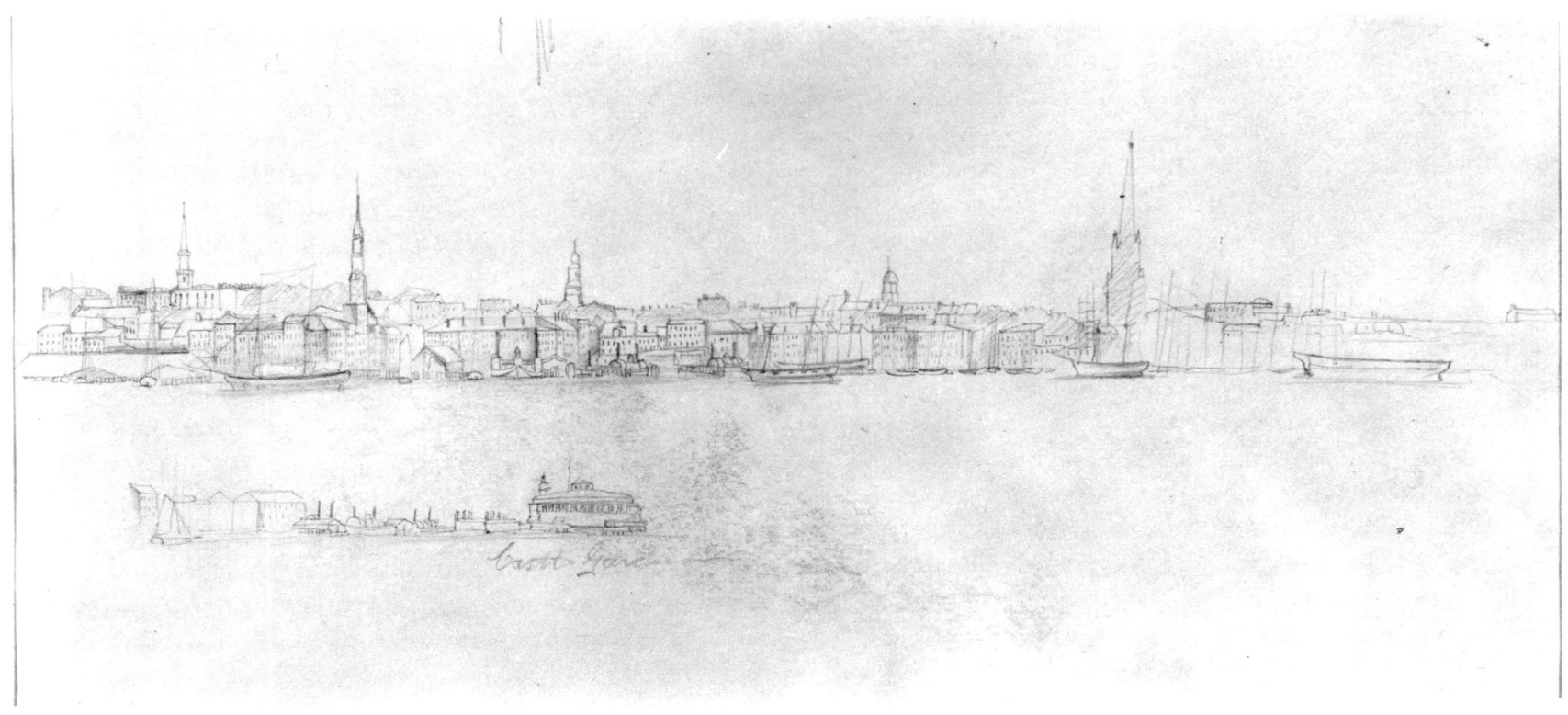

legs, and, above all, the women in their fluttering ribbons, rainbow silks, and latest Parisian fashions."[9] The Palmer family, out for a stroll on Broadway two years after their arrival, would have peered into the innovative plate-glass windows of A. T. Stewart's new marble business palace, the first American "department store," offering a variety of fine merchandise under one vast roof at bargain prices made possible by massive sales volume.

At the same time, they must have glanced nervously at the beggary on every corner. Only a short distance north of this center of conspicuous consumption was the notorious district known as "Five Points," where Charles Dickens, on his tour of America in 1842, found poverty, crime, and degradation equal to that of the worst slums in England. The couple was urgently aware of the need to establish their middle-class credentials and attract business immediately.

One of their earliest lithographs, when they were still at 55 Ludlow Street, is an undated portrait of an intelligent-looking gentleman wearing metal-rimmed spectacles, *Nehemiah Cleaveland, M.D.* (ca. 1844; p. 25). A cultivated New Englander and graduate of Bowdoin College who had earned both MD and LLD degrees, Dr. Cleaveland was at that time director of a "School for Young

20. *View of New York: From Brooklyn Heights: Study for a Lithograph; below a separate view of Castle Garden, New York City.* 1845. Graphite drawing on paper. Courtesy of the New-York Historical Society. (Checklist 4-24)

Ladies" in fashionable Brooklyn Heights.[10] The portrait, which looks as though it was adapted from a daguerreotype, could have served to introduce the Palmer's work to important people in the community. They seem to have been adept at making contact with well-connected individuals.

While the Palmers were beginning to issue lithographs, Mrs. Palmer was also seizing other opportunities to advertise her talent. In 1844, she exhibited two watercolors, a landscape and a view entitled *Snowden, North Wales*, at the annual National Academy of Design exhibition.[11] Two years later both Fanny and her sister Maria won recognition at the annual fair sponsored by the American Institute, an organization created "for the purpose of promoting and encouraging domestic industry in this State and the United States, in agriculture, commerce, manufactures, and the arts."[12] Every year this huge extravaganza, a harbinger of the oncoming

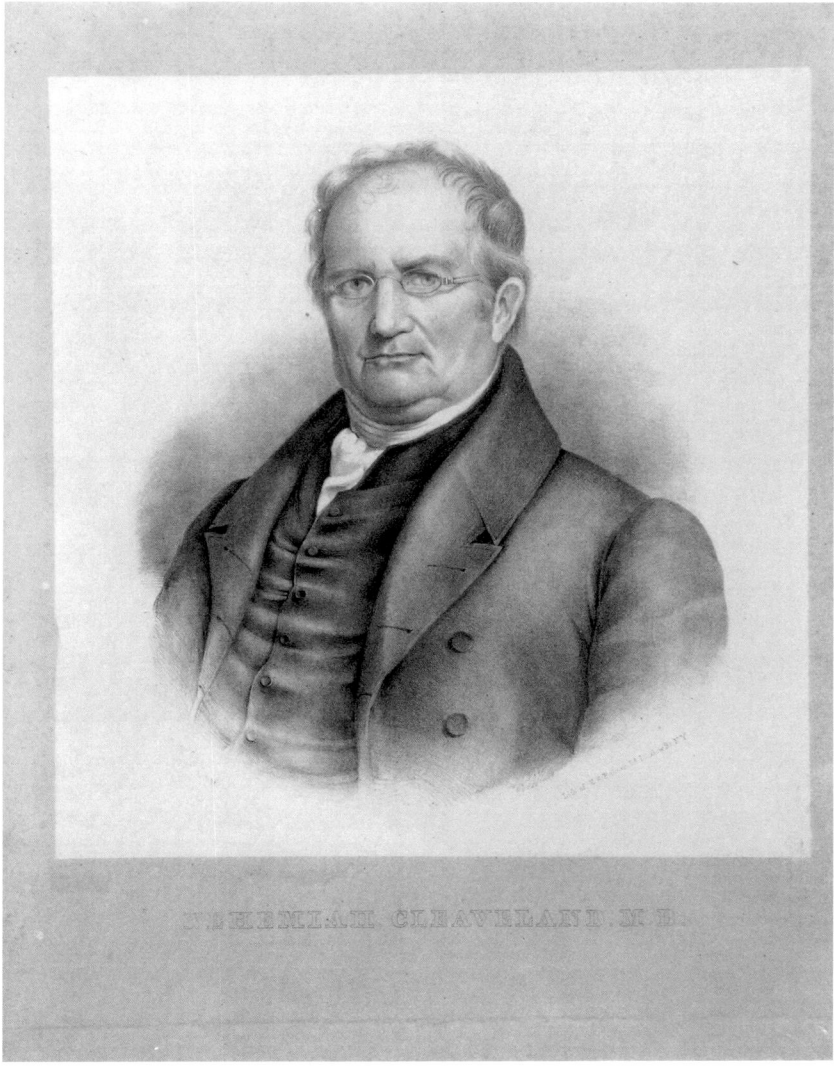

21. *Nehemiah Cleaveland, M.D.* Undated, ca. 1844. Printed and published by E. S. Palmer. (Checklist 2-3)

tidal wave of American consumerism, attracted hundreds of thousands of people from all classes of society eager to examine their nation's latest products, goods, and style trends.

Alongside the awards listed for the best cattle, firearms, fishing hooks, and other goods were those for fine arts. A diploma was awarded to "Mesdames Palmer & Bond, 230 East Broadway, for specimens of water-coloured painting." Someone named "Seymour Palmer," perhaps Mr. Palmer, also showed watercolors but did not win an award. In 1847, Mrs. Palmer alone earned a diploma at the fair for "a specimen of drawing," and in 1848 artists "Palmer and Bond" again exhibited five watercolors, but by this time the firm F. & S. Palmer was also winning awards for lithography.[13]

F. F. Palmer unfortunately did not have the luxury of indulging any yearning to be a "high" artist for very long. These efforts publicized her skills and attracted customers to the Palmer lithography business, but in those days it was difficult indeed for a woman to pursue a successful career as a painter not only because of the biases against women but also because of the kinds of contacts and associations that were necessary to secure patrons. The Sketch Club and the Century Club, for example, where artists mingled with prominent collectors and community leaders, were all-male enclaves.[14]

Whereas such notables as Asher Brown Durand, John Kensett, Fitz Henry Lane, Arthur Fitzwilliam Tait, Winslow Homer, and Eastman Johnson, all of whom had begun as engravers or lithographers, were soon devoting themselves to painting, Palmer had to keep her nose to the limestone, as it were, working incessantly on lithographs. Lithography was viewed primarily as a commercial medium and had a rather low status in the art world at that time, but even in her own modest calling she was an unusual phenomenon in the field. A number of women drew lithographs for other companies, but none had a career that came anywhere near Fanny Palmer's until later in the century.[15]

F. & S. Palmer's shop was on Ann Street, a narrow, crowded lane in the heart of the publishing district clustered around City Hall Park. Competition was fierce: printers and lithographers were located up and down Ann, Nassau, Beekman, and adjacent streets. But the Palmers were also surrounded by many businesses that might order work from them, such as the book dealer and publisher W. H. Graham in the nearby Tribune Building and the music publisher Millet. The neighborhood was also lively and stimulating. P. T. Barnum's American Museum of "Marvelous Living Human Curiosities" was a block away at the corner where Ann Street intersected Broadway; Mathew Brady's Daguerreian Miniature Gallery had just opened nearby; and New York's leading newspapers, the *Sun*, the *Tribune*, and later the *Times*, were located in buildings on adjacent streets, causing the area to be nicknamed "Printing House Square."

Around the corner and up the street at Nassau and Spruce, directly across from City Hall Park, was the retail store of F. F. Palmer's future employer, Nathaniel Currier. His lithographic publishing firm had recently risen from obscurity to fame, and he could now afford this prime location—the hub of civic life and the scene of festivities, parades, demonstrations, and protest meetings. From his front door, Currier could see the park's splashing fountain, trees, and flowers as well as City Hall itself.

The Palmers had opened their business at a favorable moment. The depression that began with the Panic of 1837 was finally lifting, and the city was emerging as a financial and commercial powerhouse with one of the busiest seaports in the world. It was also a time of nationalist fervor and expansionism. During President James K. Polk's term (1845–49), the region that is now Oregon and Washington was wrested from Great Britain by saber rattling and ultimately by treaty, and during the Mexican (Mexican-American) War Texas was annexed, and more than five hundred thousand square miles were acquired. At the same time that the country was expanding to the West, European immigrants were pouring into New York City. More than three million arrived between 1840 and 1855, among them many who were fleeing from Ireland's potato famine or seeking refuge from the failed democratic revolutions of 1848 in Germany and other nations.[16]

Because of the population explosion and the commercial boom, the city was in the midst of its usual frenzy of tearing down existing buildings and putting up new ones; the hills and varied terrain of Manhattan were being leveled and divided into a profit-making grid by developers. As warehouses, stores, hotels, and boarding houses were crammed into Lower Manhattan, well-to-do citizens moved farther and farther uptown to get away from the commercialism and din. First, they moved to Washington Square and then to Gramercy Park and Union Square. By 1844, they were beginning to erect mansions in what was still the countryside north of Thirty-Fourth Street. Former mayor Philip Hone, witnessing the demolishment of cherished old landmarks, mourned in his diary: "Overturn, overturn, overturn! is the maxim of New York. The very bones of our ancestors are not permitted to lie quiet a quarter of a century, and one generation of men seems studious to remove all relics of those which preceded them."[17]

Many of these trends are reflected in the prints of F. & S. Palmer. Soon after arriving in the United States, the couple issued a portrait of James Polk, *The Hon. James K. Polk*, around the time of his nomination as the Democratic presidential candidate in late May 1844. The Palmers cleverly sent a copy to the Democratic-leaning *Brooklyn Eagle*, which printed an enthusiastic notice of the print under the confident title "Portrait of President Polk": "E. S. Palmer, of 55 Ludlow street, N.Y., has sent up a capital lithographic portrait of the next President, James K. Polk, of Tennessee. As compared with another which we have before us, we should pronounce it a good likeness. Every Democrat will, of course, purchase a copy."[18]

Reflecting the frenzy of home construction and church building, Frances drew and Edmund printed architectural renderings that

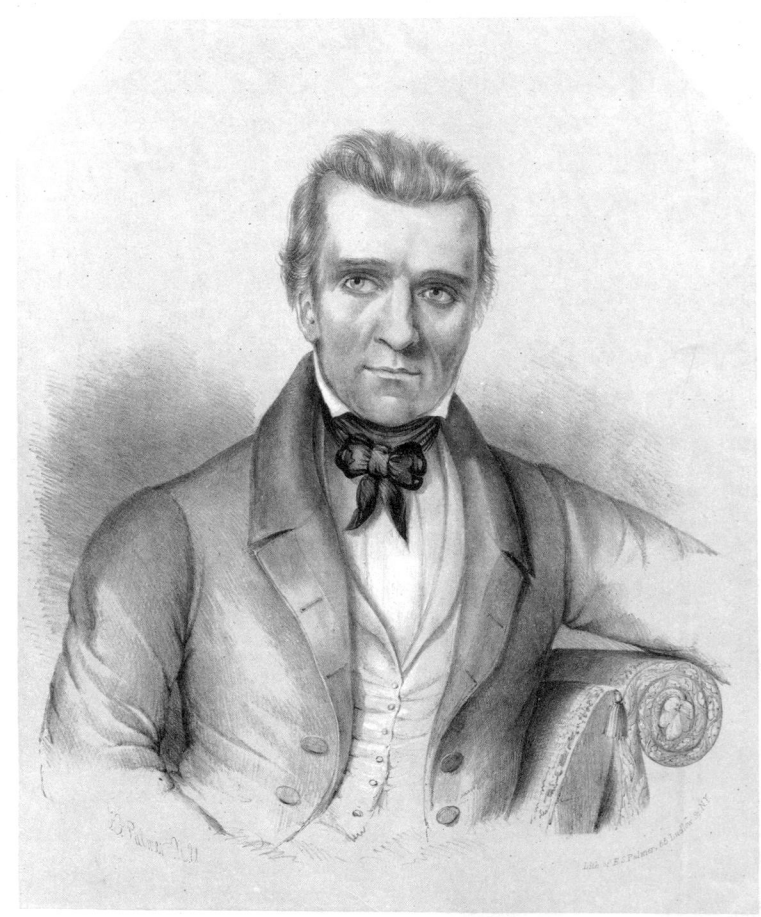

THE HON. JAMES K. POLK.

22. *The Hon. James K. Polk*. 1844. Printed by E. S. Palmer, published by J. Childs. Courtesy of the William L. Clements Library, University of Michigan. (Checklist 2-4)

ranged from modest cottages and Italianate mansions to neogothic churches. One of Mrs. Palmer's first jobs was an advertisement for an emporium selling plaster architectural ornaments (p. 27), and another was for a new kind of hot-air furnace (p. 268)—images that reflect the home-building trend. The Mexican War, the Oregon boundary dispute, and the native-born street toughs known as "b'hoys" also appear in the Palmers' early work. All in all, the art of the refined English lady with a Tory background and distant aristocratic connections had become a small mirror of the robust Jacksonian era.

Whereas in England Palmer had restricted herself largely to picturesque local and historic sites, she now drew ships, battle scenes, botanicals, landscapes, architecture, sheet-music covers, cartoons, and magazine illustrations. The five years between 1844 and 1849 became a time of thorough apprenticeship for her later role as a people's artist, one who would express—through the medium of inexpensive, mass-produced prints—the patriotic pride, the natural beauty, the yearnings for upward mobility, as well as the expansionist dreams of the young American nation. As in England, a number of her lithographs were adapted from drawings or prints by other artists, sometimes embellished with her own flourishes, but she also designed and lithographed a substantial number of original works that reveal her own style and handwriting.

The Palmers hustled for work wherever they could find it, often for other publishers but sometimes with published and copyrighted prints in their own name. The earliest dated American print that has been located is a quaint Victorian advertisement for "F. Basham, modeller, plaster, cement & scagliola worker, No. 408 Broadway, New York," showing a frontal cutaway view of a crowded, ornate showroom filled with "architectural ornaments got up to any design . . . mouldings . . . rosettes, capitols . . . statues and garden ornaments . . . busts taken from the living or the dead on the shortest notice." Copyrighted by Frederick Basham on January 24, 1844, and lithographed by the Palmers' temporary partner, Edward Jones, the image includes Mrs. Palmer's signature without any mention of her husband. She seems to have drawn it as a freelance job for Mr. Basham. The crude lettering, including a backward N in the word *cement* in the title, is uncharacteristic of F. & S. Palmer's more refined inscriptions. The fact that she secured work, shortly after arriving in New York, from Basham—a respected portrait sculptor and designer of architectural ornaments and an active leader in the American Institute—indicates how quickly she had earned the respect of leading people in the community.[19] This image, created with an added tint stone, is an early example of Palmer's use of the tint stone in the United States.

In that first year of business in America, 1844, F. & S. Palmer also lithographed one of the earliest in a long series of architectural prints, which featured the Church of the Pilgrims on the corner of Henry and Remsen Street in Brooklyn Heights (p. 28). The architect of this building, Richard Upjohn, was already working on what would become his most famous New York landmark, the richly ornamented, neogothic Holy Trinity Episcopal Church on Broadway and Wall Street. Demonstrating his versatility, his

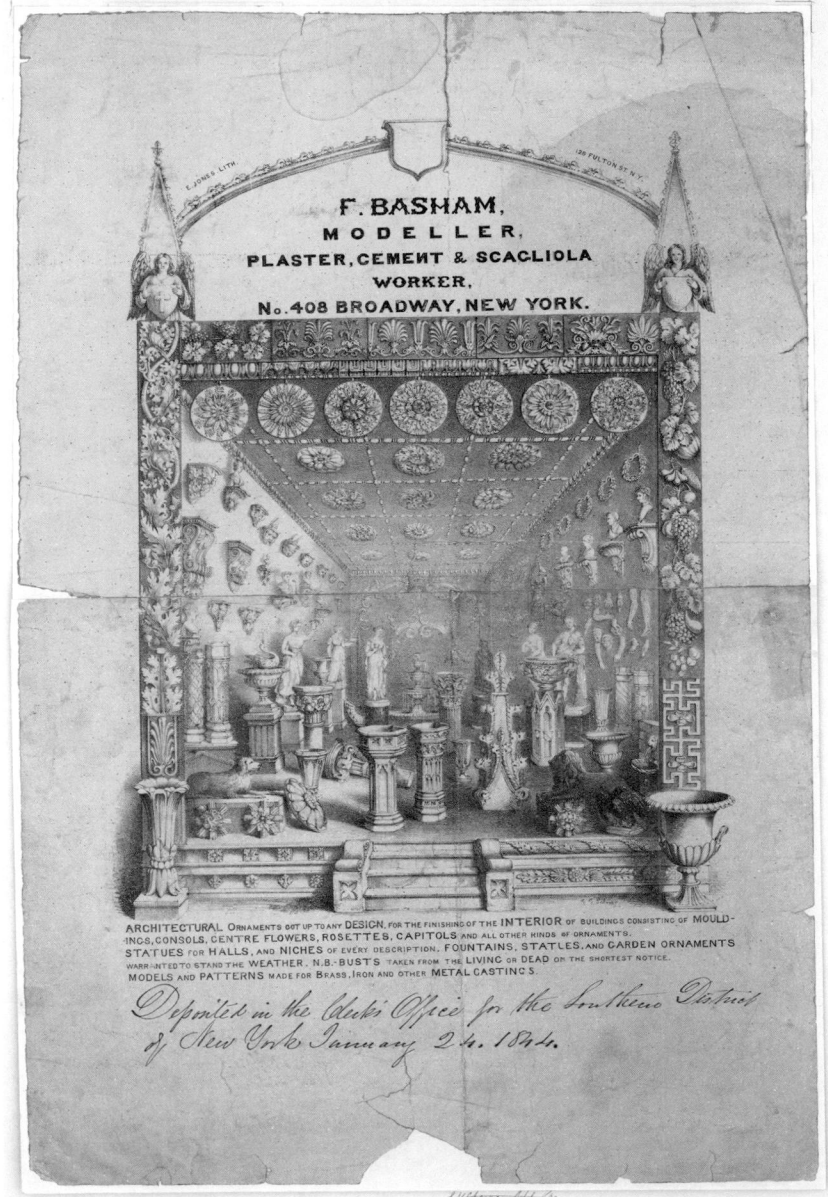

23. *F. Basham, Modeller, Plaster, Cement & Scagliola Worker, No. 408 Broadway, New York.* Undated, 1844. Printed and published by E. Jones. Courtesy of the Prints and Photographs Division, Library of Congress, LC-DIG-pga-07823. (Checklist 2-1)

design for Brooklyn's first Congregational church is a pioneering example of the simpler, more massive Romanesque Revival style that would become popular later in the century. This simplicity suited the parishioners, who eschewed ostentation and were so proud of their New England forebears that they embedded a piece of Plymouth Rock in the interior wall.[20]

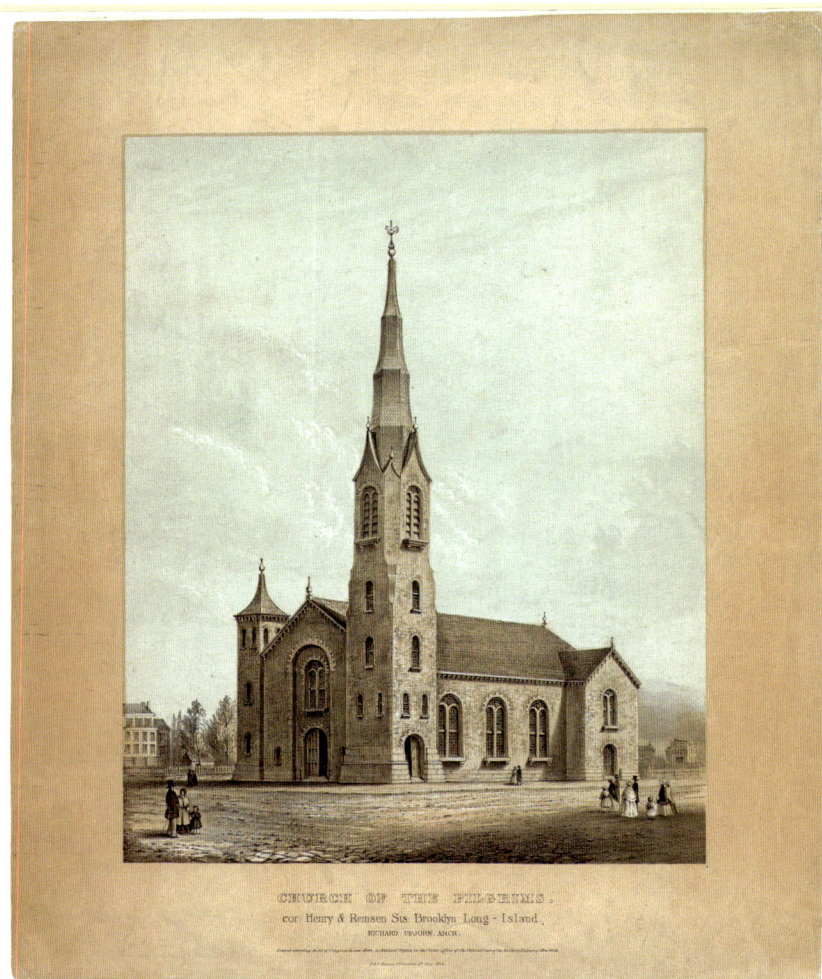

24. *Church of the Pilgrims. cor: Henry & Remsen Sts: Brooklyn, Long-Island. Richard Upjohn, Arch.* 1844. Printed by F. & S. Palmer, published by Richard Upjohn. Courtesy of the Metropolitan Museum of Art, the Edward W. C. Arnold Collection of New York Prints, Maps, and Pictures, Bequest of Edward W. C. Arnold, 1954. (Checklist 2-5)

It seems remarkable that the Palmers were already sufficiently well connected to secure work from the up-and-coming Richard Upjohn. Fanny's watercolor of his temporary studio (undated, Metropolitan Museum of Art), located behind Trinity Church during construction, suggests a personal relationship with the architect, who was, like the Palmers, one of a coterie of talented British expatriates living in New York.

In the following year, 1845, the couple produced one of their finest architectural prints, a tinted lithograph of the Episcopal Church of the Holy Trinity in Brooklyn (gallery plate 2), designed by architect Minard Lafever, another prominent gothic-revivalist. The

building was commissioned by the wealthy Brooklyn paper manufacturer Edgar Bartow, who was so eager for a church in his community to rival Upjohn's Trinity that he single-handedly paid for most of its construction (1844–47) and played an important role in its design.

The Palmers, who became members of this Brooklyn congregation, seem to have brought a special feeling to the creation of the print. A soaring sense of scale permeates the composition, taken from the architect's drawing of the building. Such prints were frequently commissioned during construction of churches to raise funds, arouse interest, and attract new members. It appears that the Palmers did indeed produce the image from Lafever's idealized rendering during the church's construction. The copyright date reads 1845, and the print itself shows a tall spire crowning the entrance—a spire that would not be erected until 1860.[21] But copyright records at the Library of Congress show that "S. Palmer" did not actually register the work until January 2, 1847. And it was only when the church was ready to hold services in April 1847 that the Palmers delivered a copy of the print to the *Brooklyn Daily Eagle*, which reported "a very neat colored lithograph of the new Brooklyn church of the holy trinity [*sic*] has been sent us from F. & S. Palmer, 55 Ludlow st. [*sic*]."[22]

No doubt buoyed by the Lafever commission, the Palmers then went after the job of lithographing the most admired project of the era, Upjohn's Trinity Church. A letter to the architect on March 13, 1846, a month before the dedication ceremony, reveals the Palmers' way of doing business.

55 Ludlow St., NY
Dr Sir
I have consulted Mrs. Palmer on the subject of Lithographing Trinity Church & beg to submit the following proposition which perhaps may meet your views as being less expense or risk to you.

I will publish the Drawing cojointly with you, furnishing you 100 impressions for your own separate use & benefit, charging you Seventy Dollars, you allowing me an equal share of the profits arising from the sale of and further number that may be issued after deducting the expense of Printing & paper. If you entertain the idea I should like to commence immediately as I shall be fully occupied after the next month.

I am Dr Sir
Yours Most Respect[fully]
S. Palmer
13 March 1846[23]

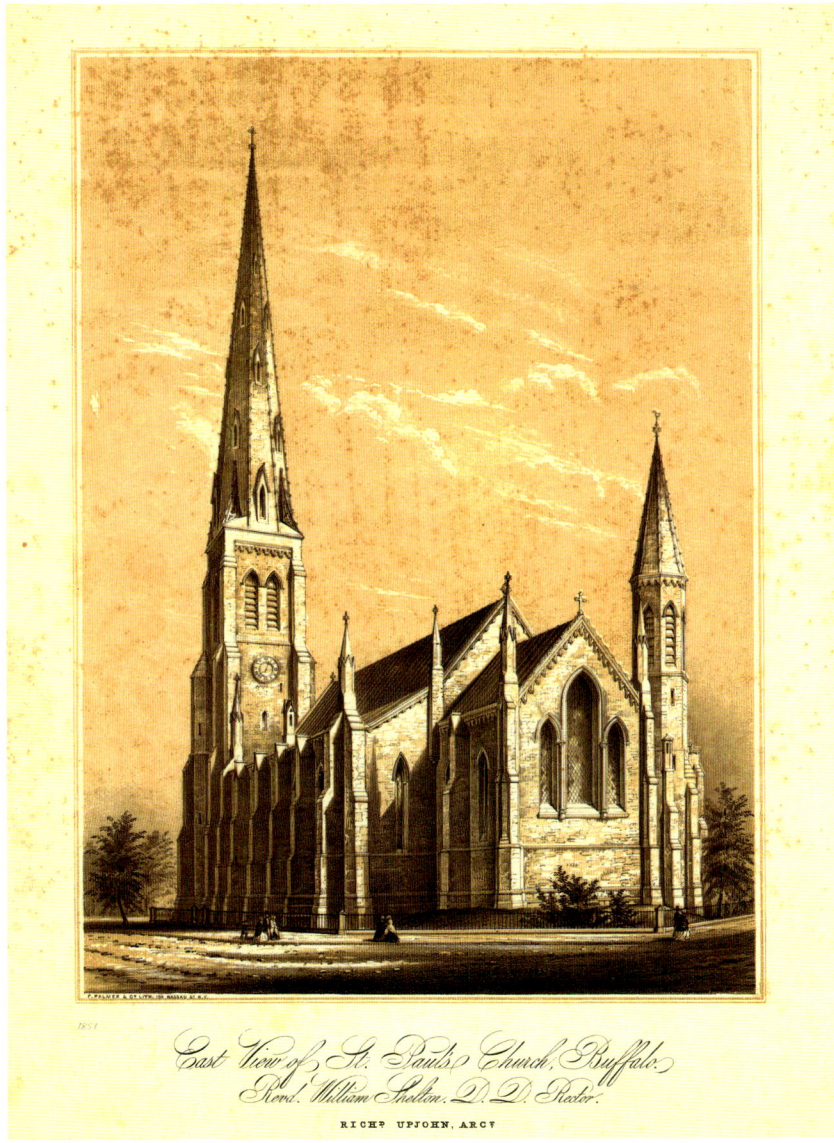

25. *East View of St. Paul's Church, Buffalo. Revd. William Shelton. D.D. Rector. Richd. Upjohn, Arct.* Undated, ca. 1851? Printed and published by F. Palmer & Co. Courtesy of the American Antiquarian Society. (Checklist 2-213)

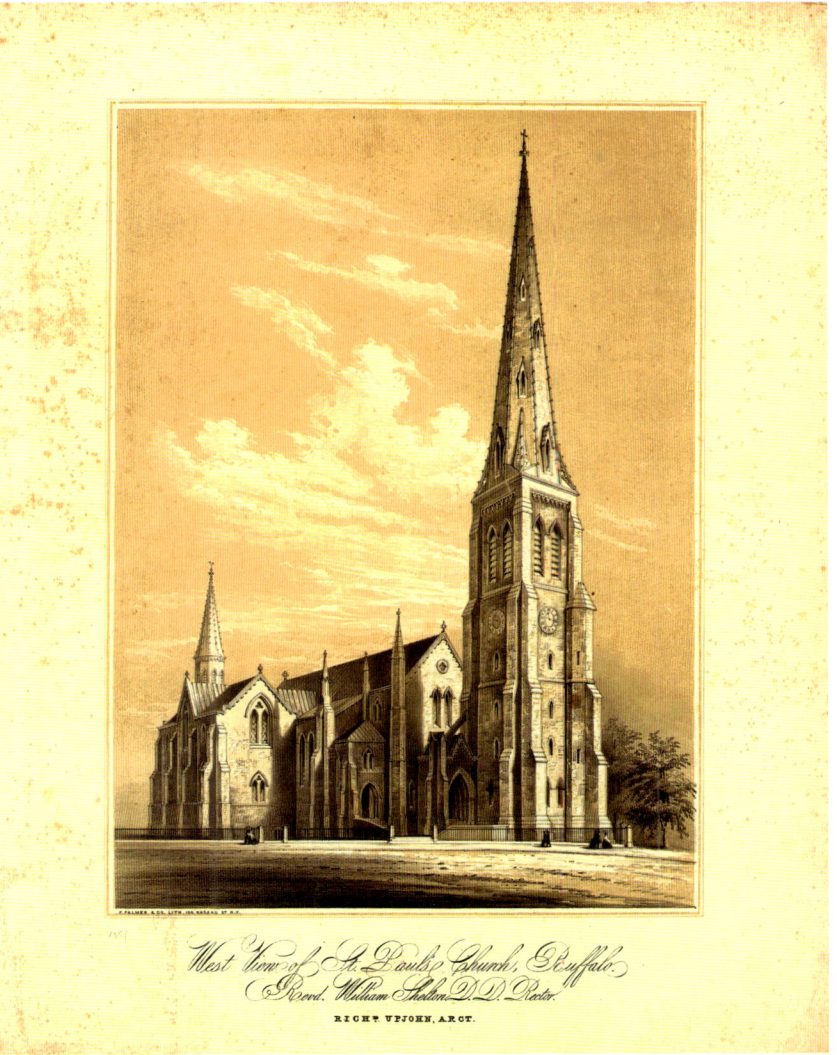

26. *West View of St. Paul's Church, Buffalo. Revd. William Shelton. D.D. Rector. Richd. Upjohn, Arct.* Undated, ca. 1851? Printed and published by F. Palmer & Co. Courtesy of the American Antiquarian Society. (Checklist 2-214)

The couple did not win this plum of a job, but F. Palmer & Co. later lithographed two views of Upjohn's imposing St. Paul's Church in Buffalo, New York (ca. 1851). The congregation commissioned her to lithograph prints of their new building under construction to raise funds for a new bell.

In the following years, F. F. Palmer continued to earn a fine reputation as a lithographer of elite church buildings; however, in 1848 she drew one that served the opposite end of the social spectrum—the plain, rugged-looking Baptist Mariners Chapel at 234 Cherry Street, built by a missionary society whose members hoped to serve and "save" the sailors and the downtrodden in the neighborhood near the East River (p. 30). In place of the well-dressed parishioners usually shown walking and riding to church in Palmer's prints, the artist animated this image with a motley crew of seamen, their families, a bent-over old man with a cane, a beggar and his dog, and several well-dressed "do-gooders" approaching the church. The pastor entering the building is taking a last glance at his sermon.

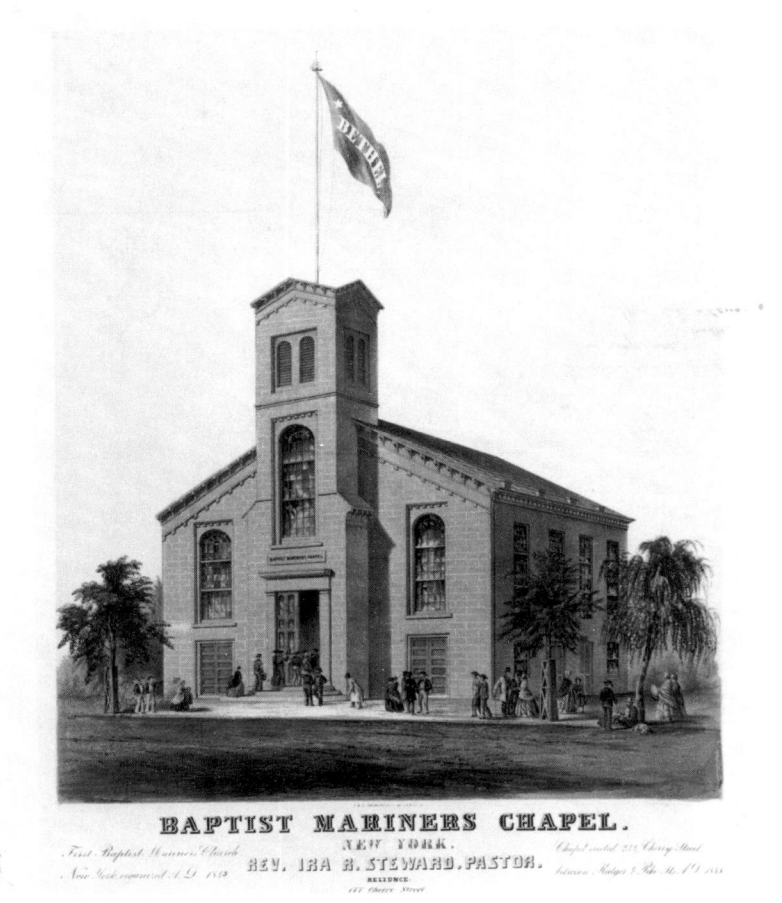

27. *Baptist Mariners Chapel. New York. Rev. Ira R. Steward, Pastor. Residence 177 Cherry Street.* Undated, ca. 1848. Printed and published by F. & S. Palmer. Courtesy of the Metropolitan Museum of Art, Gift of Mary Knight Arnold, 1974. (Checklist 2-181)

In addition to their ecclesiastical prints, the Palmers were lithographing and printing many images of secular architecture. An early subject, around 1844, was one of the most talked-about mansions of the day, designed by the trend-setting architect A. J. Davis (*Suburban Gothic Villa, Murray Hill, N.Y. City. Residence of W. C. H. Waddell, Esq.*). Located on the corner of Fifth Avenue and Thirty-Seventh Street, an area of the city that was still rural at the time, it was one of the first of the mansions to be constructed in that neighborhood. The building, referred to as New York City's first castellated gothic-revival home, was so fashionable that it was used as the setting for the novel *Fashion and*

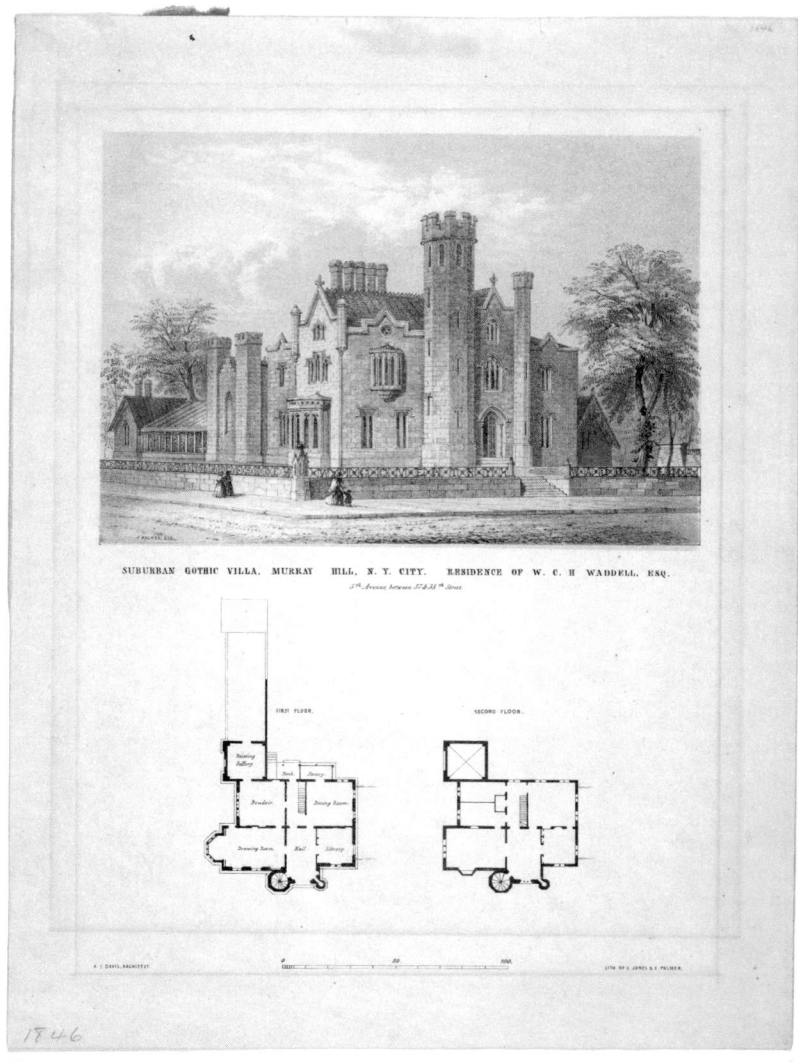

28. *Suburban Gothic Villa, Murray Hill, N. Y. City. Residence of W. C. H. Waddell, Esq. 5th Avenue, between 37 & 38th Street.* Undated, ca. 1844. Printed and published by E. Jones & E. Palmer. Courtesy of the Miriam and Ira D. Wallach Division of Art, Prints, and Photographs: Print Collection, the New York Public Library. (Checklist 2-2)

Famine (1854), written by the popular author Ann Sophia Winterbotham Stephens, who described it thus:

> It was a castellated villa in the very suburbs, standing upon a gentle swell of a hill, and commanding a fine view both of the city and the beautiful scenery that lies upon the North and East Rivers. . . . It seemed almost like the country, trees all around and green grass and rose bushes. . . . [R]ich and faultless was

the furniture that arrived from day to day after the masons and artists had completed their work. Statues of Parian marble, rich bronzes, antique carvings in wood, and the most sumptuous upholstery were arranged by the architect. . . . Grand, imposing, and unsurpassed for magnificence by anything known in our city.[24]

The tower on the left side of the mansion, in front of the conservatory and stable, was an art gallery: "Wealth was then measured by the thickness and profusion of gilt frames of all sizes and patterns. Pictures by Thomas Cole and Asher Brown Durand filled the house."[25] Another feature was the wrought-iron fence around the building, spelling out the owner's name in delicate tracery. No passerby could fail to know who owned the new mansion. Palmer carefully copied A. J. Davis's sepia, ink, and watercolor drawing of his building (1844, New York Public Library) but made it look more like part of an actual scene by adding figures of two women and a family who seem to be ogling the mansion as they stroll by. This is a good example of how the artist, even when copying someone else's work, sometimes enhanced it with her own embellishments. Printed with a pink-beige tint, *Suburban Gothic Villa* displays a technique similar to that used for Palmer's English prints.

Sometime in this period, the artist took the ferry to Staten Island, a place where wealthy New York merchants owned country homes, from which they commuted by ferry to New York and where they enjoyed boating, hunting, and fishing in their leisure hours. There she drew two entirely original views. *Elliottsville, S.I.* (undated, ca. 1844–45) shows a newly emerging neighborhood of fine homes on the north shore waterfront, with three boathouses and a pier in the foreground. The community, named after its developer, Dr. Samuel MacKenzie Elliott, a famous New York eye surgeon and ardent abolitionist who bought land and built homes there, soon attracted a number of families with similar views and became a hotbed of antislavery activity; indeed, many an Elliottsville basement became a stopping-off point for runaway slaves on the Underground Railroad.[26] Dr. Elliott's house, shown in the center background, is still lived in today, and the town, renamed Livingston, remains a charming enclave of historic homes.[27]

The second Staten Island print, Palmer's on-site rendering of Richmond Seminary from around 1847–48, portrays the ample frame building on a tree-filled hill that housed a school for girls (p. 32). A road leading up to it passes what may be the headmaster's home and stable below.[28] The school served the daughters of

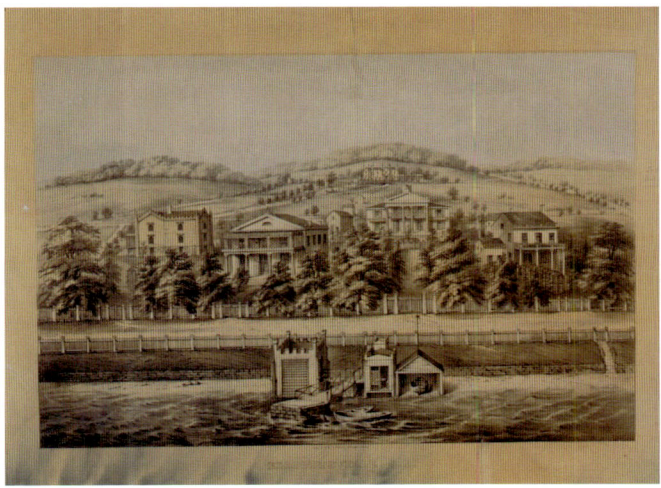

29. *Elliottsville, S.I.* Undated, ca. 1844–45? Printed and published by F. & S. Palmer. (Checklist 2-6)

families in nearby Richmond, at that time Staten Island's government administrative center, with a substantial year-round population. The lithograph is a good example of Palmer's vigorous, rhythmic use of the crayon in an entirely original early print taken directly from life.

Around this time, steam-packet boats, which first crossed the Atlantic in 1838 carrying mail, cargo, and passengers, had become a source of great national pride, and large crowds attended their launchings. Former New York mayor Philip Hone, after going with his wife and daughter to view a newly launched packet, the *Queen of the West*, enthused in his diary: "If John Bull is not 'knocked in half' by this specimen of Yankee naval magnificence and extravagance he has no sensibility. He will begin to think by and by that there may be some truth in the prediction of Monsieur De Tocqueville that 'the Americans were born to rule the seas as the Romans were to conquer the world.'" Hone proudly listed the cargo items to emphasize the number of products that Americans were now exporting to Europe.[29]

In 1845, F. F. Palmer lithographed what seems to be the first of many subsequent marine prints. Adapted from William Marsh's painting, *Henry Clay, Packet Ship* (p. 33) is signed "On Stone by F. Palmer" and published by "S. Palmer, 55 Ludlow & 128 Fulton Sts." This print was followed by at least five more marine images (*Mobile & New Orleans* [p. 271], *Crescent City* [p. 276], *New Line between Boston & New York* [p. 276], *Empire City Line* [p. 277], and *Reindeer* [p. 277]—all from around 1848–51),

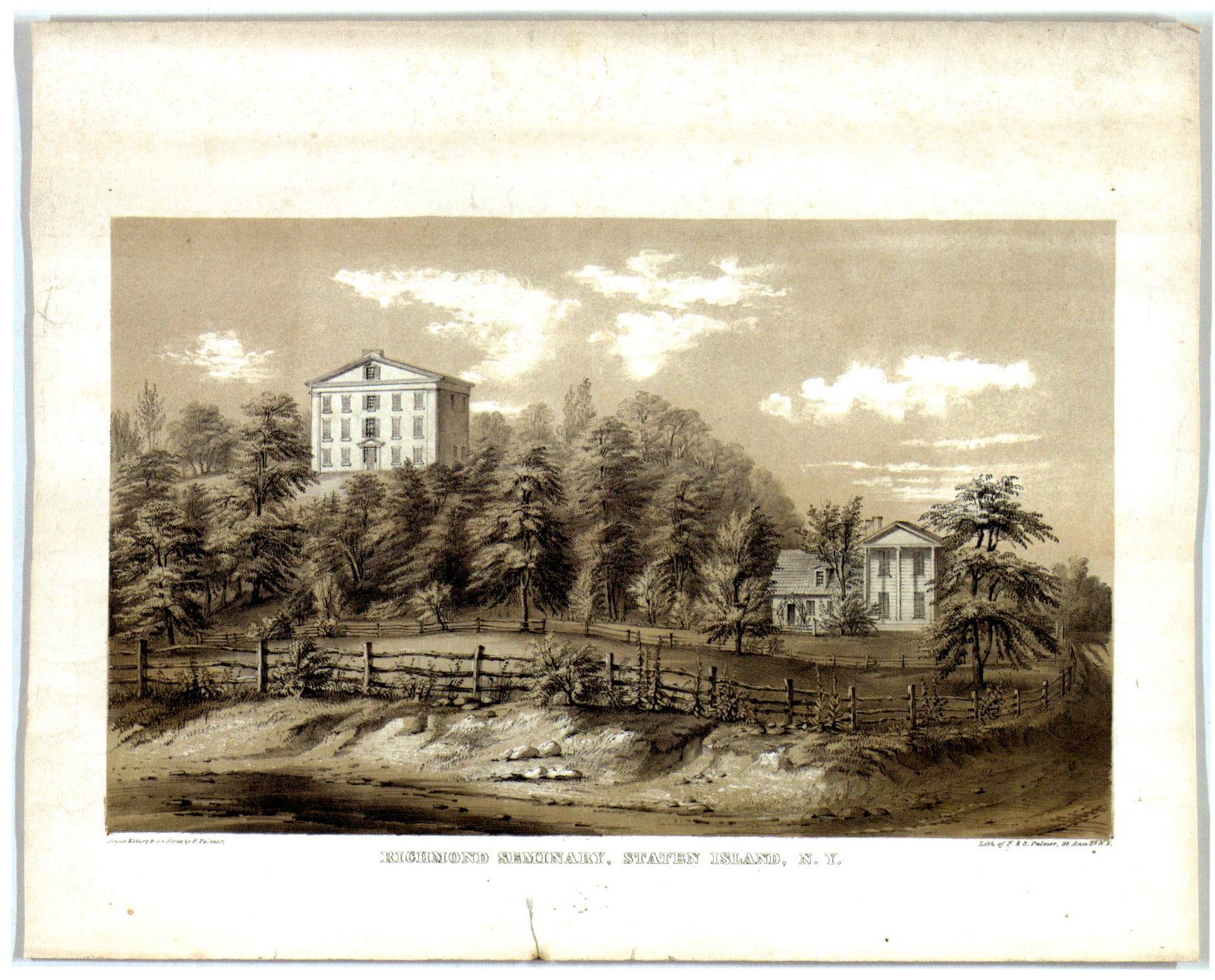

RICHMOND SEMINARY, STATEN ISLAND, N. Y.

mostly adapted from paintings by Marsh and another well-known marine painter, James Bard. Palmer would later create several fine boating prints for Nathaniel Currier.

In this same period, F. F. Palmer lithographed a nostalgic sheet music cover, *My Mountain Home* (p. 34), for music publisher William E. Millet. This time the legend below the illustration reads "Lith of F. & S. Palmer." In the foreground, a bonneted woman and her little girl gaze across a lake at a rustic cottage nestled

30. *Richmond Seminary, Staten Island, N.Y.* Undated, ca. 1847–48? Printed and published by F. & S. Palmer. Courtesy of the Metropolitan Museum of Art, the Edward W. C. Arnold Collection of New York Prints, Maps, and Pictures, Bequest of Edward W. C. Arnold, 1954. (Checklist 2-180)

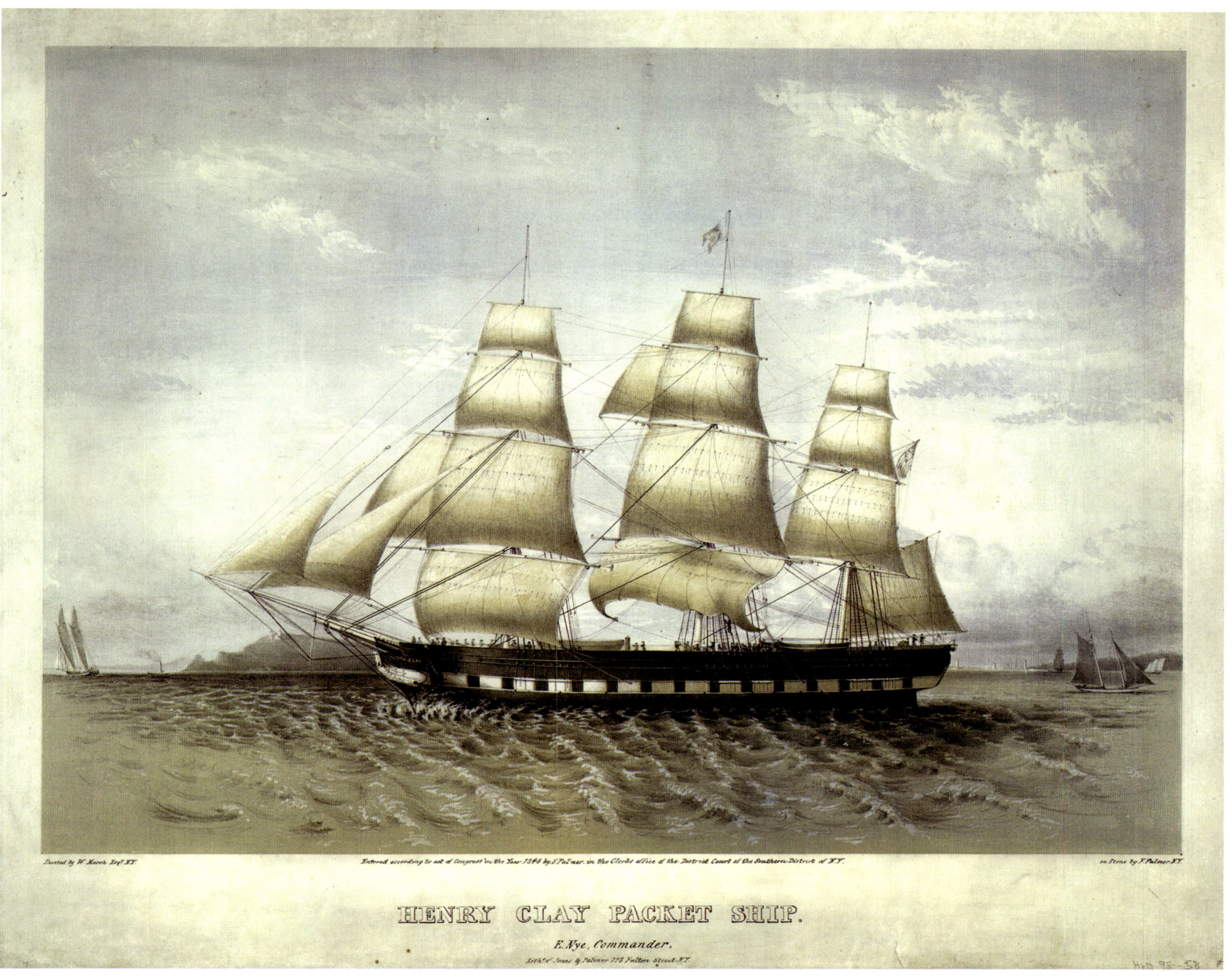

HENRY CLAY PACKET SHIP.

E. Nye, Commander.

31. *Henry Clay, Packet Ship. E. Nye, Commander.* 1845. Printed and published by S. Palmer. Courtesy of the Mariners' Museum, Newport News, VA. (Checklist 2-8)

below a mountain in the distance. The fringy trees and blocky, striated rocks, so familiar from her Leicestershire prints, reappear in this vignette. The artist continued to draw covers for Millet's firm in the following years.

In 1846, F. F. Palmer revealed a delightful and insufficiently recognized side of her artistry—her sense of humor. That year she lithographed a number of cartoons, including several depicting "b'hoys," a slang expression for a certain class of rowdy and rocks, look like Palmer's work, but the rest is in a different style from her other lithographs.[31]

Harness racing was wildly popular at that time, and it was common for young men to get out on the avenues after work or on the weekend and then repair to a tavern (and sometimes a brothel). In one print, a white "b'hoy" is catching up with a black man in overalls, driving a work cart, who looks back nervously to see who is gaining on him. The white driver scornfully taunts the African American: "Ho–Ho–Ho–Sambo—get along there what ar' you at?" (p. 200).[32] Another print, *Two of the B'hoys. No. 4 Breaking* (undated, 1846; p. 35), shows a "b'hoy" with his "g'hal" beside him in a wagon. As he suddenly pulls hard on the reins, his girlfriend is thrown forward but seems to enjoy it. The ironic title intimates that the young woman doesn't quite meet the standards of respectable femininity.[33]

We know that Palmer made quite a splash with these cartoons because Evert A. Duyckinck,[34] one of the most famous editors and literary critics of the day, wrote to his brother that he had admired her "b'hoys" in the windows of local print dealers. He added that a new humor magazine named *Yankee Doodle*, which he hoped would become "an American Punch [*sic*]," was coming out, and "the design for the cover by the lady who sketches the 'bhoys' for the shop windows is good, an embodiment of a Yankee with a hat and an axe."[35] When the first issue of *Yankee Doodle* appeared, he was even more enthusiastic: "Do you not think the Yankee something of a triumph? . . . Are not the illustrations at least good? The Yankee on the cover by Mrs. Palmer, executrix of the B'hoys."[36]

Yankee Doodle, adapted for the cover from Palmer's design by a wood engraver, is an extraordinary American icon (p. 36). Derived from "Brother Jonathan," a popular early-nineteenth-century archetype of a typical American, and a forerunner of Uncle Sam, *Yankee Doodle* is here represented as a successful gentleman farmer in top hat and striped pants, holding an ax, which he has just used to chop down trees. A description inside the magazine explains that, "having knocked down many a tall woodland in his day, with his axe, he now carries it to wield against high-headed and braggart abuses. . . . [H]e will swing it so freely and with so good effect, the day will yet come when there will not stand . . . a domineering blustering press . . . a hypocrite divine . . . nor any trickster of any class or kind staining the good name of the land[.] Long live Yankee Doodle, Master of Wise Mirth and First President of Fun!"[37]

At the top of this fanciful composition, figures representing the logos of magazines of many nations (including Britain's *Punch*) are

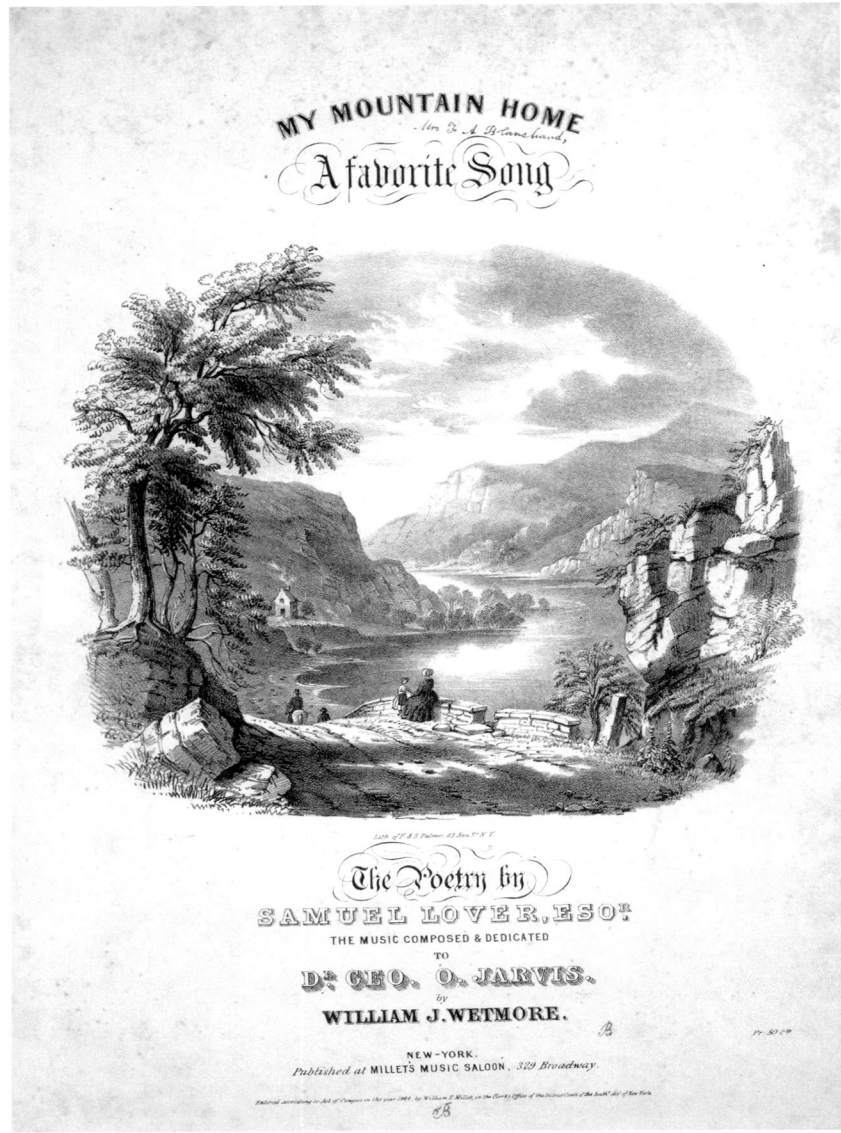

32. *My Mountain Home A favorite Song.* 1844 [ca. 1846–47?]. Printed by F. & S. Palmer, published at Millet's Music Saloon. Courtesy of the Lester S. Levy Collection of Sheet Music, Sheridan Libraries, Johns Hopkins University. (Checklist 2-12)

working-class fellows, often depicted in bright red shirts and tall hats, with greased dreadlocks. In the cartoons, the "b'hoys" boisterously race their horse-drawn sulkys (pp. 35, 253–54).[30] Six of these comic prints were entered for copyright by Thomas Odham, an unknown person who may have been the cartoonist. The prints do not carry Fanny Palmer's signature, and they may have been drawn and put on stone by Odham or another artist and printed by F. & S. Palmer. Certain details, such as the ground with stones

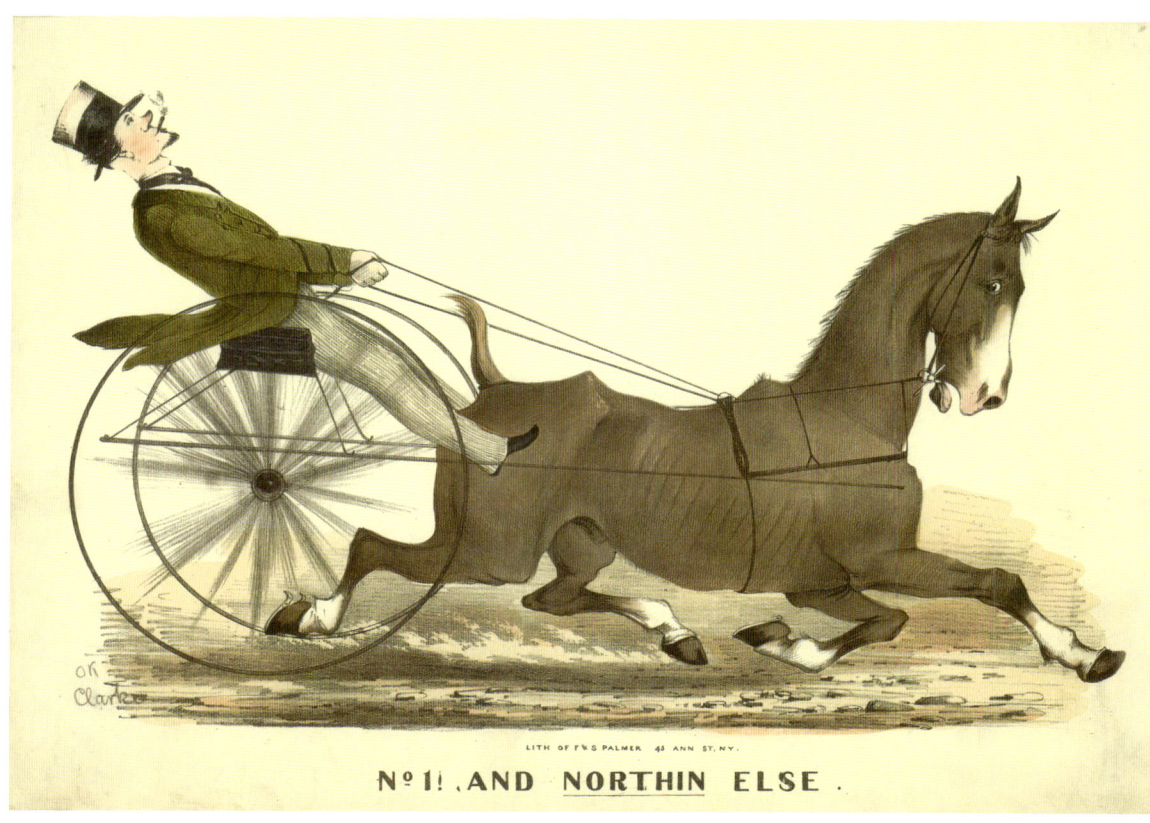

33. *No. 1! and Northin Else*. Undated, 1846. Printed and published by F. & S. Palmer. Courtesy of the New-York Historical Society. (Checklist 2-15)

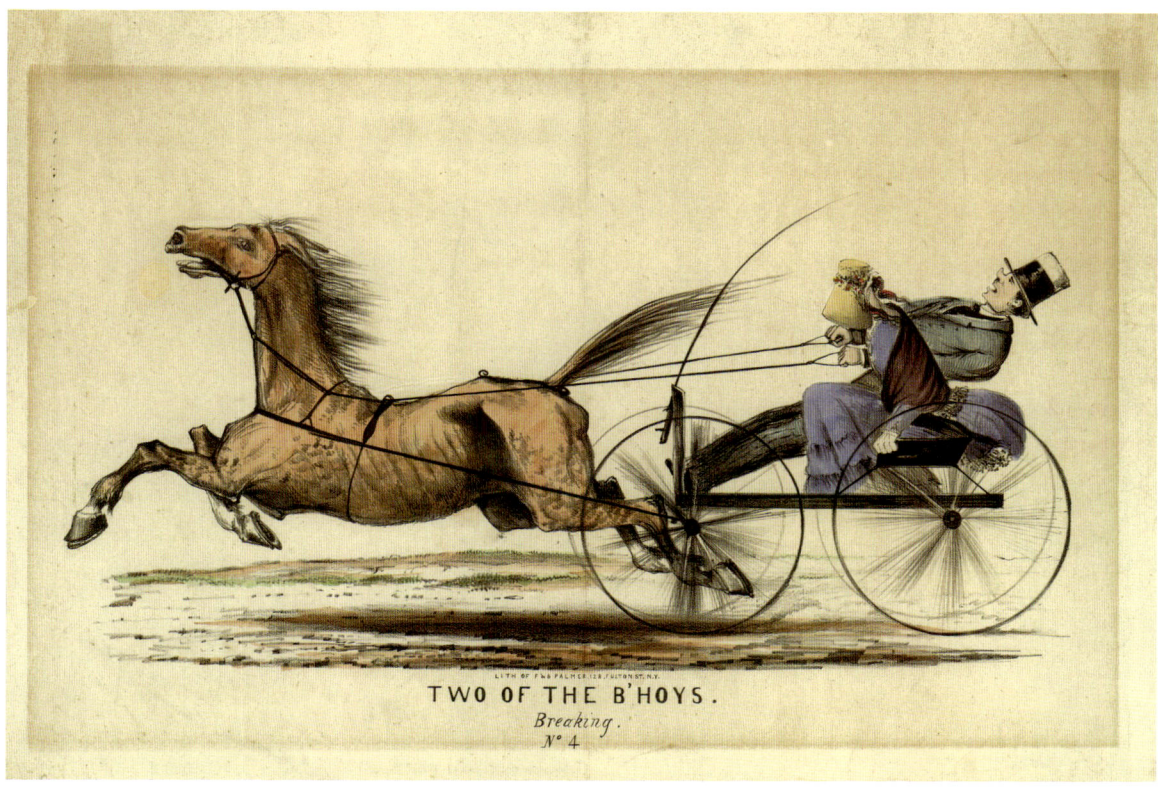

34. *Two of The B'Hoys. No. 4 Breaking*. Undated, 1846. Printed and published by F. & S. Palmer. Courtesy of the Old Print Shop. (Checklist 2-18)

35. *Yankee Doodle*. 1846. Published by William H. Graham. Courtesy of the American Antiquarian Society. (Checklist 2-23)

greeting the American newcomer as he strides confidently forward onto the world stage.

Palmer's cover was used on several subsequent issues. For the second issue, she also had the honor of drawing the magazine's first full-page cartoon, *The Naughty Boy Who Didn't Do His Errand* (October 1846), showing a Quaker woman (a symbol of the people of Pennsylvania) threatening to sweep a politician out of office with a broom for his role in a tariff bill. It is truly astonishing that in the mid-nineteenth century, Palmer was chosen by publisher William Graham and a distinguished editorial board to be their political caricaturist. Even today, few women have achieved much prominence in this field. Unfortunately, "the domineering blustering press" attacked the new publication's politics so virulently from all sides that it folded in a year.

The Palmers also produced three political lithographs under the F. & S. Palmer company name. *War! Or No War* (1846) is a wry but amiable look at democracy on the street level. Two "b'hoys" in overalls and stovepipe hats stand face to face in front of the Bowery Theater (a working-class venue), arguing about the future location of the boundary between Oregon and British Canada—a hotly debated topic at that time. While they decide the fate of the nation, a poor woman apple seller sits in the background, passively watching the men argue. In that era, women, who had no voting rights, were marginalized in images of the political process not only in prints but also in paintings—for instance, those by George Caleb Bingham, Richard Caton Woodville, and other genre painters of the era.[38]

Volunteers for Texas (1846; p. 38), copyrighted on the day the Mexican War was declared, is a humorous comment on the poor quality and unpreparedness of volunteers rushing to enlist and of their officers as well. A hodgepodge of recruits (some appear to be Irish, and one in the foreground may be a stereotype of a mulatto) in ragtag clothing (one is using a parasol as a musket) are standing at attention, while their effete, weak-chinned officer, dressed in an elaborate uniform, regards them through a monocle. Diarist Philip Hone, a member of the Whig elite opposed to the war, was keenly aware of these class differences. Mourning the loss of so many of his upper-class friends' sons, he wrote:

> One must be struck with the disparity of loss . . . between the officers and privates. In the wars of Europe . . . where the men are formed into machines to carry on the trade, their officers have only to set them in motion and keep them to their work. . . . We

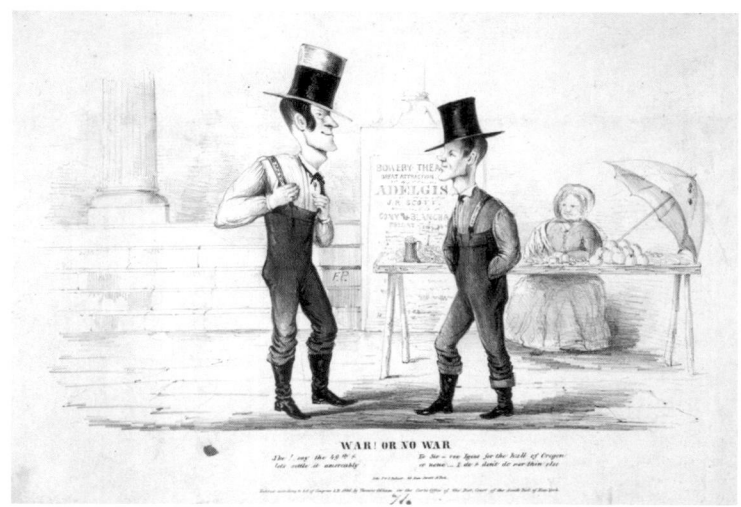

36. *War! Or No War.* 1846. Printed by F. & S. Palmer. Courtesy of the Prints and Photographs Division, Library of Congress, LC-USZC4-5745. (Checklist 2-22)

have a different kind of warfare to wage. The troops now engaged in Mexico are principally raw recruits, undisciplined and unpractised,—brave enough in battle, but governed by impulse; they require constantly the example of their officers to lead them on, and this example is never withheld. The officers are a set of the most chivalrous, daring fellows in the world. Most of them of good families, they fight for glory, and, knowing the risk attendant upon its acquirement, never hesitate to encounter it.[39]

Palmer, however, treats the subject in a less-reverential light, lampooning both the enlisted men and the officer class. Indeed, as David Tatham has pointed out, this comic theme was not new in American caricature and drama.[40] Because Americans objected to a standing army, which they associated with European monarchy and oppression, the government relied heavily on a system of poorly trained militia and raw volunteers in wartime. Edward Williams Clay, David Claypoole Johnston, and others drew hilarious scenes of the militia's "annual muster"—their brief period of training and sometimes revelry.

In another print, *The Mexican Rulers, migrating from Matamoras with their Treasures* (1846; p. 38), a monk and two leering frocked priests on horseback, each with a pretty girl and a basket of food and wine mounted behind him, are deserting (with their "treasures") the town on the Rio Grande that American troops have just occupied. Print historian Bernard Reilly points out that

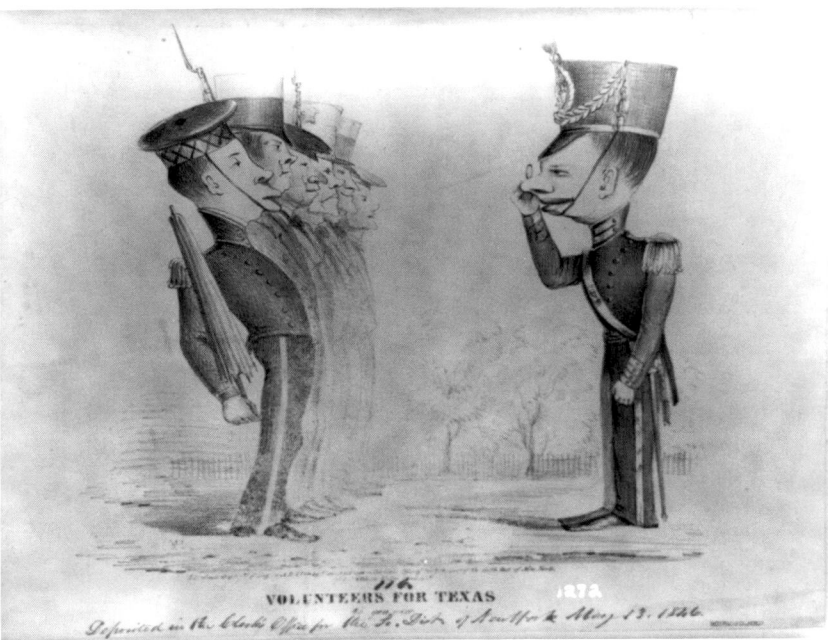

37. *Volunteers for Texas As You Were.* 1846. Printed by F. & S. Palmer. Courtesy of the Prints and Photographs Division, Library of Congress, LC-USZ62-1272. (Checklist 2-21)

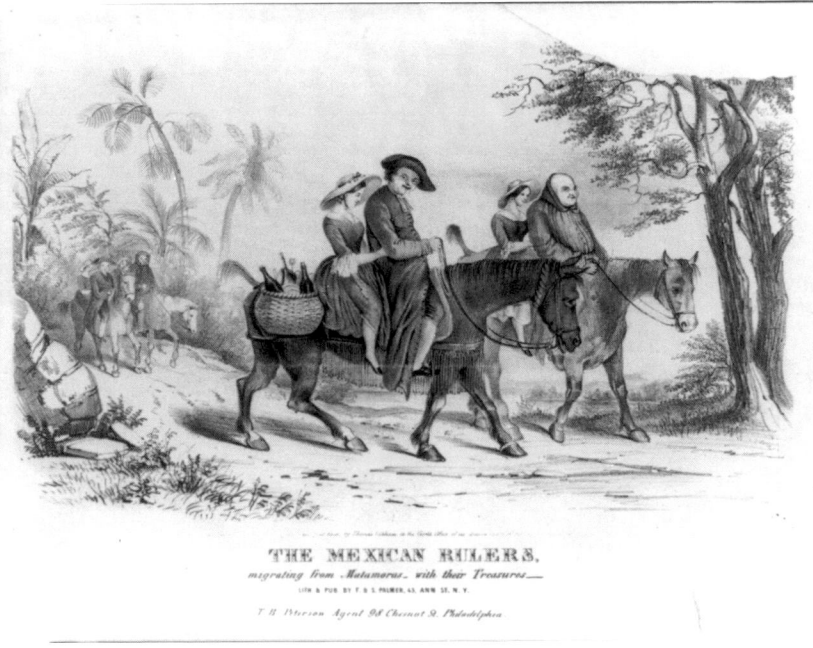

38. *The Mexican Rulers, migrating from Matamoras with their Treasures.* 1846. Printed and published by F. & S. Palmer. Courtesy of the Prints and Photographs Division, Library of Congress, LC-USZ62-35464. (Checklist 2-14)

by calling these figures "Mexican Rulers" Palmer conflates the Mexican Catholic clergy with a corrupt ruling class.[41]

At the same time that F. & S. Palmer was lampooning various aspects of the Mexican War, it, along with other lithographers, also rushed in to take advantage of the public's appetite for patriotic battle scenes. On May 28, 1846, only twenty days after the event took place, "S. Palmer" deposited for copyright in his own name the print *Battle of Palo-Alto. Charge of Capt. May's Dragoons, in which Genl. La Vega was taken prisoner* (p. 39). At a time when information traveled slowly and cameras were still unable to record the rapid motion of figures in action, lithographers often had to dream up their images from a mixture of newspaper accounts, European battle paintings, and their own imaginations, a practice that often resulted in errors. F. F. Palmer was no exception. Her print actually shows the Battle of Resaca de la Palma in which General La Vega was captured in a dry riverbed covered with chaparral. The Battle of Palo Alto, which had occurred the previous day on a flat plain without a tree in sight, incongruously appears in the background.

The artist's action-filled composition lives up to the challenge of this heroic subject, but her figure drawing is a bit naive. Note, however, that the figures drawn by her competitors are often

worse. Indeed, her print compares favorably with the crude and equally inaccurate images published by Sarony & Major and by her future employer, Nathaniel Currier (*Capture of Genl. La Vega by the Gallant Capt. May at the Battle of Resaca de la Palma, May 9th, 1846* [1846]). Currier's print has the right battle but the wrong hero: one of Captain May's soldiers, not the captain himself, captured La Vega.[42]

Palmer then lithographed the victorious Battle of Buena Vista (1847; p. 40) from a sketch by General Zachary Taylor's aide-de-camp, Joseph H. Eaton. The almost abstract exposition of the battle forces deployed in front of a huge stylized mountain lays out this pivotal campaign in a diagrammatic manner but is not in Palmer's characteristic style. She evidently copied Eaton's drawing as faithfully as possible for publisher H. R. Robinson.

In the same year, F. & S. Palmer produced two entirely original works, *The New York Drawing Book, Containing a Series of Original Designs and Sketches of American Scenery by F. Palmer*, nos. 1 and 2 (1847).[43] Taking advantage of a thriving vogue for drawing books featuring illustrations for art students to copy, the Palmers created two twenty-five-cent, four-page booklets that showcased their work.[44] The Palmers' drawing books contained

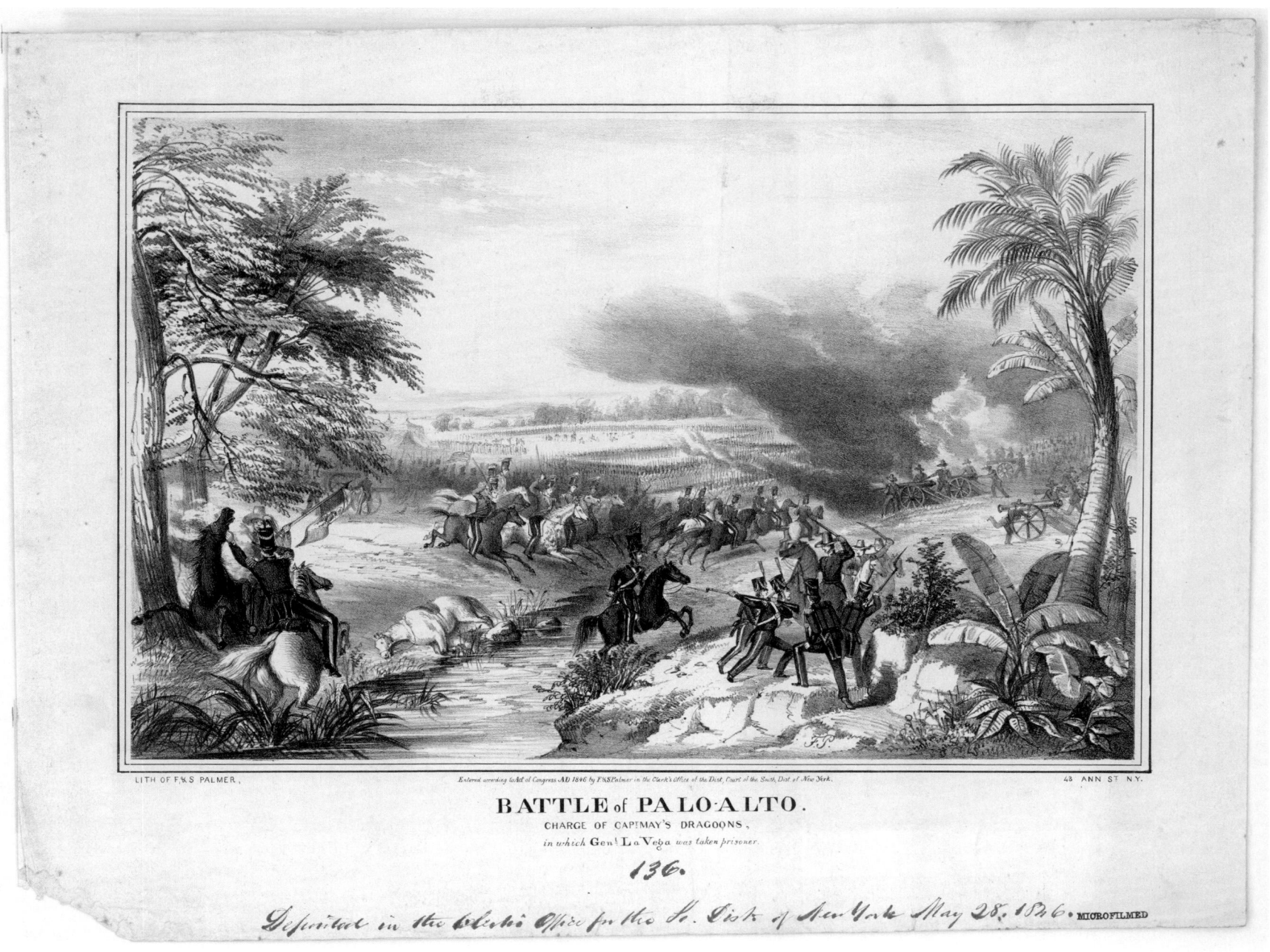

LITH OF F. & S. PALMER. Entered according to Act of Congress AD 1846 by F.&S.Palmer in the Clerk's office of the Dist. Court of the South. Dist of New York. 48 ANN ST N.Y.

BATTLE of PALO-ALTO.

CHARGE OF CAPT MAY'S DRAGOONS,

in which Genl LaVega *was taken prisoner.*

136.

Deposited in the Clerk's Office for the S. Dist of New York May 28, 1846. MICROFILMED

39. *Battle of Palo-Alto. Charge of Capt. May's Dragoons, in which Genl. La Vega was taken prisoner.* 1846. Printed and published by F. & S. Palmer. Courtesy of the Prints and Photographs Division, Library of Congress, LC-DIG-pga-07822. (Checklist 2-13)

images of landscapes, trees, farm animals, and figures that might be suitable for copy, although there is no accompanying text or instruction. Education was the ostensible purpose, but the books were also a form of promotion—a way to show the world that the Palmers could do fine lithographic work. Never missing an opportunity to drum up business, the couple plastered the back covers of both numbers with a full-page advertisement that indicated that the Palmers were ready to accept any assignment, big or small, and even sold lithograph supplies:

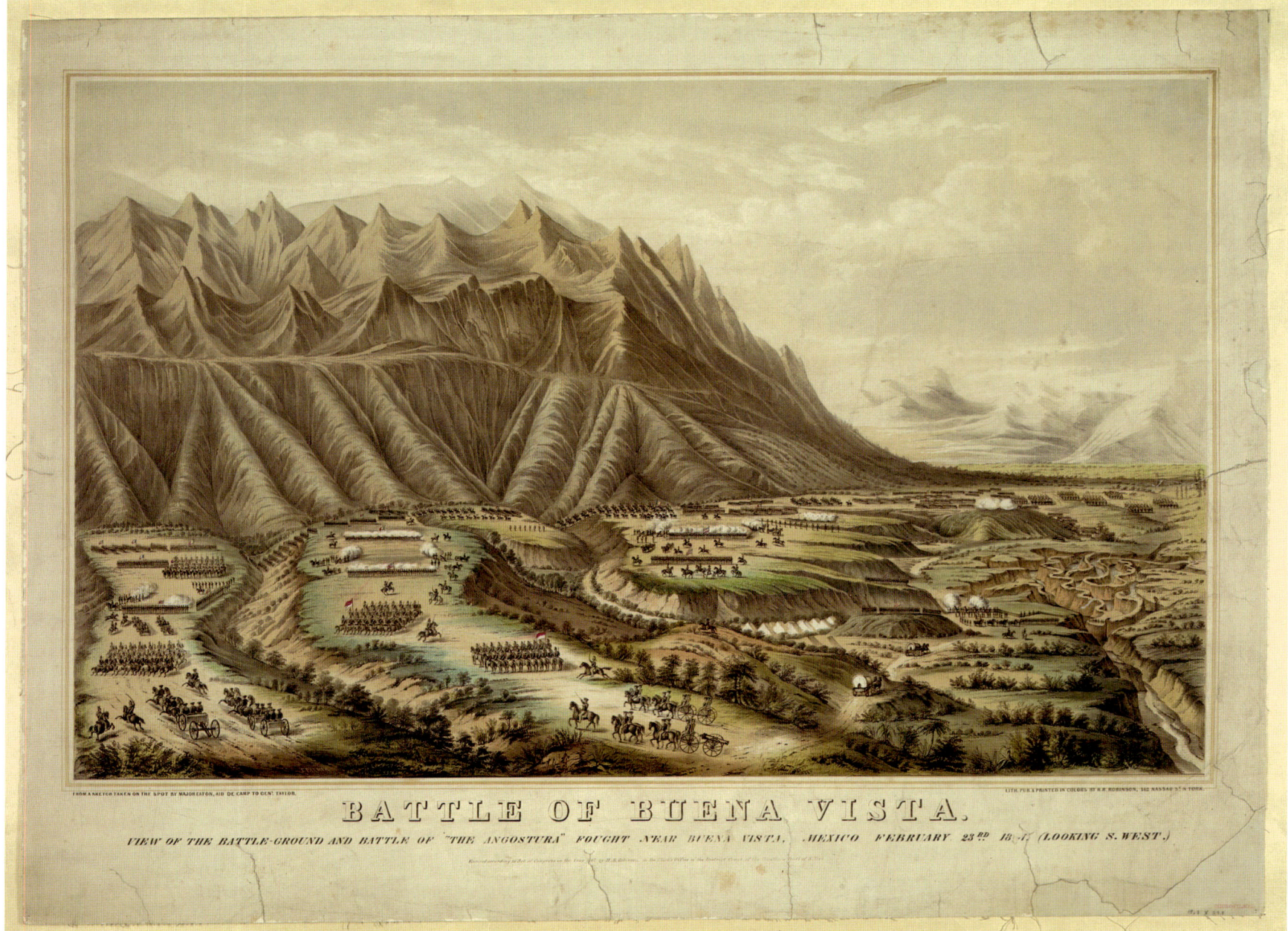

BATTLE OF BUENA VISTA.

VIEW OF THE BATTLE-GROUND AND BATTLE OF "THE ANGOSTURA" FOUGHT NEAR BUENA VISTA, MEXICO FEBRUARY 23RD 1847. (LOOKING S. WEST.)

40. *Battle of Buena Vista. View of the Battle-Ground and Battle of "the Angostura" fought near Buena Vista, Mexico February 23rd, 1847. (Looking S. West.).* 1847. Printed and published by H. R. Robinson. Courtesy of the Prints and Photographs Division, Library of Congress, LC-DIG-pga-02525. (Checklist 2-145)

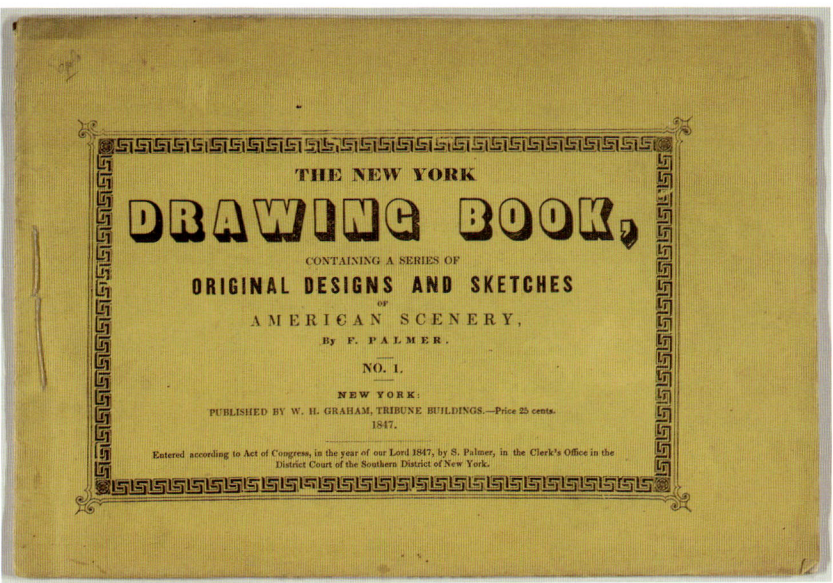

41. Cover of F. Palmer, *The New York Drawing Book*, no. 1 (New York: W. H. Graham, 1847). Courtesy of the American Antiquarian Society.

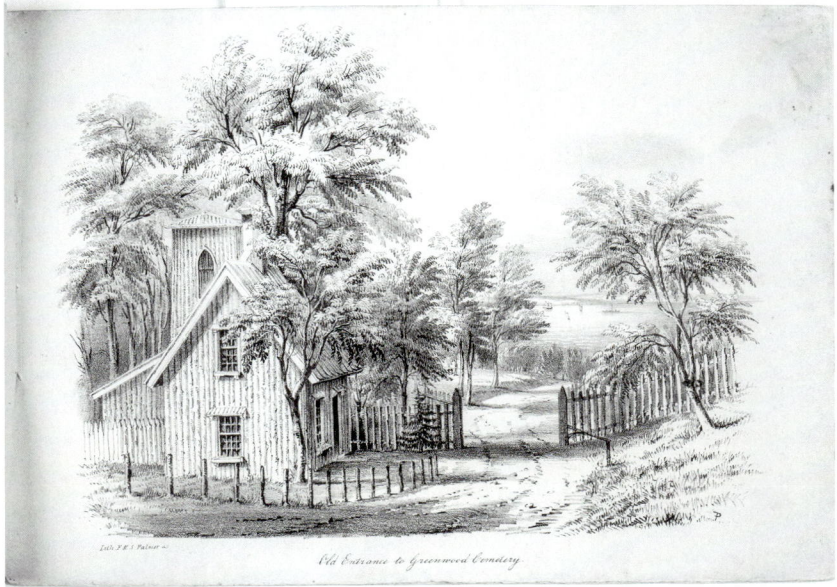

42. *Old Entrance to Greenwood Cemetery*, in F. Palmer, *The New York Drawing Book*, no. 1 (New York: W. H. Graham, 1847). Courtesy of the American Antiquarian Society. (Checklist 2-146)

F. & S. Palmer

Artists & Lithographers,
43 Ann-street, New York,
Execute every description of Lithography
in the best manner and on lower terms
than any other Establishment
PORTRAIT, ARCHITECTURAL, LANDSCAPE,
BOTANICAL, ANATOMICAL, AND MECHANICAL
DRAWINGS; MUSIC TITLES, MAPS, PLANS OF
ESTATES, RAILWAY SECTIONS, ELEVATIONS,
LAW FORMS, INVOICES, HEADS, CHECKS,
BILLS OF EXCHANGE, LABELS, FACSIMILIES,
MANUFACTURERS, PATTERN CARDS,
CIRCULARS AND WRITINGS OF EVERY
DESCRIPTION, AND IN EVERY CHARACTER.
Printing in gold and Colors,
Original Designs,
Sketches from nature and of
Residences, &c. made in every style.
Lithographic Materials, Crayons, Ink, &c.
of the best kind constantly for Sale.

The first illustration in *New York Drawing Book* number 1 is a full-page view of the "old entrance to Greenwood [*sic*] Cemetery" in Brooklyn, showing the original rustic gatehouse and picket fence before it was replaced by Richard Upjohn's massive gothic brownstone entryway. Through the half-open gate is a glimpse of the beautiful trees and one of the four lakes that continue to make this cemetery a memorable destination.

Green-Wood Cemetery was an exciting subject at that time. Modeled after the innovative Mt. Auburn "garden cemetery" in Cambridge, Massachusetts, it had opened in 1838 and immediately became one of the most popular strolling sites and burial grounds in the New York area. This was before Central Park, and, in fact, its romantic nature settings inspired Central Park. By 1866, the *New York Times* was quipping, "It is the ambition of the New Yorker to live on the Fifth-avenue, to take his airings in the [Central] Park, and to sleep with his fathers in Green-Wood."[45]

The first booklet includes vignettes of rustic cabins, a mill, a group of resting cattle, and a full-page view of Brooklyn's historic "Old Stone House" (*Sketch on the Gowanus Road, L.I.: Washington's Head Quarters*, p. 42). Erected in 1699 by one of the earliest Dutch settlers, this building was venerated in Palmer's era because it stood on the blood-soaked site of a disastrous but valiantly fought early battle of the American Revolution. The house still stands in Park Slope's Byrne Park, near the original site, reconstructed from the original stones.

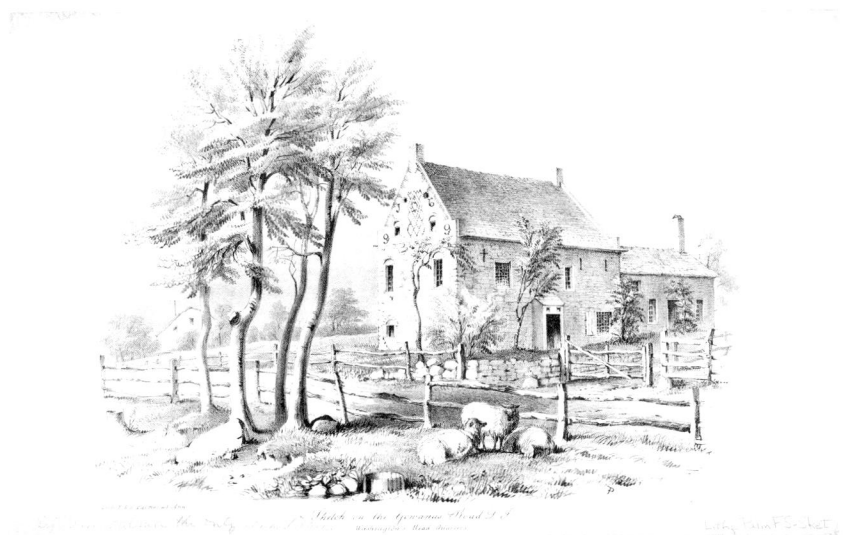

43. *Sketch on the Gowanus Road, L.I. Washington's Head Quarters*, in F. Palmer, *The New York Drawing Book*, no. 1 (New York: W. H. Graham, 1847). Courtesy of the American Antiquarian Society. (Checklist 2-149)

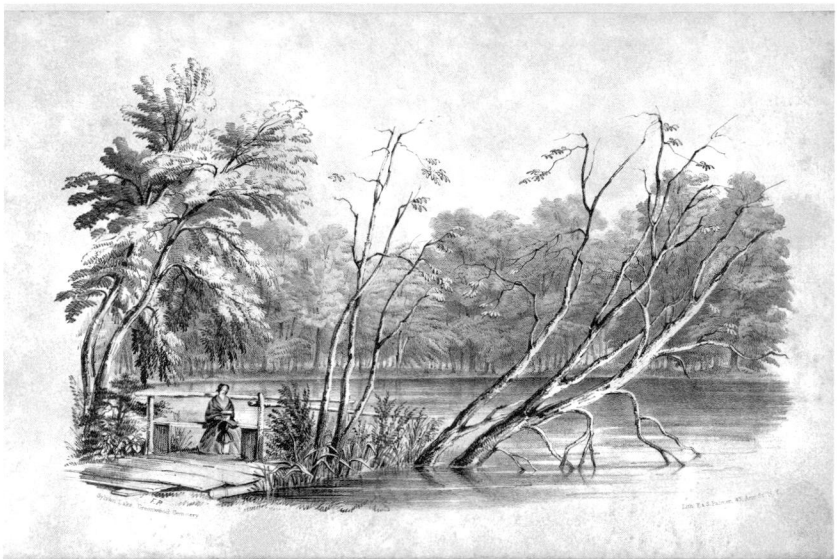

44. *Sylvan Lake. Greenwood Cemetery*, in F. Palmer, *The New York Drawing Book*, no. 2 (New York: W. H. Graham, 1847). Courtesy of the Metropolitan Museum of Art, Harris Brisbane Dick Fund, 1954. (Checklist 2-153)

The illustrations in *New York Drawing Book* number 2 continued in the style of the first booklet: idyllic views, quaint farm scenes, and, notably, Palmer's only known portrait of a woman. The first image is a landscape depicting Burdett's Landing, a wooden dock on the west bank of the Hudson River at Fort Lee, New Jersey, followed by a page of three country scenes. The Palmers returned to Green-Wood Cemetery for the booklet's final image, *Sylvan Lake. Greenwood Cemetery*, showing a woman sitting next to a standing young boy on a dock before one of the cemetery's quiet, tree-lined lakes. Although the second booklet's illustrations relied primarily on familiar subjects, the third page unexpectedly contains a half-length portrait of a young woman (p. 43). A romantic figure, the woman wears a dress of loose, flowing fabric, her long hair cascading down her bare shoulders. She clutches a bunch of flowers to her chest while looking off dreamily. The woman's proportions are unbalanced, with a small, oval head atop a long thick neck and larger body and hands that have poorly defined fingers. This image reflects Palmer's ongoing struggle to depict accurately the human figure.

Overall, though, the images in the drawing books are composed and lithographed with authority, liveliness, and charm and are imbued with the romantic landscape mood of British lithography. The vignettes are placed handsomely on the pages, with white open spaces playing through them, and the artist deftly creates a sense of distance by crisply defining details in the foreground and fading into lighter tones. Both numbers of *The New York Drawing Book* are important because they give a clear picture of the character of Palmer's original work when she wasn't copying someone else. They demonstrate that when left on her own, Palmer was a very capable artist.

Around 1847, the couple seized on additional opportunities and enlarged their eclectic repertoire still further by lithographing a number of Dr. Asa B. Strong's drawings for his botanical encyclopedia *American Flora or History of Plants and Wildflowers*. The book was so popular that it grew into four volumes, reprinted at different times by several publishers.[46] The descriptions of the plants' medical uses are amusing; a large number were purgatives, a major method of dealing with illness at that time. In order to complete such a big job speedily, the author farmed out the task of lithographing his drawings to several lithographers, including F. Michelin, W. M. Moody, and E. Whitefield. The second volume contains the Palmers' charming hand-colored frontispiece of a wreath (p. 43) and twelve botanical images (pp. 44, 273). The third volume includes four of their hand-colored images of plants as well as a frontispiece portrait of the great Swedish botanist Carl Linnaeus (p. 274), taken from an engraving of an original painting.[47] A number of the anonymous plates also look like their work. Some later editions either include their names or leave them out in an indiscriminate manner typical of the era.

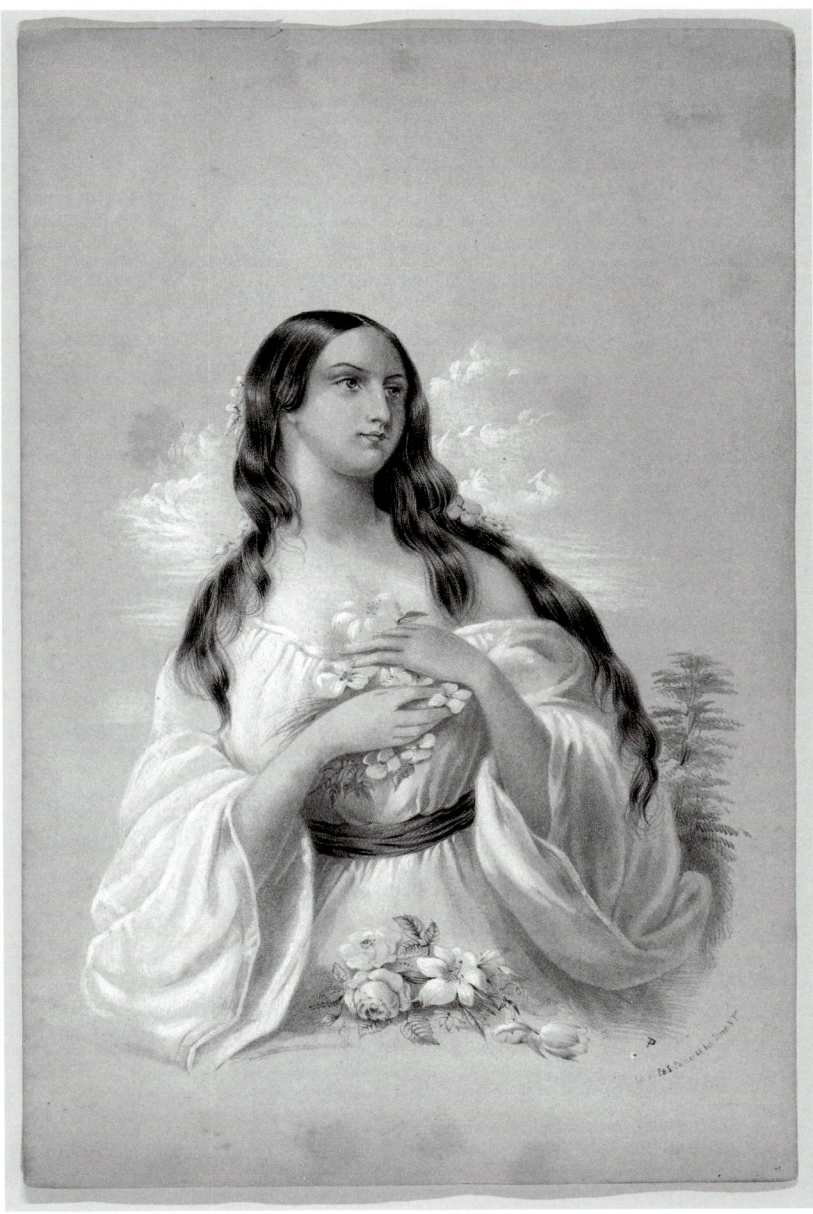

45. Page 3 of F. Palmer, *The New York Drawing Book*, no. 2 (New York: W. H. Graham, 1847). Courtesy of the Metropolitan Museum of Art, Harris Brisbane Dick Fund, 1954. (Checklist 2-152)

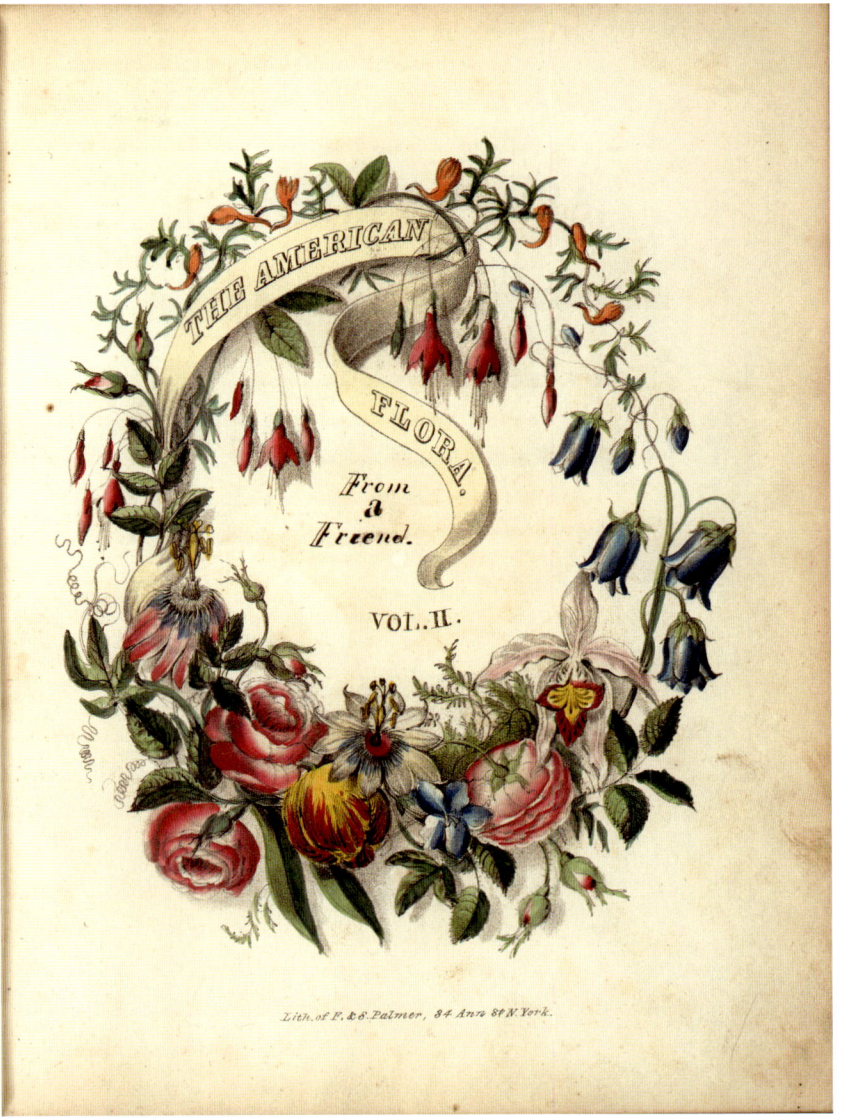

46. *The American Flora. From a Friend. Vol. II.* Illustration from *The American Flora or History of Plants and Wildflowers*, vol. 2 (New York: Green & Spencer, 1848), frontispiece. Courtesy of the Huntington Library, San Marino, CA, RB 315449 v. 2. (Checklist 2-183)

John C. Riker commissioned the couple to produce illustrations for at least four autograph albums (*Flower Tokens*, *Love and the Flowers*, *Flowers in Frolic*, and *Flowers of Loveliness*) during this time, around 1847–48. Bound in gold-embossed red, green, or brown leather and published by Riker, one of New York's finest bookbinders, such albums, often purchased as gifts for young ladies, typically included a few fanciful illustrations scattered between blank pages on which the owner, friends, and relatives could inscribe poetic, sentimental, and spiritual thoughts. The delightful images in these albums are not original; they are taken from the surreal fantasy drawings of the famous French illustrator J. J. Grandville that had been engraved as illustrations in the French book *Les fleurs animées* (1847; p. 44).[48] Each image shows one or more women morphed into the form of a flower symbolizing a human trait or emotion; for example, violets symbolize modesty, and Narcissus gazing at her own reflection in the water is vanity. These images, derived from the "language of the flowers,"

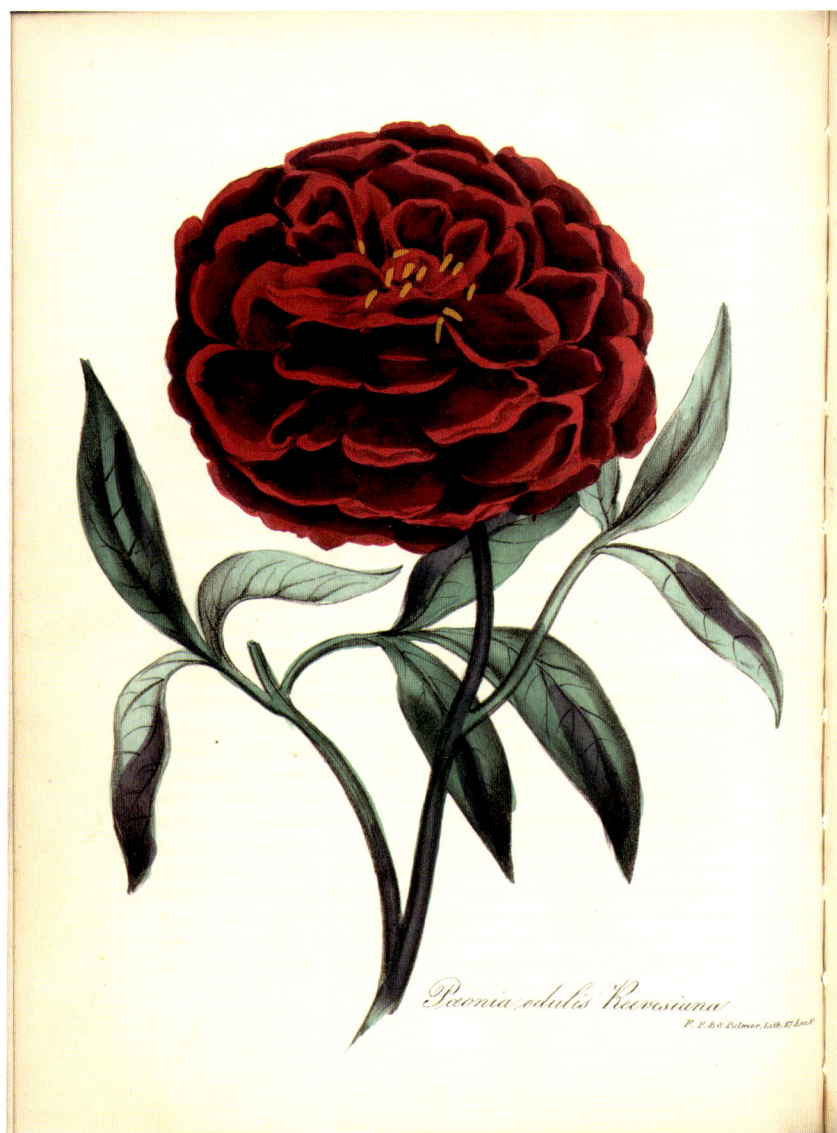

47. *Paeonia edulis Reevesiana*. Illustration from *The American Flora or History of Plants and Wildflowers*, vol. 2 (New York: Green & Spencer, 1848), between pp. 86 and 87. Courtesy of the Huntington Library, San Marino, CA, RB 315449 v. 2. (Checklist 2-200)

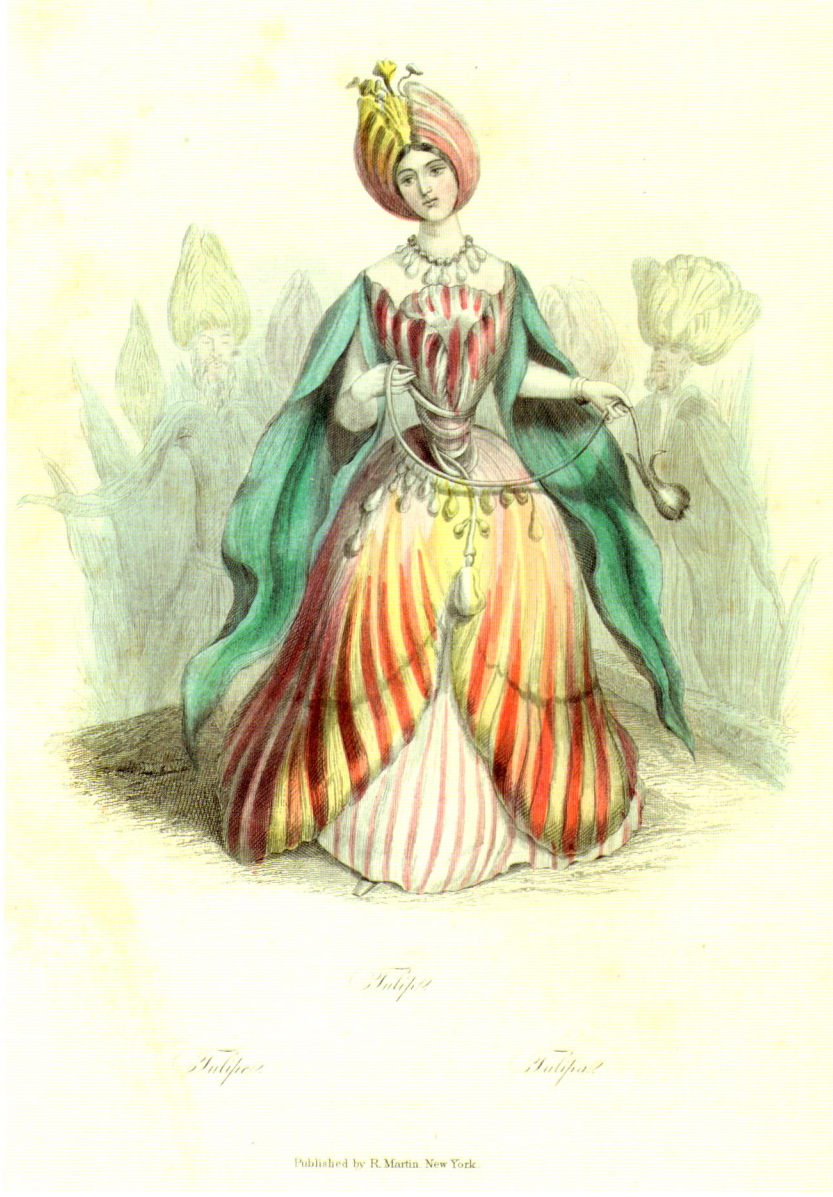

48. *Tulip*. Illustration from Nehemiah Cleaveland, trans., *The Flowers Personified: Being a Translation of Grandville's "Les fleurs animées"* (New York: R. Martin, 1847–49). Courtesy of the Huntington Library, San Marino, CA, RB 429977 v. 1.

so popular in Victorian times, became wry and satirical comments on human nature in Grandville and Palmer's hands.[49]

Palmer did not credit Grandville on her prints, nor did she claim the illustrations as her own inventions; the legend below the images simply reads, "Lith. of F. & S. Palmer, 34 Ann St." Copyright laws were weak at the time, and it was common practice for lithographers to borrow from other artists' works, especially if those works were published in another country. One must note,

however, the delicate but precise accuracy of line and tone with which Palmer adapted the engravings into lithographs, accented with discreet areas of hand-painted watercolor (p. 45).

Interestingly, in that same year author-educator Nehemiah Cleaveland, the Palmers' acquaintance, published an English translation of the Grandville book, adorned with new hand-colored steel engravings lifted from the same fantastic designs.[50] The question

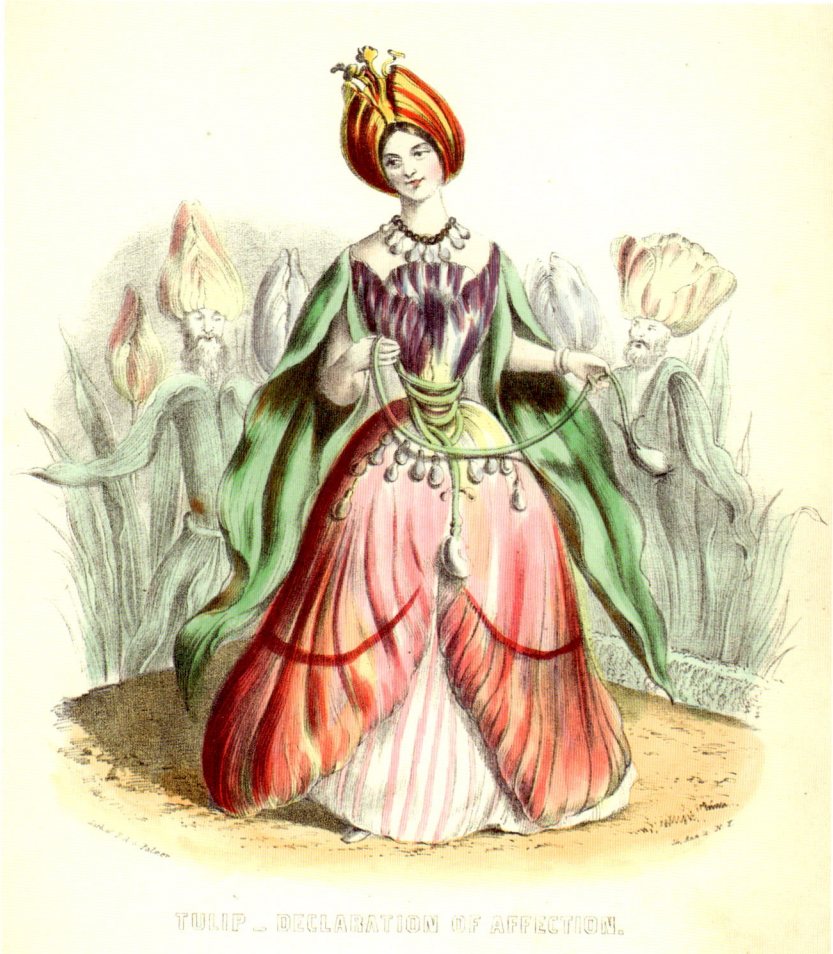

49. *Tulip—Declaration of Affection*. Illustration from *Love and the Flowers* (New York: J. C. Riker, n.d. [ca. 1847–48?]). Courtesy of the Huntington Library, San Marino, CA. (Checklist 2-176)

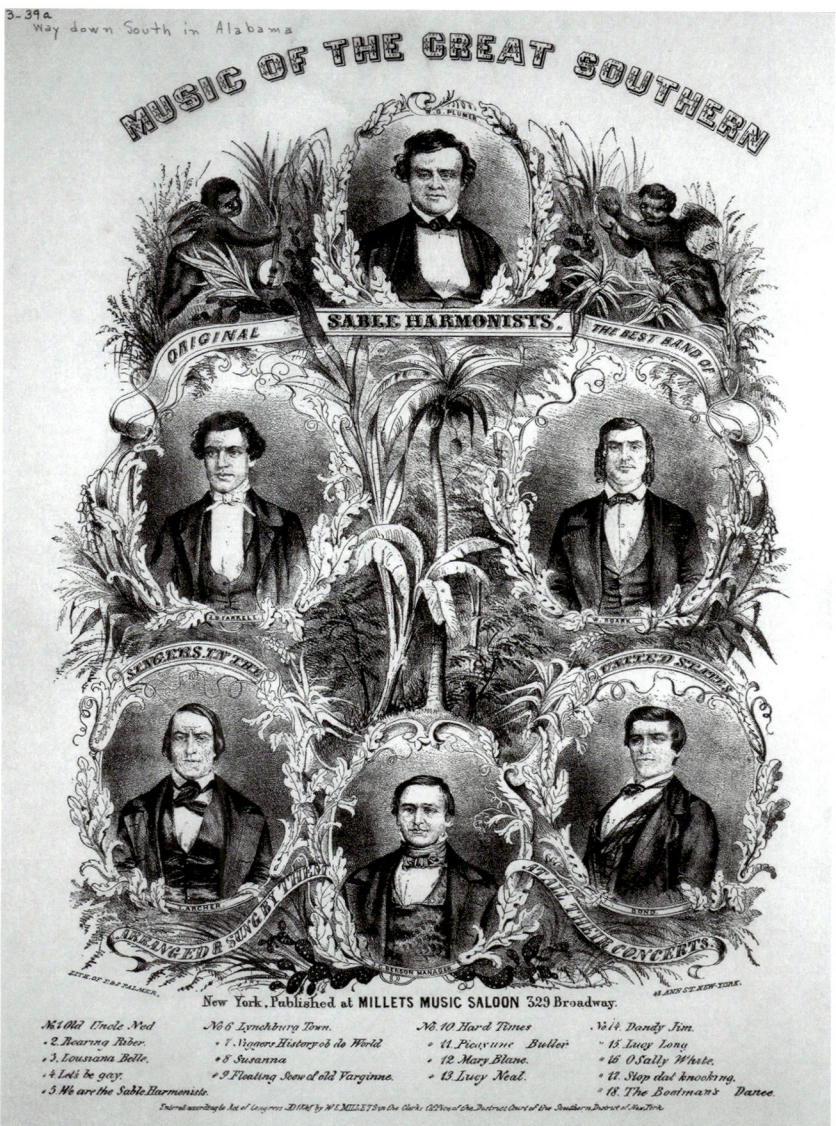

50. *Music of the Great Southern Original Sable Harmonists, The Best Band of Singers in the United States. Arranged & Sung by them at all their concerts.* 1848. Printed by F. & S. Palmer, published at Millets Music Saloon. Courtesy of the Lester S. Levy Collection of Sheet Music, Sheridan Libraries, Johns Hopkins University. (Checklist 2-203)

remains: Did Cleaveland introduce the Palmers to these enchanting images and perhaps encourage the couple to use them for their own purposes? Their paths crossed several times: Cleaveland also issued an illustrated book about Green-Wood Cemetery around the same time that Mrs. Palmer drew her picture of its front gate.[51]

A print that is interesting from a sociological point of view is a sheet-music cover for a group of minstrel singers: *Music of the Great Southern Original Sable Harmonists, The Best Band of Singers in the United States* (1848). In Palmer's print, she depicts two cherubic black angels flying overhead as the muses of the white minstrel singers below. Although her design has a more refined aura than many such designs, some of the Stephen Foster songs listed below the image sentimentalize the relationship between slaves and their masters (such as "Old Uncle Ned"). The refinement also begins to

fade when we read the title of one of the songs, "Niggers History ob de World." In contrast, a year or two later Palmer created a small head-and-shoulders portrait of the newly elected black president of Haiti, Faustin Soulouque, dressed in official regalia with military brushes on his shoulders, that would have appealed to the American antislavery crowd (*Faustin Soulouque, Président d'Haiti*, ca. 1849–50; p. 46). The French title suggests that it may have been commissioned by someone on the island.

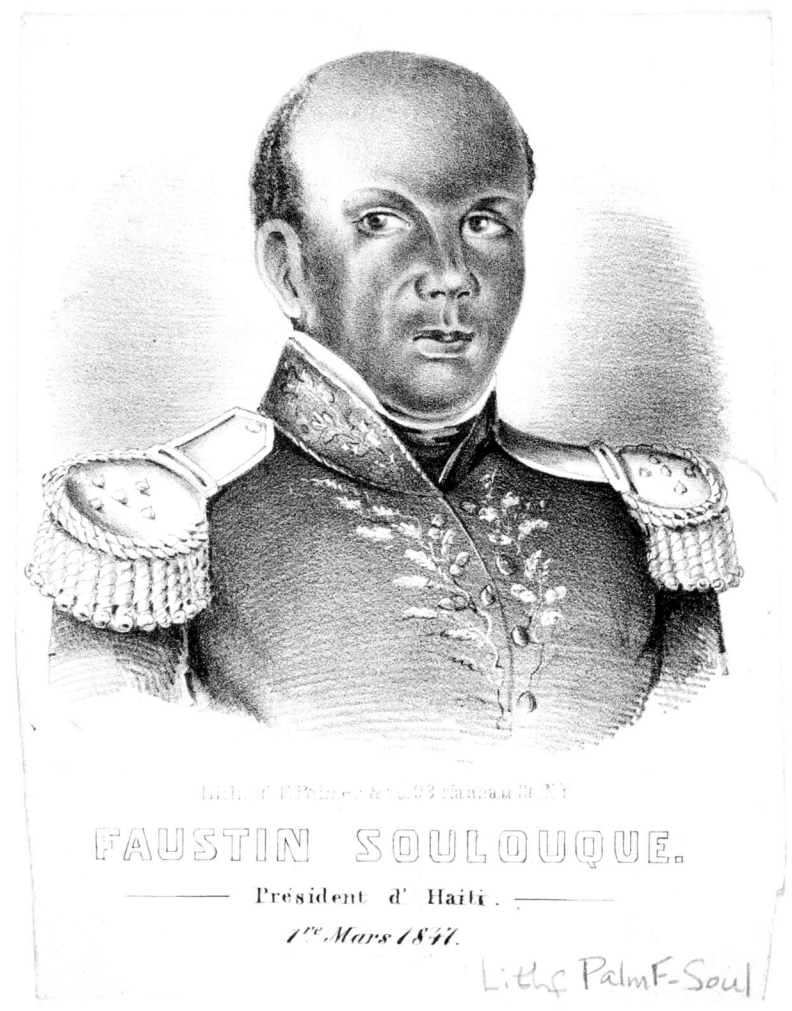

51. *Faustin Soulouque. Président d'Haiti. 1re Mars 1847.* Undated, ca. 1849–50. Printed and published by F. Palmer & Co. Courtesy of the American Antiquarian Society. (Checklist 2-211)

At this time, the Palmers were also lithographing a number of architect William H. Ranlett's illustrations for his two-volume set *The Architect, a Series of Original Designs, for Domestic and Ornamental Cottages and Villas* (1847–49; pp. 47–48, 257, 260). This was the era of the "War of the Styles," when various forms of romantic-revival architecture were competing with one another. F. F. Palmer's meticulous renderings of Ranlett's drawings, accented with a warm yellowish tint, showcase an amusingly eclectic collection of homes ranging from a rustic cottage to villas in the Anglo-Norman style, the French style, the Tudor style, the Greco-Italian style, the Italian Bracketed style—even the Persian style!

Working on these plates, Palmer became familiar with a large repertoire of Victorian architectural elements—turrets, towers, porch railings, varying rooflines, and jigsawed gingerbread ornaments—that she later put to good use when she began to create scenes of prosperous suburban life for Currier & Ives. The fine lithography and printing of these plates reveal the growing technical sophistication of both Fanny and her printer husband. Ranlett thought so highly of Palmer that he singled her out for praise in the first volume: "The volume contains 60 plates . . . the most difficult of them being executed on the stones by Mrs. F. Palmer[,] *who stands at the head of the art.* . . . The plates are from the well-known lithographic press-room of Messrs. Palmer."[52]

Ranlett's note that the most difficult plates were "executed on the stones by Mrs. F. Palmer" and the varying credit lines used by the Palmers in *The Architect* put to rest the confusion created by author Harry T. Peters when he declared in *Currier & Ives: Printmakers to the American People* that "there is no evidence that [Fanny Palmer] ever actually lithographed on stone"[53] and later in *America on Stone* that the prints by the Palmers of Ludlow Street and Ann Street and by "F. Palmer & Company" on Nassau Street were "not to be confused with Frances Flora Bond Palmer, who made so many of the Currier & Ives prints."[54]

The years 1847 and 1848 seem to have been the couple's banner years. Their work was so outstanding and prolific that the American Institute awarded F. & S. Palmer a diploma "for the second best lithography" at its annual fair in 1848. This was no mean accomplishment; within just a few years of arriving in the United States, they were being honored as second only to Sarony & Major, one of the most respected lithography companies in New York City.[55]

Ironically, it was at this very moment that the partnership of F. & S. Palmer showed the first signs of faltering. Evidence for this can be found in Ranlett's volumes. Whereas images in the first volume are signed consistently with the "F. & S. Palmer" imprint, either at 43 or 34 Ann Street, in the second volume the credit lines evolve to include "Palmer & Co.," "F. Palmer & Co.," and "F. Palmer Co." at 98 (and finally 100) Nassau Street, indicating that at a certain point Mrs. Palmer had begun to run the business under her own name and at a new address.[56] Meanwhile, the family had moved to 97 Washington Street in Brooklyn, where Edmund listed himself separately as "printer" in the Brooklyn directories of 1848–49, and Mrs. Palmer would have to commute to New York on the Brooklyn ferry.[57]

As a solo entrepreneur, Mrs. Palmer lithographed several prints under her own company name. The portrait of Faustin Soulouque,

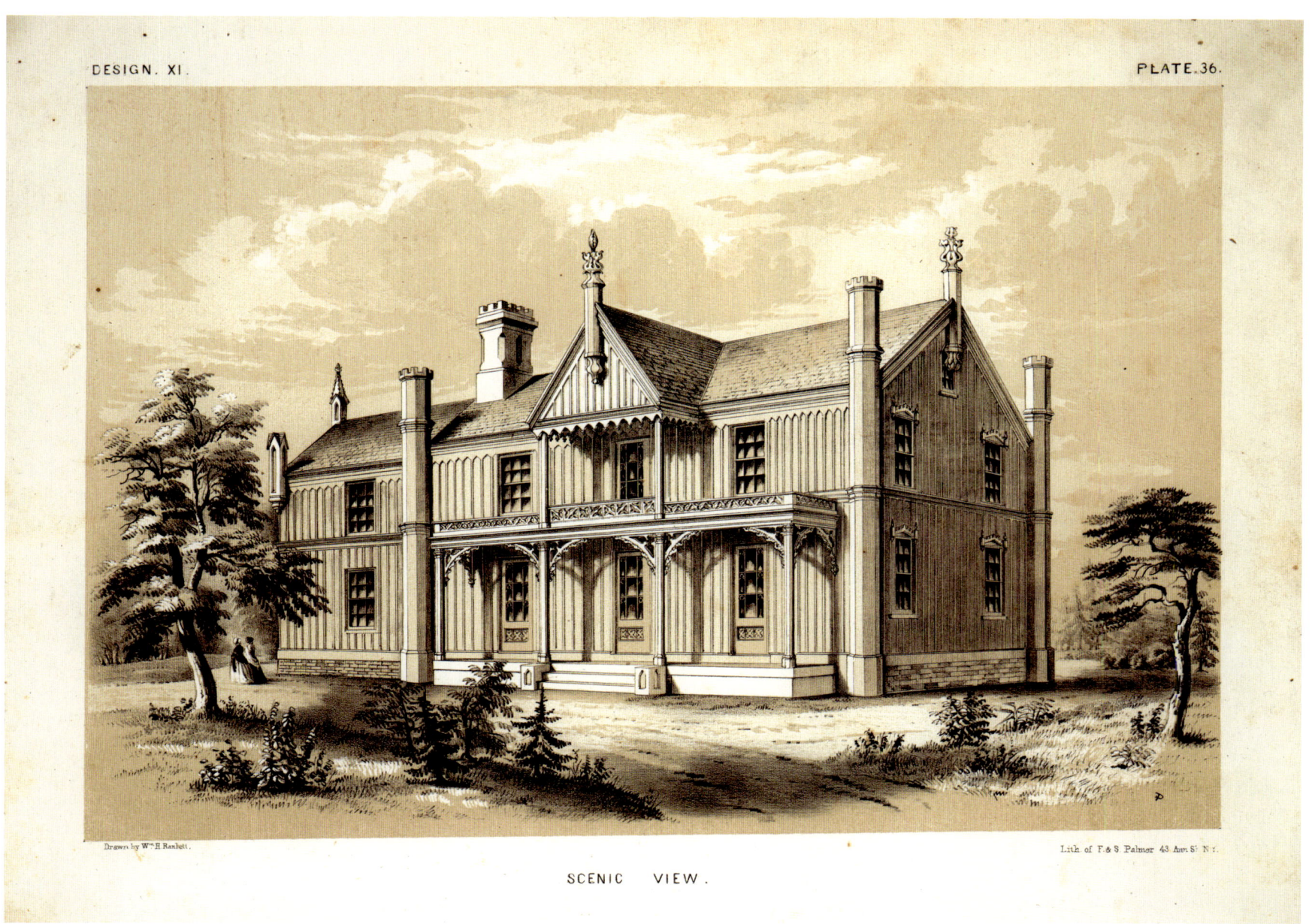

Drawn by Wᵐ H Ranlett.   Lith of F. & S. Palmer 43 Ave Sᵗ Nᵞ.

SCENIC   VIEW.

52. *Plate 36. Design XI. Scenic View.* Illustration from William H. Ranlett, *The Architect*, vol. 1 (New York: William H. Graham, 1847). Courtesy of the Huntington Library, San Marino, CA, RB 388205 v. 1. (Checklist 2-60)

mentioned earlier, is one such print. Another is an interior view of the famous Broadway Tabernacle (ca. 1849–50; p. 49). This unorthodox "free church," designed by Charles Grandison Finney, a famous evangelical pastor of liberal sympathies, was in the form of a large circular theater where he hoped to seat 2,500 people—poor and rich, black and white, together, without the customary pew payment. However, many New Yorkers were so hostile to the notion of an integrated congregation that someone set fire to the building during construction, and the Tabernacle later became the scene of bitter ideological struggle about whether the church should support abolition or not.[58]

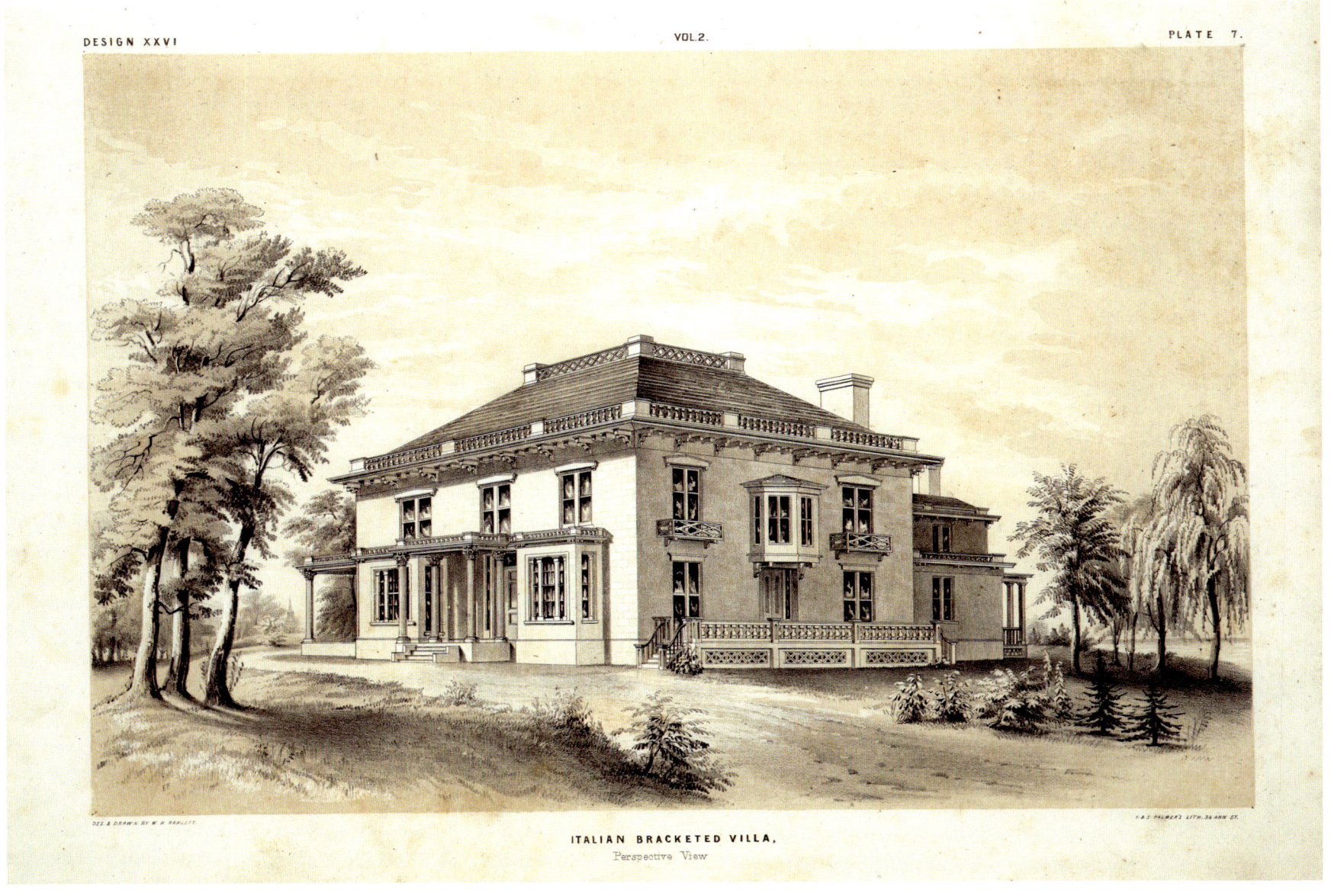

ITALIAN BRACKETED VILLA,
Perspective View

To raise income, the Tabernacle was frequently rented out for secular events. Former mayor Philip Hone wrote in his diary, "I attended, last evening, a great meeting at the Tabernacle, convened to protest against a favourite measure of the administration,—the annexation of Texas to the Union."[59] Palmer may have adapted her view of the interior architecture from a lithograph of such a secular event (*Distribution of the American Art-Union Prizes at the Tabernacle-Broadway, New York, 24th Dec. 1847* [1847]), designed by the prominent painter T. H. Matteson and lithographed by Francis D'Avignon.[60] Her print is less polished than theirs, but by reducing the size of the figures and other changes she succeeded in creating the illusion of a very large auditorium

53. *Plate 7. Design XXVI. Italian Bracketed Villa, Perspective View.* Illustration from William H. Ranlett, *The Architect*, vol. 2 (New York: Dewitt & Davenport, 1849). Courtesy of the Huntington Library, San Marino, CA, RB 388205 v. 2. (Checklist 2-91)

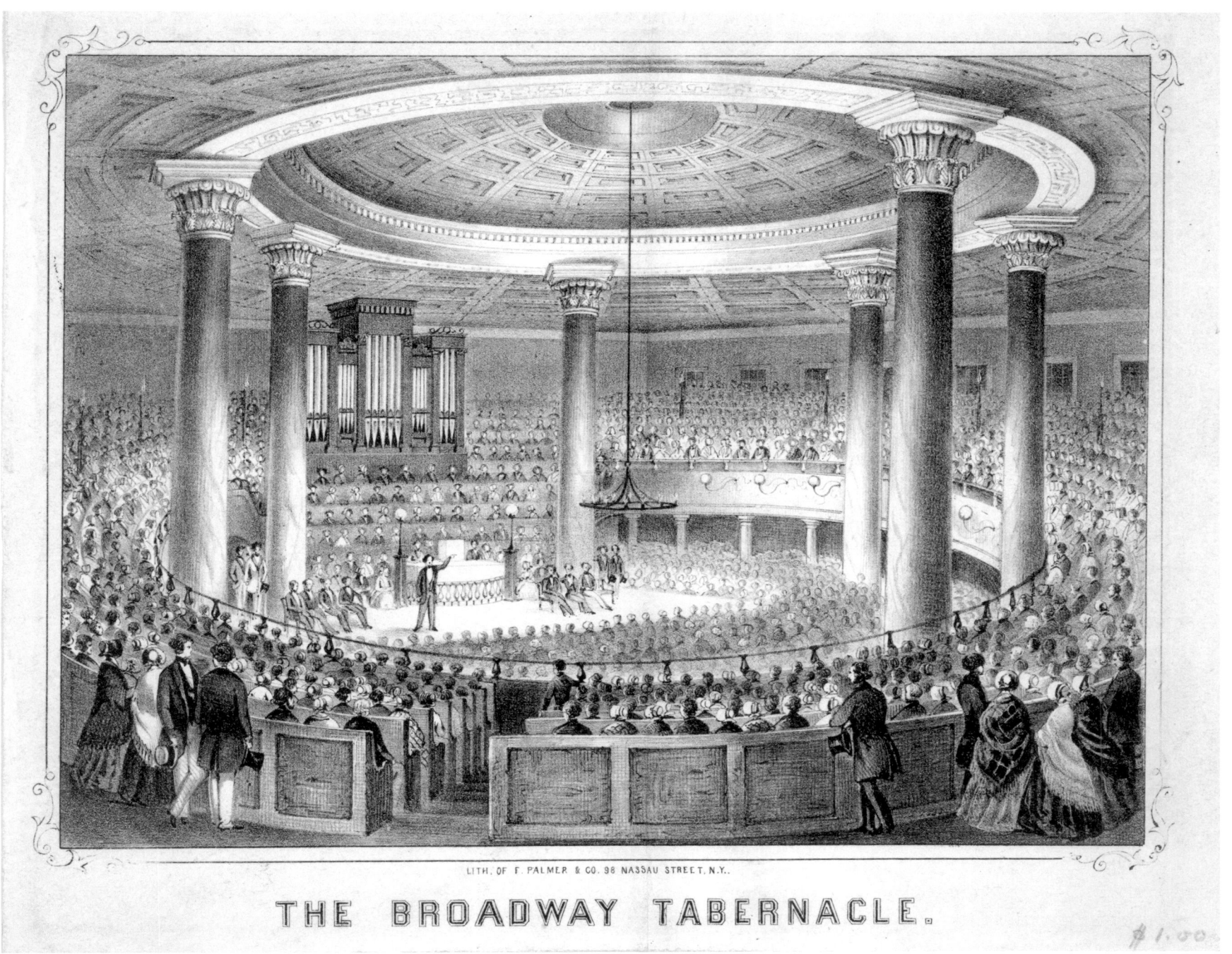

LITH. OF F. PALMER & CO. 96 NASSAU STREET, N.Y.

THE BROADWAY TABERNACLE.

54. *The Broadway Tabernacle*. Undated, ca. 1849–50. Printed and published by F. Palmer & Co. Courtesy of the Miriam and Ira D. Wallach Division of Art, Prints, and Photographs: Print Collection, the New York Public Library. (Checklist 2-210)

in which a charismatic speaker stands at the edge of the platform, holding a mesmerized audience in thrall.[61]

Precisely why Edmund and Fanny were separating their businesses at this point is still unknown. There are hints that Nathaniel Currier was already beginning to commission work from F. F. Palmer, raising prospects that she might earn more as his full-time employee than the couple had earned together in a small,

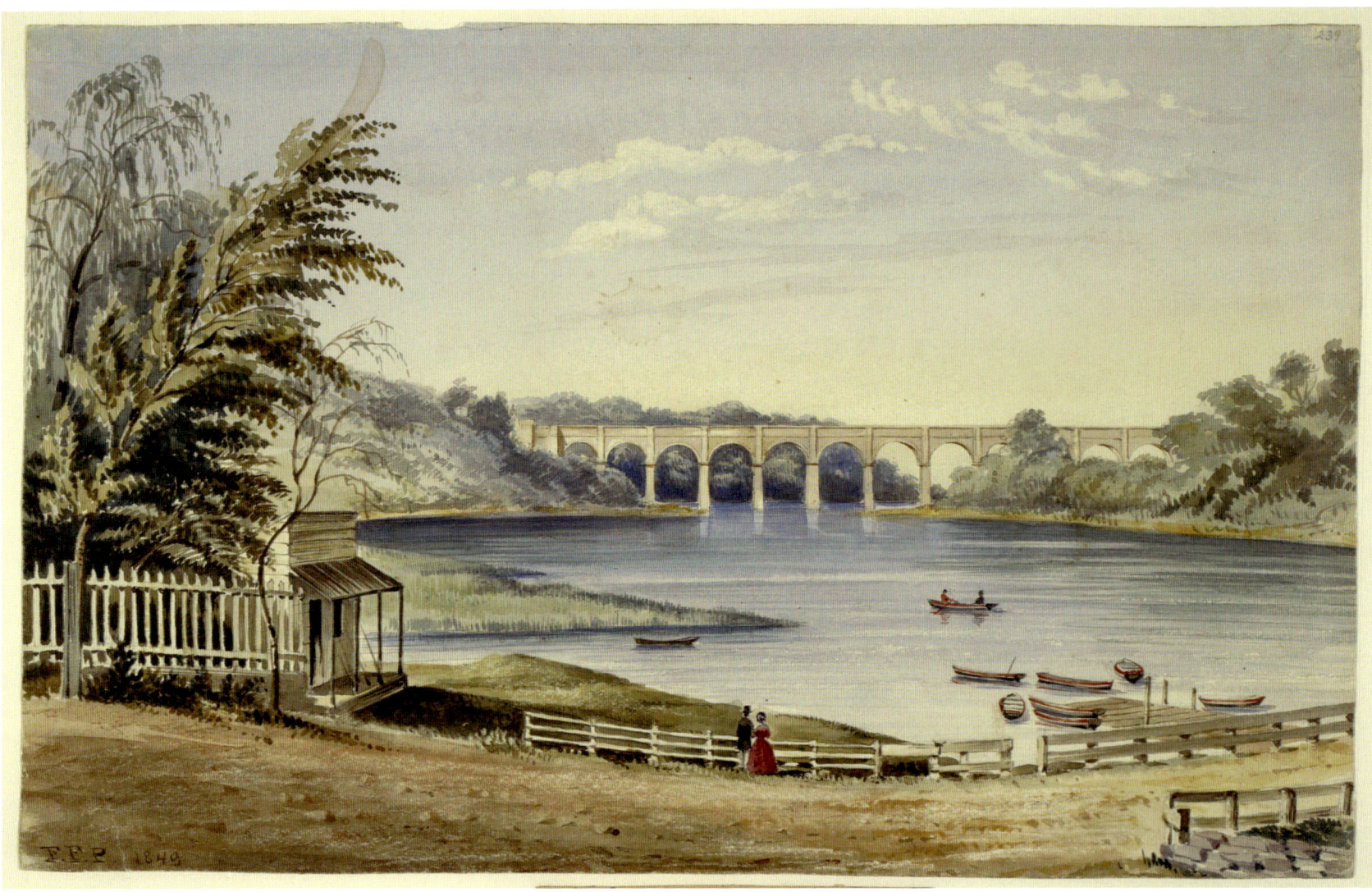

55. *High Bridge New York*. 1849. Watercolor on paper. Courtesy of the Miriam and Ira D. Wallach Division of Art, Prints, and Photographs: Print Collection, the New York Public Library. (Checklist 4-4)

struggling firm. A Currier lithograph, *The Old Stone House, L.I., 1699* (undated), closely resembles a pencil drawing she made of the same subject,[62] and the small, anonymous group of Currier prints entitled *Crayon Studies* look suspiciously like her sketches.

It is not surprising that Palmer's talent made an impression on Currier. She was now an award-winning artist whose shop was located right around the corner from his store, and her prints were being shown in the windows of local print dealers.[63] He may have dropped in to chat, or she may have approached him with samples of her work or ideas for new prints. By 1849, Currier was beginning to use Palmer's work on a regular basis. That year she painted a watercolor study of the newly constructed High Bridge (New York Public Library), taken from the approach to Macomb's Dam Bridge in the foreground. Currier added a man driving a

horse and buggy on the left and a fisherman on the right and lithographed it under the Currier label as *The High Bridge at Harlem, N.Y.* (p. 51) without crediting her for the drawing.

The new stone masonry bridge, modeled after the ancient aqueduct on the Roman Campagna, was a very exciting subject. Spanning the Harlem River in a rural area north of the city at 174th Street, it was the final link in the new aqueduct that was at last bringing an ample, safe supply of water from the Croton River to a citizenry that had long suffered from chronic epidemics of cholera

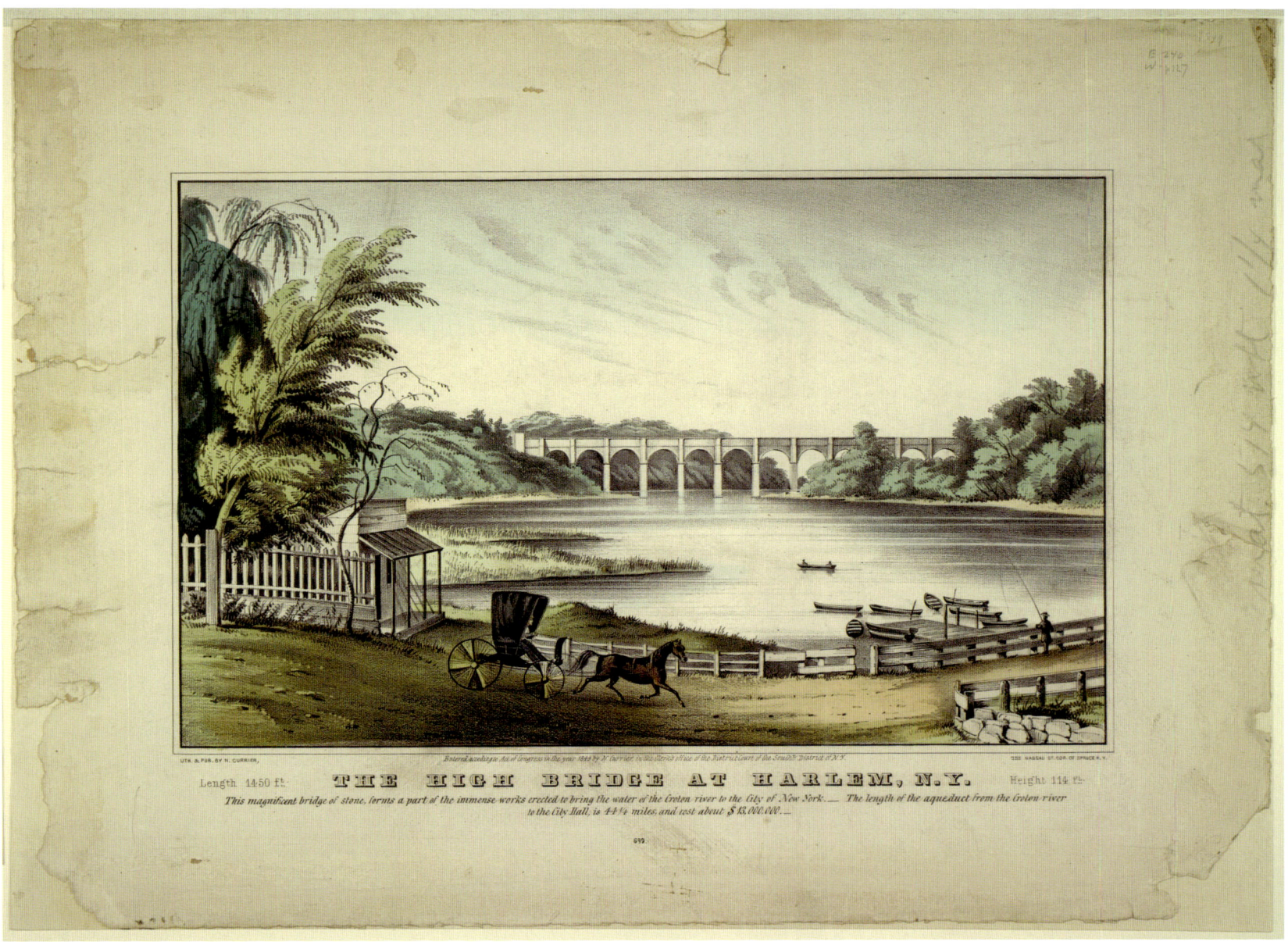

56. *The High Bridge at Harlem, N.Y.* 1849. Printed and published by N. Currier. Courtesy of the Miriam and Ira D. Wallach Division of Art, Prints, and Photographs: Print Collection, the New York Public Library. (Checklist 3A-13)

and other diseases transmitted by polluted wells and cisterns. The opening of the water system had been celebrated by the longest parade in New York history, reaching a climax when the fountain was turned on in City Hall Park. Former mayor Philip Hone wrote in his diary: "Nothing is talked of or thought of in New York but Croton water; fountains, aqueducts, hydrants, and hose attract our attention and impede our progress through the streets. Political spouting has given place to water-spouts. . . . Water! Water! is the universal note which . . . infuses joy and exultation into the masses."[64]

Soon after the bridge was completed, the pipes it carried were decked over, and it became a favorite strolling path, with

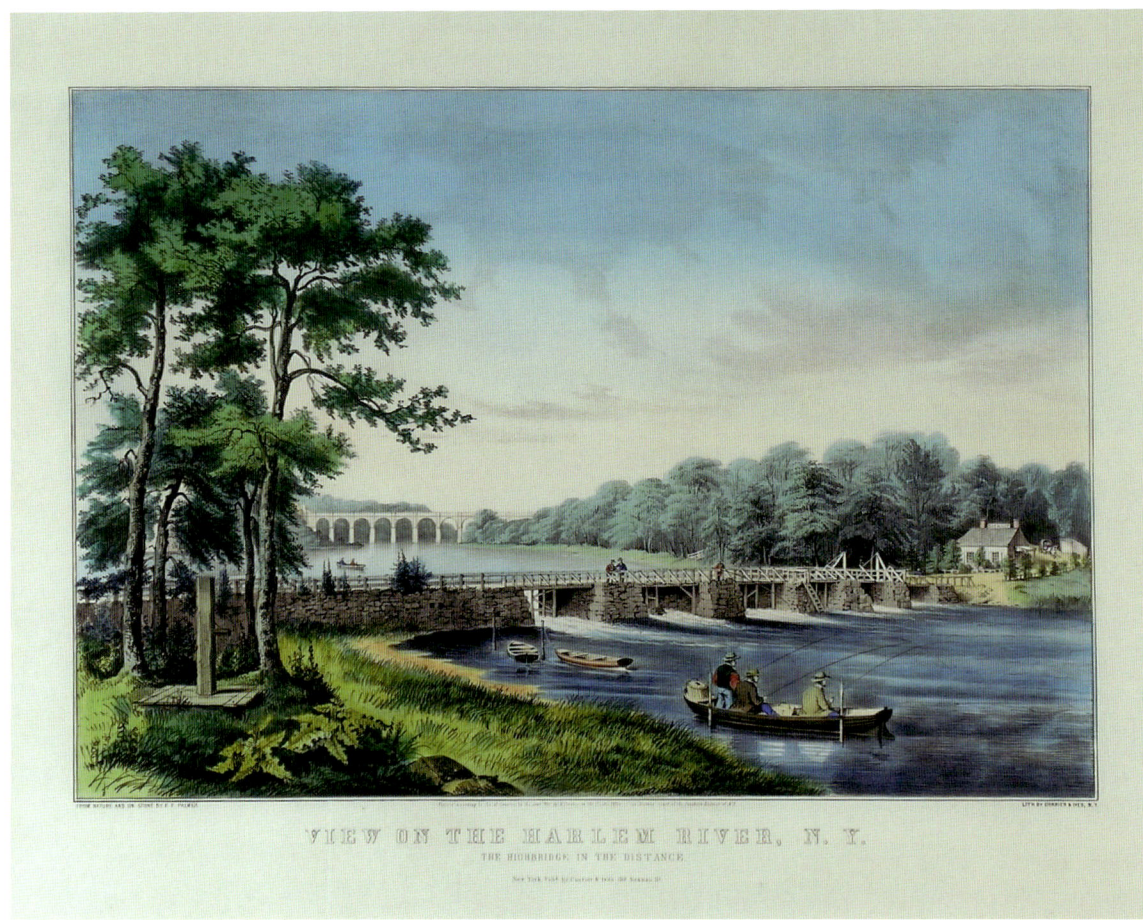

VIEW ON THE HARLEM RIVER, N. Y.
THE HIGHBRIDGE, IN THE DISTANCE.

57. *View on the Harlem River, N.Y. The Highbridge in the Distance.* 1852 [ca. 1857–72]. Printed and published by Currier & Ives. (Checklist 3-160)

parks at either end—a popular subject for artists in the following decades.[65] Palmer later included it in the background of two other Currier prints, *Bass Fishing. At Macomb's Dam Harlem River, N.Y.* (1852; gallery plate 18) and *View on the Harlem River, N.Y. The Highbridge in the Distance* (1852, ca. 1857–72), both signed "From nature and on stone by F. F. Palmer."

Although the central stone arches were later replaced with cold steel to make room for larger boats to pass under, and the surrounding area is now densely populated with apartment buildings, Palmer's print still reminds us of how rural and romantic the bridge and its setting once were. High Bridge was finally closed around 1970 for safety reasons, but a passionate group of conservationists, refusing to part with the picturesque, oldest-standing bridge in the city of New York, worked unremittingly with city and state agencies to have it restored for pedestrians and bicyclists to once more stroll across it and picnic in the parks at either end, as they did in earlier days.

The year 1849 marked a turning point in Palmer's career. Currier finally included her name below two panoramic images, *View of New York. From Brooklyn Heights* (p. 94) and *View of New York. From Weehawken* (p. 95), thus distinguishing her for the first time from the many nameless hires who cranked out anonymous prints for the company. Only a few artists received this kind of recognition.

Meanwhile, the federal census for 1850 shows that her husband had abandoned the printing trade and was working as a tavern keeper at the Abbey Hotel near the Brooklyn City Hall.[66] From this point forward, his principal role in lithography was to serve as a model for some of his wife's prints of hunters and fishermen. According to a much later and not too reliable item in the *New York Times*, the Palmer firm officially went out of business around 1851, and Currier bought out the stock.[67] At the same time, F. F. Palmer embarked on a twenty-year relationship with Currier that would carry her to the forefront of her profession.

4

The Palmers in Transition

THE PALMER FAMILY AND MARIA BOND moved to Brooklyn at a time when many of its wealthy leaders believed that their prosperous, expanding city was destined to outstrip Manhattan and become the region's dominant cultural and commercial center. Well-to-do families escaping from the crime and congestion of New York City were settling in the elegant neighborhood of Brooklyn Heights, just across the East River. As one longtime resident of Manhattan stated in 1852, he was migrating to the suburbs, "where my person and property will be safe . . . and my anxiety for the safety of my children will be entirely removed."[1]

Located on a high bluff affording a splendid view of the southeastern shoreline of Manhattan, New York's first suburb, now a National Historic District, still retains much of its charm and character. Although the Palmers were not wealthy enough to live right in Brooklyn Heights, they must have found it pleasant to stroll down the "tree-shaded streets and bluestone-paved walks lined by rows of fine old brick and brownstone houses behind decorative iron fences,"[2] built in a variety of romantic revival styles ranging from neoclassical to Romanesque and gothic.

The Palmers soon moved again from Washington Street to Smith Street,[3] near the downtown area, a neighborhood inhabited mainly by tradesmen and skilled artisans. Unlike their more successful home-owning acquaintances, they remained renters, and, like most renters, they moved frequently. Nevertheless, their financial situation seems to have improved somewhat as a result of Fanny's new position: the census of 1850 lists an "Ellen Riley," born in Ireland, living with them—undoubtedly a maid who helped with household chores.[4]

Despite their modest means, the Palmers evidently felt socially at ease in their new location. They were parishioners in the same Holy Trinity Episcopal Church that they had illustrated in a splendid print and could stroll by the Church of the Pilgrims, another church they had lithographed. They had issued a portrait of the prominent Brooklyn author-educator Nehemiah Cleaveland and

were friends of the well-known Anglo-American engraver Samuel Valentine Hunt, who settled in Bay Ridge; indeed, the Hunts and the Palmers would eventually share a grave plot at Green-Wood Cemetery.[5]

Now that F. F. Palmer was working for Currier, the Fulton Ferry made it simple to commute, when necessary, to Lower Manhattan. The ferry was, in fact, crowded with carriages and businessmen who found that it took less time to reach the financial district from Brooklyn than it had from their former uptown residences in New York City. Mrs. Palmer may occasionally have taken the same ferry as the young journalist Walt Whitman, recent editor of the *Brooklyn Eagle*, who had not yet published his odes to America, *Leaves of Grass* (1855). Both Whitman and Palmer admired the view of New York City from Brooklyn and created works of art describing it. In the years ahead, poet and artist would celebrate many of the same optimistic national themes, although Mrs. Palmer might not have regarded the bohemian Whitman as a suitable guest at her tea table.

What kind of woman was F. F. Palmer when she moved to Brooklyn and began to work for Nathaniel Currier? Author Harry T. Peters, later a friend of several elderly artists who had worked with her in their younger days, described her as "a small, frail woman with large, dark eyes and a typically English complexion, on the whole rather plain in appearance but possessing a delightful personality."[6] Louis Maurer, a colleague who joined Currier & Ives a few years after Palmer, remembered her as a "very plain, hard-working woman."[7] Mrs. Daniel W. Logan, wife of Currier's sales manager, reminisced that she "worked very hard. Was modest and subdued in dress . . . a lady-born and bred."[8] Indeed, both Fanny and her sister Maria are described by their friend Mrs. Charles Baker as "*exceedingly* refined, cultured women . . . very highly respected," who mingled with the best families in Brooklyn."[9]

Palmer and her future employer were almost the same age. Currier, a tall, slim, neatly dressed man with fair coloring and piercing blue eyes, courteous and gentlemanly—a friend of newspaper publishers, clergymen, politicians, and poets—must have been charmed by this small, genteel, but very professional woman. One senses a sympathetic bond between the somewhat introspective employer, who had worked his way up from a very poor childhood and had experienced personal tragedy (the death of his first wife and two children), and this talented artist struggling to keep her business afloat. Although Currier was a hard-driving businessman, he had a generous side; he quietly helped members of his own family and others in need. According to his nephew, he refused to allow his landlord, the American Tract Society, to drive away a poor Irishwoman ("Aunt Mary") who sold apples for a penny a piece in front of his shop and stored them in the basement. "Uncle Nat" told them "he would leave the building if they insisted on it. The matter was dropped."[10] He treated his employees with fairness and gave each one a generous gift when he retired from the company in 1880. Long after Nat Currier's death, his nephew met a former employee who told him fondly, "I'd walk on my hands and knees from the Battery to Harlem for that man."[11]

But the canny publisher never hired anyone purely out of sentiment; when it came to business, he was the soul of practicality. By this time, around 1849–50, he was thoroughly acquainted with Palmer's work and knew that she was not only a skilled draftsman and printer but also a creative artist. A respectable matron in her late thirties, a disciplined and experienced worker who had already tackled a great variety of subjects and was able to cooperate with her colleagues on every aspect of the medium, she became the firm's most versatile staff artist, whether assisting at the busy factory around the corner from the retail store or, more often, completing her assignments at home.[12]

Perhaps Currier also felt that because F. F. Palmer was a woman, she was less likely to leave and join the competition. There was a high turnover of artists and lithographers in the industry. For example, Napoleon Sarony, who did work for Currier, became a partner of Henry A. Major, one of Currier's chief competitors. Sarony ultimately became an even more serious competitor when he became a leader in portrait photography, the new medium that eventually challenged the commercial viability of lithographic prints. Both William K. Hewitt and John H. Bufford, who had worked on some of Currier's early prints, had gone to Boston, where Bufford founded his own successful company. Later, one of Currier's best artists, Louis Maurer, deciding that he could not support his future wife, Miss Sarah Stein, on a wage of twelve

dollars a week, left the company to work for twenty-five dollars at Major & Knapp, and eventually became a full partner at Heppenheimer & Co.[13]

As late as 1863, Currier told author Virginia Penny that he "cannot get enough [lithographers] in New York well qualified."[14] He also claimed that in France women had greater opportunities and were more recognized in the field; he was even thinking of importing some from that country to work for him. Of course, another advantage of hiring women was that they were expected to accept lower wages. According to Penny, Palmer earned between twelve and thirty dollars a week over the years, a decent amount for a woman in those days, but her income also included freelance assignments that she continued to carry out for a variety of other publishers.[15]

The fact that Palmer was British was no disadvantage. Lithography had first developed in Europe, and many of the best lithographers still came from abroad. Currier himself had learned to print from a French pressman at the Pendleton workshop;[16] one of his most skilled artists, Louis Maurer, had emigrated from Germany (German lithographers were particularly respected for their meticulous craftsmanship); Francis D'Avignon was Russian and French. The field was a veritable melting pot of talent.

Palmer never became an American citizen even though she spent the rest of her life in the United States. Perhaps her British upper-class origins gave her a certain cachet. Mrs. Baker reported about both Fanny and her sister: "They lived very comfortably here, but never amassed any surplus to speak of. It would have been different, of course, if the husband and son of Mrs. Palmer had not gone through everything the two women earned. No one gathered this. They suffered in silence."[17]

Fortunately, Fanny's sister Maria was enterprising. Listed as a music teacher in the Brooklyn directory, she took private pupils and at some point secured a position as a teacher of music and art at the Misses Day's girls' school in Brooklyn.[18] The women in the family enhanced their income in a variety of other ways as well: "Mrs. Palmer, Miss Bond, Mrs. Edgecombe [Fanny's daughter] went into everything artistic that was popular, such as the wax flowers, at which they could make money."[19]

Fanny's younger brother, Robert Bond, who had set himself up in Manhattan, listed his occupation as "artist" or "draughtsman" at a bewildering succession of addresses.[20] He is described as a "finished musician [in both] voice and pianoforte" as well as a landscape and still-life painter who did "very fine fruit pieces,"[21] but only a few watercolors bearing his name have thus far turned up. Robert married Mary Sutton, also from England, and in 1865 they were joined by his wife's British niece, Miss L. Shaw. According to this niece, Fanny, Maria, and Robert remained unusually devoted to one another through the years; Robert visited his sister Fanny faithfully every Sunday and often worked with her on architectural drawings.[22]

Indeed, because of the large number of prints that Palmer completed, author Harry Peters conjectured that not only Robert but also Maria and Fanny's daughter Frances must have assisted her.[23] There is, however, a much more entrepreneurial explanation for her large output. Palmer told author Virginia Penny that she had trained several young men in lithography, one of whom, after four years of apprenticeship, was paid seven dollars a week to assist her with the large number of assignments that came her way.[24] As in England, she was teaching while continuing to produce prints; she was in fact running her own small atelier. Interestingly, she appears to have never trained any women.

From this point on, the news is not good about Edmund Palmer. Fanny's colleague Louis Maurer later described Edmund as "a ne'r-do-well. Fond of pleasure, hunting, etc. and much addicted to strong drink."[25] By 1855, he no longer appeared in the business directory. According to Maria's friend Mrs. Baker, Fanny's handsome son Edmund Jr. also "fashioned himself after his father [and] was exceedingly dissipated."[26]

Perhaps it is time to reconsider the mythology surrounding F. F. Palmer and her menfolk. In those days, any middle-class married woman who had to earn money to help support her family was an object of pity, and her husband would have been regarded as an irresponsible wretch. The recollections of people who had known Fanny Palmer are colored by these Victorian mores. For example, Mrs. Baker reported that "Miss Bond and Mrs. Palmer were the bread earners of the family. They toiled incessantly—particularly Mrs. Palmer on her lithographs. I think she tried to drown or forget the sorrow her husband and son caused her by constant work at her art." However, when asked whether she had actually ever heard Fanny complain, Baker admitted that "she suffered in silence . . . always cheerful."[27] Interestingly, though, in a firsthand contemporary account, Palmer sounds quite unlike a silently suffering wife: "She has spent twenty-two years in lithographing—seventeen of them in this country. . . . She thinks one must have the talent of an artist, and great practice with the pencil, to succeed. . . . She thinks there will be employment to a few

well qualified. She has always been kept busy. The employment is not more unhealthy than any other of a sedentary kind."[28]

This is not the voice of a downtrodden laborer but rather of a quietly self-confident professional who may have chosen her career as much because she wanted it as because of financial pressures. "One must have the talent of an artist, and great practice with the pencil to succeed" is a modest way of saying, "*I* have the talent of an artist and great practice with the pencil, and that's why *I* have succeeded." And, indeed, she did succeed. Her sister-in-law's niece, Miss L. Shaw, who knew Fanny from the 1860s on, remembered that she had so much work that she sometimes had to turn jobs away.[29]

As for Mr. Palmer, in all fairness he did work as a printer during their early years—a trade requiring skill and hard labor—and their business relationship seems to have been unusually egalitarian for the era. Together they won recognition from the American Institute for their work and were mentioned with respect in the introduction to Ranlett's book on domestic architecture. Although Edmund Seymour Palmer, "gentleman," tried to continue on his own as a Brooklyn printer and then became a tavern keeper, he may have found it very difficult to compete in the hurly burly of mid-nineteenth-century America.

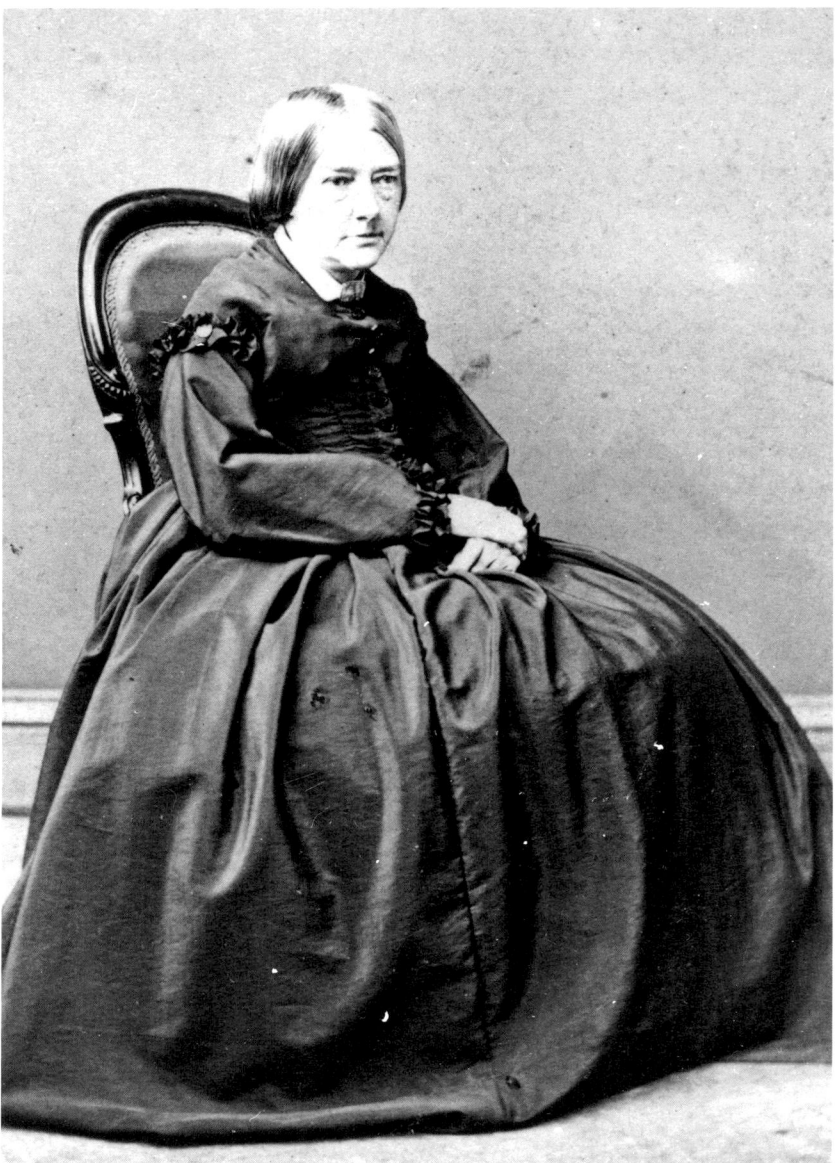

58. Frances ("Fanny") Flora Bond Palmer, ca. 1865. This is the only known image of Fanny Palmer. Harriet Endicott Waite Papers. Courtesy of the Archives of American Art, Smithsonian Institution.

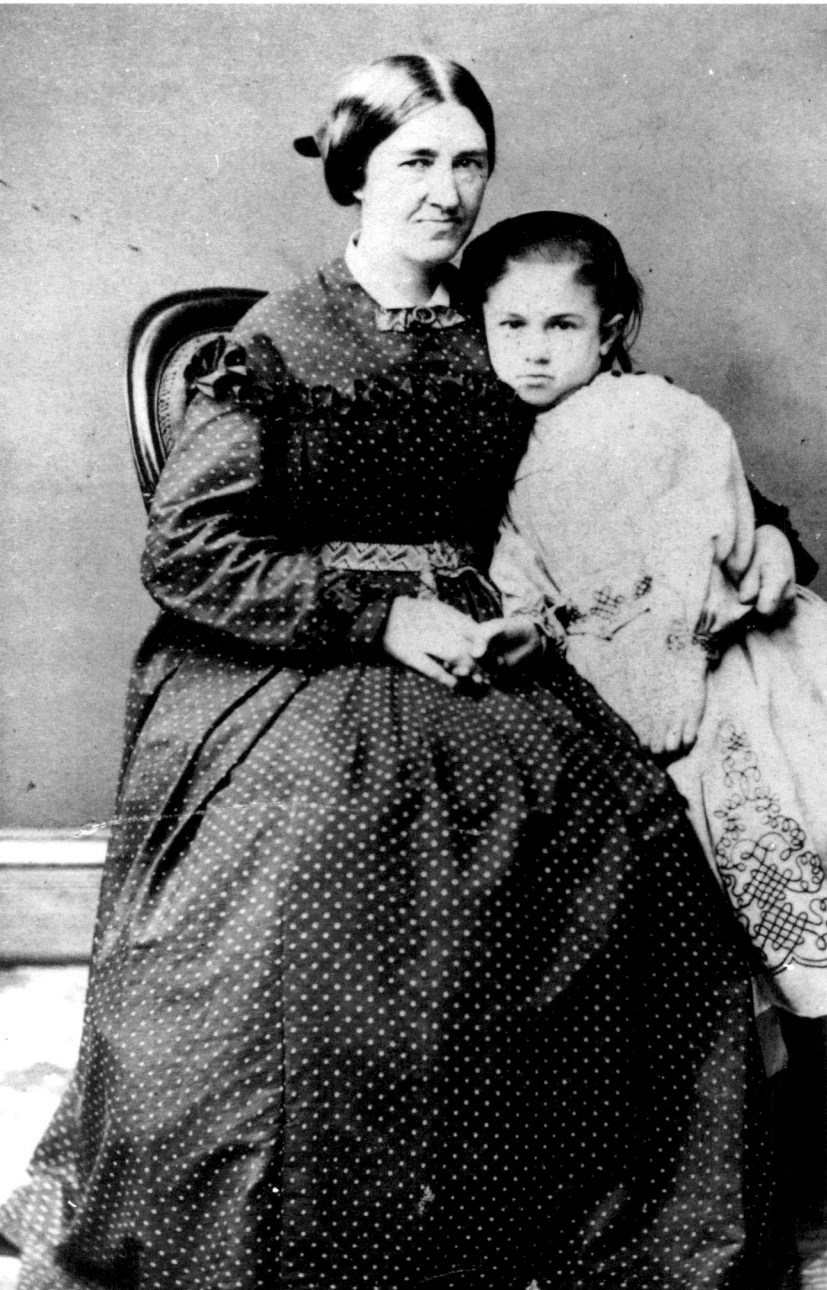

59. Maria P. Bond with grandniece Maria F. Mary Edgecombe, ca. 1865. Harriet Endicott Waite Papers. Courtesy of the Archives of American Art, Smithsonian Institution.

A Gallery of Prints
by Fanny Palmer

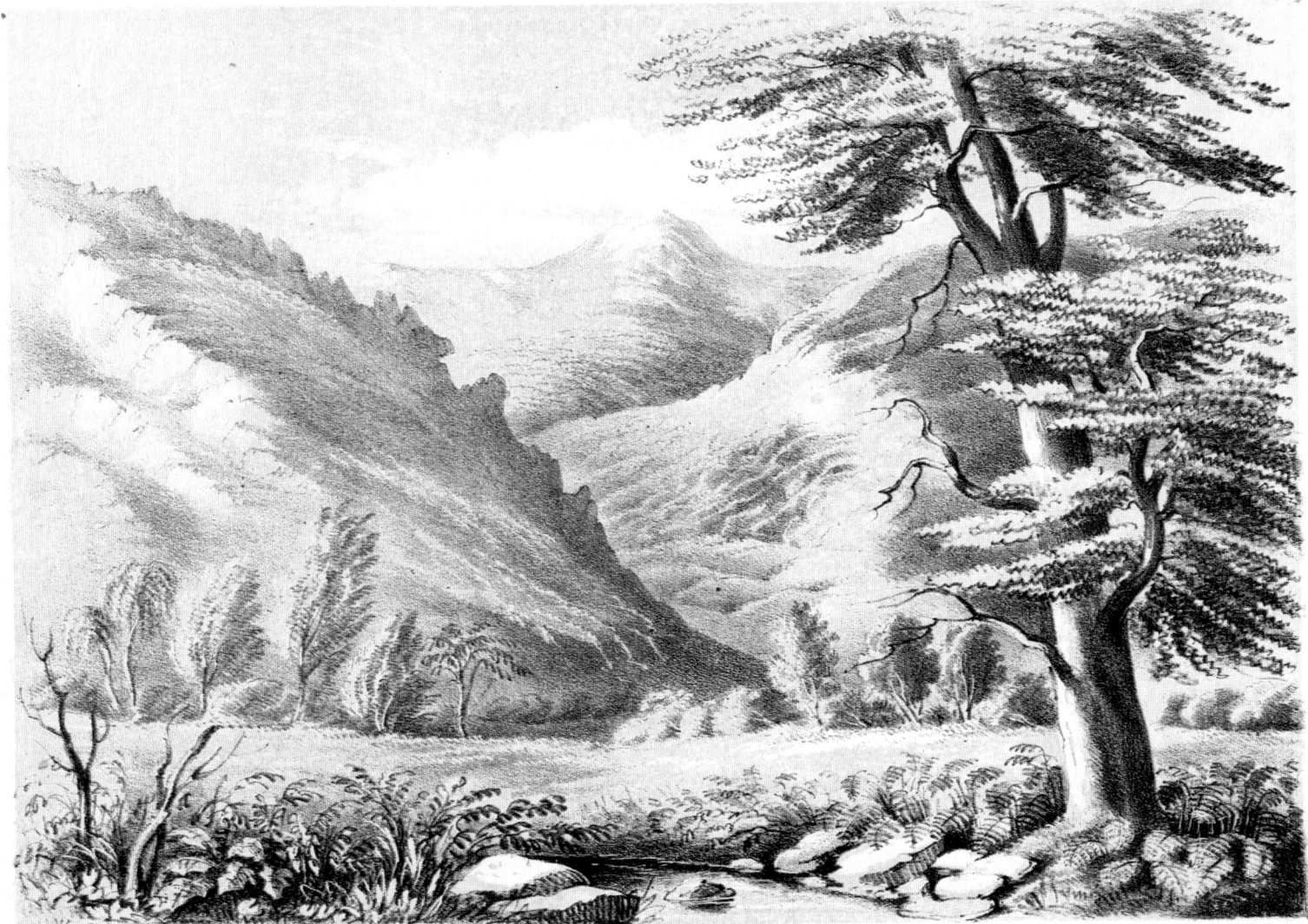

F F Palmer, litho.   Printed by ... Palmer, Leicester

HIGH CADEMAN.

Gallery plate 1
High Cademan. Illustration from T. R. Potter, *The History and Antiquities of Charnwood Forest* (London: Hamilton, Adams, Nottingham, UK: R. Allen; Leicester, UK: E. Allen, 1842). Courtesy of the Huntington Library, San Marino, CA, DA670.C44 P8. (Checklist 1-15)

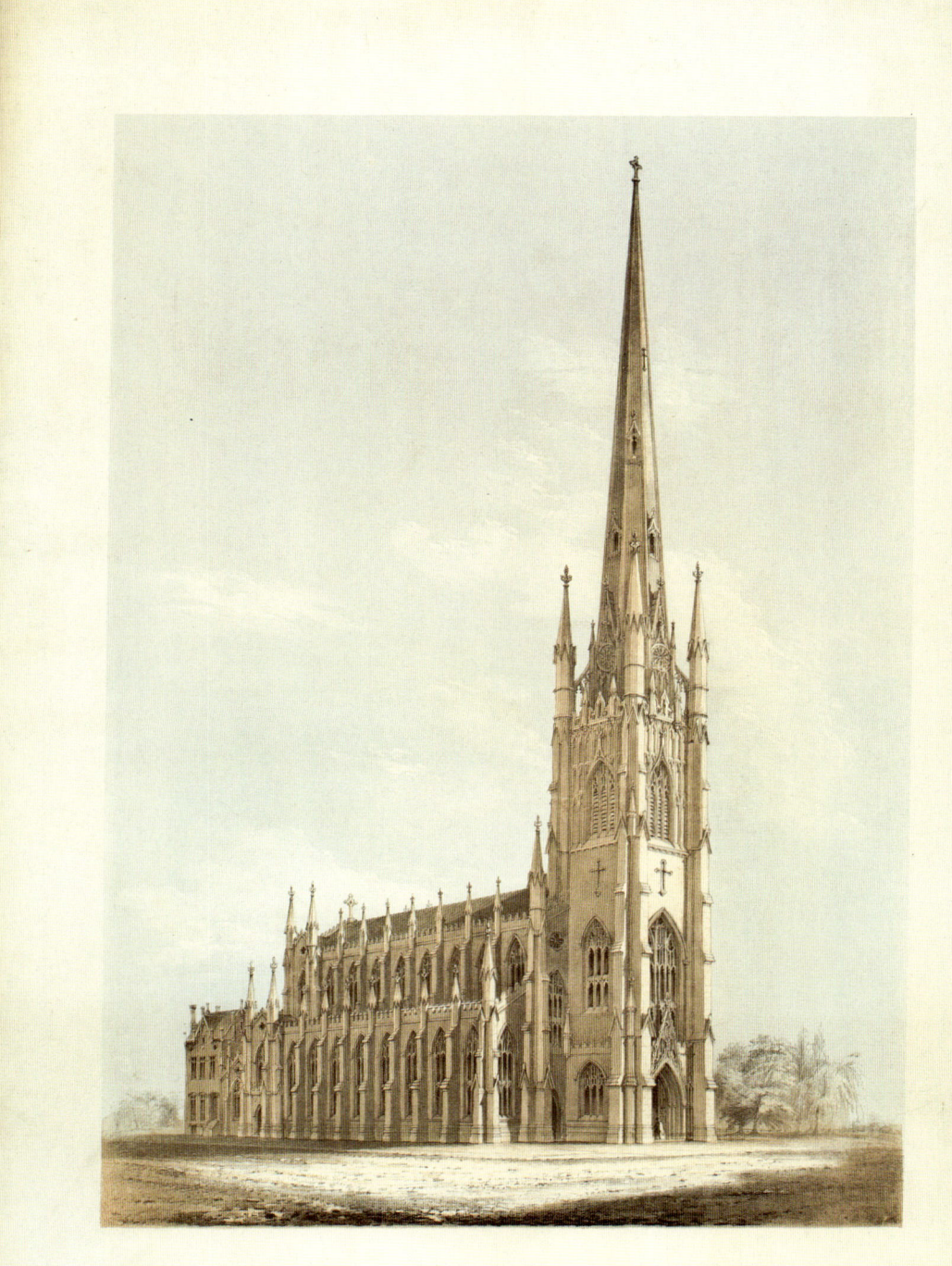

CHURCH OF THE HOLY TRINITY.

BROOKLYN HEIGHTS.

MINARD LAFEVER ARCHT.

Gallery plate 2
Church of the Holy Trinity. Brooklyn Heights. Minard Lafever Archt. 1845. Printed and published by F. & S. Palmer. Courtesy of the American Antiquarian Society. (Checklist 2-10)

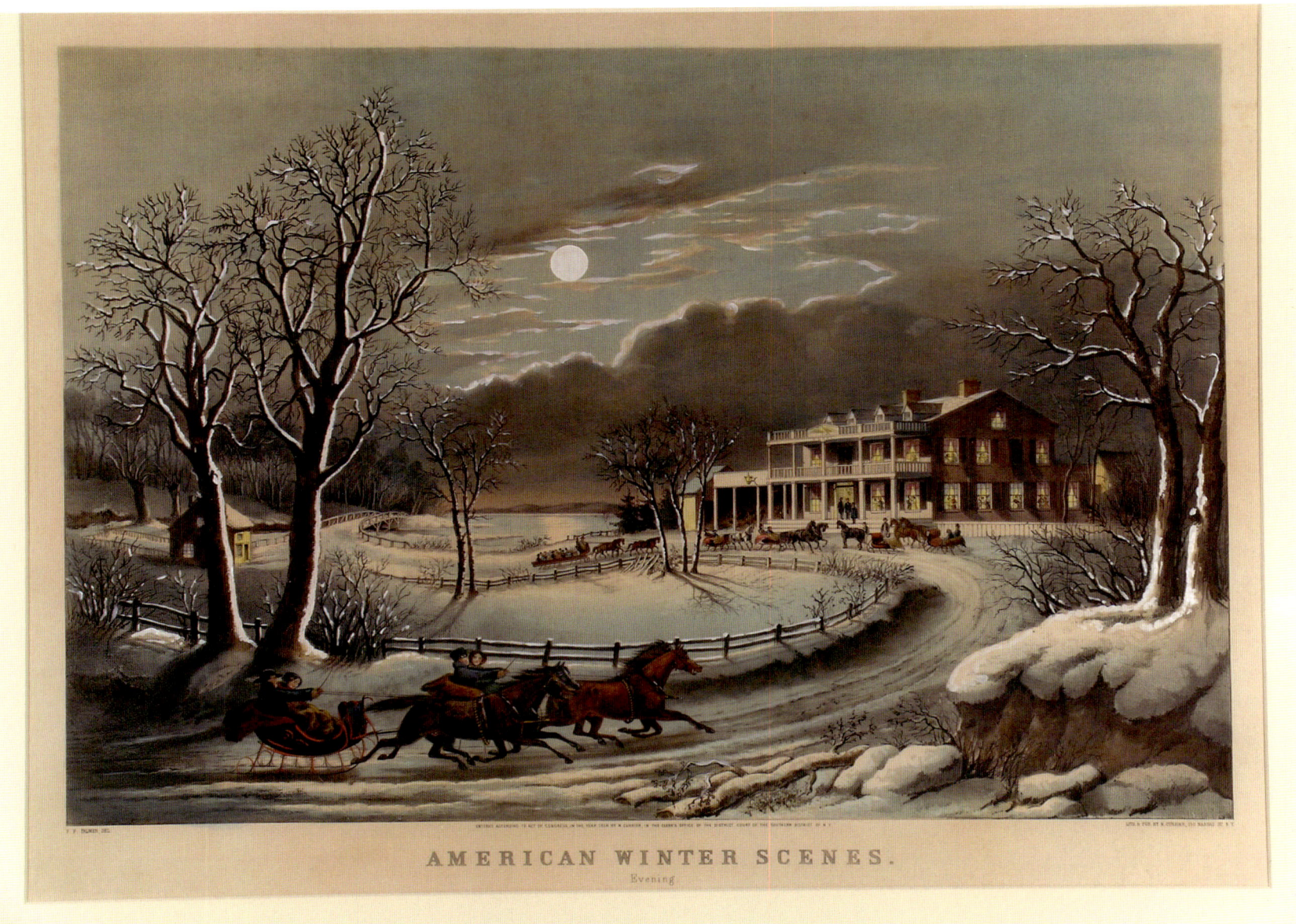

AMERICAN WINTER SCENES.

Evening

Gallery plate 3
American Winter Scenes. Evening. 1854. Printed and published by
N. Currier. (Checklist 3-19)

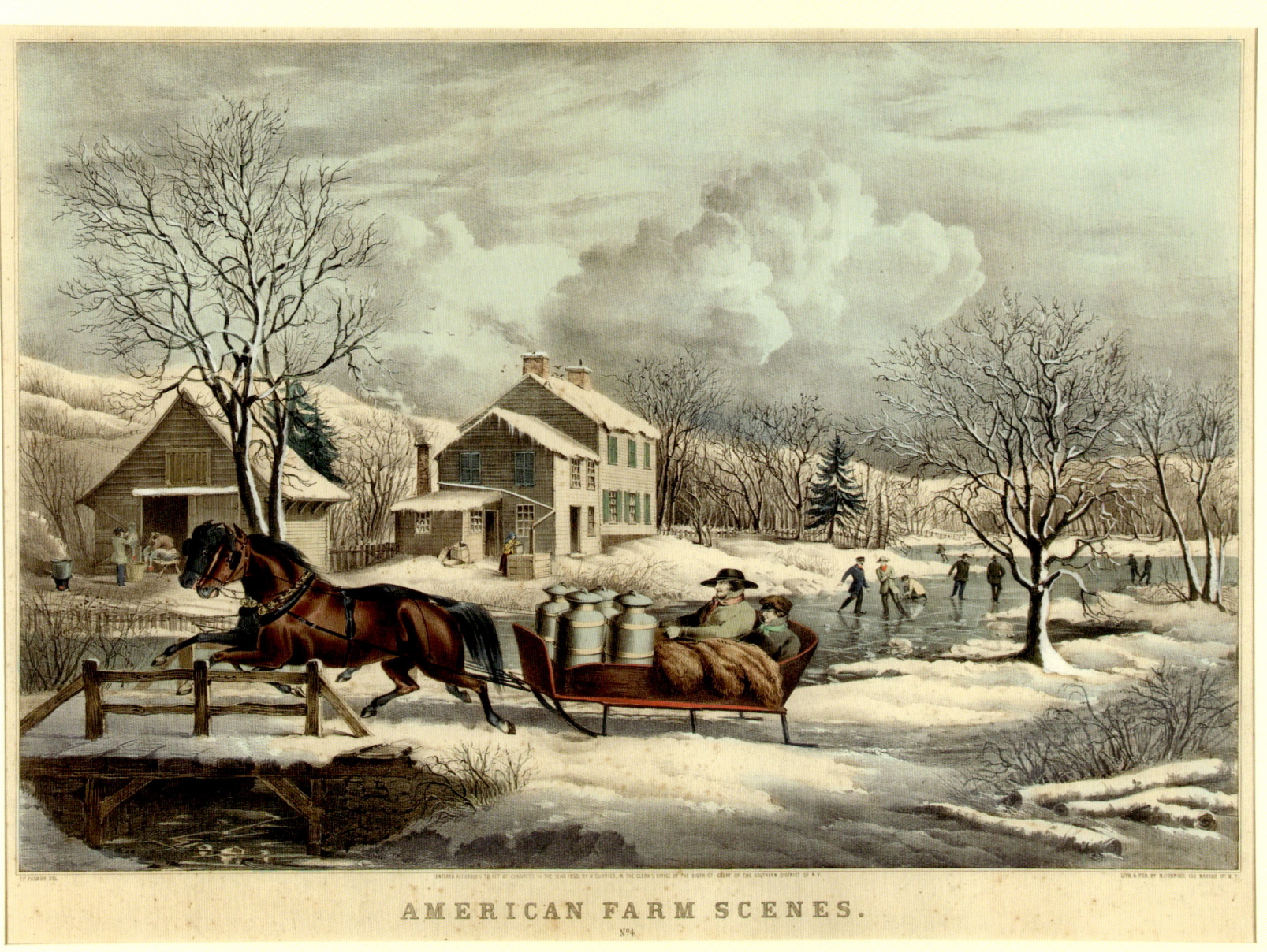

AMERICAN FARM SCENES.

Nº4

Gallery plate 4

American Farm Scenes. No. 4. 1853. Printed and published by N. Currier. Courtesy of the Yale University Art Gallery. (Checklist 3-12)

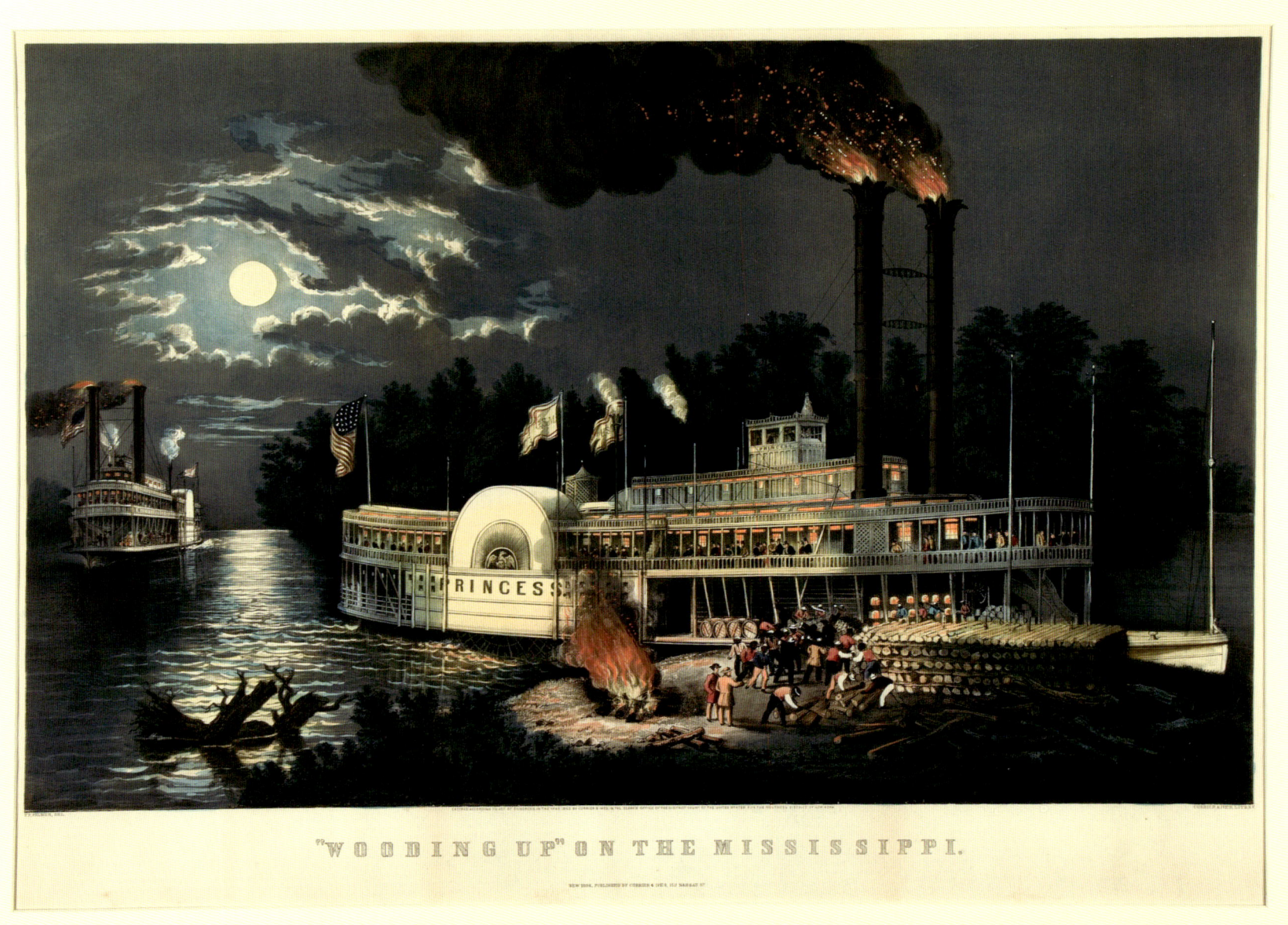

Gallery plate 5
"Wooding Up" on the Mississippi. 1863. Printed and published by
Currier & Ives. Courtesy of the Yale University Art Gallery. (Checklist
3-176)

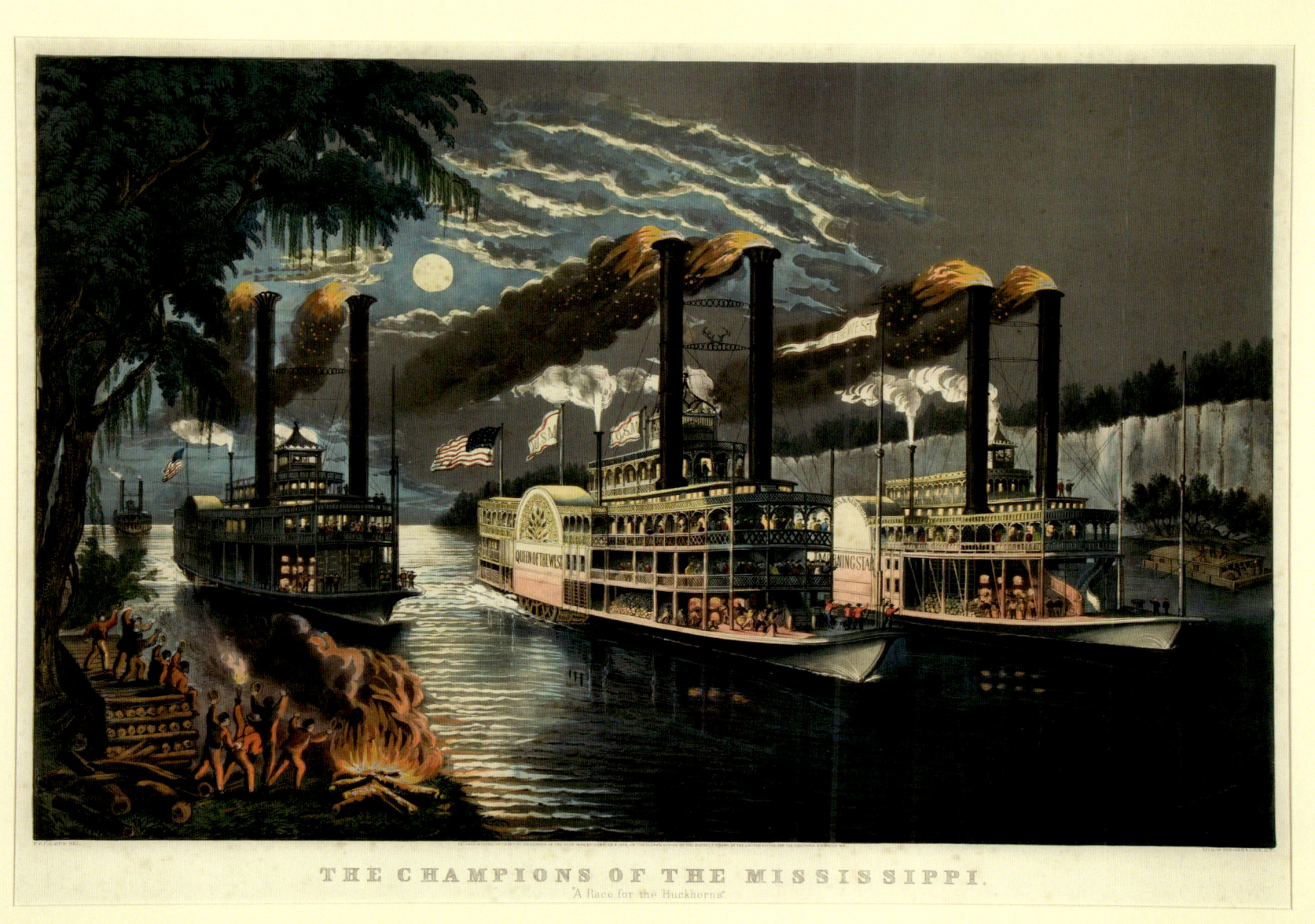

Gallery plate 6
The Champions of the Mississippi. "*A Race for the Buckhorns.*" 1866.
Printed and published by Currier & Ives. Courtesy of the Yale University Art Gallery. (Checklist 3-27)

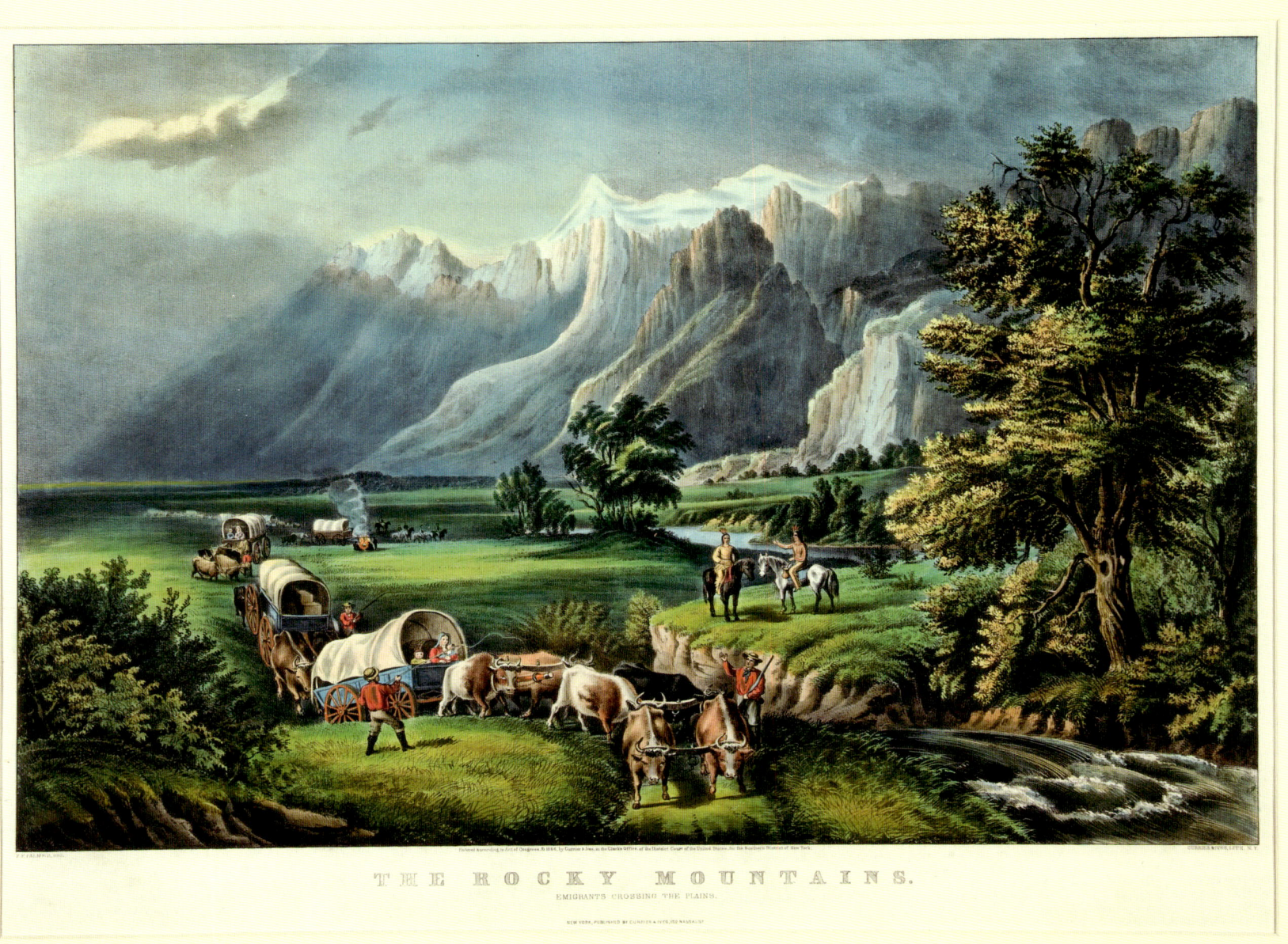

Gallery plate 7
The Rocky Mountains. Emigrants Crossing the Plains. 1866. Printed
and published by Currier & Ives. Courtesy of the Yale University Art
Gallery. (Checklist 3-117)

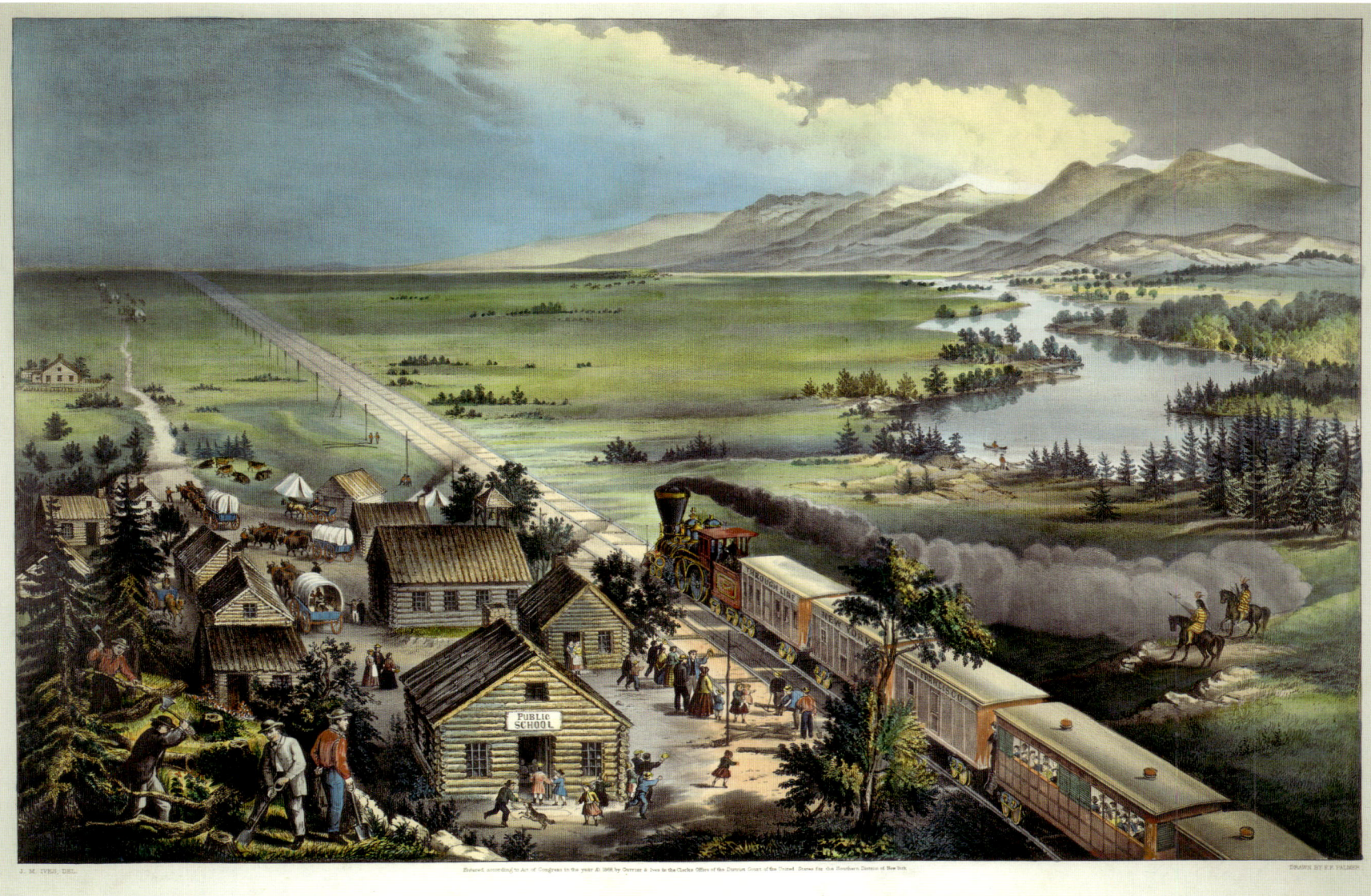

ACROSS THE CONTINENT.
"WESTWARD THE COURSE OF EMPIRE TAKES ITS WAY."

Gallery plate 8
Across The Continent. "Westward the Course of Empire takes its way." 1868. Printed and published by Currier & Ives. Courtesy of the Yale University Art Gallery. (Checklist 3-1)

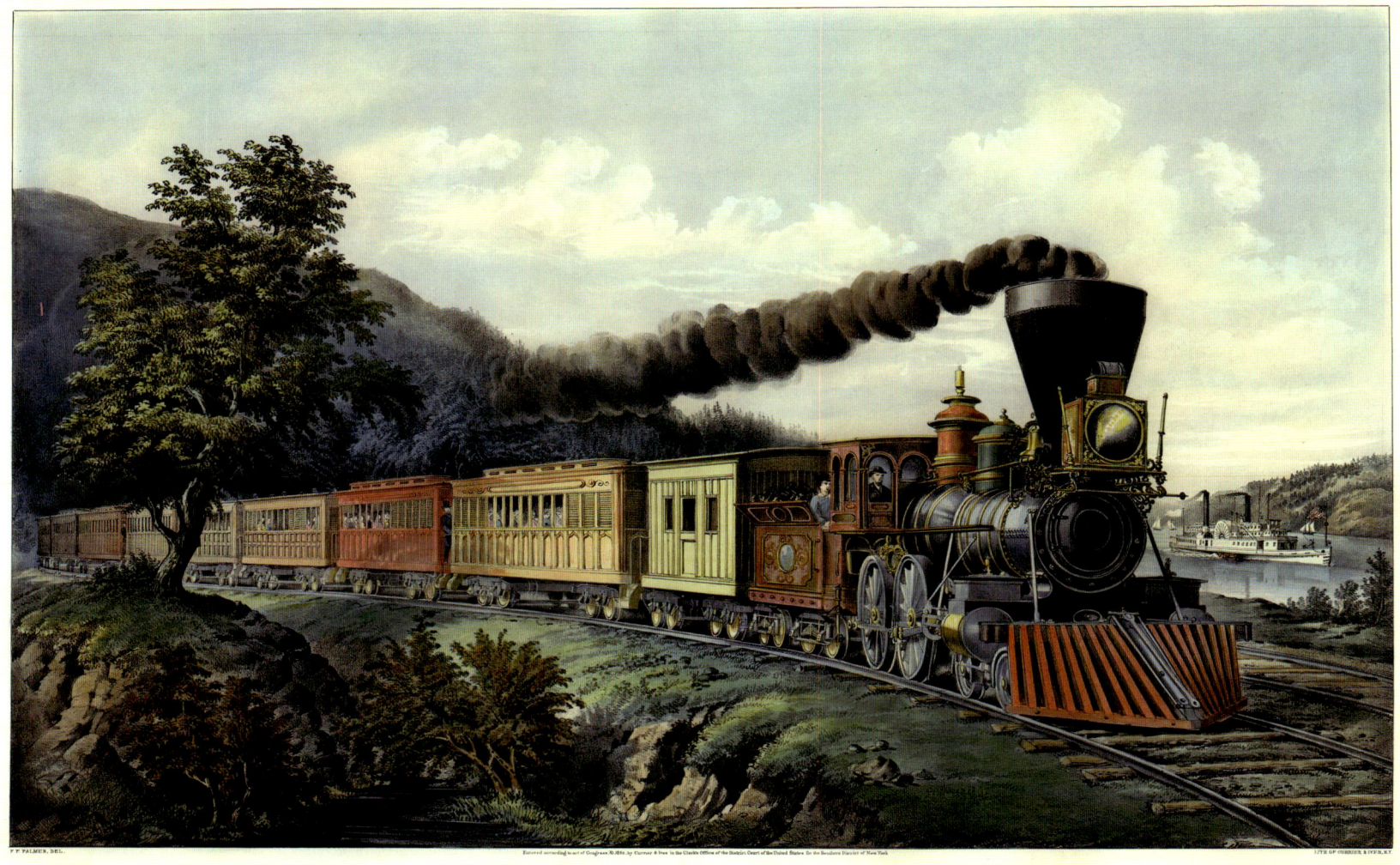

AMERICAN EXPRESS TRAIN.

Gallery plate 9
American Express Train. 1864. Printed and published by Currier &
Ives. Courtesy of the Old Print Shop. (Checklist 3-8)

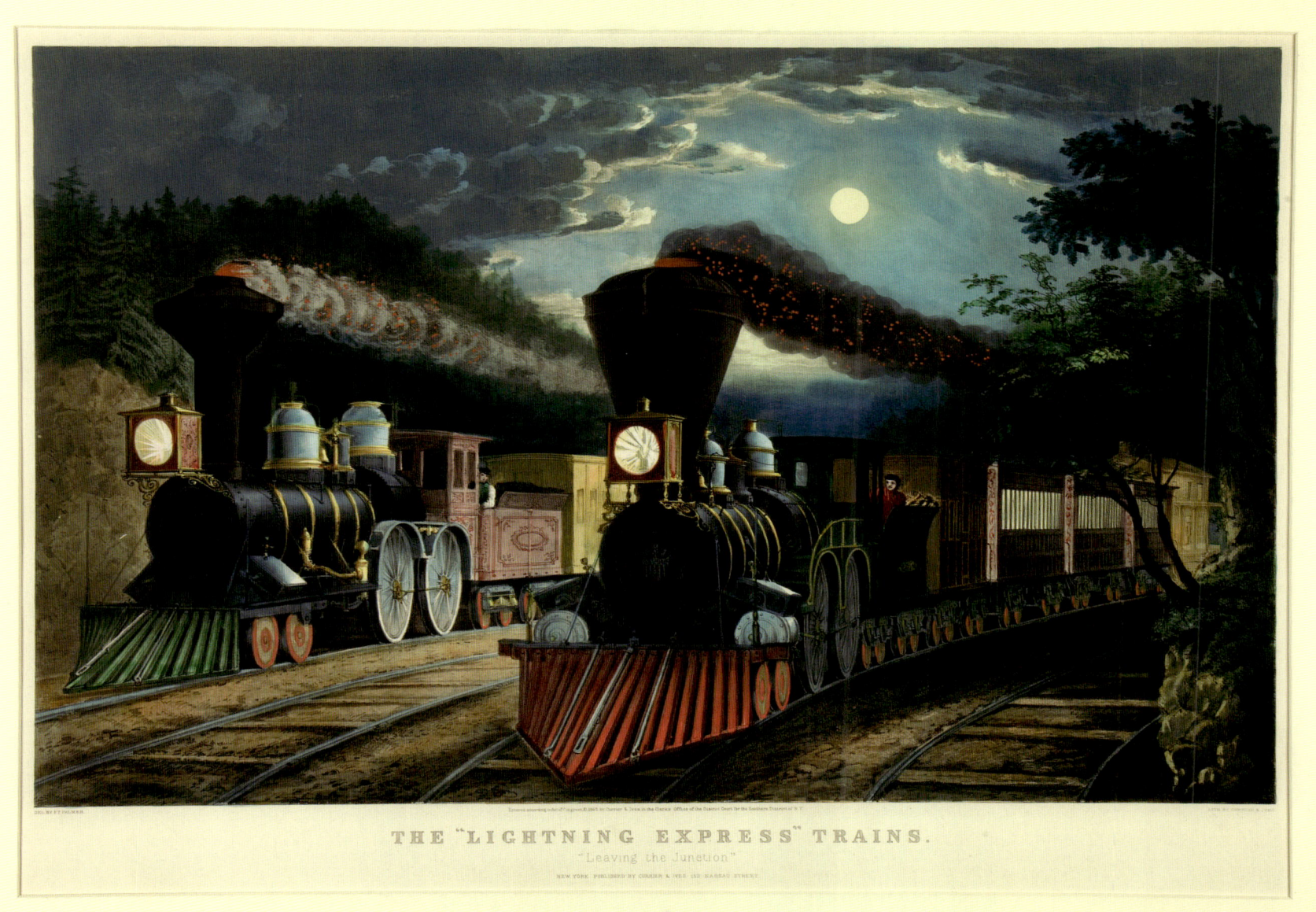

THE "LIGHTNING EXPRESS" TRAINS.

"Leaving the Junction"

NEW YORK. PUBLISHED BY CURRIER & IVES 152 NASSAU STREET.

Gallery plate 10
The "Lightning Express" Trains. "Leaving the Junction." 1863.
Printed and published by Currier & Ives. Courtesy of the Yale University Art Gallery. (Checklist 3-74)

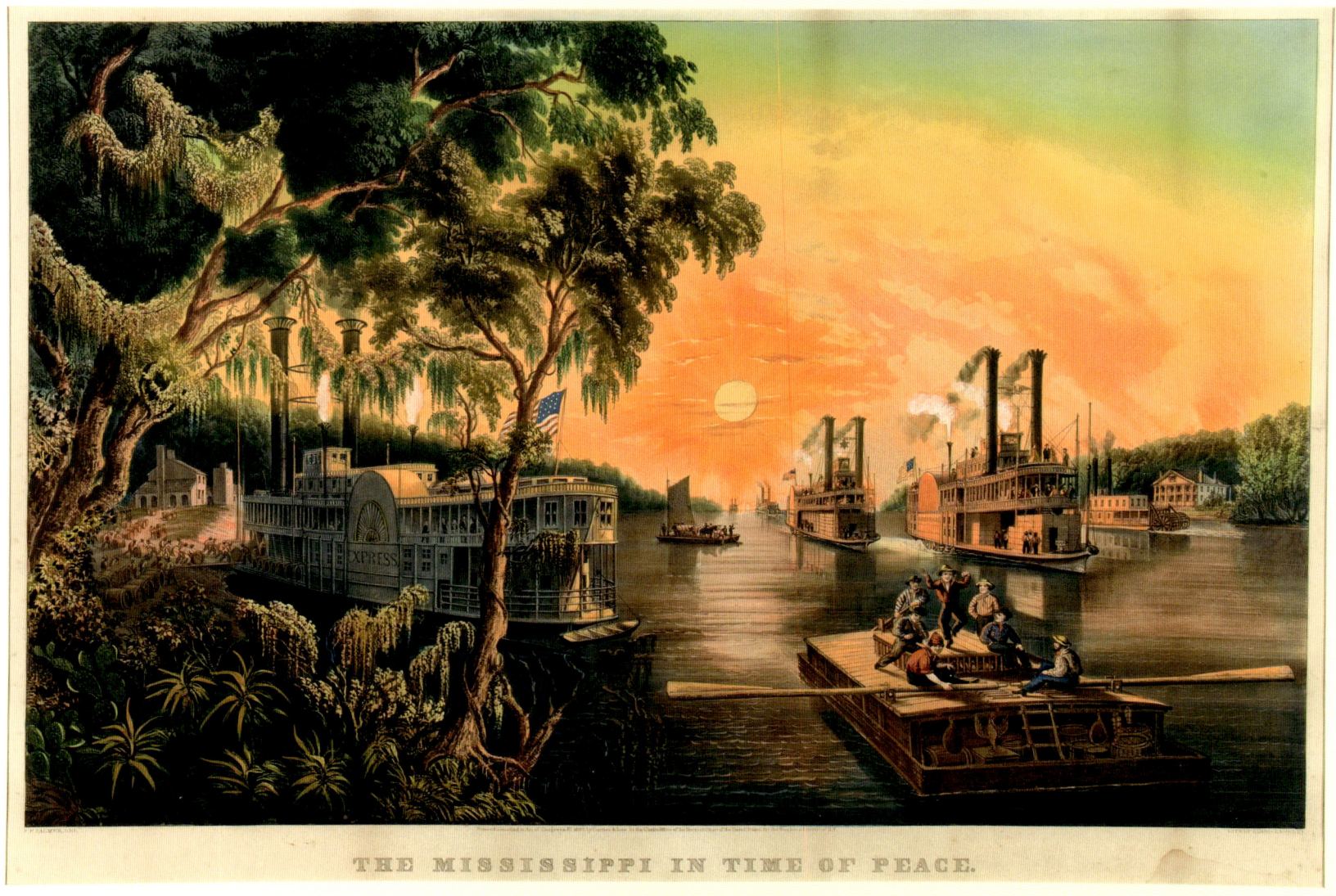

THE MISSISSIPPI IN TIME OF PEACE.

Gallery plate 11
The Mississippi in Time of Peace. 1865. Printed and published by Currier & Ives. Courtesy of the Old Print Shop. (Checklist 3-83)

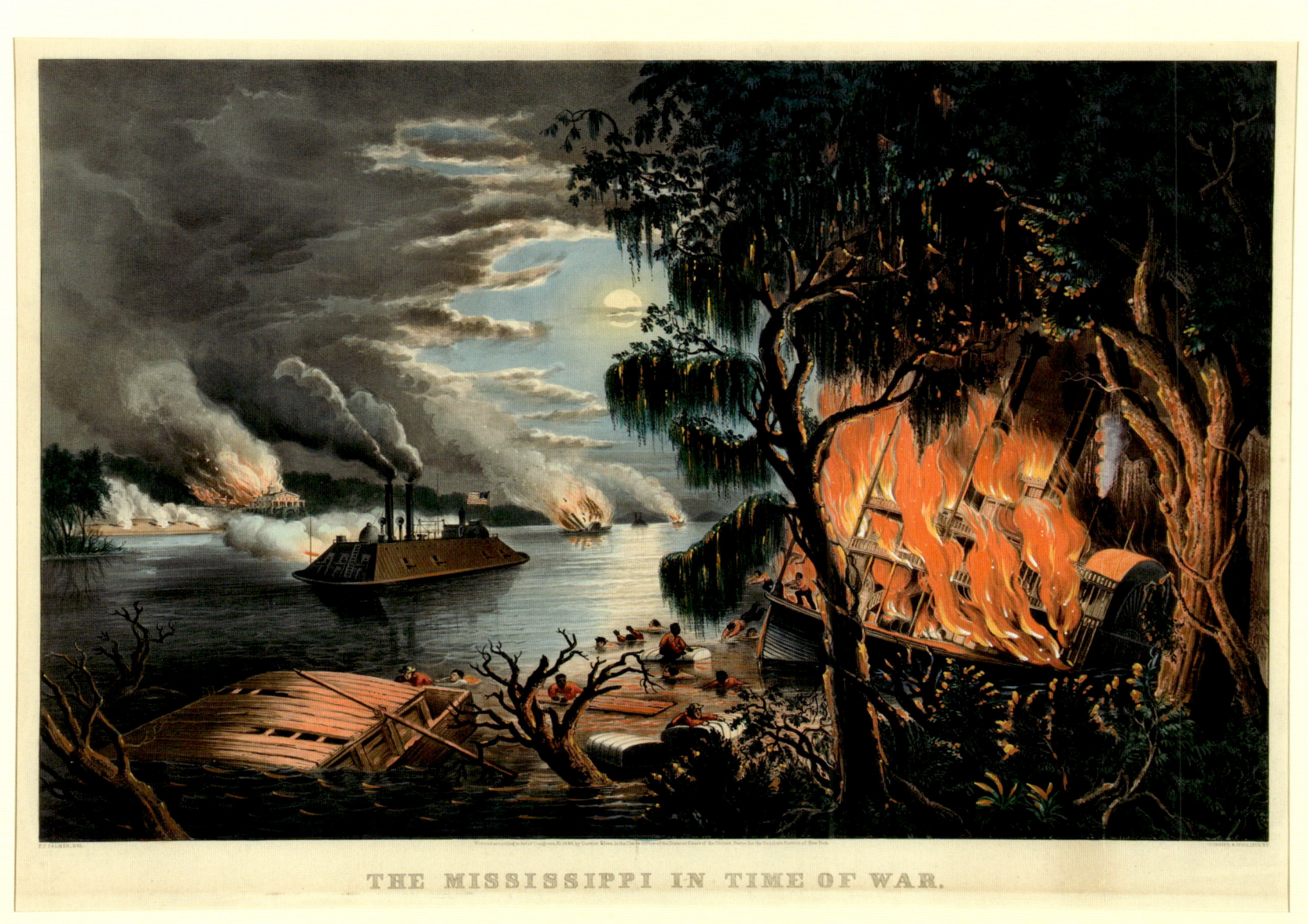

THE MISSISSIPPI IN TIME OF WAR.

Gallery plate 12

The Mississippi in Time of War. 1865. Printed and published by Currier
& Ives. Courtesy of the Yale University Art Gallery. (Checklist 3-84)

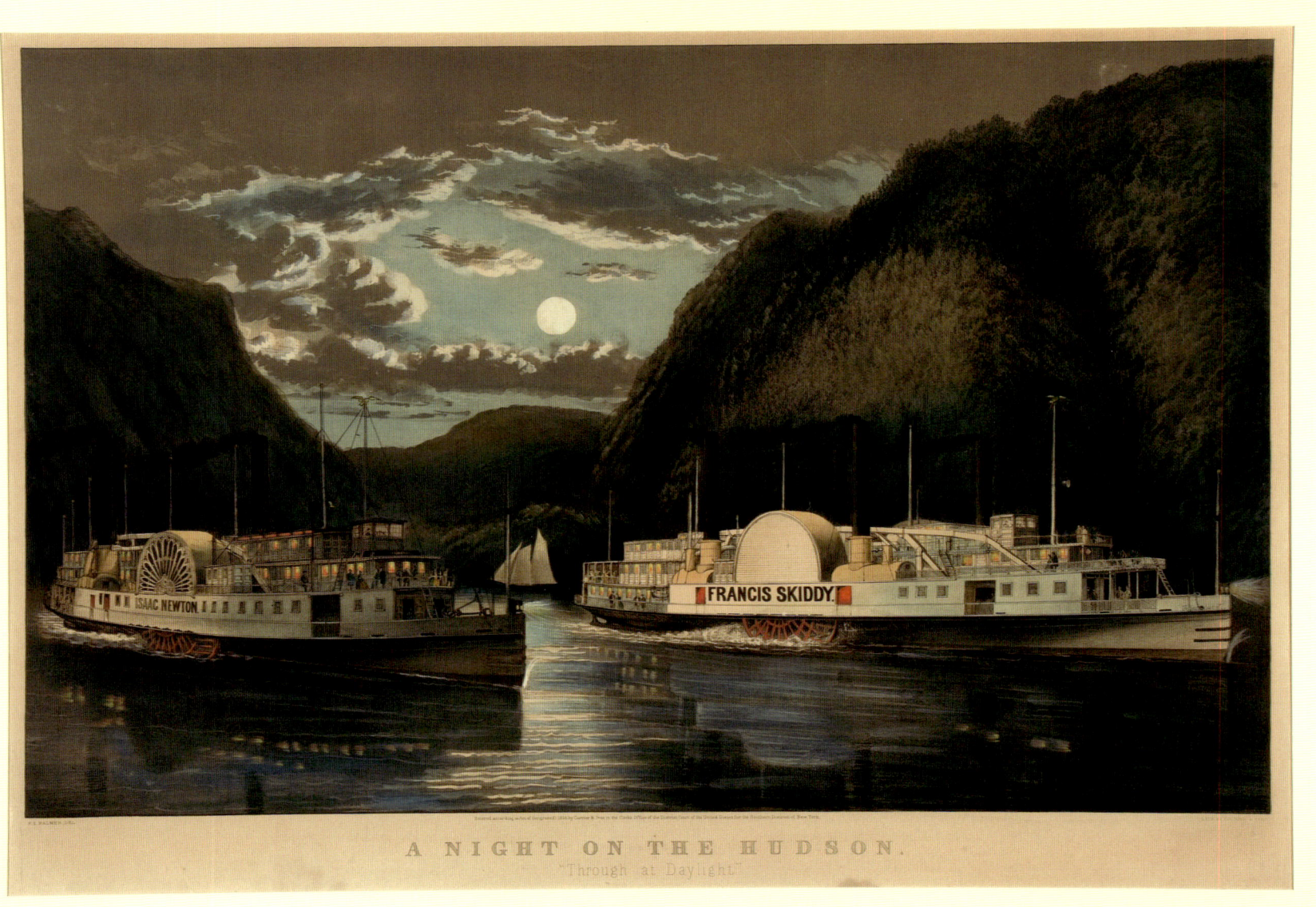

A NIGHT ON THE HUDSON.
"Through at Daylight"

Gallery plate 13
A Night on the Hudson. "Through at Daylight." 1864. Printed and
published by Currier & Ives. Courtesy of the Yale University Art Gallery. (Checklist 3-95)

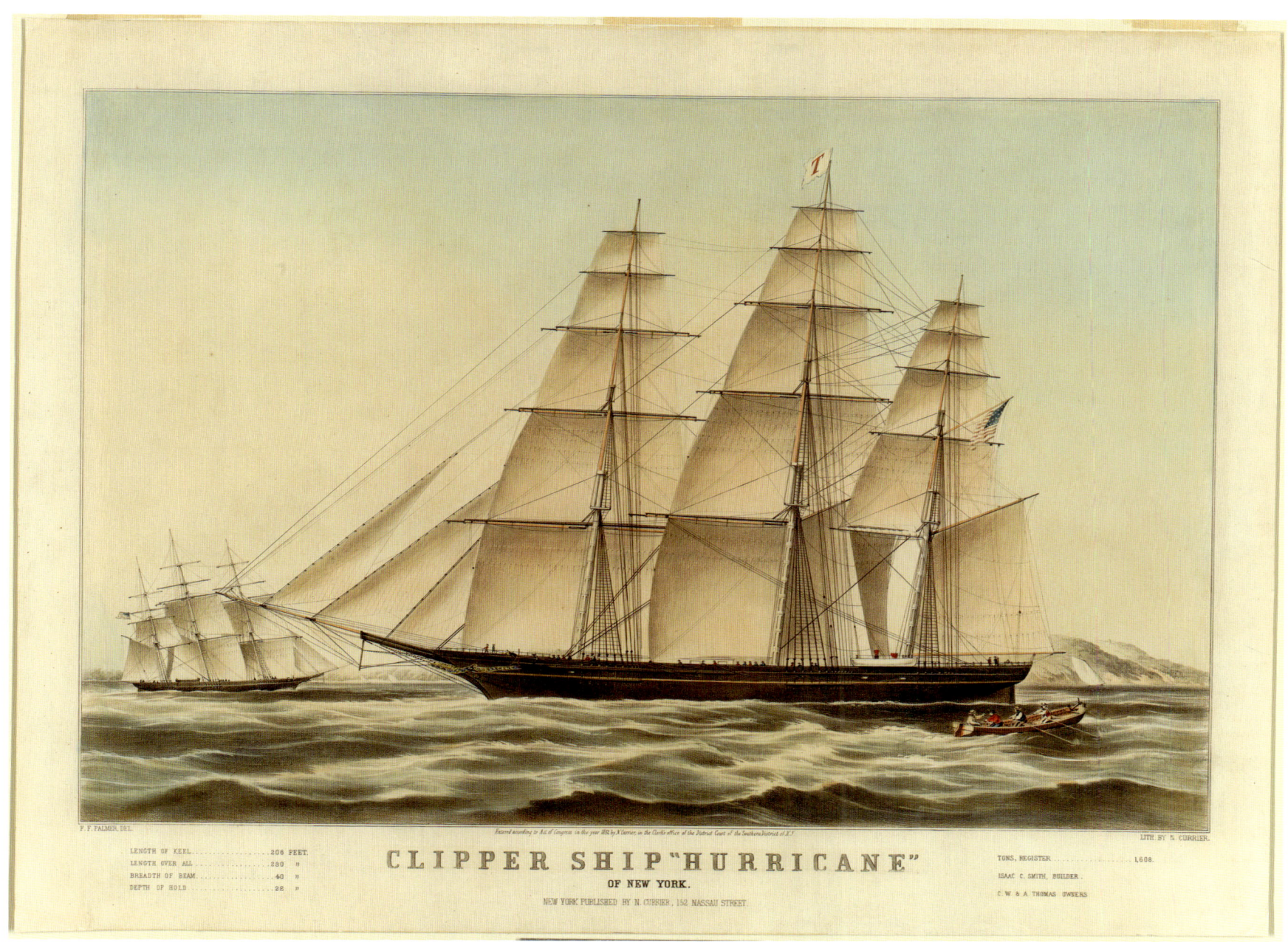

F.F. PALMER, DEL.

LENGTH OF KEEL...............206 FEET.
LENGTH OVER ALL..............220 "
BREADTH OF BEAM..............40 "
DEPTH OF HOLD................22 "

Entered according to Act of Congress in the year 1852 by N Currier, in the Clerks office of the District Court of the Southern District of N.Y.

LITH BY N. CURRIER.

TONS, REGISTER ....1,608.

ISAAC C. SMITH, BUILDER.

C. W. & A. THOMAS OWNERS

CLIPPER SHIP "HURRICANE"
OF NEW YORK.

NEW YORK PUBLISHED BY N. CURRIER, 152 NASSAU STREET.

Gallery plate 14
Clipper Ship "Hurricane" of New York. 1852. Printed and published
by N. Currier. Courtesy of the Museum of the City of New York,
57.300.36. (Checklist 3-30)

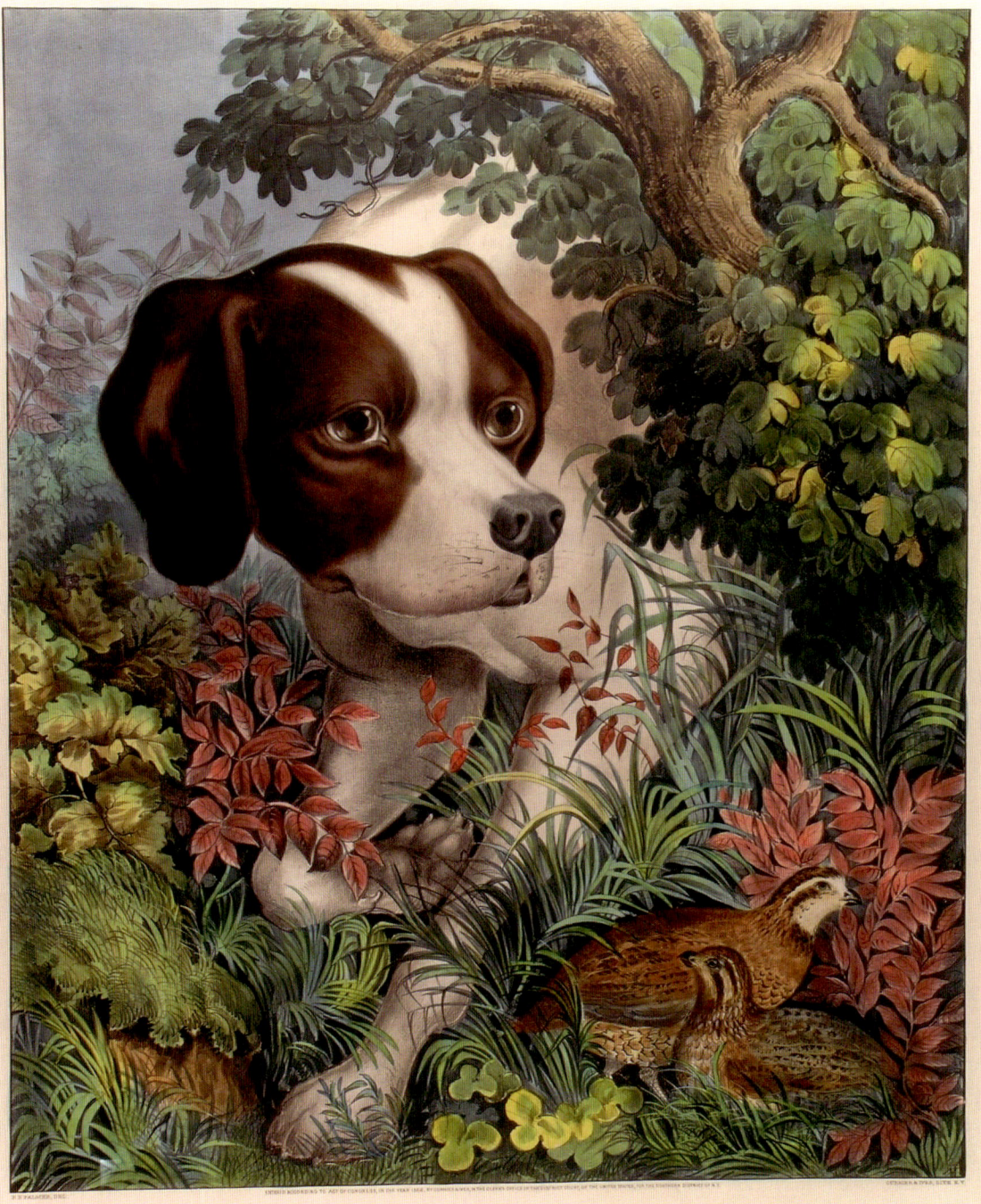

POINTING A BEVY.

Gallery plate 15
Pointing a Bevy. 1866. Printed
and published by Currier & Ives.
(Checklist 3-108)

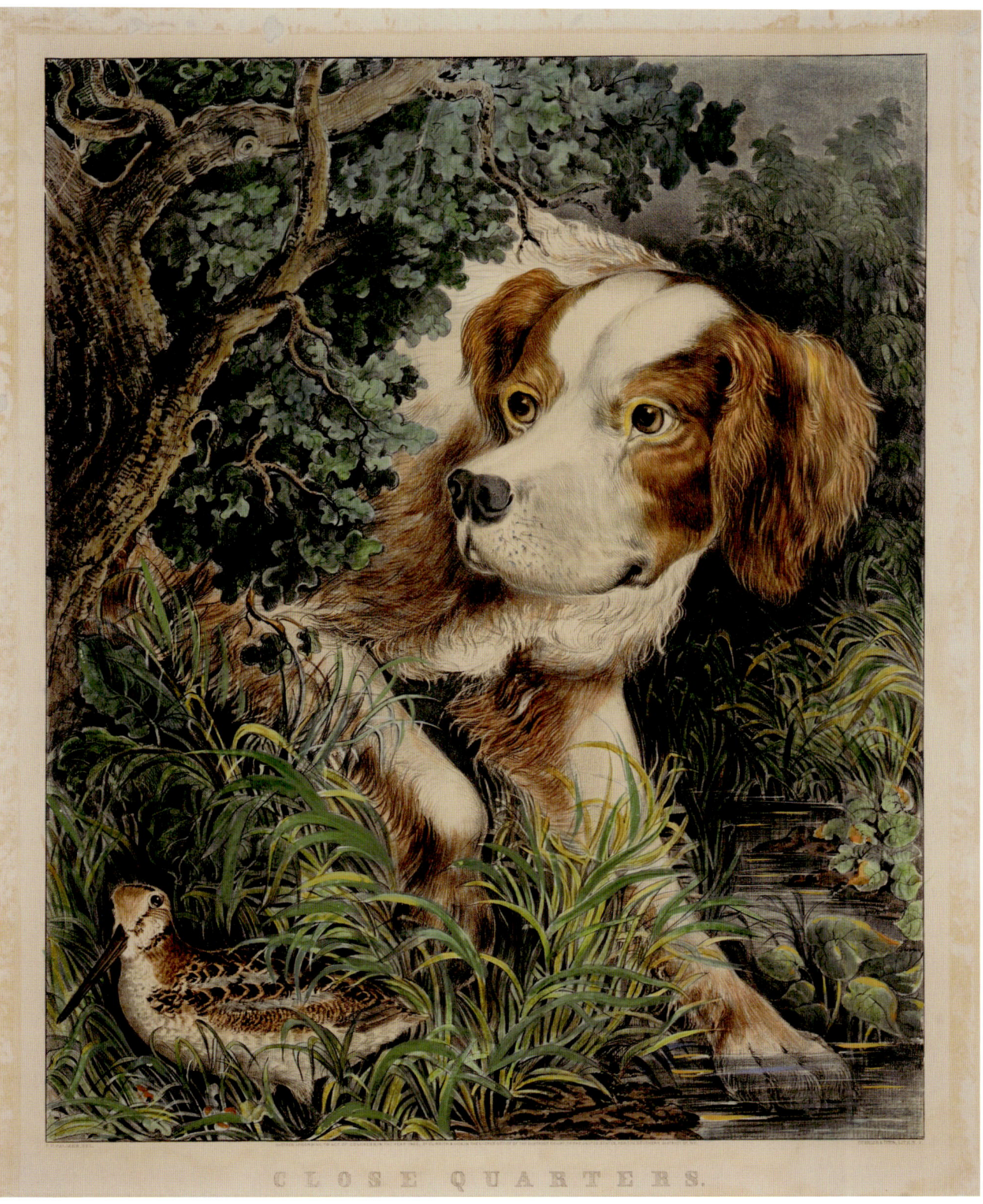

CLOSE QUARTERS.

Gallery plate 16
Close Quarters. 1866. Printed
and published by Currier &
Ives. (Checklist 3-34)

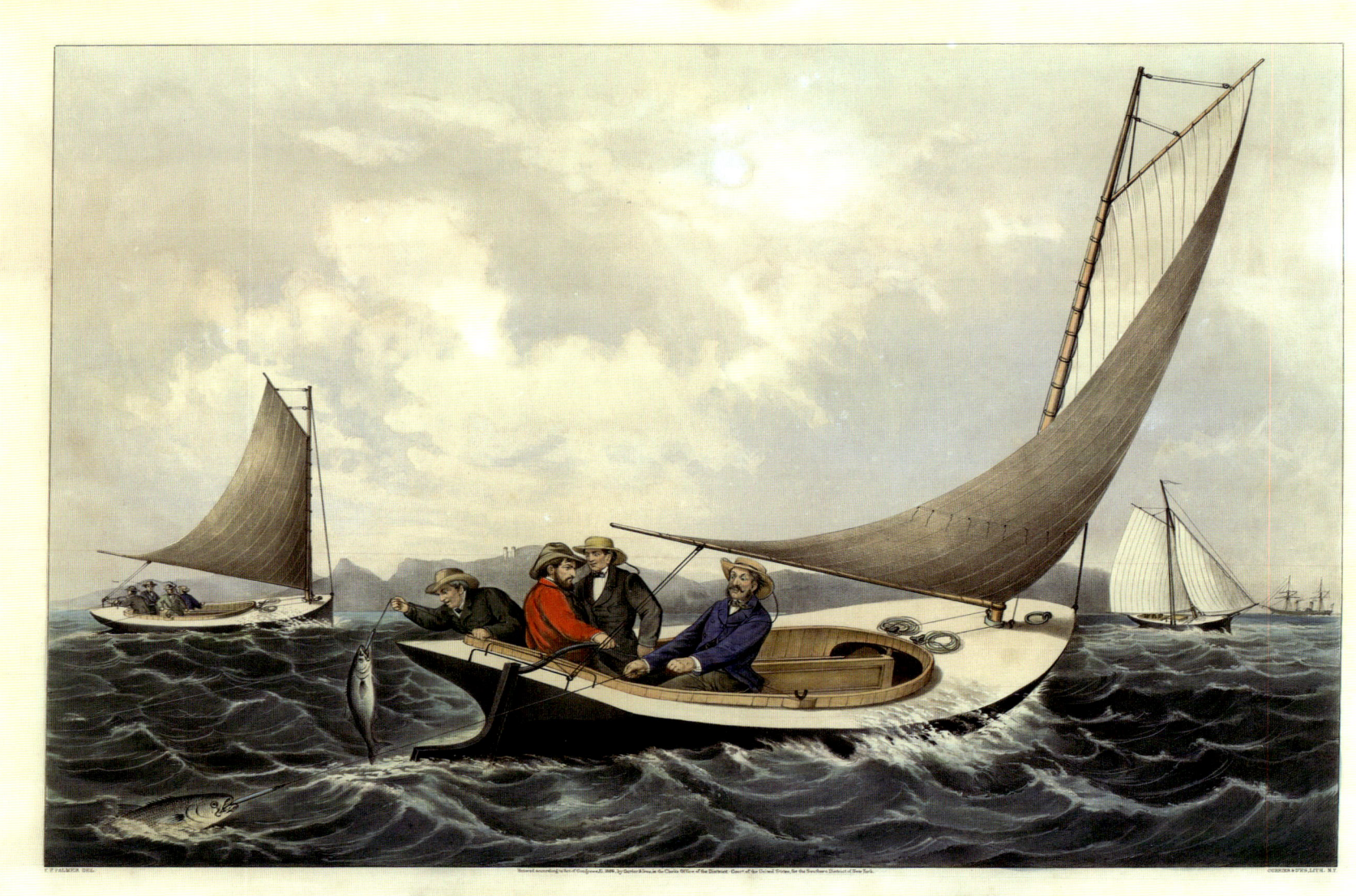

TROLLING FOR BLUE FISH.

Gallery plate 17

Trolling for Blue Fish. 1866. Printed and published by Currier & Ives.
Courtesy of the Old Print Shop. (Checklist 3-139)

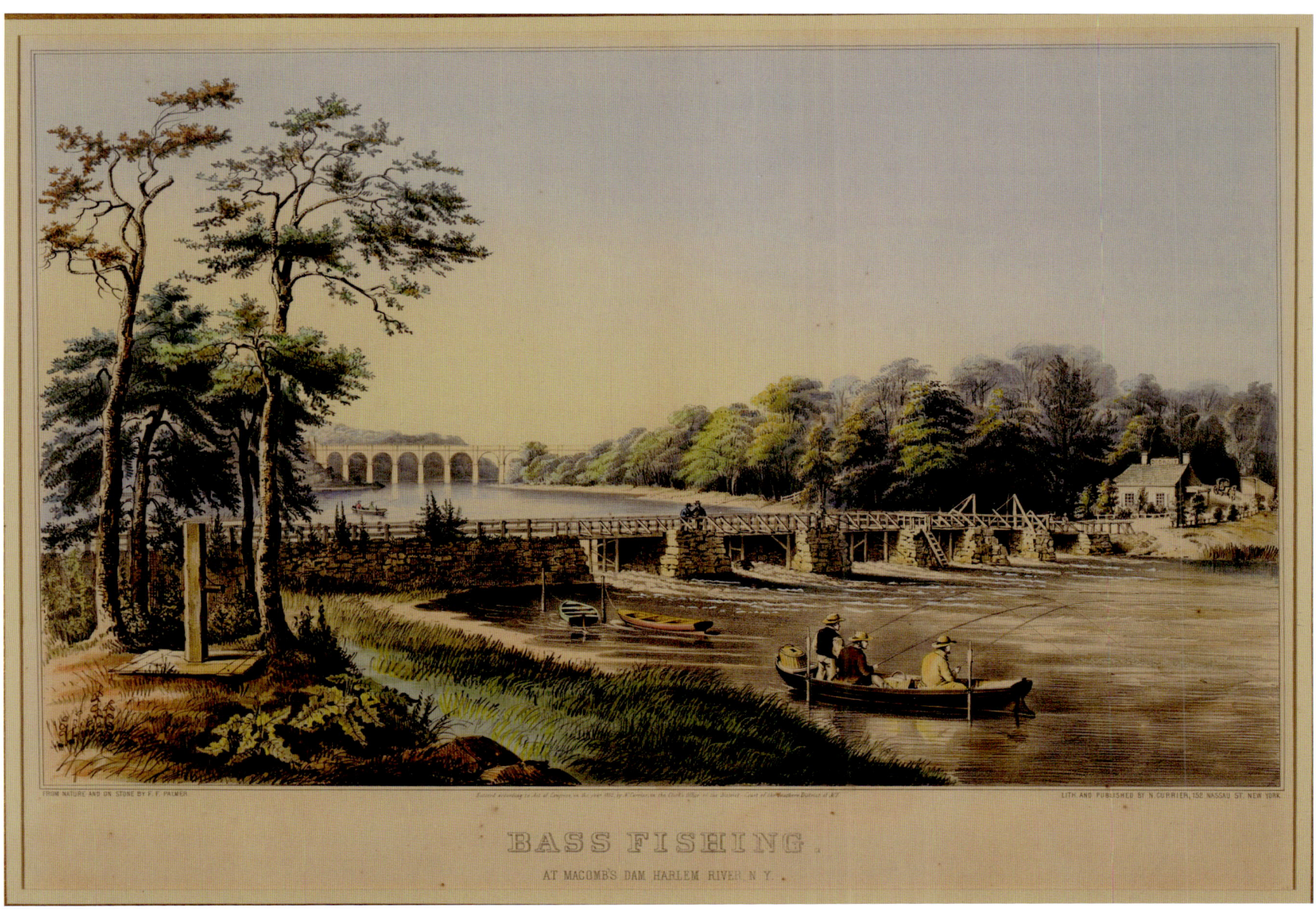

Gallery plate 18
Bass Fishing. At Macomb's Dam Harlem River, N.Y. 1852. Printed and
published by N. Currier. (Checklist 3-23)

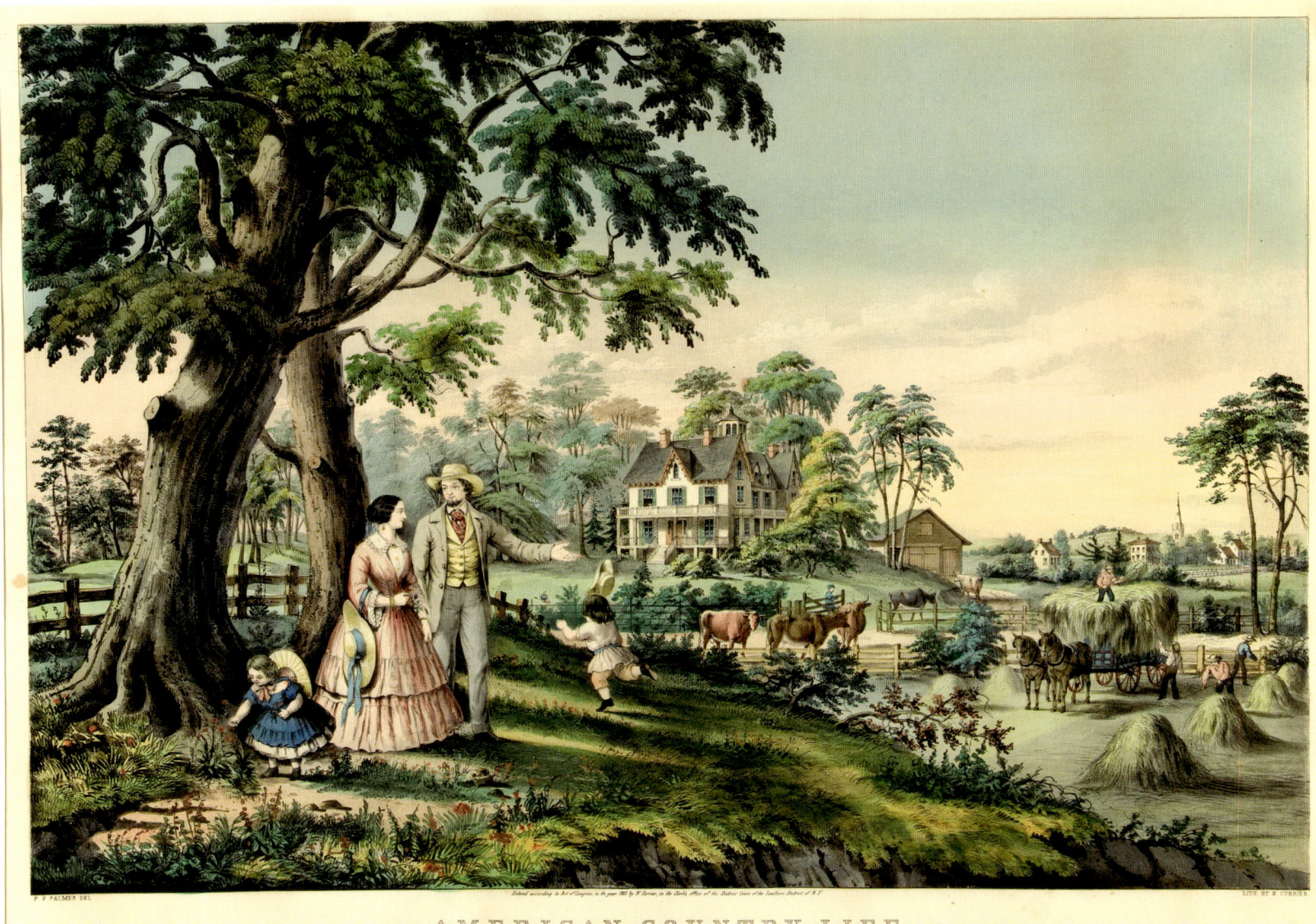

AMERICAN COUNTRY LIFE.

Summers evening

Gallery plate 19
American Country Life. Summers Evening. 1855. Printed and pub-
lished by N. Currier. Courtesy of the Yale University Art Gallery.
(Checklist 3-6)

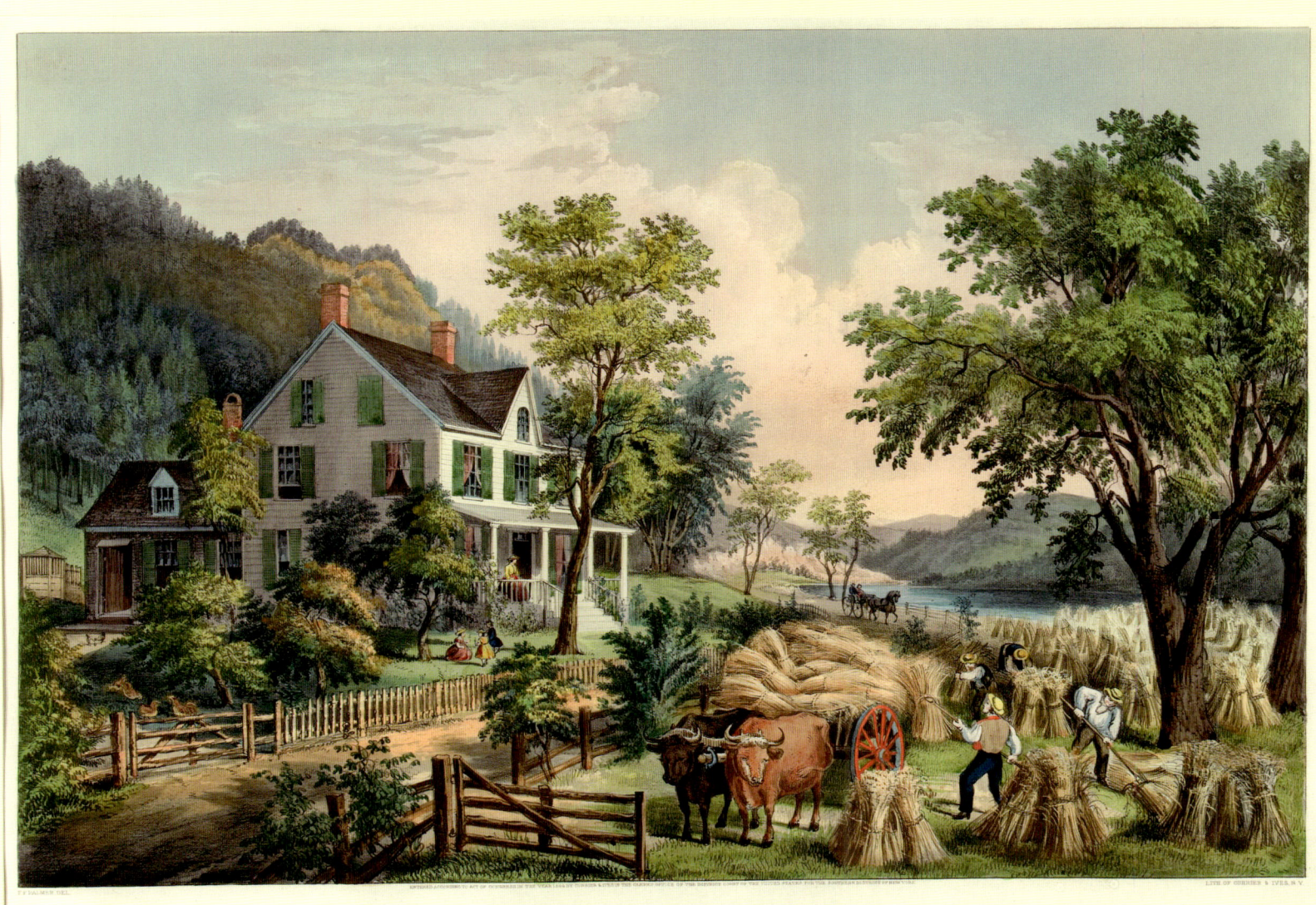

THE FARMERS HOME—HARVEST.

NEW YORK PUBLISHED BY CURRIER & IVES 125 NASSAU STREET

Gallery plate 20
The Farmers Home—Harvest. 1864. Printed and published by Currier
& Ives. Courtesy of the Yale University Art Gallery. (Checklist 3-42)

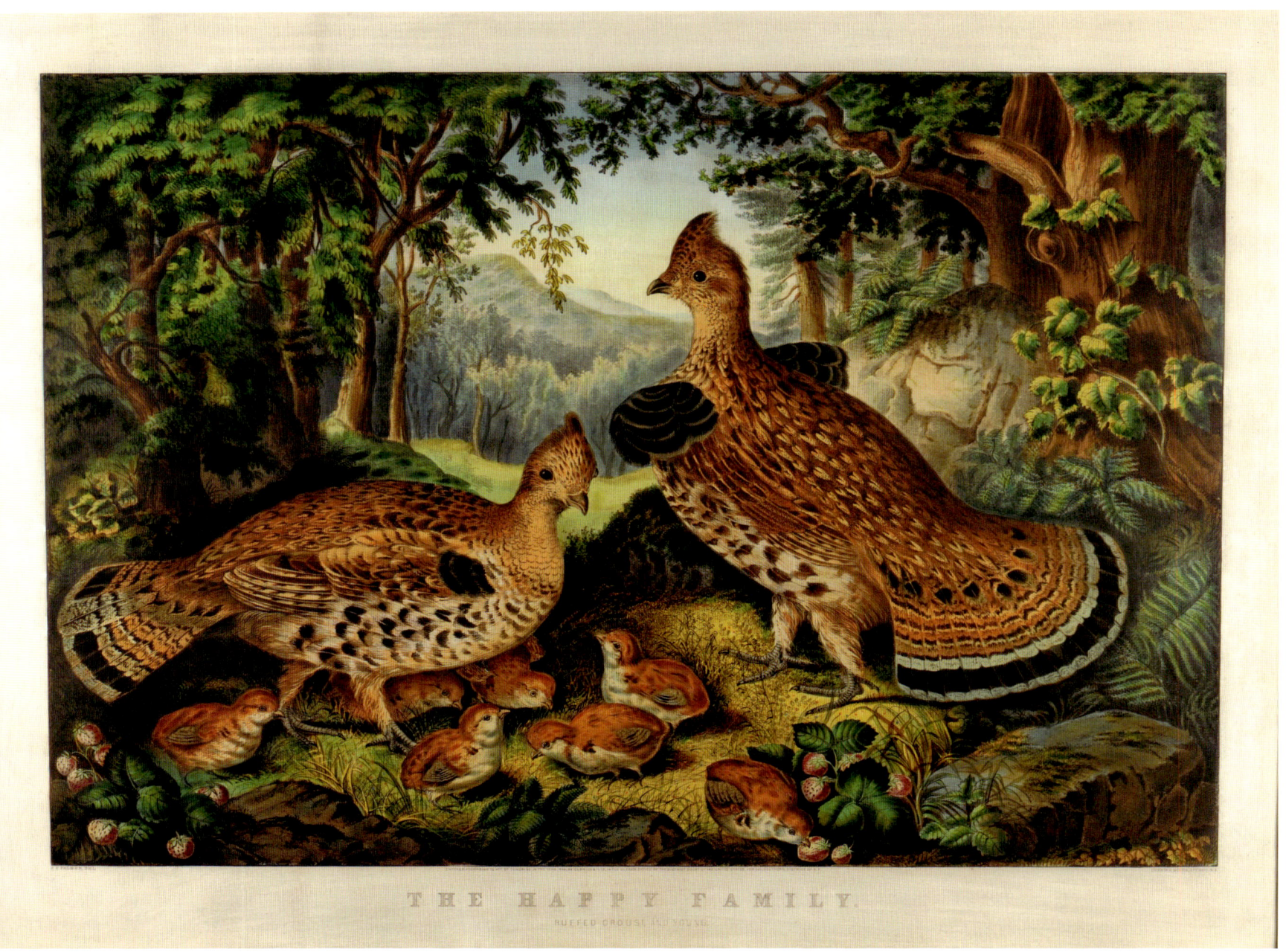

THE HAPPY FAMILY.

RUFFED GROUSE AND YOUNG.

Gallery plate 21
The Happy Family. Ruffed Grouse and Young. 1866. Printed and
published by Currier & Ives. (Checklist 3-54)

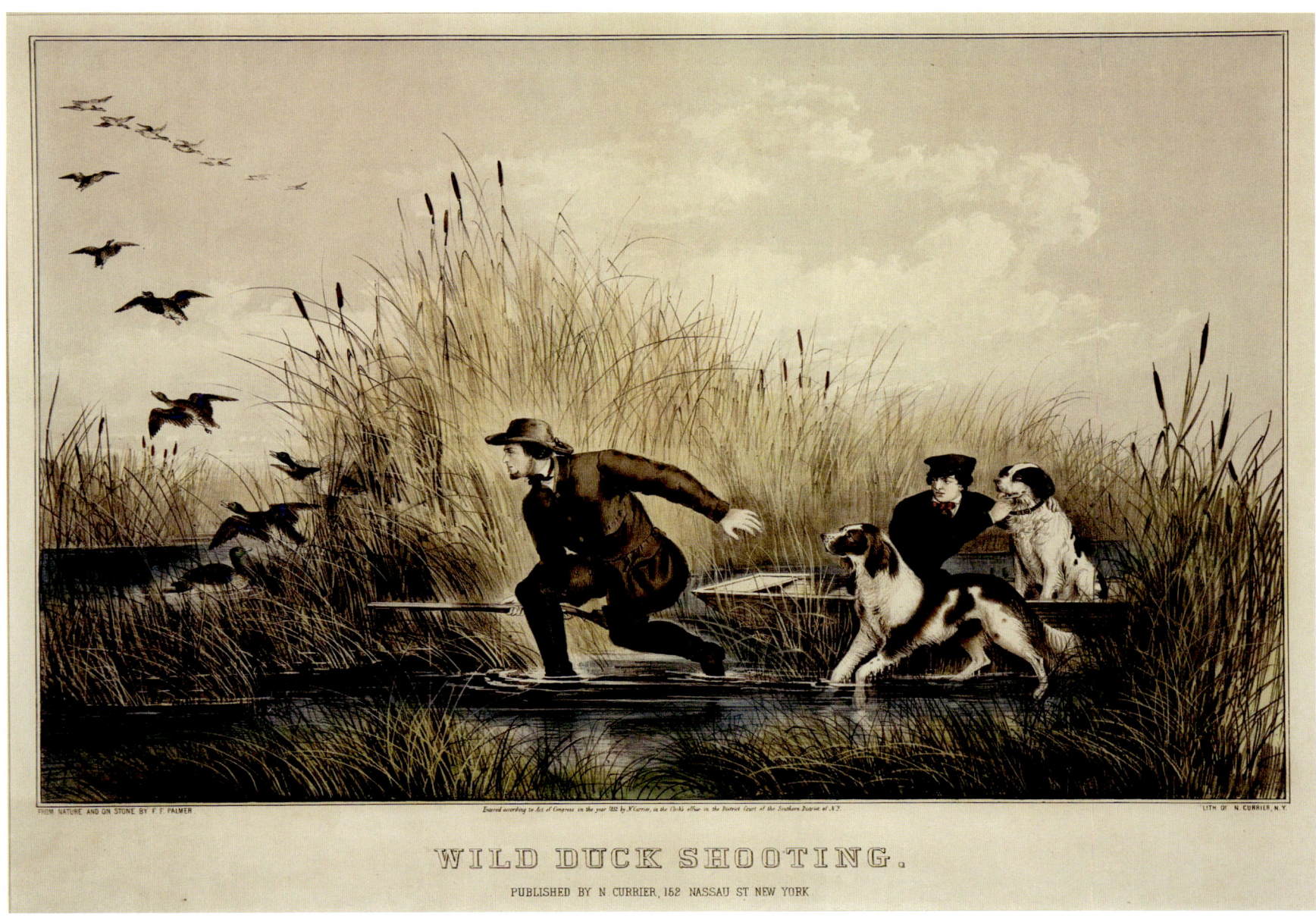

WILD DUCK SHOOTING.

FROM NATURE AND ON STONE BY F. F. PALMER   Entered according to Act of Congress in the year 1852 by N. Currier, in the Clerk's office in the District Court of the Southern District of N.Y.   LITH OF N. CURRIER, N.Y.

PUBLISHED BY N. CURRIER, 152 NASSAU ST NEW YORK.

Gallery plate 22
Wild Duck Shooting. 1852. Printed and published by N. Currier. Courtesy of the Old Print Shop. (Checklist 3-171)

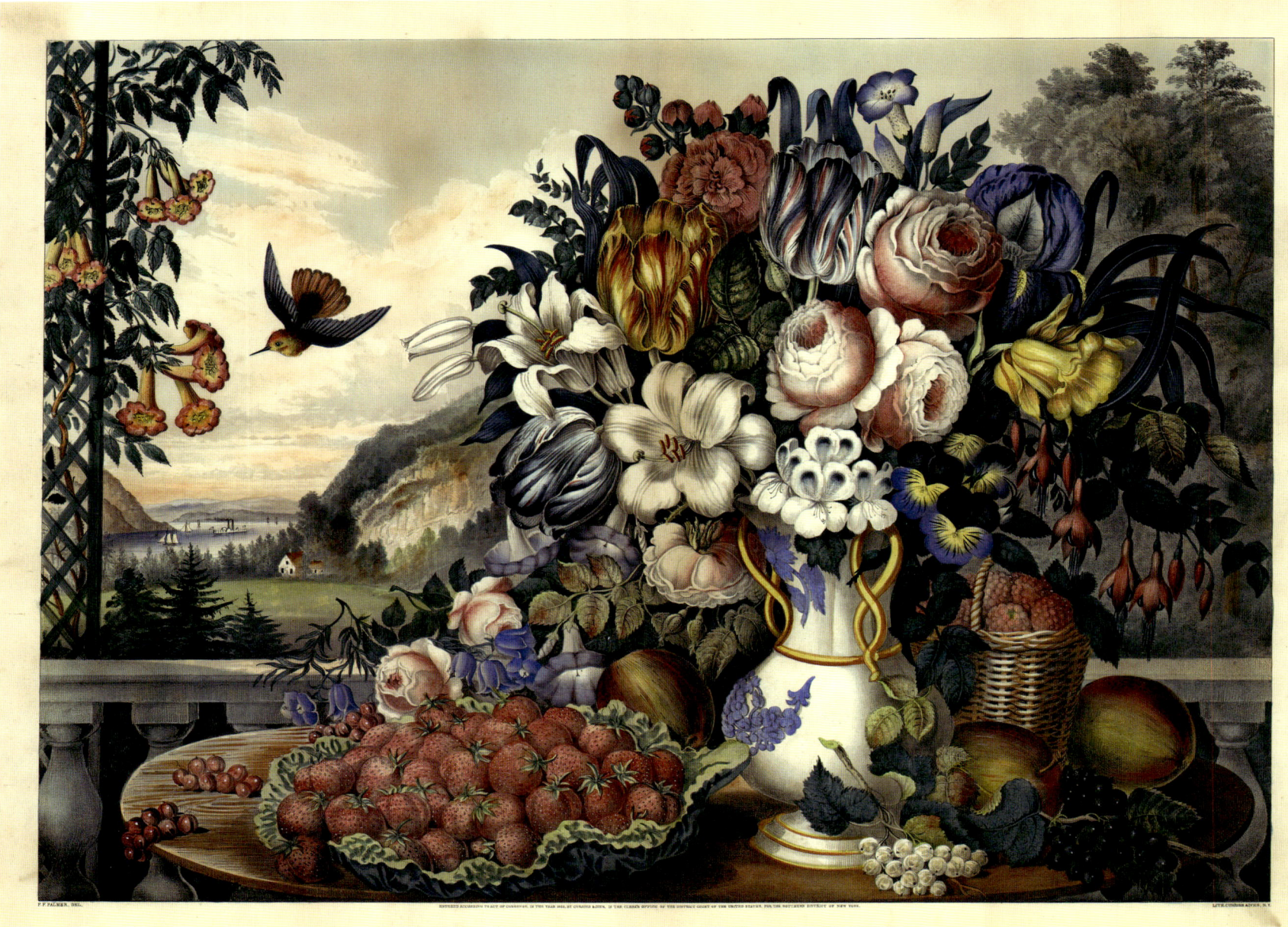

LANDSCAPE, FRUIT AND FLOWERS.

Gallery plate 23
Landscape, Fruit and Flowers. 1862. Printed and published by Currier
& Ives. Courtesy of the Old Print Shop. (Checklist 3-70)

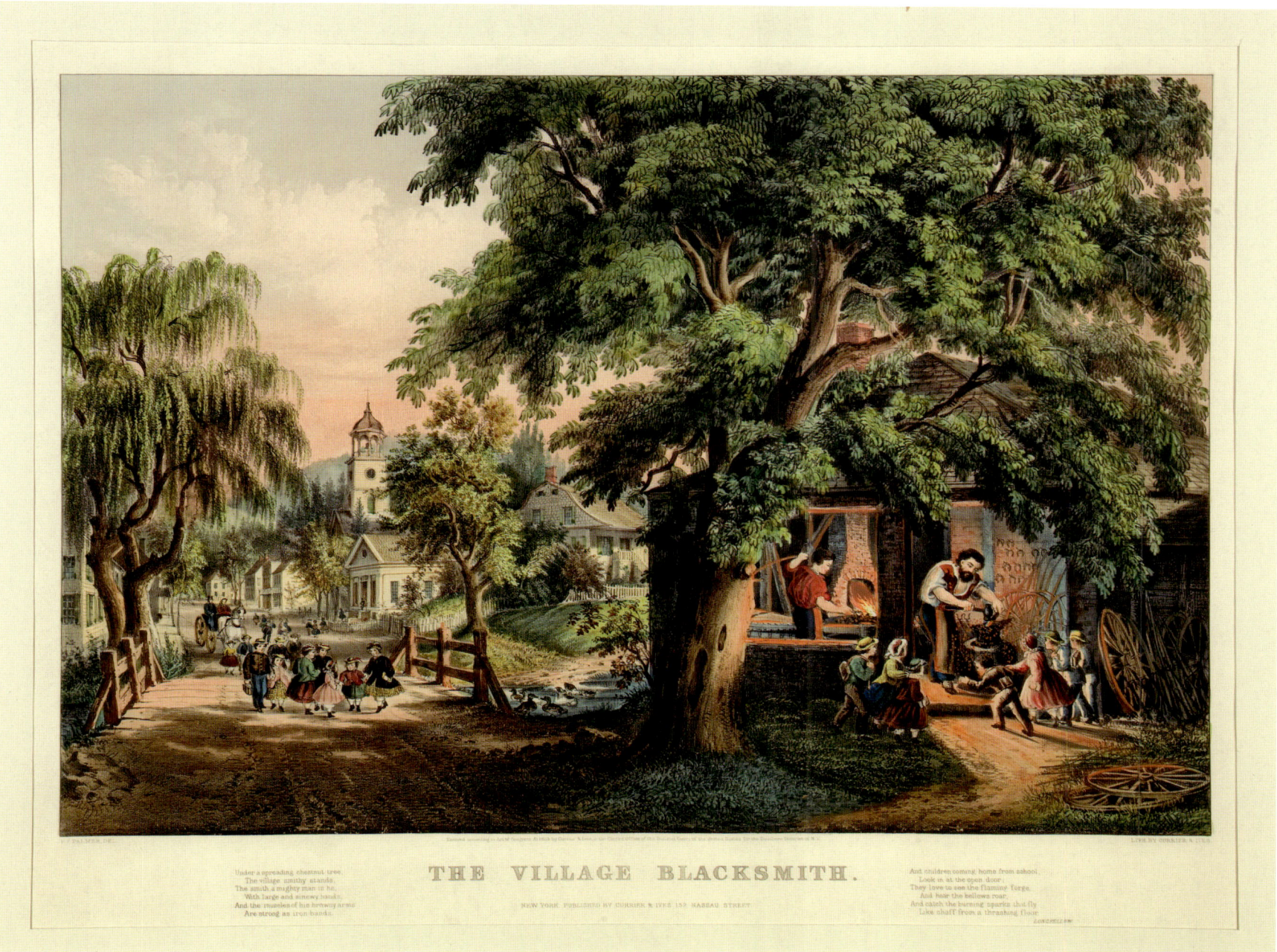

THE VILLAGE BLACKSMITH.

Gallery plate 24
The Village Blacksmith. 1864. Printed and published by Currier &
Ives. Courtesy of the Yale University Art Gallery. (Checklist 3-166)

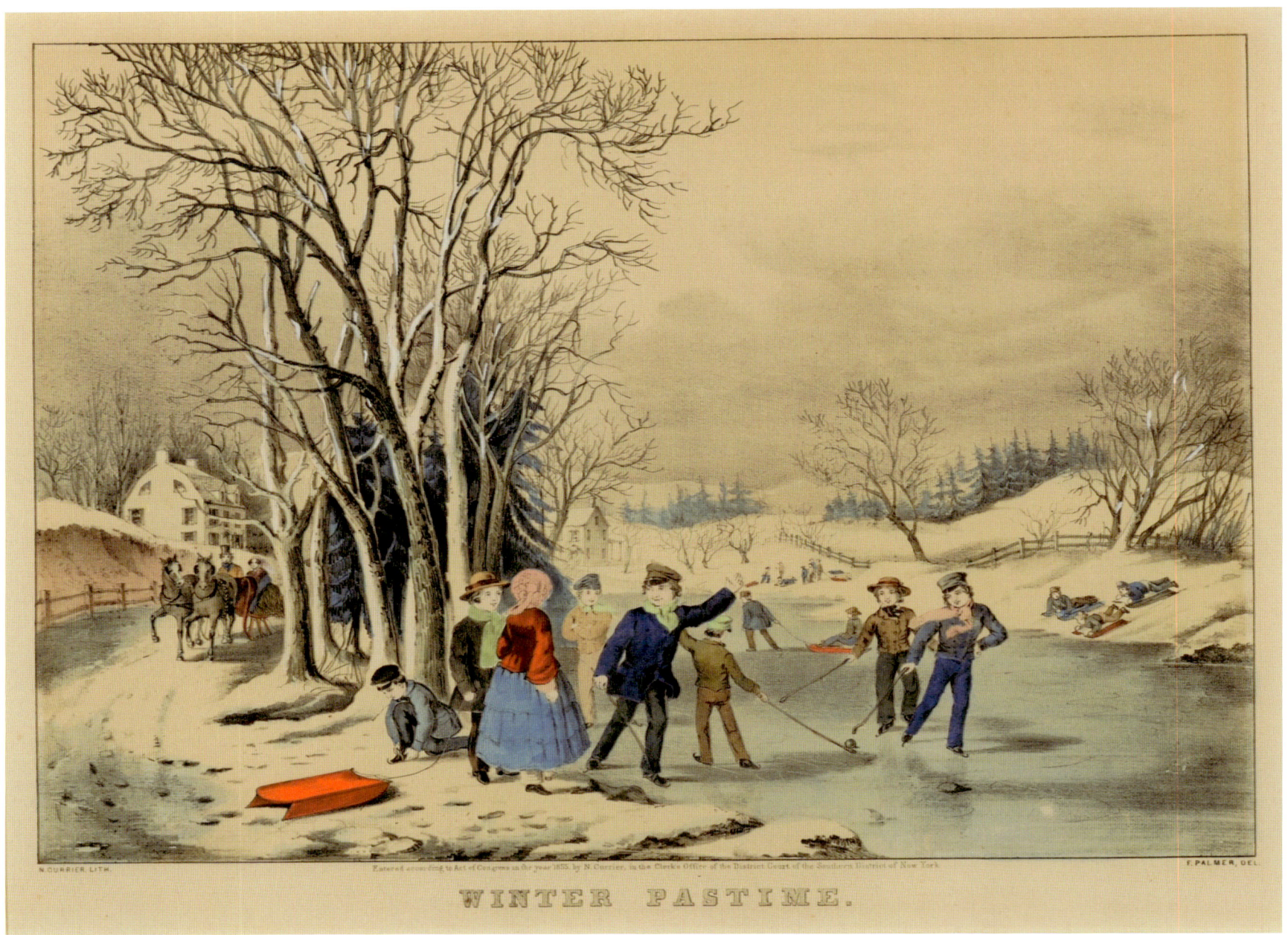

WINTER PASTIME.

Gallery plate 25

Winter Pastime. 1855. Printed and published by N. Currier. (Checklist 3-174)

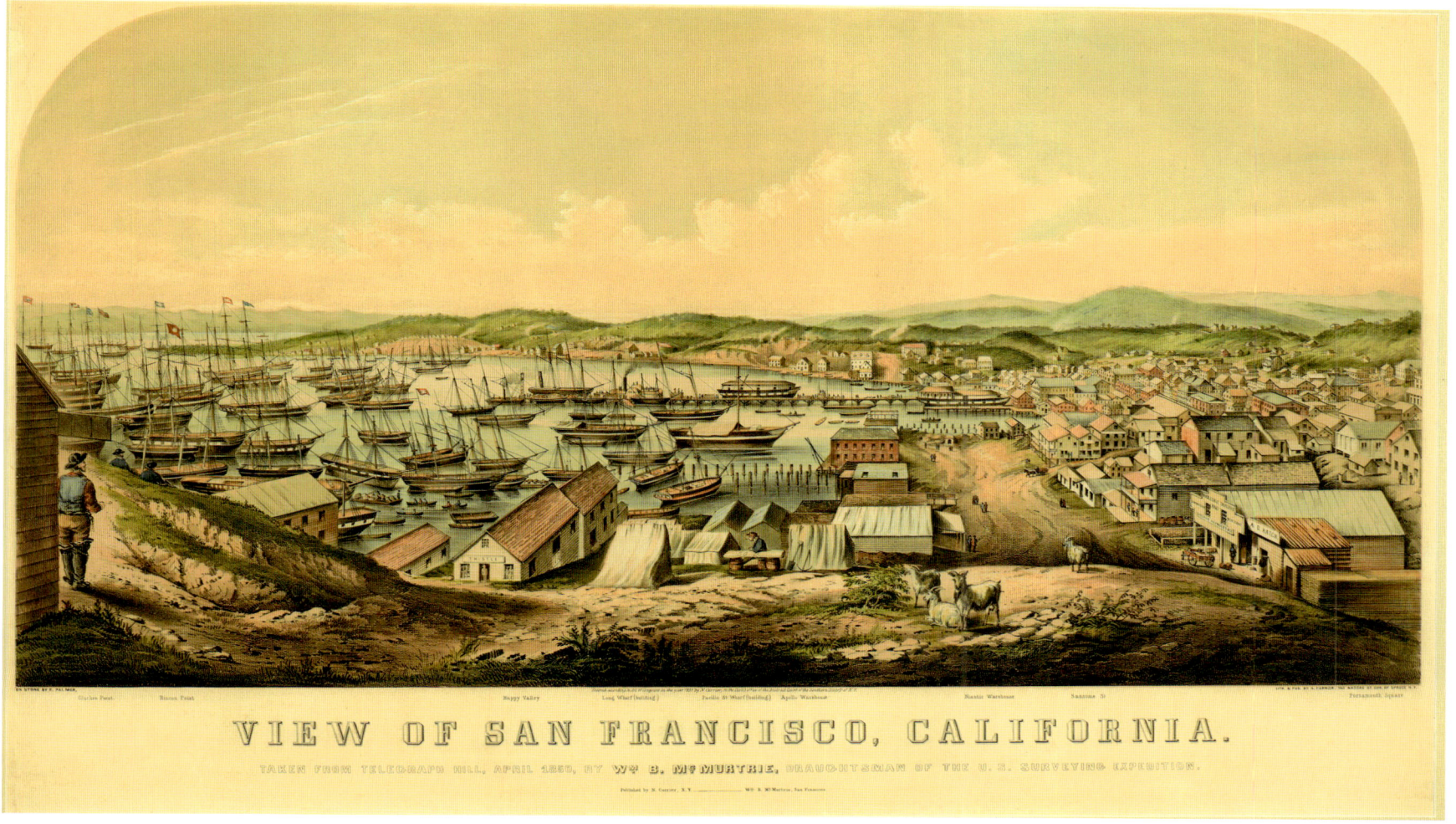

Gallery plate 26

View of San Francisco, California. Taken from Telegraph Hill, April 1850, By Wm. B. McMurtrie, Draughtsman Of The U.S. Surveying Expedition. 1851. Printed and published by N. Currier. (Checklist 3-156)

5

Life at N. Currier & Co.

WHAT KIND OF BUSINESS did Fanny Palmer join when she began to work full time for Nathaniel Currier around 1849? At a moment when the market for lithographic images was exploding, Currier was rapidly becoming the most successful publisher of lithographs in the United States. According to one estimate, his firm, at its peak, was producing more than 90 percent of the country's lithographed pictures.[1] As the population burgeoned, there was a huge demand for colorful prints to brighten up the interiors of drab homes, offices, and public buildings, and for the first time printers could meet that demand quickly in large quantities and at low prices. Lithography was a revolution in mass communication.

Nathaniel Currier's rise to prominence was a Horatio Alger classic story of rags to riches. He was born in Roxbury, Massachusetts, in 1813, but young Nat's childhood was suddenly cut short when he was eight and his father died unexpectedly. He and his older brother, Lorenzo, were forced to scramble for odd jobs in order to support their mother, sister, and baby brother, Charles.

Currier's lifelong career began in 1828, when at the age of fifteen he had the good fortune to be taken on as the first apprentice at William and John Pendleton's pioneering Boston lithography workshop.[2] John Pendleton, a copperplate engraver, had gone to Paris to master the new medium and returned with lithograph stones, transfer paper, ink, crayons, and a skilled French printer described as "the first real lithographic pressman in the United States."[3]

The enterprising Pendleton brothers recruited well-known artists to work with them, including the prominent Philadelphia painter Rembrandt Peale, who was eager to spur the development of lithography in the United States, and A. J. Davis, a fine draughtsman who was drawing Boston buildings at the start of his career as an architect. With these accomplished artists serving as role models, the Pendleton workshop became in many ways the first significant art academy in Boston—a breeding ground for new talent. In fact, several apprentices—George Loring Brown, Fitz Henry Lane, and others—went on to become nationally recognized painters. It has even been suggested that the smooth, graduated tones of the medium influenced the development of the Luminist School of painting.[4]

Young Nathaniel Currier received excellent training and was able to get in on the ground floor of what would soon become a major new industry. It is also worth noting that at an impressionable age he saw the work of a number of capable women printmakers (including Eliza Goodridge, Mary Jane Derby, Margaret Clark Snow, and others), which may have prepared him psychologically to hire later a talented woman lithographer when she showed up on his doorstep. The Pendletons even used an image of a woman drawing on a lithographic stone (taken from Charles Hullmandel's book *The Art of Drawing on Stone* [1824]) in a business advertisement. At that early stage, the company was encouraging as many people as possible to try the medium, but later, after it grew into a successful commercial operation, few women were included on the Pendleton staff.[5]

After a six-year apprenticeship, Currier took a job in Philadelphia before moving to New York City in 1834 in the hopes of joining John Pendleton, who had opened a branch there. When John Pendleton decided to go elsewhere, Currier entered into an unsuccessful yearlong partnership with Adam Stodart. In 1835, at age twenty-two, Currier bought out his partner and opened his own business on a shoestring—N. Currier's Press, at 1 Wall Street.[6]

While struggling in obscurity, taking on a variety of mundane assignments for other publishers along with some original prints, Currier began to see that there was a good market for newsworthy disaster scenes, such as *Ruins of the Merchant's Exchange* (1835) and *View of the Great Conflagration of Dec. 16th and 17th, 1835* (1836)—prints he published depicting the frightful fire that burned down much of Lower Manhattan. In 1840, he seized his big opportunity when Cornelius Vanderbilt's state-of-the-art steamboat, the *Lexington*, burned and sank on Long Island Sound, drowning almost all of its more than 140 passengers, including some very prominent citizens. The community was profoundly shocked. Currier and his friend Ben Day, editor of the penny tabloid the *New York Sun*, decided to join forces to issue a full-page color supplement featuring a vivid image of the flaming boat and the victims struggling in the water. This was one of the earliest examples of an illustrated "extra," to be hawked on street corners by shouting newsboys. Orders poured in from all parts of the country, keeping Currier's presses busy day and night.

Seeing such a sensational event in all its color and detail so shortly after it occurred created a great deal of excitement. In those days before the flowering of photojournalism, daily newspapers generally did not include pictures of news events; a few woodcuts, mostly for advertisements, were the principal illustrations. From that time forward, Currier's company had a national presence and began to flourish. No longer simply the owner of a job shop, cranking out pedestrian assignments for other publishers, he began to create, publish, and market his own line of prints for a growing audience.

Currier soon outstripped his competitors, not because of the quality of his prints—Endicott and Company and other businesses sometimes equaled or even surpassed him in quality—but rather because of his keen sense of what the public wanted and of how to rationalize production and to market his work profitably. Early on, he showed exceptional ability as an executive and businessman. Although Currier continued to supervise and give the final approval on prints, he was soon able to turn over all the actual drawing and printing to his staff and to devote himself to developing the company into a nationwide and even international operation.

Each morning at 7:00 a.m., pushcart and backpack peddlers lined up at the curb in front of N. Currier for prints to be hawked in Manhattan, Brooklyn, Hoboken, and other communities accessible by wagon or ferry. In the late afternoon, these vendors returned to Nassau Street with unsold items to settle up any refund from their deposit. In addition to his own retail outlet and a variety of other stores, such as print and decorating shops, Currier also supplied a network of peddlers who traveled on distant rural routes. Many upstate farm wives later recalled how these itinerants would come to the door and unfurl a long vertical scroll pasted up with a tempting array of colorful samples.

Currier also hired sales agents in various parts of the country and abroad and—far ahead of his time—developed an extensive mail-order business, a move that proved to be very lucrative in an era when many households were far from shops and stores.

American travelers to foreign countries were soon surprised to find Currier & Ives prints turning up in such faraway places as Australia.

During its seventy-two-year existence, the firm issued at least eight thousand different images in millions of copies and various permutations.[7] For example, a sunny scene could be transformed into a moonlit view by darkening the sky and changing the color scheme.[8] Popular subjects were often reissued later, sometimes with changes or with elements of one print combined with another. One of Currier's marketing ploys was to issue prints in pairs or sets of four, thus encouraging the purchase of more than one at a time. He also sold large quantities of black-and-white prints to schools for children to color and to amateur artists, who converted them into "paintings." An entire separate catalog advertised,

Uncolored Prints Published by Currier & Ives, No. 152 Nassau Street, N.Y. Adapted to Grecian Oil and Oriental Painting, Italian or Diaphanic Pictures on Glass, and any other of the popular methods of painting or coloring.[9]

This catalog included elaborate instructions for mixing paint, stretching paper, making varnish, and other techniques for converting cheap black-and-white prints into full-blown "masterpieces."

The publisher churned out lithographs that would appeal to a broad variety of customers: patriotic images of great leaders and historical events; prints of sporting events; views of farms, cities, and wilderness; political cartoons, election banners, and pictures of candidates; scenes of firemen racing to conflagrations; pictures of trappers, Native Americans, and covered wagons; religious themes for a variety of denominations; drawings of steamboats and trains; romantic pictures of Europe for homesick immigrants; still lifes; illustrations of poems and other literary subjects; sentimental scenes of family life; and a torrent of pictures of pretty girls—almost anything that would sell. The prints found their way into homes, hotels, schools, offices, men's clubs, yacht clubs, barber shops, stables, and saloons. In one catalog, the company even boasted that its "Cheap Colored Prints" were suitable for ornamenting "the backs of bird cages, clock fronts, or any other place where an elegant and tasteful picture is required."[10]

It is a mistake, however, to think that Currier was simply turning out prints as cheaply as possible for a mass market, with no regard for quality or aesthetics. Although the major part of his income came from masses of inexpensive "stock prints," the publisher did not overlook the lucrative, high-end customer. Advertising often in the upper-class New York weekly paper *The Spirit of the Times: A Chronicle of the Turf, Agriculture, Field Sports, Literature, and the Stage*, the clever marketer often ran a boldface headline, such as "THE TROTTING HORSES OF AMERICA," guaranteed to attract a particular niche market. Then, after listing his equine prints, he would slip in descriptions of a select group of large images, many by Fanny Palmer, of other subjects that might appeal to this wealthy audience. Note, for example, that in describing Palmer's rendering of William B. McMurtrie's drawing *View of San Francisco, California* (1851; gallery plate 26), Currier asserts that, "independent of its correctness[,] . . . it forms the most beautiful picture ever published of this 'El Dorado' of the Pacific."[11] This colored print sold for five dollars, a high price at that time.

When Palmer visited Currier's store at 152 Nassau Street for the first time, she found herself walking past tables placed out on the street, where in good weather customers examined marked-down prints guarded by a boy. Passing windows filled with a motley array of prints, she entered a doorway with a gold-lettered sign above it and looked into a busy shop, twenty-five feet wide and seventy-five feet deep, where masses of prints were piled up and spilling over center rows of tables, flanked by additional rows of crowded bins on either side. Each bin had an inventory of its contents pasted on the cover. Customers rummaging through lithographs separated by subject with cardboard dividers could select one, then fold back the lid like an easel and place the image on its rack to examine it. More prints were tacked up or hanging in frames on the walls, along with paintings that had served as models for the lithographers and were up for quick sale. Small prints, the so-called stock prints that were the mainstay of the business, sold for pennies, from five to twenty-five cents; medium-folio prints were around a dollar; and large-folio prints, created with more care by the company's best artists, ranged from a dollar and a half to three, four, or even five dollars, depending on the quality and popularity of the print.

Currier's loyal sales manager and general foreman, Daniel W. Logan, could be seen running about, supervising a staff of about five salesmen, who assisted customers or worked in the basement, framing, packing, and shipping prints all over the country and abroad. This devoted employee was known to come to work even when he was ill, claiming that he felt better in the shop than lying in bed.[12]

The aisles were often crowded with browsers; indeed, the store was something of a hangout or informal salon for a group of Mr. Currier's distinguished friends. While Nat Currier kept a sharp eye on the entire operation from a tall desk in the fifteen-foot office space at the back of the store, such famous men as Horace Greeley, editor of the *Tribune*, abolitionist preacher Henry Ward Beecher, and Hiram Woodruff, renowned horse trainer and author of *Trotting Horses of America*, dropped by to chat. Impresario P. T. Barnum sometimes strolled over from his American Museum with the popular performing dwarf Tom Thumb perched on his shoulder.

In later years, Currier's son Edward ("Ned"), who studied law at Amherst but had been groomed to eventually take over his father's place, left a vivid description of what the store was like during a hotly contested election campaign. He wrote to his recently retired father in September 1881 that there was such a crush of buyers demanding pictures of the candidates that the staff had to barricade the doors and regulate traffic to prevent the shop from becoming dangerously overcrowded. After grabbing every print, customers "yelled so for more pictures" that worried people in the neighborhood stuck their heads out of the windows to see what the noise was about.[13]

The actual manufacture of prints took place in a nearby building at 2 Spruce Street. When a newsworthy subject, such as a disaster, election, or victorious war campaign, was in great demand, the drawing would be transferred to several stones using a special transfer paper, and all the presses would be in use simultaneously. The entire staff would work day and night, while newsboys and peddlers gathered in the street waiting to get their copies.

Palmer met an interesting cast of characters when she was brought over to the production plant for the first time. Currier most likely introduced her to John Cameron, a full-time staff lithographer who, like Palmer, enjoyed a long career with the company. A skilled craftsman described as a "hunchback" with a penchant for strong drink, he collaborated with Palmer on a number of prints in the following years.[14] Perhaps she smelled liquor on Cameron's breath when he shook her hand, but that would not have been too off-putting. If we can believe reports about her husband, she was used to it. Palmer would also have noted the curvature of his back. She apparently shared this characteristic with him; her own back was described in later years as a "deformity."[15]

J. Schutz, who did much of the lettering at that time, might have been sitting near the good light of a window, squinting through a magnifying glass as he painstakingly drew the complicated titles and inscriptions in reverse on the lithograph stones with a sharp, diamond-pointed crayon or steel pen. Franz Venino, designer of many of the "pretty girl" images, and Otto Knirsch (nicknamed "the Berliner") were also in-house lithographers.

Palmer would certainly have met Currier's younger brother, Charles. Nathaniel had trained him to be a lithographer, perhaps intending to bring him in as partner, but Charles clung fiercely to his independent identity. He had a desk in the center of the third floor, where he ran his own business under his own name, producing a modest mélange of prints, including fashion advertisements for Butterick's, the company that sold sewing patterns to women. Palmer, who became Charles's neighbor in Brooklyn, later helped him develop a top-of-the-line lithograph crayon, which he at one point manufactured in his attic (much to his wife's annoyance). These crayons, called "crayolas," were regarded as superior to any in the field and ultimately provided Charles and several of his sons with a base income.[16]

In later years, one of these sons commented on the difference in temperament and physical appearance between his father and his uncle. Nathaniel was very erect, slim, and clean shaven, whereas Charles was shorter, stouter, wore side whiskers and a beard, and covered his bald pate and rim of hair with a tall white hat. A warm-hearted family man, Charles had about a dozen children, several of whom died (this same son later couldn't recall exactly how many—"family all scattered"), and after his beloved wife's death at age forty-nine, he never remarried.[17] According to another son, "Mr. Charles was more of a worldly man and Mr. Nathaniel more for business and a person of very high principles. Mr. Charles easy going. Spent his money freely, very extravagant in treating friends with wines and smokes . . . preferred spending the evenings visiting friends rather than working."[18]

Another full-time artist, Louis Maurer, a pleasant, fresh-faced young man twenty years younger than Fanny, had had some training in mechanical and perspective drawing, animal anatomy, and lithography in Germany before immigrating to New York with his family in 1851. He joined the staff a few years after Palmer did and sometimes worked on the figures in her prints. Well known for his lithographs of firemen, western scenes, and horse racing, Maurer was a colorful personality. He played and collected flutes and was an excellent horseman and a crack shot, and after retiring from his own business he became a painter of western subjects. In his last years, before his death at age one hundred, he resembled Buffalo Bill, complete with white hair and goatee.[19]

There was also a talented roster of freelance artists who worked at home or at other companies. One of the finest, Charles Parsons, a full-time employee at Endicott and Company, took on freelance assignments (especially marine prints) for Currier & Ives (the company's new name starting in 1857). Accomplished and gracious, he eventually became head of the art department at the famous book and magazine publishing house Harper & Brothers, where he was the mentor of an important group of young artist-illustrators, including Winslow Homer. His son, Charles R. Parsons, in partnership with lithographer Lyman W. Atwater, also drew marine compositions and other subjects for Currier. The waggish Thomas Worth came by with a steady stream of trotting and racing sketches, political cartoons, and satirical drawings, including in later years the scurrilous *Darktown* series ridiculing African Americans.

The well-known painter Arthur Fitzwilliam Tait sold Currier & Ives the rights to reproduce a number of his sporting and western canvases—the source of some of the company's most popular prints. His professional history provides a revealing contrast to Palmer's. Like her, Tait came from England, and, also like her, he began his career as a lithographer producing prints of the new British railway lines. But soon after arriving in the United States, he was able to become a full-time painter and by 1858 had earned the title of "academician," the highest rank at the National Academy of Design.[20]

A sportsman himself, Tait spent much of his time working from nature at his place in the Adirondack mountains, frequently inviting prominent men, some of whom he included in his paintings, to join him on hunting and fishing expeditions—a good way of bonding with potential patrons. Although nineteenth-century American male artists didn't have an easy time making a decent living (even Winslow Homer had to be helped along by his generous brother), they did have many more opportunities than women to get adequate training, circulate in the world of wealthy and powerful men, and hold office in leading art organizations.

The wide distribution of Currier & Ives lithographs gave Tait useful publicity, but he complained that the prints sometimes credited the lithographers more than the original artist and were undercutting his sales of paintings. Angered when his name was included without permission on a small, poorly executed copy of his work, he cut off his connection with the firm around 1866 and moved over to a major competitor, Louis Prang, owner of the chromolithograph business that was introducing new methods of color printing to the field.[21]

George Durrie was another painter whose poetic scenes of Connecticut farm life became the models for a very popular series of lithographs. Durrie's biographer suggests that he admired and may have been influenced by Palmer's treatment of snowy, bare-branched trees, women feeding chickens, and other motifs in her farm prints.[22]

The firm occasionally lithographed a famous work, such as Eastman Johnson's painting *Corn Husking* (1860), but doing so was expensive. More often it adapted material, not only from paintings but also from engravings, daguerreotypes, and even the lithographs of competing companies—modifying them enough to call them their own.

Currier & Ives was a commercial operation, and the art staff often worked together as a collaborative team. Palmer created many landscape and architectural backgrounds for other artists, and they in turn sometimes drew the figures in Palmer's compositions, not always with happy results. However, she entirely composed, drew, and lithographed a number of her signed prints, and some were labeled "from nature and on stone," indicating that they were sketched directly from life.[23] We must look to these prints to get a true impression of her individual style and technique.

Artists often had to dream up their fanciful inventions quickly from whatever sources they could find. For this reason, they sometimes visited the nearby Astor Library on Lafayette Place, one of the few very large New York City libraries that were free to the public, to collect visual information from its splendid collection—for example, details of American Indian costumes in illustrated books about western life. None of the staff artists was able to visit the western territories in those early days, which may be why the famous chief Sitting Bull, when shown Currier & Ives horse prints, told Louis Maurer that his colleagues were good artists "but big liars."[24]

Most important of all the individuals whom Palmer encountered in her first visits to the production plant was James Merritt Ives, who had married into the family of Nathaniel Currier's brother, Charles, and had already been working as Nathaniel's bookkeeper and industrious general assistant for some years.[25] Ives, who was himself a skilled amateur artist, proved to be so invaluable to his employer that in 1857, about eight years after Palmer joined the firm, Currier made him a partner, renaming the company "Currier & Ives." This new partner was to have a strong influence on Palmer's career and collaborated with her on a number of important prints.

In 1866, the two entrepreneurs, who had up to this point been renting the factory space at 2 Spruce Street, bought a nearby five-story building at 33 Spruce Street and moved their production facility to the three top floors, renting out the lower two. The walls of all three floors and the basement were lined with racks holding hundreds of finished stones, each numbered and ready to be pulled out at a moment's notice to meet orders for additional prints.

The third floor was taken over by presses and the actual printing operation. On the fourth floor, near the good light of the back windows, artists and lithographers developed the prints, although some artists (including Palmer) worked primarily at home and had their pieces picked up by the company wagon. Currier and later Ives maintained final authority over the artists' preliminary designs, scrawling pencil notations for suggested changes ("take out wagon, move figures"[26]). When a drawing was finally approved, it was turned over to a lithographer, who could take as much as two weeks or more to copy a complex image on stone, often modifying it to fit the space or strengthen its impact.

After the stones were inked and printed, the wet lithographs were placed on racks. When they were dry, batches of the inexpensive smaller ones were taken upstairs to the fifth floor, where the all-female assembly line (primarily German immigrants with a smattering of art training) sat at a long table applying watercolors to the images. Referring to a color model placed where they all could see it, each worker added one color to parts of the picture and passed it along to the next worker, who added another color. The first artist might wash in a blue sky and water; the next might add green grass and trees; a third would splash a dab of bright red on a wagon or a piece of fruit. Finally, a female supervisor in charge of the whole operation checked the work and added finishing touches. Stencils were often used for mass production of small prints because an entire color area could be laid in with one swoop of the brush.

In those days, women who worked in factories were for the most part outside the pale of polite society, but Currier screened his employees carefully, priding himself on his staff's good character and ability; it was prestigious to be known as a "Currier girl." However, this respectability doesn't seem to have done too much for their wages—they were reportedly paid three to seven dollars a week (which was actually a decent amount compared to the pittance earned by most women at that time). Nathaniel Currier once explained that he particularly liked to hire young girls: "[Mr. C.] finds that small girls are usually the best workers. Their fingers are more nimble, and they enter into it with more zeal. He thinks it best for them to commence at ten or twelve years of age. . . . The work requires care, and is wearisome because of sitting long and steadily."[27]

Palmer's employer sounds like an exploiter of child labor, but one must remember that Currier himself began to work at the age of eight and was already apprenticed as a lithographer at fifteen. Those were the labor conditions of the times.

Larger, more-expensive prints were handled with greater care, farmed out a dozen at a time to skilled specialists who colored the entire image at a very low piece rate (a dollar a dozen) in their own studios. This practice provided work not only for male artists (Currier claimed that only men colored the large, expensive prints for his company) but in some places also for a small army of middle-class women who needed to earn money discreetly without lowering their husbands' social status by doing it publicly. Author Virginia Penny gave an amusing description of this phenomenon in Philadelphia:

> Some [women] associate in companies, and take their work to the house of one of their number; but the greater part are educated women, who do not wish it known that they earn money by their labor: these carry the plates [i.e., black-and-white prints] to their own homes (and even have them sent to the fashionable places of resort in summer), so that many a fair damsel trips along Chestnut street [*sic*] with a roll of something, which seems to be music, but is, in fact, work.[28]

One of Palmer's ongoing tasks was to supply color models for these colorists to use as a guide. She would try out several watercolor treatments on black-and-white proofs for her employers, who then decided which one was the most effective.

It is pleasant to picture F. F. Palmer operating in this setting, the only woman artist on the staff (except for the girls on the assembly line). Her quiet English accent could be heard as she chatted with her German-accented colleague Louis Maurer about how to combine her landscape with his figure drawing or responded to Currier's New England twang as employer and employee discussed the suggested changes scrawled on her sketch. One can envision the diminutive Mrs. Palmer, her hair pulled back severely in a bun and her body stooped by a curvature of the back, walking upstairs from the fourth to the fifth floor in a dark, full-skirted dress with a modest white collar, holding a colored sample of one of the prints to serve as a model, and then giving the girls pointers about how to proceed with the job.

Palmer remained for more than a quarter of a century one of Currier & Ives's premier, all-purpose artists. In her early days with the company, Currier sent her out to rural Long Island in his carriage to gather atmospheric background material for the staff. A few examples still remain of Palmer's lively, sensitive sketches of farmhouses, barns, fences, toll gates, and other motifs, drawn directly from life in soft pencil, both sides of the paper used for economy's sake.

One can picture Palmer and a company driver returning from such an expedition, making their way through the hectic horse-drawn traffic on Broadway, passing the splashing fountain in City Hall Park, alighting in front of the Nassau Street store, and entering the shop with a sheaf of drawings. Perhaps she chatted with Mr. Currier about the sketches or about a painting by a popular Hudson River School artist whose work was on exhibition at the National Academy of Design (she sometimes adapted a composition). She might have inquired about his family or discussed a poem by Henry Wadsworth Longfellow or John Greenleaf Whittier, who was Currier's abolitionist cousin and summer neighbor in Amesbury, Massachusetts. The cultivated Mrs. Palmer was often assigned the task of illustrating literary works.

Although Fanny Palmer was highly regarded in Currier's company, she could not be part of the male bonding described in her colleagues' reminiscences. Louis Maurer spent a great deal of time with Arthur Tait, camping at his place in the Adirondacks. Thomas Worth and James Ives frequently went off to the trotting races together in search of print material and jolly companionship. Palmer seems to have done most of her work in her home studio, commuting to Nassau Street as needed.

6

Prints for the People

FOR FANNY PALMER, her new position at Nathaniel Currier's company was a liberation in many ways. Not only was she assured of steady employment without the need to hustle for jobs in competition with a plethora of struggling print shops, but she also no longer had to deal with the mess and labor of the actual printing process. And perhaps most important of all, in addition to copying the work of others, she was also hired to develop new and original compositions as a recognized *artist* as well as a lithographer, one of the few artists regarded as prestigious enough to have their names printed below the image.

Before this, in order to survive F. F. Palmer had completed an odd hodge-podge of assignments—whatever came her way. Much of her work was original, but much was also reproductive lithography, probably including a great deal of pedestrian ephemera—advertisements, labels, cards, and invoices—that have entirely disappeared. Now it took on a broader and at the same time more clearly defined scope: she became one of the Currier firm's principal purveyors of the American Dream. At the peak of her production, she delivered images of New York City, farmers in the fields, Hudson River mansions, sporting scenes, and sentimental pictures of family life to the presses at the rate of one every two weeks.[1] They flowed from her pencil, brush, and crayon in such numbers and variety that a review of her work is like witnessing a documentary film or pageant of mid-nineteenth-century American life.

The prints reflect the intense nationalism of the times. Purchasers wanted to view their rapidly expanding country through rose-colored glasses; they welcomed a new mythology for a new democratic nation. This nationalistic spirit was reflected in all the arts: in James Fenimore Cooper's novels, Ralph Waldo Emerson's essays, and William Jennings Bryant's poems as well as in visual media.

Palmer undoubtedly also visited National Academy of Design exhibitions and was influenced by painters of the dominant Hudson River School (such as Thomas Cole, Asher Durand, Frederick Church, and Albert Bierstadt), who chose as their principal subject matter the majesty of their country's unspoiled scenery. She was also influenced by the popular school of American genre painting exhibited at a gallery run by the American Art-Union, a new organization founded in 1839 by prominent and wealthy citizens intent on fostering a national school of art, and the gallery showcased scenes of everyday American life, such as those by George Caleb Bingham, William Sidney Mount, Richard Caton Woodville, Eastman Johnson, Lilly Martin Spencer, and others.[2] As one important member of this organization phrased it,

> Every nation, worthy of the name of nation, has its native soul, as well as native soil—its own peculiar views of all that makes up this life, and its own mode of uttering those views. If this be true as a general proposition, it has still more force when applied to this country. If there ever was a people on the face of the earth with peculiar and striking characteristics, it is the American people; and if we could only release ourselves from that strange infatuation about foreign arts and artists, and foreign literature, and foreign everything, and dare and love to be ourselves, we should soon have an American literature, an American school of art, as well as a peculiar form of government.[3]

Making good use of their go-getter mercantile skills, the leaders of the Art-Union promoted American talent by holding an annual lottery, a method modeled on the successful raffles held by British art unions. In return for a yearly fee of five dollars, each person who joined received one or more large engravings and was entered in a drawing for one of the artworks that the Art-Union bought, exhibited, and then distributed to lucky winners at an annual event. By 1849, the Art-Union had more than eighteen thousand members, was running exhibitions day and evening at its gallery, and was providing artists with a level of patronage they never had before. Unfortunately, in 1852 the organization was declared a gambling operation and was forced to shut down by the courts, but not before it had exerted a strong influence on American art.[4]

Palmer was undoubtedly familiar with the Art-Union exhibitions shown on nearby Broadway and was influenced by the everyday farm scenes and genre subjects that were so typically American in their content. In fact, she adapted elements from at least two Art-Union engravings—George Caleb Bingham's *Jolly Flatboatmen* (1846) and John Kensett's *Mount Washington from the Valley of Conway* (1851)—in her work for Currier.[5]

However, neither Currier & Ives nor their lithographers considered their low-priced, rapidly executed images to be in the same category as this "high art." The company advertised itself as the "Grand Central Depot for Cheap and Popular Prints."[6] Charles Parsons's family omitted from his obituary the fact that he had been a lithographer, even though he spent many years in the profession; it would have lowered his status as the distinguished head of the art department at Harper & Brothers.[7] Many years later, in the 1930s, Palmer's colleague Louis Maurer, by then almost one hundred years old, expressed astonishment that his prints now commanded such high prices. Regarding them as mere throwaways of the moment, he had given them all away.[8]

Today we value these prints highly. As in the case of cinema and jazz, what was initially considered a vulgar stepchild of the arts turned out to be an important art form. What we find in the work of Palmer and her colleagues is a vivid picture not so much of the country as it actually was but of the way in which large sections of the American people wanted to see it.[9] Although the images appear at first glance to be realistic representations (and aspects of them are), they actually reflect the fluctuating attitudes, dreams, and prejudices of their time. This variable zeitgeist was influenced, of course, by the country's leaders, who, with their own agendas, helped to shape the public's ideas through newspapers, magazines, oratory, and sermons.

Palmer dealt with several major themes, glamorizing both urban and rural life. On the one hand, city views were very popular. Tourists especially liked to bring home pictures of the vibrant, growing metropolis, with its principal landmarks keyed below the image. On the other hand, life in the city was insecure, crime-ridden, and stressful. Americans still had strong ties to their agrarian origins and viewed rural life as the bedrock of American moral values. Perhaps more than any other artist at Currier

& Ives, Palmer was responsible for the company's many nostalgic images of life on the farm and in small villages. She dramatized the nation's growing affluence in images of well-to-do citizens at leisure on the grounds of their splendid homes or engaged in such pastimes as hunting, fishing, and boating. Even farm wives and the working classes could identify with such a lifestyle by hanging an inexpensive print on a parlor wall.

Other images reflect the pride that Americans felt in their new forms of technology. Yankee know-how and Progress with a capital P were embodied in pictures of American clipper ships, steamboats, and the new railroad and telegraph lines that were rapidly connecting all parts of the country. Currier & Ives saw no contradiction between prints glorifying urban and technological development and prints reflecting a nostalgic longing for the rural past. Janus-like, the company looked backward and forward at the same time, hoping to appeal to all markets.

Certain subjects were not assigned to Palmer. After joining Currier & Ives, she never produced political cartoons, trotting and horse-racing scenes, military figures in combat, firemen racing to conflagrations, or pictures of white men fighting with Native Americans, although she had dealt with some of these themes when she was in her own business. Either the artist preferred not to treat those subjects, or her employers believed that her male colleagues were more adept at rendering them, or perhaps they were not considered appropriate subjects for a woman artist. One must add that Mr. Currier and Mr. Ives were not interested in any content that threatened the status quo. The one attempt she made to show a wife rebelling against an unfaithful husband—a funny drawing called *Love, Marriage, and Separation* (undated, Museum of the City of New York)—was never published.

From 1849, Palmer began to produce lithographs for her new employer in such numbers that from here on it is necessary to establish some broad headings of the types she produced as a framework for discussion, arranged in roughly chronological order.

City and Suburban Views

Palmer's earliest dated and signed works for Currier are two views of New York City seen from high points across the water. The city had become the leading commercial and financial center in the country, and its citizens gloried in its skyline. Walt Whitman described it from the Brooklyn ferry:

Now I am curious what sight can ever be more
    stately and admirable to me than my mast—
    hemm'd Manhatta, my river and sun-set, and
    my scallop-edged waves of flood-tide . . .
Stand up, tall masts of Manahatta!—stand up,
    beautiful hills of Brooklyn! . . .
Come on, ships, from the lower bay! Pass up
    or down, white-sailed schooners, sloops,
    lighters![10]

In Palmer's *View of New York. From Brooklyn Heights* (1849; p. 94), two families, seen from behind, stand on a treeless bluff gazing across the East River at the Lower Manhattan waterfront, fringed by the masts of docked cargo ships. The harsh, unbroken horizontal line of Palmer's print, without the softness created by the customary flanking trees, emphasizes the urban feel of the scene and the speed of the boats, flying along to left and right. Only the ferries crossing at angles to the traffic serve as *repoussoirs*, bringing the eye forward and around the composition. Keyed below the title are important landmarks, including the lighthouse and battery on Bedlow's Island, the Merchant's Exchange, the ferry landing, city hall, and Astor House. Toward the center, the spire of Trinity Church near Wall Street rises higher than the rest, suggesting that the city is a meld of commerce and the Protestant moral and spiritual ethic. There, in a church owning huge amounts of New York City real estate, the Schermerhorns, the Astors, and other wealthy and powerful parishioners met and mingled.

In the companion print *View of New York. From Weehawken–North River* (1849; p. 95), the view is from the leafy New Jersey Palisades, where Aaron Burr fatally shot Alexander Hamilton in a duel in 1804. A gentleman in a tall hat and cane points out to two bonneted ladies the landmarks across the Hudson River, while another man looks through a spyglass at a point on the opposite shore that is today's crowded midtown Manhattan. Below them on the water are sailboats, people in rowboats, and two paddle wheelers, the *New World* and the *Isaac Newton*.

In his book *The Magisterial Gaze*, Albert Boime interprets this elevated view as an expression of the new American elite glorying in its power from the heights. He quotes the poem *Fanny* by Fitz-Greene Halleck, a poet, banker, private secretary to John Jacob Astor, and member of the prestigious Knickerbocker Group, who spent weekends at a Weehawken hillside villa overlooking Manhattan. In the poem, according to Boime, Halleck spoke for

the "Wall Street crowd" when he "took the panoramic view as an extension of personal and patriotic power."

    The city bright below; and far away,
  Sparkling in golden light, his own romantic bay.
  Tall spire, and glittering roof, and battlement, . . .
    And white sails o'er the calm blue waters bent,
. . . nor lives there one
    Whose infant breath was drawn, or boyhood's days
  Of happiness, were pass'd beneath that sun,
    That in his manhood's prime can calmly gaze
  Upon that bay, or on that mountain stand,
Nor feel the prouder of his native land.[11]

Both views of Manhattan were standard stops on the grand tour of America and were illustrated by many artists and printmakers. Comparing Palmer's views to John Hill's aquatints of William Guy Wall's watercolors only twenty-six years earlier, we can see the city's rapid development in just a few decades.[12]

Turning her vision across the continent to the West Coast, where the Gold Rush was causing the raw new town of San Francisco to explode outward, Palmer lithographed *View of San Francisco, California. Taken from Telegraph Hill* (1851; gallery plate 26). The image was taken from a watercolor done in April 1850 by William B. McMurtrie, the artist-draughtsman accompanying the US Pacific Coast Survey.[13] The fact that Currier selected Palmer from his group of experienced lithographers to carry out this timely and unusually expensive print (five dollars), with the imprint "on stone by F. Palmer" shown below the image, indicates his respect for her technical skill.

In this image, a man stands high on the aptly named Telegraph Hill in front of the signal house from which he sent semaphore telegraph messages to local merchants, informing them about arriving ships and their cargoes.[14] He looks out over the bay crowded with vessels and the cluster of wharves, stores, and houses beginning to spread around the waterfront. Across the water is empty land, ripe for development—the real gold of the region.

American artists of the mid–nineteenth century often chose such a viewpoint, looking down from the heights at vistas that conjured up visions of the future.[15] The popular travel writer Bayard Taylor, a promoter of expansionism and Anglo-Saxon superiority, expressed this vision when he wrote of looking out over an undeveloped valley in northern California in 1849. Imagining a lovely

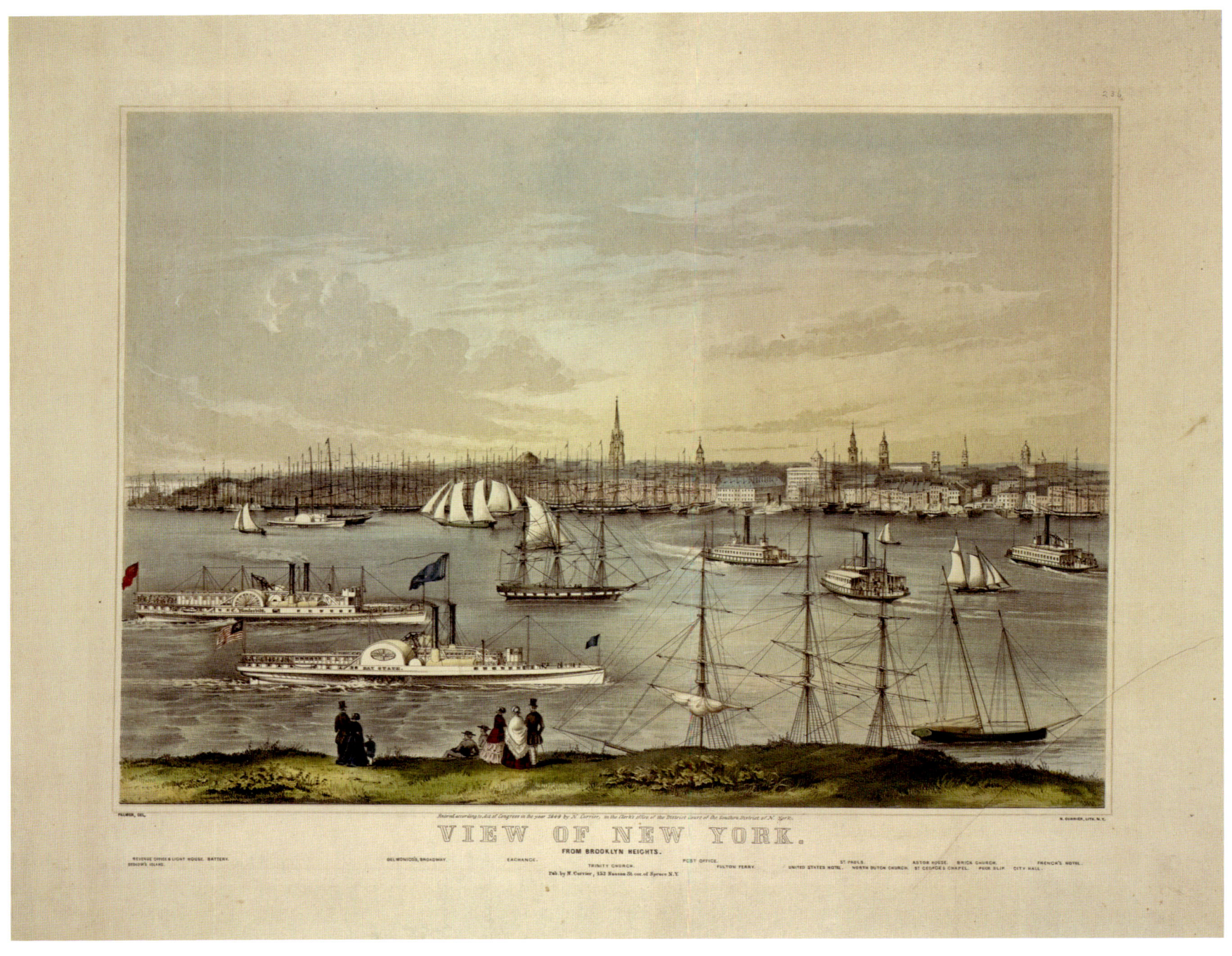

VIEW OF NEW YORK.

FROM BROOKLYN HEIGHTS.

60. *View of New York. From Brooklyn Heights.* 1849. Printed and published by N. Currier. Courtesy of the Miriam and Ira D. Wallach Division of Art, Prints, and Photographs: Print Collection, the New York Public Library. (Checklist 3-152)

city one hundred years in the future, he saw mansions as "fair as temples, with their white fronts and long colonnades . . . statues peeping from the gloom of laurel bowers . . . culture, plenty, peace, happiness everywhere. I saw a more beautiful race in possession of this paradise—a race in which the lost symmetry and grace of the Greek was partially restored."[16]

In 1853, Palmer demonstrated her virtuoso rendering of architecture with the print *New York Crystal Palace. For the*

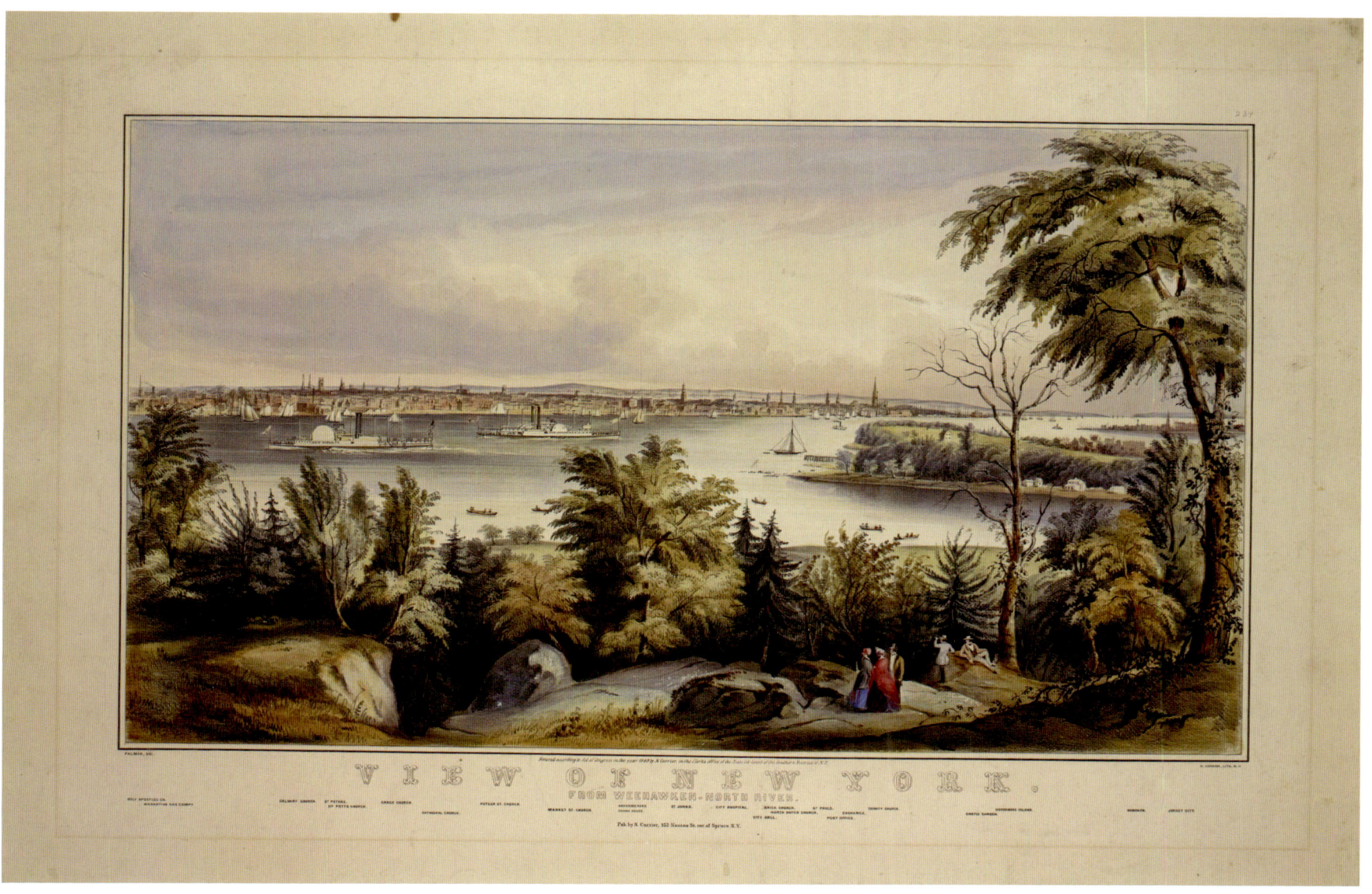

61. *View of New York. From Weehawken–North River.* 1849. Printed and published by N. Currier. Courtesy of the Miriam and Ira D. Wallach Division of Art, Prints, and Photographs: Print Collection, the New York Public Library. (Checklist 3-154)

Exhibition of the Industry of all Nations (p. 96). On open land north of the city at Sixth Avenue and Forty-Second Street (where Bryant Park is located today), this immense iron and glass exhibition hall was built to house America's first world's fair. The building, in the shape of a Greek cross, was inspired by London's Crystal Palace, built for England's World's Fair of 1851. The New York Crystal Palace enclosed almost five acres of exhibits from many countries; above all, it showcased the growing scientific, industrial, and cultural prowess of the United States—everything from steam engines to printing presses, lighthouse lenses, paintings, sculpture, even potato peelers. Hiram Powers's new statue *The Greek Slave* occupied a central position and was a *succès de scandale* because of its nudity, beauty, and veiled reference to American slavery.[17]

The fair was the highlight of the year. Walt Whitman, who returned so many times that the guards began to view him with suspicion, later wrote a poem, "The Song of the Exposition," for the American Institute, evoking a vision of such a building as the eighth wonder of the world—a symbol of American bounty and freedom:

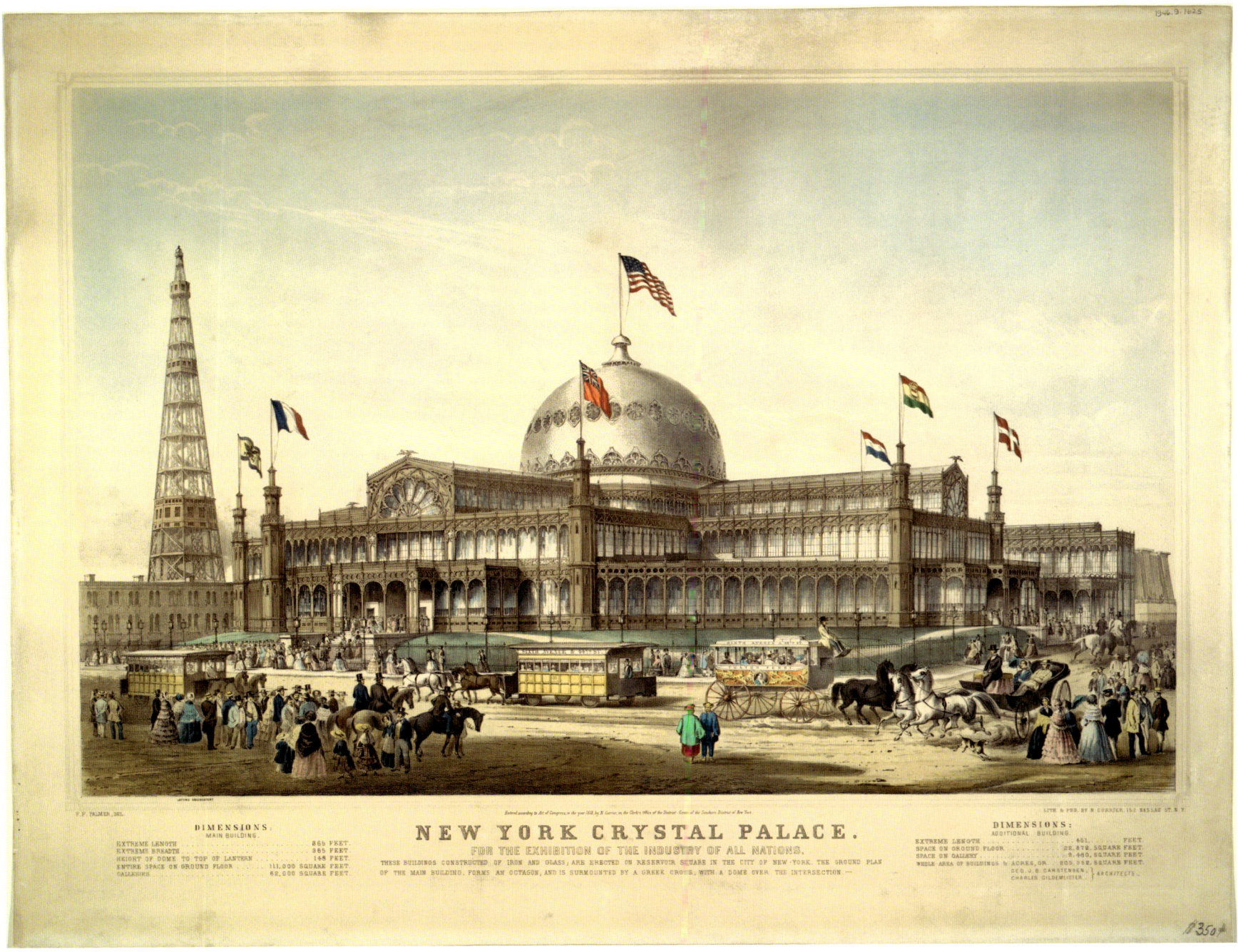

F. F. PALMER, DEL.

Entered according to Act of Congress, in the year 1853, by N. Currier, in the Clerk's Office of the District Court of the Southern District of New York.

LITH. & PUB. BY N. CURRIER, 152 NASSAU ST. N.Y.

DIMENSIONS:
MAIN BUILDING.

EXTREME LENGTH	365 FEET.
EXTREME BREADTH	365 FEET.
HEIGHT OF DOME TO TOP OF LANTERN	148 FEET.
ENTIRE SPACE ON GROUND FLOOR	111,000 SQUARE FEET.
GALLERIES	62,000 SQUARE FEET.

NEW YORK CRYSTAL PALACE.
FOR THE EXHIBITION OF THE INDUSTRY OF ALL NATIONS.

THESE BUILDINGS CONSTRUCTED OF IRON AND GLASS, ARE ERECTED ON RESERVOIR SQUARE IN THE CITY OF NEW-YORK. THE GROUND PLAN OF THE MAIN BUILDING, FORMS AN OCTAGON, AND IS SURMOUNTED BY A GREEK CROSS, WITH A DOME OVER THE INTERSECTION.—

DIMENSIONS:
ADDITIONAL BUILDING.

EXTREME LENGTH	451. FEET.
SPACE ON GROUND FLOOR	25,672 SQUARE FEET.
SPACE ON GALLERY	9,480 SQUARE FEET.
WHOLE AREA OF BUILDINGS ½ ACRES, OR	203,762 SQUARE FEET.
GEO. J. B. CARSTENSEN,	} ARCHITECTS.
CHARLES GILDEMEISTER,	

62. *New York Crystal Palace. For the Exhibition of the Industry of all Nations.* 1853. Printed and published N. Currier. Courtesy of the Yale University Art Gallery. (Checklist 3-94)

Around a palace, loftier, fairer, ampler than any yet,
Earth's modern wonder, history's seven outstripping,
High rising tier on tier with glass and iron façades, . . .
Over whose golden roof shall flaunt, beneath thy banner
    Freedom.[18]

In Palmer's print, left of the Crystal Palace is Latting Observatory, a wooden open-work conical structure—then the tallest structure in New York—in which visitors could ride the new Otis steam-driven elevator to the second floor for a thrilling view of the city. Americans were taking an early look at the invention that would soon revolutionize urban skylines. Behind the palace on the right, the sloping side of the new Croton Reservoir is seen jutting out.

Visitors on foot, on horseback, and in horse-drawn trolleys and carriages swarm around the palace building. Amid this hubbub, two Chinese men wearing braids and traditional garb chat in the foreground, lending an international flavor to the scene. The Gold Rush had brought the first influx of Chinese immigrants to the West Coast, and a few had trickled into New York City, but the all-white crowd leaves a space between themselves and the newcomers.[19] Although the virulent anti-Asian feelings that would soon develop in the United States are not yet evident in Palmer's lithograph, the newcomers are clearly depicted as "others." Around this time, P. T. Barnum was featuring an immigrant Chinese family at his American Museum of freaks and curiosities. A Currier print depicting this family, *The Living Chinese Family: Arrived in New York April 1850* (1850), begins with the following description: "Miss Pwam-Ye-Koo, aged 17 years a young lady with feet 2½ inches long."

Sometime in the mid-1860s, Palmer lithographed another urban spectacle, a dreamlike view of the Fairmount Water Works in Philadelphia (p. 98), the innovative water-pumping system that was the pride of the City of Brotherly Love. The city fathers had conceived the brilliant idea of housing the machinery in Greek Revival buildings on the shore of the Schuylkill River and surrounding the buildings with hillside walks, gazebos, and statues by Philadelphia's leading sculptor, William Rush. Crossing the river on the right is another new engineering wonder, the first successful wire suspension bridge in the United States, built by Charles Ellet Jr. in 1842.

People from many nations came to marvel at the waterworks; artists painted it; Mark Twain, Charles Dickens, and other authors described it enthusiastically.[20] The pumps stopped supplying water to the city in 1909, and the Philadelphia Museum of Art now stands where the reservoir once crowned the hill. In the 1970s, the beautiful complex was designated a National Historic Landmark and later restored with an interpretive center.

After James Ives became Currier's partner in 1857 and assumed more influence over the company's imagery, Palmer produced *New York Bay. From Bay Ridge, L.I.* (1860; p. 99). The near-bird's-eye perspective and swinging lines leading the eye back to the opposite shoreline reveal a new, dynamic spatial quality in her work. Here the artist presents us with the "good life" led by wealthy Brooklyn villa owners at a time when the suburbs still had large open spaces. A driver and two women ride forward in a carriage from a stylish neogothic mansion located on the bay front, passing the neatly trimmed grounds where a gardener is picking fruit. As in previous views, landmarks seen across the water are listed in the margin below: Bedlow's Island, Jersey City, Hoboken, Castle Garden, and so on.

In 1861, the first year of the Civil War, the artist completed *Staten Island and the Narrows. From Fort Hamilton* (p. 183). At that moment, the print had an especially reassuring and timely message because it showed that New York City was well protected. Fort Hamilton on the right and Fort Lafayette on an offshore island are guarding the Narrows of New York Harbor, while across the water Fort Richmond protects Staten Island. Fort Lafayette was also a subject of particular notoriety and hot debate in the press at this time because it was being used as a Union prison, where civilians suspected of aiding the Confederacy—many of them prominent businessmen and government officials—were incarcerated (Southerners were calling it the "American Bastille"). Currier & Ives often featured such newsworthy subjects in its prints.

In the foreground of this fine composition, a Victorian family gazes through the opening between three tall, graceful trees that frame the prison and make it a center of interest. Sailboats and steamboats ply the waters, leading the eye back into the hills. This print may have been inspired by William Bartlett's view of the same subject. If so, Palmer changed and improved Bartlett's view considerably.

Two of the artist's most admired New York views are the pair of prints *Blackwells Island, East River. From Eighty Sixth Street, New York* (1862; p. 100) and *View of Astoria, L.I. From the New York Side* (1862; p. 101). Once again, these city views are more

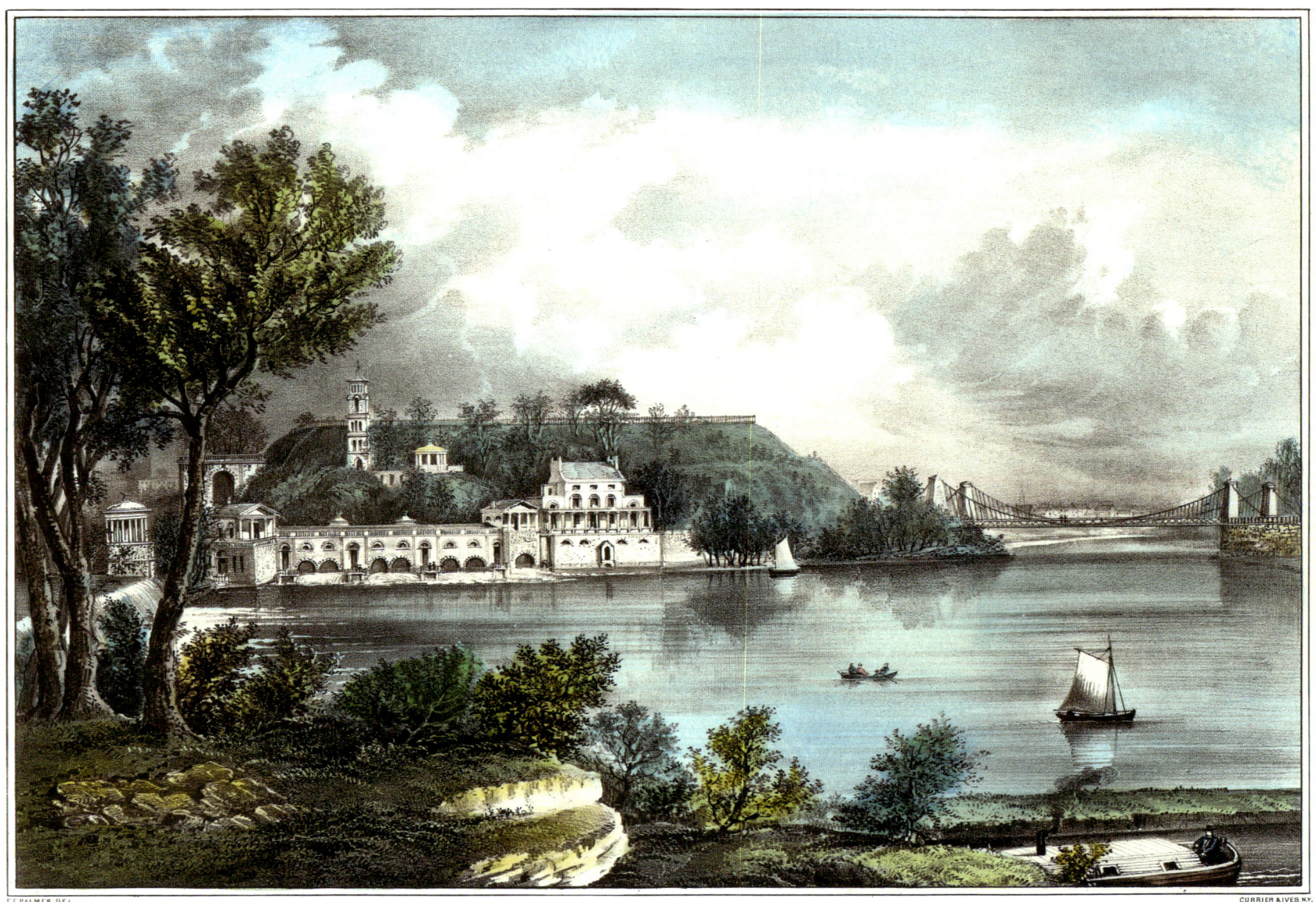

FAIRMOUNT WATER WORKS.
PHILADELPHIA.

dynamic than her earlier ones. *Blackwells Island*, for example, is viewed at an angle, and the color is luminous and brilliant. In typical Currier & Ives fashion, this print is a cheerful image of what was actually a grim subject. The pleasant sunlit buildings shown on the left housed a prison, an insane asylum, a workhouse for the indigent, and a smallpox quarantine hospital. Architect A. J. Davis had designed a progressive and humane plan for the new asylum (its famous octagon tower can be seen on the extreme left), but Charles Dickens described the reality of conditions inside

63. *Fairmount Water Works. Philadelphia.* Undated, ca. 1865. Printed and published by Currier & Ives. Courtesy of the Old Print Shop. (Checklist 3-40)

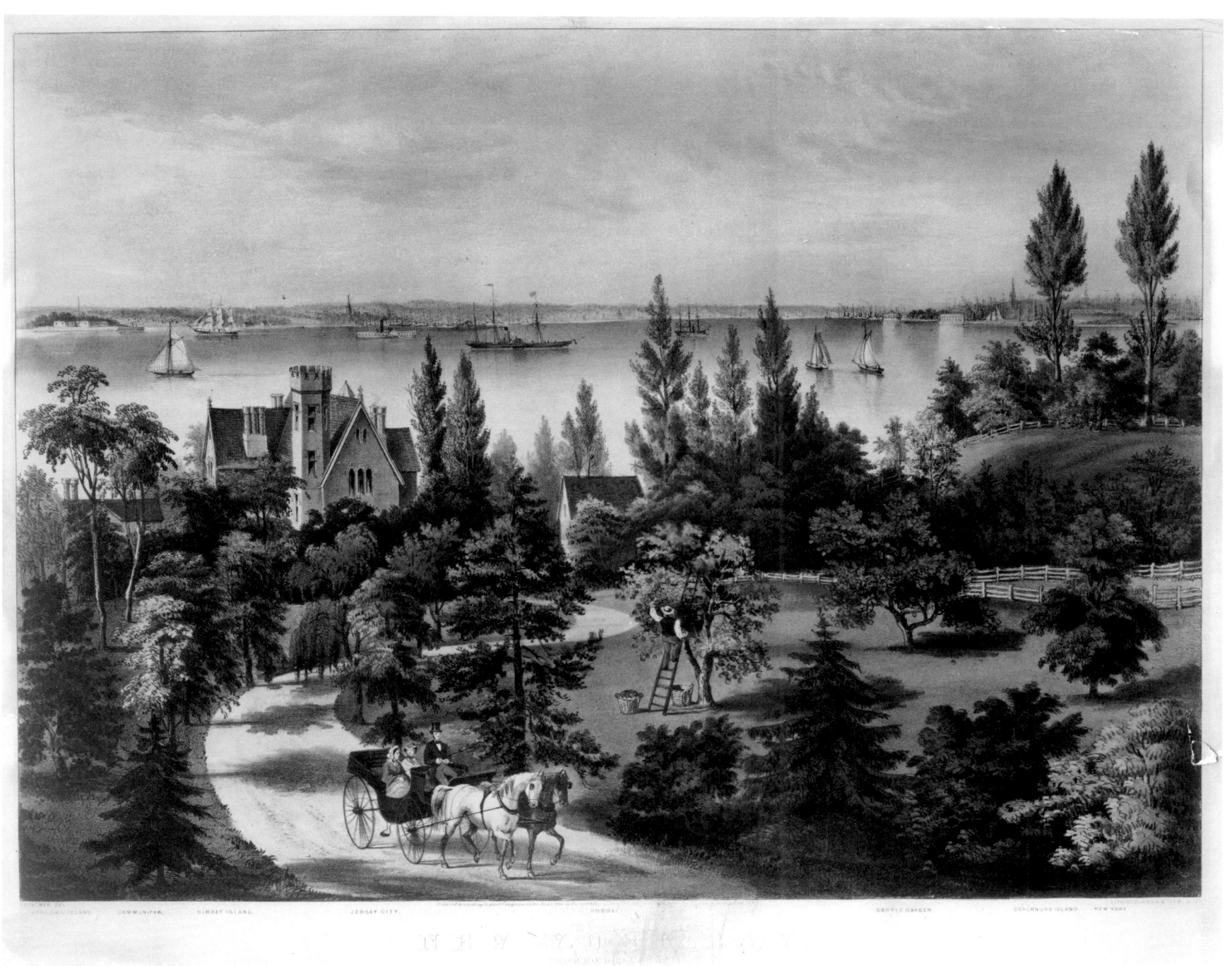

64. *New York Bay. From Bay Ridge, L.I.* 1860. Printed and published by Currier & Ives. Courtesy of the Old Print Shop. (Checklist 3-93)

after his visit there in 1842: "Everything had a lounging, listless, madhouse air, which was very painful. . . . In the dining-room, a bare, dull, dreary place, with nothing for the eye to rest on but the empty walls, a woman was locked up alone. . . . [T]he terrible crowd with which these halls and galleries were filled, so shocked me, that I abridged my stay within the shortest limits."[21]

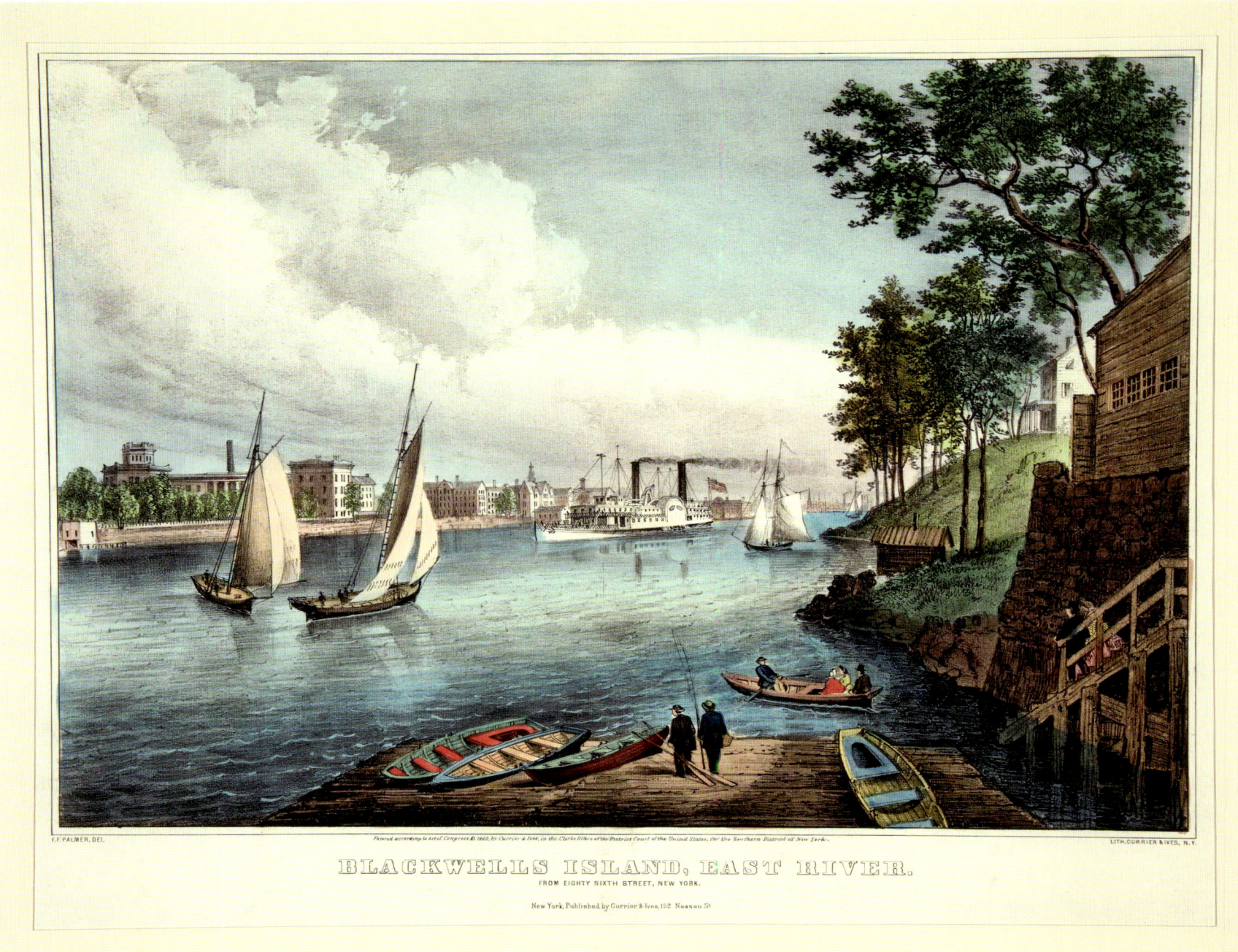

BLACKWELLS ISLAND, EAST RIVER.

FROM EIGHTY SIXTH STREET, NEW YORK.

New York, Published by Currier & Ives, 152 Nassau St

In Palmer's lithograph, the scene has been turned into one of civic pride in institutions that New York's citizens hoped would ameliorate some of the social problems of the day. Happy pleasure seekers are sailing on the river and embarking in rowboats. What is not so obvious from looking at the print is that a boat departed every hour to the workhouse from the wooden landing in the foreground.

65. *Blackwells Island, East River. From Eighty Sixth Street, New York.* 1862. Printed by Currier & Ives. Courtesy of the Yale University Art Gallery. (Checklist 3-24)

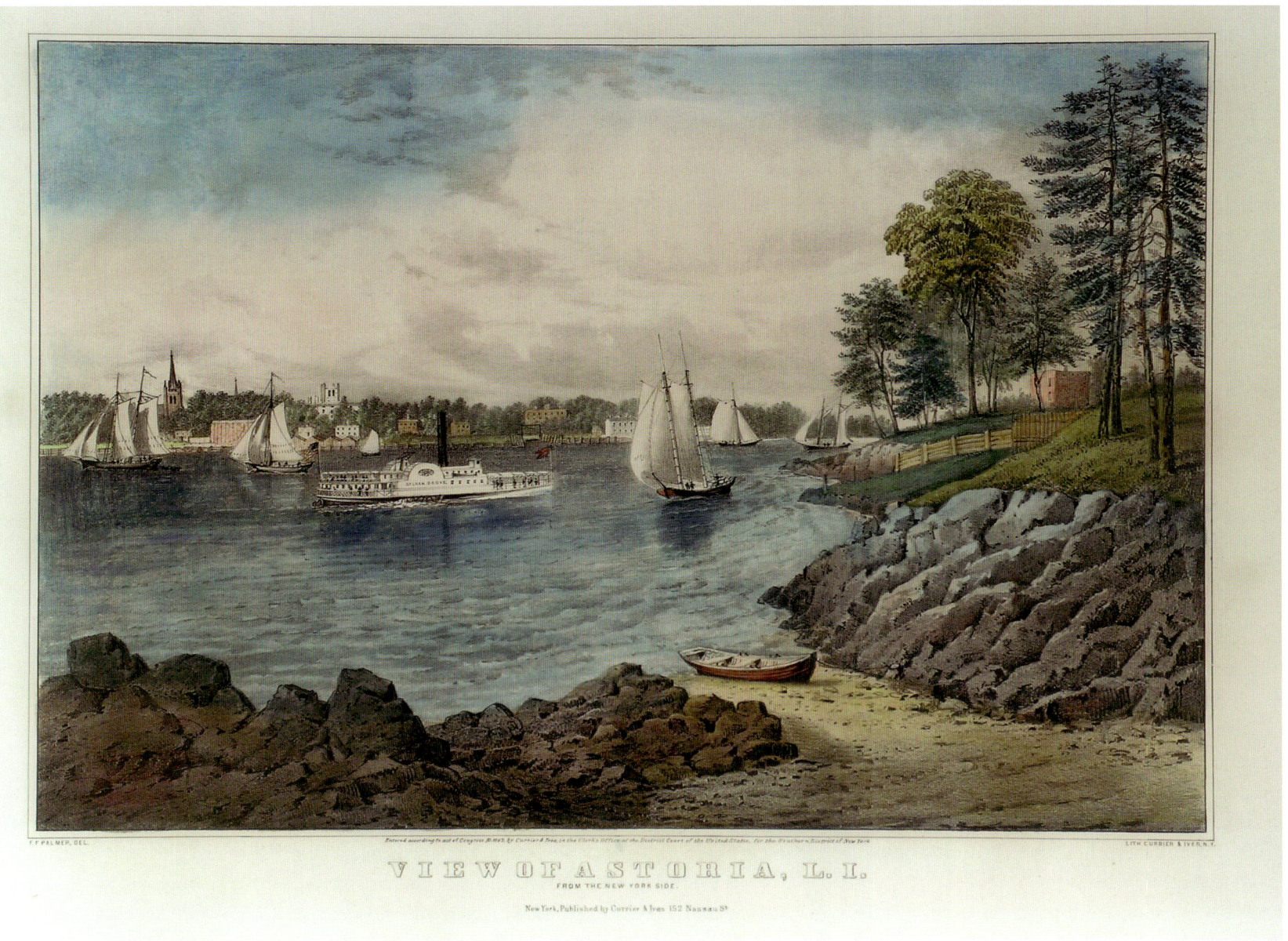

VIEW OF ASTORIA, L.I.
FROM THE NEW YORK SIDE.

New York, Published by Currier & Ives 152 Nassau St.

66. *View of Astoria, L.I. From the New York Side.* 1862. Printed and published by Currier & Ives. (Checklist 3-150)

The companion print, *View of Astoria, L.I.*, centers attention on the four-year-old paddle steamer *Sylvan Grove*, which made regular runs from Peck's Slip in Lower Manhattan to Harlem. It is shown gliding forward smoothly, in contrast with the sailboats that lean to right or left. Astoria, seen across the East River from the east side of Upper Manhattan around Ninety-Sixth Street had a pleasant, tree-filled suburban aspect in 1862.

MARINE PRINTS

Among Palmer's early works for Currier are six prints of clipper ships, so called because they sailed at such a clip. Those elegantly streamlined needle-nosed vessels, originally built in Baltimore and used against the British during the War of 1812, had gradually been enlarged and refined by American designers until in 1845 the *Rainbow* completed a round trip to China in seven months and seventeen days and was declared the swiftest sailing ship afloat.[22]

The Gold Rush of 1849 further stimulated clipper ship production. A year after the discovery of the first gold nugget, almost

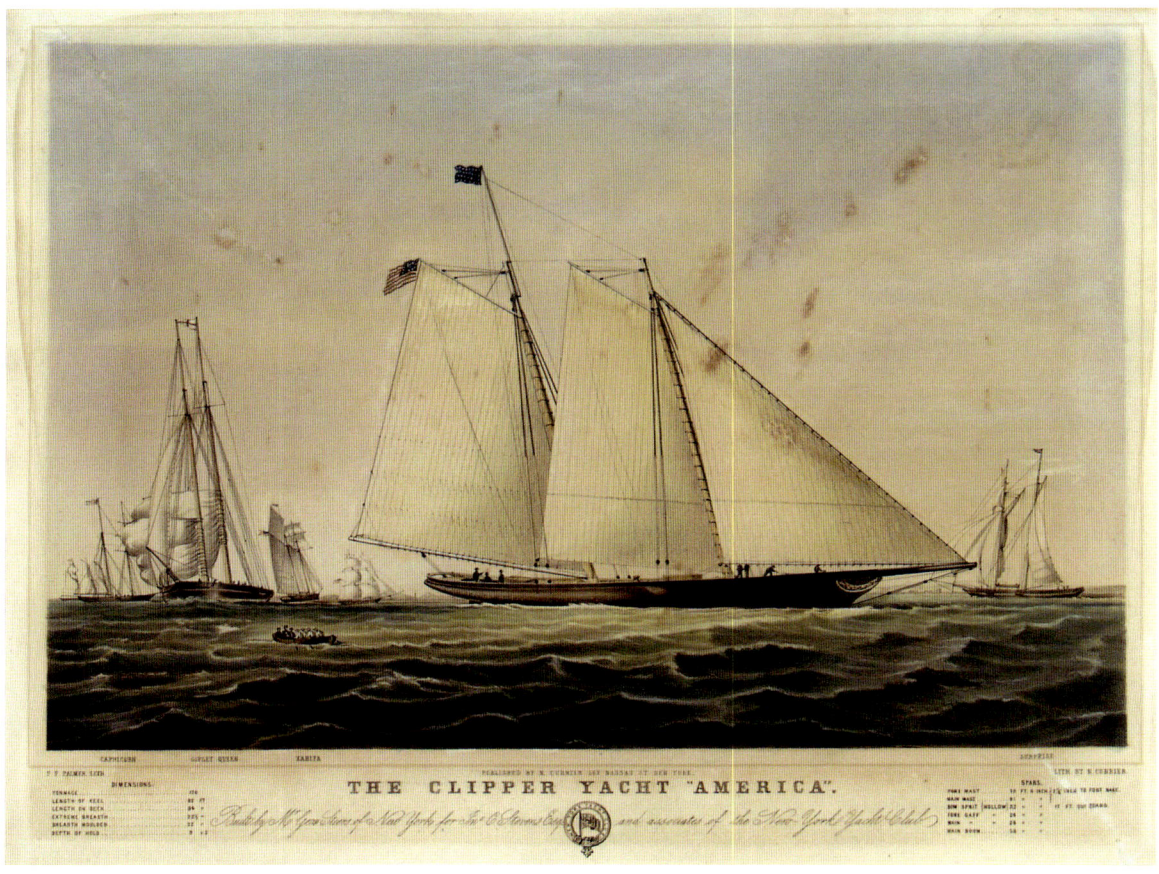

THE CLIPPER YACHT "AMERICA".

67. *The Clipper Yacht "America."* Undated, ca. 1851–52. Printed and published by N. Currier. Courtesy of the Old Print Shop. (Checklist 3-33)

sixteen thousand men and women took the arduous sailing route around Cape Horn at the southern tip of South America to San Francisco. The clippers sometimes raced each other, while an eager public compared their speeds and followed their progress in the newspapers.

In 1851, Commodore John C. Stevens and his New York Yacht Club were invited by Prince Albert and Britain's unbeaten Royal Yacht Squadron to compete against them for the first time in the All-Nations Race around the Isle of Wight. Stevens immediately ordered ship builder George Steers to construct a new state-of-the-art clipper yacht named *America*; it defeated all fourteen British ships and became a powerful symbol of the young nation's emergence as a world leader. Queen Victoria came by in her steamer yacht to congratulate the American crew. According to legend, when she asked, "Who came in second?" someone replied, "Your majesty, there was no second." Upon his return, Stevens was feted at a magnificent dinner, interrupted by resounding toasts and huzzahs, at New York's Astor House hotel on Broadway.[23] The traditional victory cup was renamed "America's Cup."

At that euphoric moment in American maritime history, F. F. Palmer drew *The Clipper Yacht "America"* (undated, ca. 1851–52), in which the *America* heads to the right under full sail, with the English yachts trailing in the distance. The seal of the New York Yacht Club appears on the inscription below the image. Nathaniel Currier advertised proudly in the weekly periodical *Spirit of the Times* that the drawing was made "under the supervision of Mr. George Steers, the builder, and may be relied upon as correct."[24]

Palmer also drew *Clipper Ship "Hurricane" of New York* (1852; gallery plate 14), *Cutter Yacht "Maria"* (1852; p. 290), *Clipper Ship "Contest"* (1853; p. 288), as well as *Clipper Ship "Young America"* (1853; p. 289) and *Clipper Ship "Sweepstakes"* (1853; p. 103)—the latter two adapted from paintings by the Anglo-American marine artist James E. Buttersworth.[25] Palmer's carefully controlled technique in the *"Sweepstakes"* print (note the finely rendered scalloped waves) can be studied on one of the few original Currier & Ives lithograph stones that have escaped destruction (in the ConAgra Collection, Omaha, Nebraska).

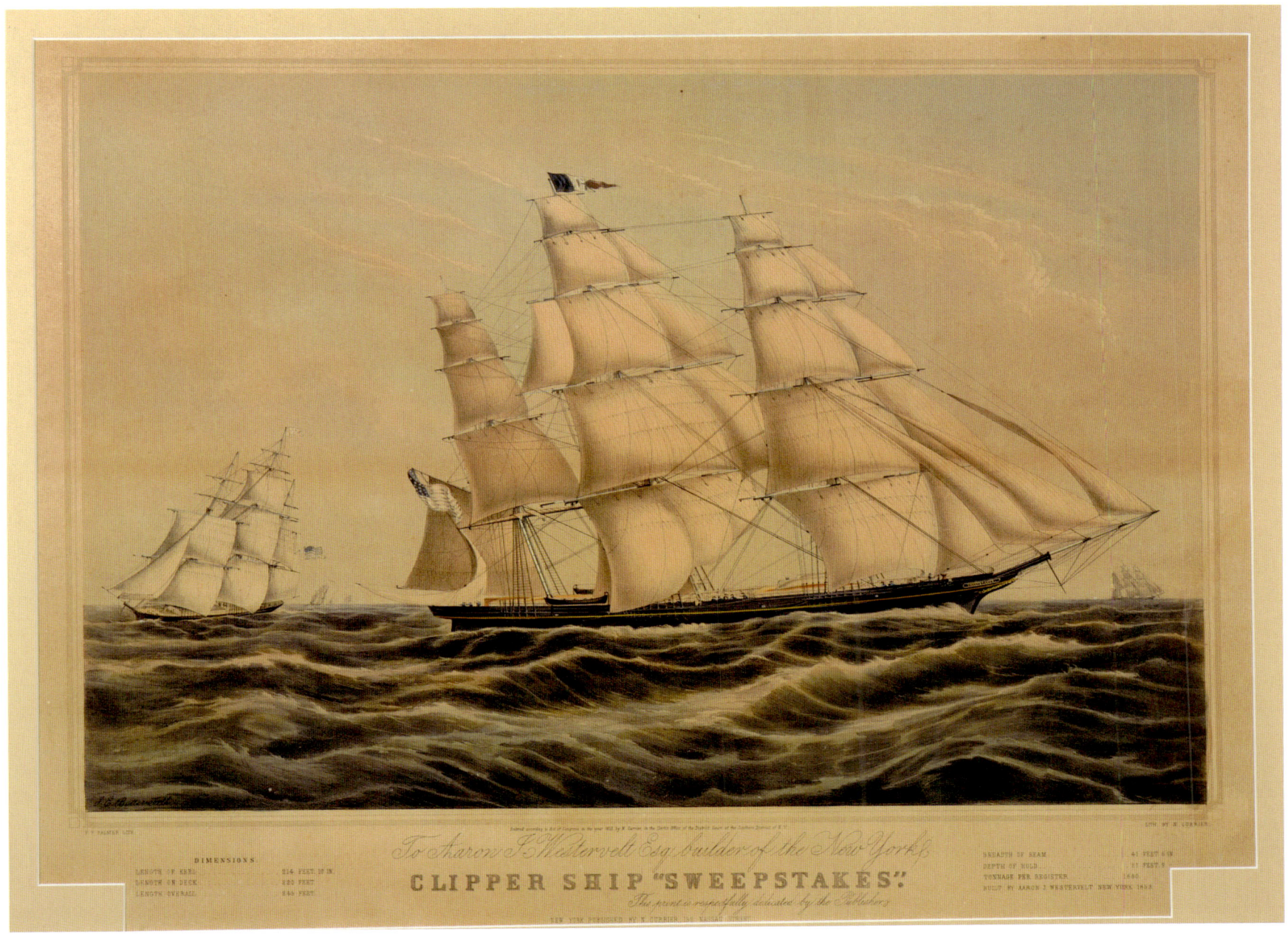

68. *Clipper Ship "Sweepstakes."* 1853. Printed and published by N.
Currier. (Checklist 3-31)

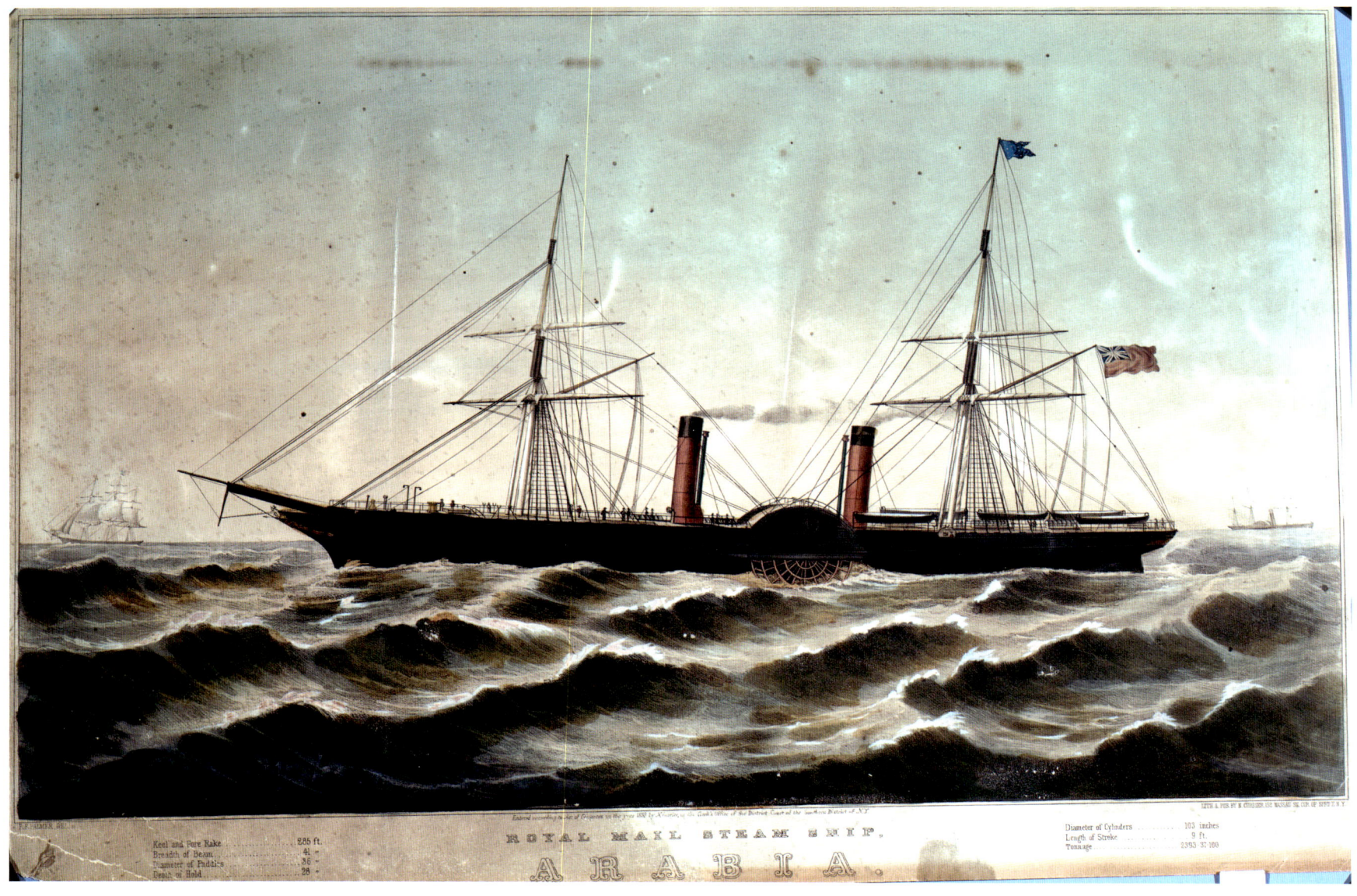

Entered according to Act of Congress in the year 1852 by N Currier, in the Clerk's Office of the District Court of the Southern District of N.Y.

LITH. & PUB. BY N. CURRIER, 152 NASSAU St. COR. OF SPRUCE N.Y.

ROYAL MAIL STEAM SHIP.

ARABIA.

Keel and Fore Rake	265 ft.
Breadth of Beam	41 "
Diameter of Paddles	36 "
Depth of Hold	28 "

Diameter of Cylinders	103 inches
Length of Stroke	9 ft.
Tonnage	2393 37/100

Dedicated to its builder, Aaron J. Westervelt, owner of the renowned Westervelt shipyard, the *Sweepstakes* turned out to be a kind of requiem for clipper ships. The boat was, in fact, the last of its kind built by the company. By 1857, the market was flooded, and a severe financial depression was destroying maritime trade. Great Britain had seized the lead in the production of iron steamships, which were now replacing wooden boats.[26]

Palmer drew and lithographed two of those steamships (in *Royal Mail Steam Ship, Asia* [1851; p. 312] and *Royal Mail Steam Ship. Arabia* [1853]), probably from daguerreotypes.[27] She would later become known for her dramatic compositions of steamboats churning down the Hudson and Mississippi Rivers.

69. *Royal Mail Steam Ship. Arabia.* 1853. Printed and published by N. Currier. Courtesy of the Mariners' Museum, Newport News, VA. (Checklist 3-119)

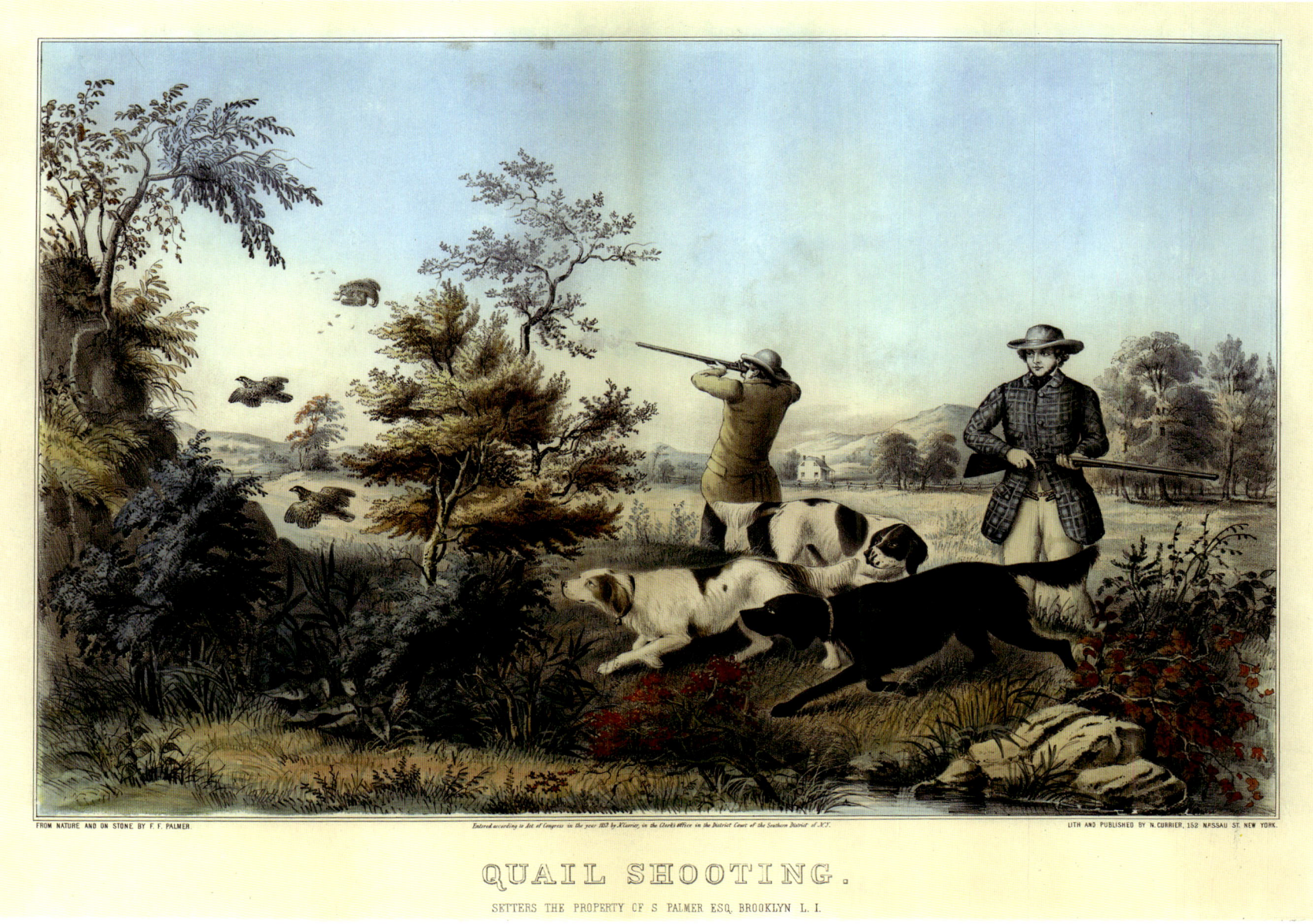

FROM NATURE AND ON STONE BY F. F. PALMER.   Entered according to Act of Congress in the year 1852 by N.Currier, in the Clerks office in the District Court of the Southern District of N.Y.   LITH AND PUBLISHED BY N. CURRIER, 152 NASSAU ST. NEW YORK.

QUAIL SHOOTING.

SETTERS THE PROPERTY OF S. PALMER ESQ. BROOKLYN L. I.

70. *Quail Shooting. Setters the Property of S. Palmer Esq., Brooklyn, L.I.* 1852. Printed and published by N. Currier. Courtesy of the Old Print Shop. (Checklist 3-109)

SPORTING PRINTS

Pictures of hunting and fishing, long a staple of British art, were becoming increasingly popular in the United States as growing middle-class wealth and leisure stimulated a new interest in those gentlemanly pastimes. In 1852, Currier published a series of Palmer's sporting prints that have always been among her most popular works. Signed "From nature and on stone by F. F. Palmer," they are known as the "Long Island Series" because they (except for *Rail Shooting. On The Delaware*, p. 309) are drawn directly from the salt marshes, farmlands, and scrubby woods of Long Island.

On May 15, 1852, Currier advertised these prints in the first sporting weekly in the United States, *Spirit of the Times*. He named Palmer as the artist and indicated that her husband was serving as the model:

SPORTSMEN, ATTENTION!

N. Currier has just published the following elegant prints . . . quail shooting, woodcock shooting, rail shooting, snipe shooting, partridge shooting, wild duck shooting. . . . Price $2.00 each plate splendidly colored. . . . [T]hey are entirely new and original in design. . . . The dogs, positions, dress, and even the ground represented have been drawn from nature by F. F. Palmer, under the supervision of that well-known keen sportsman, S. Palmer, Esq. of Brooklyn, L.I., and the dogs are portraits of those owned by him and his friends.[28]

Lettering below the image of the print *Quail Shooting* reads "Setters the Property of S. Palmer Esq., Brooklyn, L.I."[29] Notice how tactfully this is reported. It would have been demeaning to state that S. Palmer, a man, was posing for his wife. Instead, it is implied that he is instructing her in the correct positions.

Quail Shooting (p. 105), like all the prints in this series, has the fresh feel of a scene observed in the actual moment. The hunter, his smoking gun still raised, has just shot a bird, and it is pulverizing in the air, its feathers flying apart. *Wild Duck Shooting* (gallery plate 22) captures the tense excitement of the sport. A hunter wearing high boots crouches in the marshy water as wild ducks fly up in V formation from a thicket of cattails. He signals his dog to stay quiet until he can take aim, while behind him a lad in a rowboat restrains a second dog. The strong diagonal line leading the eye up to the birds causes the viewer to identify with the hunter's intense focus on his prey.[30] Currier sweetened his sales pitch for prints in this series by adding to the advertisement for it that "the above will be furnished, neatly framed in rosewood frames, with inside gilt strip, at $4 each and boxed ready for shipping free of charge."[31]

A later print, *On a Point* (1855), combines hunting with a charming Long Island farm scene. Two pointing setters in the foreground are followed by a pair of hunters in the middle distance who skirt alongside a field of wheat sheaves. A typical gambrel-roofed Long Island Dutch farmhouse can be seen farther back. These subjects were so popular that several of them (e.g.,

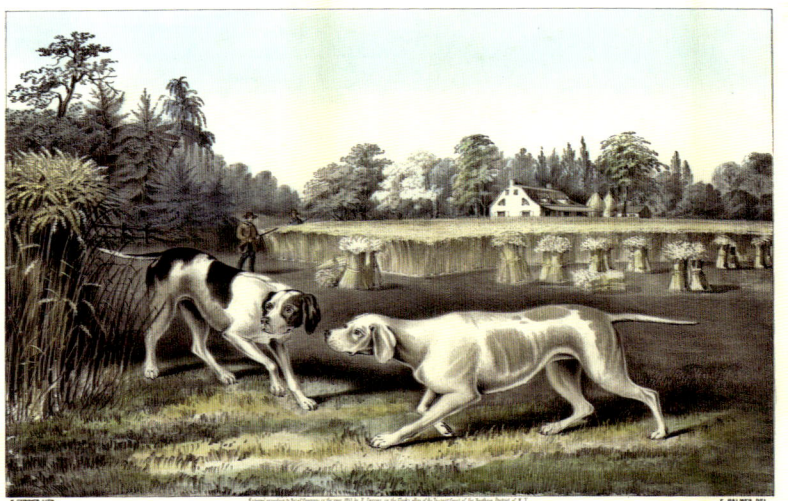

71. *On a Point.* 1855. Printed and published by N. Currier. Courtesy of the Old Print Shop. (Checklist 3-104)

Woodcock Shooting [1852; p. 107] and *Partridge Shooting* [1852; p. 307]) were repeated, with changes, after the Civil War. In Palmer's later versions, the sportsmen are more fashionably dressed, reflecting the growing affluence connected with such pursuits, and the images don't have quite the same feel of direct observation found in this earlier series.

"Man's best friend" must have been Palmer's best friend as well. She never missed an opportunity to include a dog, whether accompanying his mistress on a stroll (*My Cottage Home* [1866; p. 213]), nipping at the feet of a small boy on his way to school (*Across The Continent* [1868; gallery plate 8]), or following a farmer returning from the field (*Haying-Time. The Last Load* [1868; p. 108]). In a pair of richly ornamental "portraits" of hunting dogs sniffing out their prey (*Close Quarters* [1866; gallery plate 16] and *Pointing a Bevy* [1866; gallery plate 15]), the artist blends careful observation with fine color and decorative design.

Palmer also drew fishing scenes "from nature and on stone." In *The Trout Stream* (1852; p. 109), a fisherman's bent rod signals a nibble. Next to him, a lad, about the same age as Palmer's son at that time, holds a net, waiting attentively for the catch. The wicker creel slung across the fisherman's back and the Long Island trees, rocks, and grasses lend an Arcadian authenticity to the image. Another print, *Bass Fishing. At Macomb's Dam Harlem River, N.Y.* (1852; gallery plate 18), shows three happy-looking men dropping their

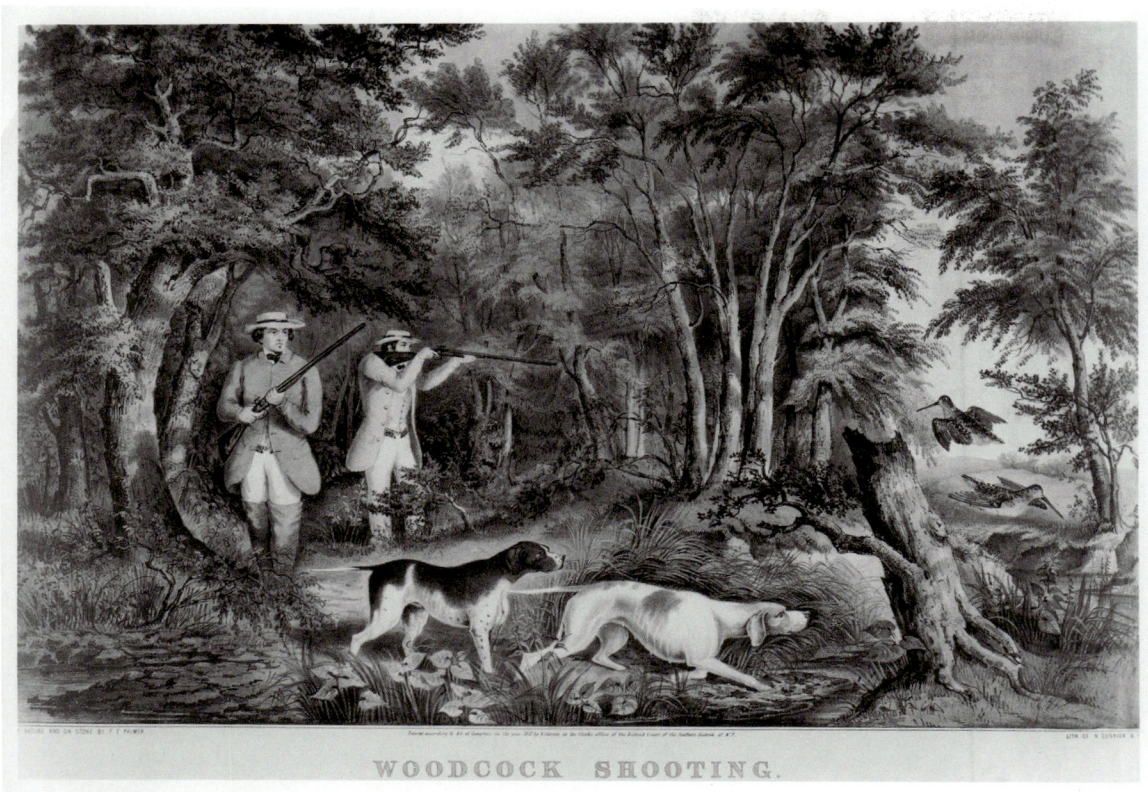

72. *Woodcock Shooting.* 1852. Printed and published by N. Currier. Courtesy of the Old Print Shop. (Checklist 3-175)

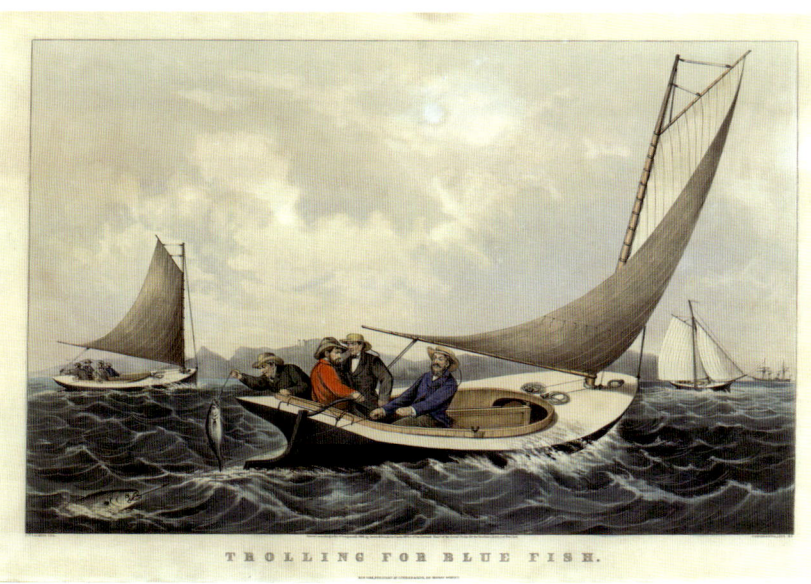

73. *Trolling for Blue Fish.* 1866. Printed and published by Currier & Ives. Courtesy of the Old Print Shop. (Checklist 3-139)

lines from a boat on the Harlem River, with the dam and the distant arches of High Bridge seen behind them. Currier advertised in *Spirit of the Times* that the image was sketched directly from nature with "all the magnificent scenery of that romantic spot."[32]

Fourteen years later Palmer revisited this theme in *Trolling for Blue Fish* (1866), a rollicking image of four men careening along in a catboat on a choppy sea in New York Bay, pulling in fish after fish. The print reminds us that the waters around Manhattan Island were once so crowded each summer with bluefish that the shores were thick with the bones of their prey.[33] A great sense of nippy fresh air, big sky, and splashing water suffuses this print. We know that Palmer enjoyed taking a rowboat across the water from Manhattan with her family and was thoroughly familiar with such sights.[34] In this case, she drew the setting and presumably, because the work bears her name, designed the composition, but Thomas Worth, who had actually sailed in this boat with the owner, Hank Haff, reportedly provided sketches of the boat and figures. Haff, the man at the tiller wearing a red shirt, had piloted some of New York's most famous racing yachts to victory.[35] Note the contrast between the skipper's heroic profile as he guides the

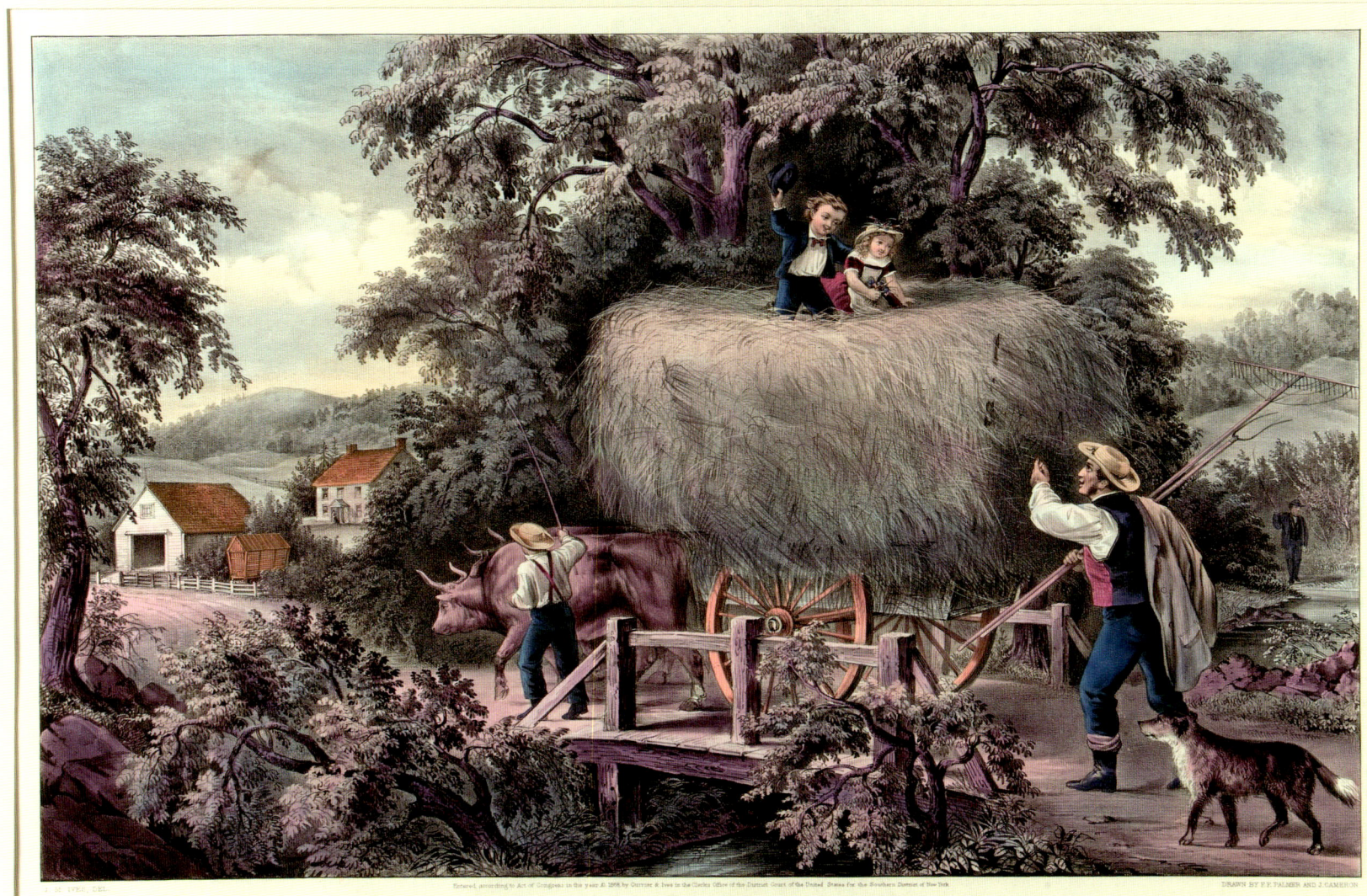

HAYING-TIME.   THE LAST LOAD.

74. *Haying-Time. The Last Load.* 1868. Printed and published by Currier & Ives. Courtesy of the Yale University Art Gallery. (Checklist 3-58)

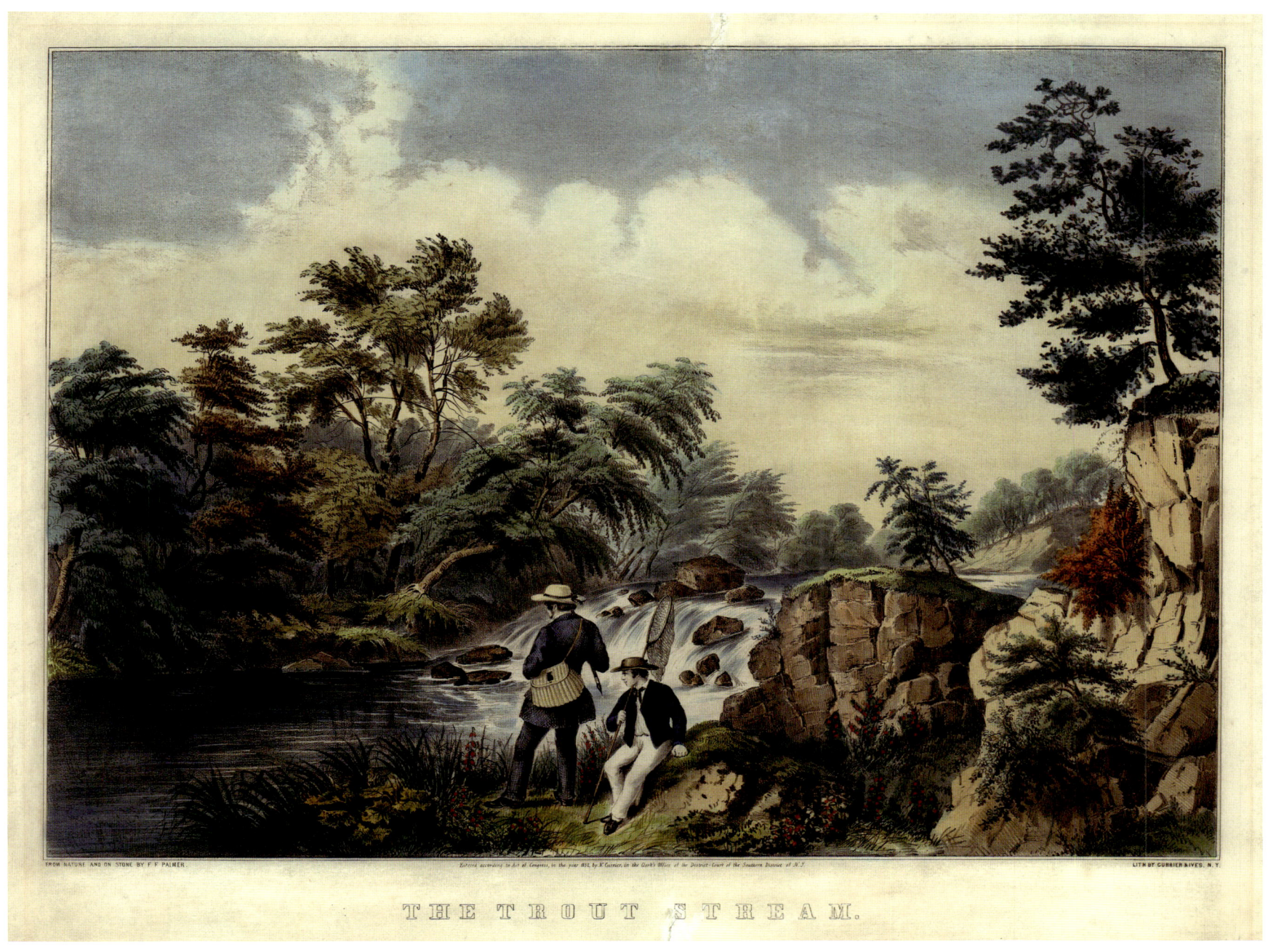

THE TROUT STREAM.

75. *The Trout Stream.* 1852 (ca. 1857–72). Printed and published by
Currier & Ives. Courtesy of the Old Print Shop. (Checklist 3-142)

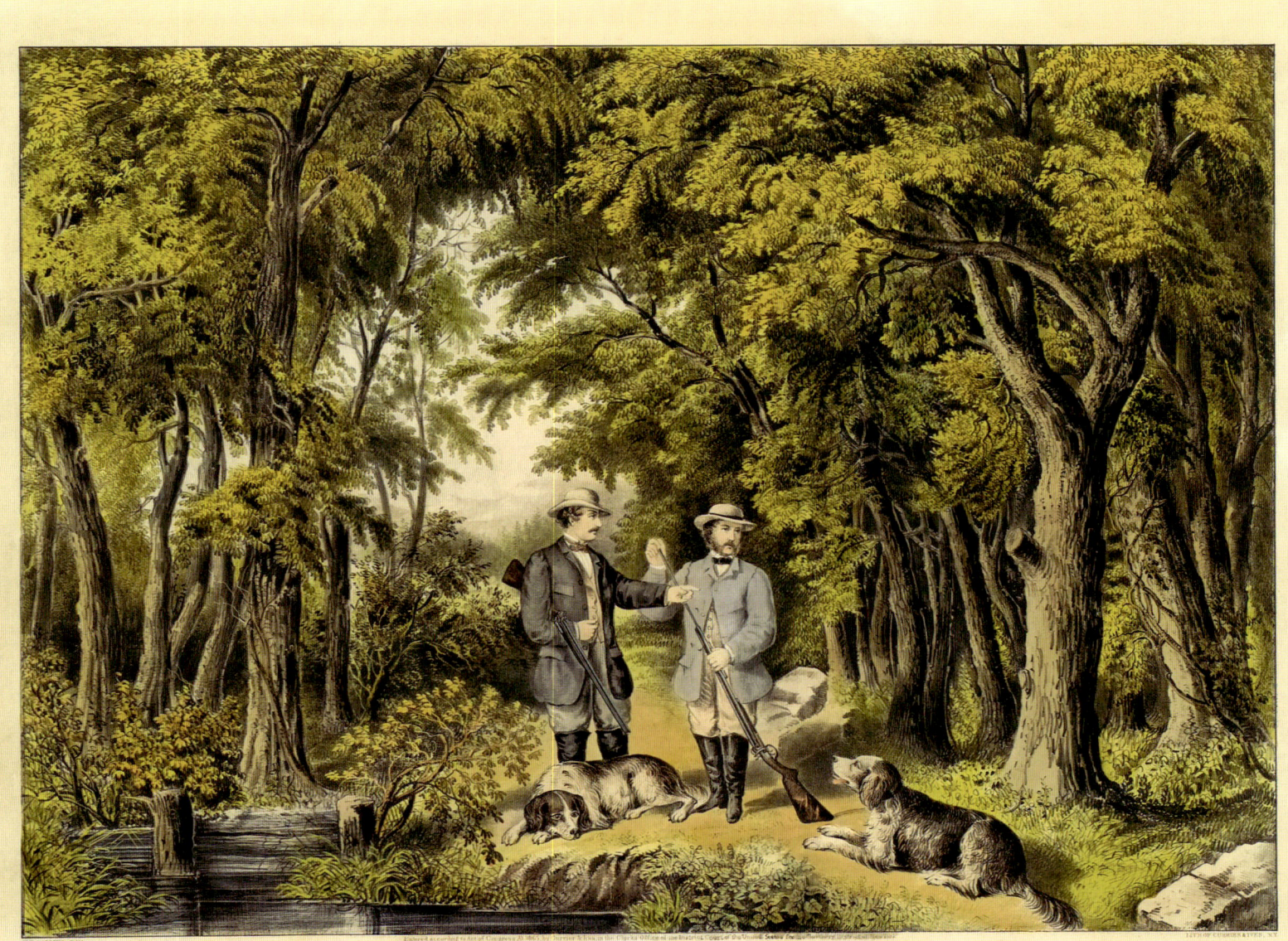

MORNING IN THE WOODS.

76. *Morning in the Woods*. 1865. Printed and published by Currier & Ives, 2004.D03.461. Courtesy of the Michele and Donald D'Amour Museum of Fine Arts, Springfield, MA. Gift of Lenore B. and Sidney A. Alpert, supplemented with Museum Acquisition Funds. Photography by David Stansbury. (Checklist 3-86)

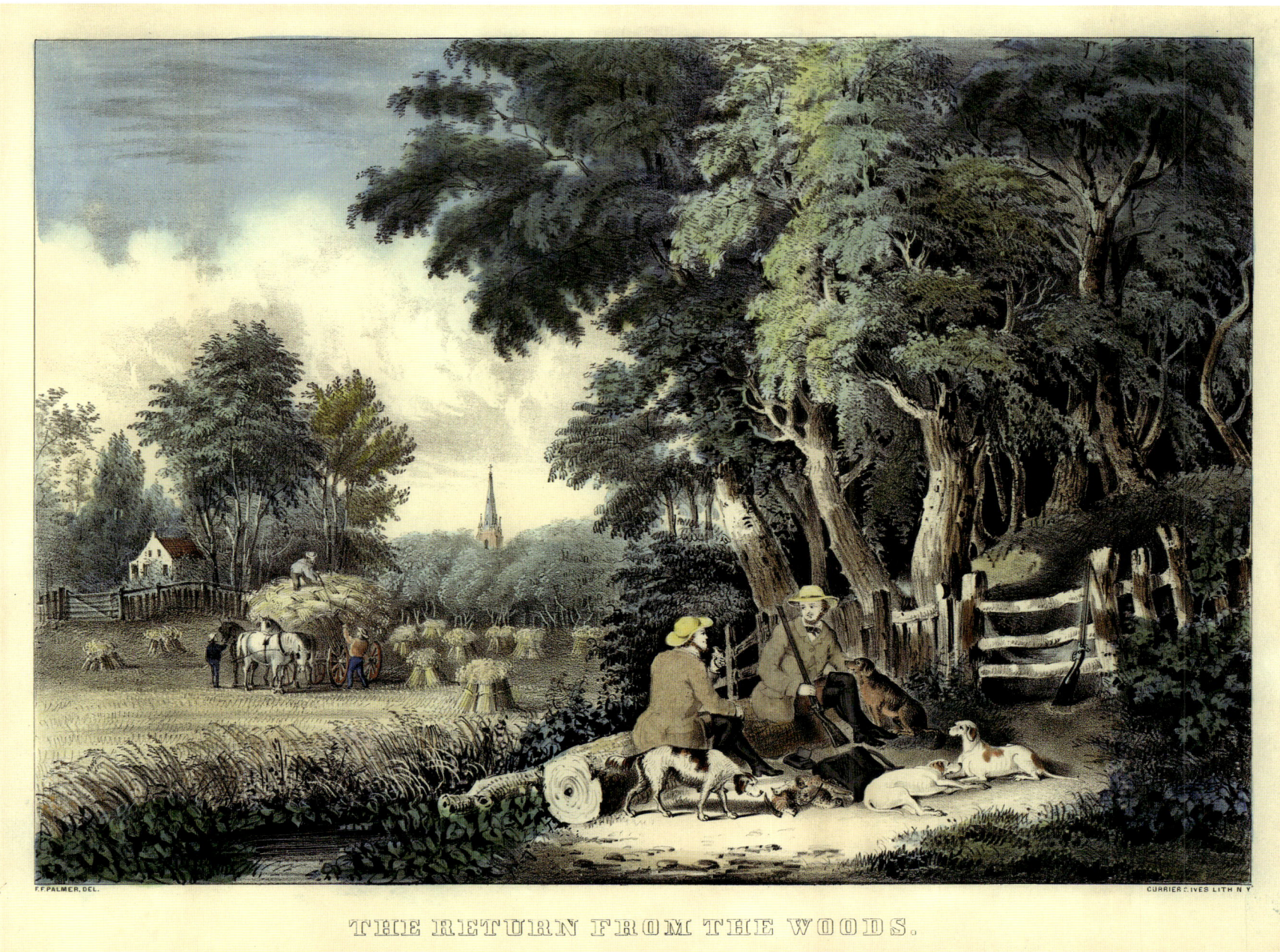

THE RETURN FROM THE WOODS.

New York. Published by Currier & Ives, 152 Nassau St.

77. *The Return from the Woods*. Undated, ca. 1857–72. Printed and published by Currier & Ives. Courtesy of the Old Print Shop. (Checklist 3-114)

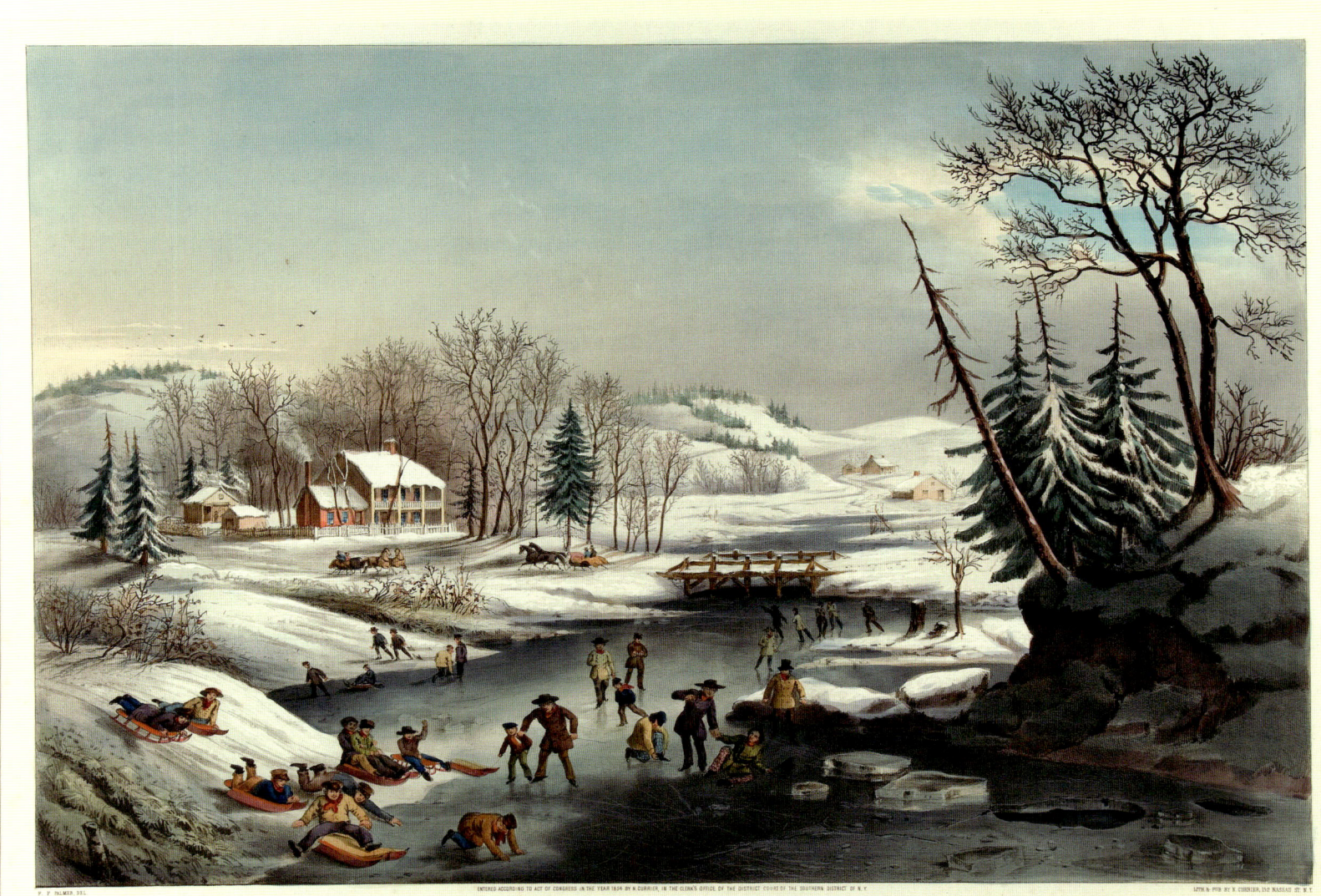

78. *American Winter Scenes. Morning.* 1854. Printed and published by
N. Currier. Courtesy of the Yale University Art Gallery. (Checklist 3-20)

boat and the pop-eyed glee of his companions, rendered with Worthian humor.

The tiny twin lighthouses on the gray hills in the background locate the scene precisely in front of New Jersey's Navesink Highlands, bordering the Lower Bay.[36] Perhaps this location was chosen because the lighthouses, which lit up the dangerous entrance to New York Harbor for many years, were in the news; they had just been rebuilt to look like a gothic brownstone fortress and were a showcase for the most modern navigational technology (and are now a New Jersey State Historic Site).

These prints of fishing and hunting are more than pleasant scenes of leisure pastimes; they are nationalist icons. For example, in *Morning in the Woods* (1852, ca. 1857–72; p. 110) and *The Return from the Woods* (undated, ca. 1857–72; p. 111), we see a blend of two kinds of Arcadian imagery—farm and forest—both of which symbolize New World abundance. In the second print, two hunters rest on a log after a day of sport, while their obedient dogs relax quietly near the dead birds spilling out of a leather bag on the ground. Behind them is the entrance to the woods where they have spent the day; on the left, the late-afternoon light shines on farmworkers in a gold-tinged meadow as they load sheaves of ripe wheat onto a wagon. A white church spire near the center suggests that God has blessed this American scene. The image also celebrates the blessings of democracy as they purportedly existed in the North; here there are no plantation owners whipping their slaves or lords whose subservient peasants work the land. The leisurely hunters and the industrious farmers are represented as free and equal citizens.

Known for her snow scenes, Palmer portrayed the joys of winter sports in *Winter Pastime* (1855; gallery plate 25) and *American Winter Scenes. Morning* (1854; p. 112), two images of boys and men sledding down hills and skating on a pond. A companion print, *American Winter Scenes. Evening* (1854; gallery plate 3), shows young partygoers racing their horse-drawn sleighs under a full moon toward a country hotel, whose lit-up windows reveal silhouettes of dancers inside.

Notice that all the hunters, fishermen, sledders, and skaters in Palmer's prints are men and boys; a girl is never shown taking an active part in these sports. Also, with few exceptions, her sportsmen seldom stray far from home; they are shooting game birds on Long Island or fishing on New York Bay and the Harlem River, returning to their families with their trophies in the late afternoon.

In contrast, her male colleagues, Arthur F. Tait and Louis Maurer, often emphasize the bonding among men who have escaped from home for an extended getaway to the Adirondacks and the North Woods, where, far from the confines of family life, they could smoke, drink, and relax around the campfire, enjoying the stimulating company of members of their own sex (Louis Maurer, *Camping Out: "Some of the Right Sort"* [1856]) or, better yet, reasserting their masculine identities by overcoming dangerous challenges such as combat with a bear (Arthur F. Tait, *The Life of a Hunter: A Tight Fix* [1861]).

FARM SCENES

In 1853, Palmer inaugurated a major phase of her career with *American Farm Scenes*, a quartet of prints portraying the four seasons. These prints were the forerunners of a long series of rural images that have delighted the public ever since and are still being reproduced on calendars and greeting cards. Like the sporting prints, they present a vision of America as the embodiment of a pastoral golden age. *American Farm Scenes. No. 1* (p. 208) is a springtime idyll. In the foreground, a boy leads two oxen pulling a plow that a farmer is pushing through the soil. On the upper left, another farmer drives a wagon past a farmhouse, and a man and woman stand chatting in front of an open barn door.

Nowhere are the muck and hardship of farm life. The substantial white farmhouse with green shutters is freshly painted. The farmer behind the plow wears a clean version of the traditional low-crowned, broad-brimmed hat, long-sleeved shirt, tie, and vest; he is an archetype of American democratic dignity. The message is one of contentment and prosperity—the soil is always fertile, the weather is good, and people are neighborly. Even the hefty red ox in the foreground, his mouth slavering from the effort as he pulls his load, looks out at us contentedly. Gender roles are clearly differentiated. Whereas in *American Farm Scenes. No. 1* a man and boy plow the field, in *American Farm Scenes. No. 2* (p. 114) a farm wife and her small daughters feed chickens and pigs close to the house.

American Farm Scenes. No. 4 (gallery plate 4; p. 115) has been described as an "ode to the New York dairy farmer." The state was a center of butter and milk production, yet few prints document this fact.[37] The snowy scene captures the light and atmosphere of winter. Under a sky heavy with lowering gray clouds, a man and his son, bundled up against the cold, are driving to market in a horse-drawn sleigh filled with four large milk cans. As the horses trot briskly onto a wooden bridge, one can almost hear the clopping of their hooves and the rattling of the cans. In the background,

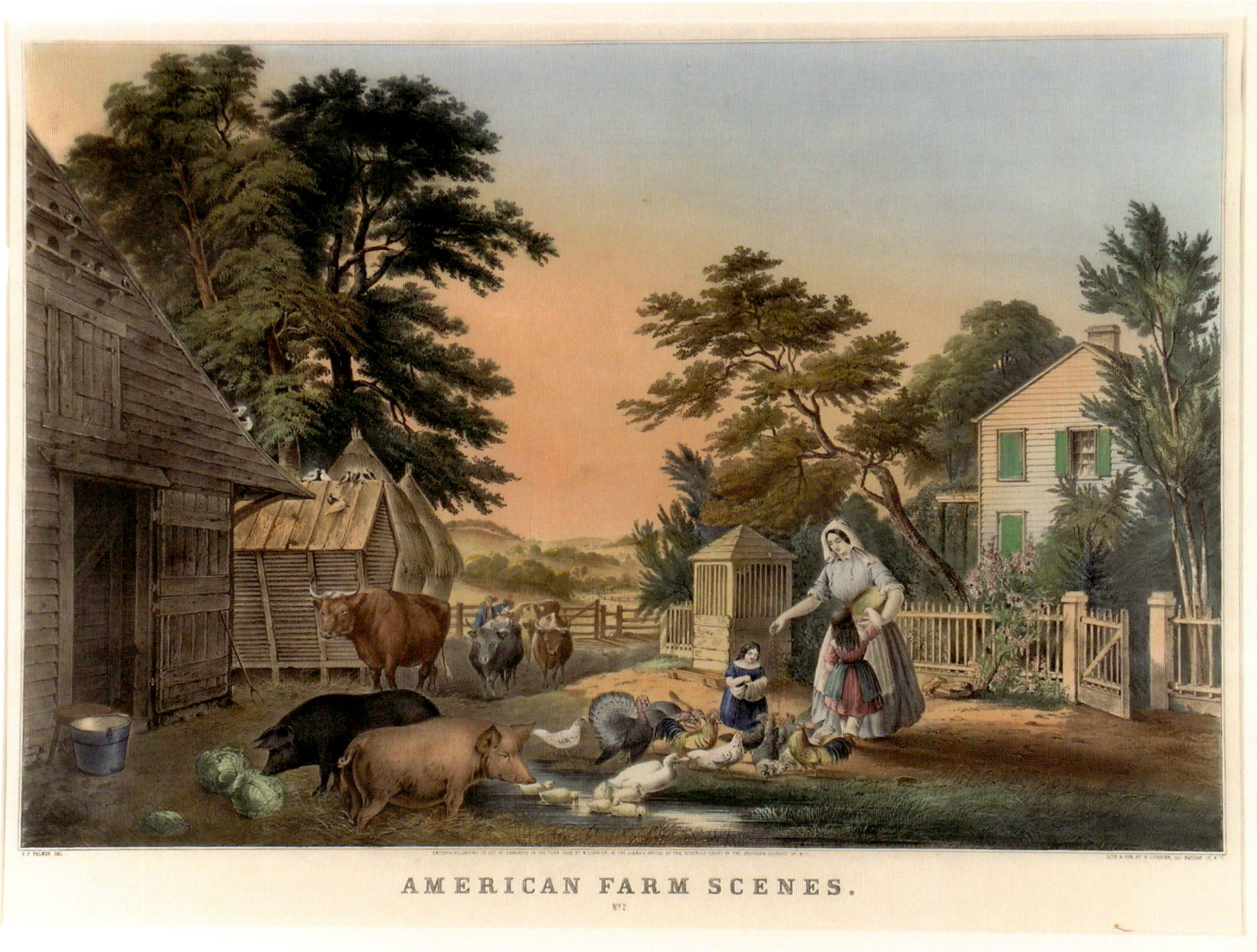

AMERICAN FARM SCENES.
Nº2

small Brueghelian figures pluck fowl for a smoking cauldron, fetch water from a well, and skate on a frozen stream. The high quality of Palmer's ever-popular print becomes evident when we compare it to a crude, cropped version issued anonymously by the company years later (*Winter Morning in the Country*, 1873; p. 115).

Perhaps Palmer's most honest renderings of rural life are two charming rustic views that appear to have been sketched directly on-site, *The Ferry Boat* (undated, ca. 1850–56; p. 116) and *View on Long Island. N.Y.* (1857; p. 117). A friend of the Palmer–Bond family reported: "[Maria] used to tell me about their crossing over from New York in row boats on a Sunday to picnic. . . .

79. *American Farm Scenes*. No. 2. 1853. Printed and published by N. Currier. (Checklist 3-10)

Her description of the thrifty little Dutch and Huguenot Farms there was fascinating to me."[38] Today the site that *View on Long Island. N.Y.* captures, known as Spinney Hill in Manhasset, is a traffic-filled urban scene.

In recent years, Sarah Burns and other scholars have gone below the surface to document just how far such farm images departed from reality. For example, in each of three prints portraying

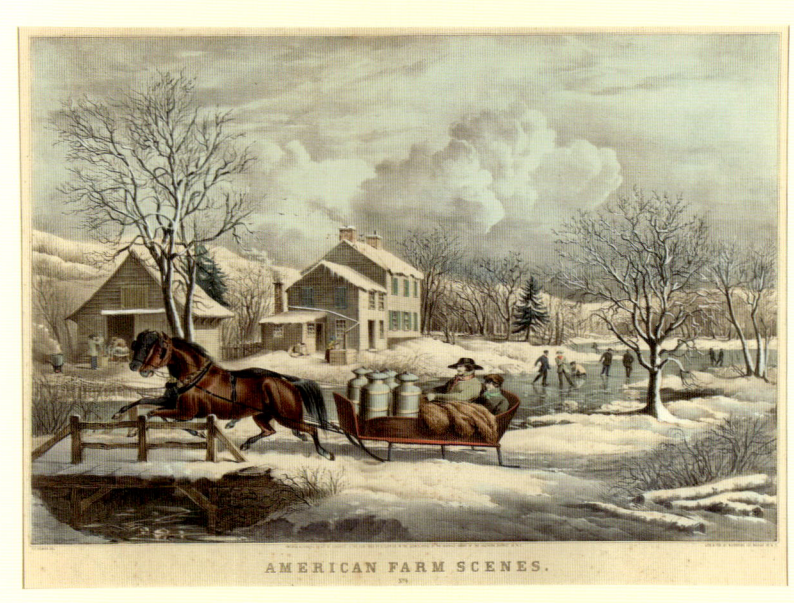

80. *American Farm Scenes. No. 4.* 1853. Printed and published by N. Currier. Courtesy of the Yale University Art Gallery. (Checklist 3-12)

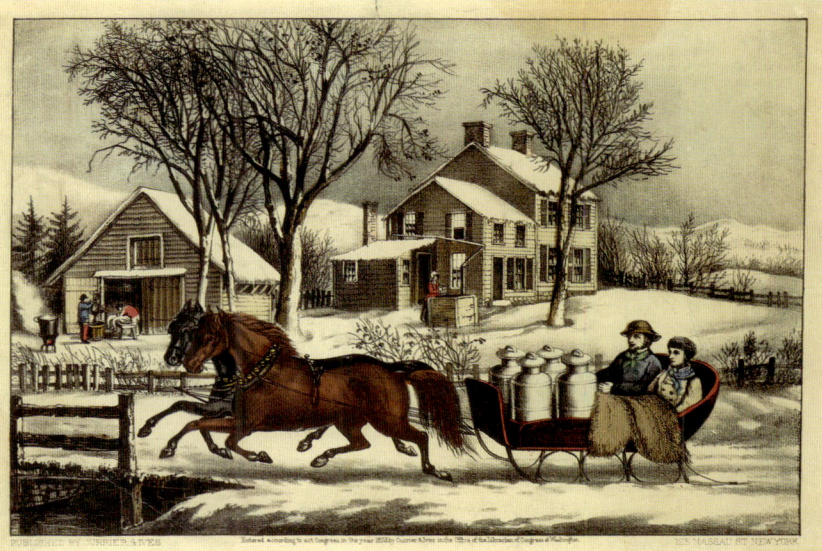

81. *Winter Morning in the Country.* 1873. Printed and published by Currier & Ives. Courtesy of the Metropolitan Museum of Art, Bequest of Adele S. Colgate, 1962.

barnyards (*American Farm Scenes. No. 3* [1853; p. 151], *American Farm Yard—Morning* [1857; p. 118], and *American Farm Yard—Evening* [1857; p. 119]), all the animals—cattle, horses, pigs, chickens, ducks, dogs, even a peacock—are lumped together in one enclosure. Although this animal melting pot makes for a lively composition, most farmers would have viewed such arrangements as sloppy husbandry; they usually separated their animals into appropriate pens and yards.[39] The images are, in fact, dreamlike catalogs of "the compleat farm" in an Arcadian never-never land.

Some farmers were contented with their lot, but in reality the farmer's life was often one of grinding toil from dawn to dark, haunted by continual fear of weather and price fluctuations that might at any moment drive him and his family off the land. Archival photographs reveal that although many farms were beautiful (especially those owned by wealthy gentlemen farmers), others were in barren, treeless surroundings. Mechanized farm equipment—horse-drawn steam threshers and hay mowers—were in use by the 1850s but never appear in Palmer's prints because they would spoil the bucolic charm of the imagery. Also, of course, large numbers of farmers were hired hands or tenant farmers rather than independent yeomen working their own land. In the Hudson River Valley around Albany and western New York, the Anti-Renters movement of the 1840s launched a rebellion that

attempted to correct the imbalance that resulted from "great land-owners who lived in aristocratic opulence by leasing millions of acres to many thousands of tenants."[40]

As for the independent farmer, that sturdy symbol of republican virtue, grounded in his attachment to the soil, he often viewed the land simply as an instrument of speculation—his goal to acquire property, improve it slightly, sell, and move on to the next investment. In his book *Walden*, Henry David Thoreau inveighed against the money-grubbing farmers around him, who, he believed, were driven only by the dollar.[41]

Not only commercial printmakers but also leading painters (as well as poets and novelists) were highly selective, choosing to depict only those aspects of rural life that met the public's agendas. And yet these images had and still have a compelling, convincing power and poetry. The fine compositions are a blend of closely observed detail and poetic editing. Burns points out that in the mid–nineteenth century the images served as a soothing escape from encroaching industrialization and the stresses and strains of the new urban society. They also performed another important function. In the decades leading up to the Civil War—a period of constant sectional conflict between the North and the South—the image of the independent farmer working his own land in peace and prosperity served as a potent symbol of "the rightness of the northern capitalist system of freehold property and free labor."[42]

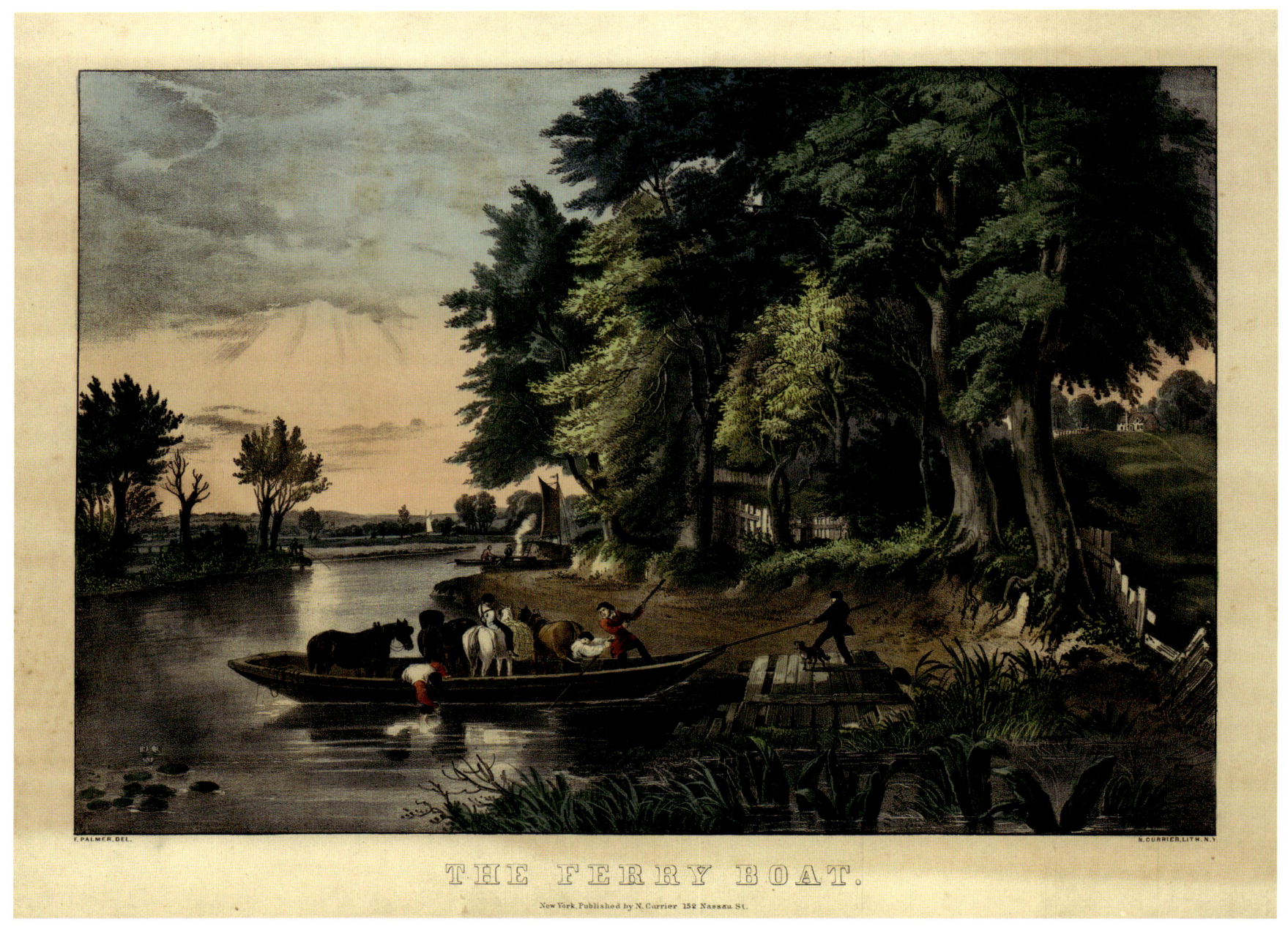

THE FERRY BOAT.

New York. Published by N. Currier 152 Nassau St.

82. *The Ferry Boat.* Undated, ca. 1850–56. Printed and published by N. Currier. Courtesy of the Old Print Shop. (Checklist 3-44)

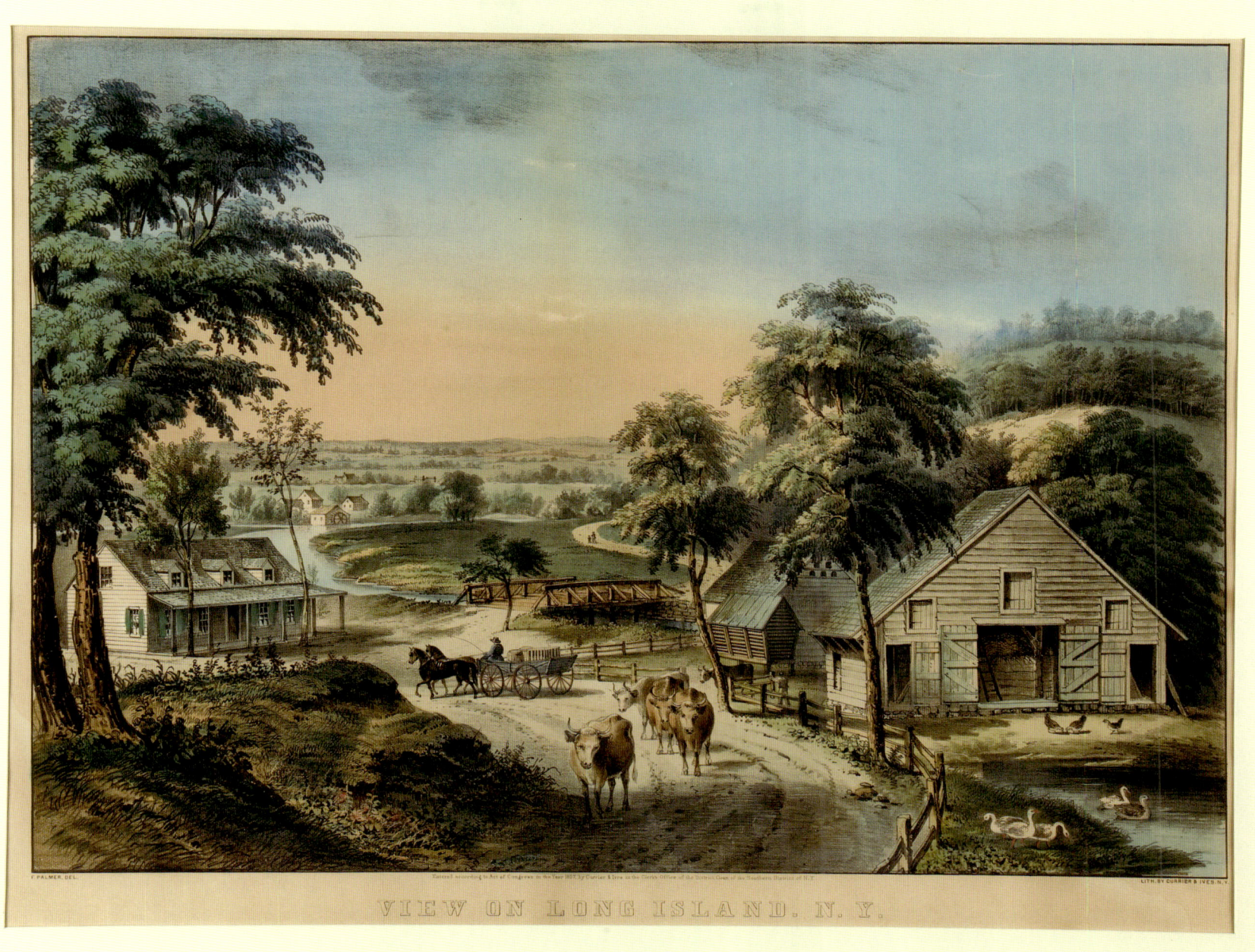

VIEW ON LONG ISLAND. N. Y.

83. *View on Long Island*. N.Y. 1857. Printed and published by Currier
& Ives. Courtesy of the Yale University Art Gallery. (Checklist 3-159)

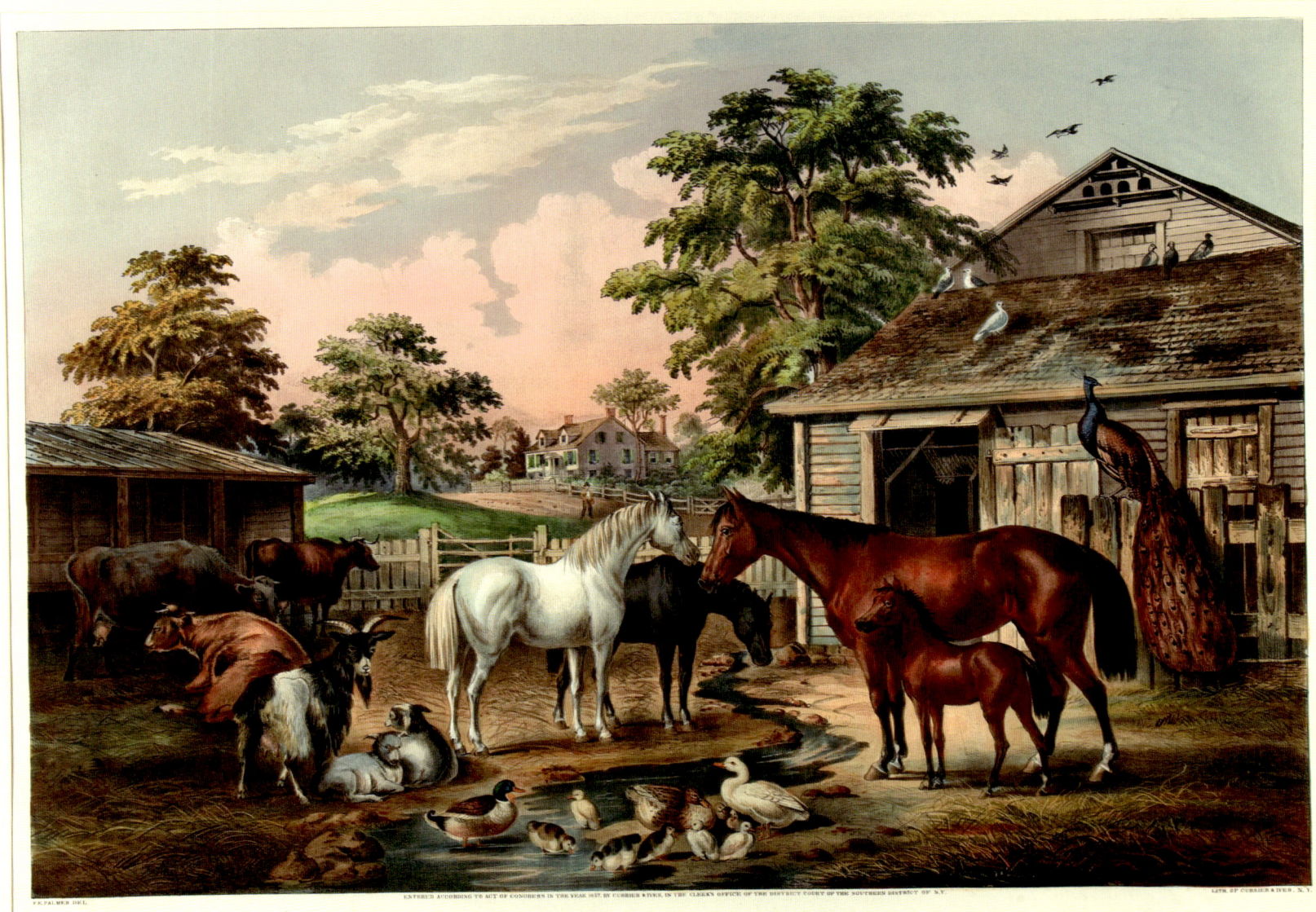

AMERICAN FARM YARD — MORNING.

84. *American Farm Yard—Morning.* 1857. Printed and published by Currier & Ives. Courtesy of the Yale University Art Gallery. (Checklist 3-14)

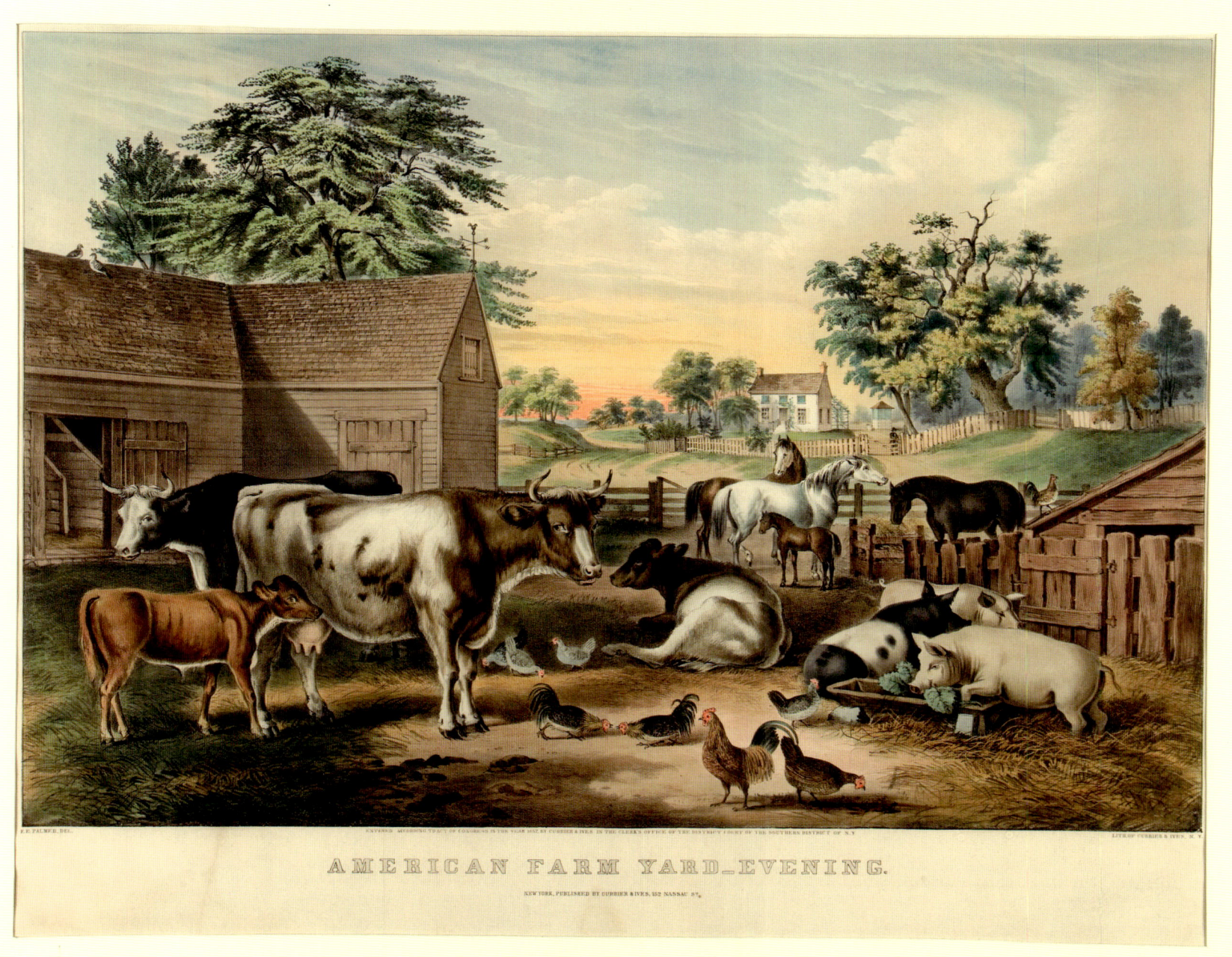

AMERICAN FARM YARD—EVENING.

NEW YORK, PUBLISHED BY CURRIER & IVES, 152 NASSAU ST.

85. *American Farm Yard—Evening.* 1857. Printed and published by Currier & Ives. Courtesy of the Yale University Art Gallery. (Checklist 3-13)

In 1855, Palmer created the *American Country Life* series: the first of many prints featuring suburban and rural mansions set amid spacious grounds, where affluent family members are shown strolling about the land, enjoying the view, riding horses, and picking flowers, while in the background their servants curry horses and farmers harvest crops. The 1850s was a decade of greatly increased wealth for the merchant class. At the same time that territorial expansion and increased trade were creating a demand for goods and products, massive waves of immigration kept labor costs low, ensuring large profit margins. Successful businessmen, finding themselves able to enjoy semiretirement at an early age, were building elegant homes on Long Island, along the Hudson River, and elsewhere. Indeed, Fanny Palmer's employer, Nathaniel Currier, spent summers at Lion's Gate, a country home in Amesbury, Massachusetts, while continuing to maintain a townhouse in New York City.

Eager to overcome a sense of American cultural inferiority and provincialism, these longtime and newly rich citizens incorporated into their domestic structures architectural elements taken from Italian, French, or British villas and castles. Neoclassical ornament lived next door to gothic filigree in an American version of architectural romanticism. Among the principal tastemakers of the period were architect A. J. Davis, a leader of the Greek and neogothic revival movements, and his mentor A. J. Downing, a landscape designer who exerted a wide influence through his books *Cottage Residences* (1842) and *The Architecture of Country Houses* (1850). Downing preached the virtues of the romantic picturesque, the idea of harmony between architecture and its natural setting, and the importance to one's moral and spiritual health of living in the country.

In his preface to *The Architecture of Country Houses*, Downing revealed his quasi-religious feeling about the importance of "Home" not only to the individual but to society as well. He viewed it as a sacred shrine, the seat of all that is good and holy:

> The mere sentiment of home, with its thousand associations, has, like a strong anchor, saved many a man from shipwreck in the storms of life. . . . All to which the heart can attach itself in youth, and the memory linger fondly over in riper years, contributes largely to our stock of happiness and the elevation of the moral character. For this reason, the condition of the family home—in this country where every man may have a home—should be raised, till it shall symbolize the best character and pursuits, and the dearest affections and enjoyments of social life.[43]

Palmer was peculiarly suited by training and background to create images of such country mansions. In England, she had drawn numerous castles, churches, and other buildings, many directly from life; and in New York City, before joining Currier's company, she had lithographed the buildings of such leading architects as A. J. Davis, Richard Upjohn, and Minard Lafever. Although the artist was not wealthy, she moved in a genteel circle and understood the outlook of the people she portrayed in the prints.

In *American Country Life*, a series described in a Currier & Ives catalog as "pleasing illustrations of the life of an American Country Gentlemen, in the four seasons,"[44] a fine home is a major motif in each image. The first home features a rectangular tower, and the second a hexagonal cupola; the third is in the Italian bracketed style, and the fourth is an elegant brownstone.

American Country Life. May Morning (1855; p. 207) shows family members enjoying a fine spring day on the grounds of an Italianate home on a hill with a view of the boat-flecked ocean. In the foreground, a country gentleman in top hat, three-piece suit, and gloves is taking a morning horseback ride, accompanied by his son on a white pony. He passes a garden where two well-dressed women pick bouquets and water flowers, while a little daughter pats her pet lamb. A farmer is plowing on the right, and a groom, almost invisible in the left background, curries a horse in front of the stable. The relative class positions of the villa owner, his wife, the farmer, and the groom are revealed clearly in this image.

In *American Country Life. Summers Evening* (1855; gallery plate 19), the proud homeowner, strolling in the countryside with his wife and their frolicking children, points out the peaceful abundance being created by the nation's farmers; and in *American Country Life. October Afternoon* (1855; p. 181), he returns home from a day of sport, with a fine catch of birds and fish, to the wife and baby who await him behind the fence of his well-kept home.

The final print in this quartet of the seasons is *American Country Life. Pleasures of Winter* (1855; p. 202). It is unusual because its central image and largest figure is an African American groom bringing a horse-drawn sleigh to the front portico of a brownstone mansion, where a family is preparing to go for a ride in the snow. The presence of such a well-dressed and pleasant-looking black servant indicates the homeowner's wealth and status. Fur blankets draped on the seats indicate that the party will be toasty and comfortable during their ride. In the background, woodsmen chop trees, and skaters circle on an icy lake.

As the father turns away to help his fashionably dressed wife down the front steps, his small son takes the opportunity to aim a snowball at the black servant. Black people were expected to accept these little "pleasantries" with good humor; they were supposed to "know their place" at a time when many Northerners were worrying about the explosive consequences of abolitionism. A description in a Currier & Ives catalog expresses the attitude of the times: "The darkey shows his ivories in evident delight at the youngster's antics," adding, "This elegant print vividly illustrates the fact that 'the country is delightful, even in the winter.'"[45]

The *American Country Life* prints have remained perennial favorites because of their fine design, atmospheric effects, and freshly observed details of rural life. Later, in the 1860s, Palmer continued to create variations on this theme. *Life In the Country. Evening* (1862; p. 122) shows the proud mistress of a hillside mansion waiting for her women friends to arrive. The year is 1862, during the Civil War. Note the oversize Union flag flying from the home's high tower and the elaborate fountain splashing on spacious grounds. This print invites envy and desire; it represents all that a (white) woman was supposed to want—a wealthy husband and a fine home in which she holds sway. Other examples of this genre are *A Home in the Country* (undated, ca. 1857–72; p. 182) and *Summer in the Country* (1866; p. 211).

The artist also created a number of pictures of happy families in more modest cottages (*The Cottage Door-Yard—Evening* [1855; p. 209] and *The Return from the Pasture* [undated, ca. 1857–72; p. 123]). Whether they were rich or poor, most Americans' dream was (and still is) to own a home, and this subject is a repeated theme in Palmer's work. Tucked away in all of these charmingly composed prints are subliminal messages about Victorian values—especially the concept of separate realms for men and women, a subject that is developed more fully in chapter 11, dealing with the ideology embedded in Palmer's work.

F. F. Palmer was now at the height of her powers, a seasoned professional who had won the respect and admiration of her employers. Proof of this is found in a Currier & Ives descriptive catalog of prints for around 1858, a brochure that supplies a great deal of information about the firm. Eight of Palmer's prints are featured on the front page, preceded by an introductory blurb enthusing, "The following described Pictures will be found very attractive to all lovers of rural scenery and occupations, and elegant ornaments

for any room in the house. *They are from original drawings made by an artist of great celebrity* in the faithful delineation of natural landscapes, and are purely American in character and incident."[46] Her name is mentioned again on page 4. Under the heading "The Dog and Gun," six hunting scenes are described as "entirely original in design, and correct in details, and give a faithful portraiture both of man and dog, as well as the native scenery . . . drawn from nature by F. F. Palmer."[47] The catalog also reveals that her employers were keenly aware of Palmer's skillful atmospheric effects ("the effect of the rich warm sunset[,] . . . tinting the house-tops and distant hills, is very fine"[48]).

Nathaniel Currier was not the only publisher aware of Palmer's talent at this time. One advantage of working out of a home studio was that it gave her great flexibility. At the same time that she was busily employed by Nathaniel Currier, she continued to carry out independent assignments for other publishers. Among them are her splendid prints *East View of St. Paul's Church, Buffalo* and *West View of St. Paul's Church, Buffalo* (both undated, ca. 1851?; p. 29), with her own imprint, "F. Palmer & Co."; *St. John's P.E. Church, Mt. Morris. Livingston Co. N.Y.* (1856; p. 124) for Sarony & Co.; *St. James Church and Rectory. Chicago, Illinois* (1856), published by Sarony, Major & Knapp; *View of Richmond Va.* (undated, ca. 1852–53?; p. 125), lithographed from John W. Hill's panorama for Smith Brothers & Co.; and the music cover *Spanish Gipsies* (undated, ca. 1852?), printed by F. Michelin for publishers Gould & Berry.

Ironically, in 1859, at this time of peak achievement, a sudden interruption occurred in her work. This was a stressful period in the artist's personal life. Edmund Seymour Palmer, at the age of forty-nine, took an unexpected and ungraceful exit from the world by falling down the stairs in the hotel where he had formerly been a tavern keeper. The *Brooklyn Eagle* carried a notice on March 7: "Coroner Horton was notified this noon by Mr. James, proprietor of the Abbey Hotel, in Fulton avenue, to hold an inquest at his house on the body of a man whose name he did not know who died last night from injuries sustained by falling down stairs." Although the coroner decided that the victim had suffered from "congestion of the brain," the general consensus among Fanny's friends and colleagues was that he had died from a drunken fall. When the news came out, James Ives made his unkind but immortal remark: "That's the best thing he ever did!"[49]

The legend of Mr. Palmer's alcoholic pratfall into oblivion has been repeated again and again, but it is, in fact, gossip related by colleagues and friends many years after the fact. Edmund might

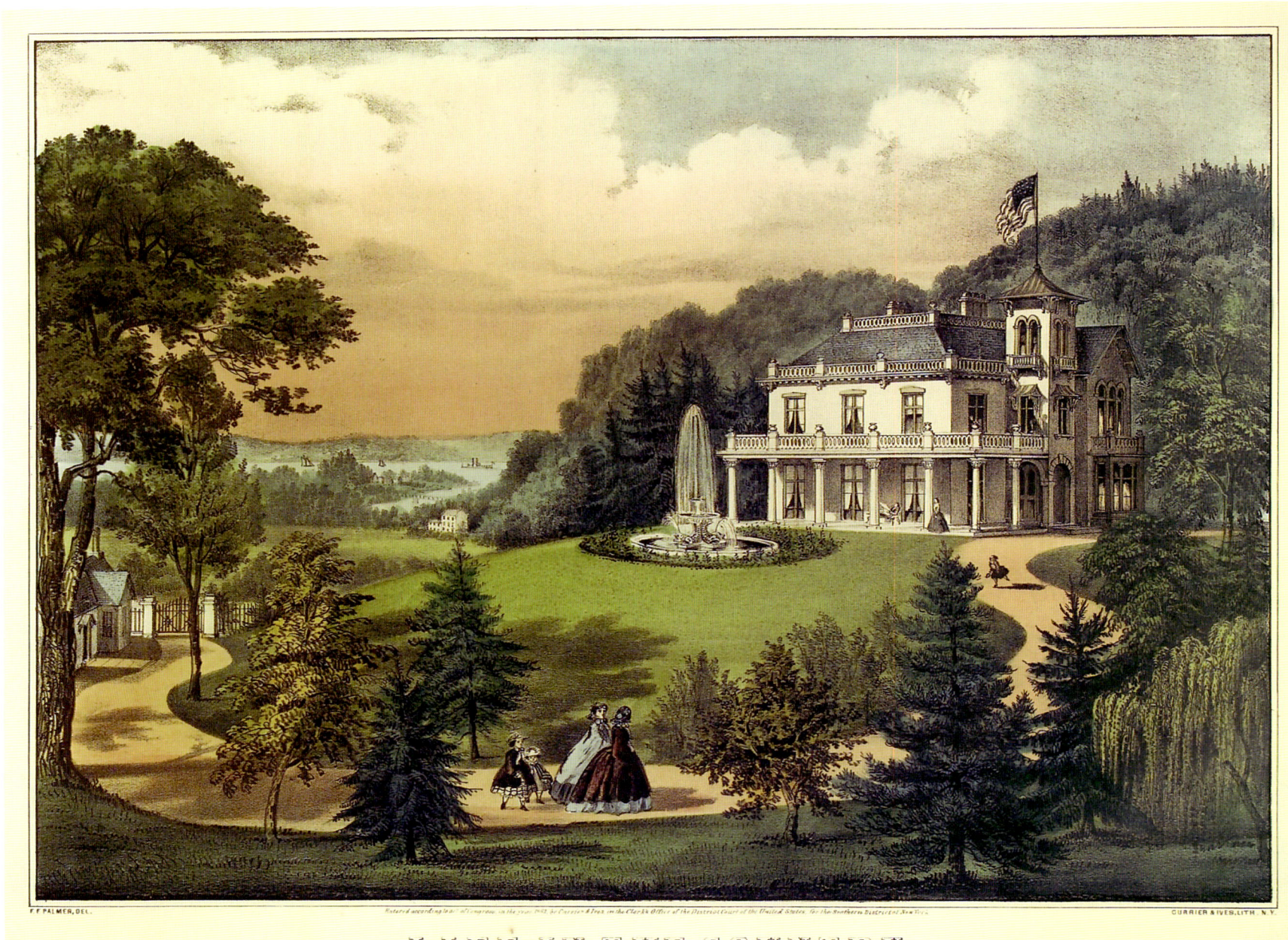

LIFE IN THE COUNTRY.
EVENING.

New York, Published by Currier & Ives, 152 Nassau St.

have had a stroke or an aneurism or might simply have lost his balance. Of course, Mrs. Palmer never complained publicly about her husband; she saw to it that despite their modest circumstances he would go out in style. Edmund's funeral service was held on March 9, 1859, in Brooklyn's Holy Trinity Episcopal Church, and he was buried at Green-Wood Cemetery. Records show that Fanny, suddenly confronted by the death of her husband, immediately

86. *Life In the Country. Evening.* 1862. Printed and published by Currier & Ives. Courtesy of the Old Print Shop. (Checklist 3-72)

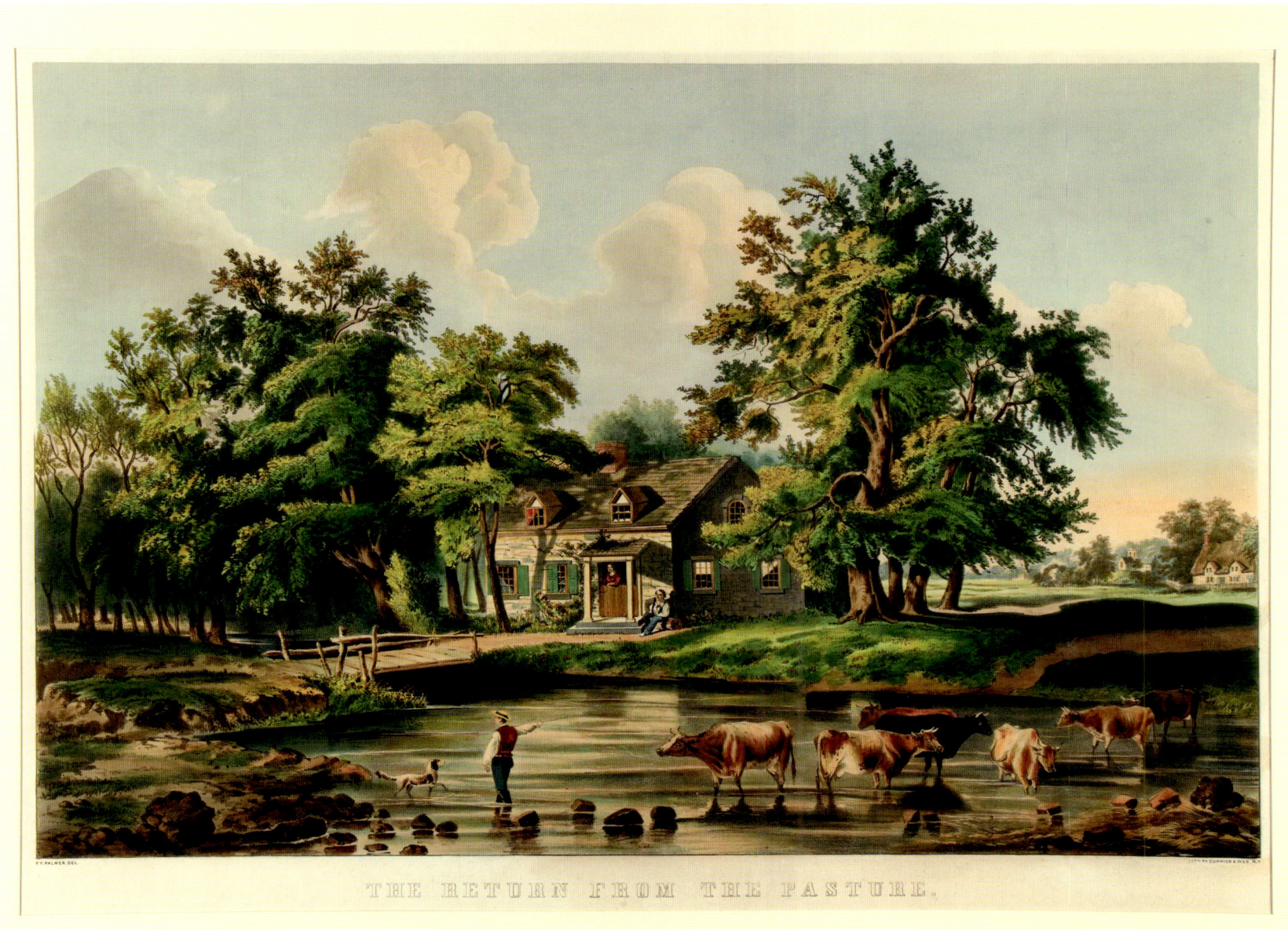

THE RETURN FROM THE PASTURE.

87. *The Return from the Pasture*. Undated, ca. 1857–72. Printed and published by Currier & Ives. Courtesy of the Yale University Art Gallery. (Checklist 3-111)

purchased a portion of grave lot 4659 from Alfred Hunt, a relative of Samuel Valentine Hunt, the Anglo-American engraver who was also later buried there with his family.[50] She and the other Palmer–Bond family members were ultimately interred alongside her husband at the most prestigious cemetery in the New York area. Nevertheless, evidence of their modest financial circumstances is the fact that no stone (except a small one erected for Robert Bond by his wife) remains to mark their resting places. If any stones were in fact placed there, they were small enough to be buried by time.

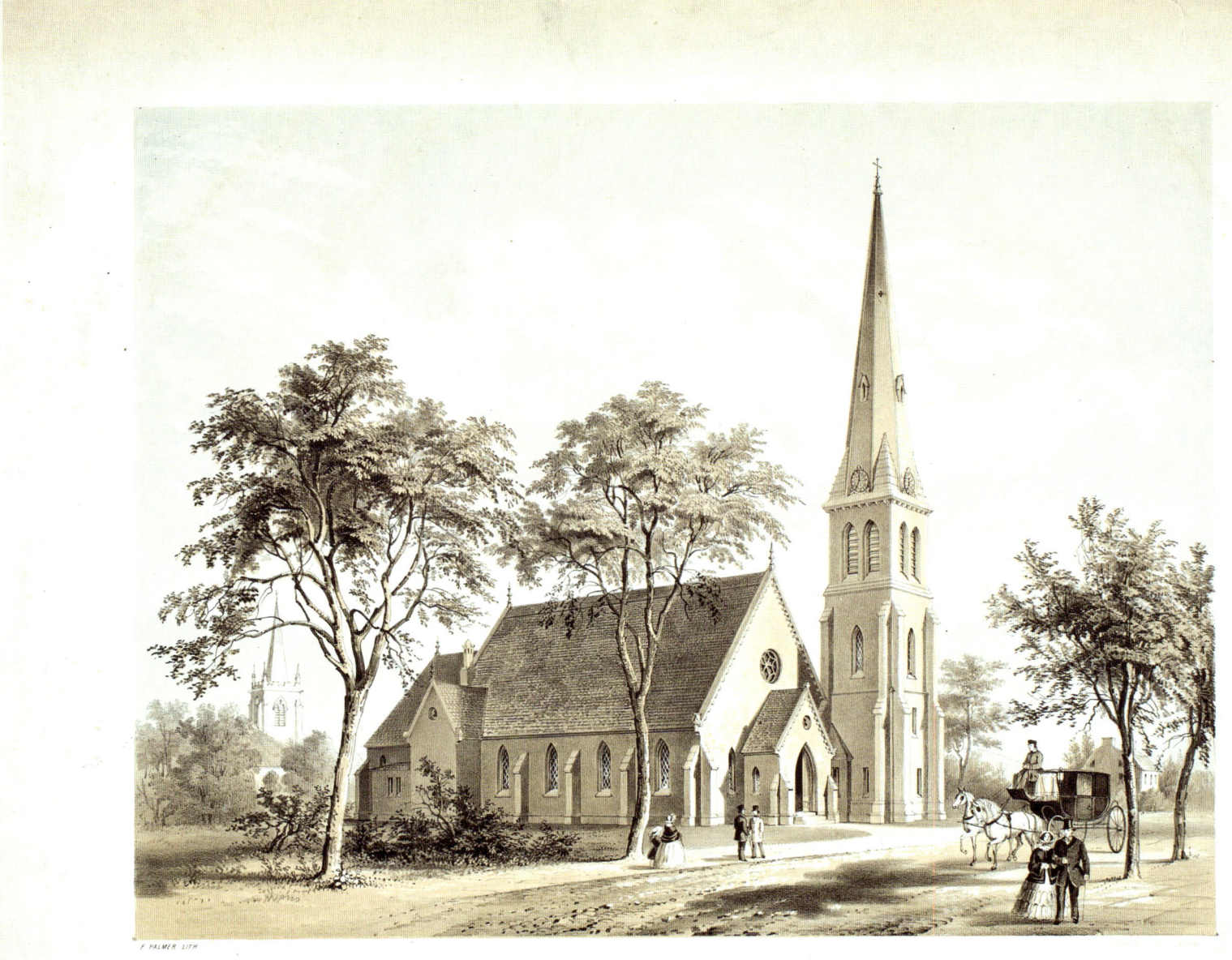

ST. JOHN'S P. E. CHURCH, MT. MORRIS.
LIVINGSTON CO. N.Y.

Cleaveland & Backus Brothers Architects, New York 1856

88. *St. John's P.E. Church, Mt. Morris. Livingston Co. N.Y. Cleaveland & Backus Brothers Architects, New York 1856. 1856.* Printed
and published by Sarony & Co. Courtesy of the American Antiquarian
Society. (Checklist 2-219)

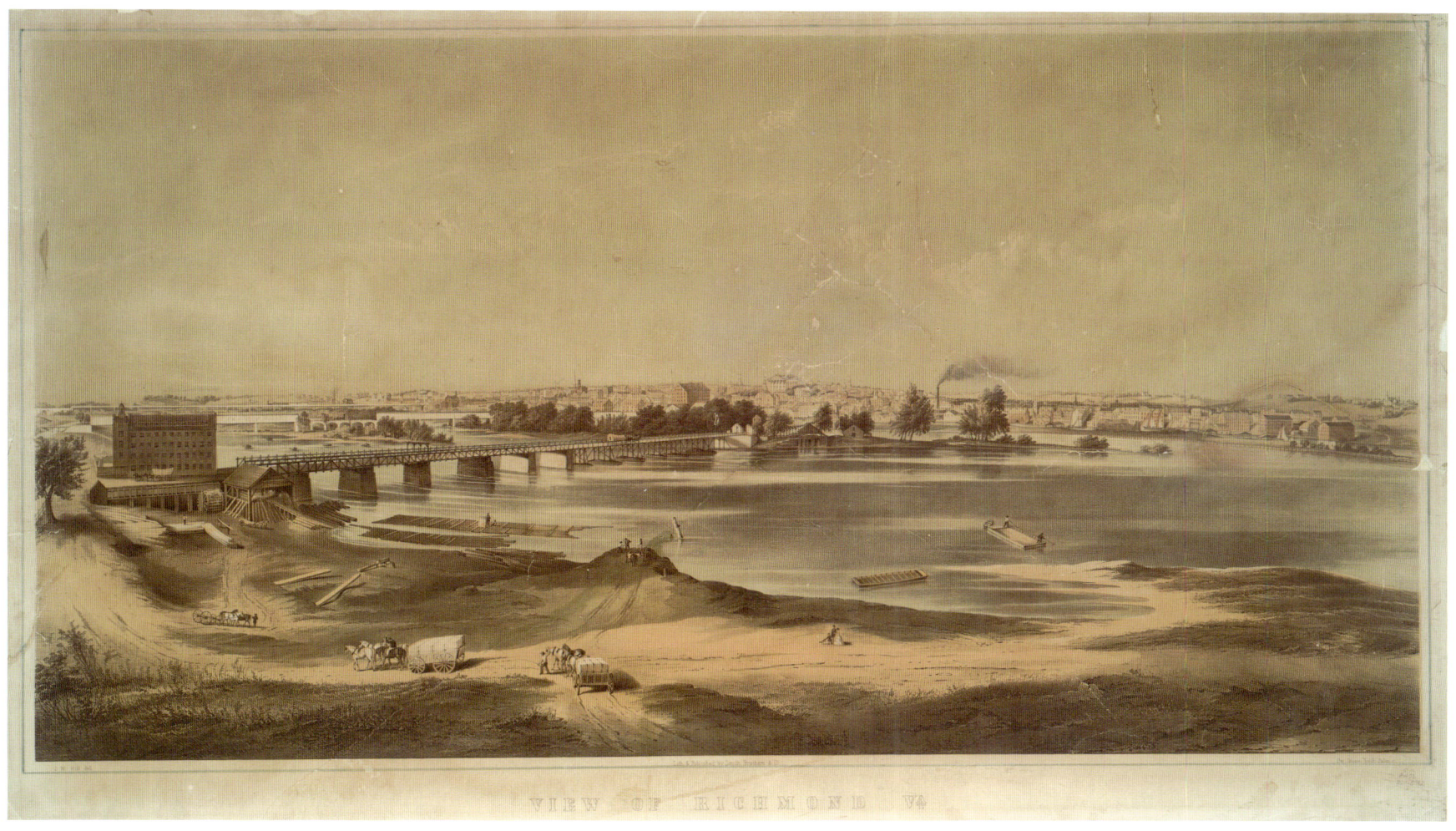

89. *View of Richmond Va.* Undated, ca. 1852–53? Printed and published by Smith Brothers & Co. Courtesy of the Miriam and Ira D. Wallach Division of Art, Prints, and Photographs: Print Collection, the New York Public Library. (Checklist 2-217)

In that same year, the artist's daughter, Frances, now married to David Edgecombe, bore a child, Maria Felicea Mary Edgecombe.[51] Mrs. Palmer may have been called upon to help with the new infant. We have no examples of her work during this difficult time.

A year after her husband's death, Fanny Palmer moved again, this time to 17 High Street.[52] Her son, Edmund Jr., is listed in the federal census for 1860 as "photographer,"[53] although all reports from friends and relatives describe him as a wastrel. No profession, however, is listed for F. F. Palmer, who was now the main support of the family. Did she feel that it would show a lack of decorum to identify herself as a professional working woman, or did the census taker subconsciously rule out this possibility?

British records show that upon her husband's death, Mrs. Palmer had, within the required six-month period, obtained Edmund Seymour Palmer's will from England, bequeathing to his "dear Wife . . . Frances Flora . . . whatever might remain of his 2200 pound trust fund . . . and any other real or personal estate that he might have acquired." In the census for 1860, Mrs. Palmer listed her assets as three hundred dollars.[54]

7

Creating an American Epic

See, vast trackless spaces;
As in a dream they change, they swiftly fill;
Countless masses debouch upon them;
They are now cover'd with the foremost people, arts, institutions, known.
. . . .
Americanos! Conquerors! . . . For you a programme of chants.
— Walt Whitman, "Starting from Paumanok," 1867

Our logrolling, our stumps, and their politics . . . our Negroes and Indians . . . the northern trade, the southern planting,
the western clearing . . . are yet unsung. Yet America is a poem in our eyes: its ample geography dazzles the imagination.
— Ralph Waldo Emerson, "The Poet," *Essays: Second Series*, 1844

AFTER FANNY PALMER returned to work in 1860 following her husband's death, the next decade proved to be extraordinarily productive. She was now, more than ever, the primary wage earner in her family, driven to produce as much as possible in order to keep them all afloat. There had also been a stimulating change at Currier's company. By 1857, Nathaniel Currier's energetic assistant, James Merritt Ives, had worked his way into partnership and had introduced a new marketing sense. In addition to his skills as a businessman, he was a rather capable amateur artist who knew how to punch up a design in order to give it more appeal and was good at combining elements from the sketches of several artists.

Ives seems to have had a vision of the company's role as a creator of images expressing the broad trends of the day, and he viewed F. F. Palmer as an artist capable of carrying out many of his big ideas. Indeed, Ives's son Fred later told an interviewer that his father "thought a great deal" of her.[1] James Ives also apparently enjoyed playing the role of "art director"; his name appears as a collaborator on eight of her prints—works that include such epic themes as the Civil War and the transcontinental railroad.[2]

HUDSON RIVER IMAGES

During the late 1850s and early 1860s, Palmer began work for the new partnership with a series of views of West Point and the surrounding Hudson River region. From the time that Henry Hudson first sailed up that river in 1609, artists and writers have admired its beauty—the rosy glow of summer's haze, the wild and flashing storms. Washington Irving, one of America's first internationally renowned authors, described his maiden voyage on it as a boy: "What a time of intense delight was that first sail through the Highlands! I sat on the deck as we slowly tided along at the foot of those stern mountains, and gazed with wonder and admiration at cliffs impending far above me, crowned with forests, with eagles sailing and screaming around them."[3]

Even a skeptical foreign visitor such as the English writer Frances Trollope, who had little good to say about American life, wrote glowingly about the Highlands:

One might fancy that these capricious masses, with all their countless varieties of light and shade, were thrown together to show how passing lovely rocks and woods and water could be. . . . For several miles the river appears to form a succession of lakes; you are often enclosed on all sides by rocks rising directly from the very edge of the stream, and then you turn a point, the river widens, and again woods, lawns, and villages are reflected on its bosom.[4]

With the opening of the Erie Canal in 1825, river towns began to thrive, and the Hudson was busy with sloops and cargo boats carrying imports from New York City to the Great Lakes region or returning to the city with cement, bricks, hogs, and other products. Its banks had over the years become the location of splendid homes with picturesque views, beginning with those of the Dutch patroons of the seventeenth century and continuing on into the Gilded Age. By the time Palmer began to create images of the region, wealthy merchants were commuting to New York on steamboats, timing their trips to accommodate business hours, and the district around West Point had become a favorite summer vacation resort for New Yorkers escaping from the city's oppressive heat.

The economic expansion during this period was accompanied by a cultural flowering. The first great movement in American landscape art, which would later be called the "Hudson River School," was at its height. Beginning with Thomas Cole, Thomas Doughty, and Asher Durand, American painters had found inspiration in the river and in American nature generally, which they regarded as God's bountiful gift to the nation. Cole, Frederick Church, and Albert Bierstadt built homes overlooking the river.

In their work, these artists and Palmer as well usually omitted factories, quarries, and other signs of industrialization that were beginning to encroach on the pristine scenery. However, steamboats were regarded as glamorous new features, sending their smoke plumes into the air, and the railroad sometimes appears in artwork, but usually as a distant, harmonious element, blending into the landscape.

Palmer completed at least fifteen prints of the area. Some of them are original, whereas others, such as *View on the Hudson* (undated, ca. 1857–72; p. 324) and *The Scenery of the Hudson. View, Near "Anthony's Nose"* (undated, ca. 1857–72; p. 128) appear to be adapted, with modest changes, from William Bartlett's illustrations in Nathaniel Willis's travel book *American Scenery* (1840).

The Hudson Highlands. From the Peekskill and Cold Spring Road, Near Garrison's Landing (1857; p. 128) is a kind of overture to the series. The viewer has come upon the crest of a hill framed by tall trees and is looking out over a vista. The road ahead leads down past cattle and a stone fence, then dips past a farmhouse and winds around a valley far below toward the distant river and highlands. This print was so popular that ten years later Palmer drew a second version (p. 296), replacing the cattle in the foreground with a couple in a horse and buggy.

Next in this series is one of Currier & Ives's finest landscape prints, *The Cattskill Mountains, From the Eastern Shore of the Hudson* (1860; p. 129), an airy, expansive view of the river. In the foreground, a farmer drives his basket-filled wagon forward on a road that winds back past farms and trees. The eye lingers over charming details of fences, haystacks, cattle, and houses, leading to the middle distance, where steamboats and sailing vessels glide on the surface of a river gleaming with reflected clouds. In the background, the Catskills loom, a scarf of clouds trailing around their peaks.

This print was published a year after the death of Washington Irving, who had peopled the region with such mythical characters as Rip Van Winkle and Ichabod Crane. Currier & Ives took advantage of a heightened market at this time to issue images of the Hudson and of Irving's home in Tarrytown. Palmer later lithographed *"Sleepy Hollow" Church, Near Tarrytown, N.Y.* (1867; p. 130), showing a family in the foreground gazing at the historic Dutch church behind which Irving is buried.

West Point

During the stressful years of the Civil War, the patriotic motif of West Point, the nation's oldest and most hallowed officer-training school, was a very appealing subject. Evidence suggests that Palmer took a steamboat up the river or rode a carriage into the region in order to gather material (*The Drive through the Highlands* [undated, ca. 1857–72; p. 130] is a result of such a trip). On the verso of a preliminary wash drawing for *The Hudson, From West Point. Grounds of the U.S. Military Academy* (1862; p. 131) are small pencil sketches by Palmer of a cannon and of visitors examining the historic chains that had been laid across the Hudson during the American Revolution in order to halt the advance of the British navy. These small notations appear to be on-site studies in preparation for a lithograph.

In *The Hudson, From West Point*, four small figures of uniformed military men, one holding a spyglass, are looking north from Trophy Point toward historic Constitution Island and at sailboats and one steamboat, flying the Union flag and speeding toward the shore. In the foreground, three large mortars and two pyramids of mortar shot from the Mexican War are symbolically guarding the site. In the middle of the Civil War, they were comforting reminders of a previous American victory.

Palmer also crossed the river and drew a pencil study of the landscape setting for her lithograph *U.S. Military Academy, West Point. From the opposite Shore* (1862; p. 132). She added the figures later when she worked on the print. The finished composition embodies a blend of reverence for the military establishment, Victorian family values, and American scenery—a mixture sure to appeal to a wide audience during the Civil War. In this image,

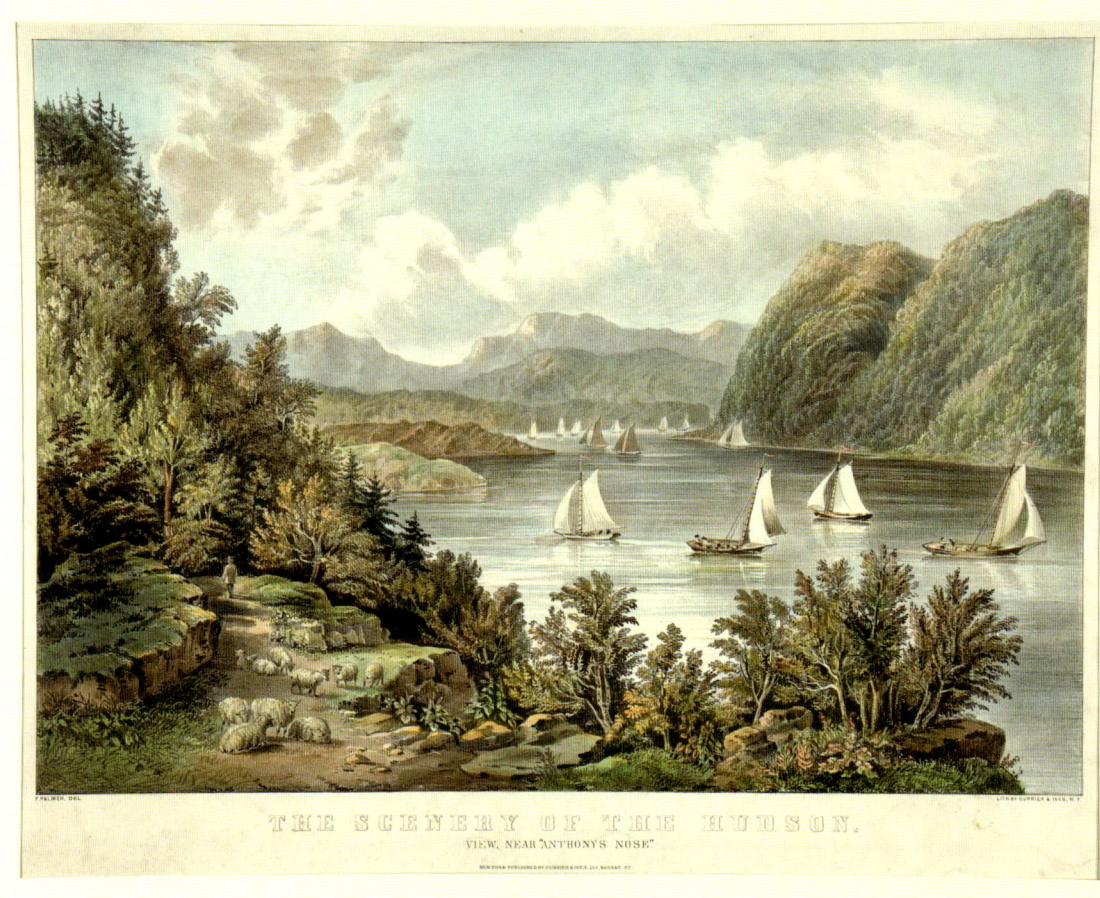

90. *The Scenery of the Hudson. View, Near "Anthony's Nose."* Undated, ca. 1857–72. Printed and published by Currier & Ives. Courtesy of the Yale University Art Gallery. (Checklist 3-123)

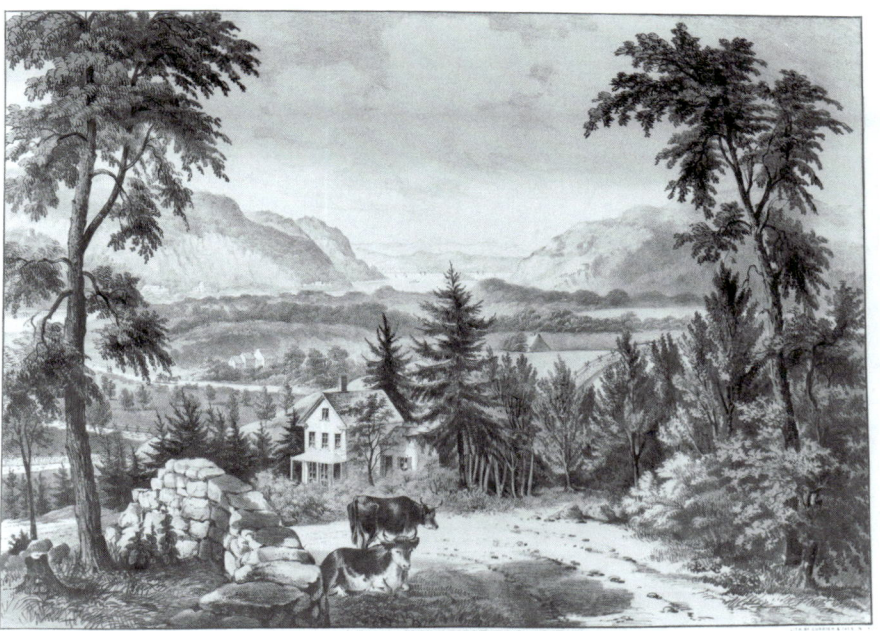

91. *The Hudson Highlands. From the Peekskill and Cold Spring Road, Near Garrison's Landing.* 1857. Printed and published by Currier & Ives. Courtesy of the Old Print Shop. (Checklist 3-63)

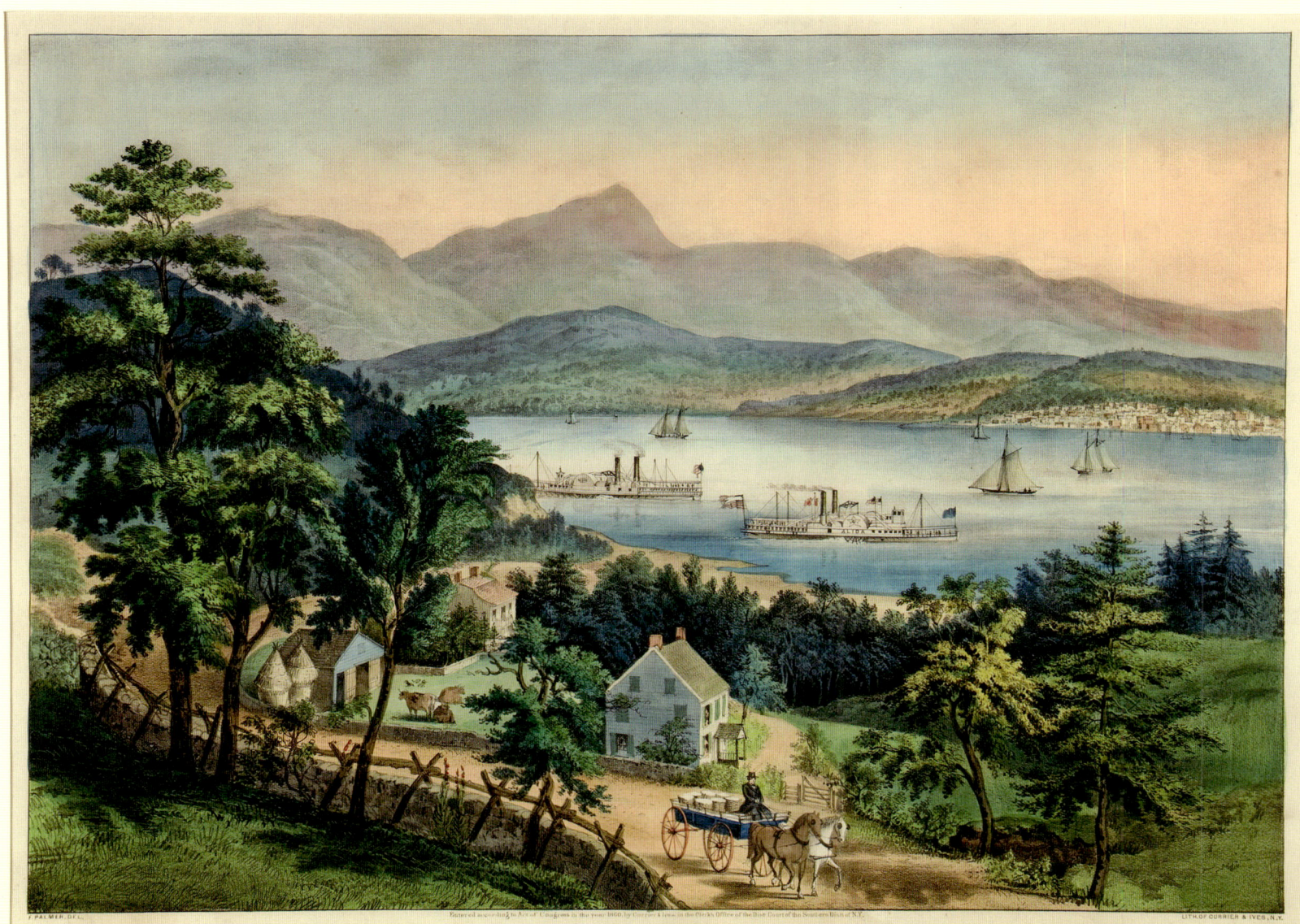

F. PALMER, DEL.   Entered according to Act of Congress in the year 1860, by Currier & Ives, in the Clerk's Office of the Dist. Court of the Southern Dist. of N.Y.   LITH. OF CURRIER & IVES, N.Y.

THE CATTSKILL MOUNTAINS,
FROM THE EASTERN SHORE OF THE HUDSON.

92. *The Cattskill Mountains, From the Eastern Shore of the Hudson.*
1860. Printed and published by Currier & Ives. Courtesy of the Yale
University Art Gallery. (Checklist 3-25)

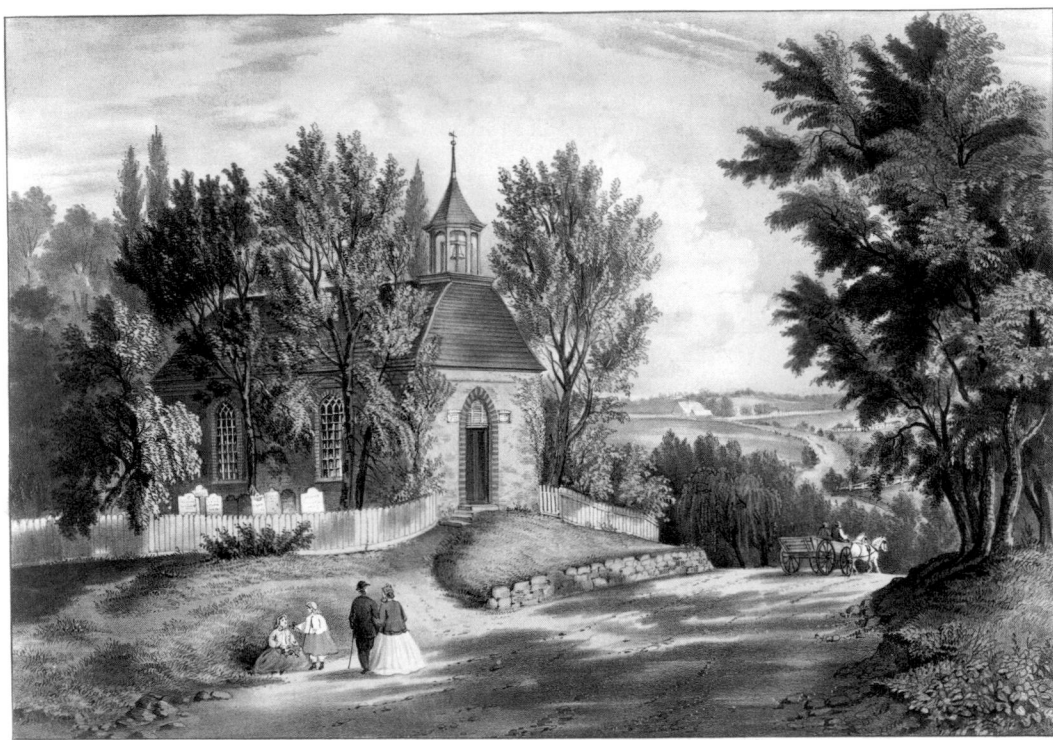

"SLEEPY HOLLOW" CHURCH.

93. *"Sleepy Hollow" Church, Near Tarry-town, N.Y.* 1867. Printed and published by Currier & Ives. Courtesy of the Old Print Shop. (Checklist 3-125)

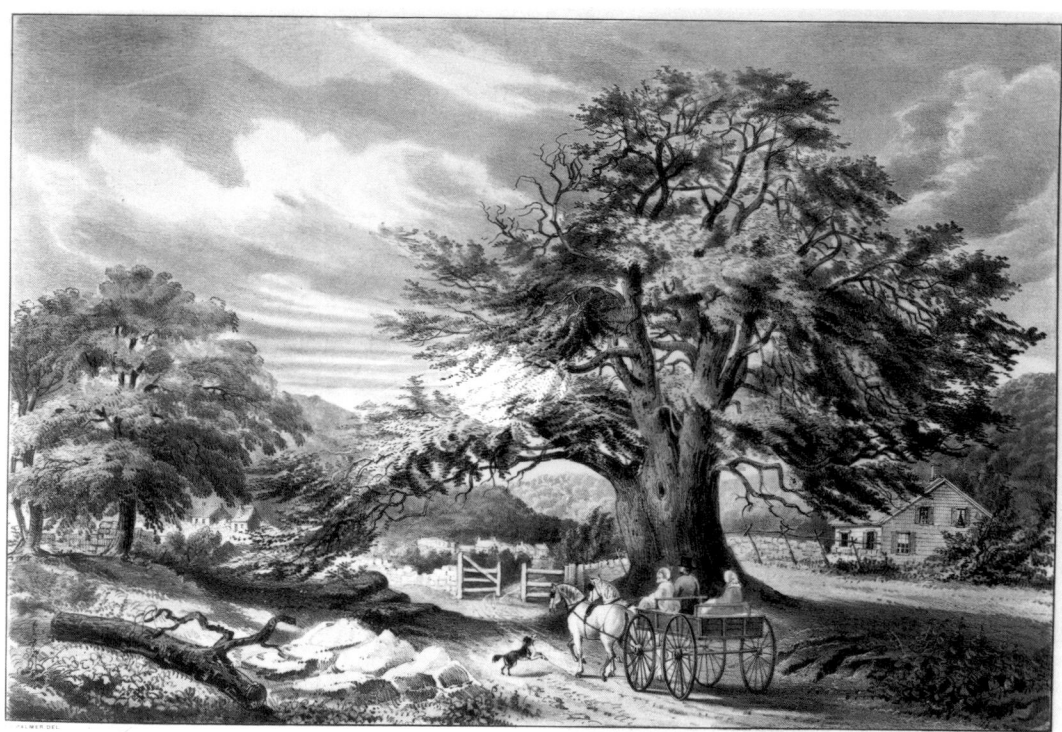

THE DRIVE THROUGH THE HIGHLANDS.

94. *The Drive through the Highlands.* Undated, ca. 1857–72. Printed and published by Currier & Ives. Courtesy of the Old Print Shop. (Checklist 3-39)

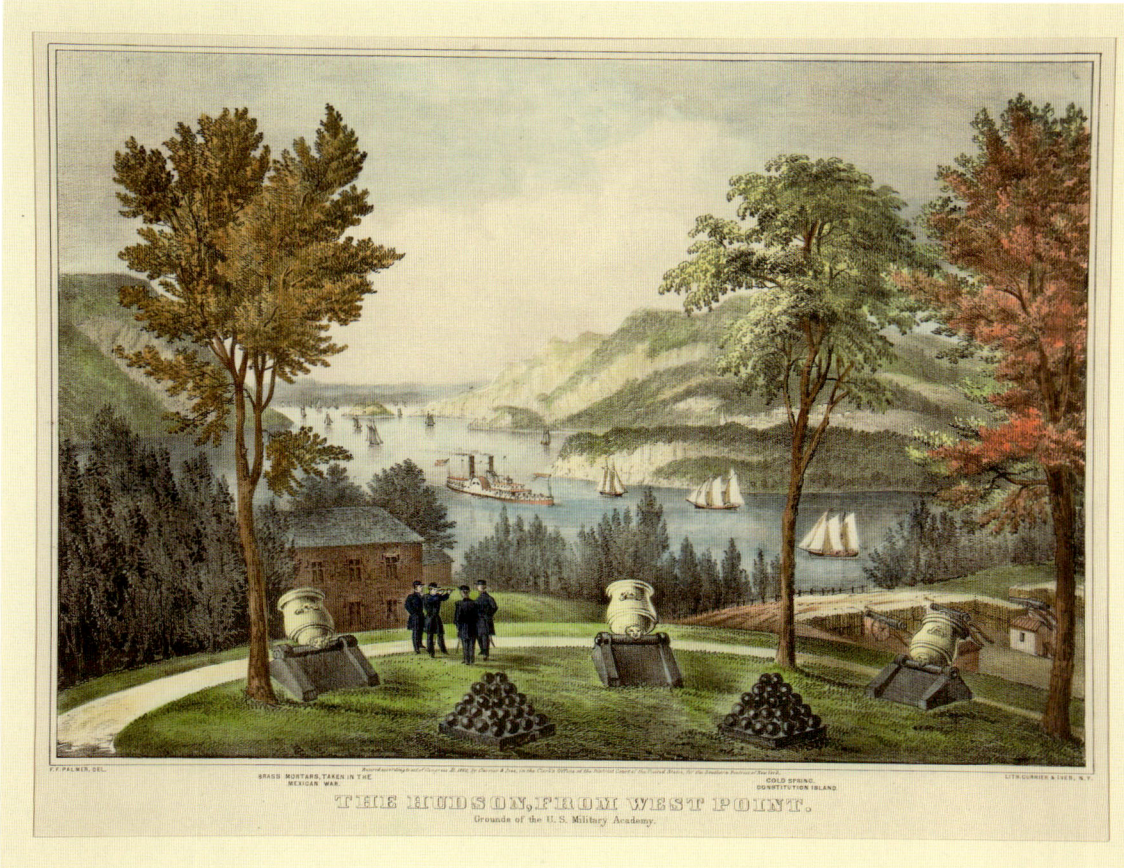

95. *The Hudson, From West Point. Grounds of the U.S. Military Academy.* 1862. Printed and published by Currier & Ives. Courtesy of the Yale University Art Gallery. (Checklist 3-62)

a father, mother, and two children, dressed for a Sunday outing, gaze across the Hudson at West Point's riding halls, barracks, and the clock tower of its academic building.[5] The young son gestures proudly toward the buildings, no doubt identifying with his future role as a soldier, while his sister listens with rapt attention.

In only one print does Palmer refer to an industrial site in the region: *West Point Foundry, Cold Spring. Hudson River N.Y.* (1862; p. 133). At first glance, one would never know that this is a picture of a major Civil War armaments factory. Two spectators are looking down over a split-rail fence at the foundry rooftops nestled amid trees and bushes. Only a smoking chimney hints at the harsh purposes of the complex of buildings in whose gloomy interiors a thousand men were producing the famous Parrott cannons for the Union army. President Lincoln visited and inspected the pouring pit in the same year that this print was published. In the distance is an alluring view of the boat-flecked river, crossed by a tiny train on a bridge.

Palmer's Arcadian image is very different from John Ferguson Weir's postwar painting *The Gun Foundry* (1866), which shows straining men pouring molten metal inside the tomblike, Piranesian

interior of the same building.[6] Nineteenth-century art historian Henry T. Tuckerman described Weir's painting as a paean to the new national industrial and economic transformation: "We know of no picture which so deftly celebrates our industrial economy."[7] Palmer's employers, in contrast, preferred to issue a pleasing country view that would disturb no one when it was framed and placed on a parlor wall. Nevertheless, viewers of the print understood from the title that they were looking at the location of one of the largest iron-forging companies in the nation, which was playing a key role in the Union cause.

Cozzen's Hotel, located three miles south of West Point on a hilltop with a splendid view of the river, was a popular resort for New Yorkers escaping from the city's summer heat and a favorite stop on the grand tour of the United States. The well-known engraver and historian Benson J. Lossing captured the ambience of this famous hostelry (torn down in the 1960s) in his book *The Hudson* (1866):

It was a place of fashionable resort from June until October, and at times was overflowing with guests, who filled the mansion

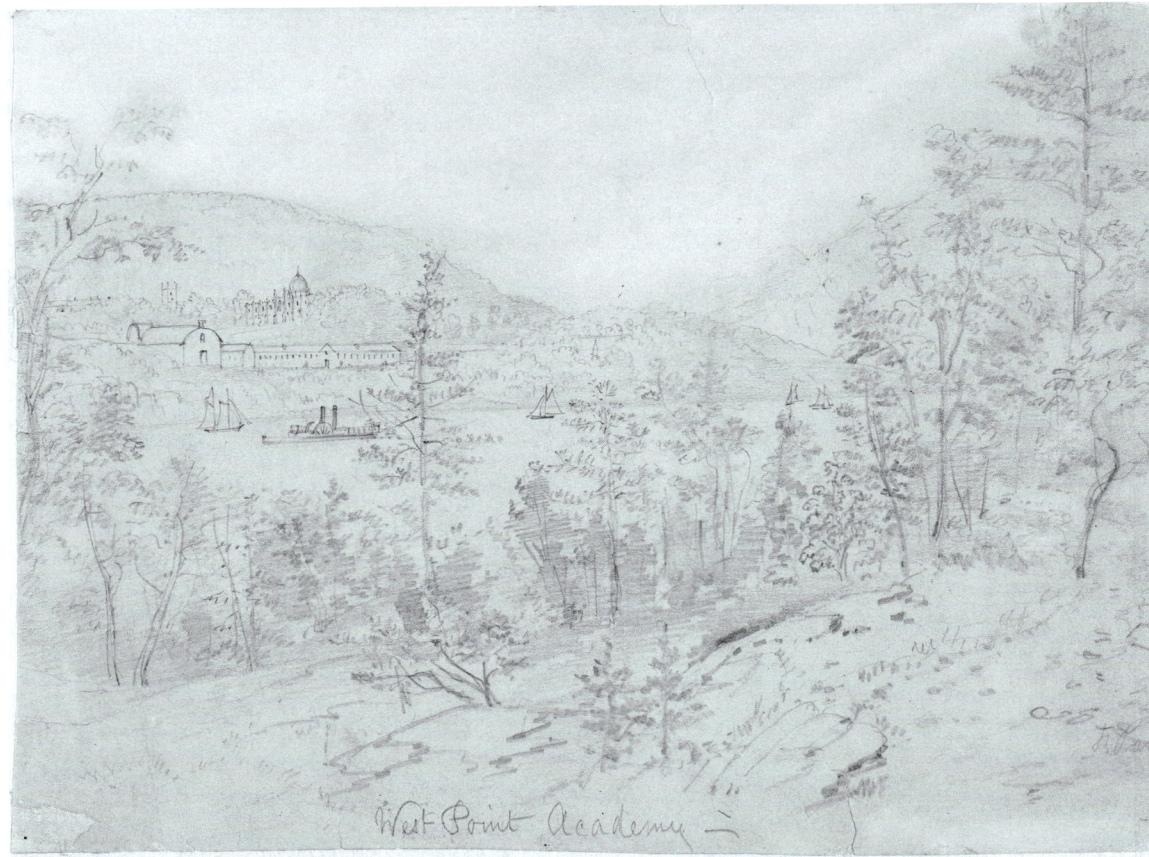

96. *West Point Academy.* Undated. Pencil drawing. Courtesy of the Museum of Fine Arts, Boston. Gift of Maxim Karolik for the M. and M. Karolik Collection of American Watercolors and Drawings, 1800–75. Photograph © 2017 Museum of Fine Arts, Boston. (Checklist 4-25)

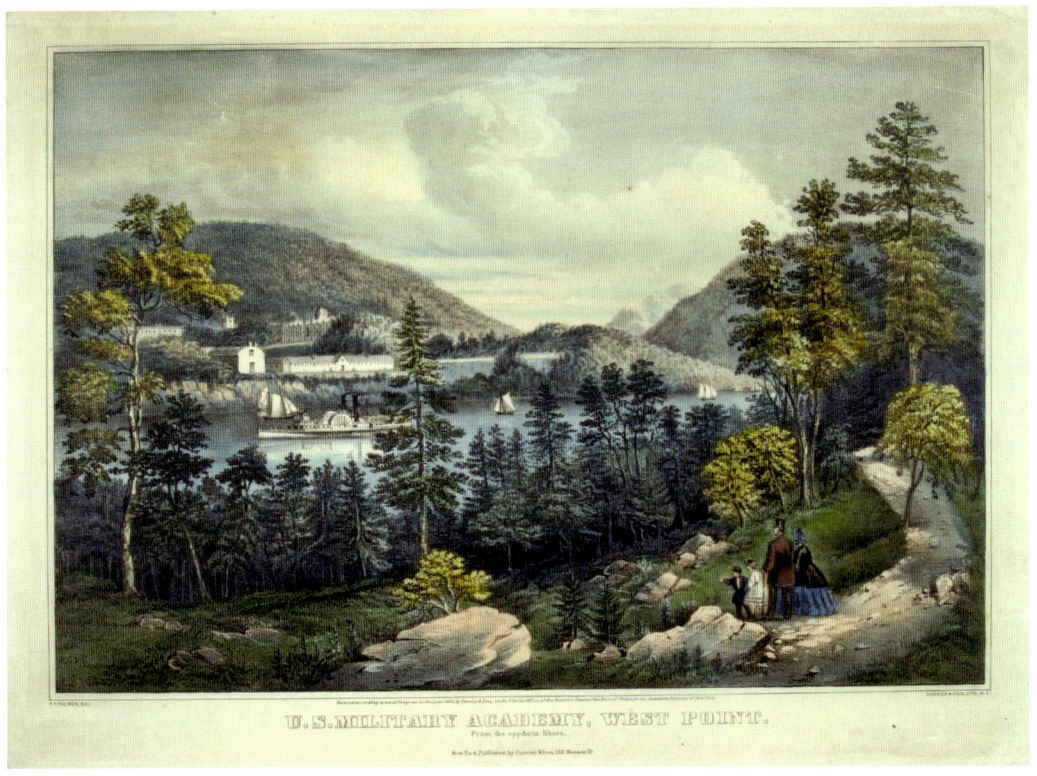

97. *U.S. Military Academy, West Point. From the opposite Shore.* 1862. Printed and published by Currier & Ives. Courtesy of the Old Print Shop. (Checklist 3-144)

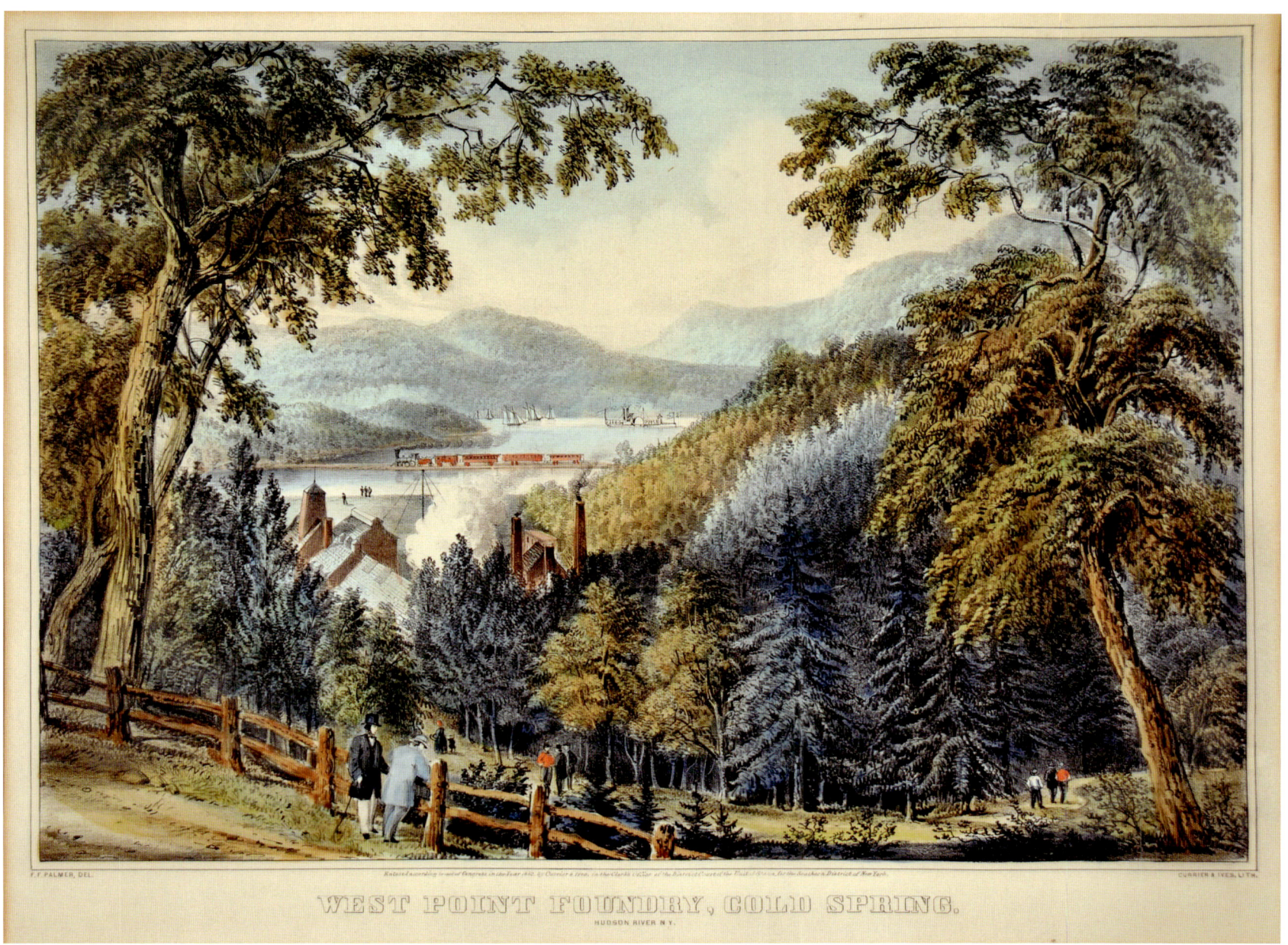

WEST POINT FOUNDRY, COLD SPRING.

HUDSON RIVER N.Y.

98. *West Point Foundry, Cold Spring. Hudson River N.Y.* 1862. Printed and published by Currier & Ives. Courtesy of the Old Print Shop. (Checklist 3-170)

and the several cottages attached to it. Among the latter was the studio of Leutze, the historical painter. Only a few days before our visit it had been the scene of great festivity on the occasion of the reception of the Prince of Wales and his suite, who spent a day and a night there, and at West Point, enjoying the unrivalled mountain and river scenery that surround them.

The pleasure-grounds around Cozzens's were extensive, and were becoming more beautiful every year. . . . All about the cliffs, on the river front of Cozzens's, are winding paths, some leading through romantic dells and ravines, or along and across a clear mountain stream that goes laughing in pretty cascades

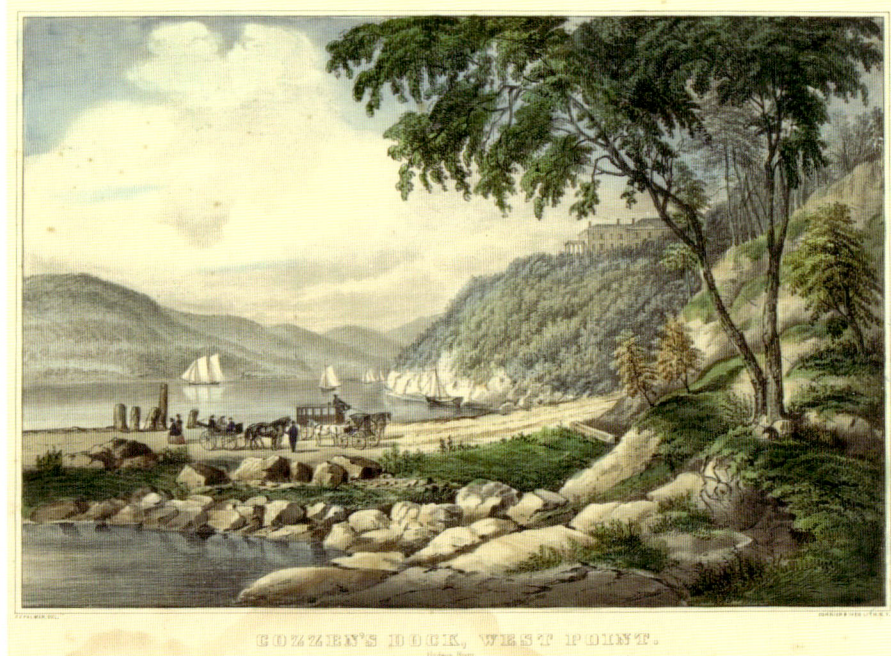

99. *Cozzen's Dock, West Point. Hudson River.* Undated, ca. 1857–72. Printed and published by Currier & Ives. Courtesy of the Old Print Shop. (Checklist 3-36)

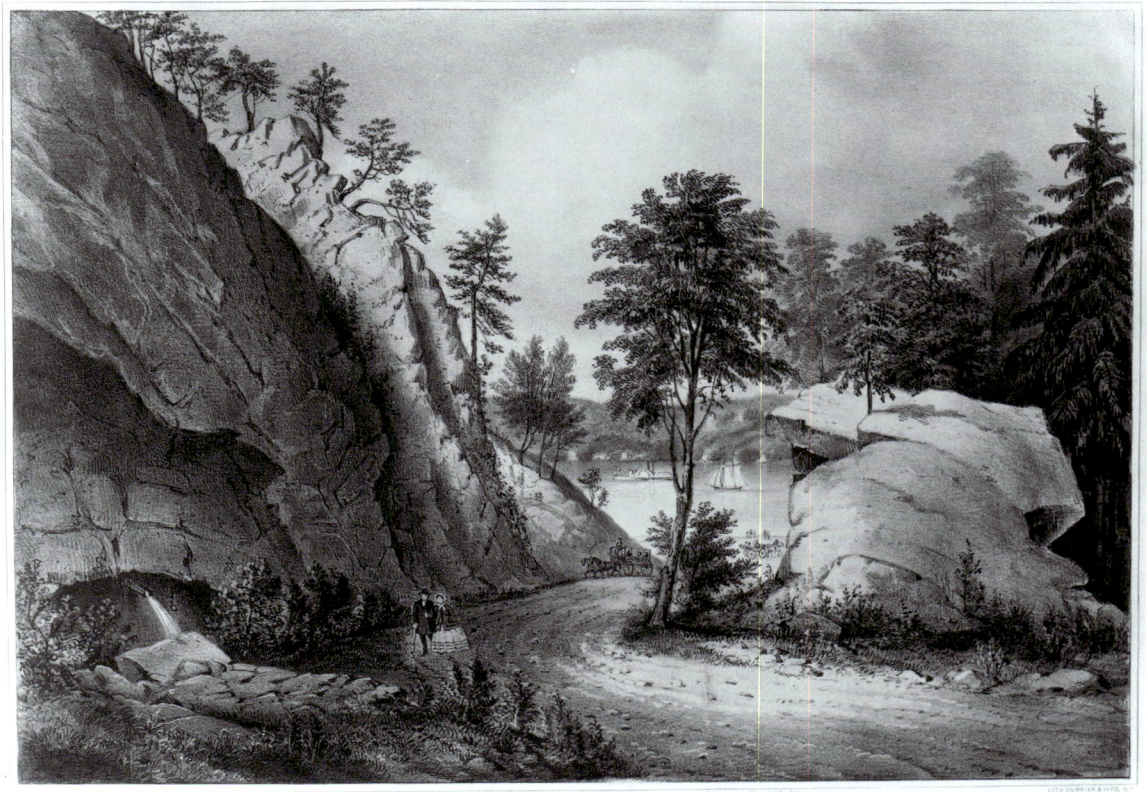

100. *The Mountain Spring. Near Cozzen's Dock, West Point.* 1862. Printed and published by Currier & Ives. Courtesy of the Old Print Shop. (Checklist 3-90)

down the steep shore to the river. The main road, partly cut like a sloping terrace in the rocks, is picturesque at every turn, but especially near the landing, where pleasant glimpses of the river and its water craft may be seen.[8]

Two Palmer prints bring this scene to life: *Cozzen's Dock, West Point. Hudson River* (undated, ca. 1857–72; p. 134) shows people and carriages waiting for a steamboat below the hill on which the hotel is perched, and *The Mountain Spring. Near Cozzen's Dock, West Point* (1862; p. 134) features a vacationing couple strolling forward past a picturesque local landmark—a stream issuing from a fissure in the hillside.

Hudson River Steamboats

After Robert Fulton launched the *Clermont* from New York to Albany in 1807, the Hudson became the first river in the world with a steamboat line. Writing in 1832 after a trip to West Point, the British actress Fanny Kemble marveled at the floating palaces: "Nothing can exceed the comfort with which they are fitted up, the skill with which they are managed, and the alacrity with which passengers are taken up from or landed at the various points along the river." Her boat, she wrote, went "bounding over the water like a race horse."[9] Over the years, the popular sidewheelers had melodramatic histories—sinkings, rammings, fires, and other disasters, such as the one shown in the *Lexington* print that brought fame to Nathaniel Currier. Great skill was required to navigate through fog and the hairpin turns of the river.

Palmer's print *A Night on the Hudson. "Through at Daylight"* (1864; gallery plate 13) evokes the drama of such a scene. As dawn breaks, two night boats, the *Isaac Newton* and the *Francis Skiddy*, glide forward between dark silhouetted mountains into the wide Hudson after a treacherous passage through the Highlands. Light hits the edges of the clouds and shines on the water. A few passengers are out on deck to see the spectacle.

A contrasting daylight scene, *The Hudson River Steamboat "St. John"* (1864; p. 189), shows the calm majesty of the river in good weather. The *St. John*, the longest and most luxurious steamboat of the era, famous for its fifteen-foot piston stroke and its magnificent interior, glides smoothly past wooded highlands, barely rippling its reflection in the glassy water. Palmer emphasizes the boat's sleek four-hundred-foot length by filling almost the entire width of the composition with its profile. A small sailboat nearby further emphasizes its great size.

Like many of its kind, the *St. John* endured disasters. When a boiler burst, a number of passengers were scalded to death; about fifteen years later it rammed and sank another steamboat but escaped damage; in 1885 it finally burned while docked off Canal Street in Manhattan.[10] But in F. F. Palmer's print it will always glide forward serenely, an image of American pride and progress in the mid–nineteenth century.

Mississippi Steamboats

The immensely wide and crooked Mississippi River had long been the highway between the Gulf of Mexico and the Great Lakes. Beginning in 1811, steamboats began to transform the river into the great trade route of the American heartland. By 1838, the former four-month canoe or flatboat trip from Louisville to New Orleans had been reduced to six days. Roughly six thousand paddle wheelers were launched on midwestern rivers between 1820 and 1880. The subject of saga and legend, they were described in 1827 by a Cincinnati newspaper editor as "rushing down the Mississippi, as on the wings of the wind . . . walking against the mighty current bearing speculators, merchants, dandies, fine ladies . . . with pianos and stocks of novels and cards and dice and flirting . . . and drinking."[11] John James Audubon, the great naturalist-artist, was less enthusiastic in his description of travel on "the filthiest . . . rat trap. . . . [When the boat got stuck on the bottom,] the ladies screamed, the babies squalled . . . the captain swore. . . . [W]hen it rained outside, it also rained within."[12]

Gleaming white, with gold trim and tall, black smokestacks folded out at the top into petal shapes, flaunting paddle-wheel covers painted with western, biblical, or other designs, these floating gingerbread palaces were hailed as a new and distinctively American architectural form described as "Steamboat Gothic." F. F. Palmer's precise draftsmanship and talent for dramatic composition made her the perfect candidate to produce eight of the firm's most important prints of this subject. In sunlight and moonshine, in flood and low tide, in war and peace, she interpreted the many moods of the river and the people living alongside it.

As the steamboats developed more and more speed, their proud captains began to set specific times for races, which became local—even national—events, accompanied by feverish betting. All excess weight was removed from the boats (it was

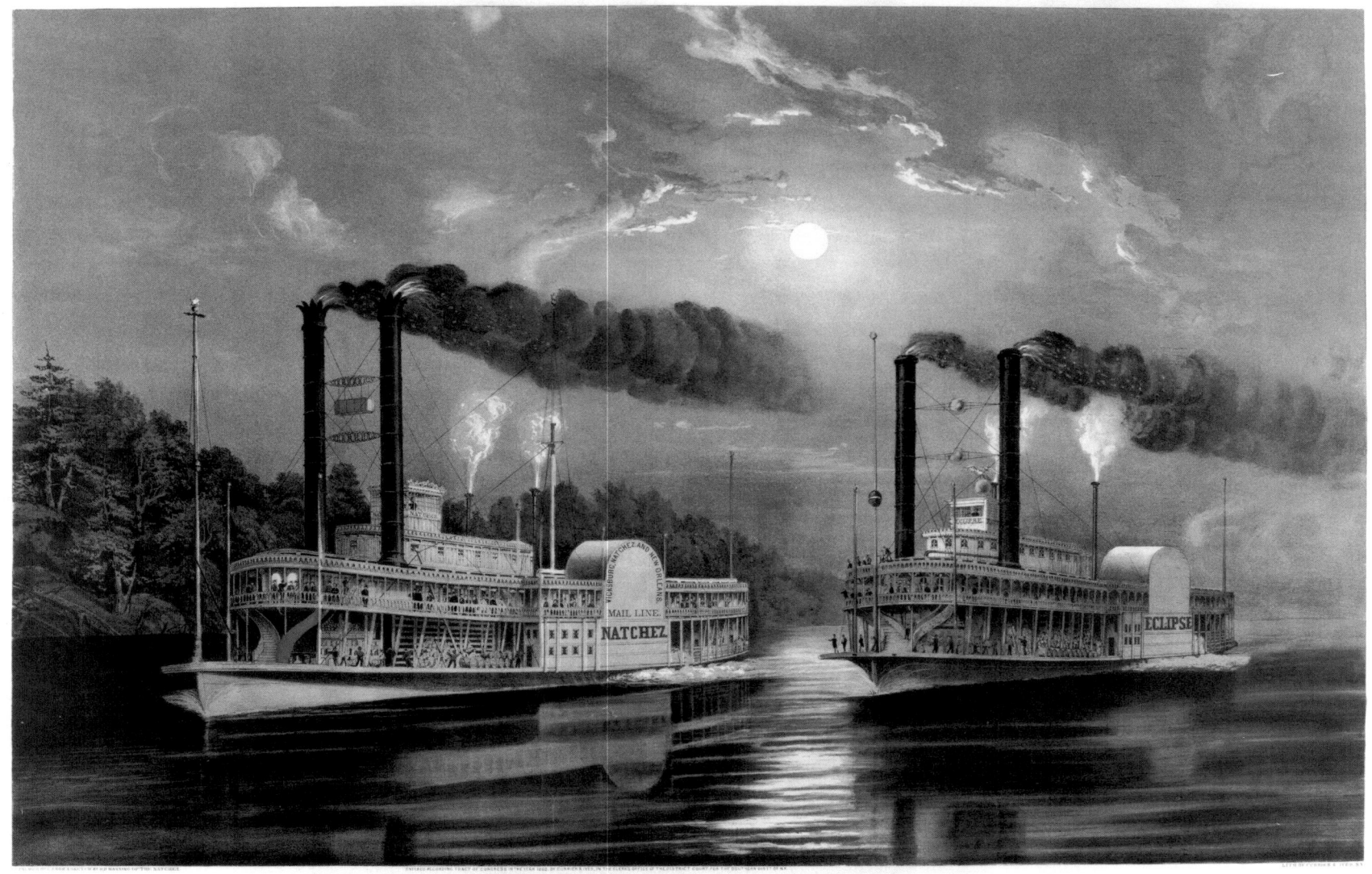

A MIDNIGHT RACE ON THE MISSISSIPPI.

said that even the gilt on decorations was scraped off). Author Mark Twain, who had once been a steamboat captain, described such an event:

> Whenever two fast boats started out on a race, with a big crowd of people looking on, it was inspiring to hear the crews sing, especially if the time were night-fall, and the forecastle lit up with the red glare of the torch-baskets. . . . [T]he two great steamers back into the stream, and lie there jockeying a moment, apparently watching each other's slightest movement,

101. *A Midnight Race on the Mississippi.* 1860. Printed and published by Currier & Ives. Courtesy of the Old Print Shop. (Checklist 3-80)

like sentient creatures; flags drooping, the pent steam shrieking through safety-valves, the black smoke rolling and tumbling from the chimneys and darkening all the air. People, people everywhere; the shores, the house-tops, the steamboats . . . and you know that the borders of the broad Mississippi are going to be fringed with humanity.[13]

In 1860, Palmer lithographed Currier & Ives's first print of this subject: *A Midnight Race on the Mississippi* (p. 136), adapted from a sketch by H. D. Manning. The *Natchez* is nosing ahead of the *Eclipse* as both glide swiftly to the left under a moonlit sky, trailing red sparks and black smoke from their stacks and white puffs from their steam vents. This print was followed six years later by an even more dramatic pair of moonlit scenes. In *"Rounding a Bend" on the Mississippi. The parting Salute* (1866; p. 185), a glittering arc of fireworks marks a boat's departure; and in *The Champions of the Mississippi* (1866; gallery plate 6), steamboats thunder toward the viewer as they "race for the Buckhorns" (a trophy awarded to the fastest boat on the river), while cheering spectators, illuminated by torches and bonfire, wave their hats from the shore. On the center boat, a flag labeled "USM," indicates that it delivers US mail.

Details in these and other prints reveal the beginnings of a man-made ecological transformation, stimulated in part by the steamboats. Because huge quantities of firewood were needed to feed the boats' insatiable furnaces, wood eventually had to be replaced with coal, a change that spurred the development of mining and steel production in Pennsylvania and Ohio. In Palmer's prints, we still see the wood yards located at frequent points along the shore and the woodpiles stacked on the lower decks of boats. In *"Wooding Up" on the Mississippi* (1863; gallery plate 5), African American stevedores are frenziedly piling wood onto the *Princess* in a well-rehearsed choreography of labor, while their white bosses look on. As Mark Twain once quipped, they worked so fast that spectators on the boat barely had time to wipe their eyeglasses before the job was done.[14]

But railroad trains soon began to outstrip the steamboats, relegating them to a secondary position. In *Life on the Mississippi*, Twain described the desolation wrought by technological change, which he saw years later during a visit to the St. Louis levee: "This was melancholy, this was woeful . . . [the] jocund steamboatman . . . he is no more. His occupation is gone, his power has passed away . . . a shorn Samson. . . . [H]alf a dozen lifeless steamboats, a mile of empty wharves. . . . [T]he towboat and the railroad had done their work, and done it well and completely."[15]

RAILROAD PRINTS

Although the steamboat had already begun to quicken the pace of American life, the steam locomotive ushered in an era of madly accelerating technological change. As Leo Marx has stated, the railroad was "the first important innovation in overland transportation since the time of Julius Caesar. . . . [T]he building of the American railroads coincided with the building of a new society and with the final phase of the European occupation of the continent. Between 1830 and 1860 . . . the line of permanent white settlements moved further [*sic*] west than it had moved in the previous two centuries."[16]

At first, the train lines were short links from cities to waterways (such as the Great Lakes) that still carried the bulk of traffic, but they rapidly spread in all directions. In 1850, there were nine thousand miles of track in the United States; by 1870, that number had increased to fifty-three thousand. A railroad mania possessed the country.

New towns sprang up along the rail lines around station stops. For the first time, farmers and merchants could ship their products quickly and cheaply across vast, difficult terrain to faraway markets. The giant railroad companies, with their geographic spread and bureaucratic levels of organization, became the pioneers of a new kind of business structure, the modern corporation. Promoters such as Jay Gould and James Fisk fought for supremacy against Cornelius Vanderbilt and other railroad titans. As everyone rushed in to buy railroad stock, market manipulations and swindles were widespread, but the public was infatuated with the new "iron horses." Trains were more than a new means of transportation; they were the symbols of a new age, representing the triumph of science and reason over raw nature, the very embodiment of the nation's dynamic future.

At first, lithographers drew locomotives in profile, like a draftsman's elevation, mostly for advertisements by train manufacturers. In artist's landscapes, they were shown in the distance, making them less intrusive on nature. However, Currier & Ives, who had "the common touch," recognized that Americans gloried in their new machines, and so the company began to show locomotives racing forward diagonally in three-quarter view, filling the picture space with their brightly colored forms—bells, whistles, headlights, smokestacks, sand domes, and cowcatchers fanning out in front to clear stray animals from their paths.

F. F. Palmer, who had already born witness to these developments in England in the 1840s when she drew sketches for the

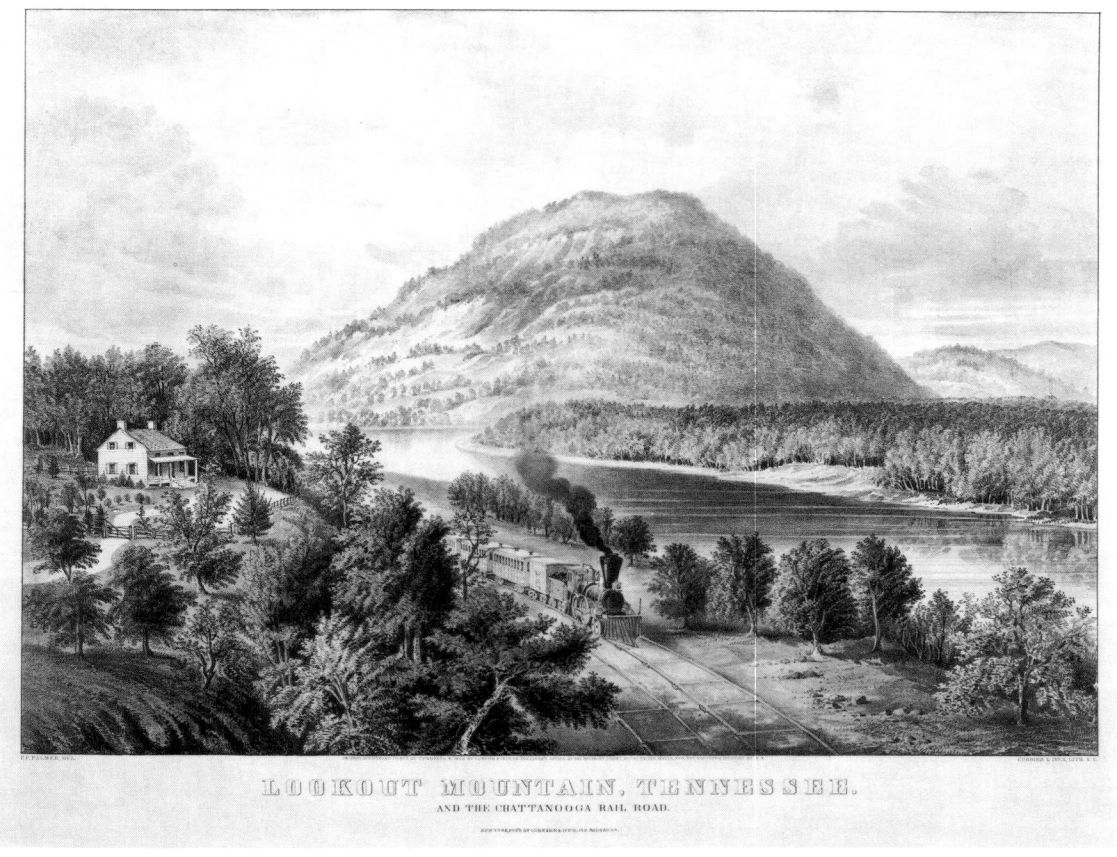

LOOKOUT MOUNTAIN, TENNESSEE.
AND THE CHATTANOOGA RAIL ROAD.

102. *Lookout Mountain, Tennessee. And the Chattanooga Rail Road*. 1866. Printed and published by Currier & Ives. Courtesy of the Old Print Shop. (Checklist 3-76)

Midland Railway line, was well prepared to create railroad images for her American employers. In 1863, she completed what many regard as the most dramatic of all the company's railroad prints: *The "Lightning Express" Trains. "Leaving the Junction"* (gallery plate 10). Two trains, their kerosene headlights glowing in the dark, their stacks trailing banners of smoke flecked with sparks, are racing forward on curved tracks past the station. The forced diagonal perspective of the trains contributes to the sense of power and speed. Circles and ovals—the white full moon, orange headlights, wheels, round engine fronts, and curved track—create a repeated rhythm. In 1863, the Civil War was at its bloody midpoint, and the railway lines had become a crucial means of rushing troops and supplies to the front; indeed, the North's superior railroad strength was a major factor in winning the war. Palmer drew the seal of the United States on the front of the nearer train, suggesting that it had been conscripted for service by the federal government. In this image, the locomotive is a symbol of Union strength and patriotism.

In a second railroad print, *American Express Train* (1864; gallery plate 9), the black-and-brass engine pulling red and yellow cars on a track alongside a river races ahead of the pale, insignificant-looking steamboat lagging behind in the water. Here the theme is the triumph of new technology over the old.

A third print, *Lookout Mountain, Tennessee. And the Chattanooga Rail Road* (1866), issued a year after the end of the war, shows another colorful train speeding through the now peaceful Southern landscape. The subtext of this print is the return of peace and transportation to a region where furious combat had taken place just a year earlier. Looming in the background is the tall cone shape of Lookout Mountain, site of the Battle above the Clouds in 1863, where Union troops had clawed their way up to victory through dense fog.

Palmer's colorful trains may appear fanciful to modern viewers, but, in fact, in the early stages of railroading companies hired specialized artisans to decorate them in appealing colors and designs. However, the trains did not always seem as glamorous to the riders as they appear in Palmer's exterior views. Charles Dickens's description of a trip in the Northeast during his visit to the United States in 1842 hints wryly at the way in which train travel reflected some of the contradictions in American life:

> There are no first and second class carriages as with us; but there is a gentlemen's car and a ladies' car. . . . As a black man never travels with a white one, there is also a negro car; which is a great blundering clumsy chest, such as Gulliver put to sea in, from the kingdom of Brobdingnag. There is a great deal of jolting, a great deal of noise, a great deal of wall, not much window, a locomotive engine, a shriek and a bell. The cars are like shabby omnibuses. . . . In the centre of the carriage there is usually a stove, fed with charcoal or anthracite coal; which is for the most part red-hot. It is insufferably close; and you see the hot air fluttering between yourself and any other object you may happen to look at, like the ghost of smoke.[17]

Years later, Robert Louis Stevenson described his trip to California in 1879 on an "emigrant train." By that time, travelers could ride in well-appointed cars with elegant diners and comfortable sleeping accommodations, but riders on this emigrant train had to put up with crowded wooden benches and such poor sanitary conditions that the odor drove Stevenson to spend much of the journey on the roof of one of the freight cars. Chinese passengers—often referred to by white passengers as "coolies" and the "dregs of Asia"—were segregated in a separate car.[18]

In Palmer's railroad prints, however, the faces of all the smiling passengers seen at the windows as well as the cheerful engineer and his young assistant, the fuel tender, appear to belong to one egalitarian, happy, white American class. Not a single brown or black face appears. Her images express the dream of a united and prosperous people rushing forward to a bright future, untroubled by ethnic or racial differences. The artist's railroad series reached a climax in Across The Continent. "Westward the Course of Empire takes its way" (1868; gallery plate 8), heralding the completion of the transcontinental railroad. This print is discussed later in the section dealing with the westward movement.

The Civil War

As noted, Palmer referred obliquely to the Civil War in a number of prints; for example, *Staten Island and the Narrows* (1861; p. 183) showed not only a famous New York view but also a reassuring image of the city's harbor defenses.[19] However, Palmer did also draw naval battle scenes. Only in recent years has her role as an artist of military subjects been recognized. In *The Union*

Image, Mark Neely and Harold Holzer write: "It is a sign of the longtime neglect of women artists in the nineteenth century and of the tendency to stereotype warfare as a province of male interest alone that [Palmer's] achievement as a war artist has not heretofore been noticed. Palmer produced a substantial part of Currier and Ives's creditable coverage of the naval war, particularly the war on the inland waterways."[20]

These authors go so far as to suggest that Palmer "barely missed becoming the most important popular image maker of the Civil War" because Currier & Ives never commissioned her to compose any land-battle scenes.[21] Although she had already drawn *Battle of Palo-Alto* (1846; p. 39) when she was in business with her husband during the Mexican War, her American employers may have felt that others on the staff would be more adept at drawing battalions of soldiers in action. She had demonstrated, however, that she was a skilled creator of marine images—clipper ships, yachts, and steamboats. Currier & Ives commissioned her to design a large-folio print of the historic first battle between ironclad warships, *Terrific Engagement between the "Monitor" 2 Guns, and "Merrimac" 10 Guns, In Hampton Roads, March 9th, 1862* (1862; p. 140).[22]

As historians have pointed out, the print is a David-and-Goliath conception in which the smaller Union ship the *Monitor*, with only two guns in its rotating round turret, triumphs over the much larger ten-gun Confederate ship the *Merrimac*.[23] The inscription at the bottom of the print exaggerates the Union triumph, "in which the Merrimac was crippled, and the whole rebel fleet driven back to Norfolk." Actually, after almost four hours of withering gunfire exchange, both ironclads left the scene relatively unscathed. The great historical significance of the event was its demonstration that the age of wooden naval boats was over. The print showed the world that the United States was in the forefront of modern naval engineering.

It was difficult to create a dramatic composition from these new iron vessels; they had none of the grace and beauty of the old sailing ships. Admiral David Farragut called them "damned teakettles." The *Monitor*, with most of its hull below water, could in fact hardly be seen—a great advantage in battle because much less surface was exposed to enemy fire. There was no glorious image of Farragut peering through his spyglass, shouting, "Damn the torpedoes! Full speed ahead!" Instead, the hideous anonymity of modern warfare was beginning to take shape.

The lively brushwork of Palmer's preliminary watercolor study for this print (p. 140; held by the New-York Historical Society) captures the drama of the encounter better than the final print.

103. *Terrific Engagement between the "Monitor" 2 Guns, and "Merrimac" 10 Guns, In Hampton Roads, March 9th, 1862. The First Fight between Iron Ships of War. In which the Merrimac was crippled, and the whole Rebel Fleet driven back to Norfolk.* 1862. Printed and published by Currier & Ives. Courtesy of the Old Print Shop. (Checklist 3-136)

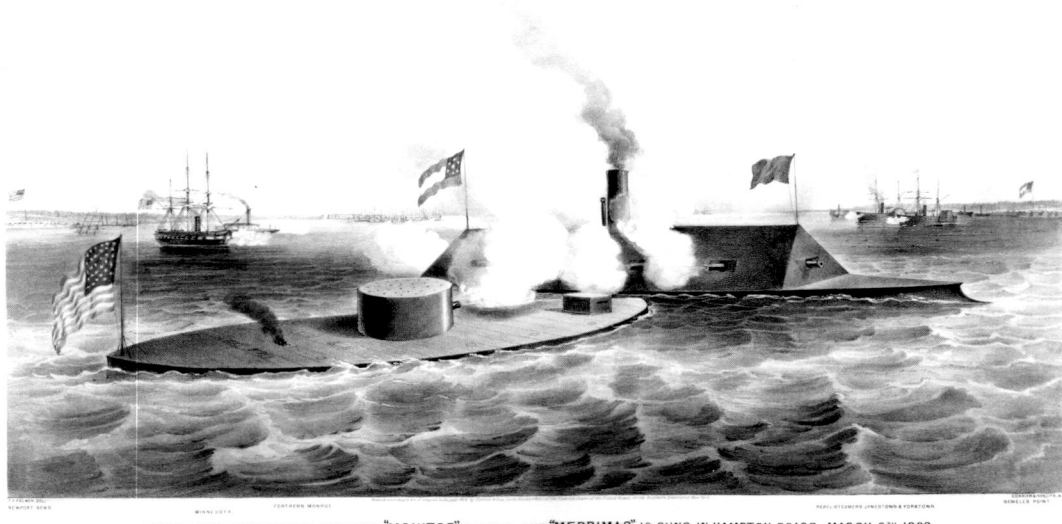

TERRIFIC ENGAGEMENT BETWEEN THE "MONITOR" 2 GUNS, AND "MERRIMAC" 10 GUNS, IN HAMPTON ROADS, MARCH 9TH 1862.
The First Fight between Iron Ships of War.
In which the Merrimac was crippled, and the whole Rebel-Fleet driven back to Norfolk.

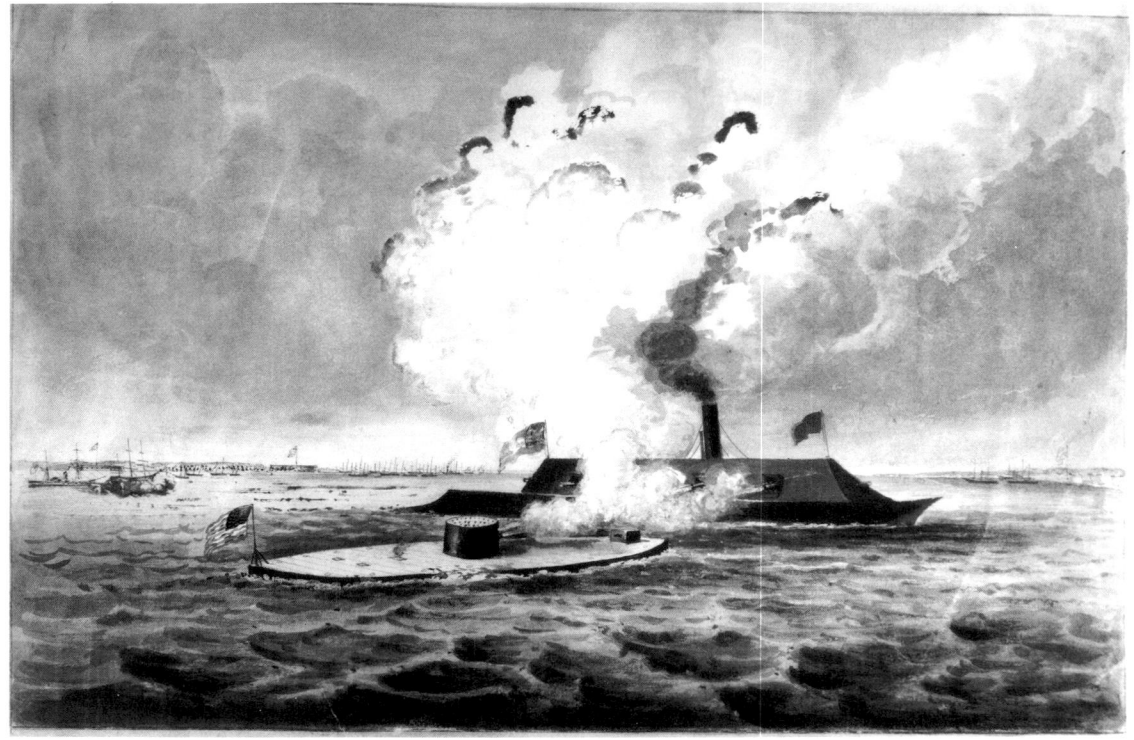

104. *Terrific Engagement between the "Monitor" 2 Guns, and "Merrimac" 10 Guns.* Undated, ca. 1862. Watercolor and graphite by Frances Flora Bond Palmer. Courtesy of the New-York Historical Society. (Checklist 4-19)

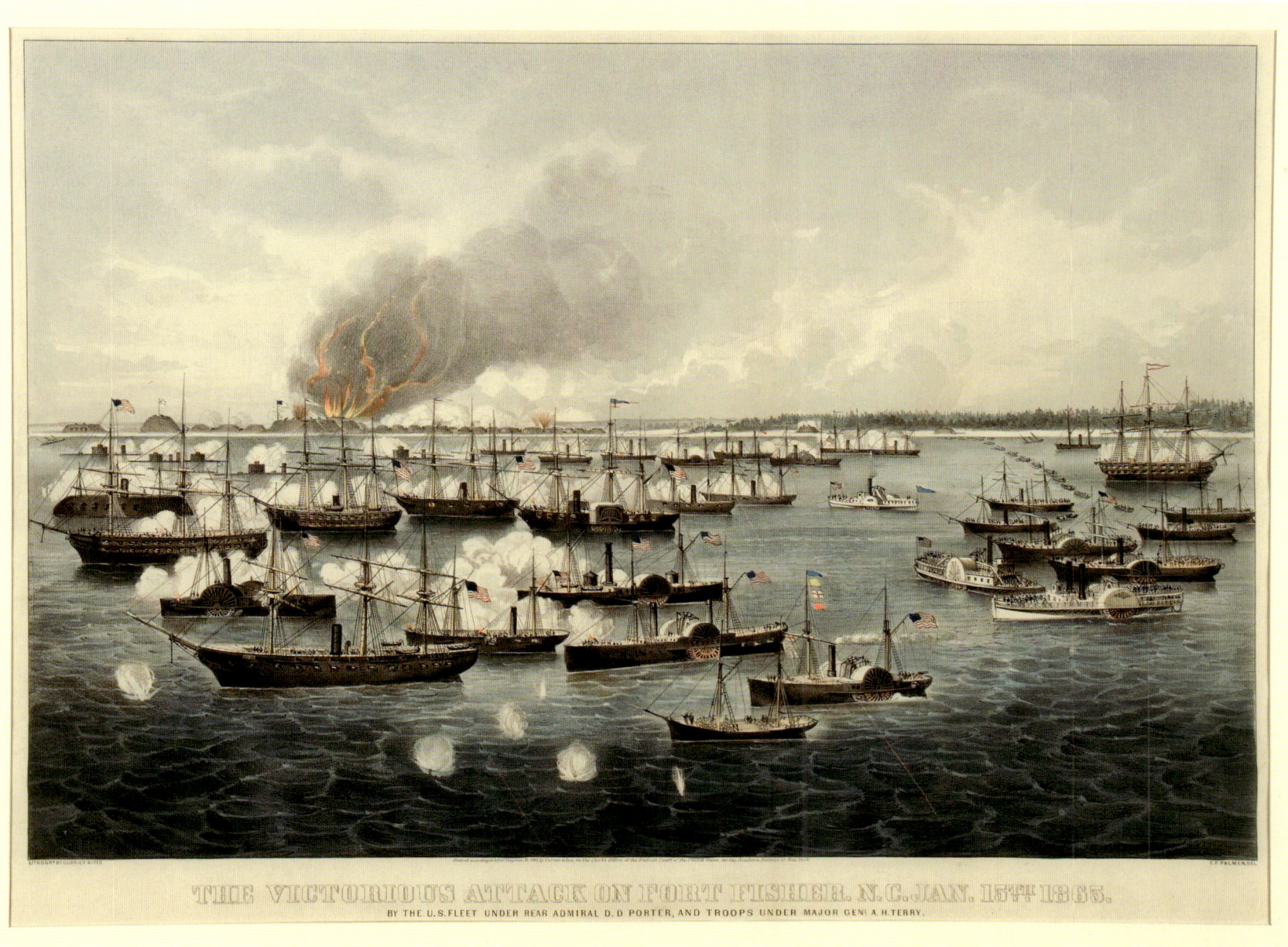

THE VICTORIOUS ATTACK ON FORT FISHER. N.C. JAN, 15TH 1865.

BY THE U.S. FLEET UNDER REAR ADMIRAL D. D PORTER, AND TROOPS UNDER MAJOR GENL. A.H. TERRY.

105. *The Victorious Attack on Fort Fisher, N.C. Jan. 15th 1865. By the U.S. Fleet under Rear Admiral D.D. Porter, and Troops under Major Genl. A.H. Terry.* 1865. Printed and published by Currier & Ives. Courtesy of the Yale University Art Gallery. (Checklist 3-146)

The *Monitor* and the *Merrimac* blast away at one another in the foreground, while in the distance warships from both sides watch the historic event. A billowing mass of white gun smoke, cut by black smoke from the *Merrimac*'s stack (symbolizing good versus evil), creates a dynamic shape across the sky.[24]

In the last year of the war, Palmer portrayed a pivotal Union triumph in her print *The Victorious Attack on Fort Fisher, N.C. Jan. 15th 1865* (1865). Fort Fisher, a giant Confederate earthworks guarding the entrance to the Cape Fear River, had persistently kept a sea lane open, enabling blockade runners to bring food and

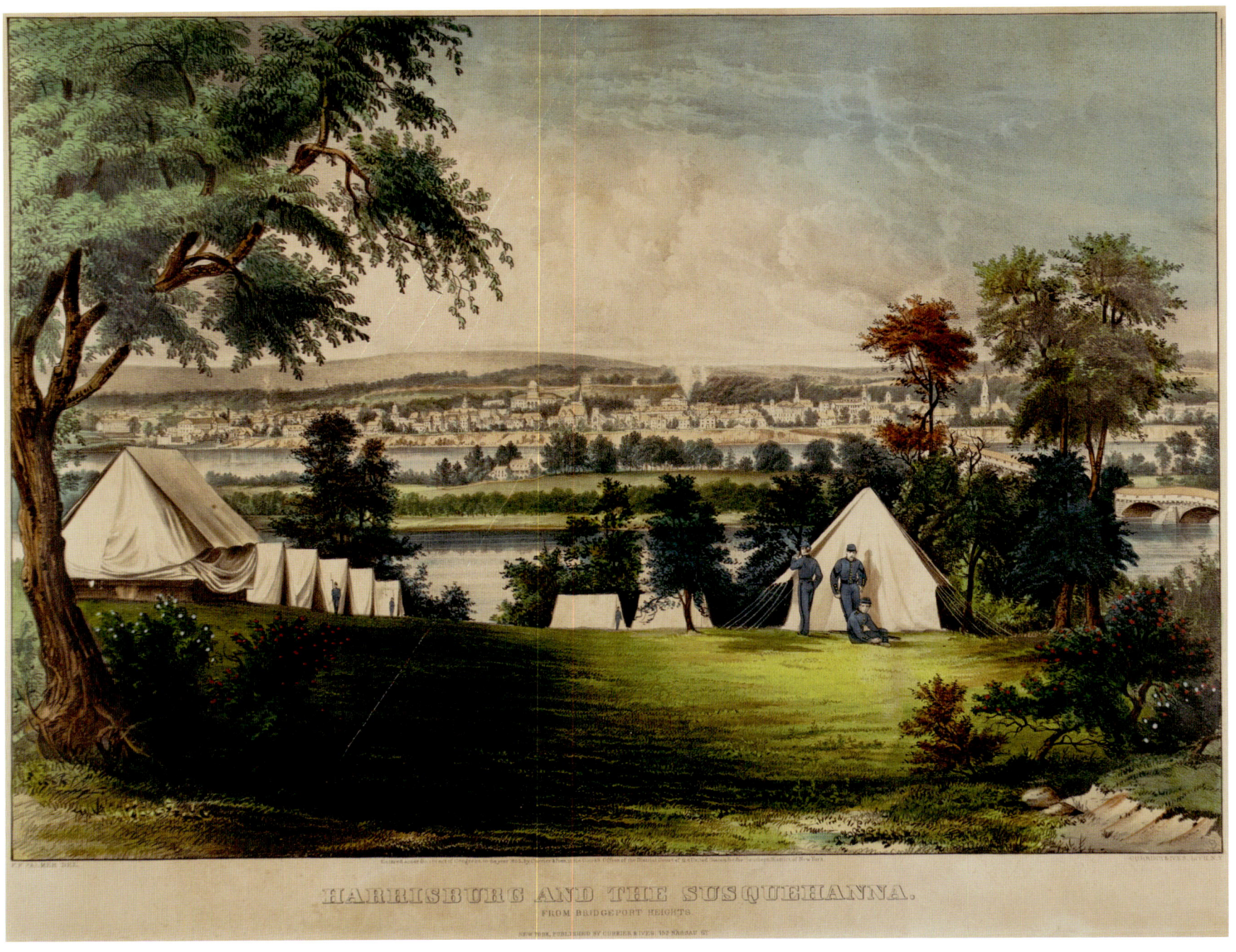

HARRISBURG AND THE SUSQUEHANNA.
FROM BRIDGEPORT HEIGHTS.
NEW YORK, PUBLISHED BY CURRIER & IVES, 152 NASSAU ST.

arms to the South. When General Ulysses S. Grant and Admiral David Porter finally coordinated a brilliantly conceived pincer attack from land and sea, the fort fell after three days, and the Confederacy, cut off from supplies, was doomed. Palmer prepared a delicate but precise pencil-and-watercolor sketch (US Marine Corps Art Collection) of the fleet of forty-four boats attacking the fortifications. Union strategy placed the Monitors closest to the shore because they were so hard to hit, while ships farther from

106. *Harrisburg and the Susquehanna. From Bridgeport Heights.* 1865. Courtesy of the Palmer Museum of Art of Pennsylvania State University. Partial gift and purchased from John C. O'Connor and Ralph M. Yeager. (Checklist 3-56)

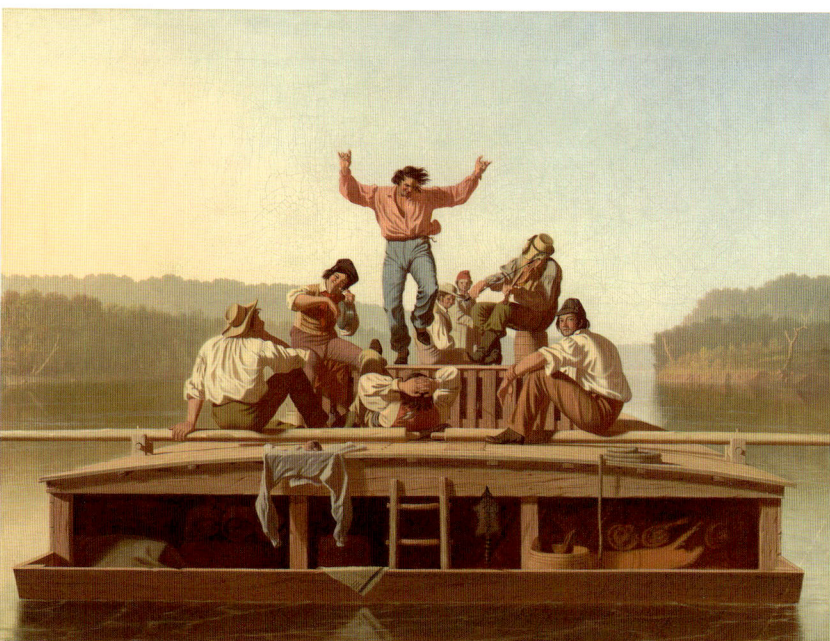

107. *The Jolly Flatboatmen.* 1846. Oil on canvas, 38⅓ × 48½ in., by George Caleb Bingham. Courtesy National Gallery of Art, Washington, DC.

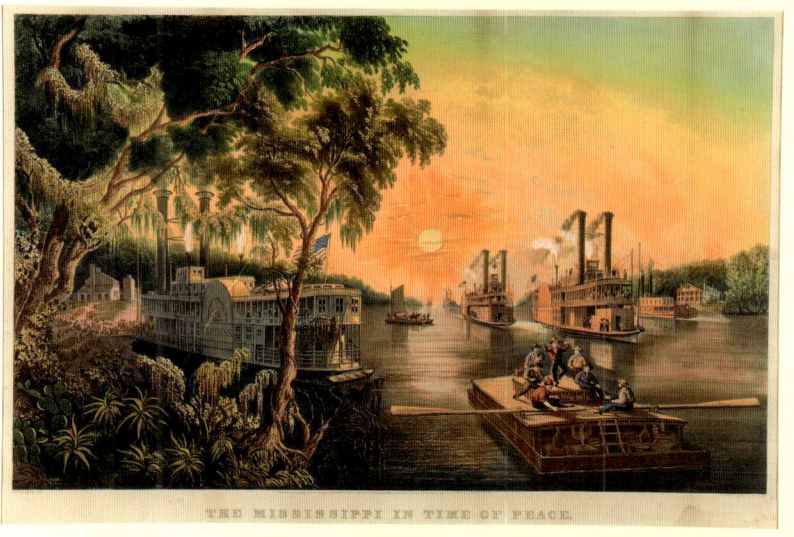

108. *The Mississippi in Time of Peace.* 1865. Printed and published by Currier & Ives. Courtesy of the Old Print Shop. (Checklist 3-83)

land are shown discharging puffs of smoke as they bombard the fort, seen burning in the distance.

The artist also drew lithographs of three Union military camps: *The Valley of the Shenandoah* (1864; p. 319); *Cumberland Valley. From Bridgeport Heights Opposite Harrisburg, Pa.* (1865; p. 290); and *Harrisburg and the Susquehanna. From Bridgeport Heights* (1865; p. 142). Orderly rows of tents in bucolic settings seem more like peaceful summer camps than military installations. Such prints soothed the fears of family members, who were, of course, worried about the condition of their absent loved ones. The fine panoramic view of Harrisburg, with the state capitol and other buildings laid out in detail, undoubtedly added to the marketability of *Harrisburg and the Susquehanna.*

Palmer's strongest Civil War images and arguably two of her finest prints are *The Mississippi in Time of Peace* and *The Mississippi in Time of War* (both 1865). Published a month before Appomattox, as the war was winding down, they are broad symbolic statements rather than pictures of specific events. Intended to be hung as a pair, the two prints, seen side by side, are framed by large trees, like proscenium stage scenery in the theater.

The Mississippi in Time of Peace (gallery plate 11) is a busy scene of river commerce glowing in the late afternoon sun. Leading

a procession toward the viewer is a flatboat and its merry crew, adapted from George Caleb Bingham's painting *The Jolly Flatboatmen* (1846), an image known to thousands at that time from the Art-Union engraving. Bingham had filled his canvas with freedom-loving pioneer types of an earlier day, paddling, jigging, and playing cards, close-up at eye level so that the viewer identified with them. Palmer, however, zooms back like a movie director, expanding the view into a broad river vista seen from some imaginary high point. The flatboat in the foreground now appears quaint and archaic, as smoke-billowing steamboats seem to charge down on it from behind. Thus, in only two decades the intimate wilderness of the river in Bingham's painting has been transformed into a wide panorama of "progress." Palmer telescopes historical time; the flatboatmen came first but are being overtaken by the technology of the modern era.

In contrast to this ode to peace and prosperity, *The Mississippi in Time of War* (gallery plate 12) is an inferno of flaming destruction. In the foreground, white and black crewmen leap into the river from a burning steamboat that has run aground, and the flatboatmen, clinging to barrels in the water, are trying to climb back onto their damaged barge. On the left, a menacing-looking gunboat is setting a plantation mansion on fire, representing "the retributive destruction to the ultimate symbol of the slaveocracy . . . [with] an ugly ironclad Union machine, the product of an advanced industrial economy, destroying the Southern plantation society."[25] The color scheme of gory red and black, the writhing moss-draped trees, the moon sending an eerie light through smoke-filled clouds—all contribute to the mood of terror.

Although the print shows no specific military engagement, it was inspired by the victorious river battles that wrested control of the lower Mississippi from Confederate forces early in the war. The Union command, recognizing the need for armored vessels to fire safely from the river, had authorized engineer Samuel M. Pook to design the first ironclad gunboats ever constructed in the Western Hemisphere. Nicknamed "Pook's Turtles" because of their shape, these vessels were essentially iron-plated, flat-bottomed stern-wheelers with guns mounted along the sides and ends.[26] Blasting their way south, the "turtles" soon destroyed Fort Henry, attacked Fort Donelson, and later in the war lay into Vicksburg. Of course, Northerners were fascinated by pictures of their new military innovation. Taken together, the images in these two Palmer prints conveyed a powerful message "that secessionists were meant never to forget."[27]

In 1868, three years after the conflict ended, James Ives, who had found Palmer to be an excellent collaborator on his visions of broad symbolic images of American life, worked with her on eight large, important lithographs. It is difficult to assess the exact nature and extent of her employer's influence on these works: the position and content of the signatures vary from print to print.

Among them is a pair of lithographs—*"High Water" in the Mississippi* and *Low Water in the Mississippi* (1868)—this time portraying the mighty river's fickle moods. The subject was particularly timely because Southern levees had been destroyed during the war, and serious flooding had occurred in 1862, 1865, and 1867. In the foreground of *"High Water" in the Mississippi* (p. 203), African American families rafting on the roof of their destroyed cabin are stoically trying to rescue a mule and salvage pieces of furniture from the water, while in the middle distance white plantation owners on the roof of their half-submerged mansion wave for help to passengers on a swiftly passing steamboat (named *Stonewall Jackson* after one of the South's greatest generals), who gawk in dismay at the scene of devastation.

The public had always enjoyed such disaster scenes; indeed, the famous print of the sinking of the steamboat *Lexington* had launched Nathaniel Currier's career. But why would the company be featuring images of African Americans as central motifs? Now in the Reconstruction period, instead of focusing on the North's victory, both black and white Southerners are seen bravely struggling to recover from the aftermath of a great flood (the Civil War?). In contrast, *Low Water* (pp. 145, 203), a peaceful scene of the river at low tide, shows a group of brightly dressed African American adults and children dancing and playing the banjo in front of their cabin, while white owners of the plantation house stroll about their land. Far below, boats come and go, leading the viewer's eye back in zigzag movements to a glowing sunset. A side-wheeler named the *Robert E. Lee* moves forward, approaching a raft carrying a store labeled "Grocery."

Scholars have critiqued Palmer's presentation in *Low Water* of childlike African Americans enjoying their lives on the old plantation—reminiscent of the "Sambo" minstrel show character.[28] In fact, both Mississippi images demonstrate how the heavy hand of her employers affected her work. Palmer had originally drawn a fully developed pencil study for *Low Water in the Mississippi* (p. 145, now at the Museum of the City of New York) in which two shirt-sleeved African American men are ferrying three white men to the other side of the river, while a group of well-dressed white people, seated at leisure in front of the plantation mansion, enjoy the view. For the final lithograph, however, someone (perhaps James Ives, who signed his name as the lithographer on the print) had removed the hard-working black boatmen and substituted the usual minstrel show clichés. What are the reasons for these changes? Unfortunately, such imagery was becoming commonplace at this time. Now, with the war over, Currier & Ives and other Northern print publishers, hoping to win back Southern customers, were issuing many prints intended to placate the bitterly wounded pride of the Confederacy (for example, *Home on the Mississippi* [1871], *The Death of General Robert E. Lee* [1870], and others).

But the reasons are more complex than that. *"High Water"* and *Low Water* were published in 1868, when, after Lincoln's assassination, a struggle was raging between Radical Republicans in Congress, who felt that freed slaves should have all the rights of citizens, and Southerners, who, like President Andrew Johnson, stubbornly resisted giving land or the vote to African Americans.[29] Unfortunately, a very large number of people in the North also felt that although freeing the slaves might have been necessary in order to win the war, the possibility that they might actually gain a degree of political or economic power was a frightening idea.

The two prints are typical of Currier & Ives's marketing strategy of appealing to all audiences. On the one hand, many purchasers simply delighted in nature's drama, enjoying all the details of Southern life: the uprooted trees, the landscape, the architecture, the steamboats, the contented African Americans, and the fine atmospheric effects for which Palmer was renowned. On the other

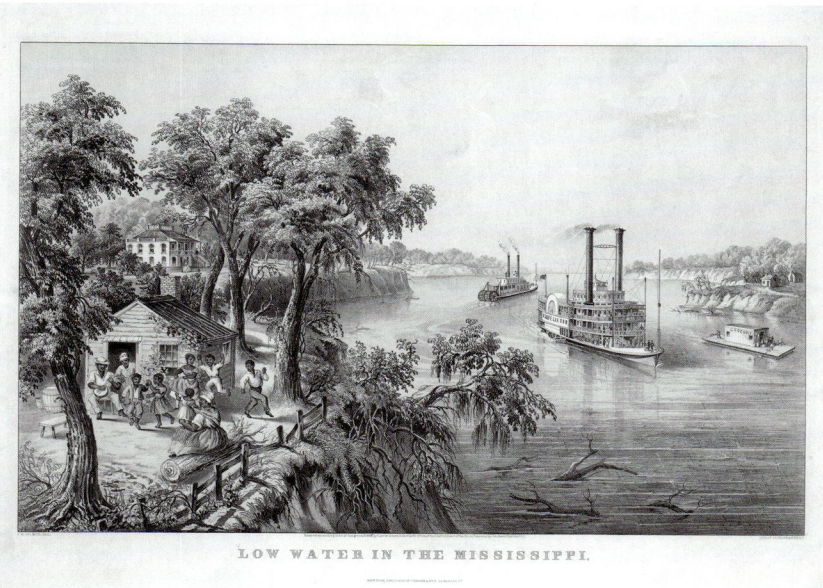

109. *Low Water in the Mississippi.* 1867. Printed and published by Currier & Ives. Courtesy of the Prints and Photographs Division, Library of Congress, LC-DIG-pga-00818. (Checklist 3-77)

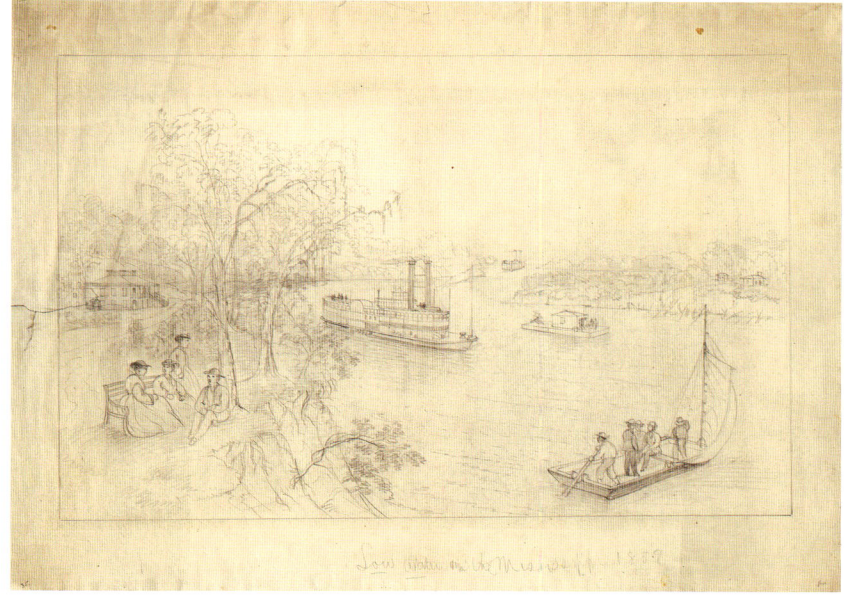

110. *Low Water in the Mississippi 1859.* 1862. Pencil drawing. Courtesy of the Museum of the City of New York, X2012.5.36. (Checklist 4-10)

hand, abolitionists and Radical Republicans could read *"High Water"* as a poignant image of newly freed slaves struggling to salvage something for their future (the "forty acres and a mule" promised to them by General Grant but rescinded by President Johnson[30]), but to white Southerners and to many Northerners as well *Low Water* suggested that everyone would be better off if freed black people went peacefully back to work for their former masters instead of demanding their own land or trying to vote and run for office.

Who was responsible for the final *Low Water* image? It may have been worked out by mutual consent, or perhaps James Ives, whose cursive signature "J.M.I. del." on the stone indicates that he was the lithographer, may have made changes when he adapted Palmer's composition to the stone. The simian faces of some of the African Americans in these prints also suggest the handiwork of intrusive collaborators. In most cases, Palmer drew African Americans with relatively unstereotyped faces (see, for example, *American Country Life. Pleasures of Winter* [1855; p. 202]).

In the years to come, as Reconstruction was abandoned and white supremacy returned to the South, racist attitudes also hardened in the North, and imagery ridiculing any attempt by African Americans to achieve parity or equality with their white counterparts became the norm. Indeed, the *Darktown Comics*, portraying

black people as stupid, ridiculous, and unsuited to share equally in American life, were among Currier & Ives's best-selling images.

PRINTS FOR THE PARLOR: FAMILY AND HOME

In 1868, James Ives also turned his epic vision on the American Victorian family. He assigned himself and some of his best artists, including F. F. Palmer and John Cameron, to work on a mythic saga—*The Four Seasons of Life: Childhood, Youth, Middle Age, and Old Age*—an idealized vision of family relationships, not so much as they actually existed but as the dominant forces in society felt they should be. The partners no doubt believed that their company was lifting the level of public morality and helping to heal the wounds of a brutal civil war by presenting an optimistic vision of family life. They also knew that there was a large market for such prints, especially among the masses of married women, who were some of the principal purchasers of lithographs for the home.[31]

But there was an additional motive for publishing the four prints at this time. Nineteenth-century stereotypes of male and female identity were beginning to be seriously challenged by the rising suffrage movement. Women had begun to organize for the right to vote as early as 1848, when the first women's rights convention was held at Seneca Falls, New York. During the Civil

War, with men away at the front, they had entered new fields of employment, and many were now seeking not only the vote but also a better education, property rights, and a wider sphere for their talents. This upsurge was regarded by the dominant political and religious leaders of the day as a fundamental threat to social order. The company issued two misogynistic cartoons, *The Age of Brass / Or the Triumphs of Woman's Rights* (1869) and *The Age of Iron / Man as He Expects to Be* (1869), showing cigar-smoking harridans taking over men's roles and leaving husbands with the babies and the laundry. For the most part, however, the partners preferred to make a more positive case for preserving the status quo by portraying the happiness and prosperity that would come to those who continued to accept the prescribed gender roles.

In order to understand the compelling force of *The Four Seasons of Life*, one must examine the changes that had come about in American society from before the war to after the war. The United States had changed from a world of farms, small shops, and cottage industries, where American men and women (and even children), although assigned different tasks, still produced many of the necessities of life at home and shared a role in the economy, to a world where products were made in factories and offices. Now, as Bryan Le Beau explains, with the rise of modern industry, the principal opportunities for men required "spending long workdays away from the rest of the family. The self-made man, the new model of manhood, derived entirely from a man's activities in the public sphere, measured by accumulated wealth and status, by geographic and social mobility. . . . The middle-class home increasingly became a female domain, cut off from business and public affairs," and the middle-class white woman was no longer supposed to work "in ways society recognized as labor."[32]

Supporting this new ideal of extreme "separate spheres" were stereotypes legitimizing these relationships. Men, it was held, were divinely (or Darwinianly) endowed with greater intellect, physical strength, and aggression and thus were suited to build the bridges and railroads, run the government, and face the competitive stresses of the workaday world. Women were supposedly weak and less intellectual but innately pious, pure, submissive, and domestic.[33] This viewpoint was bolstered by thundering from pulpit and press and supported by a host of pseudoscientific "proofs," such as the slant of a woman's forehead (phrenology) and the smaller size of a woman's brain.[34] Emotionally and spiritually, however, woman supposedly exerted an important moral influence on her rougher-edged husband. Within the confines of her home, which was her domain, she had an important role to play. As a mother,

she formed the character of the next generation. As a wife, she was to provide a comforting haven at the end of the day—the primary motivation and reward for the harried male who had to cope with the temptations and stresses of the commercial world.

The home was increasingly thought of as a kind of domestic church or sanctuary in which Christian virtues were shaped and women were its "chief ministers." Because its physical environment—furniture and decorations—were believed to influence the character of its inhabitants, the pictures women placed on their walls were important. Catherine Beecher and her sister, Harriet Beecher Stowe, coauthors of some of the most widely read books on homemaking, admonished women that "the educating influence of these works of art can hardly be over-estimated. Surrounded by such suggestions of the beautiful, and such reminders of history and art, children are constantly trained to correctness of taste and refinement of thought."[35] Urging their readers to allot one-quarter of their furnishings budget to pictures, the authors even suggested that low-income homemakers might forego a carpet and use floor matting if necessary to allow for the purchase of prints.[36] For families of modest means, low-priced lithographs filled the bill, and the ease of ordering them by mail from catalogs was a great convenience for the millions who lived far from cities and stores.

The Victorian wife and mother was cautioned to select pictures carefully. Violence (except for patriotic battle scenes and natural disasters) and any hint of immorality were abjured; history, travel, nature, nostalgic family scenes, farm and village life, and religious themes were desirable. Looking back at Palmer's total output, one can see that many of her prints fulfilled these domestic and ideological functions. Yet if we look closer, we find a slightly different edge in some of them.

In *Childhood. "The Season of Joy"* (p. 147), eight well-dressed children run out into the fields to pick springtime flowers—they themselves are in the springtime of life. Lambs graze on a nearby hill (the children, too, are little lambs of God). In the background stands a simple but substantial country home, symbol of stable family life. The message here seems to be the Wordsworthian or Rousseauian one that children "trail clouds of glory"; they are innocents fresh from heaven who should grow, free and untrammeled, under the beneficent influence of nature, in which God's spirit resides. An extremely sentimental approach to childhood had become a common theme in the postbellum era. After a fratricidal bloodbath and Lincoln's assassination, in a period of increasing industrialization and political corruption, adults saw in children their own lost innocence and their hope for the future.[37]

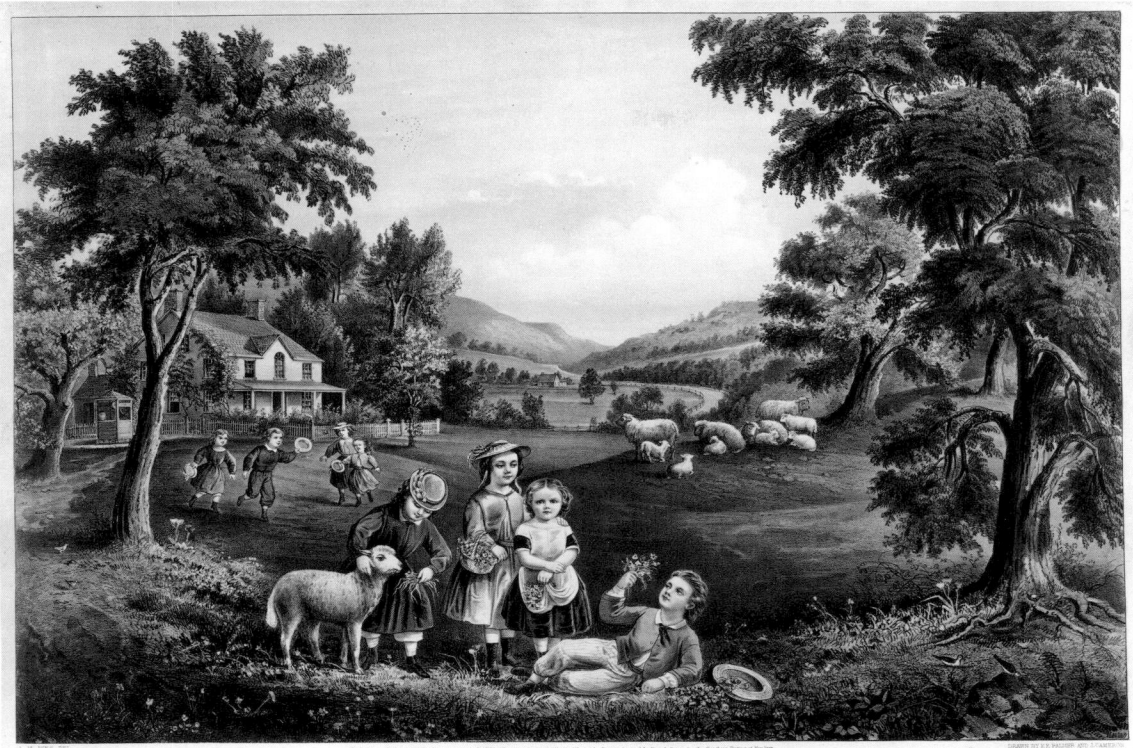

THE FOUR SEASONS OF LIFE: CHILDHOOD.
"The Season of Joy."

111. *The Four Seasons of Life: Childhood.*
"The Season of Joy." 1868. Printed and
published by Currier & Ives. Courtesy of
the Old Print Shop. (Checklist 3-47)

But there is an odd anomaly in this print. In mid-nineteenth-century paintings and prints of children playing, boys are usually more numerous than girls and certainly feistier. Yet in Palmer's print, six girls and only two boys represent that stage of life. Also, the boy in the foreground is shown lying on the ground, ecstatically sniffing a bouquet of flowers, an unusually passive male image. The oldest girl, already a "little mother" with her arm placed protectively around her small sister, finds this sensitive youth attractive and casts a shy sideways glance at him, as if to hint at the coming stages of love and marriage. Palmer seems to be pitching her concept to the women in her audience.

In the next print, *Youth. "The Season of Love"* (p. 148), two lovers walk forward on a country lane, holding hands, their other arm around their partner. The girl gazes up at her future protector, while he looks into the distance meditatively, thinking of the new joys but also of the responsibilities that he is undertaking. The girl's red dress and full bosom as well as the field of ripe summer wheat next to them hint at passion and fertility in their future married life. In the distance, a small village with its steepled church suggests that the lovers belong to a community where they

have been raised with Christian values and will pledge their troth. There is an air of energetic comradeship in the way they stride forward together.

Middle Age. "The Season of Strength" (p. 149) presents a father returning from work, greeting his family in the blooming garden in front of his home. This print is rarely reproduced because the lithograph stone reportedly broke. James Ives could easily have redrawn Palmer's design but may have decided that he wanted something more "modern," more in tune with the times, and he may also have preferred Charles R. Parsons and Lyman W. Atwater's[38] more stylish figure drawings to the rather stubby figures that someone—probably John Cameron, whose name is also listed on the print—seems to have superimposed on Palmer's composition. For whatever reason, Ives assigned the Parsons–Atwater team to redo this lithograph, so their image is the one found in most books (p. 149). It is interesting to compare Palmer's version with the one created by the men who replaced her.

In Palmer's image, the wife greets her husband outside her home, while her young son stands in the doorway behind her; their little daughter, however, has run out to join her father and

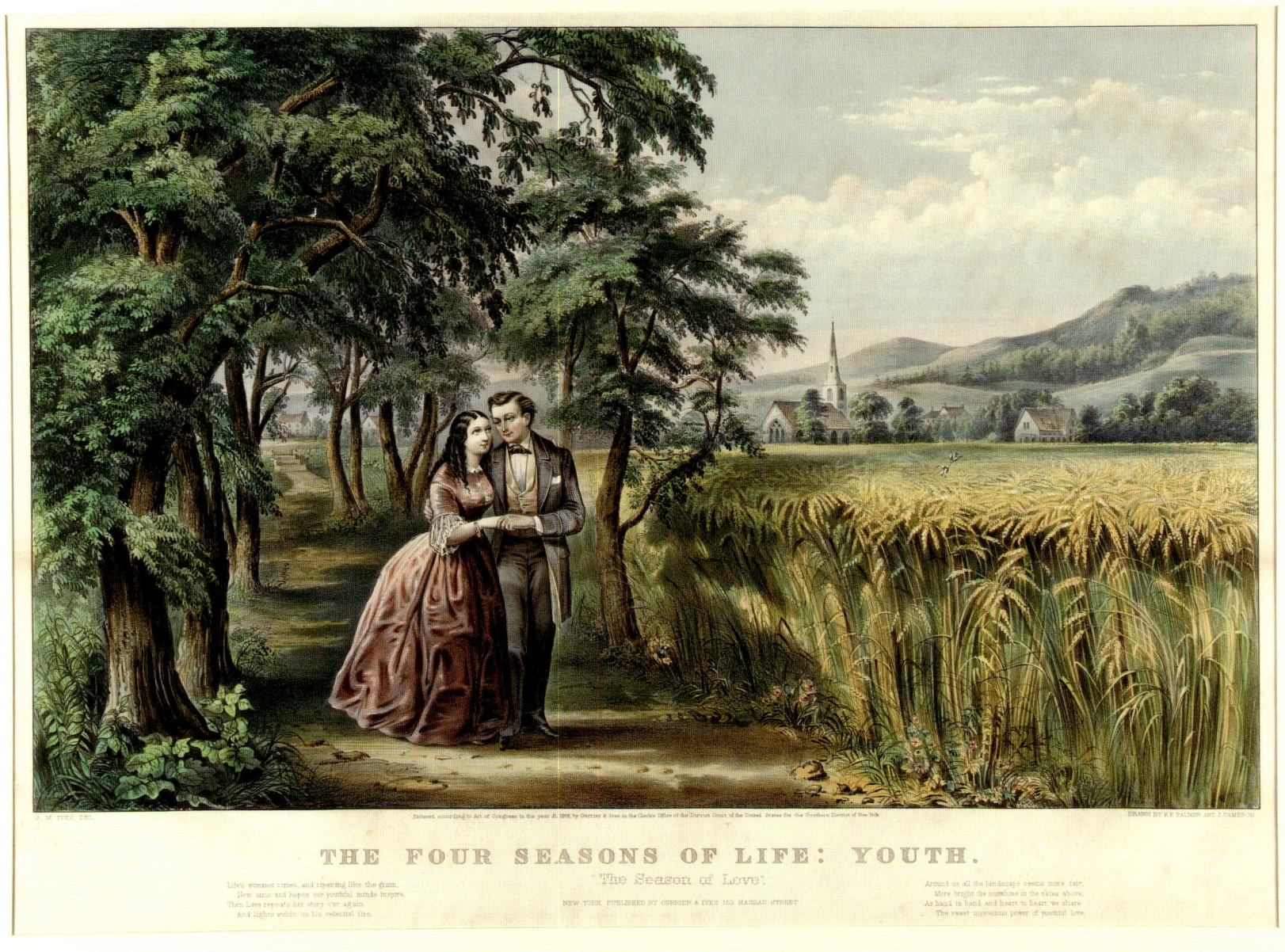

THE FOUR SEASONS OF LIFE: YOUTH.

"The Season of Love".

NEW YORK. PUBLISHED BY CURRIER & IVES 152 NASSAU STREET

holds onto his jacket as he approaches the house and lifts the baby from his wife's arms. They all look as though they might take a stroll together to the lovely lake in the background. Although the husband is returning from office or factory, the environment still feels rural; a farmer can be seen driving oxen near the gate, and garlands of flowers pour down the side of the print. Palmer's picture is a romantic, old-fashioned image of love and marriage.

In contrast, Parsons and Atwater show the wife, baby, and two daughters *inside* the home. The space is compressed, more

112. *The Four Seasons of Life: Youth.* "*The Season of Love.*" 1868. Printed and published by Currier & Ives. Courtesy of the Yale University Art Gallery. (Checklist 3-49)

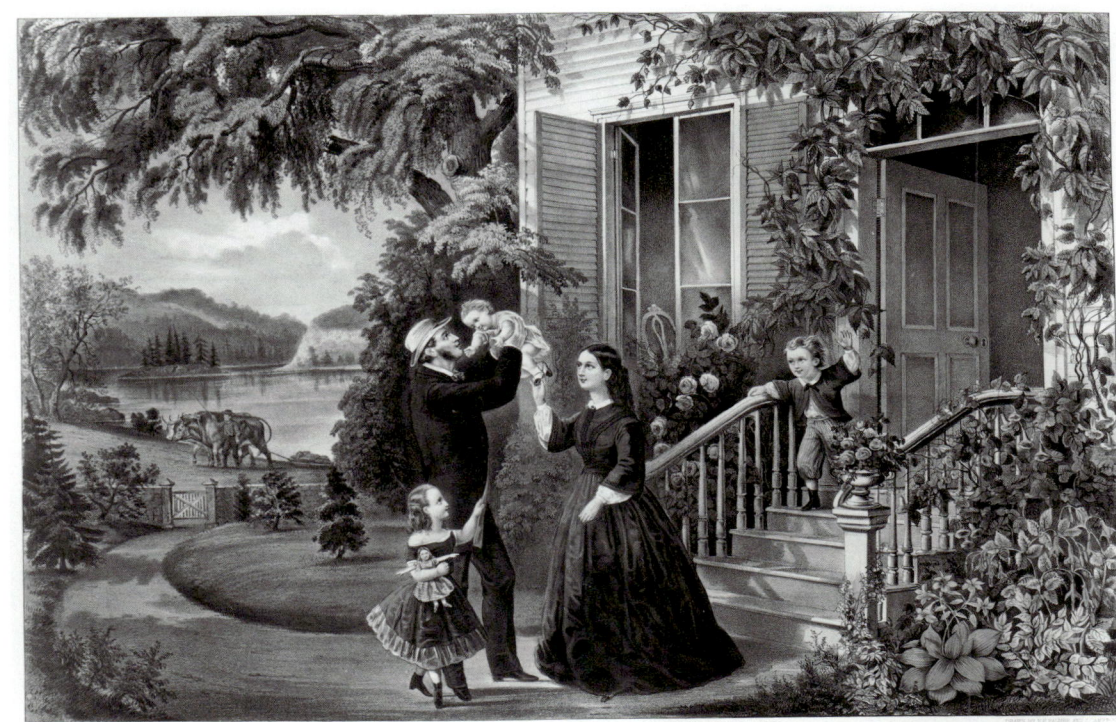

THE FOUR SEASONS OF LIFE: MIDDLE AGE.

113. *The Four Seasons of Life: Middle Age.* "*The Season of Strength.*" 1868. J. M. Ives, Del., drawn by F. Palmer & J. Cameron, printed and published by Currier & Ives. Courtesy of the Old Print Shop. (Checklist 3-48)

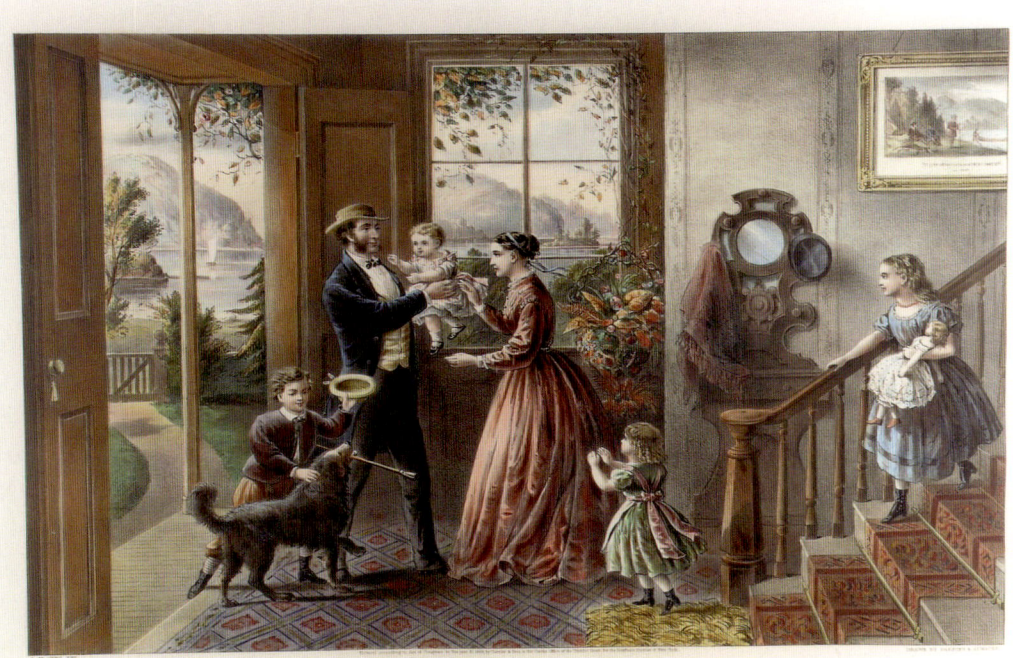

THE FOUR SEASONS OF LIFE: MIDDLE AGE.

"The Season of Strength."

114. *The Four Seasons of Life: Middle Age.* "*The Season of Strength.*" 1868. J. M. Ives, Del., drawn by Parsons & Atwater, printed and published by Currier & Ives.

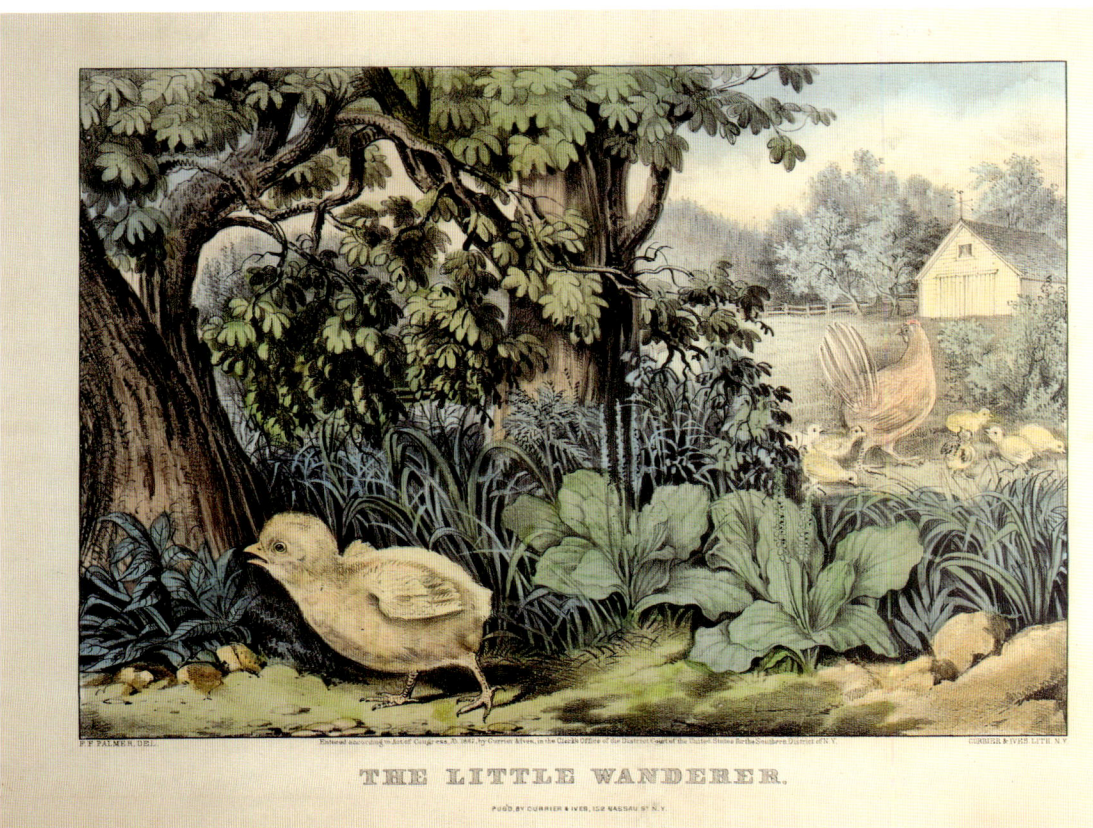

THE LITTLE WANDERER.

PUBD. BY CURRIER & IVES, 152 NASSAU ST. N.Y.

115. *The Little Wanderer*. 1867. Printed and published by Currier & Ives. (Checklist 3-75)

like a frieze. The little girls clearly identify with their mother; one walks down the stairs with her doll behind her mother, in a profile that imitates the maternal role. The young son, in contrast, is entering the house with his father and patting the dog, who holds the father's walking stick in his mouth. Thus, in spite of a surface appearance of something more "modern," the notion of "separate spheres" is actually more strongly reinforced in the revised version.

However, there is indeed something more "modern" in the way Parsons and Atwater's image reflects the new consumerism of the postwar Gilded Age. The interior is decorated with the up-to-date products being churned out at affordable prices by the burgeoning industrial society. Although cut off from earning an income, the middle-class wife has a new role as consumer in chief. Patterned wallpaper and rugs and a mirrored hat rack in the vestibule suggest that there is stylish furniture in all the rooms; and on the wall is a gilt-framed Currier & Ives sporting print. (The company never missed a chance to promote itself!³⁹) *The Four Seasons of Life: Old Age. "The Season of Rest"* (1868), also by Parsons and Atwater, shows the elderly couple enjoying a visit from their little granddaughter in a comfortable parlor, surrounded by the

accumulations of a lifetime. Prosperity, it is suggested, is the payoff for the confines of domesticity.

It is hardly necessary to remind readers that this happy allegory of traditional married life reflected the circumstances of relatively privileged, white, middle-class families. Black women never had these options; almost all of them had to work at hard, menial labor, often with their husbands in the fields, and at the end of the day had to take care of their homes and families as well. Millions of poor women, especially new immigrants, worked long hours in factories and sweatshops and lived in tenements instead of in lovely homes. All, however, could daydream of such a life by hanging a Currier & Ives print on their walls.

In addition to her direct representations of family life, Palmer designed an amusing group of anthropomorphized bird prints that embody the same values. The finest of them, *The Happy Family. Ruffed Grouse and Young* (1866; gallery plate 21), embeds a sentimental homily about gender roles (the protective father bird, the nurturing mother bird, and their happy chicks) in a splendid composition of closely observed decorative details and rich autumnal color. Other Palmer images have a whimsical quality, perhaps aimed

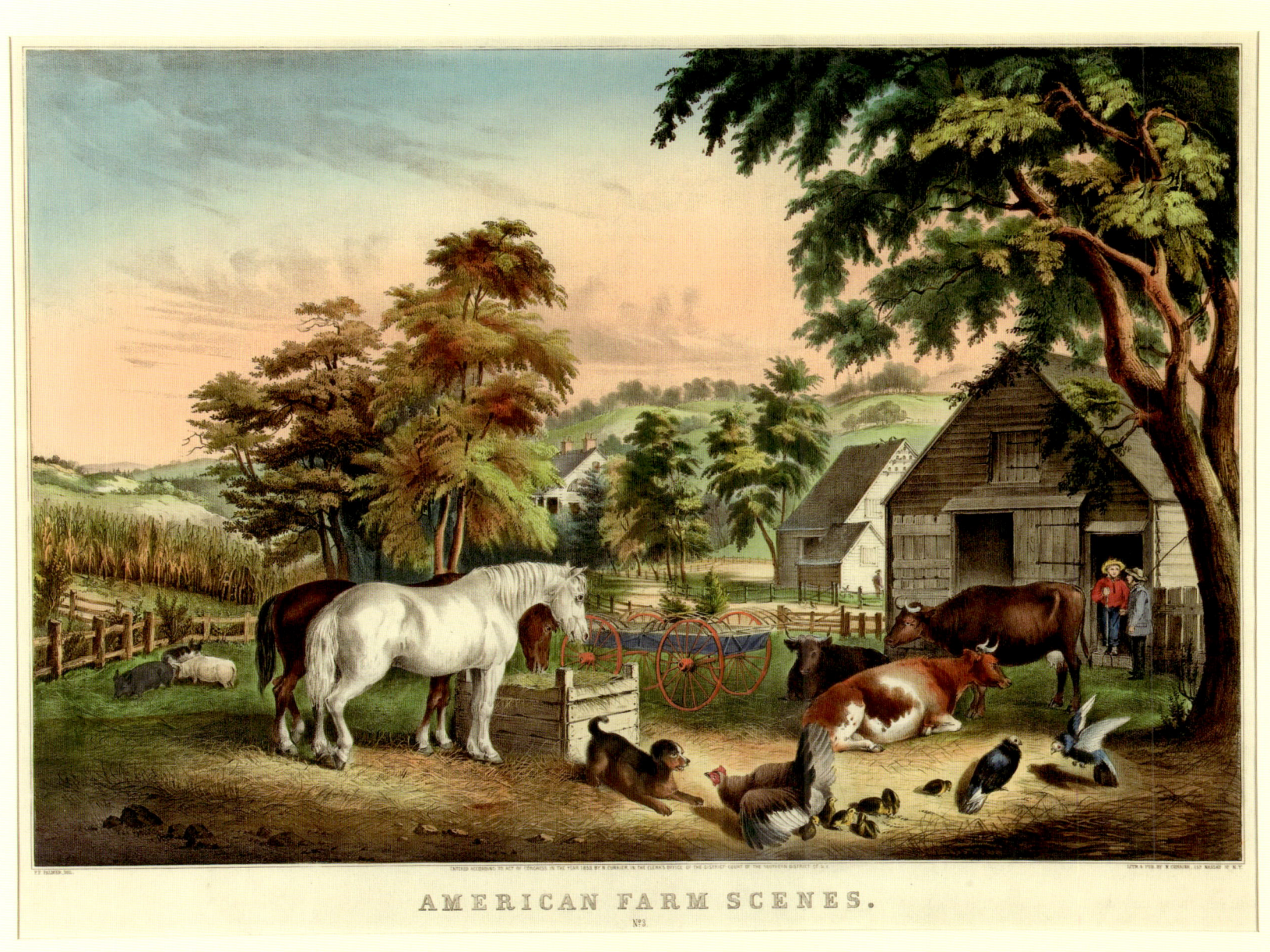

AMERICAN FARM SCENES.
Nº 3

116. *American Farm Scenes. No. 3.* 1853. Printed and published by N. Currier. Courtesy of the Yale University Art Gallery. (Checklist 3-11)

at the children's market (for instance, *The Little Wanderer* [1867; p. 150], *The Jolly Young Ducks* [1866; p. 297], *Happy Little Chicks* [1866; p. 294], *Mothers Wing* [1866; p. 303], and *Taking Comfort* [1866; p. 316]). Even a farmyard scene (*American Farm Scene. No. 3* [1853]) includes a fowl family in the foreground. Currier & Ives's catalog description explains the symbolism: "In front is a playful little dog, pretending to attack an old motherly hen, who, with ruffled feathers, seems in a terrible fright, but determined to protect the numerous little family gathered under her outspread wing."[40]

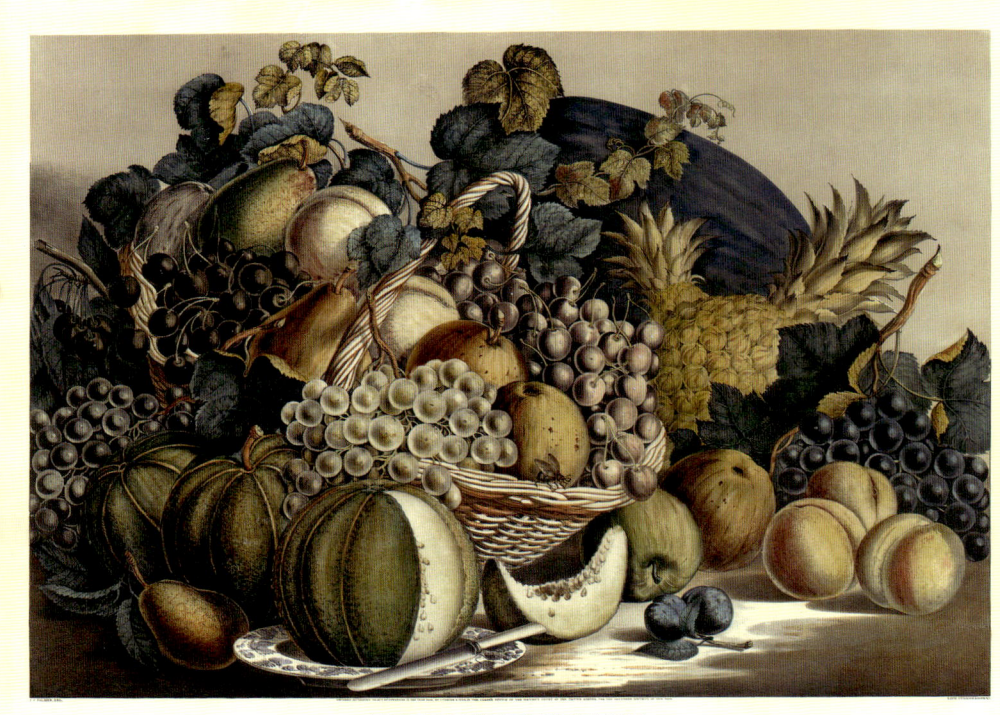

AMERICAN PRIZE FRUIT.

117. *American Prize Fruit*. 1862. Printed and published by Currier & Ives. Courtesy of the Old Print Shop. (Checklist 3-18)

STILL LIFES

It may seem odd that Palmer began a series of nine lush still lifes—works that speak of abundance and peaceful pursuits—during the bloody Civil War, but, in fact, such subjects were comforting at this time. On the home front, families clung more than ever to symbols of peaceful stability, and it was also an era when great fortunes were being amassed in the North and houses were being furnished with increasing elegance. Regarded as particularly appropriate for dining rooms, still lifes, often of fruits and flowers, evoked sentiments of pious gratitude for God's bounty, while at the same time their accouterments—ceramic and glass vases and fine wood or stone table tops—gave an air of wealth and status to a home.

These celebratory qualities are exemplified in one of Palmer's finest prints, *Landscape, Fruit and Flowers* (1862; gallery plate 23). The elaborate Victorian vase, the stone balustrade, and the spacious landscape suggest that the viewer is looking at the scene from the terrace of a luxurious home. Art historian Wolfgang Born devotes an entire page to this fine composition:

A gorgeous array of flowers and fruits is arranged in vases, bowls and baskets on a table in an open porch. A lovely view of

the Hudson River forms the background. Trumpet vines creeping up the trellis have attracted a humming bird. Although the painter records all details carefully and does not neglect the background, the painting creates a unified effect through a careful integration of all the forms . . . the lines intertwine elegantly and free themselves again without effort. This flawless composition is supported by a careful gradation of tone; and the color is equally bright and harmonious.[41]

Between 1862 and 1867, Palmer produced at least eight more still lifes of flowers, fruit, game, and fish. Instead of repeating a formula, she seems to have challenged herself with a different approach in each one—pulling out all the stops, as it were. The works share a strong decorative impulse and a feeling for pattern and color that is not quite as obvious in her other prints.

American Prize Fruit (1862) draws on some of the compositional devices and Christian symbolism of seventeenth-century Dutch still-life painting. At this time, American artists were strongly influenced by the contemporary Düsseldorf school of German painters, whose meticulously realistic work (exhibited at New York's Düsseldorf Gallery) imitated the earlier Dutch school. In contrast to the airy, open design of *Landscape, Fruit*

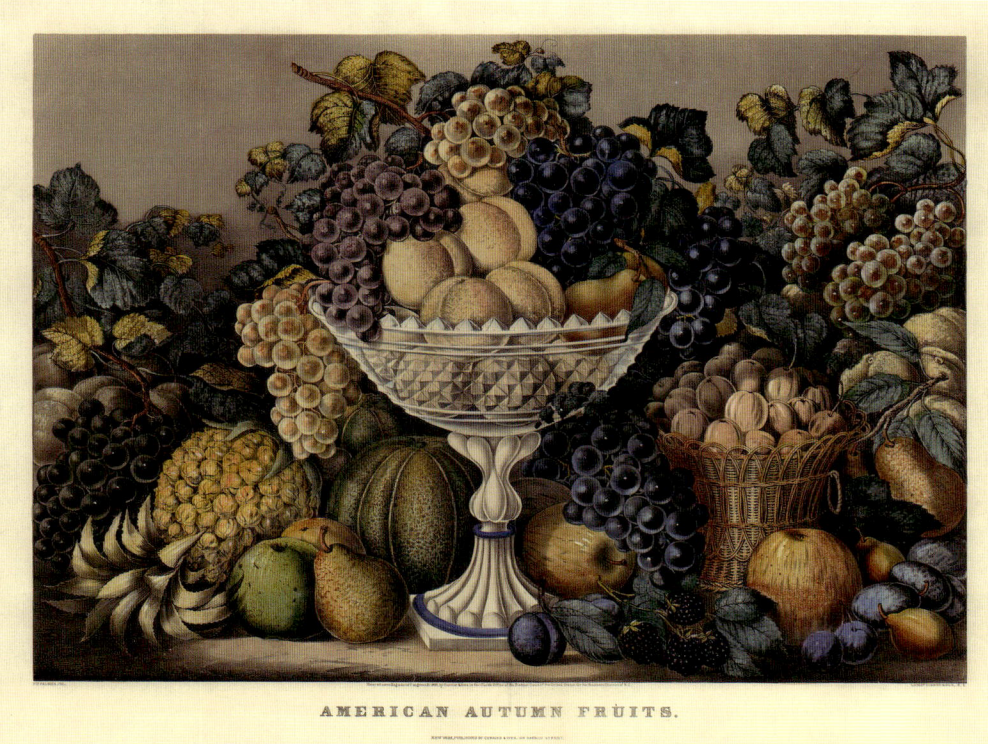

118. *American Autumn Fruits.* 1865. Printed and published by Currier & Ives. Courtesy of the Old Print Shop. (Checklist 3-2)

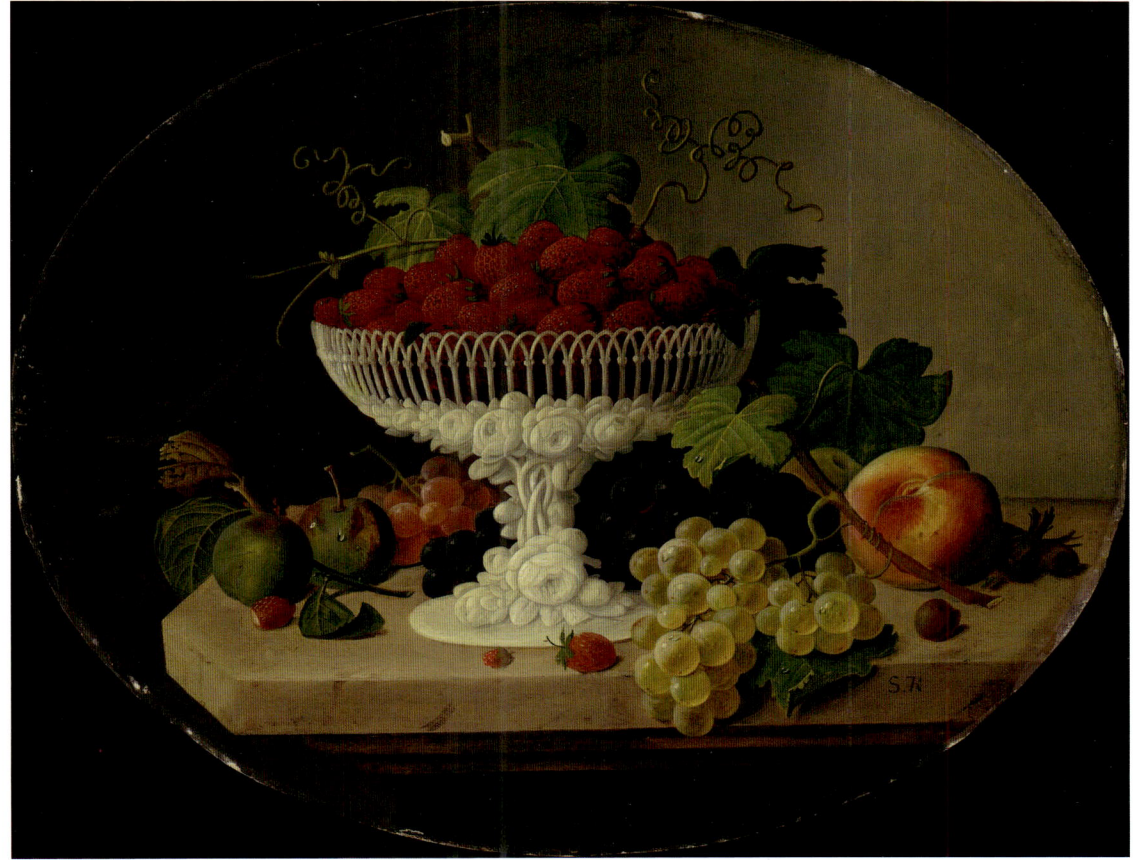

119. *Still Life: Flowers and Fruit.* 1850–55. Oil on canvas by Severin Roesen. Courtesy of the Metropolitan Museum of Art. Purchase, Bequest of Charles Allen Munn, by exchange, Fosburgh Fund Inc. and Mr. and Mrs. J. William Middendorf II Gifts, and Henry G. Keasbey Bequest, 1967.

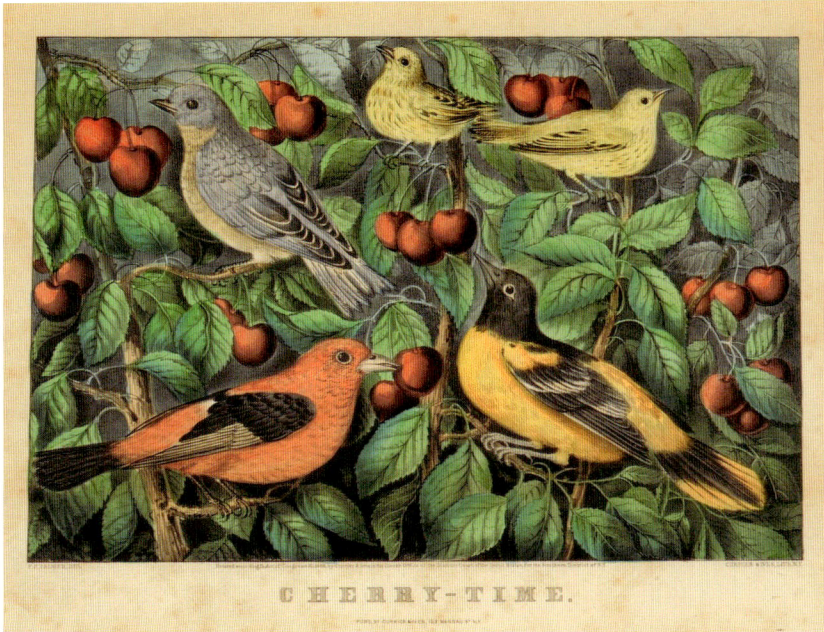

120. *Cherry-Time*. 1866. Printed and published by Currier & Ives. (Checklist 3-28)

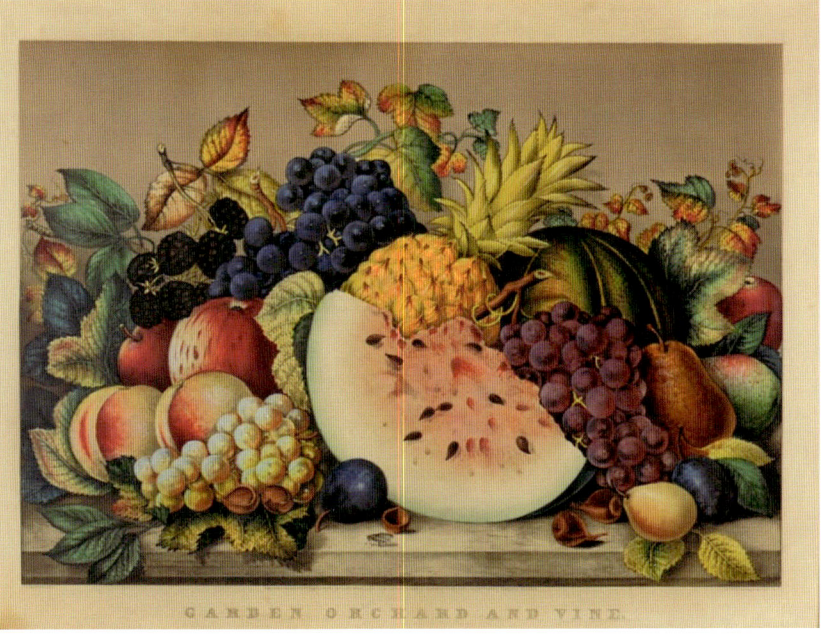

121. *Garden Orchard and Vine*. 1867. Printed and published by Currier & Ives. Courtesy of the Old Print Shop. (Checklist 3-51)

and Flowers, American Prize Fruit is dense and heavy, suggesting the weight and mass of fully ripened fruit spilling out of a tilted wicker basket onto a tabletop. In the foreground, a ripe cantaloupe on a blue-and-white Delft plate has been cut open and is dripping juice. Above it, a fly, poised on the edge of the basket, hints at the fruit's imminent decay, implying the swift passage of time and the evanescence of this life's pleasures. In the midst of our sensual existence, we are enjoined to consider the fate of our eternal souls.

American Autumn Fruits (1865; p. 153), one of the artist's few symmetrical compositions, seems to be a sophisticated version of the stenciled theorem paintings that were popular projects assigned to young ladies at girls' schools. The print may also have been influenced by the work of Severin Roesen, a much-admired German-born painter living in Pennsylvania, whose still lifes, shown by the American Art-Union, frequently included a white compote dish surrounded by fruit (p. 153). The central motif of Palmer's print is a similar pressed-glass compote filled with peaches and grapes, surrounded by a pineapple (symbol of hospitality), a basket of currants, and other fruit, all beautifully arranged on a stone ledge. The print is a technical tour de force in which a mauve background printed from a separate tint stone and jewel-like hand coloring enhance the effect of fruit shining through transparent glass.

Cherry-Time (1866) is unusual—frankly decorative in a manner not often seen in Currier & Ives prints: a flat tapestry of green leaves and branches of a cherry tree, in which colorful birds, each identifiable by its plumage, feast on the red fruit. In contrast, *Garden Orchard and Vine* (1867), with its great wedge of watermelon and other fruits on a simple tabletop, owes something to the sturdy, time-honored still lifes of the Peale family.

In 1866, Palmer also produced four prints of dead game and fish, influenced by the Pre-Raphaelite tendency to portray still lifes in their natural settings—a trend fostered by the teachings of John Ruskin. *American Dead Game* (p. 188), *American Game* (p. 284; with the same composition as *American Dead Game*), and *American Forest Game* (p. 155) variously include a turkey, a rabbit, game birds, and an antlered deer, in each case arranged on the ground among leaves and plants. In *American Game Fish* (p. 155), a variety of fish and a reel lie in front of a lake-filled landscape. These subjects appealed to sportsmen and were particularly suitable for a man's library or study. Palmer's treatment in these prints, with their emphasis on intricate patterns of feathers and fur, is less literal and more ornamental than similar compositions by Arthur Fitzwilliam Tait, who was also noted for such subjects.

Scholars conjecture that Palmer may also have designed some of the many anonymous still lifes issued by Currier & Ives. A pencil

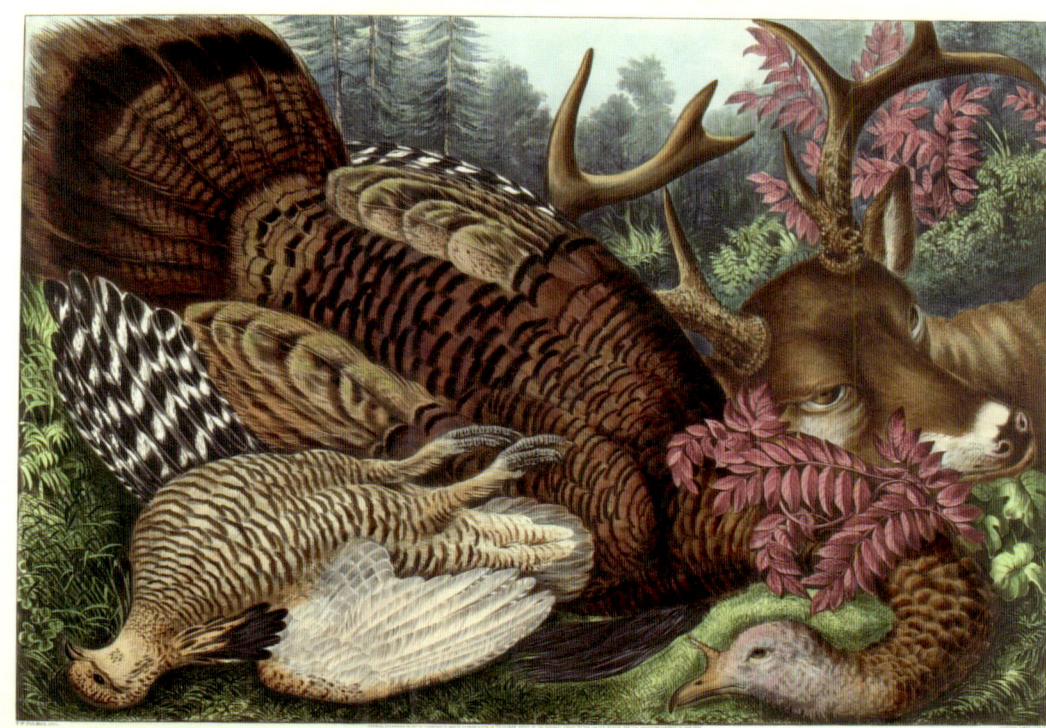

122. *American Forest Game.* 1866. Printed and published by Currier & Ives. Courtesy of the Old Print Shop. (Checklist 3-15)

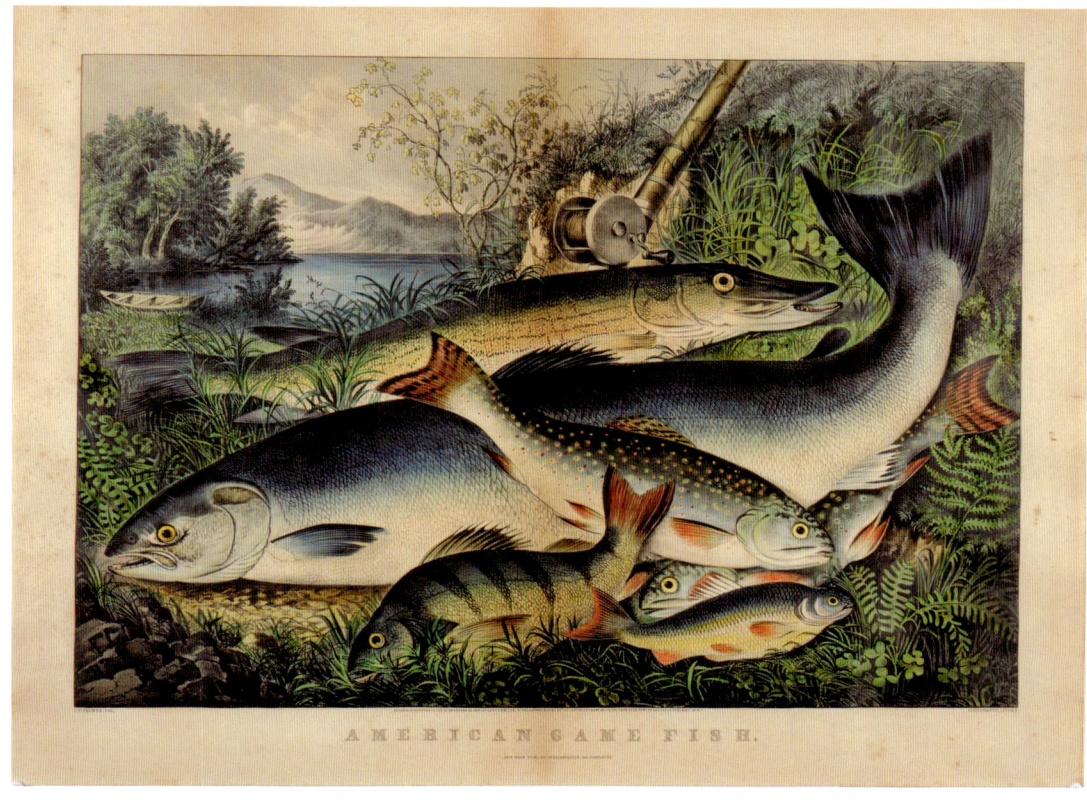

123. *American Game Fish.* 1866. Printed and published by Currier & Ives. (Checklist 3-17)

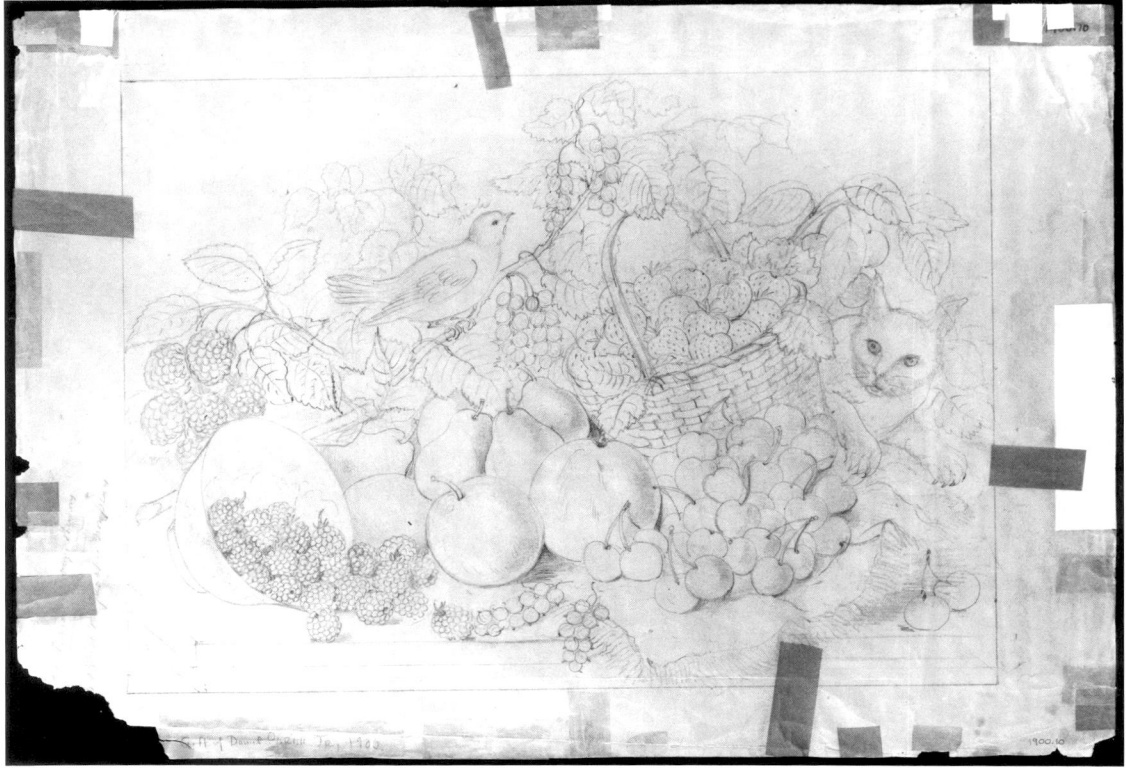

124. Contour study. Verso of *Terrific Engagement between the "Monitor" 2 Guns, and "Merrimac" 10 Guns*, watercolor and graphite by Frances Flora Bond Palmer. 1862. Pencil on paper by Frances Flora Bond Palmer. Courtesy of the New-York Historical Society. (Checklist 4-19)

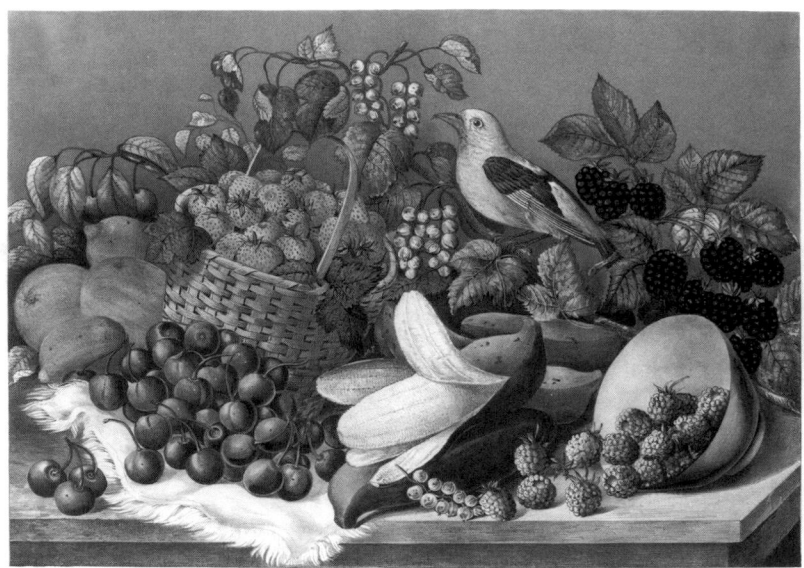

125. *Tropical and Summer Fruits*. 1867. Printed and published by Currier & Ives. Courtesy of the Old Print Shop. (Checklist 3A-27)

drawing signed by Palmer (at the New-York Historical Society)—a contour study of a tilted basket of fruit with a cat on one side and a bird on the other—seems to be a reversed image of the anonymous Currier & Ives lithograph *Tropical and Summer Fruits* (1867).

EUROPEAN ROMANTIC SCENERY AND LITERARY SUBJECTS

European romantic scenery and literary subjects were regarded as edifying themes for household pictures. This was a time of passionate interest in all things gothic and medieval, exemplified in the novels of Sir Walter Scott. Palmer, who had drawn castles, churches, and ruins directly from life in England, was well prepared to create lithographs of such themes for her American employers. They include *The Old Norman Castle* (before 1857; p. 306); *The Ruins of the Abbey* (1856; p. 312); *Melrose Abbey* (1862; p. 301); and the undated prints *Warwick Castle. On the Avon* (p. 326), *Kenilworth Castle* (p. 297), *Lanercost Priory. England* (p. 298), *Landscape and Ruins* (p. 298), and *The Banks of Doon. Burns Monument* (p. 157). One of her finest literary subjects, *Gray's Elegy. In a Country Church Yard* (1864; p. 157), captures the pensive gray and golden twilight aura of the melancholy poem.

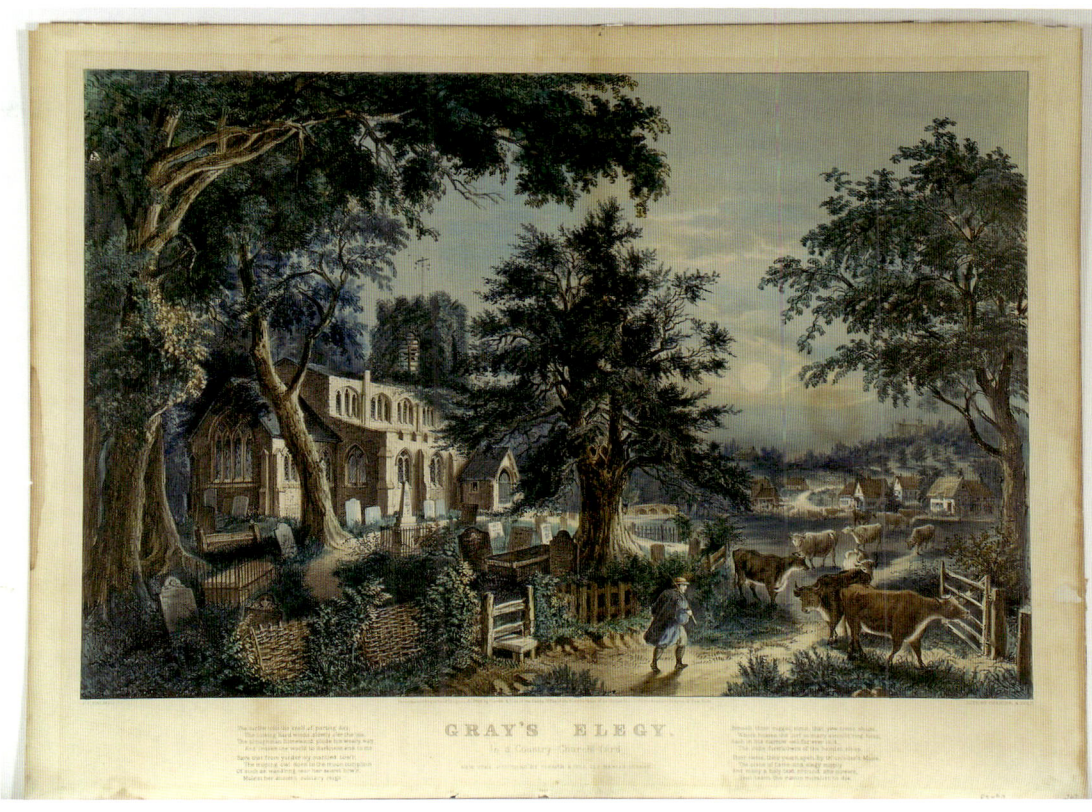

126. *Gray's Elegy. In a Country Church Yard.* 1864. Printed and published by Currier & Ives. (Checklist 3-53)

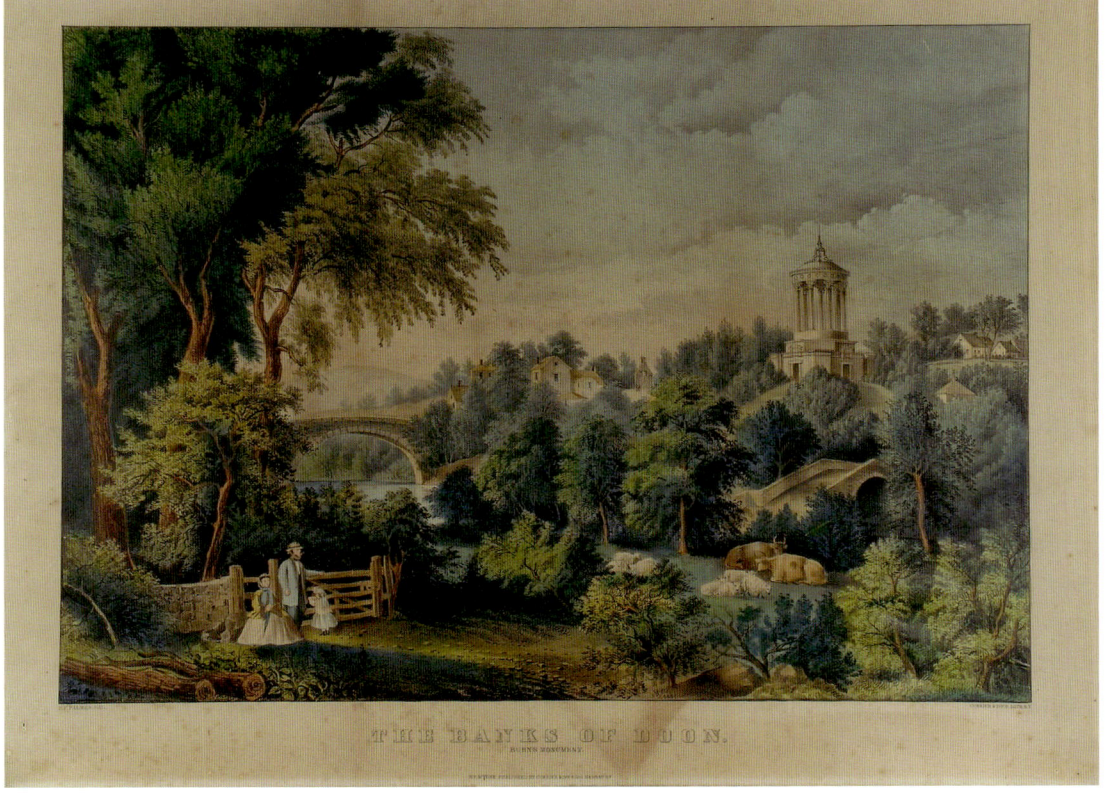

127. *The Banks of Doon. Burns Monument.* Undated, ca. 1857–72. Printed and published by Currier & Ives. (Checklist 3-22)

Before the Civil War, Palmer had lithographed two views of specific New England places: *Lake Winnipiseogee, From Centre Harbor, N.H.* (undated, ca. 1857–72; p. 159; probably adapted, with some changes, from a William Bartlett engraving) and *Mount Washington and the White Mountains* (1860; p. 179; adapted from the engraving of a painting by John Kensett).[42] Artists of this period frequently illustrated New Hampshire's White Mountains district, a favorite mid-nineteenth-century vacation destination.

After the war, however, Palmer's images of New England took on a more mythic and nostalgic character. Along with many other artists and writers, she began to glorify "olde" New England's rapidly disappearing rural past. In *Picturing Old New England* and other art history books and exhibition catalogs, art historians have analyzed the complex reasons for this trend.[43] New England emerged from the Civil War victorious in every way, not only militarily but also politically, economically, and culturally. Its abolitionist leaders, once regarded as dangerous radicals, were now hailed as liberators. New England writers—Nathaniel Hawthorne, Henry Wadsworth Longfellow, James Russell Lowell, John Greenleaf Whittier, and Ralph Waldo Emerson—had become exemplars of a well-defined American literary school. Reflecting the region's pivotal role in the triumph of the North over the South, intellectuals looked back at New England history and began to portray the region as the wellspring of national values: love of freedom, self-reliance, piety, and warm community traditions. Here, after all, was the place where the Pilgrims set foot in North America and the Minute Men fired shots heard around the world.

But there was also a darker side to this glorification of agrarian old New England. The brutality of the war, growing uneasiness about the region's rapid industrialization, and increased disillusionment with political life after Lincoln's assassination contributed to nostalgia for a seemingly simpler, nobler time. In contrast with this romantic view of rural New England, the region had in actuality become the most heavily industrialized part of the nation. During the war, manufacturing output had increased by an astonishing 60 percent. Enormous fortunes were being made, and conspicuous consumption was replacing the moderate standards of the past, while at the same time immigrant factory workers were crowding into the slums of New England's burgeoning cities. Small rural villages were becoming deserted and rundown as young people left the farms in search of opportunity in the main centers of production.[44]

Tourists, who wished to escape from the cities to scenes evoking visions of bygone civic virtue and agrarian life, were delighted with the increasingly quiet and "antique" look of places that had changed little over time. This tourism was eagerly encouraged by the city fathers of small towns and historic villages that were losing their economic base and falling into decay. Historic buildings were converted into hotels or visitor centers, and preservation groups began to transform their villages into living theme parks. Currier & Ives lost no time in taking advantage of this popular subject matter for lithographs.

Palmer's print *New England Scenery* (1866; p. 160), perhaps the archetypal image of the search for American roots in New England, is a dreamlike fantasy. Huge trees arch over a boy and girl in the foreground, who walk forward happily for a ramble in the countryside, while farther back their mother waves from her front door. Standing protectively next to their home, as if guarding the family's spiritual values, is a white-steepled church. The panoramic background includes a small village of modest but well-kept houses, a farmer driving his wagon across a distant bridge, and a river zigzagging back toward distant mountains.

Here there is no crime or vice; children can wander freely without supervision. The self-reliant little boy carries a stick, which may serve as a fishing pole, and the girl gathers wildflowers in her basket. The message is clear; this is the bastion of democracy: agrarian, white, Protestant, and native born. Here there are no smoking factories or impoverished Irish and French Canadian Catholic immigrant workers. An atavistic pride in early American bloodlines is part of this print's subtext.

In 1868, Palmer once again collaborated with James Ives and John Cameron, this time on a pair of prints illustrating the postwar vogue for New England tourism. *Haying-Time. The First Load* (p. 160) shows a city-dressed father and mother, probably on vacation, placing their boy and girl in an ox-drawn wagon for a "country experience" among farmhands who are mowing hay. In the companion print *Haying-Time. The Last Load* (p. 108), the children return from the fields in the glow of late afternoon, seated on top of a huge hay load that now fills the wagon. The little boy waves his cap exultantly to the farmer walking behind them, tired from a day's work. Like several of Palmer's late lithographs, these images seem a bit hackneyed compared to the fresher vision in earlier prints taken directly from nature. John Cameron probably added the figures to Palmer's composition, and James Ives lithographed it on stone.

Other Palmer lithographs without specifically New England titles have the same regional flavor. *The Farmers Home—Autumn*

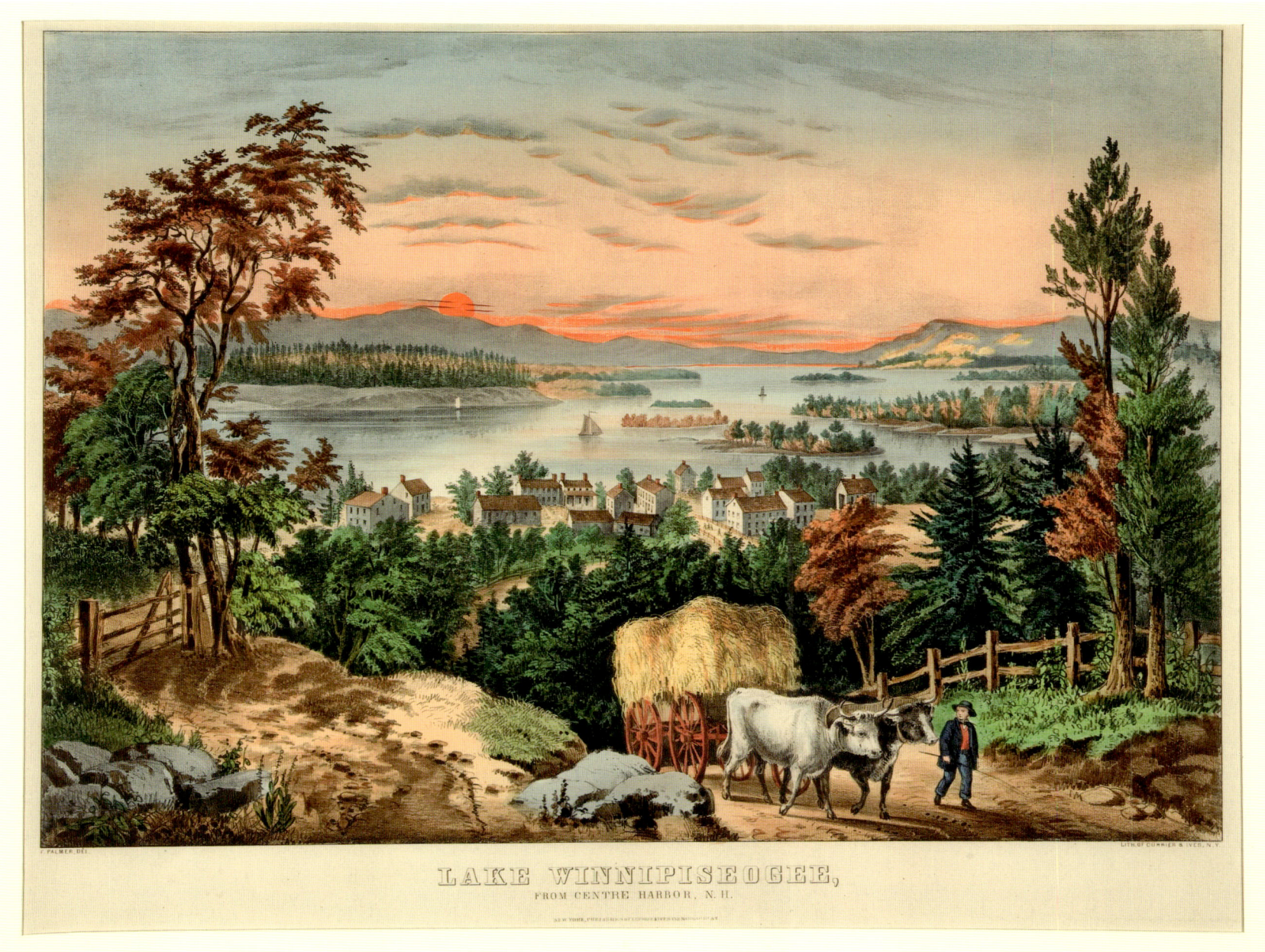

LAKE WINNIPISEOGEE,
FROM CENTRE HARBOR, N.H.

128. *Lake Winnipiseogee, From Centre Harbor, N.H.* Undated, ca. 1857–72. Printed and published by Currier & Ives. Courtesy of the Yale University Art Gallery. (Checklist 3-68)

(1864; p. 161), a view of men, women, and children harvesting fruit together, is typical of the growing vogue for nostalgic pictures of rapidly disappearing communal agricultural traditions, such as maple sugaring, corn husking, and cranberry picking.[45]

Palmer also illustrated poems by New England authors Henry Wadsworth Longfellow ("Evangeline" [p. 162], "The Wayside Inn" [p. 326], "The Village Blacksmith" [gallery plate 24]) and Samuel Woodworth ("The Old Oaken Bucket"). In Woodworth's poem, later set to music, he remembers his own childhood in Scituate, Massachusetts, where he worked on his father's farm and

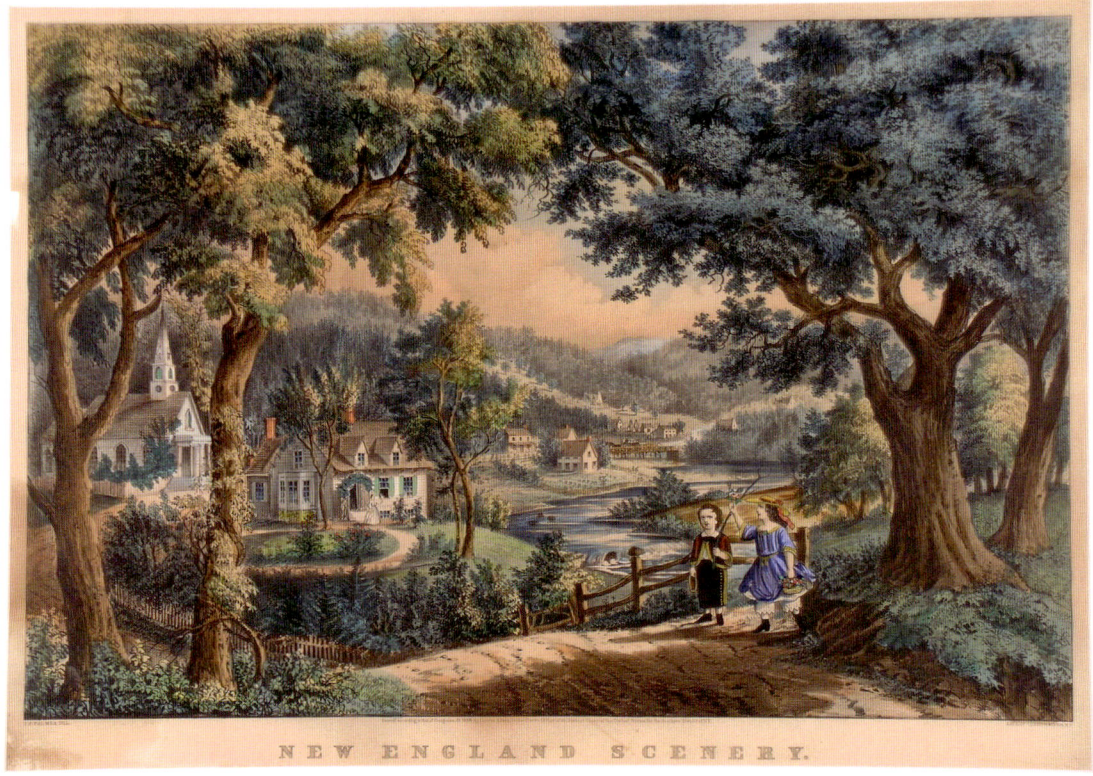

129. *New England Scenery.* 1866. Printed and published by Currier & Ives. (Checklist 3-92)

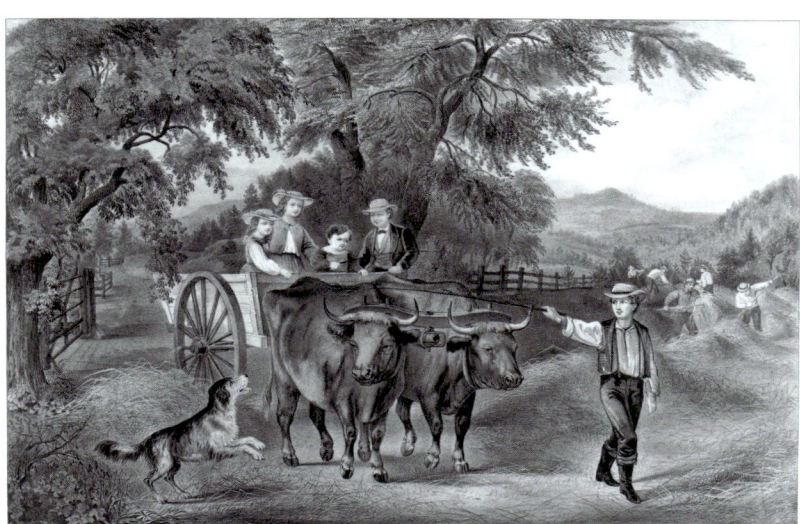

130. *Haying-Time. The First Load.* 1868. Printed and published by Currier & Ives. Courtesy of the Old Print Shop. (Checklist 3-57)

drank cool water from the oaken bucket in the heat of the day. The actual gambrel-roofed farmhouse and dairy seen in Palmer's print *The Old Oaken Bucket* (1864; p. 163) are still maintained as a National Historic Site.

In two versions of her print *The Village Blacksmith* (undated, ca. 1850–56, and 1864; p. 325 and gallery plate 24), the artist paid homage to the artisans of a handcraft that was fast disappearing from New England villages as factories began to swallow up the production of iron objects. In the later print, children trooping home from school pause to gape as the giant blacksmith sends sparks flying from his anvil. Longfellow's famous lines are printed below the image:

Under a spreading chestnut tree
The village smithy stands;
The smith, a mighty man is he,
With large and sinewy hands . . .
And children coming home from school
Look in at the open door;
They love to see the flaming forge,
And hear the bellows roar.[46]

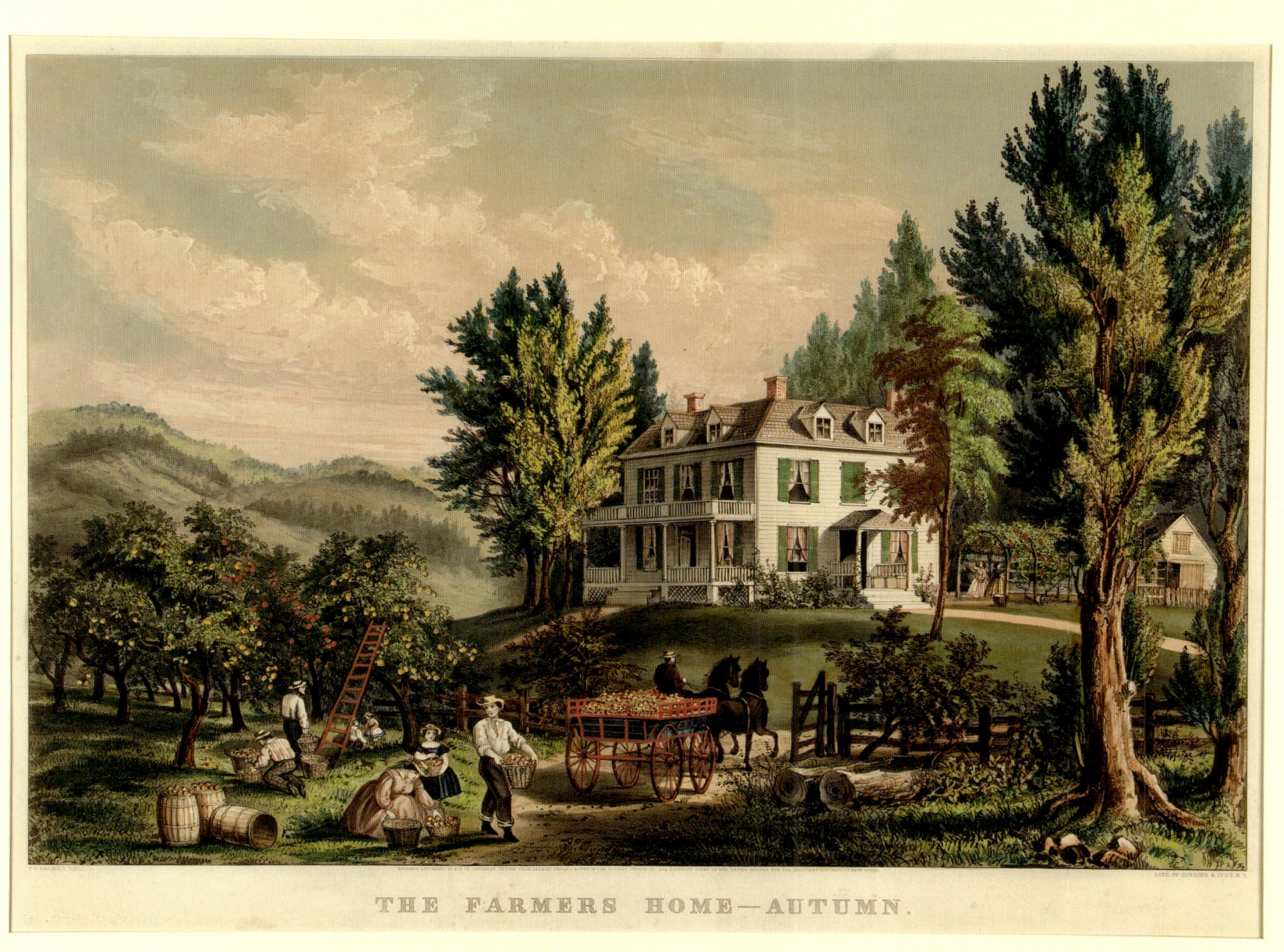

THE FARMERS HOME—AUTUMN.

131. *The Farmers Home—Autumn.* 1864. Printed and published by Currier & Ives. Courtesy of the Yale University Art Gallery. (Checklist 3-41)

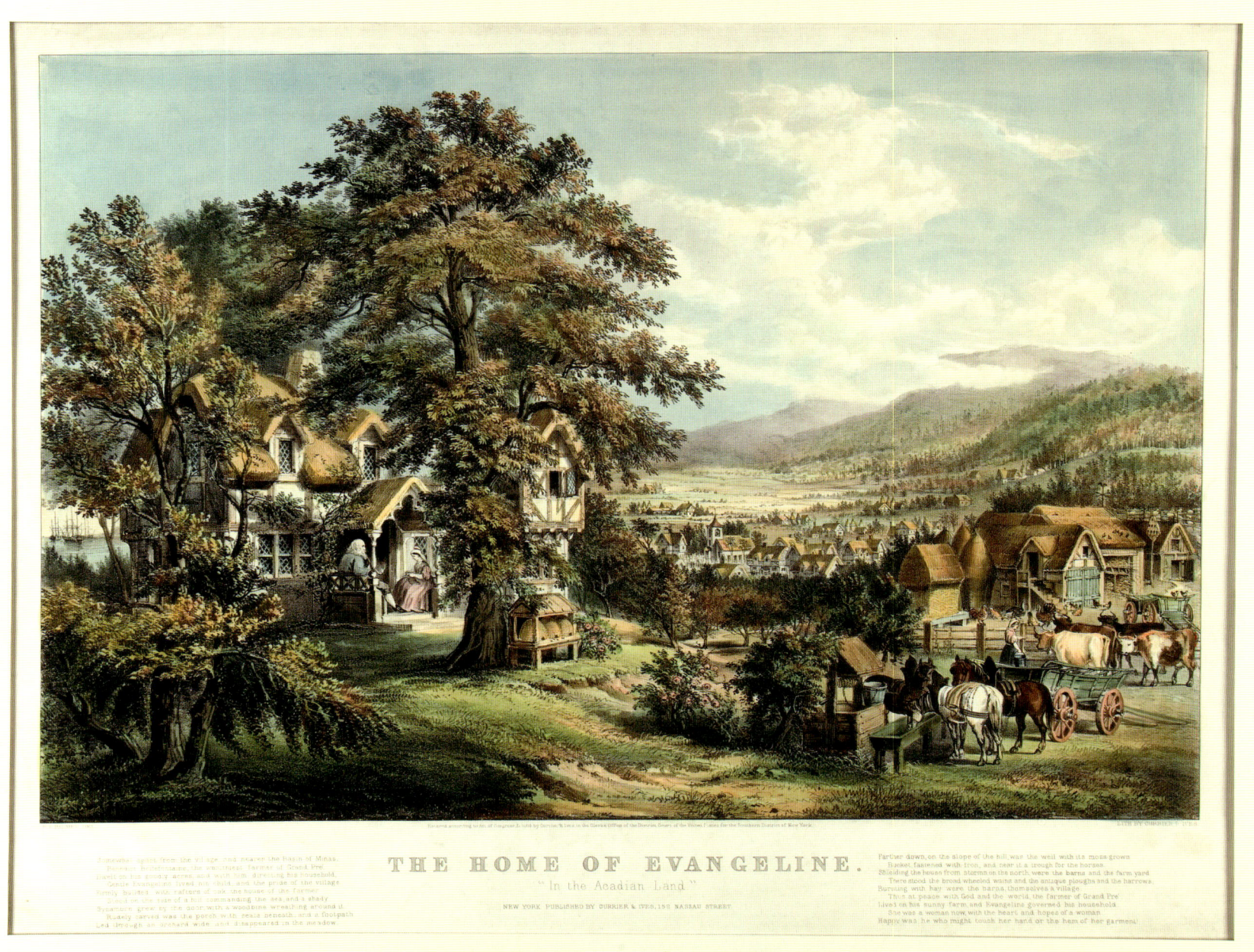

THE HOME OF EVANGELINE.

"In the Acadian Land."

NEW YORK PUBLISHED BY CURRIER & IVES, 152 NASSAU STREET.

132. *The Home of Evangeline.* *"In the Acadian Land."* 1864. Printed and published by Currier & Ives. Courtesy of the Yale University Art Gallery. (Checklist 3-61)

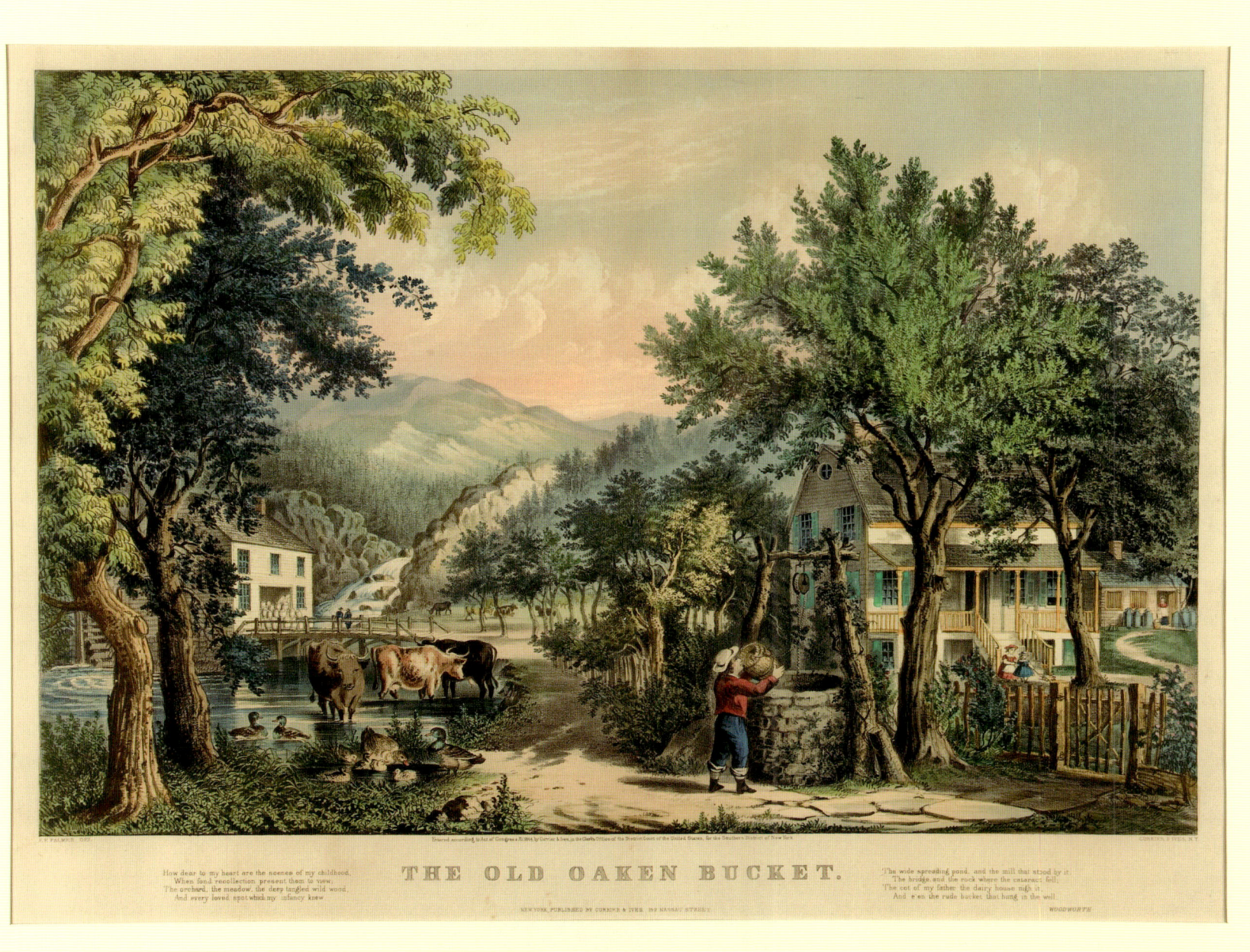

THE OLD OAKEN BUCKET.

133. *The Old Oaken Bucket.* 1864. Printed and published by Currier
& Ives. Courtesy of the Yale University Art Gallery. (Checklist 3-102)

The poem was first published in 1840. By 1864, lines that once referred to contemporary events now referenced nostalgic images from a longed-for past.

Conquering the West

In her last decade at Currier & Ives, Palmer tackled some of the boldest themes of her career: a series of prints illustrating successive stages of the westward movement. Taken together, these images document the major thrust of mid-nineteenth-century American history.

By the 1860s, this movement was entering its final climactic phase, spurred on by the ideology of Manifest Destiny—a belief that the United States was divinely destined to control the entire continent, bringing the blessings of democracy to vast new regions. A subtext was the premise that the American Indian, alas, was an incurable savage and, like the wilderness, had to make way for the advance of a new society.

Palmer began her western series around 1862, when Congress passed the Pacific Railroad Act authorizing construction of the transcontinental railroad. That year she drew her first pencil sketch envisioning the coming of the cross-country train line, but the final print was not issued until six years later. Instead, sometime in 1866–67, as construction of the railroad got under way, the artist completed a kind of catalog of successive aspects leading up to the climactic event. Although the artist never traveled far from the New York region, there was already a large body of western imagery for her to draw on. Thomas Cole had painted pioneer families in the eastern wilderness; Karl Bodmer, George Catlin, Alfred Jacob Miller, William Tylee Ranney, John Mix Stanley, Charles Deas, Albert Bierstadt, and others had gone west and brought back with them images of Native Americans, trappers, mountain men, and wagon trains.

Trappers and Mountain Men

Palmer began her westerly saga with a print showing three fur trappers relaxing around a campfire, their horses tethered to stakes in the ground (*The Trappers Camp-Fire*, 1866; p. 165). In the background, a full moon lights up snow-capped peaks and a lake. Trappers and mountain men had been among the earliest nineteenth-century explorers of the West, the vanguard of the lucrative fur trade that formed the basis of the great economic empires of John Jacob Astor and other entrepreneurs. Viewed by some (in the racist language of the era) as "white Indians"—lawless loners living halfway between society and savagery—they were admired by others as freedom-loving independents challenging the restraints and monotony of organized society. By the time Palmer worked on these prints, trappers were seen as culture heroes of an earlier day who had sometimes developed good relations with the Indians of the region, bartered trade goods for pelts, and sometimes took Native American wives. The romantic aura of Palmer's image is dramatized by the glint of firelight on the figures and horses and by the moonlit water in the background.

In the companion print, *The Trappers Camp-Fire. A Friendly Visitor* (1866; p. 205), a Native American has joined the party. He sits in aloof dignity, cross-legged, in native regalia, with his calumet (ceremonial pipe) across his knees, signaling a nonthreatening attitude. The three trappers lounge warily, holding their rifles loosely, just to be on the safe side. Palmer places the figures inside a decorative arbor of leaves and tree branches, creating a "once upon a time" aura around the encounter between "civilization" and "the wilderness"—a theme that has engaged Americans from early times to the present.

Wagon Trains and Pioneer Settlers

One of those early trader-trappers, Jedediah Smith, came back to the East in 1823 with news of the South Pass in Wyoming, a low saddleback in the daunting Rocky Mountains through which wagons could make their way to Oregon and California. By the 1840s, a trickle of emigrant families had turned into a flood of caravans heading west on the Oregon Trail, seeking land and a new life in the West. Palmer commemorated this historic migration in one of the most famous of all Currier & Ives lithographs, *The Rocky Mountains. Emigrants Crossing the Plains* (1866; gallery plate 7), an image of covered wagons lumbering forward over the plains, easily passing the Rockies on a trail alongside a rushing river. Across the river, two mounted Native Americans look on in wonder, pointing to the newcomers.

Palmer's print retained such a powerful hold on the American imagination that it is believed to have served as a source of imagery for the silent movie *The Covered Wagon* (1923), directed by James Cruze, a pioneer of Western films. In her portrayal, the grueling hardships of the journey have been minimized and the romance maximized. The pioneers are shown traveling through a verdant valley, even though much of their journey actually traversed barren and rocky terrain. The Native Americans are

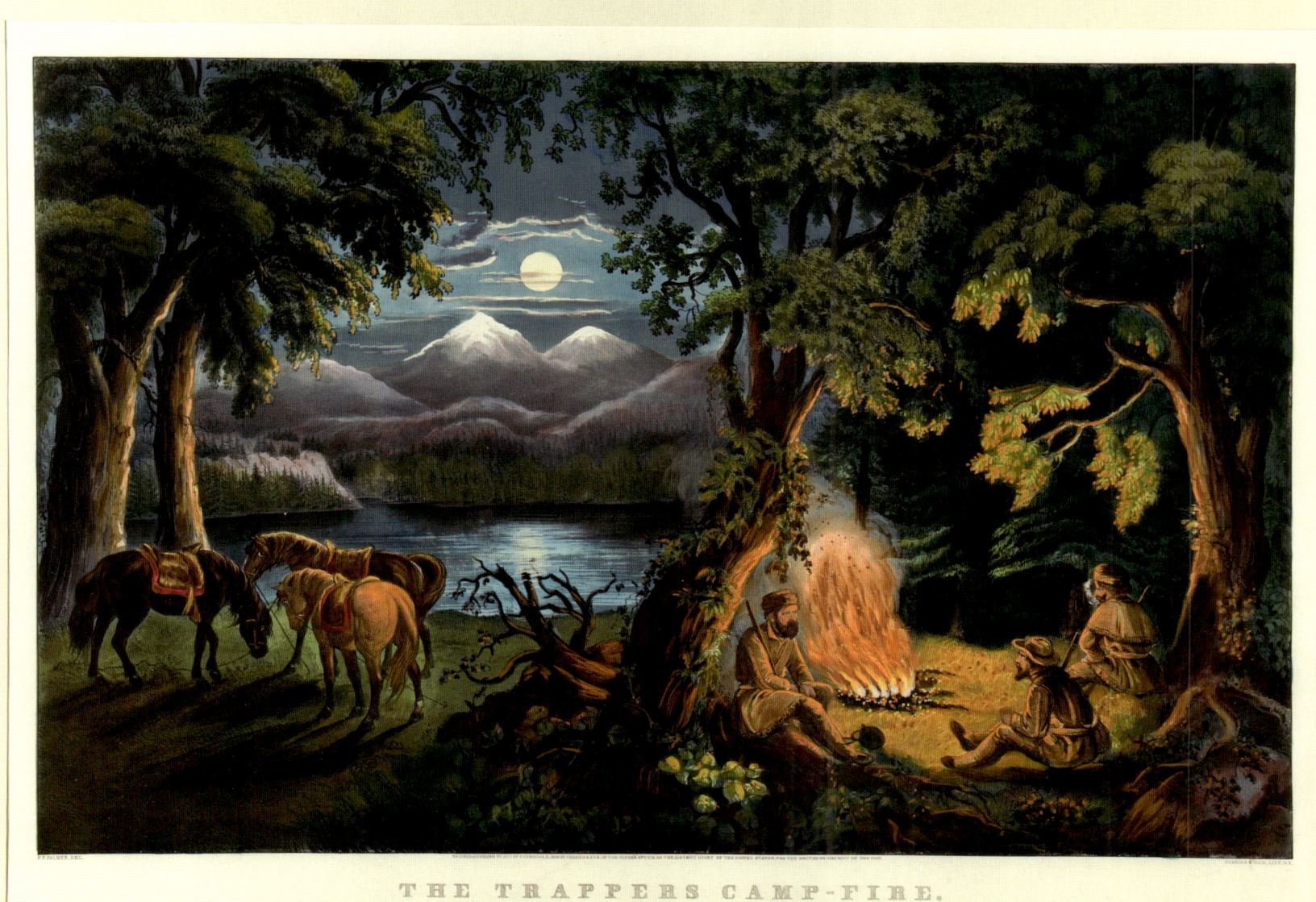

THE TRAPPERS CAMP-FIRE.

134. *The Trappers Camp-Fire.* 1866. Printed and published by Currier & Ives. Courtesy of the Yale University Art Gallery. (Checklist 3-137)

passive and accepting, whereas in truth many fought back against the invasion of their territories. The Madonna-like mother and the children seated in the nearest wagon lend a "Holy Family" aura to this archetypal icon of Manifest Destiny—a common motif in paintings of pioneer families traveling West.[47] The snow-capped peaks bear some resemblance to those in Bierstadt's paintings and are perhaps more Alpine than western.

Palmer's next Western print, *The Pioneer's Home. On the Western Frontier* (1867; p. 166), shows the emigrants carving out a Garden of Eden in the wilderness. In the foreground, two pioneer

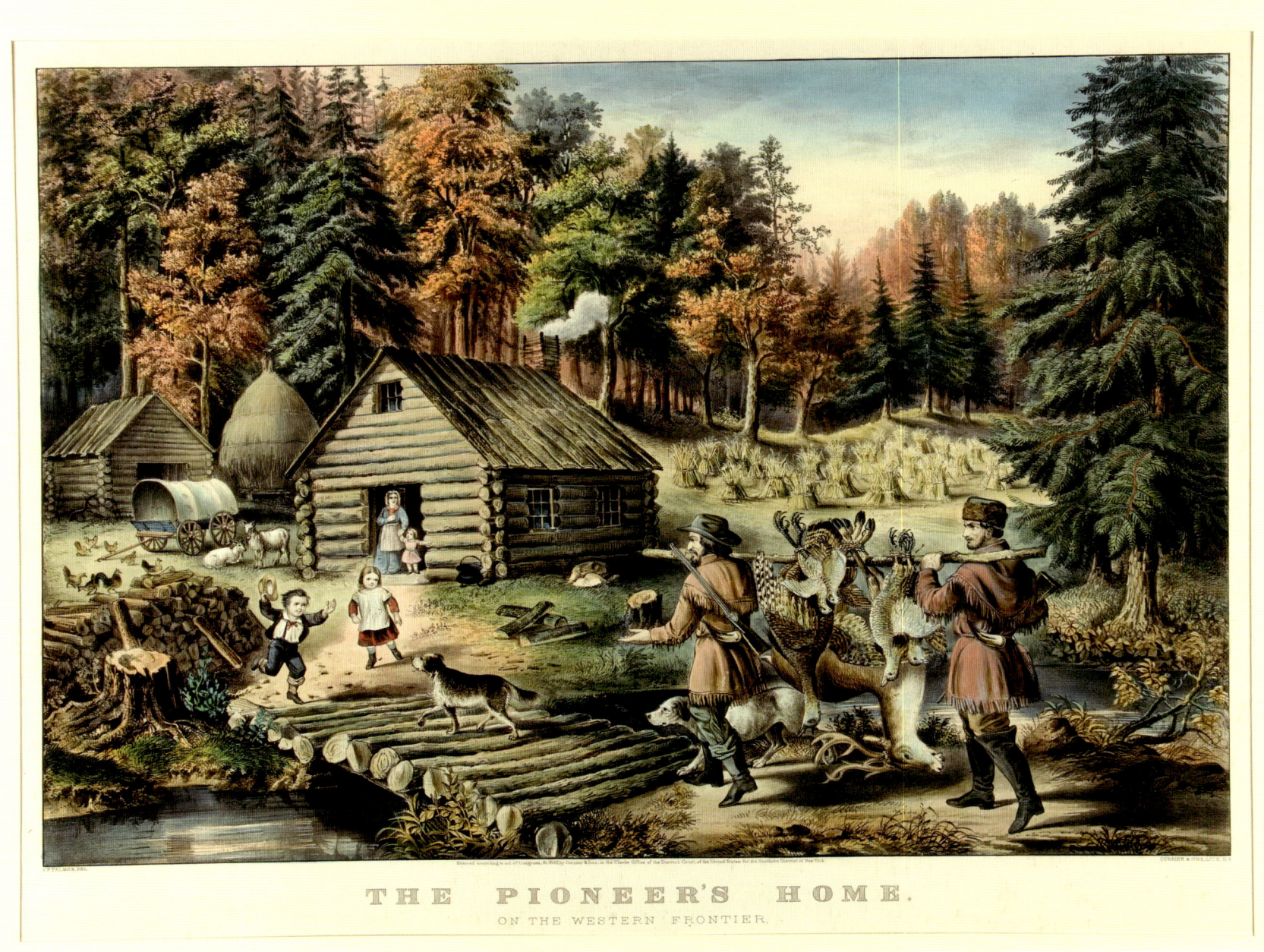

THE PIONEER'S HOME.
ON THE WESTERN FRONTIER.

hunters are returning home, carrying between them a pole strung with a dead deer and game birds. This motif echoes the Old Testament episode in which two Israelite spies, sent ahead by Moses to search out the promised land of Canaan, return with examples of the bounty to be found there: "And they came unto the brook of Eshcol, and cut down from thence a branch with one cluster of grapes, and they bare it between two upon a staff" (Numbers 13:23, King James). The biblical allusion suggests that the pioneers have found a new "land of milk and honey" in the American West.[48]

135. *The Pioneer's Home. On the Western Frontier.* 1867. Printed and published by Currier & Ives. Courtesy of the Yale University Art Gallery. (Checklist 3-107)

A boy and girl run out to greet the hunters, while a mother and small child wait in the doorway of their log cabin. In the clearing around the cabin, chickens, goats, tidy rows of wheat sheaves, and a large haystack manifest the industry of the new settlers; the covered wagon, unhitched beside the barn, reminds us of the perilous journey, now safely concluded; and a background screen of brightly colored autumnal trees looks more like a park than the dense, dangerous forest of the frontier. The wilderness is being tamed.

Palmer may have adapted the general motif for *The Pioneer's Home* from Thomas Cole's painting *A Hunter's Return* (1845, Amon Carter Museum), an earlier image of two hunters returning with dead game to their family and log cabin, as art historian Dawn Glanz notes,[49] but Palmer's approach to the subject is different. Cole, an ardent environmentalist distressed by the ongoing damage to the wilderness, shows the devastation of beautiful old trees strewn across the foreground, chopped down in order to clear the land and build the cabin, and he sets his small figures and house in the midst of an immense mountain scene, a vision of God's earthly paradise, not yet destroyed.[50] However, in Palmer's image the figures are much larger; they dominate the scene. The emphasis is on the industrious settlers, not on the landscape. Her print clearly belongs to the booster movement for westward expansion.

Mountain Ranges of the West

As the transcontinental railroad got under way, railroad companies and real estate developers, eager to arouse the interest of tourists and potential settlers by advertising the glories of scenery along the route, were encouraging and sometimes subsidizing photographers and artists to portray the awe-inspiring landscapes. Albert Bierstadt, who had accompanied Frederick Lander's expedition to the Rocky Mountains, was astonishing visitors to the New York Sanitary Fair of 1864 with his six-by-ten-foot canvas *The Rocky Mountains, Lander's Peak* (p. 168).[51] Photographer Carleton E. Watkins was exhibiting his photographs of Yosemite at Goupil's Gallery in New York City, and his stereoscopic images of Bridal Veil Falls and other mountain scenes were being peered at in parlors everywhere. Americans saw that their country possessed awesome mountain scenery rivaling the Alps and other sublime peaks of the Old World.

At that moment, when public curiosity and reverence for the unspoiled beauty of such scenery was at a peak, F. F. Palmer dreamed up two popularized, romantic views of the Sierra Nevada. In *Yosemite Valley—California. "The Bridal Veil" Fall* (1866; p. 169), she included an encampment of American Indians along the river, complete with canoes and tepees. Such images of indigenous Americans were frequently employed by painters and printmakers to symbolize nature in its primitive, uncivilized state. Her figures seem disproportionately large, somewhat out of scale with the landscape, making the awesome, frightening wilderness seem more cozy and inhabitable.

It must be noted in passing that Palmer was not the only one who took liberties with the western landscape. Even Bierstadt created many of his huge canvases in a studio in Switzerland, pastiching elements from on-site sketches and photographs and dramatizing storms and other effects to such a degree that Mark Twain, who knew the West, declared the light and atmosphere in the artist's paintings to be "altogether too gorgeous. . . . It is more the atmosphere of Kingdom-Come than of California."[52] But that is precisely what artists such as Bierstadt, Thomas Moran, and, of course, F. F. Palmer were aiming at.[53]

In Palmer's second Sierra view, *The Mountain Pass. Sierra Nevada* (1867; p. 217), a black bear in the foreground, looking more like a giant teddy bear than a fearsome creature of the wilderness, is clambering across a fallen tree trunk toward a river fed by a waterfall. One tiny Native American, high on a distant mountain ledge, holds a bow and arrows as he looks down at his prey. The sky is blue, tall pines thrust upward, and El Dorado beckons.

The Sierra Nevada was of particular interest to Americans at this time. In 1867, on the western side of the mountains near the Donner Pass, thousands of immigrant Chinese laborers in their blue cotton garments and basketry hats were swarming over the immense hillsides, blasting tunnels through rock with gunpowder and nitroglycerine, an engineering feat unprecedented in history. Supervised by Charles Crocker (one of the "Big Four" directors of the Central Pacific Railroad), the "celestials," as they were called, worked in shifts around the clock, pushing the western half of the transcontinental railroad inch by inch through the summit tunnel. Uncounted numbers of workers were covered by avalanches, frozen in the snow, or injured in explosions, and thousands of tall trees were felled to build bridges, trestles, and miles of snow sheds. A US Army general traveling in the region marveled at track laid on grades so steep that it seemed literally to "[spring] into the air over immense trestle-work bridges or along the dizzy edges of precipices."[54]

In the following year, 1868, F. F. Palmer's print *Across The Continent* (gallery plate 8) would herald the soon-to-be completed transcontinental railroad.

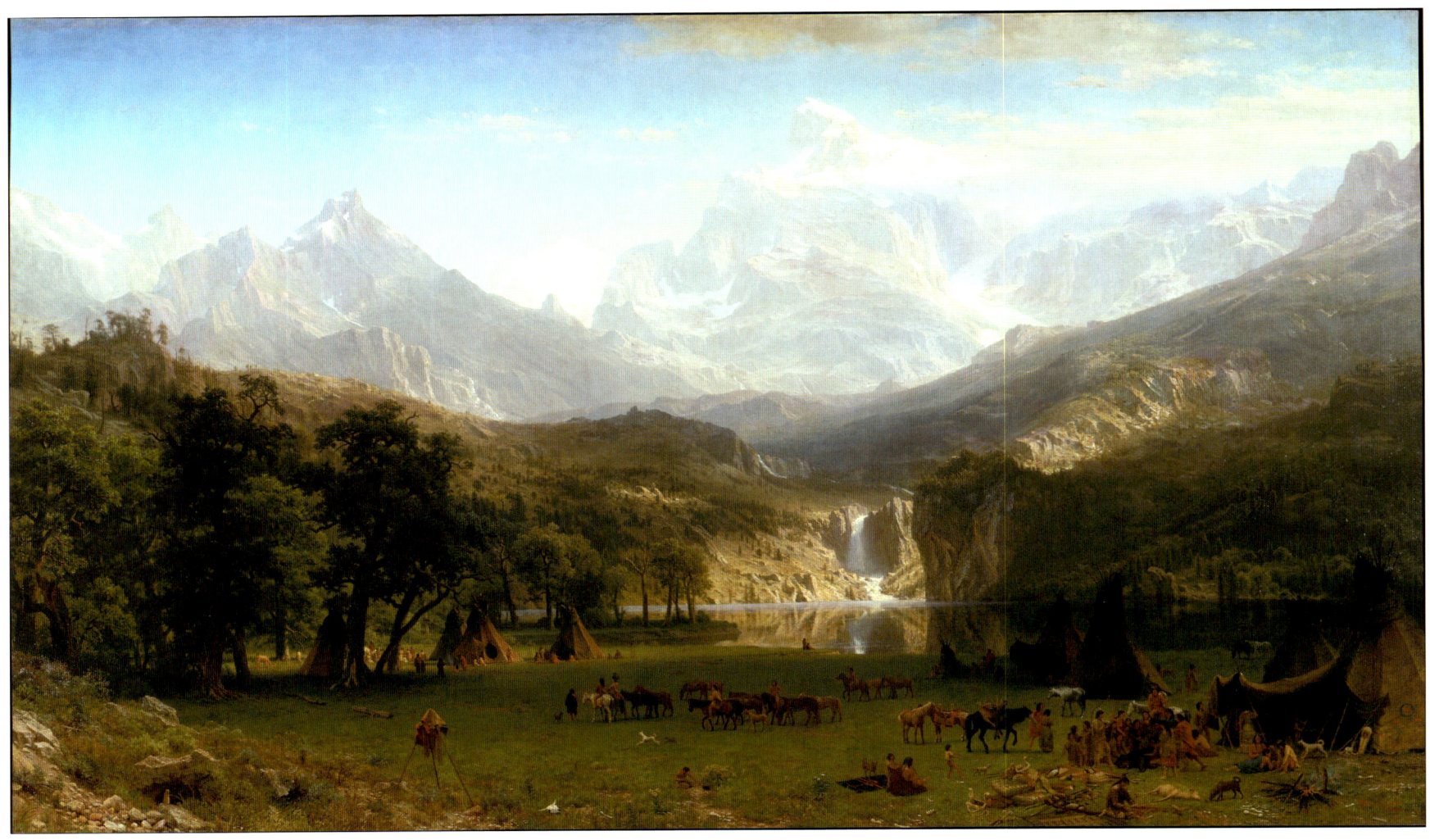

The Transcontinental Railroad

Beginning in the 1830s, visionaries had begun to dream of a transcontinental railroad that would unite the nation, bring vast wealth from trade with Asia, and turn the western plains into "the garden of the world."[55] The demand for such a railroad intensified in the 1840s and 1850s as emigration and the Gold Rush sent millions on long, perilous journeys around Cape Horn or across the malaria-ridden Panama Isthmus to California. Senator Thomas Hart Benton thundered, "There is the East! there is India!," as he sought to persuade Congress that a cross-country train line would actualize Columbus's dream of a route to the Orient and lead the nation to its culminating peak of prosperity.[56] But Northern and Southern congressmen fought bitterly over the route, recognizing that the new line would bring pivotal political and economic power to the region in which it was built.

136. *The Rocky Mountains, Lander's Peak.* 1863. Oil on canvas by Albert Bierstadt, 73½ × 120¾ in. Courtesy of the Metropolitan Museum of Art, Rogers Fund, 1907.

The moment of decision came during the Civil War, when, with no Southerners to block him in Congress, President Lincoln, an ardent advocate of the railroad and now concerned about protecting the country's Western flank from invasion by Confederate troops, was able to push through the Pacific Railroad Act of 1862 and thus to establish a northern route. That very year Palmer drew her first rough sketch of the subject.

As the Union Pacific Railroad began to lay track westward from Omaha, and the Central Pacific drilled and blasted eastward from Sacramento, Americans breathlessly followed newspaper and magazine accounts describing every detail of the race to join

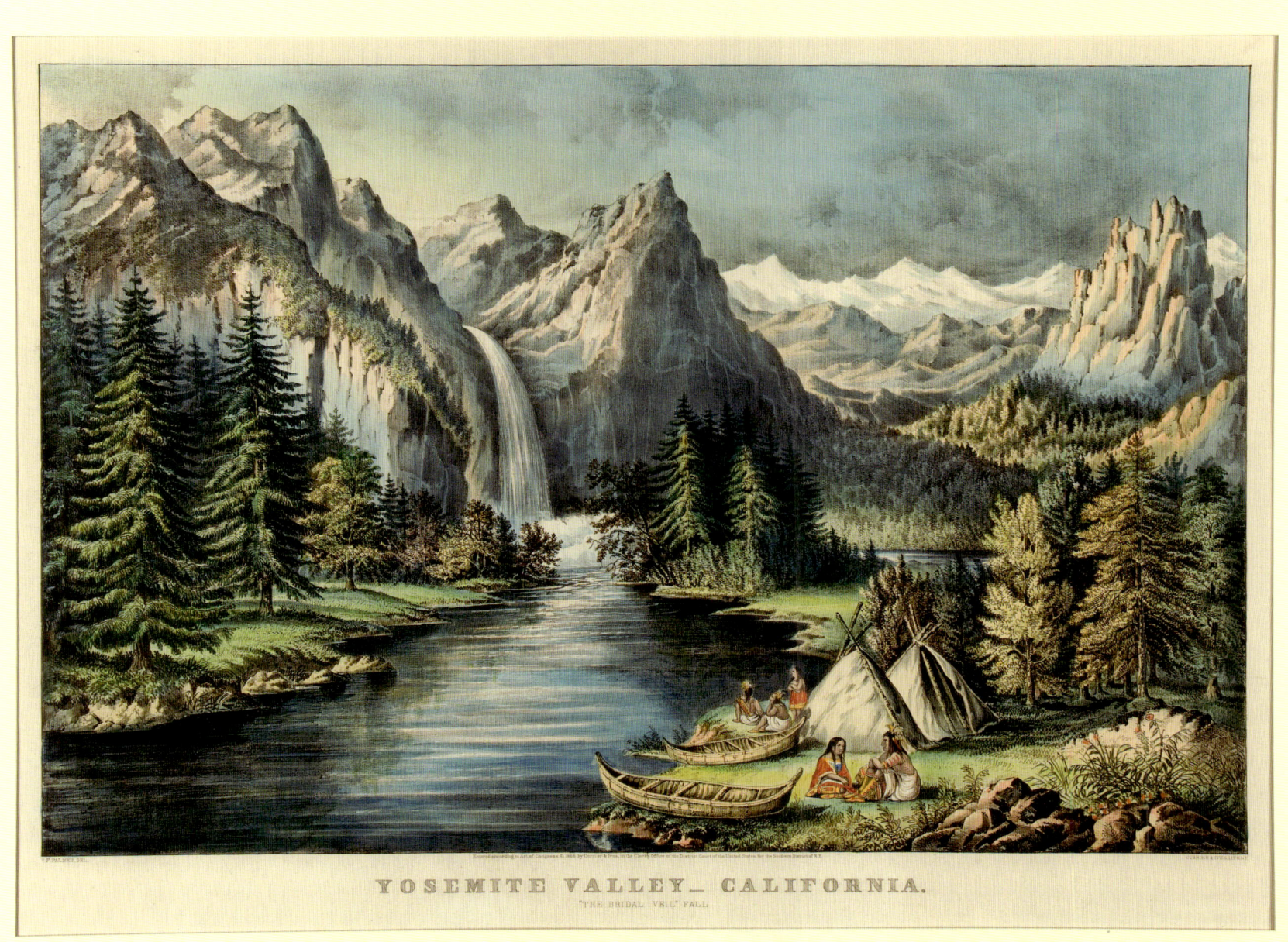

YOSEMITE VALLEY — CALIFORNIA.
"THE BRIDAL VEIL" FALL

137. *Yosemite Valley—California*. *"The Bridal Veil" Fall*. 1866.
Printed and published by Currier & Ives. Courtesy of the Yale University Art Gallery. (Checklist 3-177)

the two lines—a race spurred on by each company's desire to control the longest amount of track; by the government's award of land grants and forty-three thousand dollars for every mile laid; and—at the least—by the sheer fury of competition. In a final bravado gesture, Charles Crocker won a bet with his competitor by pushing his workers to lay ten miles of track in a single day, a feat reportedly never equaled.[57]

In 1868, a year before the two lines were finally linked on a windy plateau in Utah, Currier & Ives, which had cannily postponed

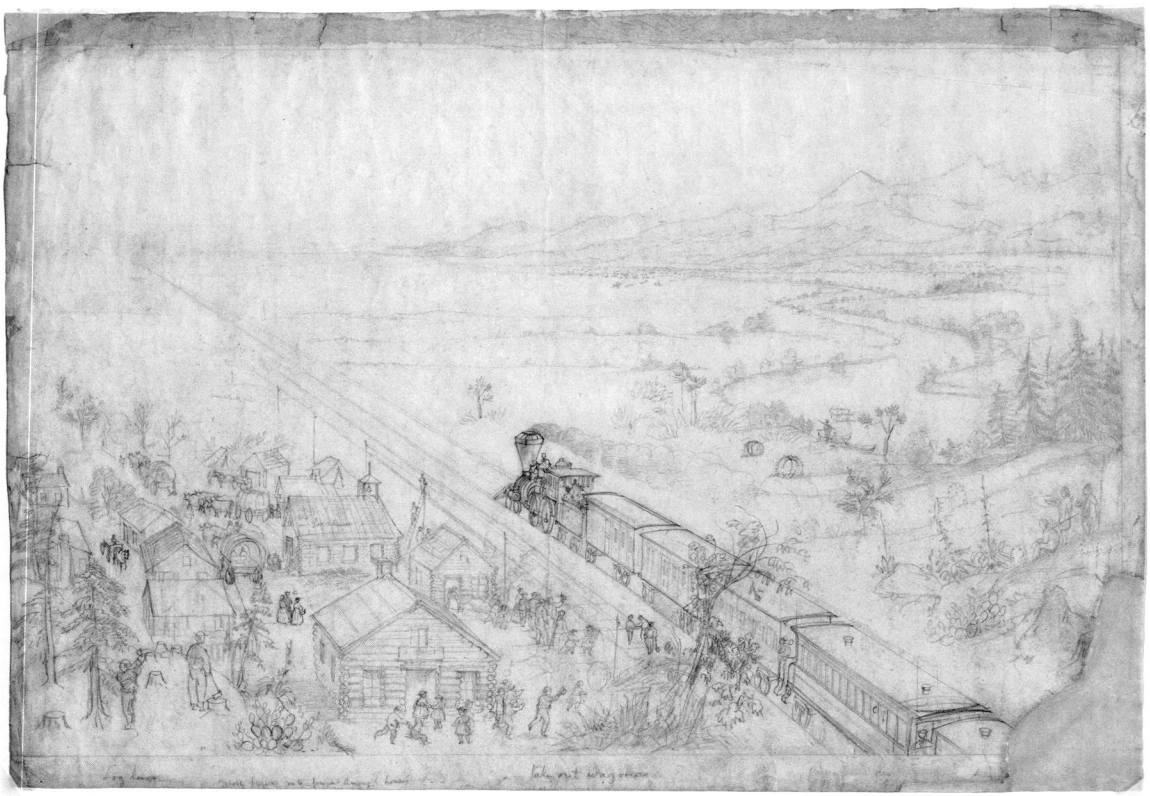

issuing Palmer's print until the moment when public interest was at its height, published *Across The Continent: "Westward the Course of Empire takes its way"* (gallery plate 8). Palmer's lithograph is the ultimate expression of the expansionist spirit that had seized the United States at midcentury. A bird's-eye view shows the new train roaring diagonally into deep space on a track running from the lower-right corner toward the upper left, an almost phallic expression of the power of western civilization as it thrusts across the yielding plains. Whereas Palmer's earlier Western prints hinted at biblical references to the Holy Family, the Promised Land, and a new Garden of Eden, this image glorifies the driving force of American technology in building a new civilization.[58]

It is illuminating to study the evolution of the print from the artist's initial sketch in 1862 to the final lithograph published in 1868. In an early pencil drawing (1862, at the Museum of the City of New York), Palmer envisioned the western plains as an arid desert, a popularly held view derived from early travel writers. A group of Native Americans are next to some cactus plants, passively watching the train go by. The new settlement rising along the tracks is rather ramshackle, something like a pioneer stockade, with thatched-roof houses, a tent, campfires, a school, and a few cattle roaming about. The railroad is taking a winding path through distant mountains all the way to a harbor on the Pacific Ocean.

James Ives, who seems to have played a major role in the print's conception, penciled in various instructions for modifying the composition. In the final print, the plains are green and fertile, waiting for settlers to transform them into profitable farms; the mountains in the path of the train (the enormous Rockies and the Sierra Nevada) have been flattened to the horizon, allowing the railroad to advance unimpeded over level terrain; and the new town springing up alongside the station is a well-built, well-organized outpost of civilization. All these features were part of the propaganda of the day, to make the trip seem easy in order to encourage travel and settlement.[59]

The lithograph *Across The Continent* is, in fact, a celebratory allegory expressing how the country's leaders and most of the American people viewed the forces at work on the eve of the railway's completion. In the left foreground, woodsmen are chopping down trees to be made into buildings. One leans on his shovel, gazing at the oncoming train and at the result of his handiwork, a thriving frontier town. Children troop into the public school (the dominant building, viewed as the principal source of civilizing influences). Behind it stands the second instrument of acculturation, a log church with a steeple bell. People rush out of log houses to wave to the oncoming train, emblazoned with the words "Through Line: New York San Francisco."

Alongside the track, workers string telegraph poles, connecting communications from coast to coast. On the extreme left, covered wagons still straggle to the horizon on the bumpy overland trail; they had opened the West but are now made obsolete by the new form of transportation. On the right side of the track, the old world of unspoiled nature still spreads out toward the horizon, a seemingly unlimited area awaiting development. Instead of the passive Indian spectators in Palmer's original sketch, two mounted, armed Indians rear backward as the onrushing train blows a cloud of smoke into their faces. In the far distance, barely visible, a few Native Americans can be seen chasing buffalos. Both the natives and the buffalos appear to be vanishing as civilization encroaches.

In its day, Palmer's print was enthusiastically received as a herald of the inevitable advance of a great civilization about to occupy and make productive a vast new territory, a view of it that remained current all the way into the 1920s and 1930s. During the Great Depression, such prints fit right in with the regionalist school of Thomas Hart Benton and others who were attempting to restore the national spirit.

When abstract art and formalism began to reign supreme in the 1940s, art historian Wolfgang Born preferred to analyze the print's composition from the point of view of its spatial sense. A European, he wrote in his book *American Landscape Painting*:

> The space-feeling of an American who moves freely in his vast continent is necessarily different from that of a citizen of a European nation who is hemmed in by the narrow boundaries of his country. . . . In order to convey the idea of the gigantic extension of the new railroad from coast to coast the artist chose an imaginary elevated point of view. . . . [E]verything appears in bird's-eye perspective, and the horizon is close to the upper rim of the picture. . . . The extension of the prairie to the side is emphasized by the simple but effective device of cutting it sharply by the vertical borders of the picture.[60]

Born treated the formal aspect of the composition effectively but was blind to the message embodied in it—the unstoppable drive of a new technological civilization, uniting the continent and sweeping aside any obstacles in its path.

There is no doubt that the design of Palmer's print *Across The Continent* does its job brilliantly. A blue sky arches over a green expanse as morning light hits the eastern sides of buildings, announcing the dawn of a happy new era. Comparing this image to an earlier work with a similar title, Emanuel Leutze's mural in the US Capitol, *Westward the Course of Empire Takes Its Way* (1861),[61] we see that the muralist shows a previous stage of the westward movement. In his image, there are no trains or telegraph poles. The pioneers have reached the top of a rugged mountain after an arduous journey and are hailing the distant plains—America's Promised Land. Leutze's composition is comparatively static; the pyramidal design blocks entry into deep space in a manner entirely different from the onrushing diagonal in Palmer's print. Her image represents a later phase of the westward movement.

Beginning in the 1970s, socially oriented scholars analyzed *Across The Continent* from a different perspective. They studied the social and economic underpinnings of this vast movement, investigating the ways in which such imagery was used to further the interests of real estate developers, railroad companies, and other commercial and political groups that stood to benefit from the expansion. In *The West as America: Reinterpreting Images of the Frontier* (1991) and other books and articles, scholars have shown how artists and photographers were subsidized to accompany government and private survey parties in order to publicize the wonders of the West.[62] They note the racist portrayal of the American Indians. Behind the arrogant dismissal shown in Palmer's print was a brutal struggle taking place between two civilizations, the emerging industrial society and the indigenous peoples whose food supply and way of life were being destroyed.[63]

Just a few years before the publication of Palmer's print, the unprovoked massacre of Native American men, women, and children at Sand Creek by a group of American soldiers was followed by the Indians' reprisals at Julesburg. In 1868, the very year that Palmer's print was issued, a band of young Sioux warriors, infuriated because they had been tricked into forced exile from their sacred lands, derailed a train at Plum Creek, Utah, killing the engineer and others. Federal troops were called in to guard the construction sites, stamp out insurrections, and herd the Native populations into bleak reservation areas.

Nowhere to be seen in Palmer's print are the Irish and Chinese immigrants who constituted much of the workforce that actually built the railroad. The workers shown stringing telegraph lines and laying ties are homogenized, creating the impression that they all are white, Anglo-Saxon Protestants. In this homogenization,

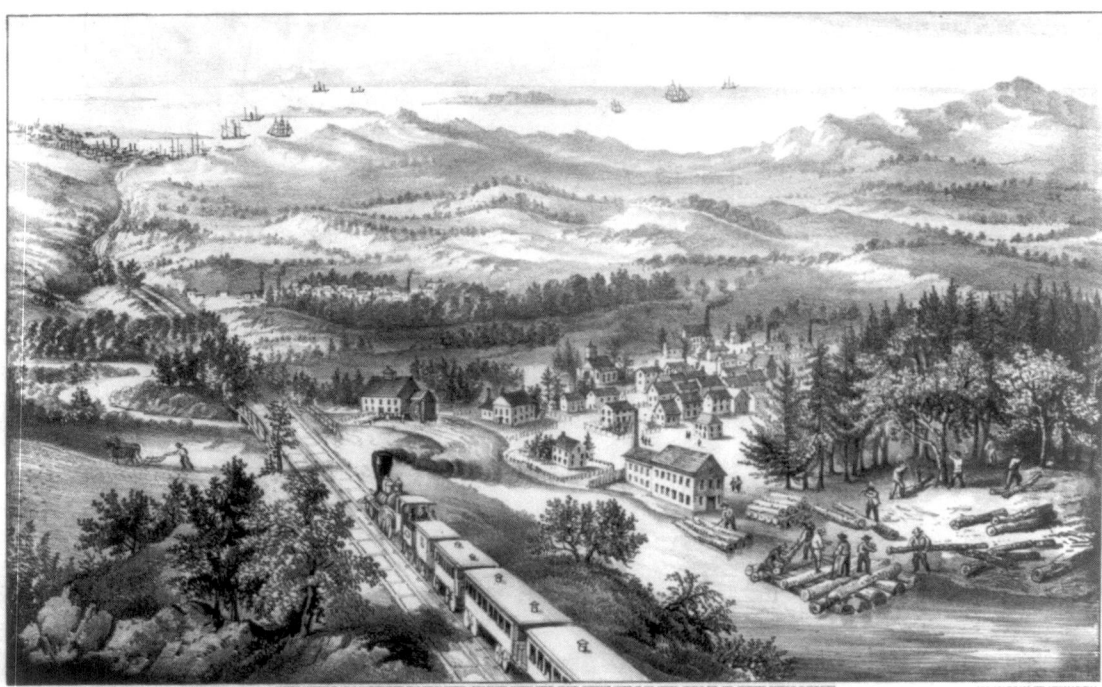

THROUGH TO THE PACIFIC.

139. *Through to the Pacific.* 1870. Printed and published by Currier & Ives. Courtesy of the Prints and Photographs Division, Library of Congress, LC-USZ62-25.

Palmer was no different from most of the painters and even many of the photographers of her day. As for the glorified vision of wholesome, respectable new cities rising on the plains, in reality the frontier towns that sprang up around the station stops (for example, Ogallala, Nebraska, and Laramie, Wyoming), described at that time as "hell on wheels," often resembled the sites of brawling, gambling, and prostitution that later became the clichés of western films.[64]

To twenty-first-century environmentalists writing about Palmer's print today, the smoke blowing from the train into the Native Americans' faces presages the ubiquitous gray smog of factories, cars, and planes.[65] Others interpret the bird's-eye viewpoint as the expression of greedy eyes lusting for land and profit, and, indeed, to thousands of immigrants the untouched plains in Palmer's print held out hope of claiming free land offered by the Homestead Act of 1862. As for profit, a few years after the completion of the railroad, when the initial euphoria had worn off, the press was filled with stories of how the directors of both the Union Pacific and the Central Pacific had plundered the taxpayers and the government through various scams, stock manipulations, and bribery of congressmen and of how the "Big Four" (directors of the Central Pacific) emerged from the transcontinental endeavor with

immense personal fortunes—prototypes of the robber barons of the Gilded Age.[66] As Congress began to investigate these scandals, Walt Whitman, the bard of the railroad, sent a mournful poem, "Nay Tell Me Not To-day the Publish'd Shame," to the *New York Daily Graphic*, and it was published on March 5, 1873.[67]

These insights of recent scholarship give us a less-glorified view of some of the historical forces at work behind the print, yet in its own day and even today *Across The Continent* continues to stir viewers with the recollection of a period of enormous optimism, when most Americans felt that the nation was moving ahead into its greatest era. The Civil War was over, and the train line was a healing symbol of national unity. As the ceremonial gold and silver spikes were finally pounded in at Promontory Point, cannons boomed, fireworks sizzled, church choirs broke out in song across the land, and preachers declared the new line to be the final embodiment of biblical prophecy. James Campbell, superintendent of the Central Pacific's rolling stock, expressed the feelings (and prejudices) of the moment in a farewell speech to his workers, delivered in a railroad car:

Little you realize what you have done. You have this day changed the path of commerce and finance of the whole world. . . . Where we now stand . . . but a few months since could be seen nothing but the path of the red man or the track of the wild deer. Now a thousand wheels revolve and will bear on their axles the wealth of half the world, drawn by the Iron Horse, darkening the landscape with his smoky breath and startling the wild Indian with his piercing scream. Philosophers would dream away a lifetime contemplating this scene, but the officers of the Pacific Railroad would look and exclaim: "We are a great people and can accomplish great things."[68]

In the millennial year 2000, historian Stephen E. Ambrose looked back and concluded: "Next to winning the Civil War and abolishing slavery, building the first transcontinental railroad . . . was the greatest achievement of the American people in the nineteenth century. . . . [T]he Americans did it first. And they did it even though the United States was the youngest of countries."[69]

It is interesting to compare Palmer's lithograph to an anonymous print of the transcontinental railroad issued only two years later.[70] In her version, the vast, empty plains and the track disappearing on the horizon suggest a boundless frontier, but in *Through to the Pacific* (1870; p. 172), published by Currier & Ives after the line was completed, the terrain alongside the new track is already beginning to fill up, not only with farms but also with factories and cities. The end of the frontier, the Pacific coastline, is visible. Although we see more of the intervening territory, space seems to be shrinking because the limits of continental expansion are apparent. Boats sailing to and from the western rim forecast that the United States would soon extend its influence overseas to the Philippines, Hawaii, Puerto Rico, Cuba, the Panama Canal, and elsewhere.[71]

8

The Last Years

WHILE PALMER was laboring on these epic themes, her personal situation was deteriorating. In 1867, her son, Edmund Seymour Jr., died of tuberculosis at the age of thirty-three. Robert Bond's niece-in-law reminisced: "The son never did work of any kind. Just lived the life of a gentleman of leisure. Was fond of hunting, etc. and kept dogs. He died when he was a young man . . . was the great spender of the family. Very fine looking young man."[1]

As of this writing, there are no confirmed prints by F. F. Palmer after 1868.[2] She is described in later years as a small, gray-haired woman whose back had become deformed either from osteoporosis or from stooping incessantly over her drawings.[3] Like her son, Palmer contracted tuberculosis, and she undoubtedly must have been concerned about the threat to the health and financial situation of her daughter, granddaughter, and sister.

In her last years, a growing number of address changes are listed in the Brooklyn directory for Palmer: 92 Hall Street (1867–69), 122 Ryerson Street (1870), 111 Hamilton Street (1871), and, finally, 123 Hamilton Street (1872–76).[4] She had moved from downtown Brooklyn to the newly developing Fort Greene neighborhood. She was still listed in the Brooklyn directory as a lithographer or artist between 1868 and 1876, but the federal census of 1870 nevertheless described her as "keeping house," and Maria Bond—listed in the Brooklyn directory as a music teacher—appears in the census as "at home."[5]

Palmer's widowed daughter had returned to her mother's house and is recorded in the same census—oddly—as "Fanny Bond, 37," instead of under her married name (Edgecombe). Her child, Maria, now twelve, was "attending school."[6] After the death of two husbands and a son, the family had become a household of four women.

F. F. Palmer died of tuberculosis on August 20, 1876.[7] On August 22, the *Brooklyn Eagle* published a six-line death notice with no mention of her long career:

DIED

PALMER. In this city, on Sunday, August 20, Mrs. FRANCES FLORA PALMER, relict of Edmund S. Palmer, of Leicester, England, aged 64 years.

Relatives and friends of the family are respectfully invited to attend the funeral on Wednesday, August 23, at two o'clock P.M., from her late residence, 123 Hamilton st. [*sic*].[8]

Nathaniel Currier's son Edward and sales manager Daniel W. Logan were among the pallbearers.[9] We can guess from this that other members of the company may have been present to show their regard for the colleague who had worked so long and diligently for the firm. Note, however, that whereas Fanny saw to it that her husband had a funeral service at the Holy Trinity Episcopal Church, her death was memorialized in a modest service at home.

F. F. Palmer was buried that day in Green-Wood Cemetery alongside her husband and son.[10] Two years later, on March 2, 1878, her daughter, Frances Edgecombe, who had been listed as a "widow" and a florist and wax-flower maker in the 1876 and 1877 Brooklyn directories,[11] joined her mother at Green-Wood, a victim of the same disease. Palmer's brother, Robert Bond, died on June 13, 1887, and her granddaughter, Maria F. Mary Edgecombe, an artist and writer who had been living with her aunt Maria, also succumbed, on October 16, 1888, to the "white plague" that devastated so many in the nineteenth century. Only Fanny's stalwart sister Maria, taller and hardier, "her dark brown hair . . . only slightly touched with gray,"[12] outlived her siblings and niece, dying on February 11, 1896, in her early eighties.[13] The last survivor of the family, Robert Bond's English-born wife, Mary Sutton Bond, joined her in-laws eleven months later, on January 31, 1897.[14]

Although F. F. Palmer's prints hung on the walls of a huge number of nineteenth-century homes and offices, her death was barely noticed by the general public. Her grave is unmarked; only her brother's modest monument, erected by his wife, remains visible. Nearby are the substantial gravestones of Nathaniel Currier and James Ives. In a final irony, a number of Palmer's works also may have disappeared. Her colleague and neighbor Charles Currier, who was the only person who had kept a complete inventory of all of the Currier & Ives prints, unfortunately stored them in a damp basement area of his home, under the front steps. By the time the three boxes were opened after his death, almost all the prints had disintegrated.[15] Since then, collectors and scholars have been engaged in a treasure hunt to reassemble a complete collection of the company's works. As of this writing, the total has risen to roughly eight thousand prints, with no end in sight.[16]

It is impossible to discuss all the prints that we know the versatile artist F. F. Palmer created for Currier & Ives over a quarter of a century. The reader is encouraged to browse through the following two chapters and the appendixes for information about many that have not been touched upon here. Suffice it to say that F. F. Palmer created a documentary of mid-nineteenth-century American life in images that sometimes have the freshness of observed reality and other times are mythic inventions. She lived from the War of 1812 to the centennial in 1876, a period of enormous growth in the United States, and mirrored many aspects of her adopted nation's tumultuous history. Indeed, one can reasonably ask which other nineteenth-century American artist, whether "high" or "low," portrayed so many of those aspects. She also lived through the meteoric rise and flowering of lithography as a primary mass printing medium. By the time she completed her last prints, lithographs printed on hand-cranked presses and colored by hand were already being superseded by chromolithographs printed in multiple color separations on steam presses and soon after that by photographic methods of reproduction.

9

The Vicissitudes of Taste

IN THE CENTURY after F. F. Palmer's death, Currier & Ives prints, like so many works of art, endured the vicissitudes of taste. When Nathaniel Currier retired in 1880, his place was taken for a time by his son Edward ("Ned"), and after the deaths of both of the original partners, Edward and Ives's son Chauncey ran the business together, but it declined steadily, producing mostly horse-trotting and *Dark-town* prints at the end. After illness forced Edward to resign, Chauncey gradually began to sell off the inventory. Their longtime sales manager, Daniel W. Logan, and his son finally acquired the company, but it limped along in smaller quarters, eventually ending up on one floor in the factory building at 33 Spruce Street until it was finally dissolved in 1907. The remaining lithograph stones were sold by the pound, and most of the images were ground off, except for those for the *Darktown Comics*, which were bought as a group for reprinting because they were still so popular.

By the 1880s, the tastes of cosmopolitan Americans of the Gilded Age had changed; they were looking to European models for inspiration. The United States was emerging as a major power on the international scene, and the Aesthetic Movement brought an interest in French paintings, Italian bronzes, Japanese prints, and the "high art" of signed, limited-edition etchings instead of mass-produced "chromos." In an age of robber barons and bloated fortunes, home decors, with their elaborately festooned window treatments, wall hangings, and bronze sculptures, left far less room and little desire for the kind of "cheap and popular" colored prints that Currier & Ives produced,[1] and the folksy American subject matter in Currier & Ives prints seemed crude and garish. Regarded as valueless mass-produced items, they were thrown out or left to molder in attics.

REVIVAL: 1920–1940

It was not until the mid-1920s that a new interest in all forms of "Americana" emerged. Early modernists began to rediscover in Currier & Ives prints some of the same direct and honest qualities that they admired in "primitive" and folk art. During the Great Depression of the 1930s, when painters of the American scene (such as Grant Wood, John Steuart Curry, and Thomas Hart Benton) were attempting to revive the national spirit, collectors began to pursue the previously scorned lithographs that now seemed to embody the roots of American values. By that time, the prints had become relatively rare due to their wholesale destruction, and so their value began to rise.

Collectors scoured yard sales, flea markets, attics, and barns. Frank Weitenkampf, print curator at the New York Public Library, wrote about Currier & Ives. Harry T. Peters, a wealthy New York coal merchant, amassed the country's largest collection, gathered information about the firm's artists, and produced a pioneering two-volume limited edition entitled *Currier & Ives: Printmakers to the American People* (1929–31). It was so well received that a mass-market abridged version followed in 1942. Peters eventually bequeathed much of his collection to the Museum of the City of New York, the Smithsonian Museum of American History, and the California Historical Society.

Credit must also be given to Harriet Endicott Waite, owner of a New York gallery specializing in Americana, who carried out a great deal of laborious research for Peters, combing through archives; unearthing dates, addresses, and copyright information; and hunting down and interviewing many of the few remaining people (such as Louis Maurer) who had known Palmer and her colleagues during their days at Currier & Ives. The papers Waite collected in the course of her research, for which she received little remuneration, are now housed in the Smithsonian's Archives of American Art and remain a major source of information about the company and its employees.[2]

In 1932, Harry Shaw Newman, proprietor of the Old Print Shop in New York, and eleven other prominent collectors and aficionados eager to promote Currier & Ives decided to select a list of the "best-fifty" large-folio Currier & Ives prints. Twenty percent of this list turned out to be works by F. F. Palmer.[3] A member of this committee—the antiques editor of the *New York Sun*—then came up with the idea of featuring one of the "best fifty" in his paper each day for fifty successive days.[4] This series caused such a surge of interest that the group followed up with a list of "best-fifty" small-folio prints. Only one of Palmer's lithographs, *Winter Morning* (1861; p. 186), was chosen for this series, for a simple reason: Currier & Ives had employed her talents almost entirely on the larger, more-expensive, signed works. Nevertheless, the men who wrote about her at this time, blinded by the attitudes of the period, often referred to her in somewhat patronizing tones as not quite up to the level of her male colleagues.[5]

1941–1960

After World War II, when abstract art dominated the scene, realism and narrative art fell out of favor, and the avant-garde viewed Currier & Ives prints as sentimental kitsch and consigned them to the dust bin of art history. However, a steady interest continued among those who collected or studied American historical prints and among the masses of people, who ignored the dictates of the cognoscenti and continued to enjoy them. One art historian, Wolfgang Born, was perceptive enough to recognize Palmer's importance and included full-page entries on her work in his books *Still Life Painting in America* (1947) and *American Landscape Painting* (1948).

1960 to the Present

In 1962, hoping to redress the neglect of an important American lithographer, historian Mary Bartlett Cowdrey published the first substantial appraisal of F. F. Palmer's work in a ground-breaking essay included in the collection *Prints: Thirteen Essays on the Art of the Print*.[6] Soon after this, in the turbulent 1970s—a period of rising interest in women artists and the social and historical context of art—Palmer's prints, along with popular prints in general, became the object of close scrutiny. Whereas only a few art and art history books had previously mentioned her, in the following decades examples of her work were singled out for discussion in more than fifty books and articles, and her images were increasingly recognized as quintessential icons of nineteenth-century American life.

In 1990, the American Historical Print Collectors Society (composed of art historians, curators, collectors, and dealers) decided to update the list of the best-fifty large-folio Currier & Ives prints for an exhibition at the Milwaukee Art Museum. This time, after an elaborate and broad-based selection process, 30 percent of the "new best fifty" turned out to be Palmer prints—more than for any other artist.[7]

10

The Art of F. F. Palmer

TODAY, when the work of women artists is viewed with greater fair-mindedness and the so-called popular arts are recognized as important expressions of an era, we can at last properly evaluate the work of Fanny Palmer. What has been surprisingly lacking thus far is sufficient attention to its aesthetic qualities. Palmer is still treated primarily as a storyteller, when, in fact, she was also a splendid designer who used the plastic elements—space, line, color, dark and light—for their formal beauty and at the same time to reinforce thematic content in a very compelling way.

Viewed as a whole, her work follows a trajectory from the relatively provincial early prints in Leicester to the increasingly polished and versatile prints she made as an independent entrepreneur in New York City and finally, after joining Currier's company, to a peak of accomplishment between 1849 and 1865, the period in which she showed the freshest and most immediate response to her new American environment.

THE CLAUDIAN LANDSCAPE

Palmer's early exposure to British art familiarized her with the formulas of the seventeenth-century French painter Claude Lorrain that were still widely used in Europe and later applied to American landscapes by Thomas Cole and other American artists in order to produce an effect of "elevation and grandeur" by imposing European models of the ideal onto the American scene.[1] These time-worn structural forms typically included large trees framing the picture on one or both sides; a dark foreground area; a body of shining water or a rural village in the middle ground; and serpentine paths meandering back toward a distant mountain or sea. Often a small figure or group in the foreground, seen from the rear, gazes at the view—the rapt spectator with whom the viewer identifies. This form of composition helped to express the reverent attitude that Americans brought to their native landscape, but Palmer made the lofty Claudian formula homier and

more accessible to the average American by including folksy and familiar elements from daily life.

Compare John Kensett's painting *Mount Washington. From the Valley of Conway* (1851) to the lithograph that Palmer adapted from James Smillie's engraving of that painting, *Mount Washington and the White Mountains, From the Valley of Conway* (1860; p. 179).[2] Kensett's tiny sheep, almost lost in the distance, are replaced by a group of larger cattle standing and resting in the foreground. In Palmer's print, the houses are larger and more conspicuous instead of hidden amid trees. The Arcadian shepherd gazing at the distant mountain has been replaced by a man walking sideways with a fishing pole. At the same time, Palmer's image is more exaggeratedly theatrical and dramatic. Taller trees frame the picture on either side, and serpentine lines lead the eye deep into the scene, snaking toward an immense snow-capped peak.

Palmer used the Claudian format variously to emphasize a range of feelings, from the nostalgia in *New England Scenery* (1866; p. 160) to the *terribilita* of warfare in *The Mississippi in Time of War* (1865; gallery plate 12). The Claudian mode can be found in some of her earliest prints in the United States—for example, in the nostalgic sheet music cover *My Mountain Home* (1844; p. 34)—and she continued to employ these devices for Currier & Ives in *Staten Island and the Narrows* (1861; p. 183), *View in Dutchess County, N.Y.* (undated, ca. 1857–72; p. 180), *The Hudson Highlands. From the Peekskill and Cold Spring Road* (1857; p. 128), *Gray's Elegy. In a Country Church Yard* (1864; p. 157), and many other works.

Not every artist who worked for Currier & Ives used these strategies. Arthur F. Tait, whose paintings of sporting and rural scenes were often the models for the company's lithographs, usually employed a more straight-on naturalistic approach, cropping the scene as in a photograph. Indeed, a critic derided him for chopping off the upper parts of the trees in a painting that Currier

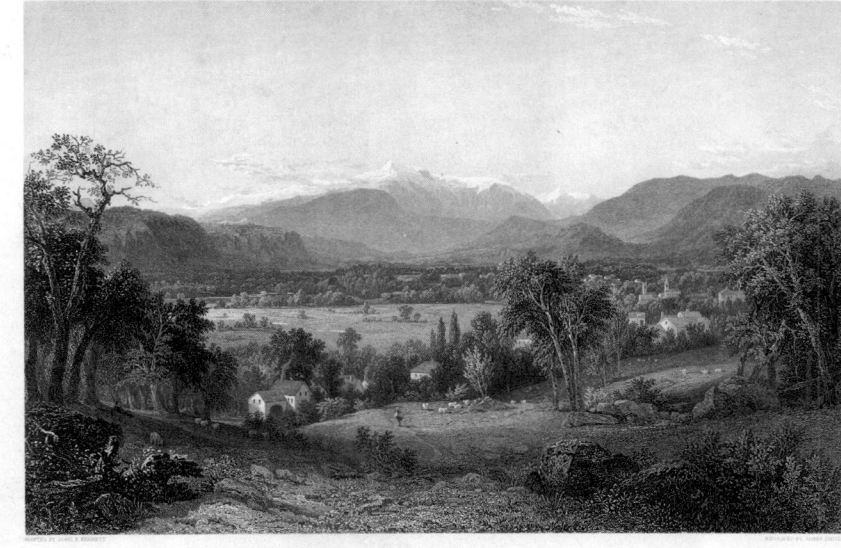

140. *Mount Washington. From the Valley of the Conway.* 1851. Painted by John F. Kensett, engraved by James Smillie, printed by J. Dalton. Courtesy of the Prints and Photographs Division, Library of Congress, LC-DIG-pga-08354.

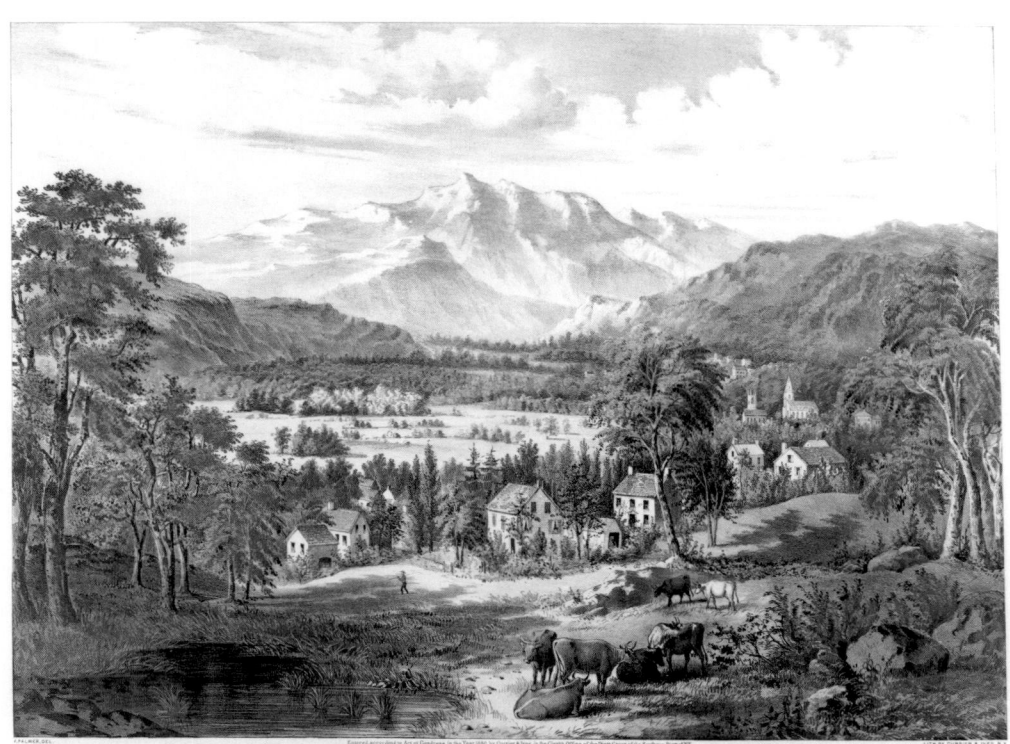

141. *Mount Washington and the White Mountains, From the Valley of Conway.* 1860. Printed and published by Currier & Ives. Courtesy of the Old Print Shop. (Checklist 3-88)

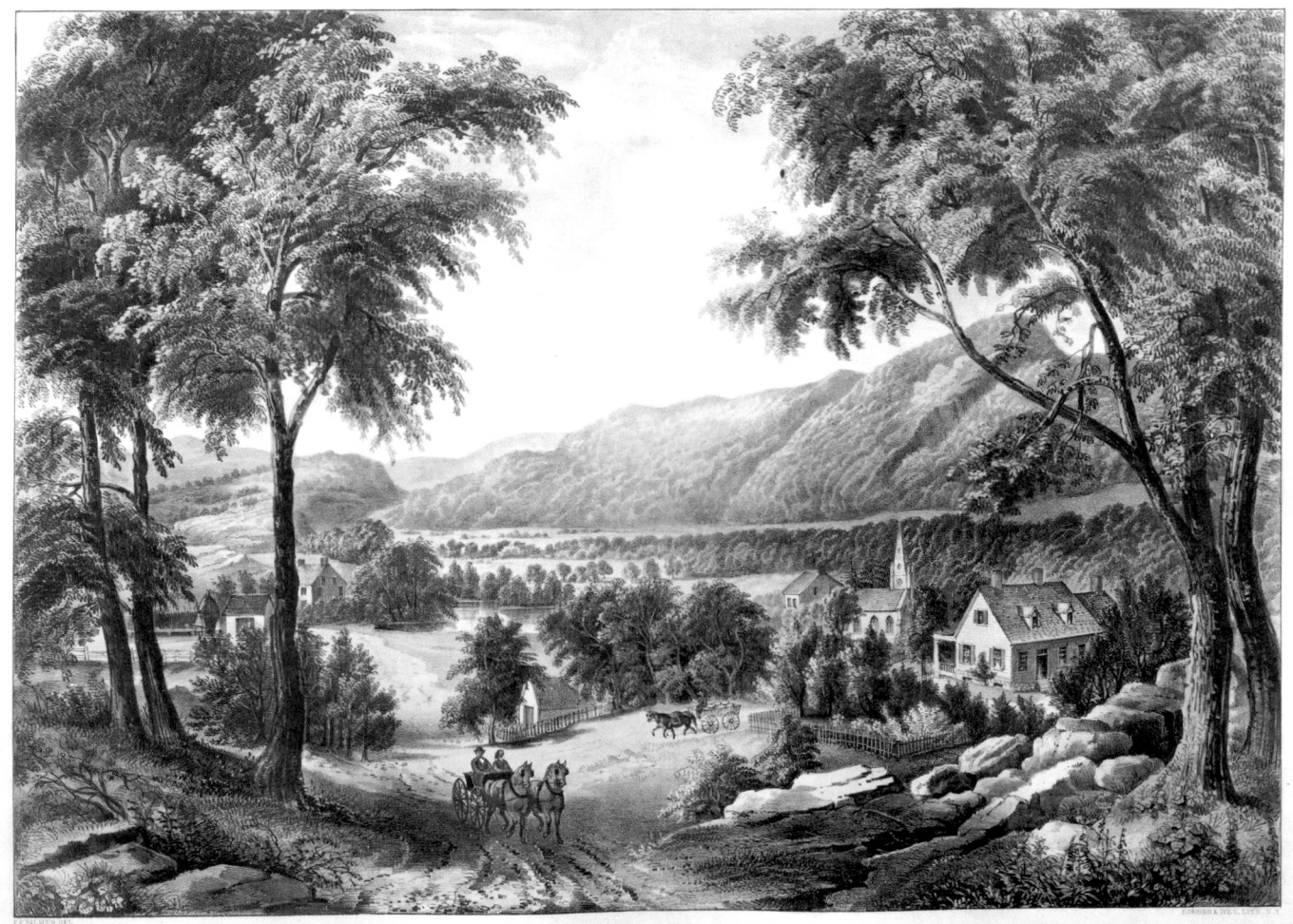

VIEW IN DUTCHESS COUNTY, N.Y.

142. *View in Dutchess County*, N.Y. Undated, ca. 1857–72. Printed and published by Currier & Ives. Courtesy of the Old Print Shop. (Checklist 3-148)

& Ives lithographed, *American Forest Scene. Maple Sugaring* (1856): "If Mr. Tait means to be an artist, he must not allow himself to suppose that a grove of maple trees with the tops cut off by his frame can make a picture."[3] George Durrie, in contrast, used overlapping planes—a more flattened effect—rather than the picturesque paths into deep space that characterize Palmer's work.

Note that Palmer herself sometimes abandoned the Claudian mode when she was emphasizing modern aspects of American life. For example, her print *New York Crystal Palace* (1853; p. 96), of the building that housed America's first world's fair and featured advances in science and manufacturing, is devoid of these artistic devices. In *Across The Continent* (1868; gallery plate 8)—an image of modern technology racing into the future—only

a few scrawny pine trees appear at the left as vestiges of the Arcadian past.

COMPOSITION

In Palmer's own day, her audience was interested primarily in the narrative content of her work, and she carefully planned her compositions to accommodate this demand. In most of her pictures, the viewer is immediately attracted to a strong center of interest, then is led around and through the image from point to point in a succession of "episodes." In an era without motion pictures and television, viewers created their own motion as their eyes panned the scene, lingering with delight over a multitude of details along the way.

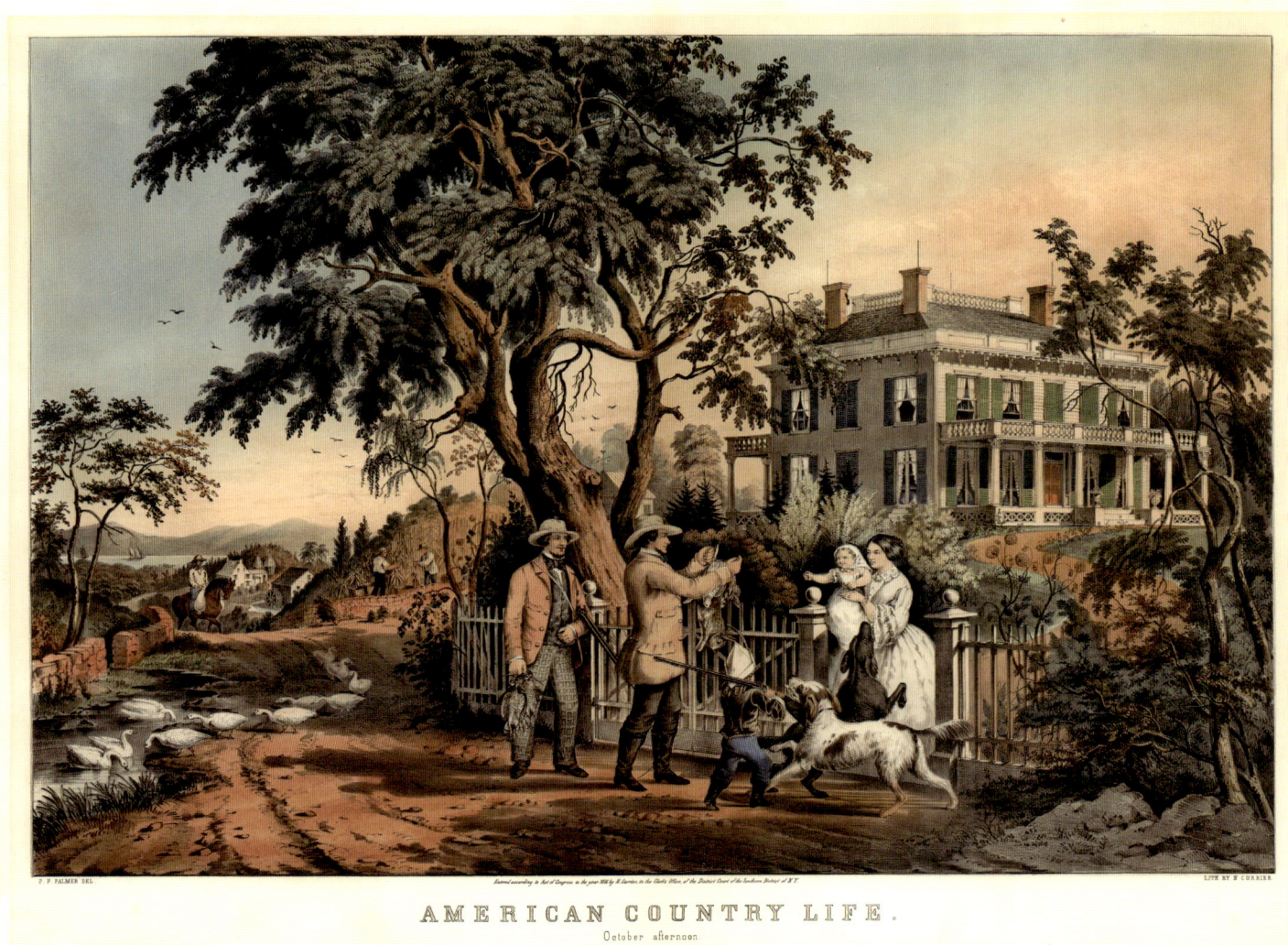

AMERICAN COUNTRY LIFE.
October afternoon.

For example, in *American Country Life. October Afternoon* (1855) we are immediately drawn to the central image of a sportsman returning with his trophies to his family. Then we follow a visual path through the garden to their house and up and around to the left side of the print, where a country road winds down into the distance, leading us past a delightful parade of geese marching into a stream, two farmers harvesting crops, a man riding a horse, a grist mill, a distant glimpse of a sailing vessel on a body of water, and a flock of autumn birds flying south. This much information could result in clutter, but Palmer organized the material into a harmonious design.

Beyond the simple organization of subject matter, however, Palmer also used the plastic elements of space, line, dark and light,

color, and pattern with great skill. An analysis of a few of her best-known prints reveals how she organized them for both expressive and aesthetic purposes.

In *American Winter Scenes. Evening* (1854; gallery plate 3), she used sonorous S-curves to express the coming together of people for a joyful community event. Note how the curves and countercurves of the roadway converge at the front door of the hotel and are carried up to the edge of the clouds and moon, then brought down through the curving tree branches. The theme—the joy of community life—is also reinforced with color. A vista of cold moonlight shining on bluish-white snow and an icy lake reveals the indifference and loneliness of nature, while the yellow lights in the windows of the hotel beckon with human warmth.

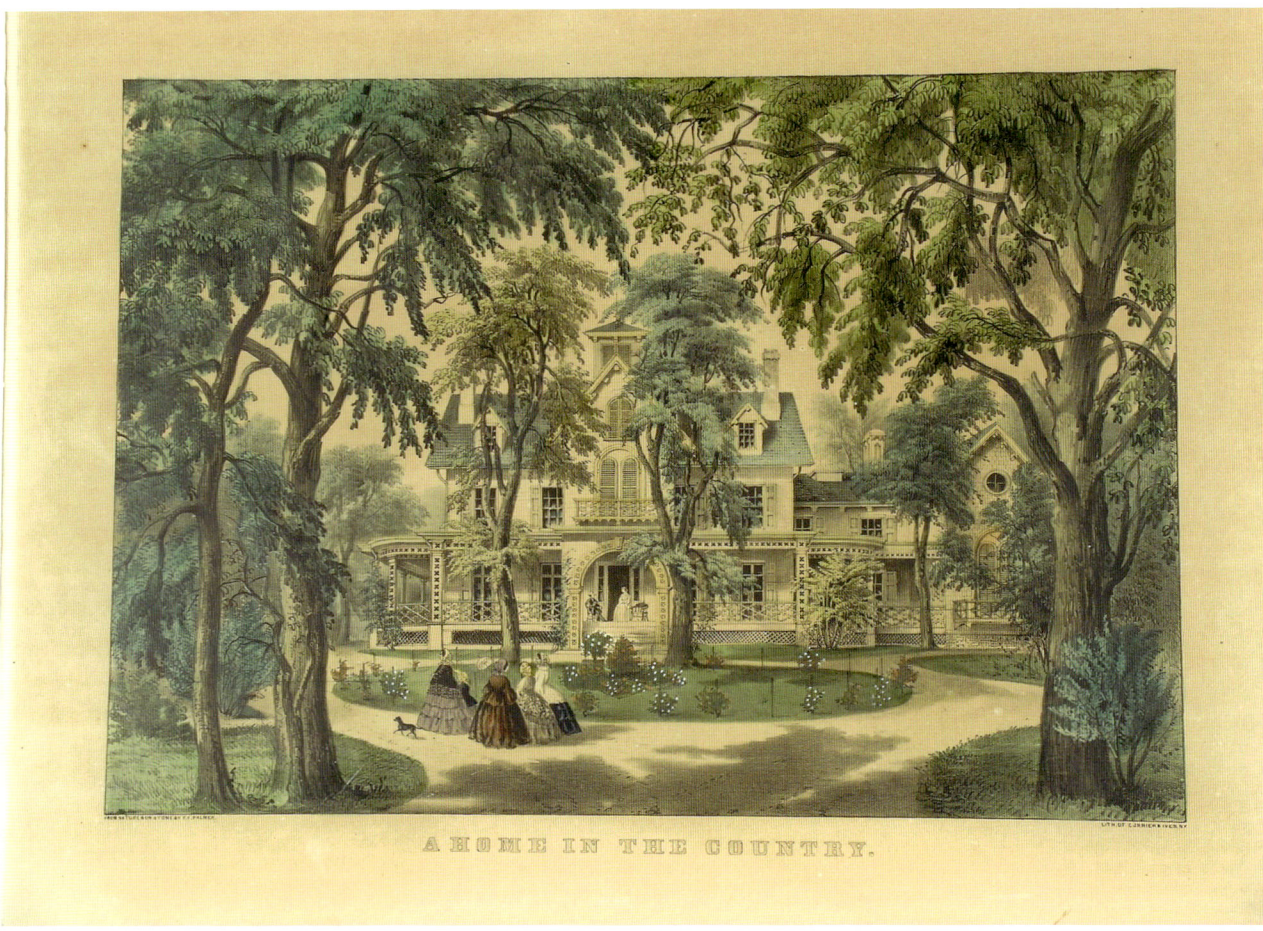

144. *A Home in the Country.*
Undated, ca. 1857–72. Printed
and published by Currier & Ives.
(Checklist 3-60)

In contrast to these galloping rhythms, *A Home in the Country* (undated, ca. 1857–72) is an image of symmetrical stability. Repeated arches formed by tall trees and the front entrance frame the lady of the house, who sits on her porch as in a shrine, while her women friends come to worship at her altar. The home is like a church, and, indeed, in that period the home was glorified as a kind of cathedral of social stability and morality. The vertical center line of the house, rising up to a tower, intersects the horizontal line of the porch roof all across the building, transforming the entire structure into a subliminally stated cross.

This seemingly simple design yields many small delights. Several motifs play against each other: the verticals of trees and house against the horizontal porch line; the curves of tree branches, archways, ladies' skirts, and circular window against the diagonal front roadways, roof lines, latticed porch rails, and jig-sawed ornament. The staging of the entire image, seen through openings between tall old trees, lends glamour to the scene, suggesting

the wealth of the owner who can afford such splendid landscaping. Indeed, the entire image is an ode to the ultimate status symbol—"a home in the country."

Perhaps the clearest illustration of Palmer's use of design elements can be found in the pair of prints that together made a strong statement about the Union's triumph and the dangers of secession and war. In *The Mississippi in Time of War* (gallery plate 12), a sword play of diagonal movements and a color scheme of murky black and fiery red emphasize the feeling of violence and conflict, whereas in the contrasting companion print, *The Mississippi in Time of Peace* (1865; gallery plate 11), repeated horizontals and verticals and orangey sunset colors emphasize the stable, joyous mood.

Note the canny way Palmer wove these images together, so that when hung together side by side they create one unified composition. Directing the eye almost cinematically, in and out, forward and back in an accordion movement, she created a continuous

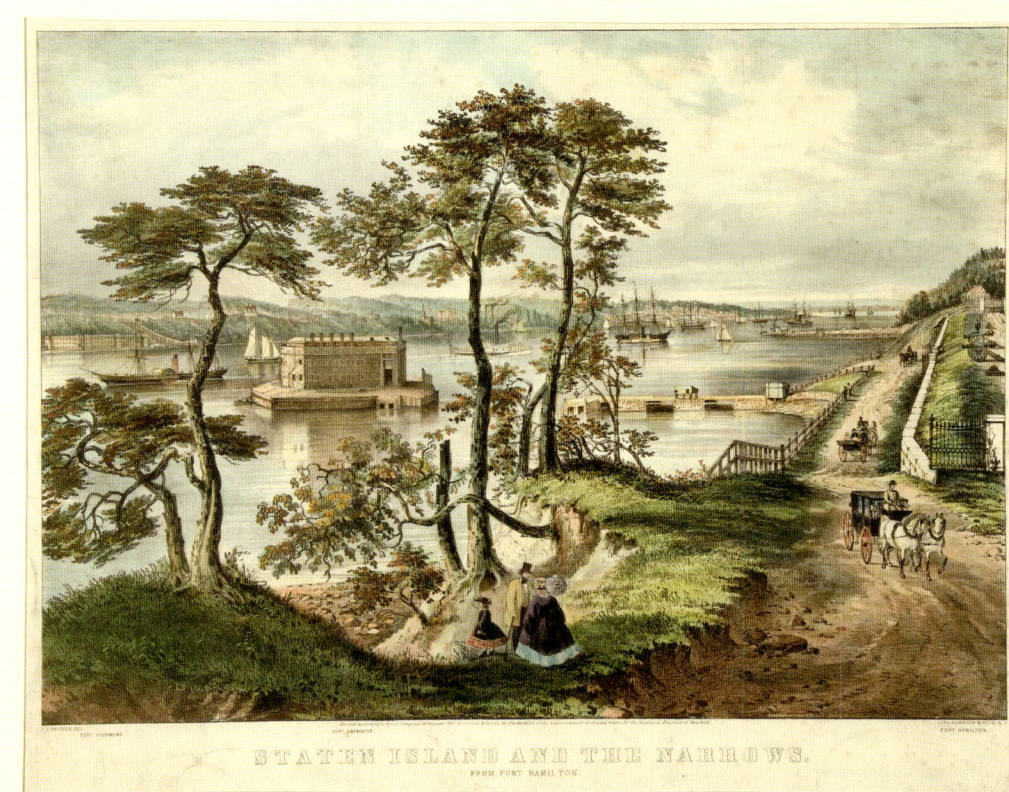

145. *Staten Island and the Narrows. From Fort Hamilton.* 1861. Printed and published by Currier & Ives. Courtesy of the Yale University Art Gallery. (Checklist 3-128)

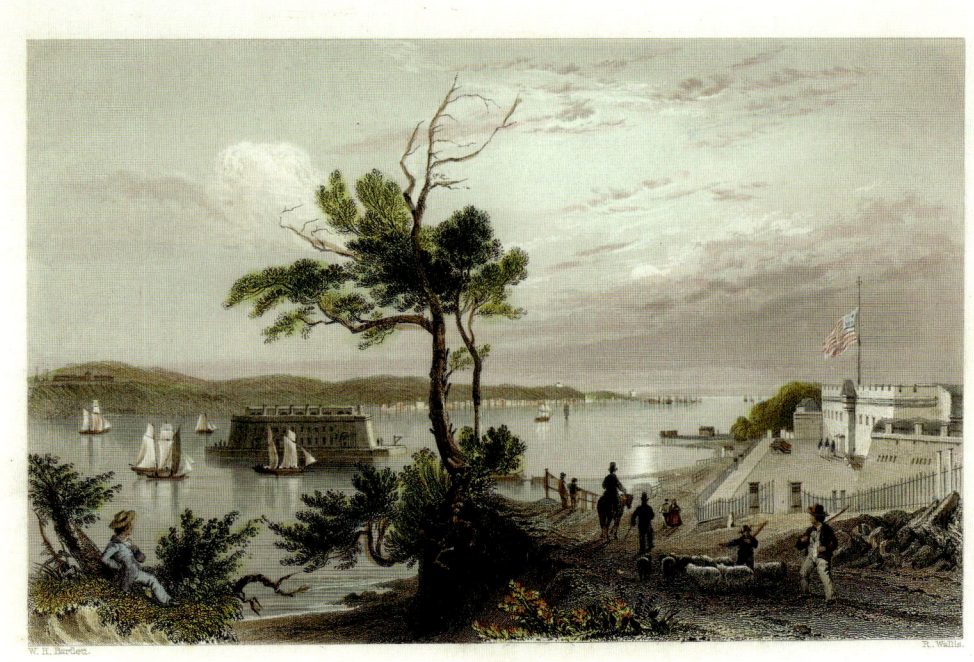

146. *The Narrows. (From Fort Hamilton.).* 1838. Steel plate engraving by R. Wallis after an illustration by William Henry Bartlett. Courtesy of the Old Print Shop.

mural-like composition. One can see how carefully this composition was planned by studying the preparatory watercolors at Boston's Museum of Fine Arts. In the study for *Peace* (1865; p. 194), the flatboat and its crew appear to be headed straight toward the viewer, more or less on the center line of the image. In the final lithograph, however, they have been tilted toward the right and are closer to the right side of the picture in order to counterbalance the lines of the ironclad and steamboat in the companion *War* print. This is just one of several small adjustments that strengthened the final diptych.

Palmer's fine sense of design becomes evident when we compare her lithograph *Staten Island and the Narrows. From Fort Hamilton* (1861; p. 183) to William Bartlett's earlier version of the same subject, *The Narrows. (From Fort Hamilton)* (1838; p. 183). Her skillful organization of space in *Staten Island* becomes obvious; she has tightened the entire composition. The exaggeratedly tall foreground trees are carefully designed to carve out interesting, harplike negative shapes and to serve as a frame for Fort Lafayette, a subject of particular interest at that time. The viewer focuses on the family group in the foreground and is then led around from point to point, while other elements are pruned and subordinated.

Light and Dark

Palmer was adept at massing or linking large light and dark shapes, often joining background and foreground areas so that they read as forms simultaneously on the flat surface and in space, creating a strong, unified design. This technique can be seen very obviously in *The Mississippi in Time of War* (gallery plate 12), in which a large arrowhead shape of light is surrounded by the dark forms of smoky sky, trees, and foreground shrubbery. Within the light area, the eye focuses on the dark silhouette of the ironclad blasting the shore. Other examples of this bold massing of light and dark are *A Night on the Hudson* (1864; gallery plate 13), *The "Lightning Express" Trains* (1863; gallery plate 10), and *The Trappers Camp-Fire* (1866; p. 165).

In some prints, the linkage is more subtle; in *The Happy Family. Ruffed Grouse and Young* (1866, gallery plate 21), the dark shapes of the background trees are linked with foreground darks, and the light of the background sky drifts down into the breast feathers of the birds in the foreground. The light opening of sky also serves to silhouette the proud profile of the father bird,

emphasizing his role as head of the family. Note that Palmer uses the formal elements for both aesthetic and expressive purposes, which, in fact, are inseparable.

Palmer also created lighting effects that enhance the drama of her compositions. For example, in *"Rounding a Bend" on the Mississippi. The parting Salute* (1866; p. 185), four different light sources illuminate the image: cold moonlight shines on the water and brightens the edges of clouds; red flames and sparks issue from smokestacks; boat windows glow with artificial yellow light; and a rainbow of fireworks marks the boat's departure. *A Night on the Hudson* also employs four different light sources. *The Trappers Camp-Fire* features a dramatic interplay between cold moonlight on snowy peaks and the reddish tones of a campfire illuminating men and horses.

A great sense of air, atmosphere, and deep space permeates many of Palmer's prints; the weather and time of day are often keenly observed. In *American Farm Scenes. No. 4* (1853; gallery plate 4), for example, the crisp, cold air is beautifully suggested in lowering gray skies over snowy expanses. In *Gray's Elegy. In a Country Church Yard* (p. 157), the somber mood of descending dusk is captured in a harmony of gray and golden tones. Spring, summer, autumn, and winter as well as early morning, noon, late afternoon, and night are artfully evoked in Palmer's work. *Winter Morning* (1861; p. 186), with its masses of snow on roofs and pine branches and its cattle footprints in a slushy barnyard, almost has the character of a Japanese woodcut. Currier & Ives catalog descriptions show that the partners were keenly aware of Palmer's fine use of atmospheric effects (using, for example, the descriptions "the sky empurpled with the rich tints of the rising sun" and "a vivid representation of autumnal sky and foliage"[4]).

Color

It was not easy to obtain fine color effects with crude mass-production methods of applying hand-painted watercolor over black-and-white prints; the colors had to be simplified in order to publish prints in large quantities at low prices. But Palmer used her thorough knowledge of printmaking to create rich effects with simple means. In *Winter Morning*, for example, the key black-and-white print establishes both the outline and areas of gray, leaving large white spaces bare for snowy areas. A pale-blue tone is used for sky, shutters, shingled barn roof, and shadows on white snow. Linked areas of brown, beige, and gold connect the

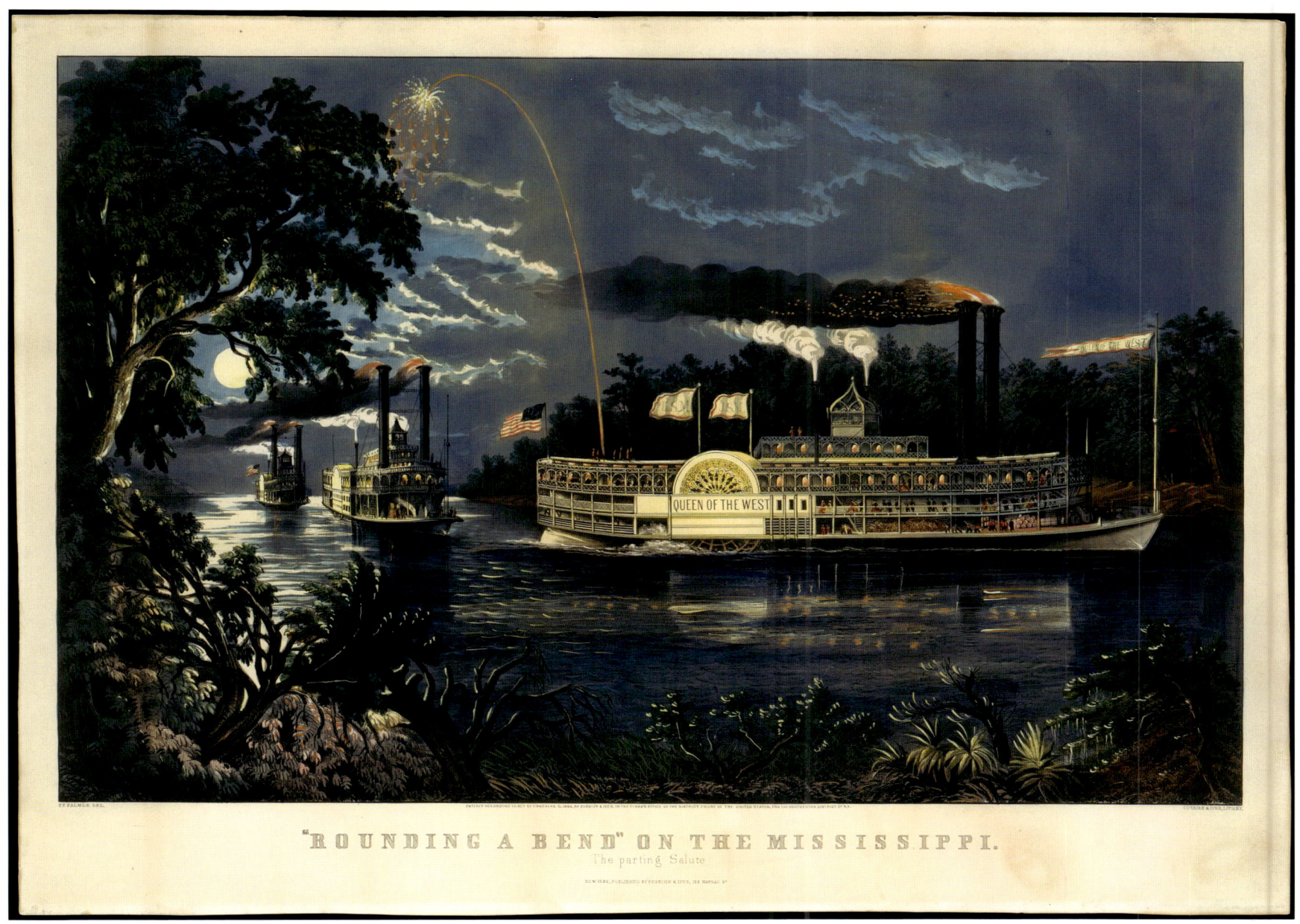

"ROUNDING A BEND" ON THE MISSISSIPPI.
The parting Salute

147. *"Rounding a Bend" on the Mississippi. The parting Salute.*
1866. Printed and published by Currier & Ives. Courtesy of the Old
Print Shop. (Checklist 3-118)

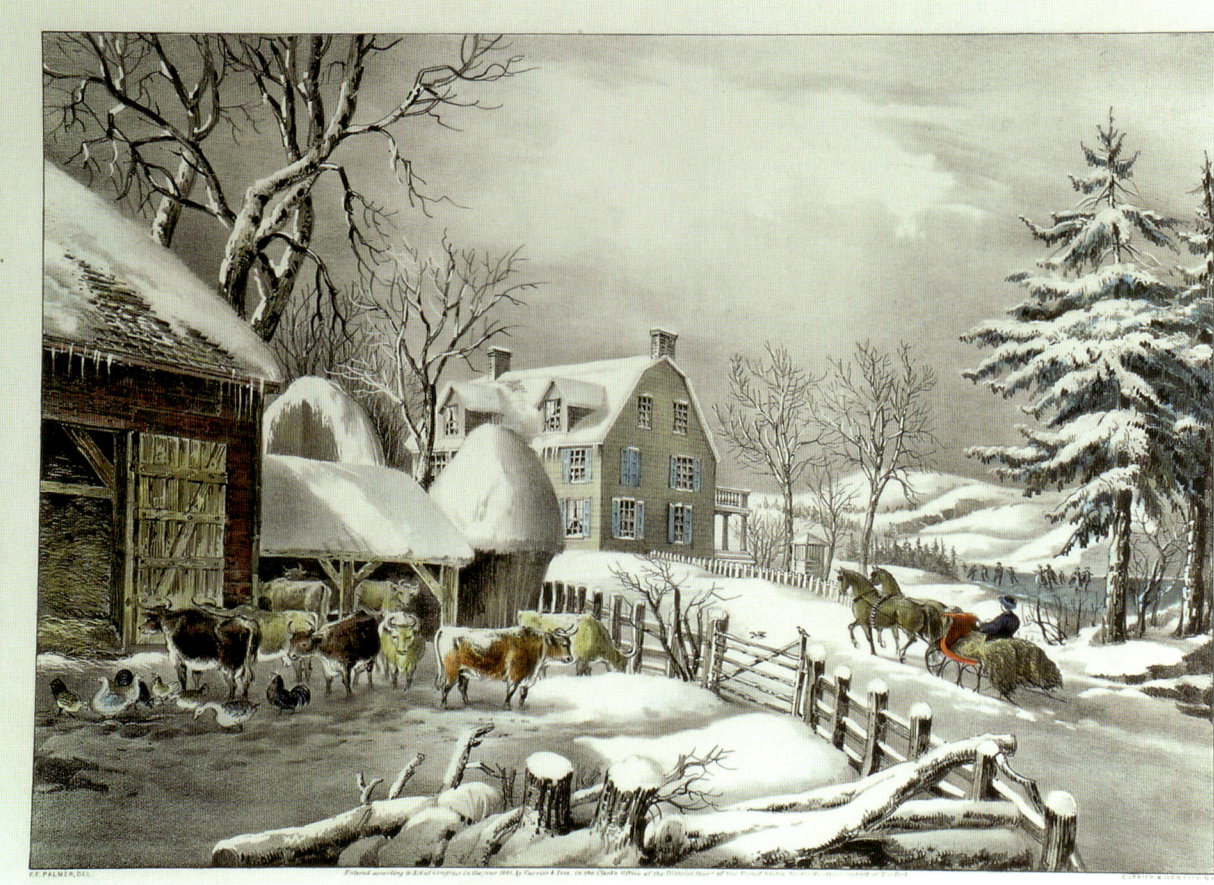

148. *Winter Morning.* 1861. Printed and published by Currier & Ives. (Checklist 3-173)

barn, animals, house, horse, and driver; a small bright accent—a touch of red—appears on the sleigh. This is a standard method of organizing color in her compositions, using relatively quiet hues throughout and then introducing accents of red, blue, or other color in the clothing of her figures or on another focus of interest. An obvious example is *Trolling for Blue Fish* (1866; gallery plate 17), in which the red shirt of the man at the helm shines out against a scheme of blues, greens, and grays. In a number of prints, highlights of opaque white gouache and the shiny transparent gloss of gum arabic were added in places to enhance the richness of colors.

On the whole, the color in Palmer's prints, which in the early years was sometimes a bit thin—more like a tinted drawing—later increased in richness and saturation. In *The Happy Family. Ruffed Grouse and Young* (gallery plate 21), deep woodland tones of green, brown, and rust are heightened by the bright-red accents of a few berries. In *Landscape, Fruit and Flowers* (1862; gallery plate 23), she orchestrates a glowing, interwoven bouquet of colors in a fine balance of warm and cool tones.

It is necessary to point out, however, that despite the painted models that Palmer provided for the company's artists to copy, the color in the prints is far from uniform. Each of the skilled hand colorists who worked on the larger, more-expensive compositions had a slightly different touch. It is possible, for example, to examine two prints of *The Four Seasons of Life: Childhood* (1868; p. 147) and find that in one the wild flowers in the foreground are outlined in red and white gouache and in the other are painted in transparent red and purple without an outline. In a way, this is part of the charm of these prints; no two are exactly alike.

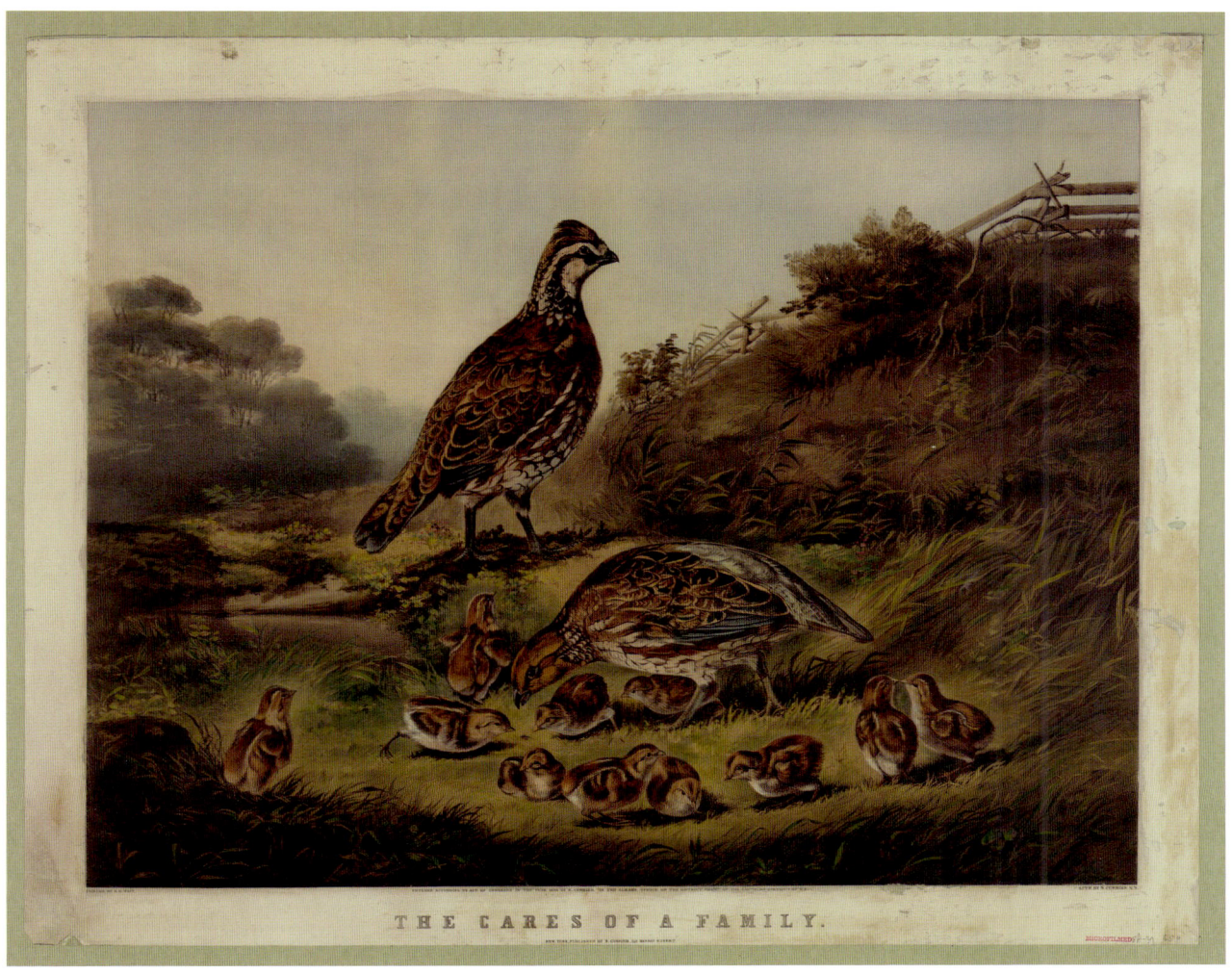

149. *The Cares of a Family.* 1856. By A. F. Tait. Printed and published by N. Currier. Courtesy of the Prints and Photographs Division, Library of Congress, LC-DIG-pga-00625.

Some print dealers have further complicated the situation by occasionally adding their own colors to faded or black-and-white prints; a reliable dealer will inform the purchaser if the color has been enhanced. And of course there is color variation owing to fading and deterioration from exposure to light and moisture, improper framing, and poor restoration. One cannot assume that any individual print shows the precise colors that Palmer intended. It is necessary to look at many copies of the same print as well as examples in carefully preserved museum collections in order to determine the artist's original color vision.

Thousands of schoolchildren also colored black-and-white prints in classrooms, and amateurs bought them to paint as they fancied. This practice was encouraged in a company catalog list of uncolored prints, which included amusingly elaborate instructions for transforming them into "Grecian Oil Paintings," "Diaphanic

Pictures or Paintings on Glass," or watercolors. To make a watercolor from a print, that catalog instructed, "it will be necessary to size them [i.e., coat the paper], so that the colors will remain on the surface and not sink into the paper. . . . Dissolve ¼ pound of best glue in one gallon of water over night. Put it in a kettle and warm (not boil) up, and add ½ an ounce of alum."[5] Needless to say, the results of these amateur efforts varied widely.

PATTERN AND DECORATION

More than any other staff artist at Currier & Ives, Palmer emphasized decorative rhythms in her compositions. This can be seen most obviously in her still lifes, but it is a characteristic that runs through her work. If we compare her images of game and fish to Arthur Tait's more naturalistic ones, their ornamental character

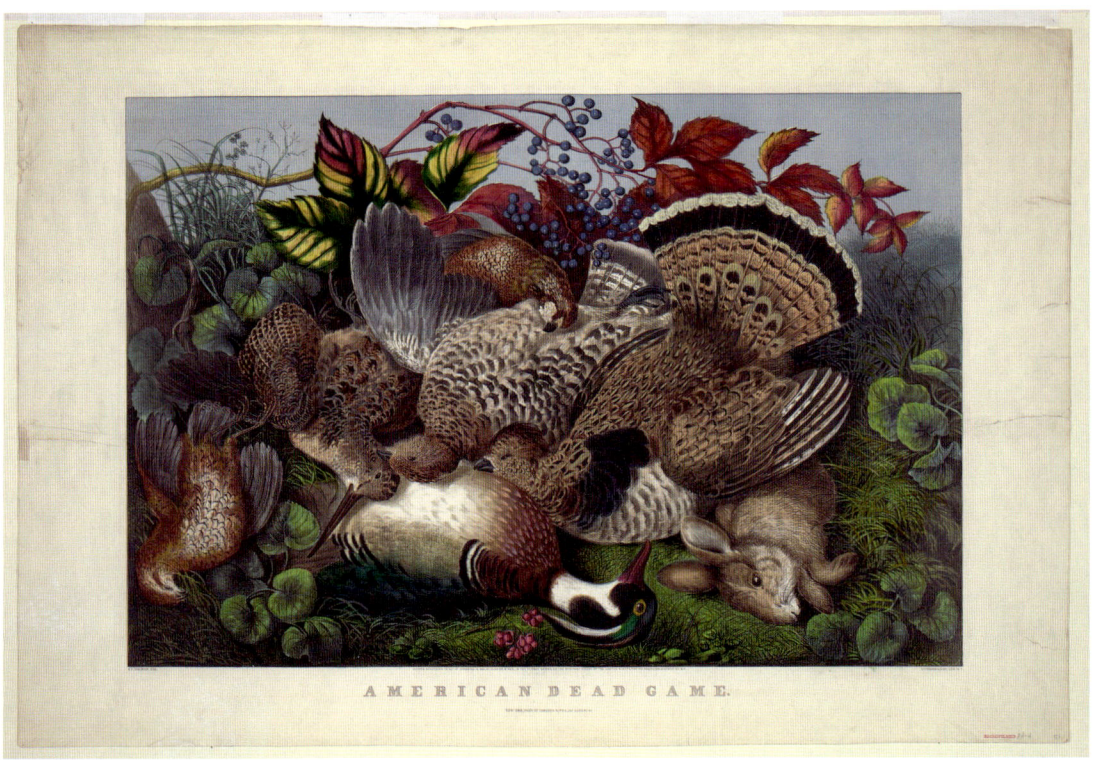

AMERICAN DEAD GAME.

150. *American Dead Game*. 1866. Printed and published by Currier & Ives. Courtesy of the Prints and Photographs Division, Library of Congress, LC-DIG-pga-00591. (Checklist 3-7)

becomes obvious. Note the fine patterning of feathers and leaves in *The Happy Family. Ruffed Grouse and Young* (gallery plate 21) and the pattern on pattern in *American Forest Game* (1866; p. 155). This patterning even gets a bit out of hand in *American Dead Game* (1866), where she almost abandons reality, caught up in a frenzy of patterned feathers, grasses, and furry pelts.

Palmer delighted in the patterns and textures of flowers, leaves, and grasses in the foregrounds of landscapes. In *The Trappers Camp-Fire. A Friendly Visitor* (1866; p. 205), a decorative arbor of trees and leaves around the figures lends a fairy-tale aura to a romantic image of the early West. In *Close Quarters* (1866; gallery plate 16) and *Pointing a Bevy* (1866; gallery plate 15), each one a close-up of a hunting dog sniffing out a game bird in the brush, she combines close observation of the animals with an almost art deco stylization of form, set against a tapestry-like background of grasses and wildflowers. *The Pioneer's Home. On the Western Frontier* (1867; p. 166), an image that might have been treated more literally by her colleagues (i.e., Tait and Maurer), reveals an interplay of patterns in the log cabin, piled logs, log bridge, leafy forest trees, haystacks, and feathers and pelts of dead game.

In general, one can also say that whereas several of her colleagues attempted to emulate the smooth look of oil paintings, her work consistently emphasizes the graphic line of the printmaker.

LITHOGRAPHIC TECHNIQUE

Intimately acquainted with every phase of production, Palmer knew how to squeeze the most out of the lithographic process. She enriched the textures and dark-and-light values in her prints by playing off lively scribbled strokes on plants, leaves, and tree bark against smoothly rendered areas such as the sides of buildings and distant mountains. She often scraped or blocked out parts of the greasy ink on the tint stone to create white areas such as clouds or scratched white highlights into dark crayon tones with a sharp instrument. This scratched calligraphy can be seen, for example, in the grasses of sporting scenes (e.g., *Wild Duck Shooting* [1852; gallery plate 22]), in traces left by skaters on the ice in *American Winter Scenes. Morning* (1854; p. 112), or in the texture of the bear's fur in *The Mountain Pass. Sierra Nevada* (1867; p. 217). *The Hudson River Steamboat "St. John"* (1864; p. 189) illustrates her use of scraped or dragged crayon tones to create reflections

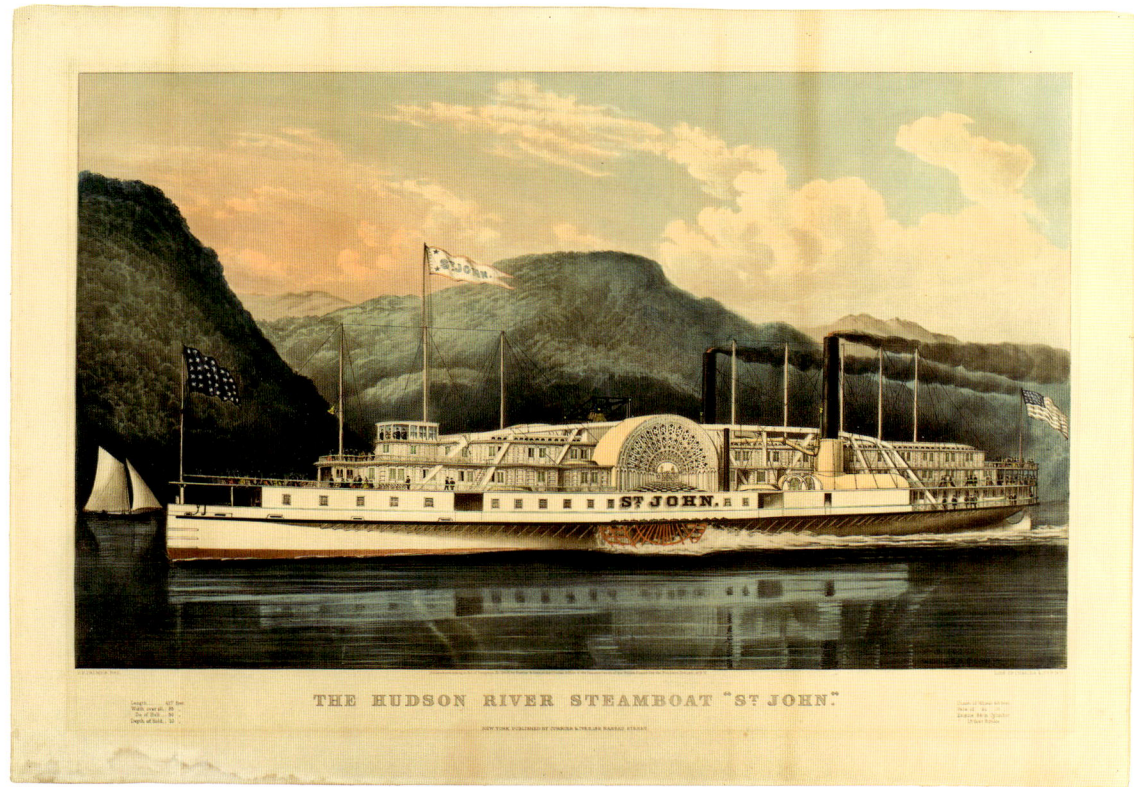

151. *The Hudson River Steamboat "St. John."* 1864. Printed and published by Currier & Ives. Courtesy of the New-York Historical Society. (Checklist 3-65)

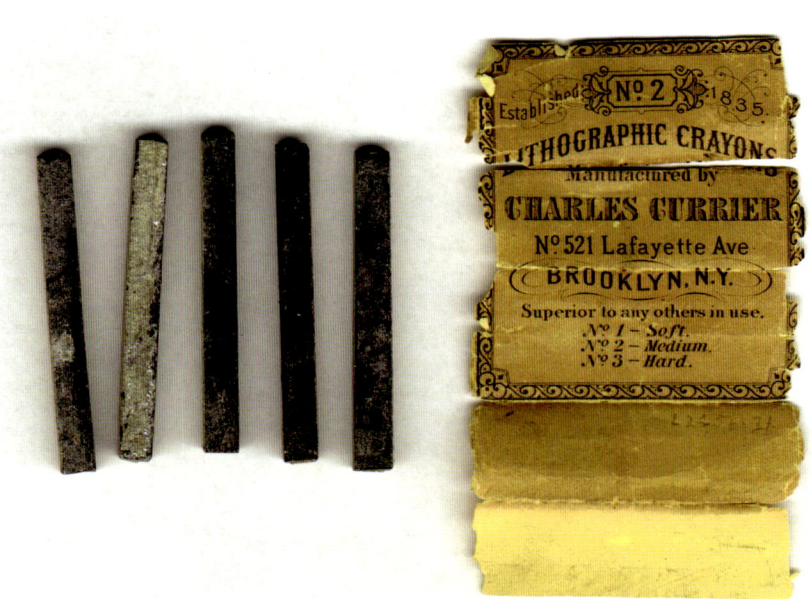

152. Package of No. 2 Lithographic Crayons manufactured by Charles Currier. Louis Maurer Collection. Courtesy of the American Antiquarian Society.

in the water. The artist occasionally made fine lines with a pen dipped in lithograph ink.

Although not the first to use a tint stone in the United States—William Sharp and Francis Michelin had employed them by 1840—Palmer was certainly early in doing so. Currier had published a few tinted prints before Palmer became a full-time employee around 1849, but she was one of the earliest to use the method at his company on a regular basis, in some cases laying down two colors from two separate stones under the black-and-white print.

A fine example of her use of a tint stone is the mauve background in *American Autumn Fruits* (1865; p. 153), leaving the paper bare where the white glass compote holds the fruit. After printing the black-and-white key print over the background tint, hand-painted watercolor was added, giving a rich effect of color shining through glass. In other prints, she used tinted areas for blue skies and green foregrounds or warm overall background tints to create the glowing effects of sunset and other atmospheric tonalities. Final touches of white gouache and a coating of gum arabic in places made highlights sparkle and colors richer.

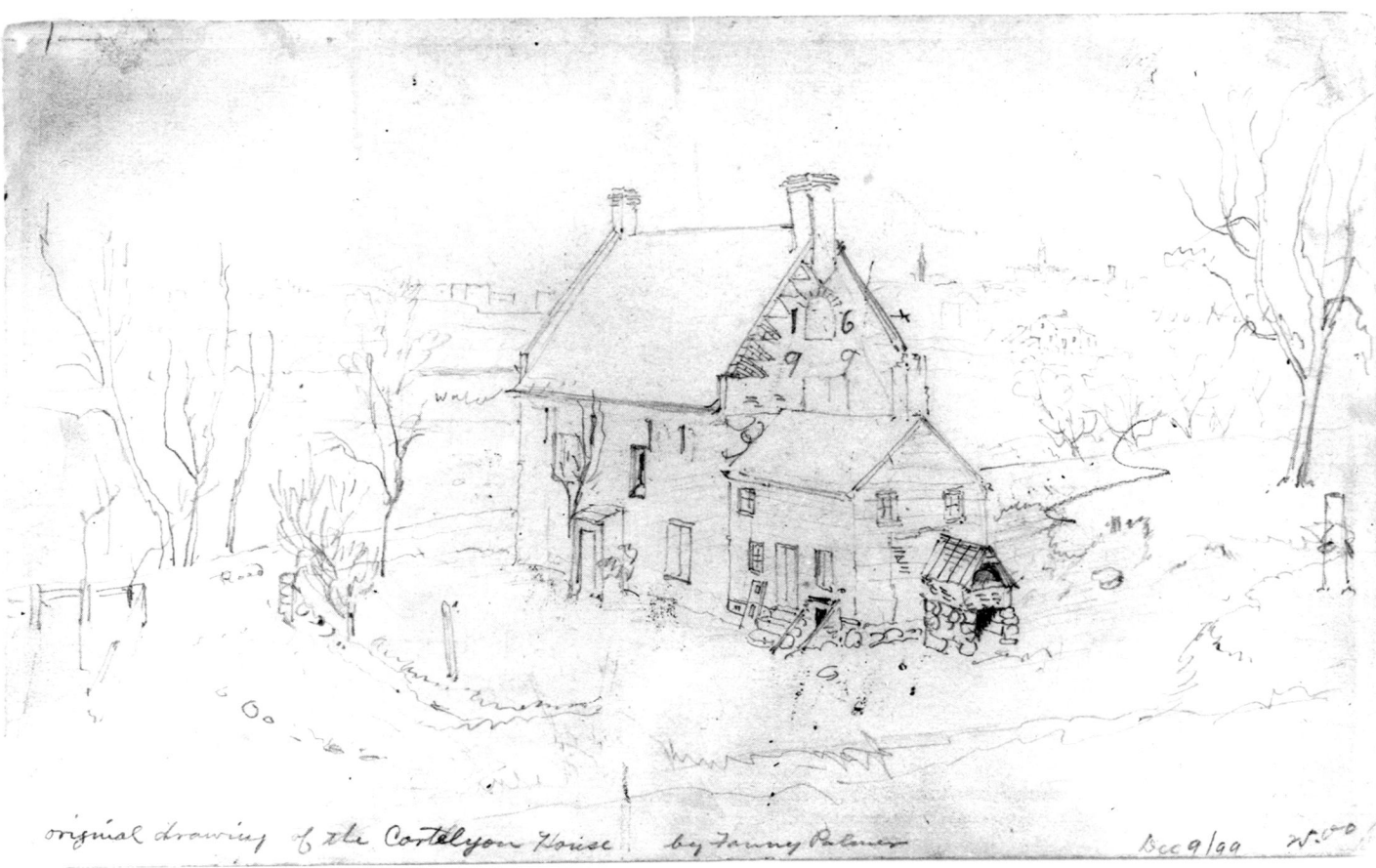

original drawing of the Cortelyou House   by Fanny Palmer   Dec 9/00   N.00

153. *Vechte-Cortelyou House, Gowanus, Brooklyn*, N.Y. Undated. Graphite on paper. Courtesy of the New-York Historical Society. (Checklist 4-21)

Because of Palmer's great knowledge of the medium, Charles Currier, who at one point lived near her in Brooklyn, enlisted her aid when he was developing an improved formula for his lithograph crayon. While he modified the proportions in his witch's brew of heated ingredients (wax, soap, suet, lamp-black, shellac, etc.), she tested the final product. They were an odd couple, the free-wheeling brother of Nathaniel Currier and the disciplined woman artist—colleagues differing in personality but bound by an intense search for an improved methodology in their field. The resulting crayons, regarded as superior to the finest French imports, were used exclusively by Currier & Ives. The only problem was that Charles didn't produce them fast enough. Exasperated, Nathaniel once offered to supply his brother with all the raw materials he needed if he would only turn out the crayons in larger quantities, but Charles, in his usual independent way, preferred to make them at his own pace. The manufacture of these crayons provided a basic income for Charles and several sons, but Mrs.

Palmer doesn't seem to have made any money from her participation in developing the new crayons. Her contribution to this effort is an example of the generosity toward her fellow artists described by those who knew her.[6]

DRAWINGS

Palmer undoubtedly made hundreds of drawings during her long career in the United States, but few have survived. Almost all that have turned up are preparatory studies for prints, usually sketched in soft pencil on both sides of the paper for economy's sake. As a result, many are rather faint, smudged by time and handling. They range from rapid on-site notations to large contour drawings, ready for transfer to the stone.

Her early drawings in England were competent but relatively pedestrian. Pencil drawings for wood engravings in *The Midland Counties' Railway Companion* (1840) already show a sturdy,

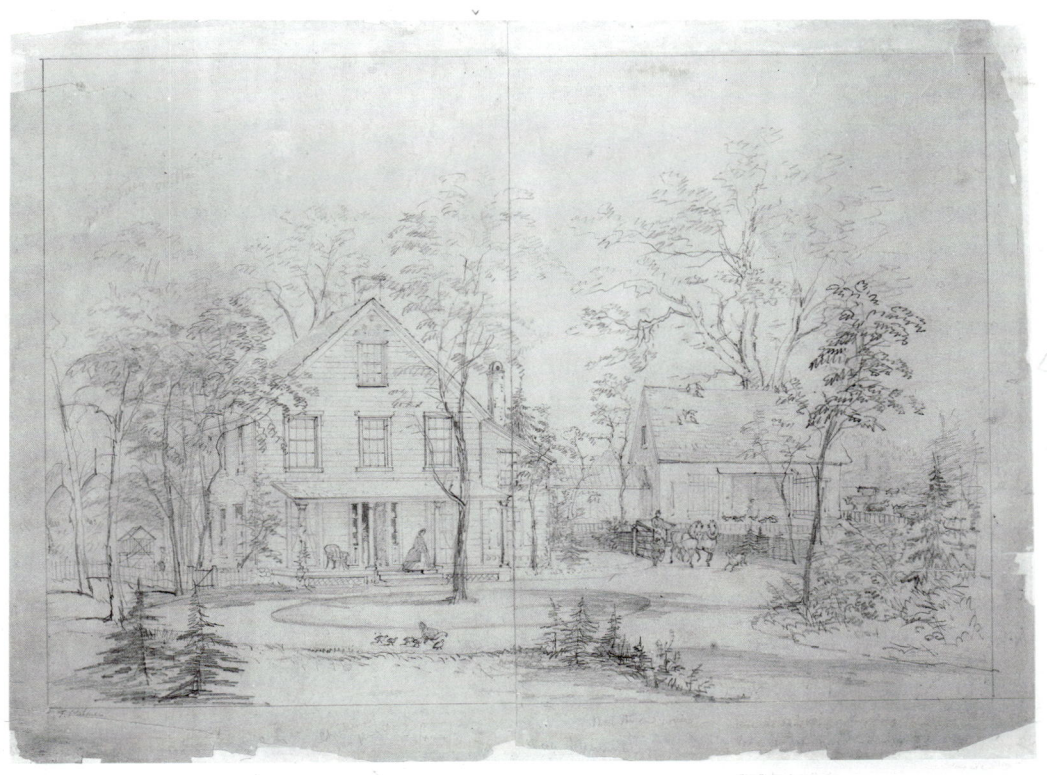

154. *Farmers Home—Summer.* Undated, ca. 1864? Pencil drawing, 19 × 25⅞ in. Courtesy of the Museum of Fine Arts, Boston. Gift of Maxim Karolik for the M. and M. Karolik Collection of American Watercolors and Drawings, 1800–1875. Photograph © 2017 Museum of Fine Arts, Boston. (Checklist 4-3)

155. *The Farmers Home—Summer.* 1864. Printed and published by Currier & Ives. Courtesy of the Yale University Art Gallery. (Checklist 3-43)

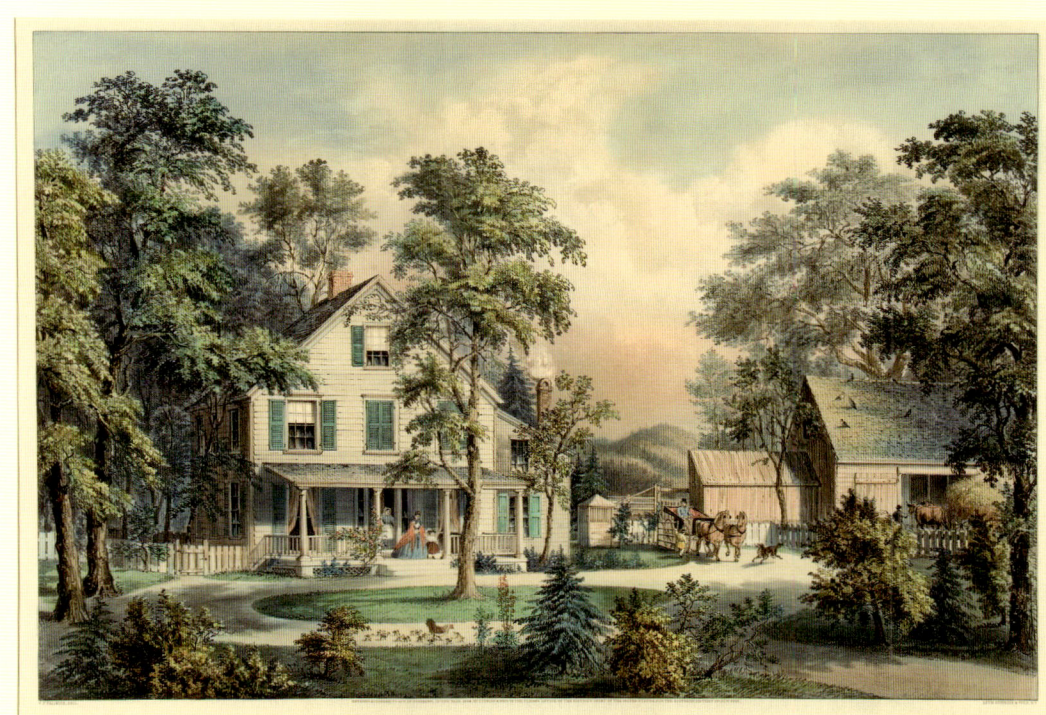

THE FARMERS HOME — SUMMER.

confident, but rather hard line (pp. 9, 342). By the time the artist and her husband began to publish the Sketches in Leicestershire series in 1842, her technique was becoming more sophisticated. After immigrating to New York City, Palmer developed the springy line and characteristic handwriting or calligraphy shown in feathery leaves on trees, striated rocks, textured grasses and plants in foregrounds, and velvety tones on the backs of animals, walls, and other smooth surfaces.

A quick notation of the lower New York skyline and a small sketch of Castle Garden below it on the same sheet (New-York Historical Society; p. 24) show her ability to capture the essentials in a few lines. In a full-page drawing of the Vechte-Corte-lyou House (New-York Historical Society; p. 190), Palmer's changing pencil pressure accents the worn details of the picturesque old ruin in contrast to the faint skyline of the distant city; the notations "road" and "water" are there to remind the artist of these details if she were to attempt to transform the subject into a print. Another sketch, *West Point Academy* (Museum of Fine Arts, Boston; p. 132), evidently drawn from life to use as the background for her lithograph *U.S. Military Academy, West Point* (1862; p. 132), shows how she set up a landscape to which she or a colleague could later add figures. In her study for *Low Water in the Mississippi* (1868; p. 145) (Museum of the City of New York), a graceful contour line encloses a spacious, airy scene of boats coming and going on the great river.

Several drawings document the artist's interaction with her employers. Perhaps the most elegant example of a Palmer pencil drawing is her preparatory contour study for *The Farmers Home—Summer* (1864; p. 191) in the collection of the Museum of Fine Arts, Boston. The artist, then at the height of her powers, drew a lady and her little girl on their front porch awaiting a carriage being driven out of the barn. With a free, lively, and economical line, she delicately but precisely suggests an entire environment, including trees and shrubs framing the house, a hen and chicks pecking on the circular driveway, the driver and pair of fine horses, cattle in the field, haystacks, pigeons on the roof, and other details of country life. Her employer's pencil notations are all over this drawing. On the lower right, there are scribbled notes: "move the barn," "leave out cattle," "let a load of hay be driving to Barn," and on the upper left, "more trees on this side." After crossing out a rear chimney, the word *smoke* was added to another chimney; a well was crossed out on the left and inscribed, "well this end [right side] of house." All of these instructions were carried out in the

final print, resulting in a tighter, more-compressed composition, framed by large masses of trees. However, some of the freshness and delightful detail in the original composition was lost.

Palmer was especially noted for her rendering of architecture and won praise for the accuracy and precision of her railroad trains, sailing ships, steamboats, and other technological subjects. But she was recognized above all for landscapes and country scenes, many of which featured animals—cows, oxen, birds, sheep, and especially dogs.

The artist's weak point was the human figure. When Palmer drew directly from life, as seems to be the case in the view of *Loughborough from Cotes Hill* (1842; p. 19) and in her early sporting prints for Nathaniel Currier, the results were better. In certain works, she seems to have used stock figures of the kind that appeared in fashion and ladies magazines. They function successfully, especially when they are used to show upper-class ladies sauntering in full skirts and bonnets and gentlemen in tall hats. One must note, however, that the Currier & Ives practice of having other artists draw the figures in some of her compositions did not always produce happy results. Even in instances where figures drawn by the artist herself seem a bit naive, they are more in harmony with the graphic line and character of her work than, for example, some of the stubby figures added by John Cameron in later prints.

PAINTINGS AND WASH DRAWINGS

With one exception, Palmer's surviving wash drawings are, like the pencil drawings, preliminary studies for lithographs rather than finished works intended to be viewed on their own. They are sometimes broadly blocked in, using a casual style suited to the visualization of a print.

In a study for *View of Astoria, L.I. From the New York Side* (1862; p. 193) (New-York Historical Society), Palmer used a few deft strokes to flick in the boats, trees, and opposite shoreline, and washed in the main masses of dark and light, indicating the changing ribbons of water as they ripple from midstream to shore. The prow of an anchored sailing vessel on the left was later omitted from the final print, probably to focus more attention on the image of the steamboat *Sylvan Grove*, a subject of particular interest to the public at that time.

Other preliminary watercolor sketches include the vigorously brushed *Terrific Engagement between the "Monitor" 2 Guns,*

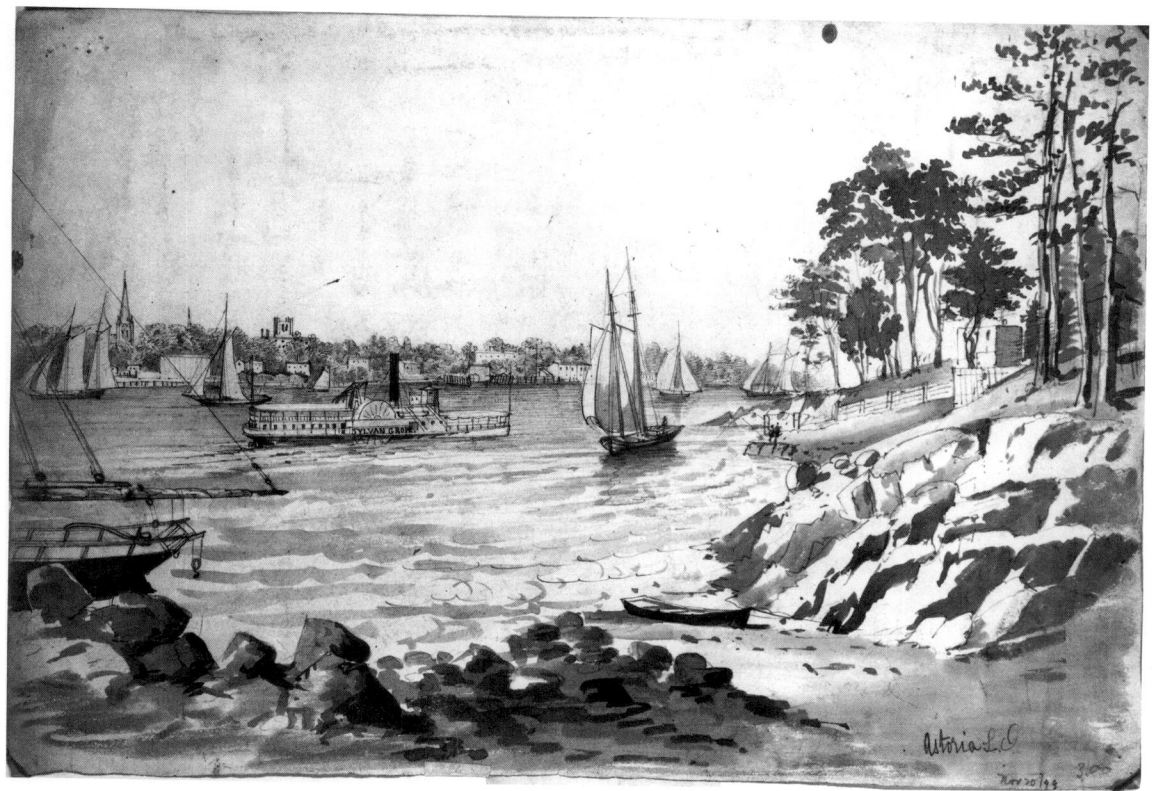

156. *View of Astoria, Long Island From the New York Side.* Undated, ca. 1862. Water and pencil on paper. Courtesy of the New-York Historical Society. (Checklist 4-23)

157. *Hudson from West Point, N.Y.* Undated, ca. 1862. Watercolor on paper. Courtesy of the New-York Historical Society. (Checklist 4-6)

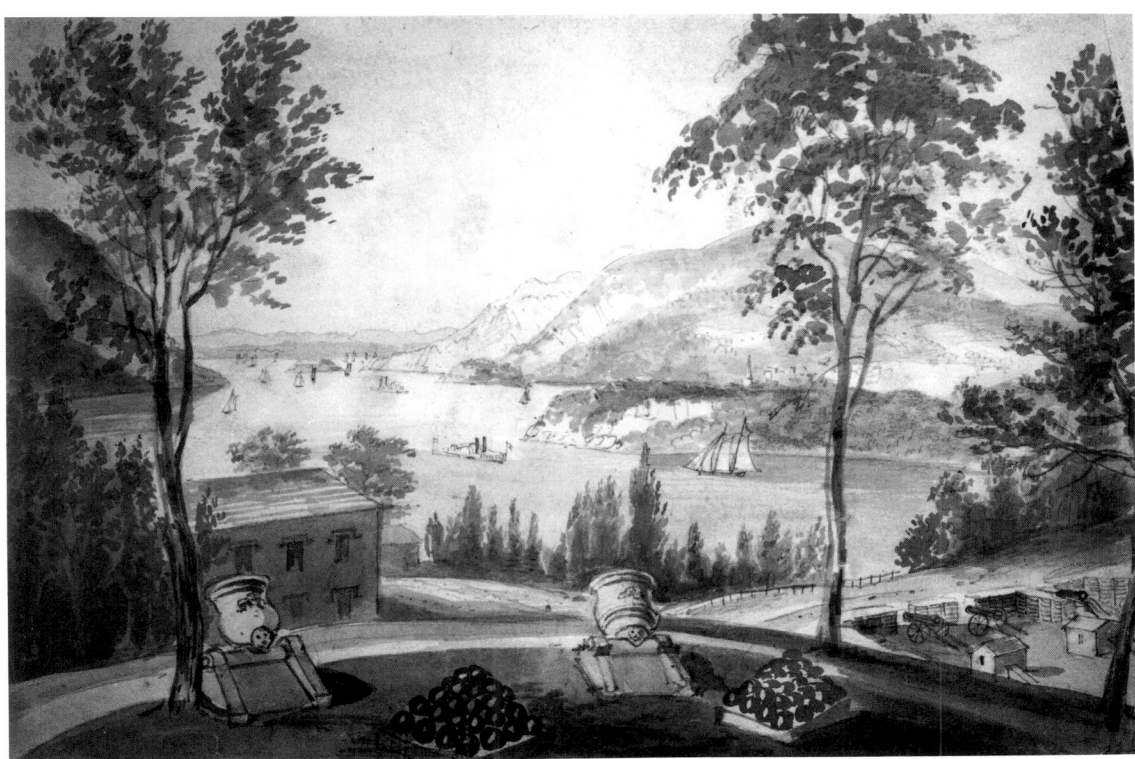

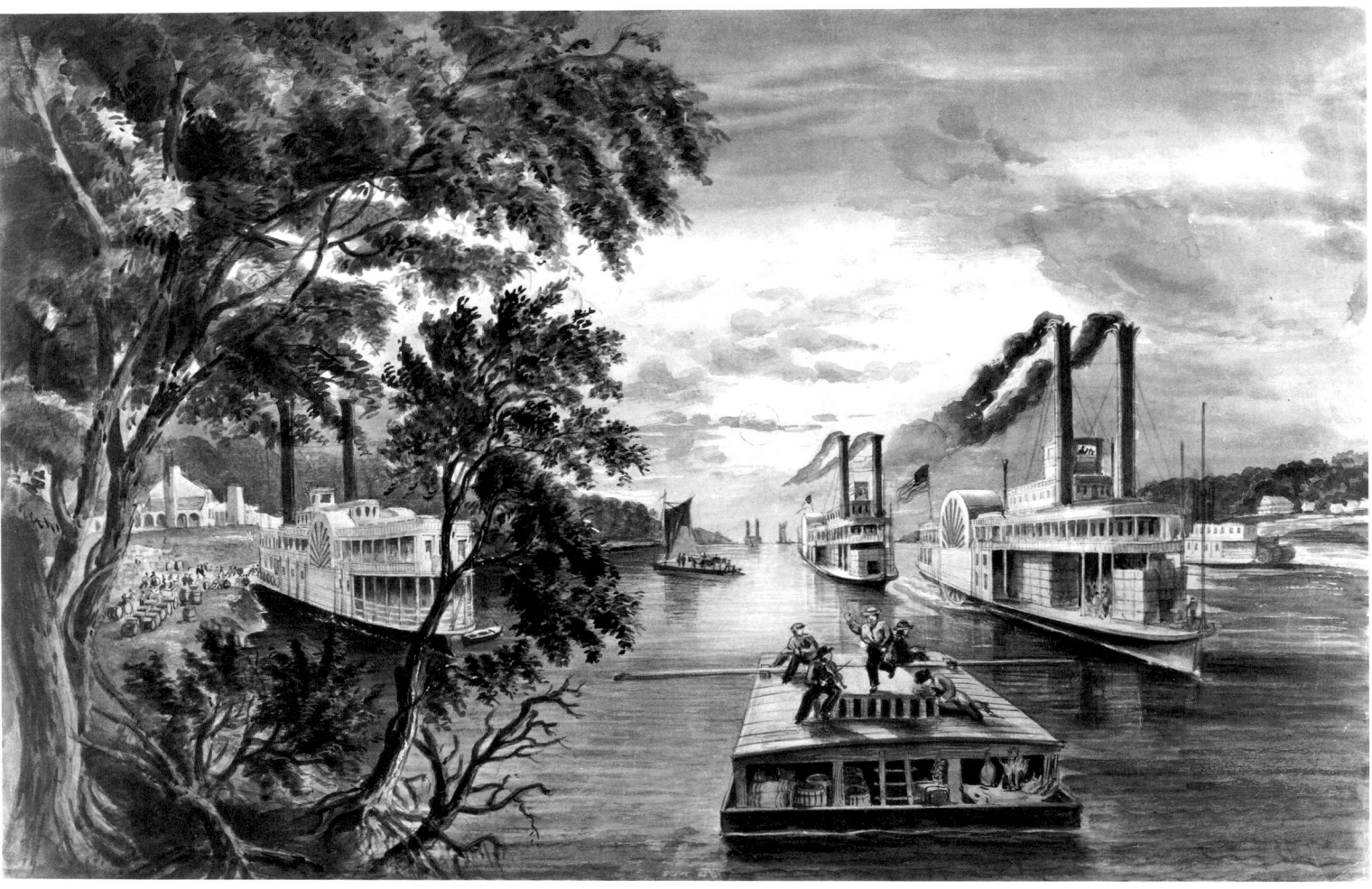

and *"Merrimac" 10 Guns* (undated, ca. 1862, New-York Historical Society; p. 140), *Hudson from West Point, N.Y.* (undated, ca. 1862, New-York Historical Society; p. 193), *The Old Farm Gate* (undated, Museum of the City of New York), and several loose, washy studies of horses and cattle in the countryside. In contrast, the pencil-and-watercolor study of the naval attack on Fort Fisher, *Landing at Fort Fisher* (1865, US Marine Corps Museums Art Collection), includes delicate but precisely rendered details (with a pale suggestion of added color) of each boat and ironclad vessel in the large flotilla firing on the fort.

Of those that have survived, Palmer's richest and most fully realized preparatory paintings are unquestionably *The Mississippi in Time of Peace* and *The Mississippi in Time of War* (1865 and 1862, Museum of Fine Arts, Boston; pp. 194–95). The artist seems to have put her whole heart into developing this pair of watercolors as completely as possible. Sue Welsh Reed and Carol Troyen have analyzed her style and sources of inspiration for these two works:

Palmer's watercolor technique is rather conventional, and reflects both her early exposure to the British landscape tradition and the requirements of commercial practice. Thin translucent washes cover the whole of the sheet; some textural variety

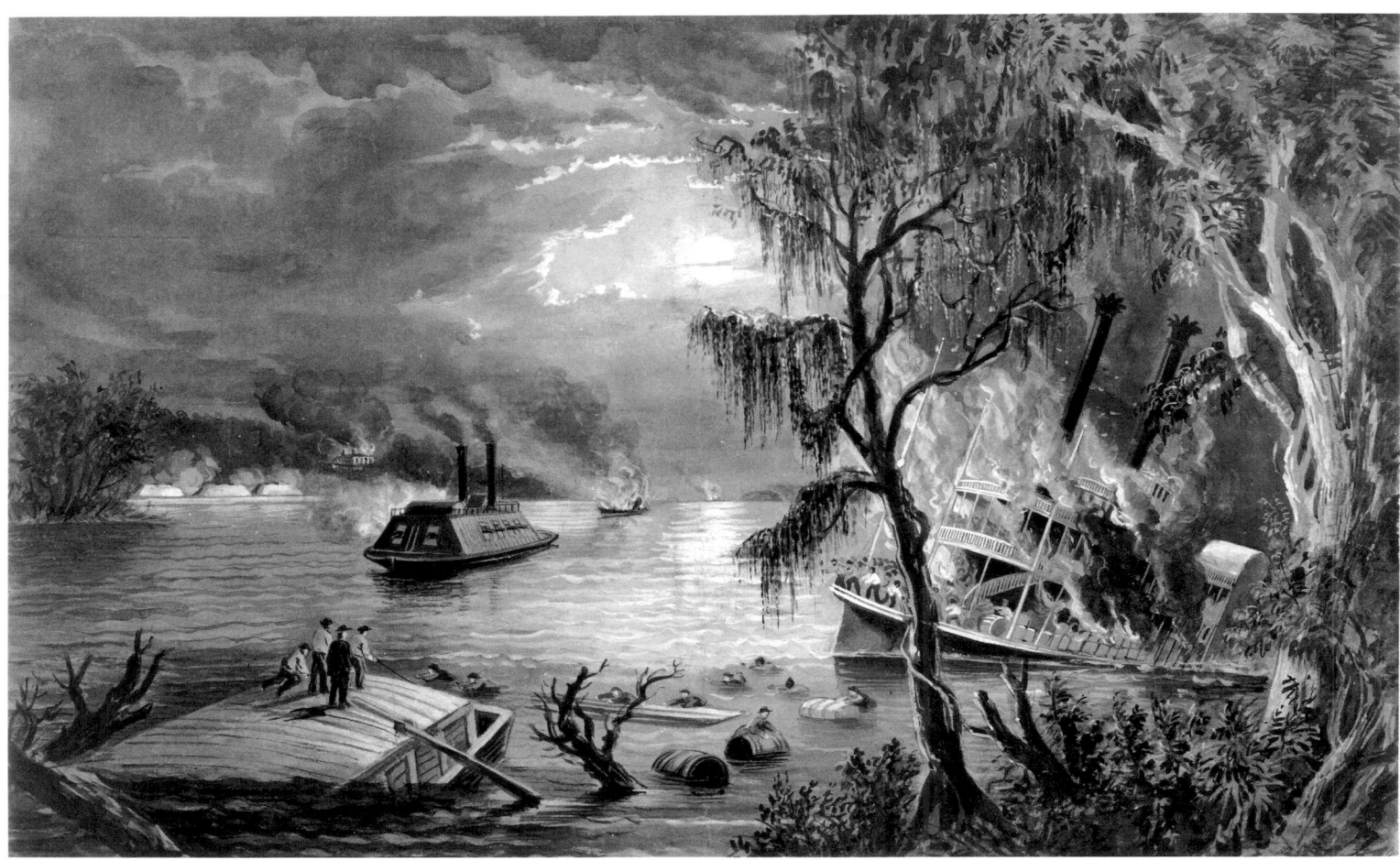

159. *The Mississippi in Time of War.* 1862. Watercolor, colored crayons, and pencil on paper. Courtesy of the Museum of Fine Arts, Boston. Gift of Maxim Karolik for the M. and M. Karolik Collection of American Watercolors and Drawings, 1800–1875. Photograph © 2017 Museum of Fine Arts, Boston. (Checklist 4-12)

is provided by short, dense, fringelike strokes, alternating with wavy ribbons of color, especially in the foliage, and by opaque white in such areas as the masts of the foundering boat and the underbellies of the clouds. . . . *The Mississippi in Time of War* is painted almost in grisaille, with accents in the acid, electric colors beloved of an earlier generation of topographical painters in watercolor, among them Nicolino Calyo and Michele Felice Corné. This dramatic palette, unusual for Palmer[,] . . . demonstrates her adaptability: although most of the subjects she

painted are picturesque, charming views, here she successfully employs the ingredients of the horrific sublime. Her colors are the violent tones of Vesuvius erupting; her trees are a shocked and shattered reflection of the human cataclysm; and her sky, eerily animated by the full moon, is heavy with clouds.[7]

Only one watercolor, *Samuel Fleet Homestead* (undated, ca. 1850s, Brooklyn Museum), seems to be a finished painting with no connection to a print. Perhaps commissioned by the owner of the fine property on the corner of Fulton and Gold Streets in Brooklyn, this carefully rendered view of a mansion on parklike grounds, with carriages and well-dressed pedestrians animating the streets around it, reveals Palmer's "deft touch and control of the watercolor medium and her eye for detail."[8] Indeed, each tree seems to be an individual portrait rendered in varying feathery strokes. The artist reflects the trend at midcentury to imitate oil

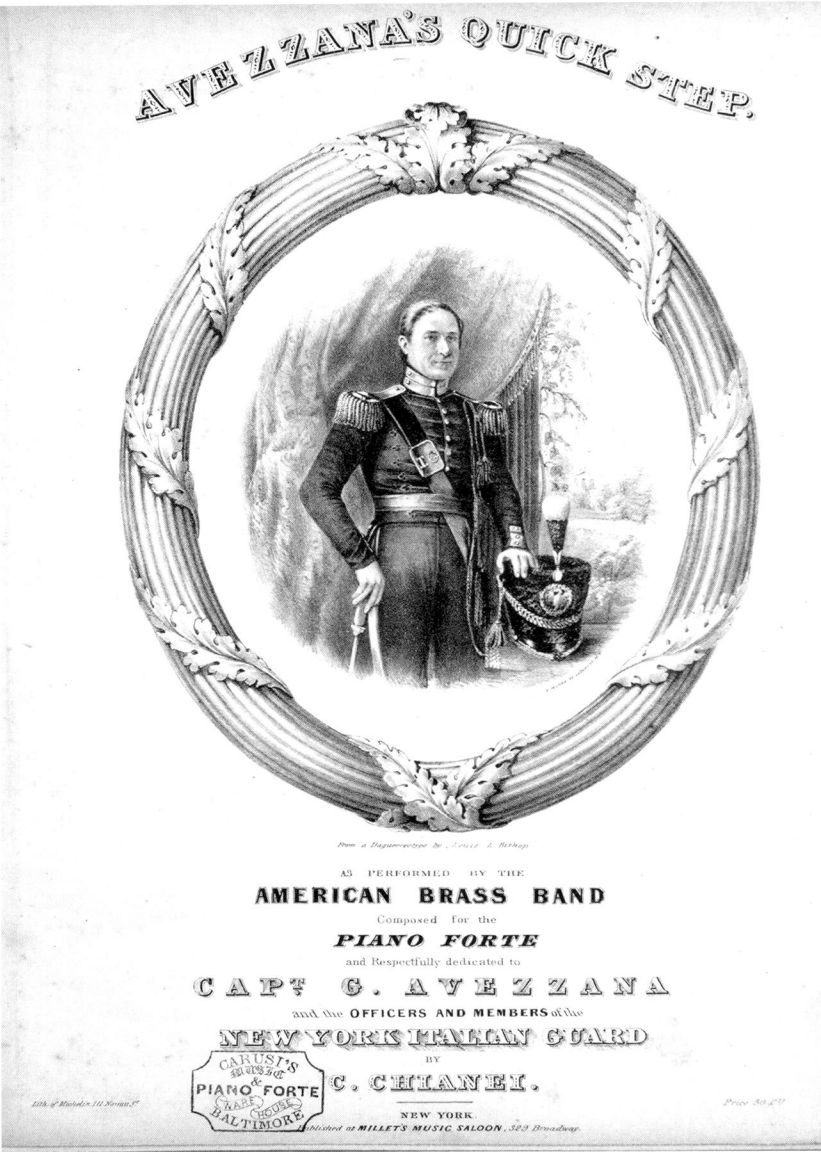

160. *Avezzana's Quick Step. As performed by the American Brass Band Composed for the Piano Forte and Respectfully dedicated to Capt. G. Avezzana and the Officers and Members of the New York Italian Guard by C. Chianei.* 1845. Printed by Michelin and published by Millet's Music Saloon. Courtesy of the Lester S. Levy Collection of Sheet Music, Sheridan Libraries, Johns Hopkins University. (Checklist 2-9)

painting in watercolor, building up the tones with opaque paint rather than aiming for transparent washes and luminosity.

As far as we know, Palmer never produced any oil paintings. The ones purporting to be hers that surface from time to time have thus far turned out to be copies of her prints, mostly by amateurs.

Daguerreotypes as Sources

Photography was already beginning to influence the work of both fine and commercial artists by the time Palmer was producing lithographs for Currier & Ives. In an advertisement, Nathaniel Currier states that a number of steamboat pictures were lithographed from daguerreotype images, including several by Palmer.[9] The portraits of Nehemiah Cleaveland (p. 25) and Faustin Soulouque (p. 46) may also be derived from photographic sources.

In several cases, Palmer combined photo imagery with hand-drawn elements. An inscription on her music-sheet cover *Avezzana's Quick Step* (1845) informs us that the dashing image of bandleader Captain G. Avezzana was taken from a daguerreotype by Louis L. Bishop, to which the artist added an ornamental frame. The six heads of minstrel singers on the cover for *Music of the Great Southern Original Sable Harmonists* (1848; p. 45) also appear to be drawn from daguerreotypes, entwined with the artist's decorative inventions of angels and southern flora.

11

Ideology in the Art of Fanny Palmer

As Stephen Daniels has stated, "It is hard to overestimate the role of Currier and Ives in the pictorial culture of the time."[1] Although the partners were responding to the demands of their customers, they also shaped public opinion by bringing a flood of images into millions of homes, schools, and workplaces. Carolyn Oldenbusch, curator of the first one-person exhibition of Palmer's art, points out:

> The vision of American life [Currier & Ives] created was as important to the mid–nineteenth century as television was to become a hundred years later. For the first time the ideals and aspirations of the middle class were mirrored back at these consumers of culture, in the form of mass popular imagery . . . an optimistic and idealized narrative of American identity still potent today. . . . Their work both celebrated industrial progress and responded to the demand for a torrent of reassuring images of rural America in which nature was always hospitable and the social order stable.[2]

The movers and shakers of society—politicians, businessmen, religious leaders—were well aware of the power of such imagery. Through the media and as patrons and sponsors of organizations, they actively promoted the patriotic expansionist spirit in art. A prominent member of the American Art-Union expressed this trend clearly in 1845:

> There can be no greater folly than that committed by our statesmen, when they treat art and literature as something quite aside from great national interests. . . . Art is too often looked upon as an abstract thing, designed only for men of taste and leisure. . . . Every great national painting of a battlefield . . . every engraving, lithograph and wood cut appealing to national feeling and rousing national sentiment—is the work of art; and who can calculate the effect of all these on the minds of our youth?[3]

What were these "national interests" and "national sentiments" that works of art should promote? The basic premise was that the United States was becoming one of the most advanced nations on earth. Its expansion from coast to coast was considered inevitable and divinely willed, the final stage of the great movement westward of civilizations that had begun in the ancient East and then traveled across Europe and that would ultimately encompass the North American continent all the way to the Pacific.[4] All this was made possible by America's democratic system; the people's ability to elect their own representatives would unleash the initiative and enterprise of every citizen and bring freedom and prosperity to all.

One has only to read a descriptive catalog sent out by Currier & Ives to feel this patriotism resonating in every line. Palmer's print *View on the Hudson* (undated, ca. 1857–72; p. 324), the company stated around 1858, is "a glimpse of the magnificent scenery for which the noble Hudson is world-renowned." Her series of country views is "purely American in character and incident."[5] The subject headings in Currier & Ives catalogs included "American Country Life," "American Farm Scenes," "American Field Sports,"—and even "American Firemen." Under the heading "Ships, Steamers, and Marine Subjects," we read: "The most . . . important sign of our unequalled national advancement, is the great improvement constantly made in the art of Ship-building. Nowhere has there been as much enterprise displayed . . . in this line of art as among American Ship-builders."[6]

F. F. Palmer's prints are layered with a patriotic sense of history in ways that modern viewers may not fully perceive. For example, *Staten Island and the Narrows* (1861; p. 183) simply looks like a charming New York view to us today, but mid-nineteenth-century viewers knew that on July 4, 1776, Fort Hamilton was the site from which an American cannon damaged one of the British battleships convoying troops to suppress the American Revolution and that

Fort Richmond was the place from which the British crossed the Narrows hoping to ambush George Washington's troops in the bitterly fought Battle of Long Island. In 1861, people could still remember their grandfathers describing what the revolution was like. Fort Lafayette (originally known as Fort Diamond) evoked memories of the great French marshal for whom it was renamed after his triumphant return tour of the United States in 1825.

Even a seemingly simple print, *Old Blandford Church. Petersburg Virginia* (undated, ca. 1857–72), conjured up the ghosts of soldiers who bloodied its grounds in three wars: the American Revolution, the War of 1812, and the Civil War, during which the church's ruins served as a field hospital. Thirty thousand veterans of these wars are buried in the adjacent Blandford Cemetery. So hallowed was this building that Louis Comfort Tiffany was later commissioned to design fifteen stained-glass windows for it as part of its restoration.

But along with this noble patriotism, some of the company's prints also reflect the less-uplifting aspects of American life. Foreign visitors in particular noted the gap between democratic theory and practice in the United States. British author Frances Trollope wryly observed, "You will see them with one hand hoisting the cap of liberty, and with the other flogging their slaves. You will see them one hour lecturing their mob on the indefeasible rights of man, and the next driving from their homes the children of the soil [i.e., Native Americans] whom they have bound themselves to protect by the most solemn treaties."[7] Robert Louis Stevenson, during a journey west on an emigrant train, was shocked by the unreasonable bias of white Americans against the Chinese, segregated in a separate car: "Of all stupid ill-feelings, the sentiment of my fellow-Caucasians towards our companions in the Chinese car was the most stupid and the worst. . . . They declared them hideous vermin, and affected a kind of choking in the throat when they beheld them."[8]

We cannot know precisely what Nat Currier and James Ives's private opinions were about these and other divisive issues of the day. Before the Civil War, they probably saw the world from the viewpoint of Northern businessmen who were concerned about the spread of slavery into western territories but who preferred compromise to a possible breakup of the Union. However, Currier and Ives were not primarily propagandists; they were in business to make money. Their objective was to sell as many prints as possible by appealing to the tastes of as many segments of the buying public as possible. During election campaigns, the firm printed banners, cartoons, and portraits of candidates for opposing parties, and in cases where Currier feared that he might be sticking his neck out

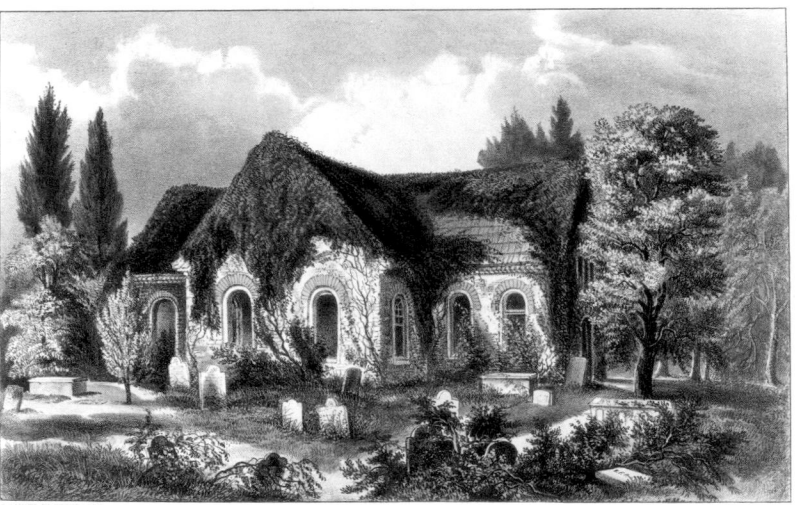

OLD BLANDFORD CHURCH.

161. *Old Blandford Church. Petersburg Virginia.* Undated, ca. 1857–72. Printed and published by Currier & Ives. Courtesy of the Old Print Shop. (Checklist 3-96)

a bit too far on some issue, he substituted the pseudonym "Peter Smith" for the publisher's name on prints or omitted it altogether, including only the factory address.[9] Over the years, the company flipped back and forth in response to their customers' fluctuating attitudes toward race, gender, and other volatile subjects.

The partners also pitched their products to various niche groups, no matter what their private opinion of those groups might be. For example, romantic scenes of Ireland and pictures of the pope and of Daniel O'Connell, leader of Irish independence, were addressed to Irish Americans, a market too large to be ignored. In other prints, however, responding to anti-Catholic sentiment, Irish immigrants were presented as thuggish louts or tools of corrupt Tammany Hall politicians.[10]

F. F. Palmer, of course, had little opportunity to express an independent viewpoint in her work. She probably submitted ideas for prints from time to time, but they always had to be approved by her employers and, as we have seen, were sometimes modified to meet their demands. Thus, for the most part her lithographs express the same shifting values being promoted between 1849 and 1873. Within that general framework, she was assigned the role of representing all that was regarded as respectable, moral, upbeat, and optimistic in American life: images of traditional happy families, wholesome leisure activities, glorious scenery, triumphant American technology.

Is Palmer's art, therefore, simply a reflection of her employers? Does her work ever divulge her own attitudes, shaped by her unique position as a woman artist far ahead of her time? Close study sometimes reveals a subtle difference of viewpoint. It peeks out at the edges and can be seen in some of the sketches she submitted before her employers made changes. In one drawing, *Love, Marriage, and Separation* (undated, Museum of the City of New York; p. 212), she even challenged the traditional view of love and marriage, but, tellingly, a print was never published.

RACE AND ETHNICITY

African Americans

Mid-nineteenth-century American art as a whole reflected the assumption in both the North and the South that "Anglo-Saxon" white Protestants belonged to a superior group destined to lead the country to its highest level. All other groups were viewed in descending order, with African Americans and at one point Asians at the bottom. Typical of the rhetoric of the day was Cyrus Mason's "Oration on the Thirteenth Anniversary of the American Institute" at the Broadway Tabernacle on October 15, 1840. Praising the productivity and inventiveness of Americans, so evident at the American Institute, he attributed these characteristics to them: "First of all, we are indebted to our ancestry. We are descended from the Anglo-Saxons and the Normans, the most free, constant, and enterprising race of men on the face of the earth. We inherit their sobriety, their patience, and their indomitable love of home, of country, and of freedom. . . . Let us never disown . . . that inheritance . . . which is one pledge of our success in the experiment we are making of enlarged civil liberty." After all this praise of freedom and "enlarged civil liberty," he added, in the next lines, without any awareness of a contradiction, that "we are also indebted to our [temperate] climate," whereas, he claimed, the laziness of African Americans was due to the fact that their race developed in a hot region.[11]

Even among the many Northerners opposed to slavery, most whites viewed black people as lacking the necessary qualities to participate as full equals in society. Northern artists usually portrayed them on the edges or in the background of paintings and prints, as menials and servants who added a bit of American flavor to the compositions or indicated their employers' wealth, but this portrayal fluctuated with the changing times—for example, during and after the Civil War.

Early in his career, Nathaniel Currier, a friend of leading abolitionists, attempted to show the evils of slavery in the print *Branding Slaves: on the Coast of Africa Previous to Embarkation* (1845). It was a powerful statement, but it sold so poorly that he never went near the theme again.[12] The subject was too touchy. Although the abolitionist movement was growing, on the whole people in the North were not eager to confront issues of slavery and race. Many Northern businessmen were prospering from trade with the South, and white workingmen had no desire for freed slaves to migrate North and compete with them for jobs. Beginning in the 1840s, the wild popularity of minstrel shows further entrenched the stereotypes of black people as inherently childlike, lazy, and "natural."[13]

Frances Palmer may have shared some of these prejudices, but there are hints that she did not harbor the most vicious attitudes of the period. This becomes evident when we compare her prints with those of her contemporaries. While still in her own business, where she had some control over the content of her work, Palmer produced three relatively benign images of African Americans. In the comic print *Ho–Ho–Ho–Sambo—get along there* (1846; p. 200), a white "b'hoy" in a racing sulky is attempting to overtake a black man driving a work cart. This image encapsulates Northern white workingmen's scornful attitude toward their black counterparts. Fearing competition for jobs, they barred African Americans from unions and skilled fields of work, referring to them as "coons" and "niggers." However, in Palmer's image the black man's face, as he looks back at the white man gaining on him, is humanized, not stereotyped. Indeed, the white "b'hoy," chomping on a cigar and asserting through his teeth that no black "Sambo" can keep up with him, comes off looking less appealing. Compare her print to Edward Jones's version of a similar subject published in the same year, *Wake Up There! What'r Ye 'Bout?* (p. 201),[14] in which an open-mouthed, microcephalic caricature of a black man is shown as a figure of total incompetence, with legs hanging out of the stirrups as he struggles to control his collapsing nag. Meanwhile, his fleet white competitor gallops ahead.

Palmer's respectful portrait of the black president of Haiti, *Faustin Soulouque* (ca. 1849–50; p. 46), dressed in military regalia was probably addressed to those antislavery customers who looked forward to an example of a democratic regime led by a black man. Unfortunately, Soulouque crowned himself emperor and was later savagely caricatured in the American press.

The third example, *Music of the Great Southern Original Sable Harmonists* (1848; p. 45), differs from the many demeaning images

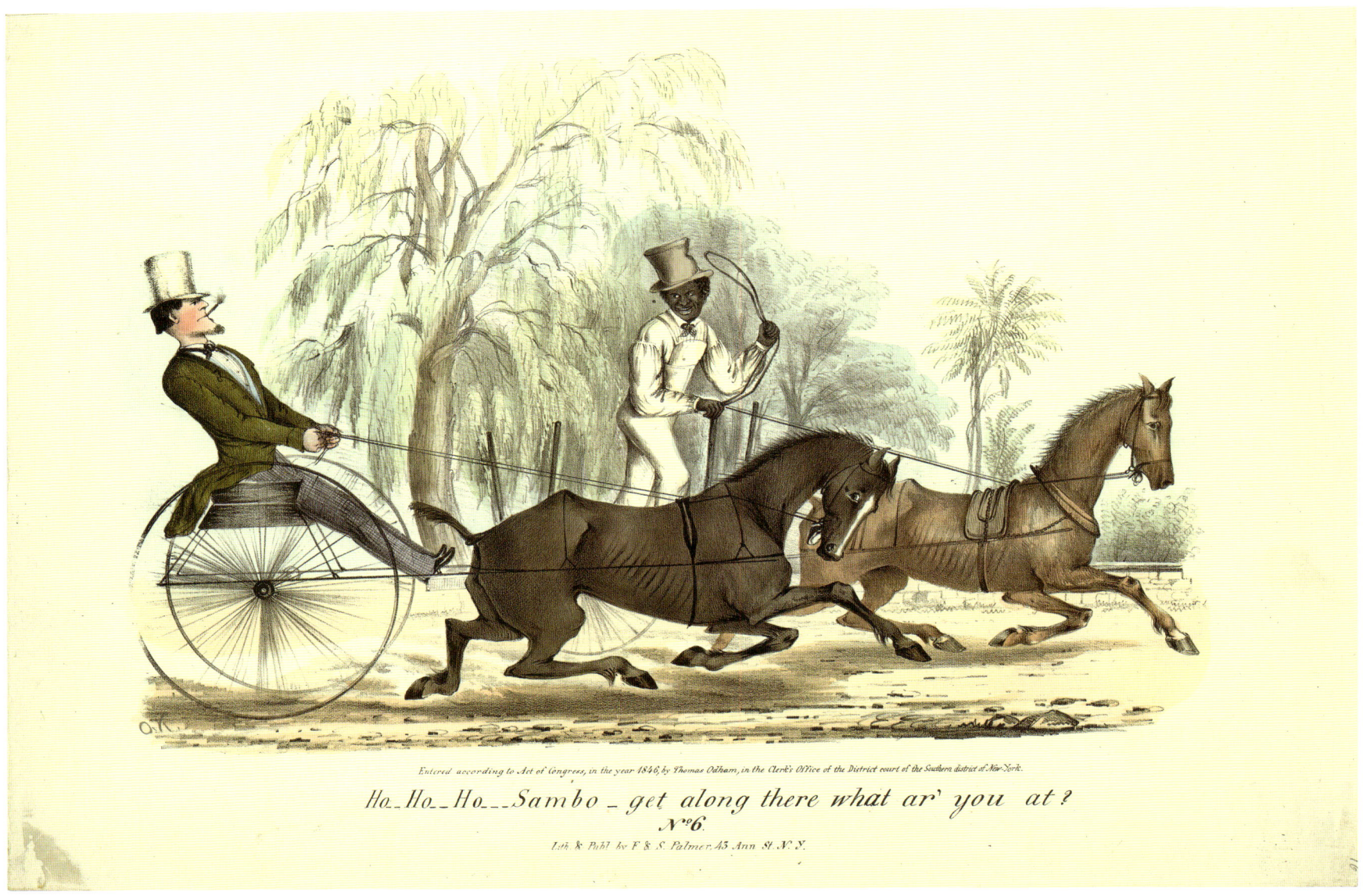

Entered according to Act of Congress, in the year 1846, by Thomas Odham, in the Clerk's Office of the District court of the Southern district of New York.

Ho_Ho_Ho___Sambo _ get along there what ar' you at?
Nº6.

Lith & Publ by F & S Palmer 45 Ann St. N. Y.

of African Americans found on the covers of minstrel sheet music. In her design, two appealing black angels or cherubs holding musical instruments are shown as the inspiration of the six white singers below them. For contrast, compare Palmer's cover with the grotesques on Nathaniel Currier's music-sheet cover *The Crow Quadrilles* (1837). To those who can decode the meaning of Palmer's entire design, though, the gentility fades. The Sable Harmonists, like all minstrel groups at that time, consisted of white men who blackened their faces and sang their "sable" songs either in comic minstrel shows or in concerts. Why, then, does Palmer's cover portray white singers and their manager *without* blackface makeup, with each one's real name listed below the image? The publisher was reassuring his customers that the troupe really consisted of

162. *Ho–Ho–Ho–Sambo—get along there what ar' you at? No. 6.* 1846. Printed and published by F. & S. Palmer. Courtesy of the New-York Historical Society. (Checklist 2-20)

Caucasians. At that time, no African Americans were allowed to perform in minstrel shows—it would have been regarded as an insult to the audience—nor could they attend these performances. In fact, it was common practice for the performers to wipe off their burnt-cork makeup and come out during intermission to show the audience that they were white.[15]

After joining Currier & Ives, Palmer drew a small white boy aiming a snowball at his family's black groom in *American*

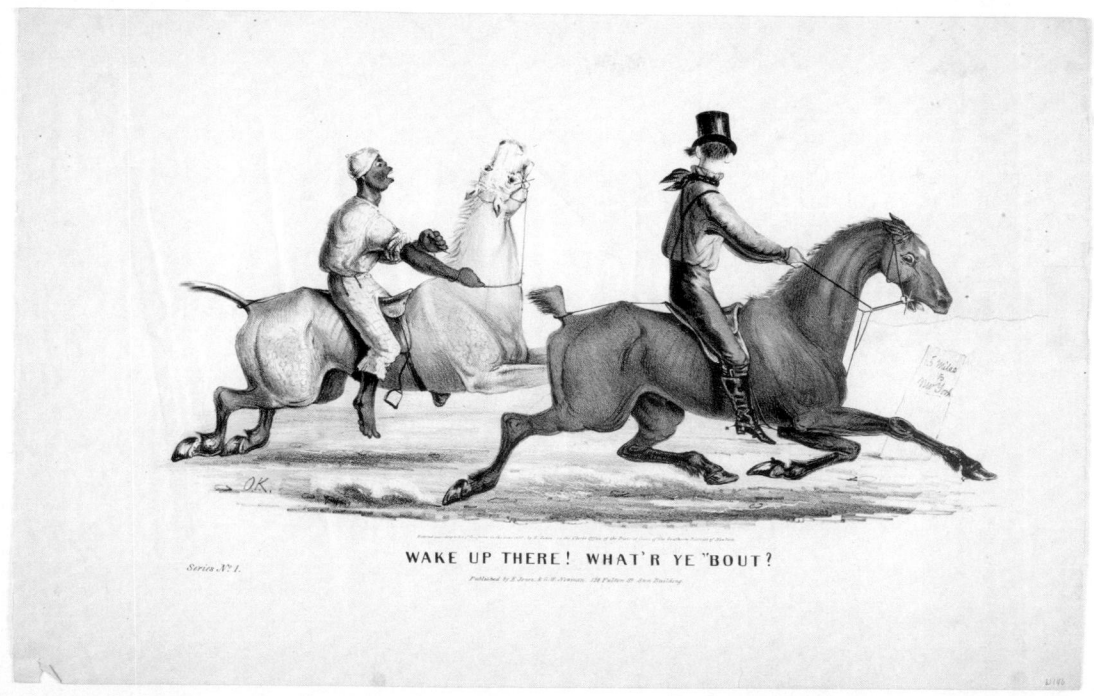

WAKE UP THERE! WHAT'R YE 'BOUT?

163. *Wake Up There! What'r Ye 'Bout?*
1846. Lithograph. Printed and published
by E. Jones & G. W. Newman. Courtesy of
the American Antiquarian Society.

Country Life. Pleasures of Winter (1855; p. 202). The motif of white urchins teasing black men was all too common in the art of the day, but her lithograph differs in tone from such prints as Currier & Ives's *The Ambuscade* (anonymous, undated). In her version, a good-looking, decently dressed black servant smiles benignly as he lifts his arm to ward off the blow. Surprisingly, the groom is the central and largest figure in the composition,[16] perhaps to show him as a status symbol signifying the wealth of his employer, the country gentleman. Liveried black servants for the growing class of nouveau-riche merchants flaunting their wealth and building new mansions on Long Island were referred to snidely (and with some envy) in the street slang of the day as "Long Island niggers."[17]

Currier probably regarded this print as an enlightened image. A catalog description even refers to the groom as "a negro man," a rather egalitarian designation at that time, but then reverts to the prejudices of the day by referring to him a few lines later as a "darkey."[18] Patronizing as Palmer's image may be, it is far more humanized than, for example, the monkeylike caricatures of black men drawn by Palmer's colleague Louis Maurer in the period leading up to the election of Abraham Lincoln in 1860 (*An Heir to the Throne* [1860], *"The Nigger" in the Woodpile* [1860], and *Republican Party Going to the Right House* [1860]) or the

pinheaded version of a black man presented as the evolutionary "missing link" in a Currier & Ives print of a P. T. Barnum freak exhibition (*What Is It?—or "Man Monkey"* [undated]). Following the publication of *On the Origin of Species* in 1859, Darwinian evolutionary theory was soon distorted to support sexism, racism, and slavery even though Darwin himself was an ardent abolitionist.[19]

With the outbreak of the Civil War, Currier & Ives rallied behind the Union, issuing stirring images of Northern victories. During this period, Palmer portrayed Southern black people rather honestly, as segregated and engaged in the hard labor of the South. In *"Wooding Up" on the Mississippi* (1863; gallery plate 5), black workers load wood onto a steamboat while their more formally dressed white masters stand around, supervising the task. In *The Mississippi in Time of Peace* (1865; gallery plate 11), small, distant figures of black stevedores load barrels (most likely of molasses) from a factory onto a paddle wheeler, and in *The Mississippi in Time of War* (1865; gallery plate 12), black and white crew members share a democracy of terror as they jump from a flaming steamboat.

Around the time of emancipation, when African American men were being recruited to fight in the Union army, and during early Reconstruction, there was a brief upsurge of respect for

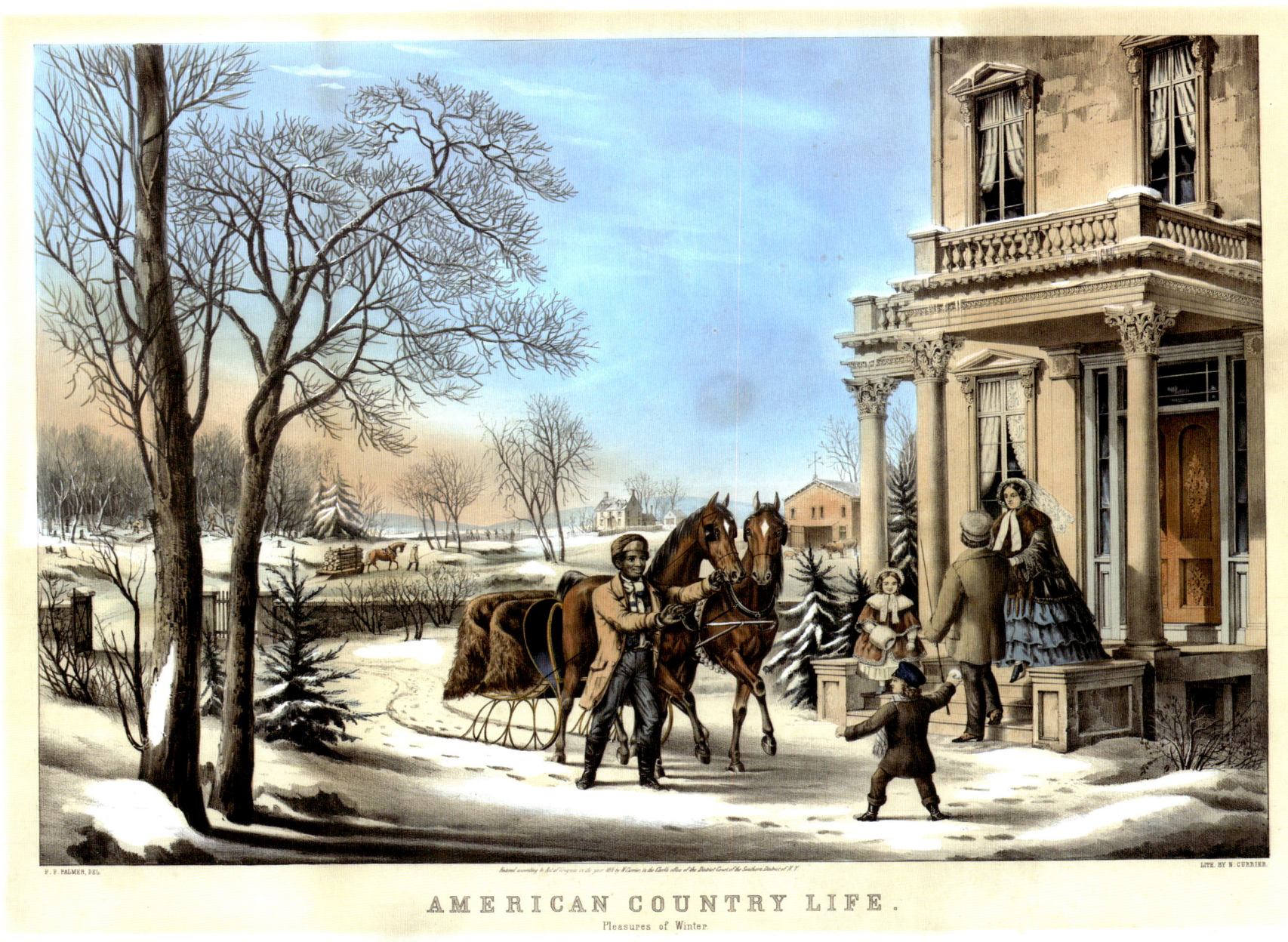

AMERICAN COUNTRY LIFE.
Pleasures of Winter
NEW YORK, PUBLISHED BY N. CURRIER, 152 NASSAU STREET.

black people in the North, and Currier & Ives issued a few small prints addressed to antislavery sympathizers and a small African American audience. Among them (none by Palmer) are *Freedom to the Slaves* (undated); *Frederick Douglass, the Colored Champion of Freedom* (undated); *The Gallant Charge of the Fifty-Fourth Massachusetts (Colored) Regiment* (1865); and *The First Colored Senator and Representatives in the 41st and 42nd Congress of the United States* (1872)—rare images of empowered black men playing a role in public life.

164. *American Country Life. Pleasures of Winter.* 1855. Printed and published by N. Currier. Courtesy of the Old Print Shop. (Checklist 3-5)

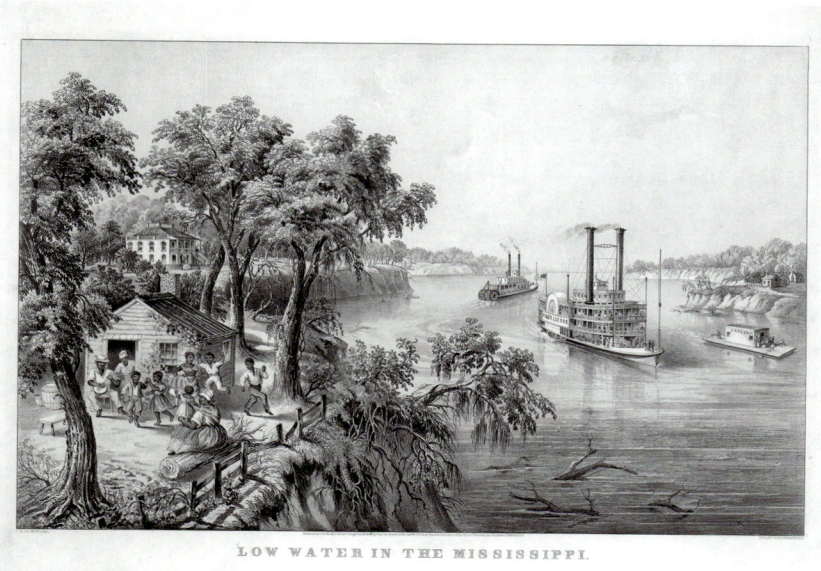

165. *Low Water in the Mississippi.* 1867. Printed and published by Currier & Ives. Courtesy of the Prints and Photographs Division, Library of Congress, LC-DIG-pga-00818. (Checklist 3-77)

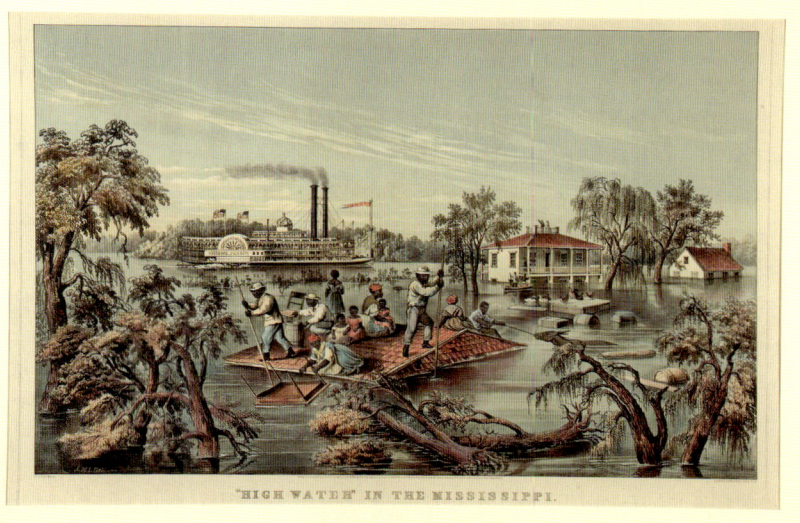

166. *"High Water" in the Mississippi.* 1868. Printed and published by Currier & Ives. Courtesy of the Yale University Art Gallery. (Checklist 3-59)

But a few years after the war, eager to take advantage of a wide-open new market in a region where the publishing business had largely been destroyed, Currier & Ives and other Northern publishers began to issue lithographs romanticizing the Old South and depicting the slave system with sentimental nostalgia.[20] Palmer's print *Low Water in the Mississippi* (1868; pp. 145, 203), picturing black people happily dancing to banjo music on the old plantation, seems to fall into this category. However, as we have seen, Palmer's initial sketch for the print (p. 145) was different from the final lithograph: it showed black men hard at work for their leisured white masters. This is believed to be one of the rare cases in which James Ives, who played an increasing role in the production of Palmer's later prints, seems to have drawn the final images on the stones. His initials "J. M. I., Del." appear on the image, and "F. E. [*sic*] Palmer" is lettered below it.

The companion print, *"High Water" in the Mississippi* (1868), appears at first glance to be simply an image of black and white people coping courageously with a natural disaster. But in the Reconstruction era, depending on the audience, the print could be read as a sympathetic portrayal of freed slaves bravely embarking on a precarious new life or of white Southerners struggling to survive in the destroyed South. Currier & Ives often created prints that would appeal to all constituencies.

In the following decade, the company continued to publish many lithographs sympathetic to the feelings of the defeated South; in fact, the company leaned over backward so far that one postwar catalog listed pictures of seven Confederate military leaders and only four from the Union forces.[21] By the late 1870s, Reconstruction was being totally dismantled. Southern whites, who had never given up their determination to regain power, had formed white militias (the Ku Klux Klan, the Knights of the White Camellia, and others) and were creating a reign of terror, turning African Americans out of elected office, disenfranchising them with legalistic tricks, and forcing them back onto the plantations as sharecroppers, barely a notch above slavery.[22] Meanwhile, people in the North had grown weary of the struggle. Facing a severe postwar economic depression, they were succumbing to a barrage of propaganda about supposed barbaric behavior and corruption in office by freed blacks. Racism hardened in the North, and Thomas Worth's *Darktown Comics*, ridiculing African Americans, became among the company's best-selling works (one print reportedly sold seventy-three thousand copies[23]).

One must add in passing that racist attitudes were not restricted to the ignorant, uneducated public; they were pervasive in all classes of society and continued far into the twentieth century. For example, in Harry T. Peters's landmark book *Currier & Ives: Printmakers to the American People* (1929–31), cartoonist Thomas Worth—by that time an old man reminiscing about "the good old days"—describes an episode in which James Ives made a black man the butt of a practical joke. As he and Ives were leaving the shop one day, a crowd stood laughing at the *Darktown* pictures displayed in the window. However, one well-dressed black man took offense, declaring that "he would like to just once get hold of the fellow who drawed dem 'scanlous' pictures of de poor colored man." According to Worth, Ives immediately responded to this slur against his best-selling line of prints by engaging in a prank. Telling "the coon he would give him an introduction to the artist," he ran down into the basement where a huge, muscular white man was packing prints and brought him upstairs to "the complaining coon," who "took one look at him, sneaked off and vanished around the corner of Ann Street in a hurry, without getting hold of the man who 'drawed dem pictures.'"[24] This description of a powerful white man putting a black man in his "place" is typical of the era. Whether the story is true or false, it seems shocking that as late as 1929 an author could repeat this incident as a source of innocent humor.[25] One of the insights gained by a study of Currier & Ives prints is the realization of how universal and deeply ingrained racist attitudes were before the civil rights movement of the 1960s.

Native Americans

Native Americans were viewed variously—depending on the time, place, and circumstance—as noble savages, cruel and bloodthirsty barbarians, or pitiable victims doomed to extinction. Palmer employed some of the milder stereotypes of Native Americans found generally in nineteenth-century American art. *The Trappers Camp-Fire. A Friendly Visitor* (1866; p. 205) refers nostalgically to an early period when trappers and American Indians sometimes traded and cooperated as they roamed the forest. In this image, an Indian has joined a group of trappers around a campfire and sits cross-legged, holding a ceremonial pipe while the trappers lounge about, loosely holding their guns. The ambivalent attitude behind this seemingly peaceful encounter is expressed in George Ruxton's book describing his experiences with Native Americans during his travels in the Rocky Mountains: "[The trapper's] nerves must ever be in a state of tension. . . . All the wits of the subtile [*sic*] savage are called into play to gain an advantage over the wily woodsman; but with the natural instinct of primitive man, the white hunter has the advantages of a civilized mind, and, thus provided, seldom fails to outwit, under equal advantages, the cunning savage."[26]

Another cliché was the image of Native Americans as powerless, helplessly accepting their coming demise. Albert Boime explains, "One of the favorite visual tropes of the period is that image of the stupefied savage confronting the signs of civilization on the march. It appears on bank notes as well as in the high art manifestations of painters."[27] In Palmer's print *The Rocky Mountains. Emigrants Crossing the Plains* (1866; gallery plate 7), two Native Americans on horseback gaze in passive wonder as they point to the wagon trains passing through their territory.

In her twin images of western mountain ranges, Palmer employs a third cliché of the Native American as the noble savage, a Rousseauian vision of the innocent primitive uncorrupted by civilization but, alas, destined to disappear. *The Mountain Pass. Sierra Nevada* (1867; p. 217), features a lone Native American on a distant mountain peak, carrying a bow and arrow, a romantic symbol of the wilderness. *Yosemite Valley—California. "The Bridal Veil" Fall* (1866; p. 169) shows an idyllic Indian encampment at the edge of a river fed by the Bridal Veil waterfall. Here, as in the paintings by Albert Bierstadt and other artists of the period, the indigenous people are included as symbols of nature in its primeval state (i.e., the opposite of "civilization").

However, the actual history of the southern Sierra Miwok and other Yosemite Indians was not as peaceful as these images suggest. The Gold Rush first brought Anglos into the region, provoking local tribes to fiercely resist incursions on their territory and way of life. Government troops were mustered to put down the insurrections; in 1851, Major James Savage led the Mariposa Battalion into the magnificent valley in order to root out and remove the native inhabitants to a reservation near the Fresno River. The tribes never accepted their relocation, though, and were later allowed to return, their numbers reduced but not destroyed.[28]

Palmer's successive images of the transcontinental railroad, from the initial sketch to the final print, trace the fluctuating view toward the Native American during this period as well as the influence of her employers on her work. Whereas her first pencil sketch *Across the Continent* (1862, Museum of the City of New York) shows a group of Native Americans passively observing the onrushing train, six years later, in the final lithograph, they are mounted and holding weapons. Smoke blowing in their faces from the train's smokestack signals that the hostile "savage" must give way to the onrush of a superior civilization.

These changes reflect the escalating conflict; federal troops under General Sherman had been called in to guard train-line construction sites and were engaged in battles with desperate tribes

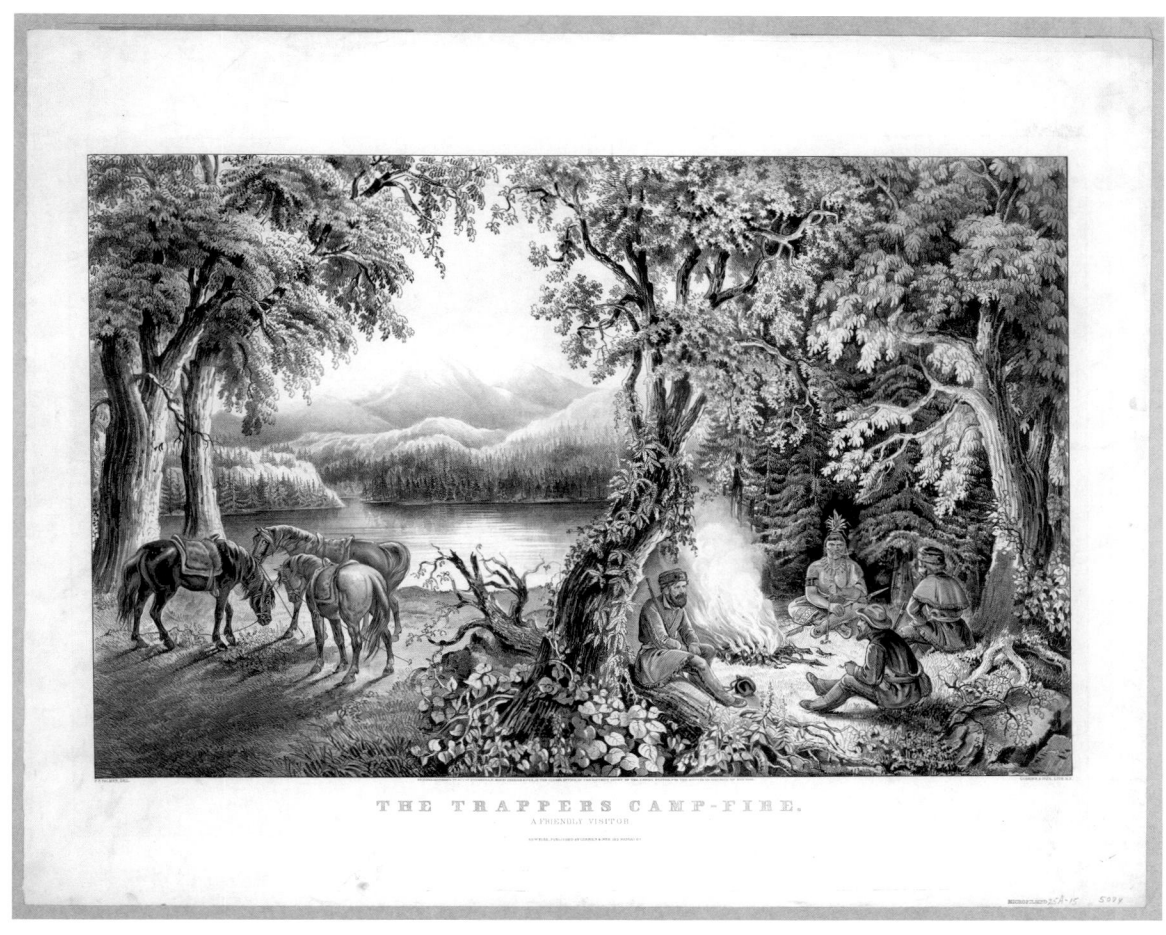

THE TRAPPERS CAMP-FIRE.
A FRIENDLY VISITOR.

167. *The Trappers Camp-Fire. A Friendly Visitor.* 1866. Printed and published by Currier & Ives. Courtesy of the Prints and Photographs Division, Library of Congress, LC-DIG-pga-00935. (Checklist 3-138)

fighting for survival. In the year the print was published, 1868, Chief Red Cloud and General Sherman were negotiating the Treaty of Fort Laramie, forcing the Sioux onto a barren reservation.

Note, however, that Palmer's images are very different from those of her male colleagues Arthur Tait, Louis Maurer, and John Cameron, who drew Native Americans as violent savages attacking and slaying white men or white men killing Native Americans (*The Last War-Whoop* [1856], *The Pursuit* [1856], etc.).

Irish, Asian, and Other Immigrant Groups

At least one Irish man appears in Palmer's early oeuvre, lining up for enlistment in her cartoon *Volunteers for Texas* (1846; p. 38). He appears to be an illiterate, impoverished buffoon, obviously with no military training, but so do all the other enlistees. Even the foppish officer examining his new recruits through a monocle fares no better as the object of Palmer's satire. After she joined Currier & Ives, one image of Asians appears in her art. In *New York Crystal Palace*

(1853; p. 96), two traditionally dressed Chinese men stand isolated in the crowd around the building that housed America's first World's Fair. The lure of "Old Gold Mountain" had brought the first migration of Chinese men to the United States in 1849. Historian Stephen E. Ambrose summarizes the treatment they received in California: "The state did all it could to degrade them and deny them a decent livelihood. They were not allowed to work on the 'Mother Lode.' To work the 'tailing' they had to pay a 'miner's tax' . . . [and many other taxes]. If Chinese dared to venture into a new mining area, the whites would set on them, beat them, rob them, sometimes kill them. Thus the saying, 'Not a Chinaman's chance.'"[29]

A few of these new immigrants had trickled into New York City, where around the time of Palmer's print they were still viewed more as curiosities than as a hated threat. Later, because of an extreme shortage of labor, the company building the western half of the transcontinental railroad reluctantly hired thousands of Chinese men to help lay tracks and blast tunnels through the Sierra Nevada under conditions of great hardship. The company's directors were soon forced to admit that their new employees were intelligent, skillful, and industrious; indeed, the Central Pacific could never have met its deadline without them. But like most artists and even many photographers of the day, Palmer did not include any images of Chinese laborers in her pictures of the transcontinental line.[30]

Except for the two Chinese men mentioned earlier, no immigrants at all appear in Palmer's images. Although the streets of New York and other cities were crowded with newcomers from many countries, the vision she helped to create is of a homogeneous white America. These omissions came in part from a growing fear in the mainstream community that an influx of unwashed ignorant foreigners was polluting American society. The "Know-Nothing" political movement back in the 1850s had called for restrictions on immigration and citizenship and had even led to riots and attacks on Irish Catholics in Philadelphia and other cities.

REPRESENTATIONS OF SOCIAL CLASSES

When Fanny and Edmund Palmer were still in their own business and had some independence in their choice of subject matter, they produced images of working-class "b'hoys," a poor woman apple vendor, ragged enlistees for the Mexican War, and a beggar with his dog. But after joining Currier & Ives, F. F. Palmer never focused on such subjects again.[31] She was meeting her employers' demand for idealized pictures of the nation, and that ideal did not include crowded slums, women and children working thirteen hours a day in factories, or beggars scavenging in the garbage. These subjects were sometimes dealt with in the black-and-white wood engravings of the pictorial press—the illustrated magazines that were becoming so popular at this time.[32] Not until the turn of the century would the so-called "Ashcan School" of artists transmute such subjects into poetry and would photographers such as Jacob Riis and Lewis Hine reveal the dire realities.

In all of Palmer's prints for Currier & Ives, only one figure is ragged;[33] even the bonneted pioneer women and their children on their arduous journey in covered wagons are neatly dressed. Pictures of affluent families, as in *American Country Life. May Morning* (1855; p. 207), are studies in fashion. The ladies of the house pick flowers in elegant dresses, wearing broad-brimmed hats to protect their skin, and the small daughter with blond curls is fetching in an off-the-shoulder dress, a popular style for little girls that embodied the veiled sensuality attached to them in the Victorian era.[34] The well-to-do country gentleman canters along

in his shiny top hat, elegant three-piece suit, and white gloves. In other prints, hunters return from the field in natty sporting attire, and farm hands and grooms wear practical clothing, but no one is really shabby. The unspoken message is that Americans live in a society where if they work hard and have decent habits, they all can look forward to a prosperous existence.

GENDER

F. F. Palmer's enchanting prints of family life—images of men, women, and their adorable children riding in carriages, strolling about, or greeting each other lovingly at the end of the workday—present a vision of enviable gender harmony and contentment, of seemingly permanent values as inevitable as the four seasons in which they are often portrayed. Palmer's employers were in business to sell prints, and such comforting portrayals sold well.

In reality, it was a time of fluidity and change from early in the century, when both sexes were still sharing the workload on farms, to midcentury, when the Industrial Revolution caused men increasingly to spend their days away in factories and offices while wives were expected to stay at home. But whether men were at home, on the farm, or anywhere else, the fundamental reality had always been and still was that they ran the country. Women could not vote or run for office, had limited property rights and inferior educations, and were largely barred from entering the professions. Even that progressive supporter of women's education Catherine Beecher declared "that in the domestic relation [a wife should] take a subordinate station, and that, in civil and political concerns, her interests be entrusted to the other sex, without her taking any part in voting, or in making and administering laws."[35]

Women's isolation from the political process is revealed in an early Palmer cartoon, *War! Or No War* (1846; p. 37). While two workingmen in the foreground argue about a hot political issue of the day, a woman apple vendor sits in the background, quietly watching the debate; she is an impotent spectator. This marginalization in scenes of political life was a recurring motif in genre paintings and prints of the day.[36]

Palmer's prints do reflect the changing position of men and women in relation to production and the economy. In her pictures of farm life, men, women, and children, although assigned different tasks, are still shown working together on the home site. Notice, however, that tasks done by women are close to the house, whereas men are out in the fields or driving wagons. The farm wife and her small daughters feed pigs, ducks, chickens, and turkeys

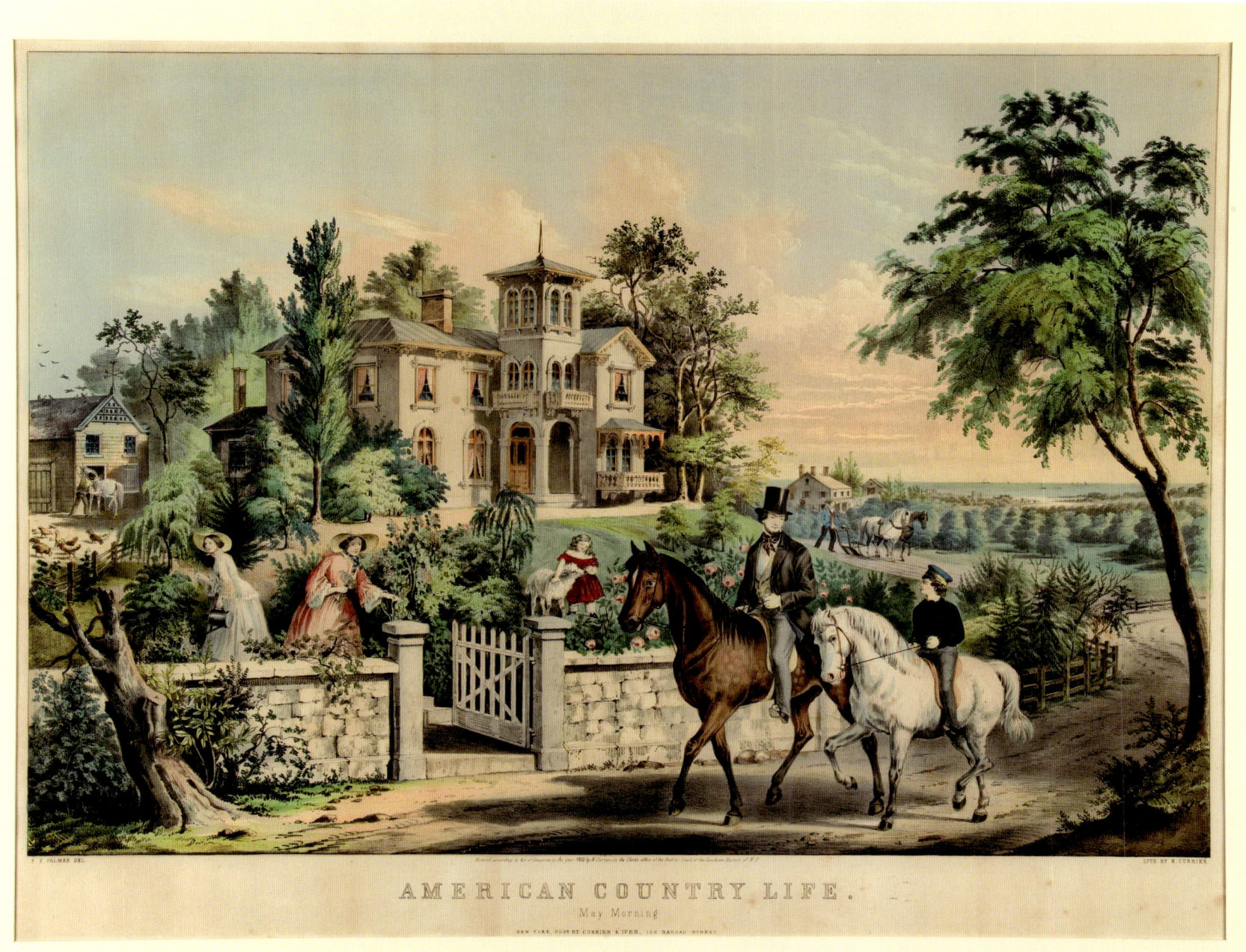

AMERICAN COUNTRY LIFE.

May Morning

NEW YORK, PUBD BY CURRIER & IVES, 152 NASSAU STREET

168. *American Country Life. May Morning.* 1855. Printed and published by N. Currier. Courtesy of the Yale University Art Gallery. (Checklist 3-3)

near the house (*American Farm Scenes. No. 2* [1853; p. 114]); a woman draws water from a well close to the house (*American Farm Scenes. No. 4* [1853; gallery plate 4]); a milkmaid emerges with a pail of milk from the dairy adjacent to the house (*The Old Oaken Bucket* [1864; p. 163]). But a young son helps his father plow the soil out in the fields (*American Farm Scenes. No. 1* [1853; p. 208]), and another goes off to town in a wagon with his father, bringing milk cans to market (*American Farm Scenes. No. 4*).

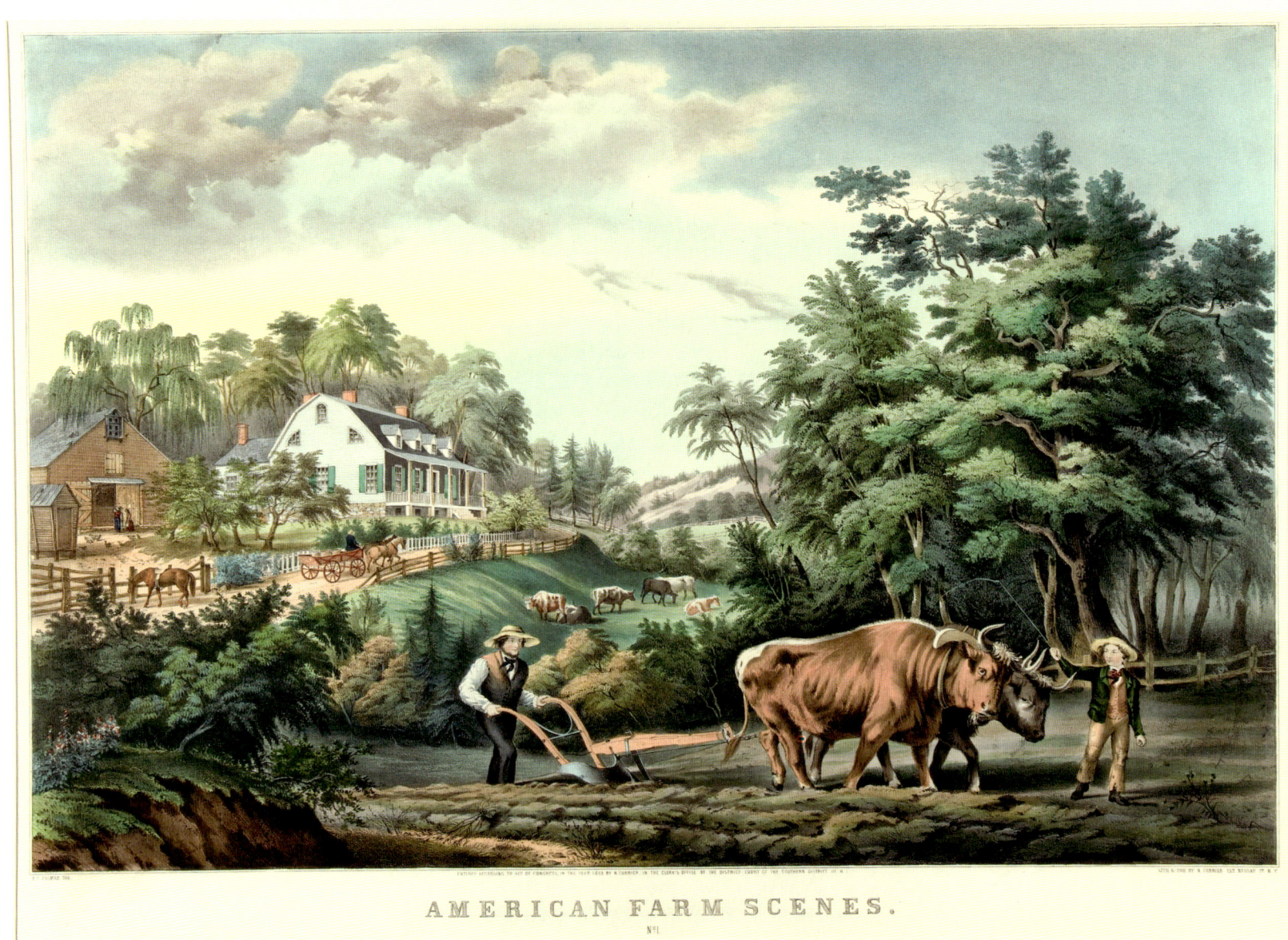

AMERICAN FARM SCENES.

Interestingly, when Palmer was in her own business in England, she drew farm wives raking hay alongside their husbands (*Ulvescroft Priory* [1842; p. 21]). In her Currier & Ives prints, however, only men plow, rake, and scythe. American farmers (in the North) equated women in the fields with the oppression of female peasants in European societies and with slavery. They assured foreign visitors that they would never allow their wives to perform the backbreaking jobs of pitching hay or plowing the soil.[37]

169. *American Farm Scenes. No. 1.* 1853. Printed and published by N. Currier. Courtesy of the Yale University Art Gallery. (Checklist 3-9)

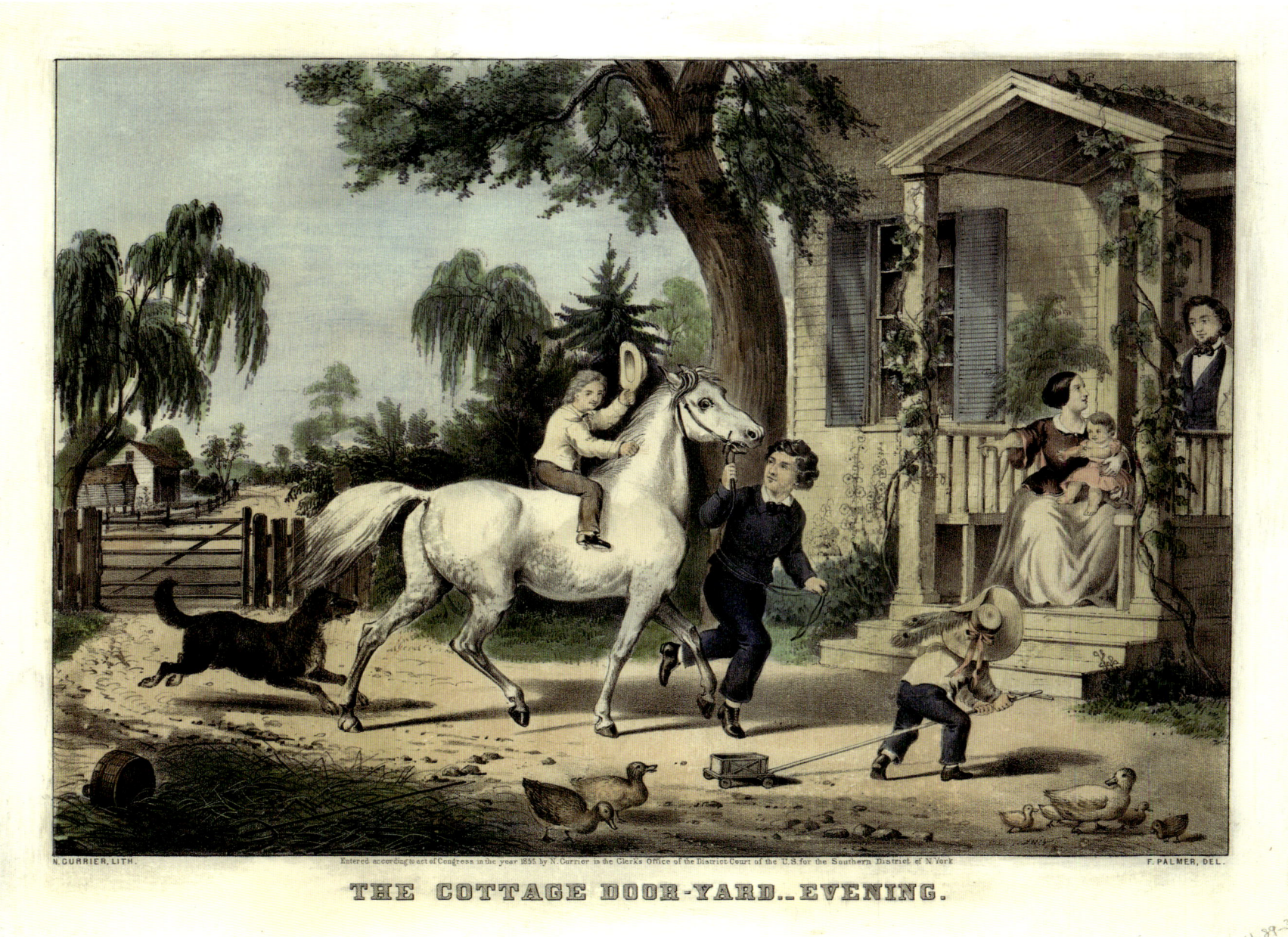

N.CURRIER, LITH.

Entered according to act of Congress in the year 1855 by N. Currier in the Clerk's Office of the District Court of the U.S. for the Southern District of N York

F. PALMER, DEL.

THE COTTAGE DOOR-YARD.—EVENING.

170. *The Cottage Door-Yard.—Evening.* 1855. Printed and published by N. Currier. Courtesy of the Old Print Shop. (Checklist 3-35)

But American women's farmwork seems to have been backbreaking enough. British author Frances Trollope's firsthand description bears no resemblance to the rosy-cheeked version shown in Palmer's lithographs. She wrote that the condition of the farmer's wife and daughters was "incomparably worse [than their husband or father's]. . . . It is they who are indeed the slaves of the soil. . . . [T]he life [the farmer's wife] leads is one of hardship, privation and labour. It is rare to see a woman in this station who has reached the age of thirty, without losing every trace of youth and beauty."[38]

But by midcentury, as men went off to create the new American empire, build railroads and bridges, and work for wages in offices or factories, the new social ideal demanded that men of any decent status were supposed to support their families; a wife who worked for money outside the home demeaned her husband. The role of the "angel in the house"—supposedly weaker and less intellectual but more nurturing, pure, and spiritual than her husband—was to provide a softening and civilizing influence, an antidote to the corrupt commercial culture, by promoting religious and moral ideals in the home ("shining her vestal light . . . into the naughty world of men"[39]).

It is not surprising, therefore, that in Palmer's lithographs the husband is shown again and again returning from work to his wife, who is confined to the hearth and the care of their children (*Four Seasons of Life: Middle Age* [1868; p. 149]); farmers bring their cattle home at dusk to wives who wait in the cottage doorway (*The Return from the Pasture* [undated, ca. 1857–72; p. 123]); even the pioneer wife on the frontier waits for her mate to "bring home the bacon" to their log cabin so that she can cook his dinner (*The Pioneer's Home* [1867; p. 166]). There are no Annie Oakleys in Currier & Ives prints.

Nor are there any female household servants in these prints. Most middle-class women employed African American or Irish immigrant women—in fact, the federal census of 1850 lists an "Ellen Riley" from Ireland at the Palmer address[40]—but they are absent from Palmer's scenes of suburban mansions because the presence of Irish and black women domestics would interfere with the myth of a classless society, introducing a jarringly unrefined note to the picture of married bliss. The cooking and cleaning appear somehow to be performed magically. The one exception seems to be *The Farmers Home—Summer* (1864; p. 191), in which an aproned figure, dimly seen in the doorway, may be a servant. Interestingly, Palmer never depicts women indoors or in the kitchen.[41] Indeed, middle-class women seem to do very little except hold babies and wait at the door or garden gate for their husbands' return.

Most striking of all is the extreme degree to which "the weaker sex" is left out of representations of hard physical effort or sports. Despite reports that Palmer herself enjoyed fishing,[42] one searches in vain for a woman casting her line. Instead, the sportsman's wife serves as the admirer of her husband's prowess when he returns with his haul (*American Country Life. October Afternoon* [1855; p. 181]). In boating scenes, men row and women are passengers (*Blackwells Island, East River* [1862; p. 100]), and, most significantly, no Palmer image shows a woman, regardless of class or

station, driving a carriage or wagon. This prohibition would be the equivalent today of being unable to drive a car.[43]

Many details in Palmer's prints reveal the power relationship that lay behind these gender roles. Beginning with an early print in England (*Hanging Stone, near the Oaks Church* [1842; p. 230]), a repeated motif is of a man pointing to the view and lecturing to his quietly listening wife or female companion (as in *American Country Life. Summers Evening* [1855; gallery plate 19] and *View of New York. From Weehawken* [1849; p. 95]). The one exception is *The Cottage Door-Yard—Evening* (1855; p. 209), in which a young wife with a baby in her lap looks up at her husband while pointing proudly to the treasures she has given him: a trio of lively young sons romping in their front yard. Men point to the wide world, whereas women point to their children.

FEMALE BONDING

Palmer completed several prints showing female bonding. In a homocentric society in which men frequently spent time in their own clubs or pubs and went out together at night to eat, socialize, and attend meetings, women sought companionship in each other's company. They gave each other support during times of stress—pregnancy, childbirth, widowhood—and developed intense friendships in which they kissed each other, expressing eternal love.

Two images portray women receiving visits from their female friends. In *Life In the Country. Evening* (1862; p. 122), the woman of the house waits expectantly as two visitors and their young daughters walk up the road toward the front door. The woman's little girl runs down to greet her visiting girlfriends. The husband, however, sits on the porch, reading a newspaper, indifferent to his wife's social group. He reads because, unlike her, he is involved in politics and the outside world and is not interested in the domestic prattle of his wife and her friends. In *A Home in the Country* (undated, ca. 1857–72; p. 182), four women and a little girl seem to be visiting the proud mistress of a fine country home. Once again, this woman's husband sits reading a newspaper, paying no attention to the arrivals. These images of a man reading while a woman knits or performs some other domestic act are familiar tropes in works of the period, symbolizing man's greater intellect, education, and participation in political life.

In *The Sunset Tree* (undated, ca. 1857–72; p. 211), three young women are resting under a tree after a companionable walk in the countryside. In the distance, the shadowy figure of a man can be seen approaching. One girl looks up in his direction with anxious

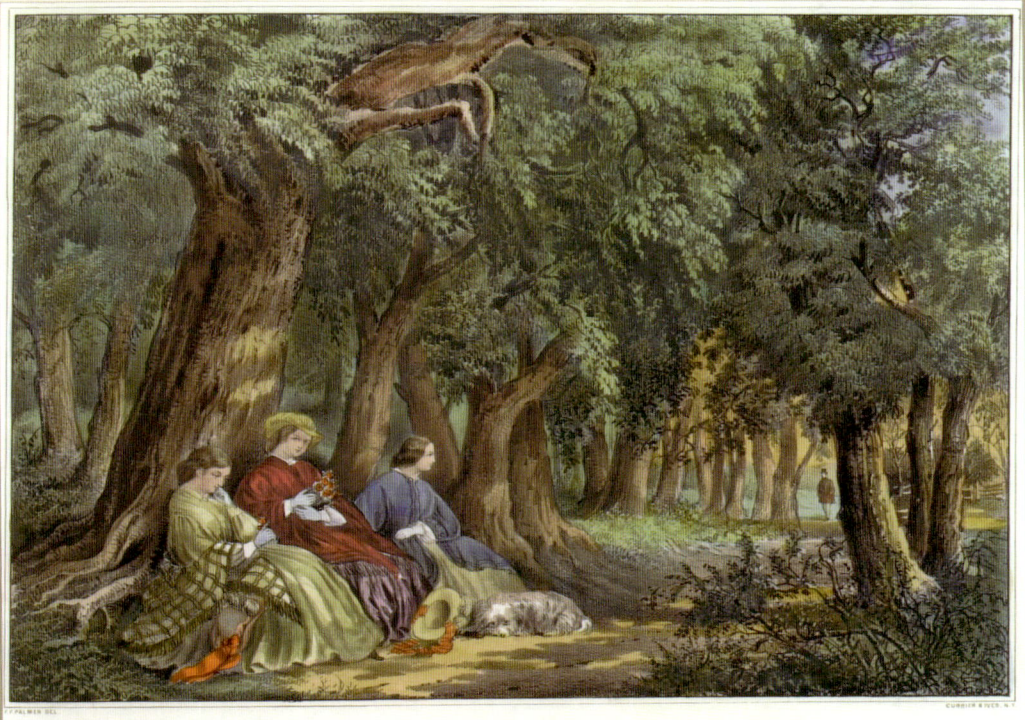

171. *The Sunset Tree.* Undated, ca. 1857–72. Printed and published by Currier & Ives. Courtesy of the Old Print Shop. (Checklist 3-134)

172. *Summer in the Country.* 1866. Printed and published by Currier & Ives. (Checklist 3-130)

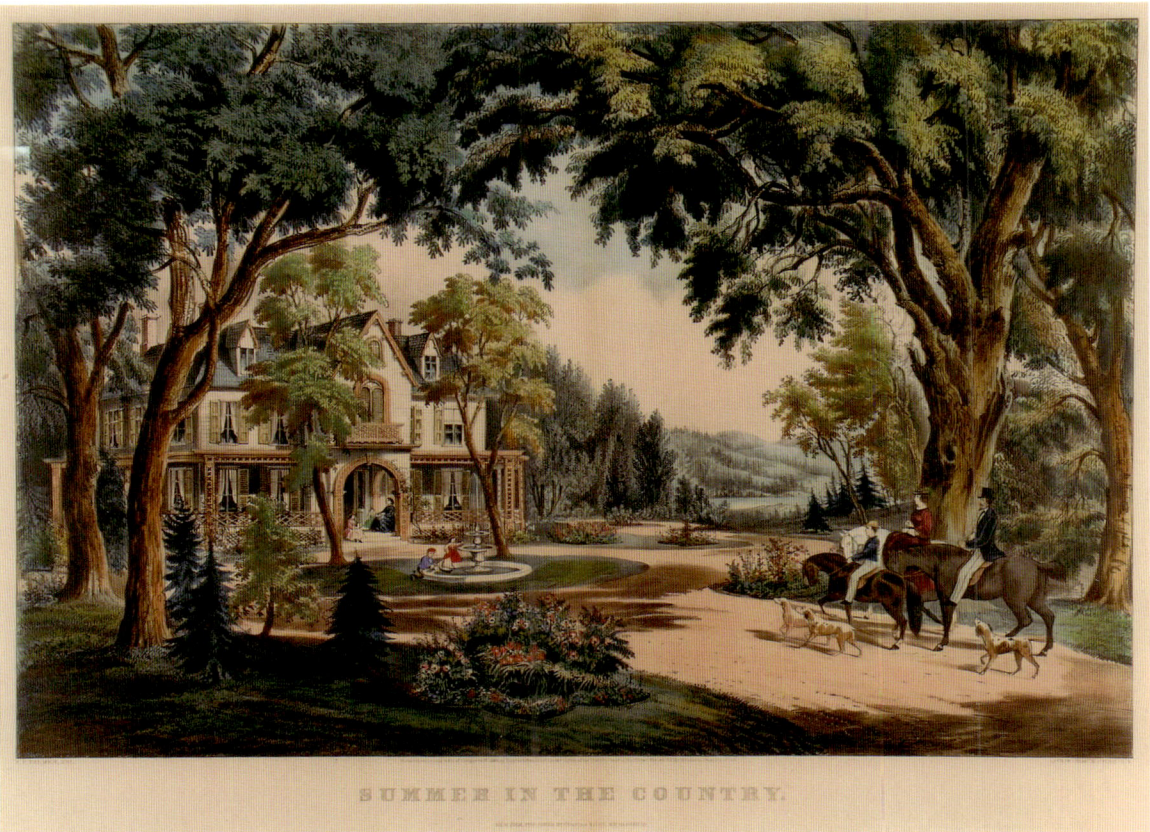

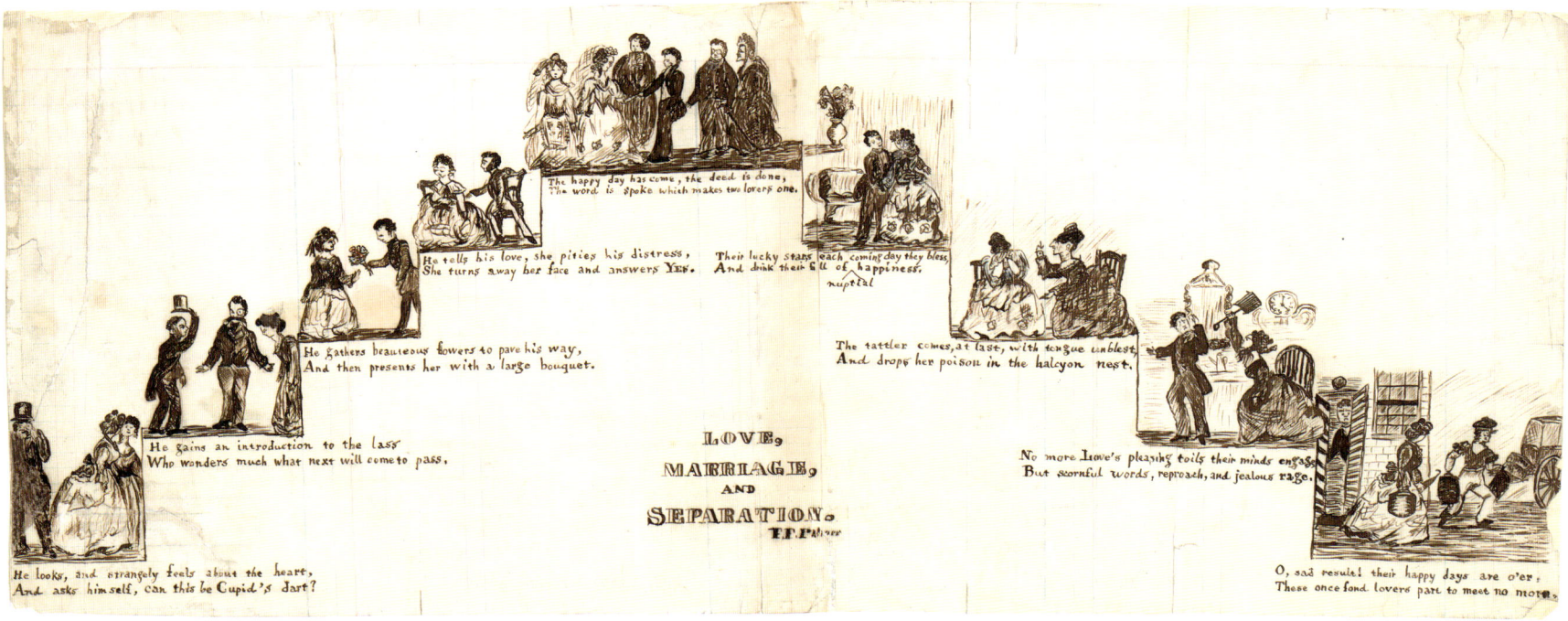

The happy day has come, the deed is done,
The word is spoke which makes two lovers one.

He tells his love, she pities his distress,
She turns away her face and answers YES.

Their lucky stars each coming day they bless,
And drink their fill of happiness.

He gathers beauteous flowers to pave his way,
And then presents her with a large bouquet.

nuptial

The tattler comes, at last, with tongue unblest,
And drops her poison in the halcyon nest.

He gains an introduction to the lass
Who wonders much what next will come to pass.

LOVE,

MARRIAGE,

AND

SEPARATION.

F. Palmer

No more Love's pleasing toils their minds engage,
But scornful words, reproach, and jealous rage.

He looks, and strangely feels about the heart,
And asks himself, can this be Cupid's dart?

O, sad result! their happy days are o'er,
These once fond lovers part to meet no more.

173. *Love, Marriage, and Separation.* Undated. Pen-and-ink drawing. Courtesy of the Museum of the City of New York, X2012.5.34. (Checklist 4-9)

expectation, while the other two seem to be meditating on their own social lives. A Currier & Ives catalog describes the print as "a picture of three beautiful girls who have been taking a walk on a summer afternoon and are reclining at the foot of a large tree. One of them seems to be looking earnestly in the distance, as if she expected her beau to come and see her home."[44] This image reveals two aspects of nineteenth-century female existence: the bonding among women and the degree to which their entire fate hung on being chosen by a man.

In *Summer Morning* (undated, ca. 1857–72; p. 220), a group of little girls are fashioning wildflowers into wreaths amid a beautiful setting of trees, village, and water. One girl hands flowers to the weaver, while two others look on with their arms around one another. This image suggests that the mutual support among women begins at a young age. If we examine *Winter Morning* (1861; p. 186) carefully, women and men can be seen skating together in the distance, and *Summer in the Country* (1866; p. 211) includes an elegantly dressed woman riding a horse (sidesaddle, of course) along with her son and husband.

None of these images shows the millions of poor women—especially immigrants, women of color, and widowed or abandoned wives who were laboring in factories and sweatshops (often with their children alongside them) or as street vendors, seamstresses, and, far too often, prostitutes. These women could only look wistfully at these pictures of strong, protective men supporting their wives and children in fine style. Also absent is any reference to the remarkable strides that women were making toward equality.

By 1861, Matthew Vassar was funding the first substantial woman's college; Elizabeth Blackwell, the first woman to earn a medical degree (in 1849), opened a training program and a hospital staffed entirely by women. Those "scribbling women" whom Nathaniel Hawthorne so abhorred were churning out successful novels; a daring group of American women sculptors were in Rome, creating marble monuments that still stand today in American parks and public buildings; everywhere, women were beginning to push aside the silk curtain that kept them from realizing their full potential.

And what about F. F. Palmer herself? Can we assume that she approved of the view of extreme separate spheres that she portrayed so often? Not necessarily. Somewhere along the way she created an ink drawing entitled *Love, Marriage, and Separation* (p. 212) that subverts the idyllic view of married bliss promoted in most Currier & Ives lithographs.[45] Designed in a series of steps going up and down (the customary format for images portraying successive stages

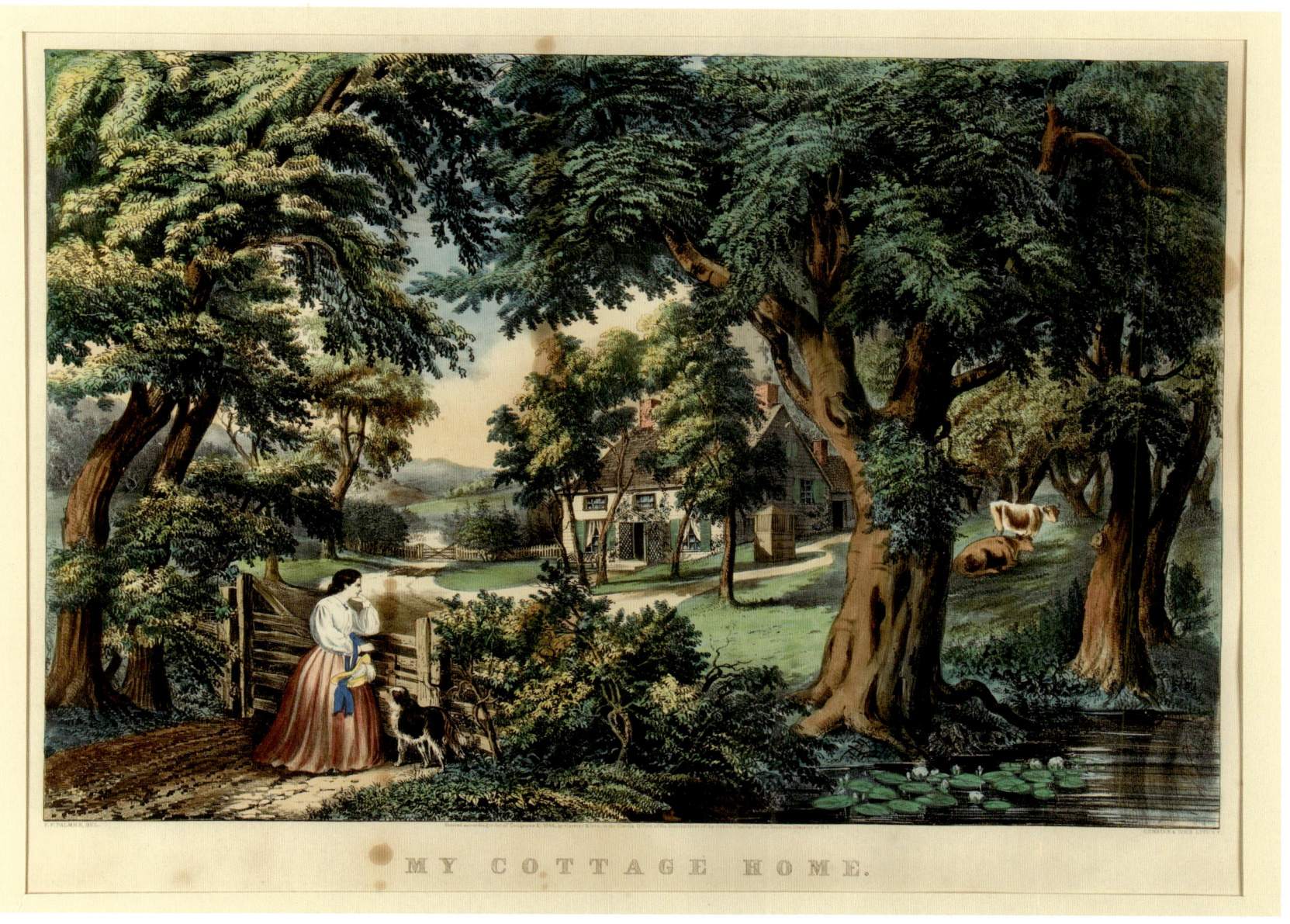

MY COTTAGE HOME.

of life), Palmer's wry, quirky drawing shows a young man worship-fully courting a girl on the lower rungs. They marry in an epiphany at the top. From that point on, family life is all downhill. The young wife hears from a gossip that her husband has been unfaithful and ends up hitting him with a fireplace shovel. On the bottom level, they both rush out of their rented flat in a rage, headed in different directions, while the landlord looks on in bewilderment.

Note that unlike the artist's idealized scenes of suburban and country life in which everyone owns a home, this young couple lives in a rented apartment. In fact, the majority of city dwellers at the time were tenants, many of them forced to move regularly on May 1 when their leases expired because landlords took advantage

174. *My Cottage Home.* 1866. Printed and published by Currier & Ives. Courtesy of the Yale University Art Gallery. (Checklist 3-91)

of this opportunity to raise the rent. Former mayor Philip Hone described the annual bedlam on the streets of New York: "Straw beds are cast into the streets; pots, pans, and kettles are seeking a new sphere of usefulness; women scold, children cry, and the head of the family begins to find that his notions of personal importance are of little consideration in the turmoil of May day."[46] Palmer her-self was part of this frequent migration—she moved at least eight times during her thirty-two years in New York and Brooklyn.

Currier & Ives never published *Love, Marriage, and Separation*, perhaps because the company viewed it as too subversive and unmarketable.[47] It did print one Palmer lithograph that has a slightly independent edge. In *My Cottage Home* (1866; p. 213), a self-sufficient, comfortably dressed woman returning from a solitary walk pauses to gaze fondly over the gate at her family home. Although the picture falls into the large category of sentimental prints about "the old homestead," it has a different feel from the torrent of simpering images of elaborately dressed and coiffed women, often shown in tight-waisted, décolleté clothing, which were listed under the Currier & Ives catalog heading "Figures and Portraits of Beautiful Girls."[48] Instead of serving as the object of the male gaze, this woman seems to be gazing at what may be her own property.

It would, of course, have been impossible for Palmer to remain in her job if her work showed any support for the rapidly growing suffrage movement. Early in his career, Nathaniel Currier had dared to issue an image of a bold young beauty in a red dress driving her carriage and galloping horses down the road (*The Star of the Road* [1849]) and another of a charmer wearing the radical bloomer costume (*The Bloomer Costume* [1851]); but as the suffrage movement gathered force in the period leading up to and after the Civil War, the company issued cartoons portraying suffragists and feminists as hatchet-faced hermaphrodites grinding their husbands into subjection, whorish vixens destroying the moral fiber of the nation, and homely spinsters longing for a little free love (see Louis Maurer's prints *The Republican Party Going to the Right House* [1860], *The Age of Brass or the Triumph of Woman's Rights* [1869], and *The Age of Iron. Man as he Expects to Be* [1869]).

CHILDREN

Pictures of boys and girls in nineteenth-century art usually show them being socialized into these same adult roles. Currier & Ives tells us exactly how it viewed children and the entire family in its catalog description of Palmer's print *American Country Life. October Afternoon* (p. 181):

OCTOBER AFTERNOON.—Represents a happy husband and his bachelor friend returning from a hunting excursion. They are met at the garden gate by the wife, with a little one in her arms, holding out its tiny hands and smiling a welcome to its father. *Another sprightly urchin has relieved his father of his gun, with which he proudly marches in advance, in paper cap and feather, a consequential hero.*[49]

The boy identifies with his father and with male aggressive roles, while the mother and baby wait quietly behind the gate.

Boys are usually active protagonists, whereas little girls are relatively passive. Boys sleigh down hills and play ice hockey, but girls stand at the edge of the lake (*Winter Pastime* [1855; gallery plate 25]); boys ride ponies, while girls pet a lamb behind the fence; a little rogue throws a snowball at the groom, while his sister stands smirking on the doorstep with her hands in a muff. In *U.S. Military Academy, West Point* (1862; p. 132), a family's young son points to the buildings of West Point and expounds on the academy's role, while his sister listens quietly to his spiel. In *Haying-Time. The First Load* (1868; p. 160), the father hands his small son the whip so that he can pretend to be driving the hay wagon, while the older daughter, who would presumably be far more capable of such a task, remains a passenger in the back of the cart. In *The Farmers Home—Summer* (p. 191), a woman and her young daughter wait quietly on the porch while her little son runs out to open the gate as his father drives their carriage out of the stable.

Particularly intriguing is the transformation of *The Old Farm Gate* from sketch to print. In Palmer's preliminary watercolor sketch for this print (undated, Museum of the City of New York), a boy rides on the gate along with the two girls, but in the final print (1864; p. 215) two boys are pushing the gate, giving two girls a ride in the same way that their fathers drive carriages or wagons, while their mothers are passengers. Was this change dictated by Palmer's employers?[50]

After the Civil War, unsettling changes in the new urban industrial society[51] gave rise to extreme nostalgia toward childhood; parents saw their own lost innocence and hopes for a better future in sentimental pictures of little boys and girls roaming freely in nature (*The Old Oaken Bucket* [p. 163] and *New England Scenery* [1866; p. 160]).

The customers who bought Palmer's prints wanted nostalgic images of happy childhood, and so a harsher nineteenth-century reality never appears in any of them—child labor in factories and gangs of homeless boys roaming city streets. In an entry for July 7, 1851, the perceptive diarist George Templeton Strong gave a grim picture of a certain class of little girls he encountered daily on the streets of New York:

No one can walk the length of Broadway without meeting some hideous troop of ragged girls, from twelve years old down, brutalized already almost beyond redemption by premature vice,

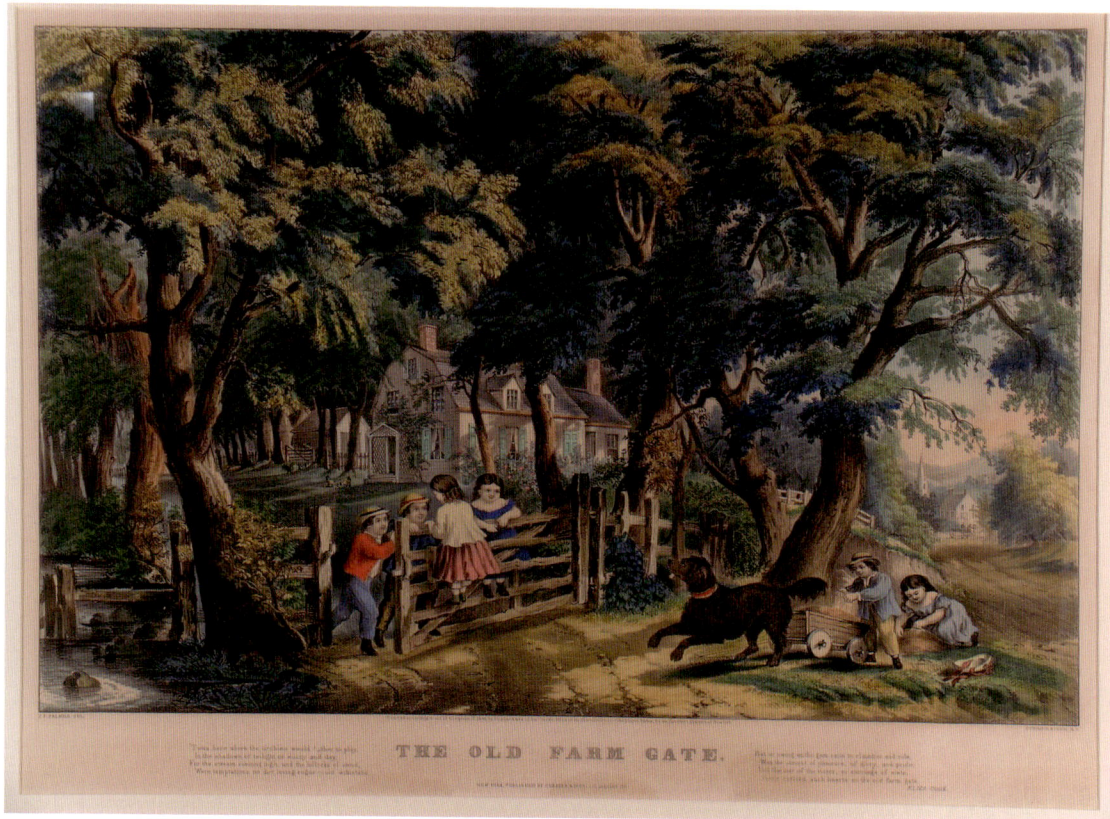

THE OLD FARM GATE.

175. *The Old Farm Gate.* 1864. Printed and published by Currier & Ives. (Checklist 3-97)

clad in the filthy refuse of the rag-picker's collections, obscene of speech . . . with thief written in their cunning eyes and whore on their depraved faces, though so unnatural, foul, and repulsive in every look and gesture, that that last profession seems utterly beyond their aspirations. . . . They haunt every other crossing.[52]

Manifest Destiny

Many aspects of Manifest Destiny have been discussed in the section dealing with Palmer's prints of the West. Here we explore some visual strategies that she and other artists employed to express the themes of expansion and progress, so dominant in American mid-nineteenth-century thought.

In contrast to European artists' pictures of nostalgic ruins of the past or of mountains seen with awe from below, nineteenth-century American artists typically present a panorama seen from the heights that often fades off into undeveloped land. This expansionist vision expresses the outlook of a people who are masters of the future—who hope to explore, conquer, settle, own, and imprint their civilization on a vast new territory.[53]

In Palmer's prints, we see this panoramic viewpoint expanding in the passing decades of her work from such relatively modest vistas in *View of New York. From Brooklyn Heights* (p. 94) in 1849 to an apogee in *Across The Continent* in 1868 (gallery plate 8). In *Across The Continent*, the great expanse melting into an infinite distance is a tabula rasa on which citizens and immigrants could picture their future. The homesteader could imagine his free land becoming a fine family farm, while large landowners could envision vast industrial farms worked with power machinery; industrialists could dream of factories and mines; preachers could see steepled churches; real estate speculators could envision instant cities rising on the plains. This sense of the future is emphasized by the way the train is just beginning to rush into the scene, cut off by the bottom edge of the picture, creating a sense of pent-up energy—of force being propelled forward.

In contrast, in Palmer's images of the Old World (*The Ruins of the Abbey* [1856; p. 312], *Melrose Abbey* [1862; p. 301], *Lanercost Priory* [undated, ca. 1857–72; p. 298], *Landscape and Ruins* [undated, ca. 1857–72; p. 298], *Kenilworth Castle* [undated, ca. 1857–72; p. 297]), the viewer is often looking up from below, a humble worshipper of awesome nature and relics of the past.

The Axe and the Stump

Art historians have pointed out that the ax and tree stump are significant motifs in nineteenth-century American art.[54] They symbolize progress and improvement—the taming of the wilderness as forests are cut down to clear the land for farms, houses, and factories; the efforts of a free people to bring about an ideal balance between the abundance created by human industry and the seemingly limitless expanse of splendid, wild nature bestowed by God upon his chosen land. Walt Whitman expressed this theme eloquently in "Song of the Broad-Axe":

> The axe leaps!
> The solid forest gives fluid utterances,
> They tumble forth, they rise and form, . . .
> Cornice, trellis, pilaster, balcony, window, turret, porch . . .
> The shapes arise!
> Shapes of factories, arsenals, foundries, markets . . .
> Shapes of Democracy total.[55]

In another Whitman poem, "Song of the Redwood-Tree," the magnificent thousand-year-old giant redwoods cheerfully accept the woodsman's ax on behalf of

> a superber race . . .
> A swarming and busy race settling and organizing
>   everywhere . . .
> Clearing the ground for broad humanity, the true America . . .
> To build a grander future.[56]

Today, however, as environmental issues have come to the forefront, some scholars read the recurrent motifs of the ax and the stump as early signs of human industry beginning to ravage nature. Indeed, F. F. Palmer unwittingly left a record of this process in her prints. In one of her earliest pre-Currier commissions, a cover for the new humor magazine *Yankee Doodle* in 1846 (p. 36), Palmer portrays the confident Yankee, symbol of the American nation, as a successful gentleman farmer, who, having succeeded extremely well in converting nature into cash (a cornucopia on the right is filled with fruits and vegetables metamorphosing into coins), is now about to wield the ax he formerly used to cut down trees as a weapon against all forms of political corruption and humbug. The ax is conflated with free speech and democracy.

Nine years later, in 1855, the ax reappears in the background of *American Country Life. Pleasures of Winter* (p. 202). In the middle distance, a snow-covered field is being cleared, leaving stumps. On the extreme left, woodsmen chop trees, suggesting that endless forests still remain beyond the frame. Toward the center, a man leading a horse-drawn sled piled high with logs suggests that more fine homes with warm fireplaces will soon cover the shorn land.

Palmer's Mississippi steamboat pictures show the accelerating inroads of the ax. Whereas George Caleb Bingham's paintings of the 1840s pictured flatboatmen on the Missouri River paddling between banks of dense untouched forest, nearly two decades later in Palmer's print *"Wooding Up" on the Mississippi* (gallery plate 5) African American laborers are loading wood onto a smoking paddle wheeler. Because huge quantities of wood were needed to feed the boats' insatiable furnaces, the banks of the Mississippi were being stripped of trees, and coal would soon take the place of wood—a change that spurred the development of mining and steel production in Pennsylvania and Ohio. In *The Champions of the Mississippi. "A Race for the Buckhorns"* (1866; gallery plate 6), cheering men on the left bank sit atop woodpiles, warmed by a wood bonfire, as the racing steamboats come by, loaded with stacks of wood on their lower decks.

The Mississippi in Time of Peace (gallery plate 11) shows the effect of all this "wood-butchering."[57] Bathed in rosy light, this scene celebrates the prosperity of the region in peacetime but also reveals growing congestion: the river is crowded with commercial boat traffic, and the forests on the left bank have thinned somewhat, making way for a factory.

Palmer's prints of the westward movement continue over time to feature the ax and the stump as optimistic motifs of progress. In *The Pioneer's Home* in 1867 (p. 166), a heavy, insistent rhythm of logs is repeated in the bridge, cabin, and barn. In the foreground, a giant stump and pile of firewood foretell the leveling of the surrounding forest and the development of the region into large, agricultural holdings.

Finally, in *Across The Continent* (gallery plate 8) in 1868 (the last known year Palmer produced lithographs), a few woodsmen wield their axes in the left foreground amid stumps of fallen trees. From their high point, they see the result of their labor: the log school, log houses, and log church of a thriving new town. In this print, no leafy trees arch overhead; denuded trees have instead become telegraph poles and railroad ties racing across the span of North America.

Palmer and the Conservation Movement

For the most part, the American people cheered on the developers and celebrated the growth of the railroads, but not everyone

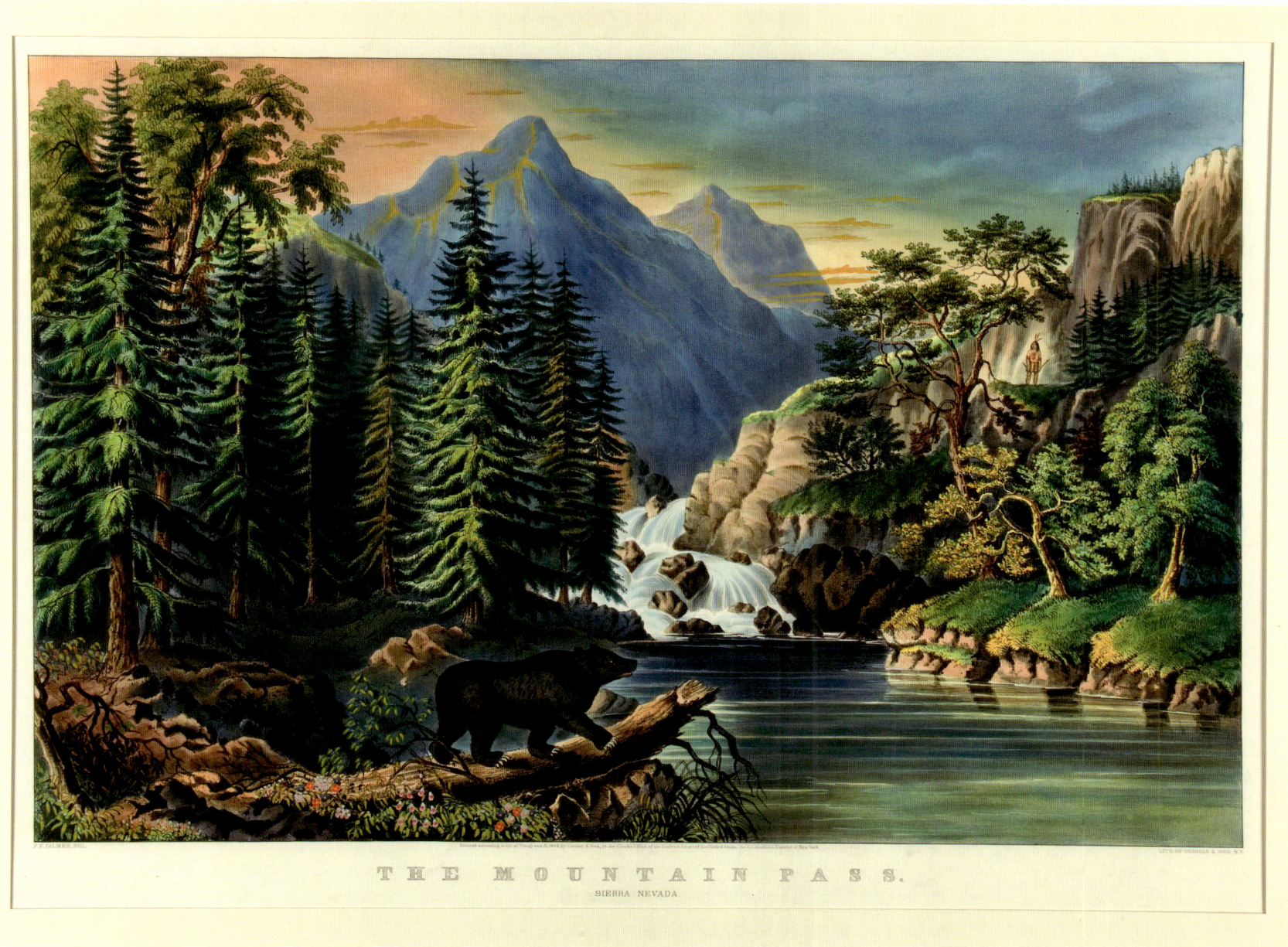

THE MOUNTAIN PASS.

SIERRA NEVADA.

went along wholeheartedly with the accompanying intrusion of industrialism on scenes of matchless beauty. In *The Machine in the Garden*, Leo Marx documents the forebodings expressed by mid-nineteenth-century intellectuals such as Nathaniel Hawthorne, Herman Melville, and Henry David Thoreau about the assault on the American pastoral way of life.[58] A countermovement was beginning to take shape.

As Alan Wallach and other scholars have pointed out, Thomas Cole, a principal founder of the Hudson River School of landscape painting, was one of the earliest artists to mourn the passing of

176. *The Mountain Pass. Sierra Nevada.* 1867. Printed and published by Currier & Ives. Courtesy of the Yale University Art Gallery. (Checklist 3-89)

the wilderness. In 1841, when the builders of a small railroad line in his neighborhood ruined the view he had so often painted, he inveighed against the "copper-hearted barbarians" in a lecture to his fellow townsmen in Catskill, the Hudson River village where he lived:

> Among the inhabitants of this village, he must be dull indeed, who has not observed how, within the last ten years, the beauty of its environs has been shorn away; year by year the groves that adorned the banks of the Catskill wasted away. . . . This is a spot that in Europe would be considered as one of the gems of the earth; it would be sought for by the lovers of the beautiful, and protected by law from desecration. But its beauty is gone, and that which a century cannot restore is cut down; what remains? Steep arid banks, incapable of cultivation. . . . Where once was beauty, there is now barrenness.[59]

The impending opening of the West by the transcontinental railroad caused early environmentalists such as Frederick Law Olmsted (codesigner of Central Park) and others to fear that even the sublime wonders of Yosemite and the Sierras would be heedlessly overrun and their beauty destroyed. They pressured President Lincoln and Congress to sign an edict in 1864 securing a ten-square-mile area of Yosemite in perpetuity for the people, the beginning of the great state and national park systems. Palmer's two views of California mountain regions, *Yosemite Valley—California. "The Bridal Veil" Fall* (p. 169) and *The Mountain Pass. Sierra Nevada* (p. 217), reflect the public's growing reverence for these majestic regions and a desire to protect them. In her romanticized images, no stumps or axes scar the scene; the trees grow thick and tall.

At the same time, these prints promoted the burgeoning tourism that soon became a source of income for the railroads and other business interests. In contrast to the wild and stormy landscapes by Albert Bierstadt, Thomas Moran, and others, F. F. Palmer's mountain views are like well-designed parks. Not a leaf is out of place; the images show a grand but comfortable and accessible-looking region welcoming the traveler into its naively stylized, almost abstract depths.

Summary

Readers may mistakenly construe the preceding analysis of the ideology reflected in Palmer's art as an attempt to minimize her work or the contribution by Currier & Ives to American culture, but, in fact, nothing could be further from the truth. On the contrary, scholars' investigations from the 1970s to the present have deepened our understanding of the multilayered way in which her prints and those of her colleagues express the attitudes of her day—often departing from realism to engage in what Patricia Hills has called "persuasive imaging."[60] Insight into the social context has added meaning to these prints, which so richly reflect the glory, the dreams, and some of the problems of nineteenth-century American culture.

12

F. F. Palmer's Contributions to American Art

No other woman lithographer quite matched Fanny Palmer in productivity and fame,
although dozens of women are known to have drawn lithographic prints.
—Helena E. Wright, *With Pen & Graver:*
Women Graphic Artists before 1900

FRANCES PALMER is finally being recognized as an important people's artist. Like the twentieth-century illustrator Norman Rockwell, who created magazine covers for the ubiquitous *Saturday Evening Post*, she produced prints that entered the homes of thousands of everyday Americans and found their way into offices, public buildings, schoolrooms, men's clubs, taverns, stables, yacht clubs, and elsewhere. She had a larger audience than most of the famous male artists of her day. But whereas Rockwell was promoted as a household name and even became world famous, Palmer has had relatively little name recognition. Nevertheless, her work has endured and has a growing audience. What, then, is her contribution to American art, and why do her prints continue to have such broad appeal?

The Enduring Appeal of Palmer's Prints

The lasting quality of Palmer's prints is based first of all on their formal excellence—fine design, expert lithographic technique, and the way in which she captured the light, atmosphere, and drama of her subjects. Another source of Palmer's continuing popularity is surely the way in which she captured the variety and sweep of the American scene at midcentury. One or two artists who worked for Currier & Ives (John Cameron, for example) had a hand in a few more signed prints than she did, but no one approached the range and scope of her imagery. A list of her prints reads like a grand tour of the United States. From Mount Washington in New Hampshire to Harper's Ferry, West Virginia; from Lookout Mountain, Tennessee, to the Fairmount Water Works of Philadelphia; from San Francisco to Harrisburg, Pennsylvania; and from

the New York shoreline to the mountains of the Far West, Palmer gave us a pageant of America. Indeed, nineteen of her prints begin with the word *American*, and at least fifteen of her subjects are now designated as National Historic Sites.[1]

Taken together, Palmer's lithographs are a clear mirror of the attitudes of her day, showing both the hopes of a people trying to build a great democracy and, inadvertently, some of the flaws and undercurrents that accompanied this vision. To study her prints is to study the nation. But the aesthetic content of her work and her pageant of the past are not the only reasons for their enduring appeal; there are subtexts in Palmer's art that exert a powerful hold on the American psyche *today*, even though our social outlook has changed so much. The emotional pull of her images continues to draw us in because many of the same longings and anxieties that haunted nineteenth-century Americans are still with us; indeed, they have become more intense.

In the mid–nineteenth century, many Americans, disturbed by the rapid change from rural to urban industrial life, sought comfort in pastoral images. Today, Palmer's scenes of river and countryside call to us still. They conjure a time of clean air and water, of homes nestling in broad meadows, of sportsmen in forests filled with game, of marshes and rivers teeming with birds and fish, of technology that still seems benign—has not yet overpowered the landscape—and seems to exist in harmony with it. Today, when marine life is being decimated, *Trolling for Blue Fish* (1866; gallery plate 17) reminds us that the waters around our cities once teemed with so many fish that an angler was kept breathless pulling them in. At a time when most of us, especially our children, are captives of television and computers, living increasingly in a

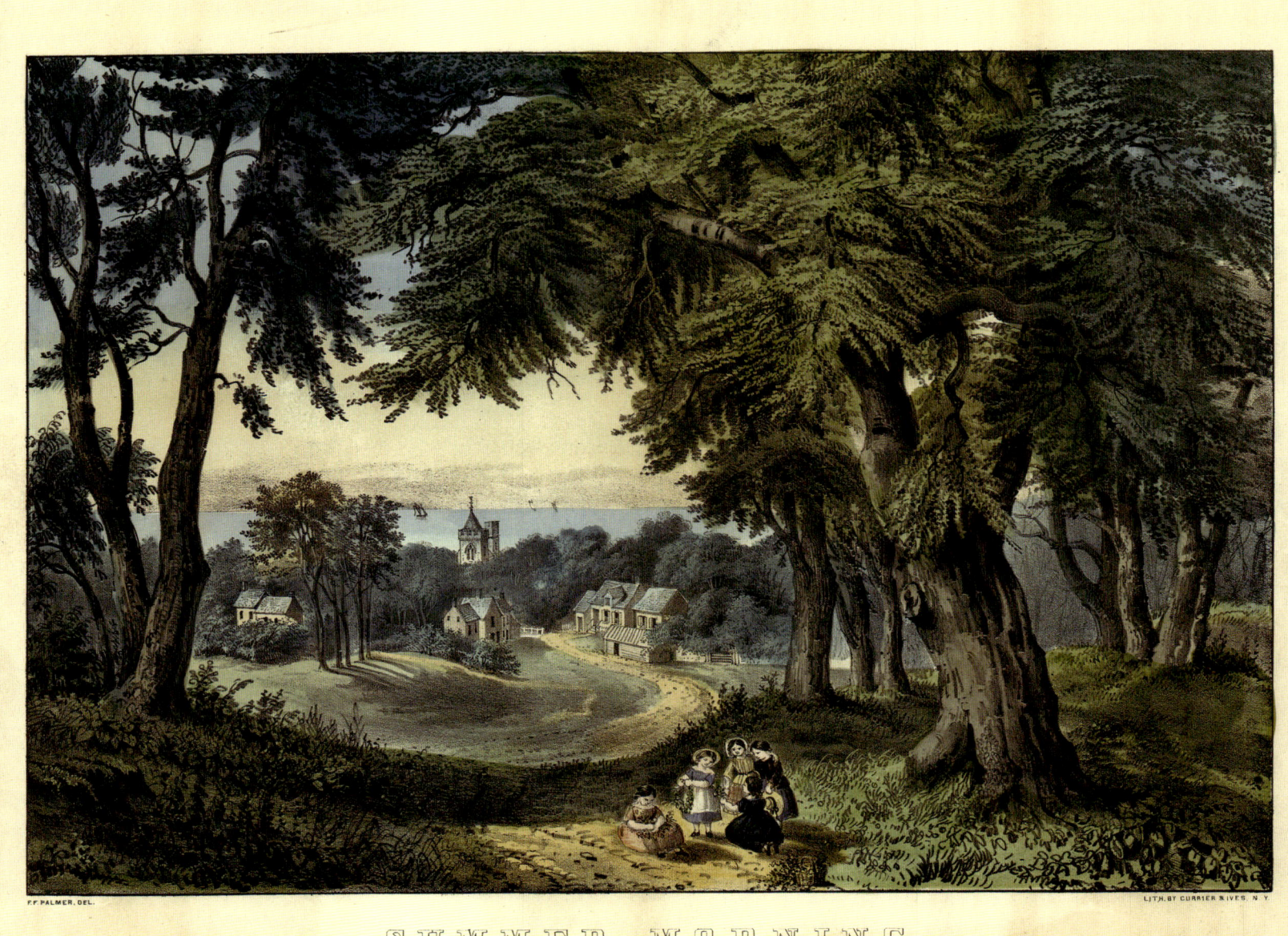

SUMMER MORNING.

New York, Published by Currier & Ives, 152 Nassau Street.

F.F. PALMER, DEL.

LITH. BY CURRIER & IVES, N.Y.

virtual world, we look in wonder at such images as the *Four Seasons of Life: Childhood* (1868; p. 147), a picture of boys and girls chasing butterflies and picking flowers in a meadow, and *Summer Morning* (undated, ca. 1857–72), an image of little girls weaving wreaths out of the natural materials around them.

Aspects of her imagery also tug at feelings of loss in human relationships. In the present era of increasing alienation, Palmer's images of peaceful domesticity and happy families may amuse us, but at the same time they touch us. Although few Americans want to return

177. *Summer Morning.* Undated, ca. 1857–72. Printed and published by Currier & Ives. Courtesy of the Old Print Shop. (Checklist 3-131)

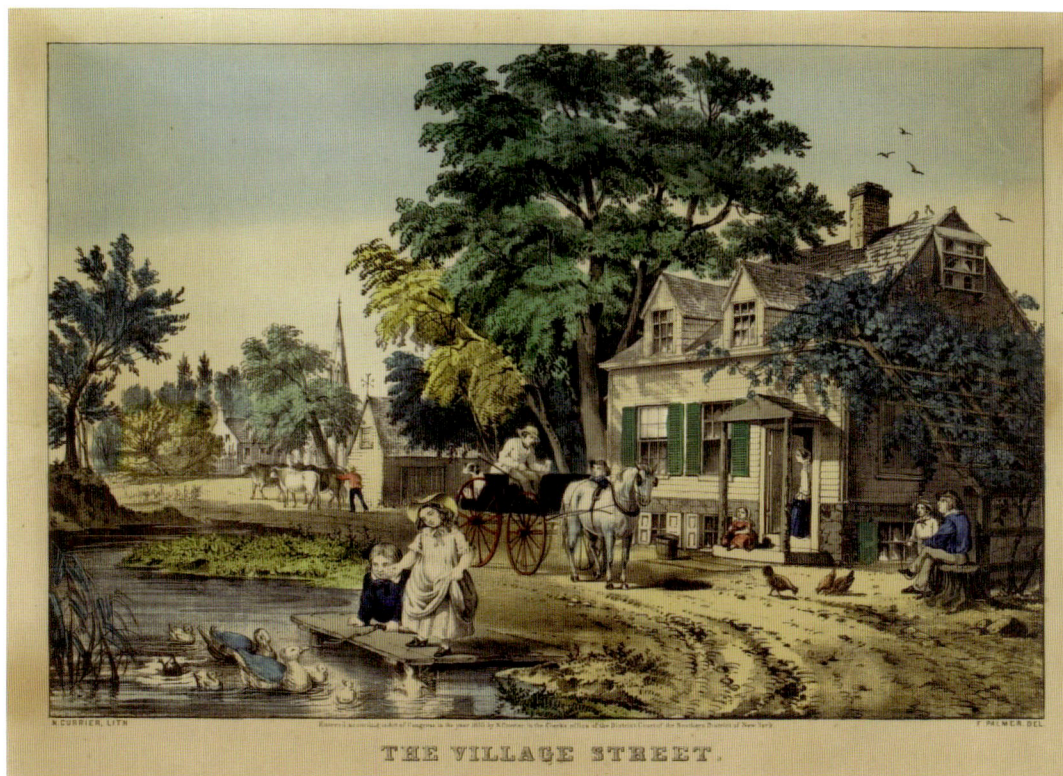

THE VILLAGE STREET.

178. *The Village Street*. 1855. Printed and published by N. Currier. Courtesy of the Old Print Shop. (Checklist 3-167)

to a time when women had little opportunity to participate in political and economic life, we still long for a world of loving families living in safe communities where people know and care for one another. We have instead suburban streets that are often spookily empty because the world has become so seemingly dangerous that families are afraid to allow their children to play outdoors without supervision. It is truly poignant, therefore, to look at images such as *The Village Street* (1855) and *The Village Blacksmith* (1864; gallery plate 24)—pictures of children playing under the friendly eyes of neighbors or walking home from school in perfect safety.

We stare at Palmer's image of the public school in *Across The Continent* (1868; gallery plate 8), presented as the bulwark, the very foundation, of an expanding democracy, and reflect that our schools often fall short of that goal. The vision of universal public education providing all with equal opportunity is increasingly being replaced by a system in which well-to-do citizens send their children to private academies, while the less affluent receive inadequate public educations. We read of gun violence in schools, guards patrolling the school halls, rape on college campuses. Viewed from this perspective, much of Palmer's work, like that of the Hudson River School of painters, points not only to the past but to the future as well. It is an unintended exhortation to restore some

of the balance between humans and nature as well as between humans and humans.

Some of these subtexts can even be found in a still life such as *Landscape, Fruit and Flowers* (1862; gallery plate 23). The viewer seems to be looking out from the porch of a home, gazing over the top of a sumptuous still life at a lovely meadow and distant river dotted with boats. Today, when thousands of red-roofed imitation "Italian villas" are springing up in the suburbs, crammed together with little space between them, and millions of people are trapped in crowded city apartments amid traffic and noise, Palmer's images of homes and cottages in ample rural settings still touch a responsive chord. They present a vision of life as it might be but most of the time is not. As philosophers have pointed out, art not only shows the present in all of its beauty or ugliness but may also present a utopian vision that draws humanity forward— an image of the possible.

Of course, Palmer's vision of American life didn't tell the whole truth. Even in her own day, much of that vision was colored with nostalgia and illusion. Author Edgar Allan Poe, rowing around Manhattan in 1844, mourned that the city's new grid plan was about to destroy a shoreline of beautiful homes in rural settings.[2] The White Mountains and Adirondacks were already beginning to be overrun by tourists and hotels, and suburban development was creeping into the Brooklyn and Long Island countryside. Not all farmers were prosperous; slums and factory conditions were oppressive; slavery and discrimination against minority groups made life a torment for millions. It is the glimpse of what we long for in the future, not in the past, that is still so compelling in Palmer's work. In Thomas Cole's words, we long for "freedom's offspring—peace, security, and happiness."[3]

PALMER'S ROLE AS PIONEERING WOMAN ARTIST

Finally, this book cannot end without reflecting on the contribution that F. F. Palmer made to the history of women artists and women in general. Although a number of women, many of them semiamateurs, worked in the field of American lithography in the mid–nineteenth century, none approached her achievement. Because she was a consummate professional, one of the premier artists at the largest American lithographic publishing house of her day, her employers entrusted her over a period of two and a half decades with many of their most important assignments— images that embody the major symbols and myths of the era.

One cannot help admiring the audacity of her reach. At a time when it was unheard of for a woman to become a leading commercial artist, she walked down the gangway into a new country, with a husband and two young children in tow, and immediately submitted her work for exhibition, won awards at the American Institute Fair, and began to carry out assignments for leading architects. But there was nothing brash or abrasive in her approach. In her dealings with friends and colleagues, she is described as soft-spoken, respectable in dress and demeanor, cheerful, cooperative, cultivated, disciplined, and extremely hard working. She quietly and cannily put herself forward, tiptoeing around the constraints placed on middle-class wives. In the business directories, she was often identified as "F. F. Palmer," but to census takers she still remained "Frances Palmer," listed as "keeping house." Although she was a leading commercial artist, her obituary in the *Brooklyn Eagle* called her "the relict of Edmund Seymour Palmer," without a word about her career. It is time at last for everyone to know her name. F. F. Palmer deserves long overdue recognition as a major lithographer of the mid–nineteenth century and a pioneer in the history of women artists.

Checklists

Notes

Bibliography

Illustration
Credits

Index

Checklists of the Work of F. F. Palmer

These APPENDIXES contain all prints and drawings that Fanny Palmer is known to have worked on in her capacity as an artist, lithographer, and printer as well as those involving her husband, Edmund Seymour Palmer.

Every entry contains the item title, copyright date (when known), image size (vertical by horizontal dimensions in inches), the publication or credit information transcribed from the item, and, when needed, any additional notes about the print. The capitalization and punctuation of titles is as given in the prints. Forward slashes in the title indicate line breaks in the print. Supplied dates and corrected dates are provided in square brackets. When known, circa dates have been added to undated prints; in cases where a date is uncertain or a conjecture, the year is followed with a question mark. Unless otherwise indicated in the entry, the items are lithographic prints. For the lithographic prints, the use of tint stones has not been indicated owing to the complexity in tracking variations, notably for Currier & Ives prints.[1]

The publication information for each print is always arranged in the following order (when present on the print), regardless of where it physically appears on the item: artist, lithographic artist, abbreviated copyright note, printer, and publisher.

Entries are assigned two numbers separated by a hyphen. The first number is the appendix number, the second the number of that entry within that appendix. In appendix 1, reissued prints are listed with the entry number of the original print placed within square brackets.

Owing to the rarity of many of the prints produced by Palmer in England and in the United States before she joined Currier & Ives, the entries in appendixes 1 and 2 include one holding library for each print. Holding institutions have not been listed for appendix 3. Location information for Currier & Ives prints in this appendix can be found in Gale Research Group, *Currier & Ives: A Catalogue Raisonné* (Detroit: Gale Research, 1984).

Prints Produced in England

The Midland Counties' Railway Companion, with Topographical Descriptions of the Country through Which the Line Passes; and Time, Fare, and Distance Tables . . . Published by the proprietors, R. Allen, Nottingham, and E. Allen, Leicester; Hamilton, Adams, and Co. London, 1840.

11 × 8½"

Holding institution: Huntington Library

F. F. Palmer drew twelve out of twenty-five of the illustrations included in this book, more than any other artist who contributed to the project. Three of her original drawings have been located, but we know that she also made nine others because she is named as the artist in the handbook's list of illustrations. All but one of Palmer's images were adapted from drawings by Palmer into black-and-white woodcuts by someone named Vizetelly (probably Henry Vizetelly). As in all of the other woodcuts in the *Railway Companion*, the printmaker has converted the drawings into vignettes, providing a more interesting shape on the page of printed text.

1-1 *The Trent Bridge* (page 44 in *Railway Companion*)
Woodcut adapted from a pencil drawing by F. F. Palmer.

1-2 *St. Ann's Church* (page 53)
Woodcut after an unlocated F. F. Palmer pencil drawing.

1-3 *Stanford Hall* (page 58)
Woodcut after an unlocated pencil drawing by F. F. Palmer.

1-4 *View of Loughborough* (page 61)
Woodcut after an unlocated pencil drawing by F. F. Palmer.

1-5 *Mountsorrel* (page 65)
Woodcut after an unlocated pencil drawing by F. F. Palmer.

1-6 *Sileby* (page 67)
Woodcut adapted from a pencil drawing by F. F. Palmer.

Courtesy of the Huntington Library, San Marino, CA, RB 4516.

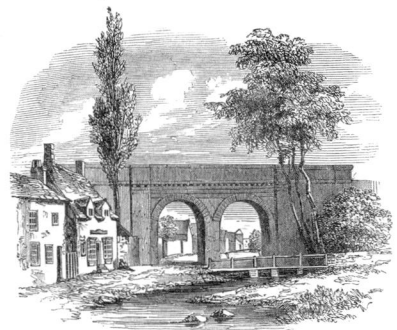

SILEBY.

1-7 *Humberstone Road Bridge* (page 72)
Woodcut after an unlocated pencil drawing by F. F. Palmer.

1-8 *Leicester Station* (facing page 73)   Illustrated, p. 10
Palmer, del. Radclyffe, Sc. Published by Richd. Allen, Nottingham, and E. Allen,
    Leicester.
Full-page steel engraving after an unlocated pencil drawing by F. F. Palmer.

1-9 *New Union Workhouse* (page 75)
Woodcut after an unlocated pencil drawing by F. F. Palmer.

1-10 *The New County Lunatic Asylum* (page 93)   Illustrated, p. 11
Woodcut after an unlocated pencil drawing by F. F. Palmer.

1-11 *Ullesthorpe Station* (page 99)   Illustrated, p. 8
Woodcut adapted from F. F. Palmer's drawing.

1-12 *Railway Inn, at Rugby* (page 101)
Woodcut after an unlocated pencil drawing by F. F. Palmer.

The History and Antiquities of Charnwood Forest by T. R. Potter. London: Hamilton, Adams, and Co. Paternoster Row. R. Allen, Nottingham; E. Allen, Leicester, 1842.

11 × 8½"

Holding institution: Huntington Library

There are a great many confusing discrepancies in the signatures, tints, and pagination found in different printings of this book, which suggests that the volumes may have been made up to order as needed, with illustrations somewhat casually placed in varying locations. The pages listed reflect the pagination of the author's copy of the book.

In many cases, the imprints of F. F. Palmer and E. S. Palmer appear in one copy, notably the copy at the Houghton Library, Harvard University, but are left out in others, and the tint color varies from book to book as well, with a print sometimes tinted in green and at other times golden buff or beige. However, all of the lithographs include one overall tint in the background, with an image printed over it in black and highlights hand-painted in white gouache. Only plates where the author has seen at least one version carrying Palmer's name are included in this catalog, but several anonymous plates may also be the work of F. F. Palmer.

1-13 *Ulvescroft Priory* (frontispiece)
Black-and-white steel engraving, image 4 × 5¾"
F. F. Palmer. del. R. Allen. Sc.

Illustrated, p. 14

1-14 *Rock Near Beaumanor* (title-page vignette)
Black-and-white steel engraving, image 3¾ × 4½"
Palmer, del. Allen, Sc.

Courtesy of the Huntington Library, San Marino, CA, DA670.C44 P8.

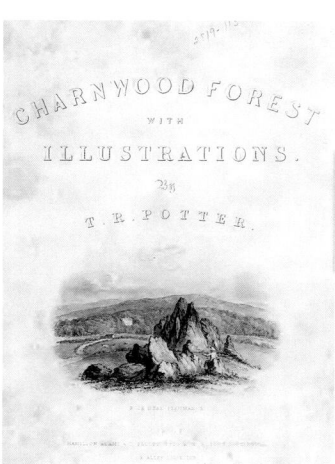

1-15 *High Cademan* (opposite page 9)
Image 5¾ × 7¾"
F. F. Palmer, Litho. Printed by E. S. Palmer, Leicester.

Illustrated, gallery plate 1

1-16 *Copt Oak* (opposite page 10)
Image 7¾ × 5¾"
F. F. Palmer, Litho. E. S. Palmer, Printer, Leicester.

Courtesy of the Huntington Library, San Marino, CA, DA670.C44 P8.

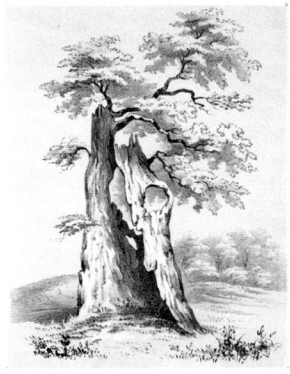

1-17 *The Oaks Chapel* (opposite page 39)
Image 5½ × 7½"
F. F. Palmer, lith. Printed by E. S. Palmer, Leicester.

Courtesy of the Huntington Library, San Marino, CA, DA670.C44 P8.

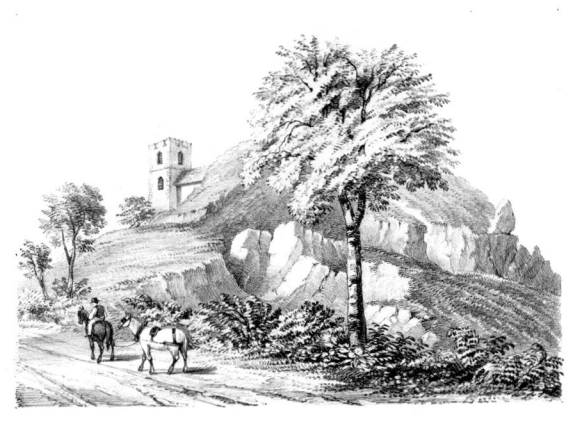

1-18 *Hanging Stone, / near the Oaks Church* (opposite page 41)
Image 7½ × 5½"
F. F. Palmer, Lith. Printed by E. S. Palmer, Leicester.

Courtesy of the Huntington Library, San Marino, CA, DA670.C44 P8.

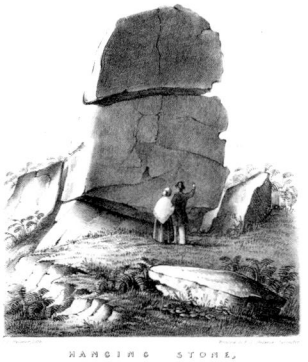

1-19 *Hanging Stone Near Beaumanor* (opposite page 73)
Image 5¾ × 7¾"
F. F. Palmer Litho. E. S. Palmer, Printer, Leicester.

Illustrated, p. 15

1-20 *Woodhouse-Eaves Chapel* (opposite page 89)
Black-and-white steel engraving, image 4⅛ × 5¾"
Palmer del. Allen sc. Published by R. Allen, Nottingham and E. Allen, Leicester.

Courtesy of the Huntington Library, San Marino, CA, DA670.C44 P8.

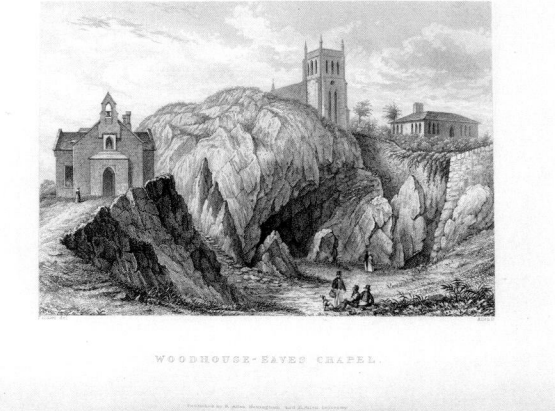

1-21 *Charley Hall* (opposite page 104)
Image 5½ × 7½"
F. F. Palmer, Litho. E. S. Palmer, Printer, Leicester.

Courtesy of the Huntington Library, San Marino, CA, DA670.C44 P8.

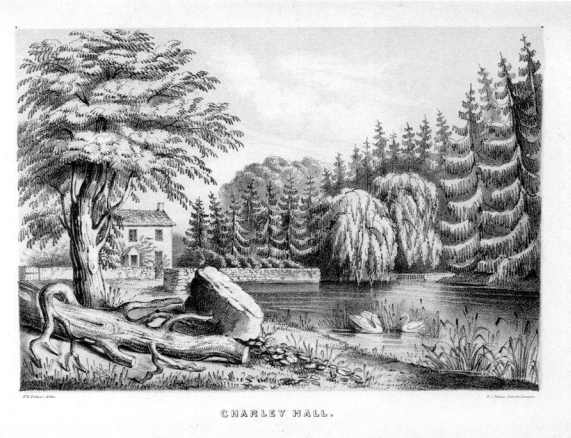

1-22 *Ruins in Bradgate Park* (opposite page 120)
Black-and-white steel engraving, image 4 2/16 × 5⅝"
Palmer del. Allen sc, Published by R. Allen Nottingham and E. Allen, Leicester.

Courtesy of the Huntington Library, San Marino, CA, DA670.C44 P8.

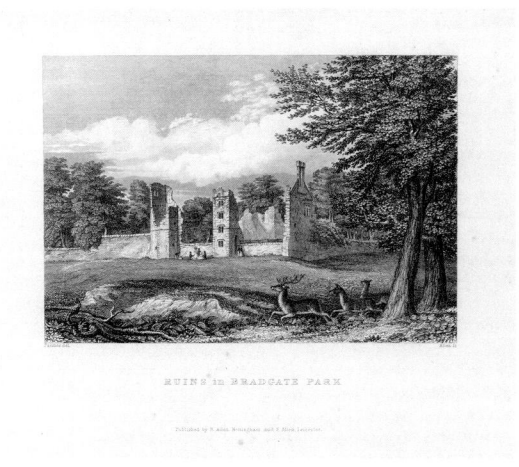

1-23 *Pelder Tor Near Whitwick* (opposite page 151)
Image 5½ × 7½"
F. F. Palmer, Litho. E. S. Palmer, Printer, Leicester.

Courtesy of the Huntington Library, San Marino, CA, DA670.C44 P8.

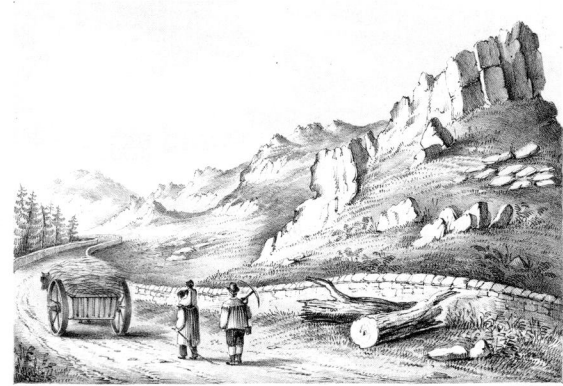

1-24 *Whitwick Church* (opposite page 154)
Image 7⅝ × 5¾"
F. F. Palmer, Litho. E. S. Palmer, Printer. Leicester.

Courtesy of the University of Pittsburgh.

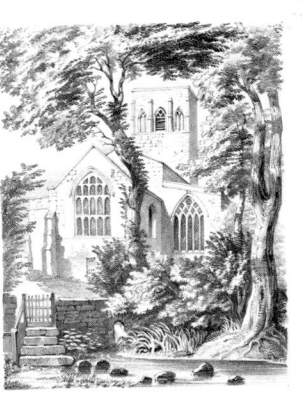

1-25 *Bardon Hill* (opposite page 160)
Black-and-white steel engraving, image 4⅛ × 5⅝"
F. F. Palmer del. R. Allen sculp. Published by R. Allen, Nottingham, and E. Allen,
     Leicester.
A Palmer lithograph of this image appears as plate 1 in *Eight Views of Charnwood*
     (p. 233).

Courtesy of the University of Pittsburgh.

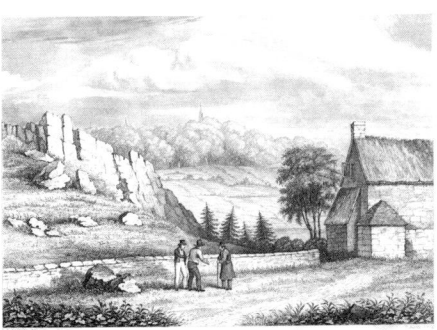

1-26 *Long Cliff* (opposite page 187)
Image 5¾ × 7⅝"
F. F. Palmer, Litho. E. S. Palmer, Printer, Leicester.

Courtesy of the Huntington Library, San Marino, CA, DA670.C44 P8.

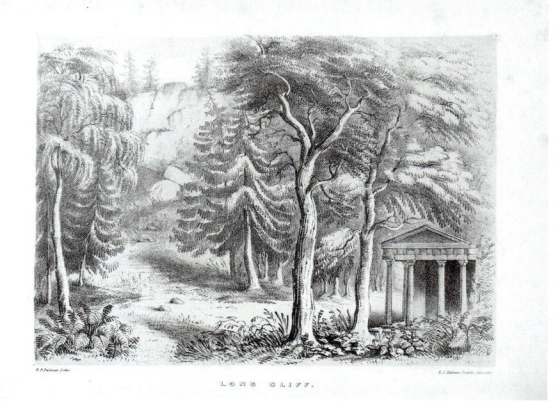

1-27 *Cursorius Isabellinus* (title page for an appendix titled "Ornithology of
    Charnwood Forest")
Lithograph vignette, hand painted in transparent watercolor, Image 5½ × 5½"
F. F. Palmer, Litho. E. S. Palmer, Printer, Leicester.

Courtesy of the Huntington Library, San Marino, CA, DA670.C44 P8.

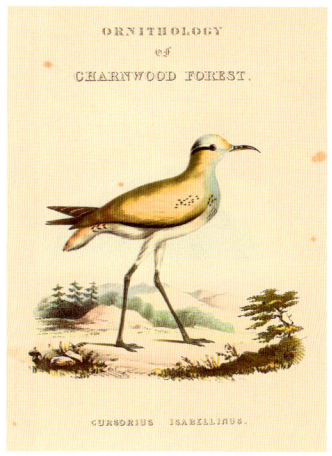

Eight Views of Charnwood (Loughborough: R. Griffin & Son, ca. 1840).
An album of eight tinted F. F. Palmer lithographs, with a thin green paper cover that reads:
"Eight Views of Charnwood, Price 1s. sold by R. Griffin & Son, printers, booksellers and
stationers, Loughborough." Several of the images closely resemble Palmer's illustrations in
Potter, *History and Antiquities of Charnwood Forest* (pp. 229–33).

Holding institution: Yale Center for British Art

1-28 *Bardon Hill* (plate 1)
Undated, ca. 1840–42
F. F. Palmer, Litho. Printed by E.S. Palmer, Leicester.

Courtesy of the Yale Center for British Art, Paul Mellon Fund.

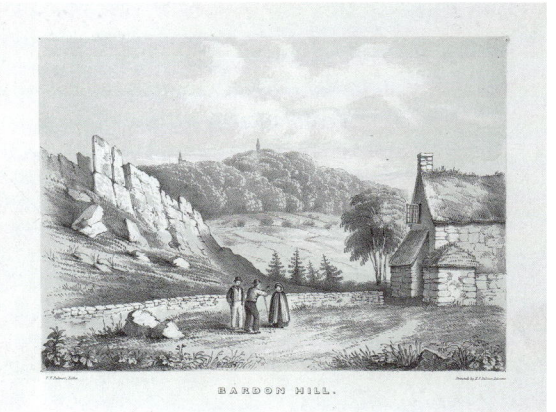

1-29 *The Monastery of Mount St. Bernard* (plate 2)

Undated, ca. 1840–42

Sketched by T. F. Lee, Esqr. F. F. Palmer, Litho. Printed by E. S. Palmer, Leicester.

Palmer's lithograph is similar to an engraving by the same name, sketched by her
    Leicester colleague J. F. Lee and engraved by R. Allen, in Potter's book *History
    and Antiquities of Charnwood Forest*. The figures are very different, but the
    landscapes are almost identical, with slight changes. Palmer also drew a view of
    the monastery in one of the Palmer series of lithographs Sketches in Leicestershire
    (pp. 239–46).

Courtesy of the Yale Center for British Art, Paul Mellon Fund.

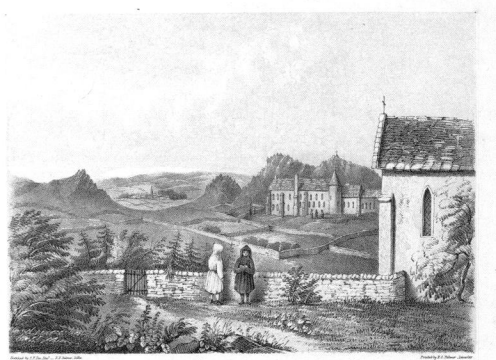

1-30 *Ruins in Bradgate Park* (plate 3)

Undated, ca. 1840–42

F. F. Palmer, Litho. E. S. Palmer, Printer, Leicester.

This lithograph closely resembles but is not identical to the engraving with the same
    title by Allen after a design by F. F. Palmer in Potter's book *History and Antiqui-
    ties of Charnwood Forest* (p. 231). Palmer's lithograph does not include figures;
    the clouds are different; the baby deer's head is turned forward; and the tree on
    the right is shaped differently.

Courtesy of the Yale Center for British Art, Paul Mellon Fund.

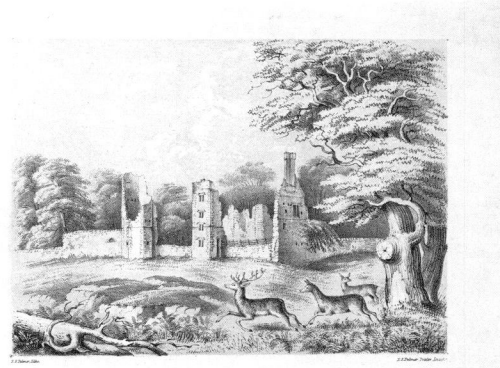

1-31 *Ulvescroft Priory* (plate 4)

Undated, ca. 1840–42

F. F. Palmer, Litho. E. S. Palmer, Printer, Leicester.

The architecture in this print is almost identical with the image by the same name in
    Potter's book *History and Antiquities of Charnwood Forest* (a steel engraving by
    R. Allen, adapted from F. F. Palmer's design [p. 229]). The engraving substitutes
    well-dressed, upper-class gentry for the simple folk in Palmer's lithograph.

Courtesy of the Yale Center for British Art, Paul Mellon Fund.

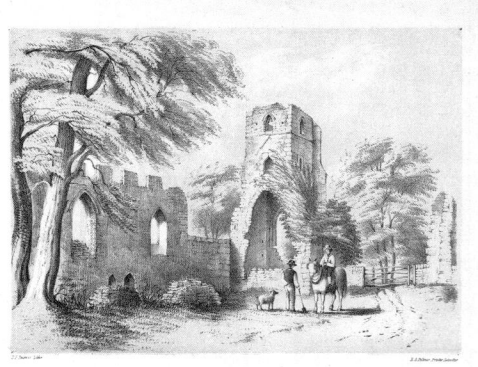

1-32 *The Oaks Chapel* (plate 5)
Undated, ca. 1840–42
F. F. Palmer, Litho. Printed by E. S. Palmer, Leicester.
This lithograph closely resembles an anonymous one carrying the same title in Potter,
  History and Antiquities of Charnwood Forest (p. 230). Slight differences in the
  branches of the tree on the right and the plants fringing the side of the road sug-
  gest that it was drawn on a different stone.

Courtesy of the Yale Center for British Art, Paul Mellon Fund.

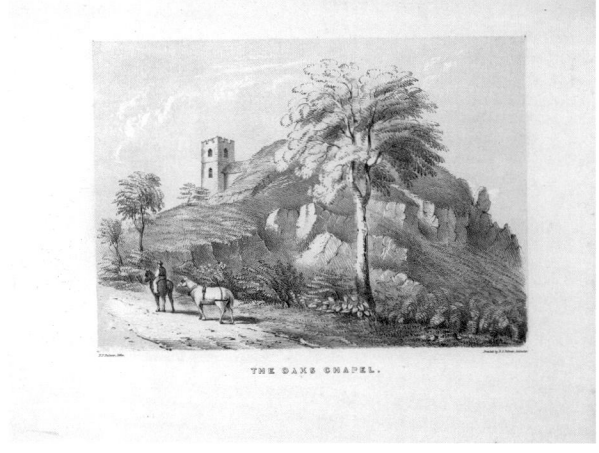

1-33 *Lower Cliff, Beacon Hill* (plate 6)
Undated, ca. 1840–42
F. F. Palmer, Lith. Printed by E. S. Palmer, Leicester.
This print is almost identical with the anonymous, identically titled lithograph facing
  page 90 in Potter, *History and Antiquities of Charnwood Forest*.

Courtesy of the Yale Center for British Art, Paul Mellon Fund.

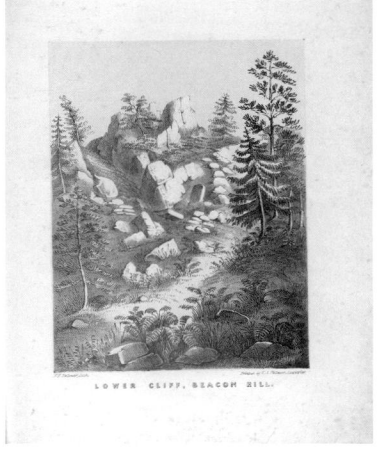

1-34 *Hand Mill / Celt* (plate 7)
Undated, ca. 1840–42
F. F. Palmer, litho. (printed below the hand mill on the image).
A similar, anonymous image faces page 42 in Potter, *History and Antiquities of
  Charnwood Forest*. This is an example of a work signed in one place by
  F. F. Palmer but unsigned in another location.

Courtesy of the Yale Center for British Art, Paul Mellon Fund.

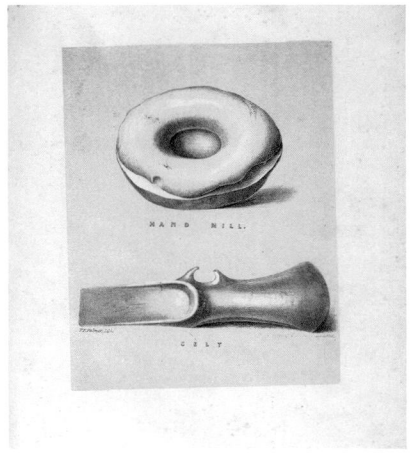

1-35 *Copt Oak* (plate 8)
Undated, ca. 1840–42
F. F. Palmer, Litho. Printed by E. S. Palmer, Leicester.

Courtesy of the Yale Center for British Art, Paul Mellon Fund.

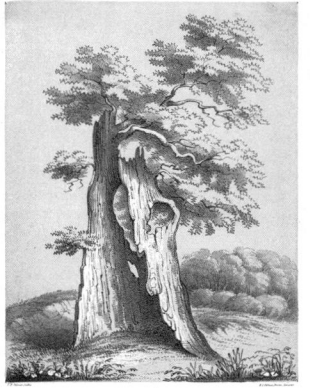

Views in Leicestershire

8⅔ × 11"

An album of fourteen F. F. Palmer tinted lithographs with a thin tan paper cover that reads, "Views in Leicestershire. Price One Shilling." Most of the images are the same as in *Eight Views of Charnwood Forest*, with the addition of *Long Cliff, Woodhouse-Eaves Church, Charley Hall, Woodhouse Church, High Cademan, Pelder Tor near Whitwick,* and *Whitwick Church* and lacking *Hand Mill Celt.*

Holding institution: University of Leicester

[1-28] *Bardon Hill* (plate 1)
Undated, ca. 1840–42
F. F. Palmer, Litho. Printed by E.S. Palmer, Leicester.

1-36 *Long Cliff* (plate 2)
Undated, ca. 1840–42
F. F. Palmer, Litho. E. S. Palmer, Printer, Leicester.

Courtesy of the University of Leicester.

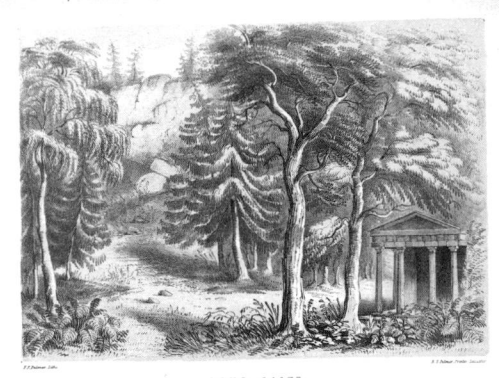

[1-30] *Ruins in Bradgate Park* (plate 3)
Undated, ca. 1840–42
F. F. Palmer, Litho. E. S. Palmer, Printer, Leicester.

[1-29] *The Monastery of Mount St. Bernard* (plate 4)
Undated, ca. 1840–42
Sketched by T. F. Lee, Esqr. F. F. Palmer, Litho. Printed by E. S. Palmer, Leicester.

[1-35] *Copt Oak* (plate 5)
Undated, ca. 1840–42
F. F. Palmer, Litho. Printed by E. S. Palmer, Leicester.

1-37 *Woodhouse-Eaves Church* (plate 6)
Undated, ca. 1840–42
F. F. Palmer, Lith. Printed by E. S. Palmer, Leicester.

Courtesy of the University of Leicester.

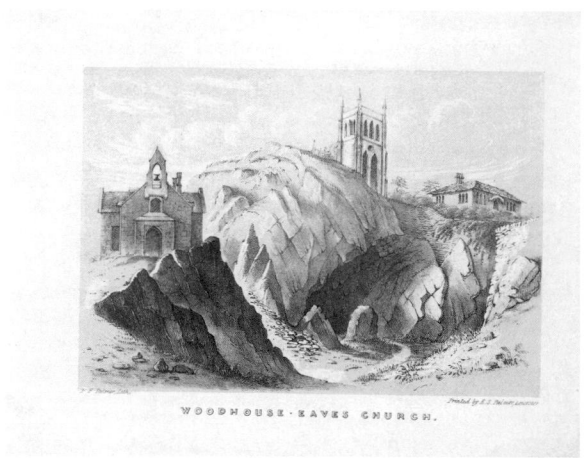

1-38 *Charley Hall* (plate 7)
Undated, ca. 1840–42
F. F. Palmer, Litho. Printed by E. S. Palmer, Leicester.

Courtesy of the University of Leicester.

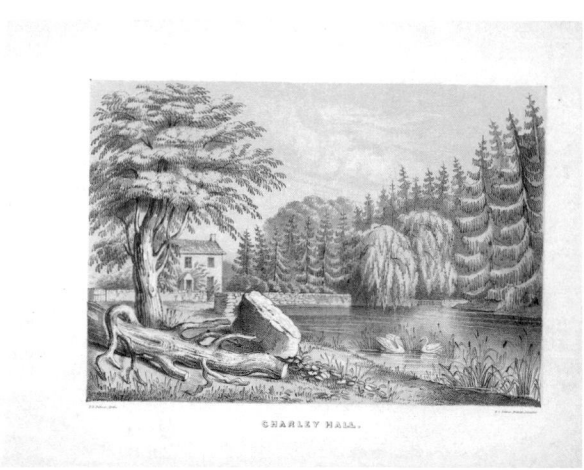

[1-32] *The Oaks Chapel* (plate 8)
Undated, ca. 1840–42
F. F. Palmer, Litho. Printed by E. S. Palmer, Leicester.

1-39 *Woodhouse Church* (plate 9)
Undated, ca. 1840–42
F. F. Palmer, Lith. Printed by E. S. Palmer, Leicester.

Courtesy of the University of Leicester.

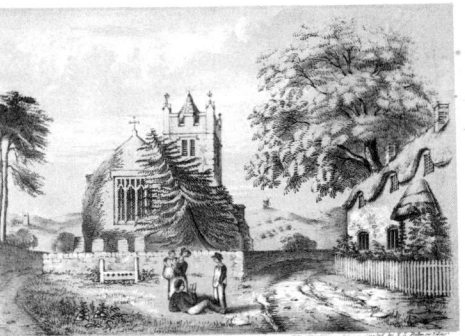

1-40 *High Cademan* (plate 10)
Undated, ca. 1840–42
F. F. Palmer, Litho. Printed by E. S. Palmer, Leicester.

Courtesy of the University of Leicester.

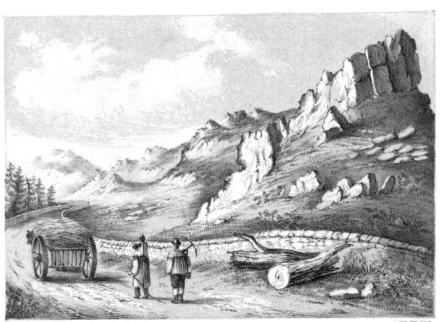

[1-33] *Lower Cliff, Beacon Hill* (plate 11)
Undated, ca. 1840–42
F. F. Palmer, Lith. Printed by E. S. Palmer, Leicester.
This print is almost identical with the anonymous, identically titled lithograph facing
    page 90 in Potter, *History and Antiquities of Charnwood Forest*.

1-41 *Pelder Tor near Whitwick* (plate 12)
Undated, ca. 1840–42
F. F. Palmer, Litho. E. S. Palmer, Printer, Leicester.

Courtesy of the University of Leicester.

1-42 *Whitwick Church* (plate 13)
Undated, ca. 1840–42
F. F. Palmer, Litho. E. S. Palmer, Printer, Leicester.

Courtesy of the University of Leicester.

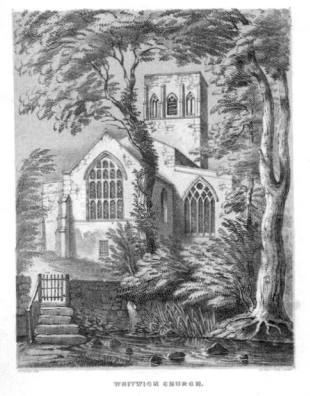

[1-31] *Ulvescroft Priory* (plate 14)
Undated, ca. 1840–42
F. F. Palmer, Litho. E. S. Palmer, Printer, Leicester.

1-43 *Leicester General News Rooms & Library*
May 1842
F. F. Palmer, lith. Flint, architect. This View is dedicated by permission to the Sub-
    scribers / By their obliged Servant / E. S. Palmer, Princess Street Leicester.
This print was later included as a frontispiece in J. F. Hollings, *Sketches in Leicester-
    shire: From Original Drawings with Historical and Descriptive Notices* (Leices-
    ter, UK: John Sydney Crossley, 1846), a bound reprint.

Sketches in Leicestershire
This series of five-pence folios of local scenes began to appear monthly beginning in June
1842. They were eventually supposed to include thirty views. The cover on each of the
numbers published over the following months is not the work of F. F. Palmer but was
designed and drawn by local artist B. F. Scott and printed by Edmund Seymour Palmer
with the imprint "B.F.S. Inv: et del: E.S. Palmer Litho." Each part of the series contained
three lithographs, often tinted and some with accents of white gouache, each on sheets
approximately 11 × 15" in size.

Sketches in Leicestershire, Part I

1-44 *Hanging Rock* (title page)
June 1842
F.F.P. (initials in squared capital letters on a small rock in the left foreground).
    Printed & Published by E. S. Palmer, Leicester. June 1st 1842.

Courtesy of the University of Leicester.

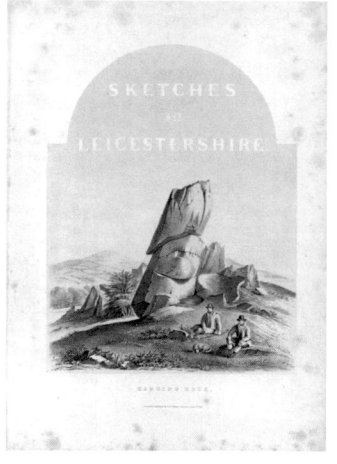

1-45 *St. Mary's Church. From the S.W.*   Illustrated, p. 17
1842
F. F. Palmer Lith. from a sketch by B. F. Scott.

1-46 *Granite Rocks, Beacon Hill.*   Illustrated, p. 17
June 1, 1842

Sketches in Leicestershire, Part II

1-47 *St. Margaret's Church, Leicester*   Illustrated, p. 1
July 1842
F. F. Palmer Lith.
After a sketch by B. F. Scott.

1-48 *Ruin in Bradgate Park.*
(Monogram of B. F. Scott in lower corner; not by Palmer.)
Do not confuse this image with Palmer's earlier print *Ruins in Bradgate Park*
    (p. 234), a different composition.

Courtesy of the University of Leicester.

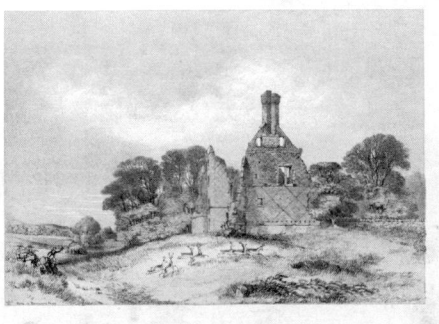

1-49 *Loughborough from Cotes Hill*   Illustrated, p. 19
July 1842
F. F. Palmer, del & lith. Printed & Published by E. S. Palmer, Leicester.
    1st July, 1842.

Sketches in Leicestershire, Part III

1-50 *Ashby De La Zouch Castle from the S.*   Illustrated, p. 20
August 1, 1842
F. F. Palmer del et lith.

1-51 *Monastery of Mount St. Bernard, Charnwood Forest*
August 1842
F. F. Palmer, del et lith. Printed & Published by E. S. Palmer August 1st 1842.

Courtesy of the University of Leicester.

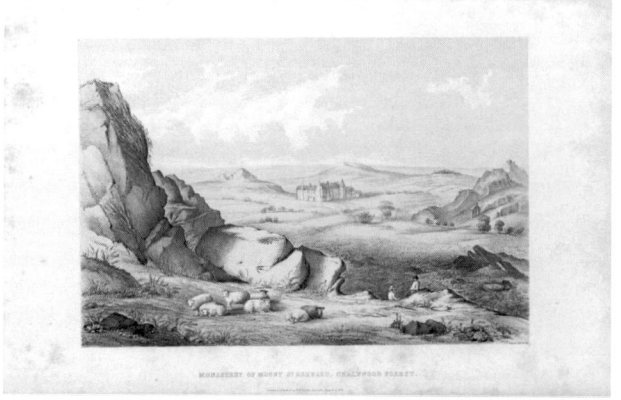

1-52 *Old West Bridge, Leicester*
August 1842
F. F. Palmer Lith. Sketched by J. F. Lee 24th March 1841. Printed & Published by
    E. S. Palmer, Leicester, August 1st 1842.

Courtesy of the University of Leicester.

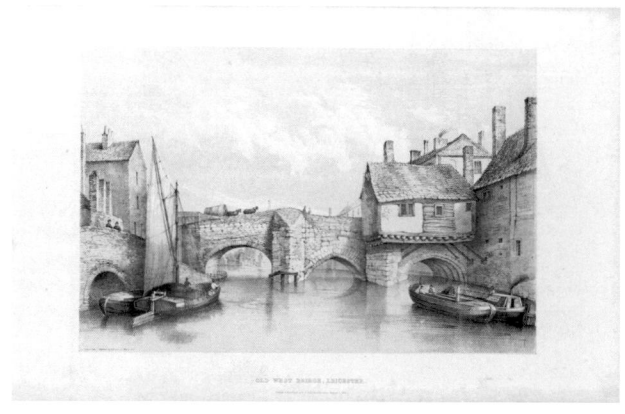

Sketches in Leicestershire, Part IV

1-53 *W. Front of Quenby Hall*
September 1842
F. F. Palmer Lith. From a sketch by B. F. Scott. Printed & Published by
    E. S. Palmer September 1st 1842.

Courtesy of the University of Leicester.

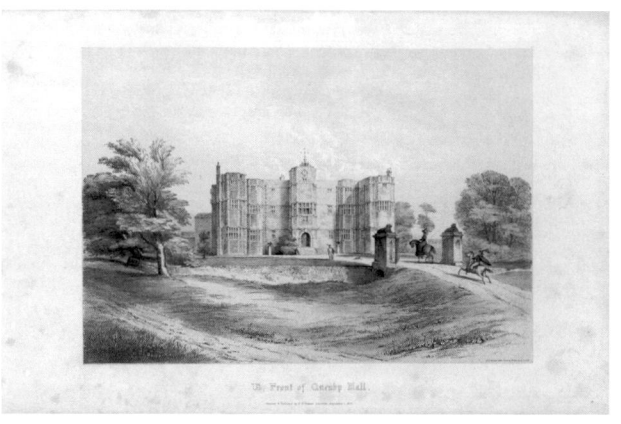

1-54 *Ulvescroft Priory*   Illustrated, p. 21
September 1, 1842
F. F. Palmer, del. et lith. Printed & Published by E. S. Palmer, Leicester, September
    1, 1842.

1-55 *Doorway of Belgrave Church; Doorway of All Saints Church, Leicester*   Illustrated, p. 18
Undated [September 1842]
F. F. Palmer, lith. from sketches by T. F. Lee.
Two architectural details side by side on one page. No printed title outside of the
    images; the titles are written at lower right on the images.

Sketches in Leicestershire, Part V

1-56 *Forest View. Bradgate Park*
October 1842
B. F. Scott, del et lith. (not by Palmer).

Courtesy of the University of Leicester.

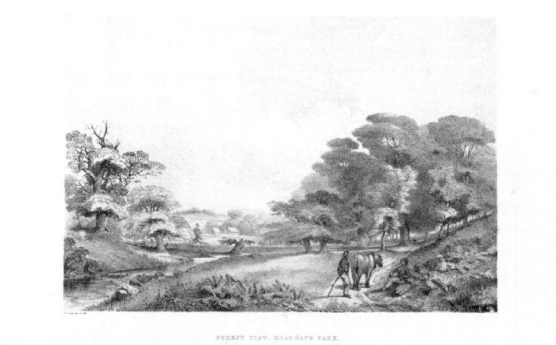

1-57 *Rice Rocks, and Bardon Hall*
October 1842
F. F. Palmer, lith. from a Sketch by W. Parsons. Printed & Published by
    E. S. Palmer, Leicester, October 1st, 1842.

Courtesy of the University of Leicester.

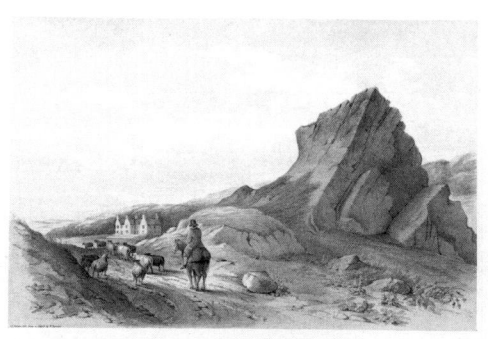

1-58 *Leicester Abbey*
October 1842
F. F. Palmer, del et lith. Printed & Published by E. S. Palmer, Leicester,
    October 1st, 1842.

Courtesy of the University of Leicester.

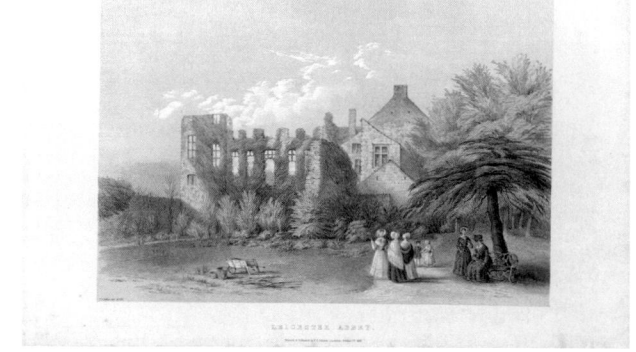

1-59 *Slate Quarry at Swithland*
November 1842
F. F. Palmer, lith. from a Sketch by B. F. Scott. Printed & Published by
    E. S. Palmer, Leicester, Nov. 1st, 1842.

Courtesy of the University of Leicester.

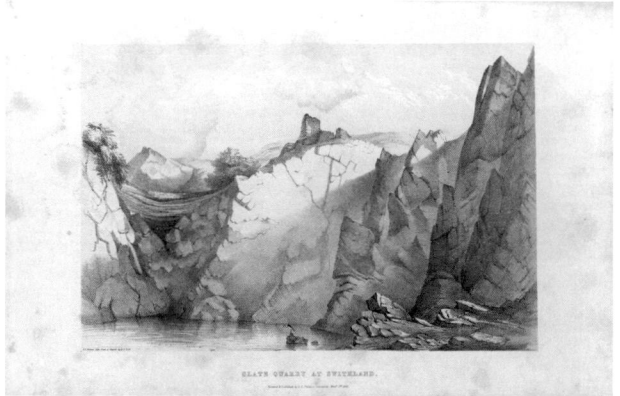

Sketches in Leicestershire, Part VI

1-60 *Hallaton Church*
December 1842
F. F. Palmer, del et lith. Printed & Published by E. S. Palmer, Leicester,
    December 1842.

Illustrated, p. 2

1-61 *Rakedale Hall*
1842
F. F. Palmer del et lith.

Courtesy of the University of Leicester.

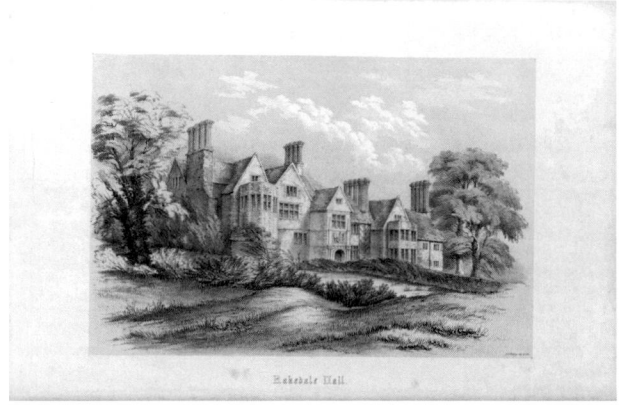

1-62 *The Old Blue Boar Inn, Leicester*
December 1842
F. F. Palmer lith from a Sketch by W. Parsons. Printed & Published by
    E. S. Palmer, Leicester, December 1842.

Illustrated, p. 21

*Sketches in Leicestershire, Part VII and VIII (exact order
of publication not established)*

1-63 *Kirby Castle*
1842
B. F. Scott del et lith. (not by Palmer).

Courtesy of the University of Leicester.

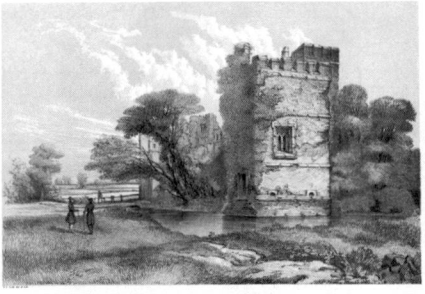

1-64 *Gracedieu Nunnery*
Undated, ca. 1842–43
F. F. Palmer, lith. from a Sketch by Ambrose Lisle Phillipps, Esq.

Courtesy of the University of Leicester.

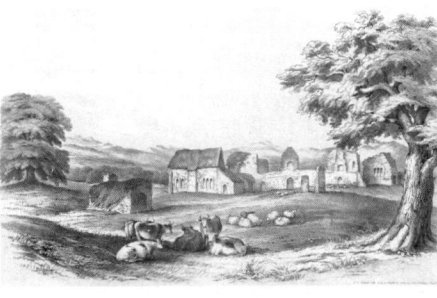

1-65 St. *Mary's Church, Leicester; Ashby Folville Church*
Undated, ca. 1842–43
Each image is 10½ × 6 9/10" sheet 15 × 22"
St. F. F. Palmer, del et lith.
Two architectural details of windows placed side by side on one page. No printed
    title outside of the images; the titles are written at lower left on the images.

Illustrated, p. 18

1-66 *Ruins of Hemington Church*
Undated, ca. 1842–43
F. F. Palmer, del et lith.

Courtesy of the University of Leicester.

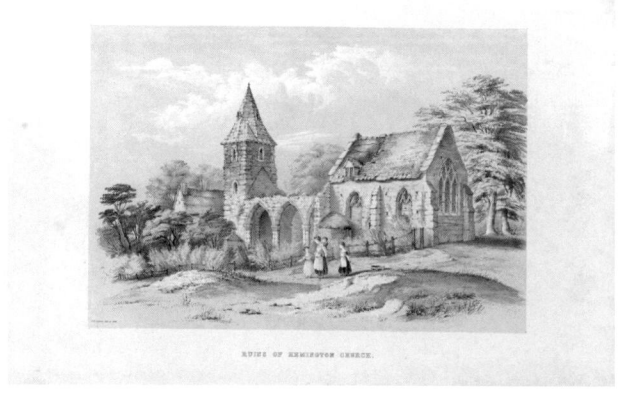

1-67 *Gaddesby Church*
Undated, ca. 1842–43
F. F. Palmer del et lith.

Courtesy of the University of Leicester.

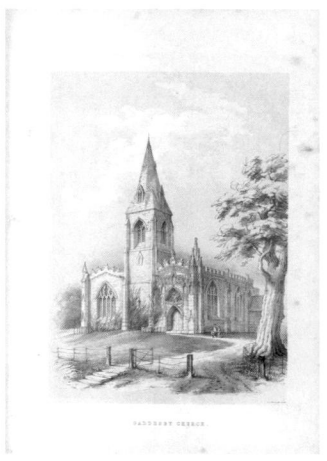

1-68 *Ashby de la Zouch Castle, from the N.*
Undated, ca. 1842–43
F. F. Palmer, del et lith.

Courtesy of the University of Leicester.

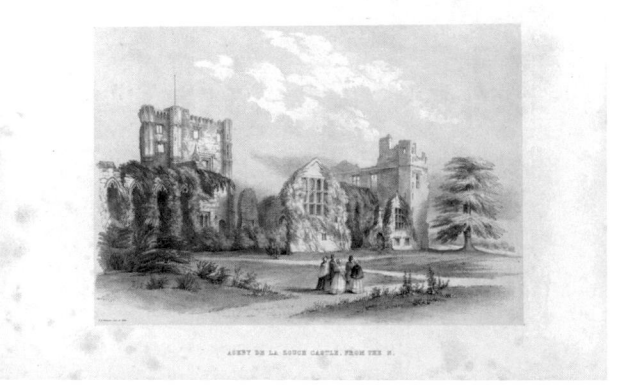

1-69 *Higham Church*
Undated, ca. 1842–43
F. F. Palmer, lith from a Sketch by W. Parsons.

Courtesy of the University of Leicester.

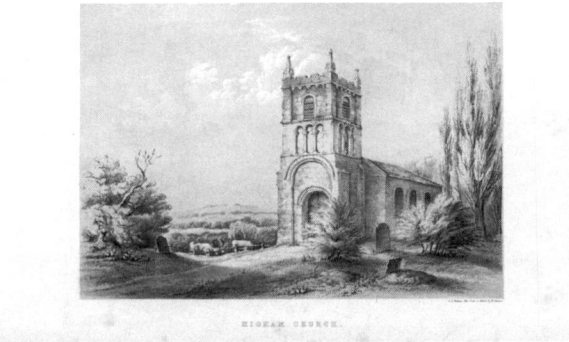

1-70 *Doorway of Bagworth Church; Doorway of Horninghold Church*
F. F. Lee, del. (at left of left image) J. Payne, del. (at left of right image)
   (not by Palmer).
Two architectural details placed side by side on one page. No printed title outside
   of the images; the titles are written at lower right on the images.

Courtesy of the University of Leicester.

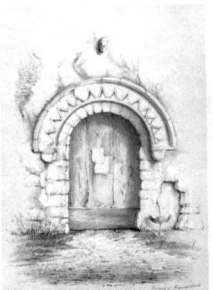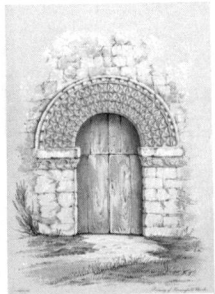

Sketches in Leicester: From Original Drawings with Historical and Descriptive Notices
by J. F. Hollings (Leicester: John Sydney Crossley, 1846).

15½ × 21¾"

Holding institution: University of Leicester

In 1846, two and a half years after the Palmers left for the United States, this bound
volume of Palmer's prints was published in Leicester by John Sydney Crossley. J. F.
Hollings, Leicester historian and headmaster of the Proprietary School, wrote lengthy
explications, printed in letterpress type, to accompany each print. In his preface, he
praised the work of Mrs. Palmer. The book includes twenty-five tinted lithographs, and
they are listed here in order of their placement in the volume.

   [1-44] *Hanging Rock* (title page)
   [1-56] *Forest View. Bradgate Park*
   [1-57] *Rice Rocks, and Bardon Hall*
   [1-46] *Granite Rocks, Beacon Hill*
   [1-59] *Slate Quarry at Swithland*
   [1-52] *Old West Bridge, Leicester*
   [1-62] *Old Blue Boar Inn, Leicester*
   [1-58] *Leicester Abbey*
   [1-54] *Ulvescroft Priory*

[1-64] *Gracedieu Nunnery*

[1-66] *Ruins of Hemington Church*

[1-63] *Kirby Castle*

[1-48] *Ruin in Bradgate Park*

[1-68] *Ashby de la Zouch Castle, from the N.*

[1-47] *St. Margaret's Church, Leicester*

[1-45] *St. Mary's Church. From the S.W.*

[1-65] *St. Mary's Church, Leicester; Ashby Folville Church*

[1-55] *Doorway of Belgrave Church; Doorway of All Saints Church, Leicester*

[1-70] *Doorway of Bagworth Church; Doorway of Horninghold Church*

[1-67] *Gaddesby Church*

[1-60] *Hallaton Church*

[1-69] *Higham Church*

[1-53] *W. Front of Quenby Hall*

[1-61] *Rakedale Hall*

[1-51] *Monastery of Mount St. Bernard, Charnwood Forest*

Prints Produced in the United States as Freelance Assignments, Other Than for N. Currier or for Currier & Ives

This list contains all of the known works that Fanny Palmer as well as her husband, Edmund Seymour Palmer, were involved in after their arrival in the United States in the early 1840s that were not for Nathaniel Currier or Currier & Ives. Most of these prints were completed before F. F. Palmer joined Nathaniel Currier's firm, but some were carried out for other publishers even after she began to work for Currier. Many of the prints are entirely her creation, whereas others are adapted from drawings, engravings, and daguerreotypes by other artists.

The list is organized chronologically as can best be determined. Some of the prints are undated, and approximate dates for these prints are based primarily on the years the Palmers were associated with certain addresses in New York City:

1844–45	55 Ludlow St. and 128 Fulton St.
1846–47	43 Ann St.
1847–48	34 Ann St.
1848–49	43 Ann St.
1849	27 Ann St.
1849–50	98 Nassau St.
1850–51	100 Nassau St.

Two prints incorrectly attributed to Edmund S. Palmer are listed at the end of this appendix.

2-1 *F. Basham, / Modeller, / Plaster, Cement & Scagliola / Worker, / No. 408 Broadway, New York*

Illustrated, p. 27

Undated, 1844

Image 14⅓ × 11" sheet 21 × 13¾"

F. F. Palmer (signature on stone, bottom right of image). E. Jones, Lith., N.Y. 128 Fulton St. N.Y.

Holding institution: Library of Congress

The copy held by the Library of Congress bears the handwritten note "Deposited in the Clerk's Office for the Southern District of New York, January 24, 1844."

2-2 *Suburban Gothic Villa, Murray Hill, N. Y. City. Residence of W. C. H. Waddell,*
Esq. / 5th Avenue, between 37 & 38th Street   Illustrated, p. 30

Undated, ca. 1844

Sheet 13 1/5 × 10⅓"

F. Palmer, lith. (signature on stone, bottom left of image). A. Davis, Architect. Lith. of
E. Jones & E. Palmer.

Holding institution: New York Public Library

The New York Public Library holds a wash drawing by Davis of the building from 1844,
showing only the plan for the first floor. Palmer's print has floor plans for both the first
and second floors. The print was purportedly reissued by Nathaniel Currier.[2]

2-3 *Nehemiah Cleaveland, M.D.*   Illustrated, p. 25

Undated, ca. 1844

Image 11 × 9 7/17" sheet 16⅞ × 13"

F. F. Palmer (signature on stone, lower left of vignetted image). Lith. of E. S. Palmer, 55
Ludlow St. N.Y.

Holding institution: Peabody Essex Museum

This print is likely dated to 1844 because of the Ludlow Street address and the signature
"Lith of E. S. Palmer," which is similar to the way Mr. Palmer indicated that he was the
printer in Leicester, England. The couple soon changed their company signature to "F. &
S. Palmer, lith." This smoothly rendered portrait looks as though it may have been adapted
from a daguerreotype.

2-4 *The Hon. James K. Polk*   Illustrated, p. 26

1844

Image 15¾ × 10⅝" sheet 18½ × 14"

F. F. Palmer (signature on stone). Entered . . . 1844 by E. S. Palmer. Lith. of E. S. Palmer,
55 Ludlow St. N.Y. Publ. by J. Childs, No. 4 Wall St. N.Y.

Holding institution: William L. Clements Library, University of Michigan

2-5 *Church of the Pilgrims. / cor: Henry & Remsen Sts: Brooklyn, Long-Island. / Richard*
Upjohn, Arch.   Illustrated, p. 28

1844

Image 13 13/16 × 10⅝" sheet 18¼ × 18¼"

F & S. Palmer, 55 Ludlow Street, N.Y. Entered . . . 1844, by Richard Upjohn.

Holding institution: Metropolitan Museum of Art

2-6 *Elliottsville, S.I.*

Undated, ca. 1844–45?

Sheet 13⅝ × 18 5/16"

Lith of F & S Palmer, 55 Ludlow St. N.Y.

Holding institution: Museum of the City of New York

This print looks as if it was transcribed from a Palmer watercolor painted directly from life.

Illustrated, p. 31

2-7 *The Peace of Home, / a Favorite Song, / as sung by / R. G. Paige, / the Poetry by / G. Lindley, Esq. / Composed by / Jules Benedict*

Undated, ca. 1845

F. F. Palmer. Lith of Lewis & Brown, 37 John St. N.Y. Published at Millet's Music Saloon 329 Broadway.

Holding institution: Lester S. Levy Sheet Music Collection, Johns Hopkins University

In its issue for January 25, 1845, *The Anglo American* periodical reported the recent publication of this music by Millet.[3]

Courtesy of the Lester S. Levy Collection of Sheet Music, Sheridan Libraries, Johns Hopkins University.

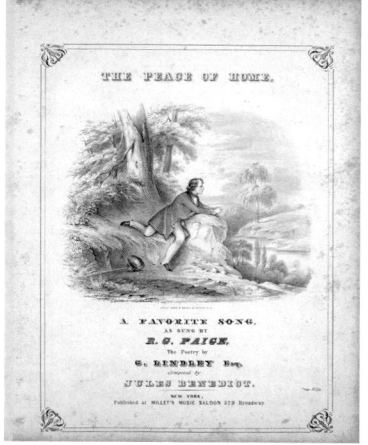

2-8 *Henry Clay, Packet Ship. / E. Nye, Commander*

1845

Image 13⅞ × 19¼"

Painted by W. Marsh, Esqr. N.Y. On Stone by F. Palmer. Entered . . . 1845, by S. Palmer . . . Published by S. Palmer, 55 Ludlow & 128 Fulton Sts. N. York.

Holding institution: Mariners' Museum

Illustrated, p. 33

2-9 *Avezzana's Quick Step. / As performed by the / American Brass Band / Composed for the / Piano Forte / and Respectfully dedicated to / Capt. G. Avezzana / and the Officers and Members of the / New York Italian Guard / by / C. Chianei*

1845

Sheet 13½ × 10¼"

Illustrated, p. 196

F. Palmer, 55 Ludlow St. N.W. From a Daguerreotype by Louis L. Bishop. Lith. of Michelin, 111 Nassau St. Published by Millet's Music Saloon, 329 Broadway. Entered . . . 1845 by Wm. E. Millet.

Holding institution: Lester S. Levy Sheet Music Collection, Johns Hopkins University

A sheet-music cover lithographed or printed by Michelin; Mr. Palmer did not play a role in this print.

2-10 *Church of the Holy Trinity. / Brooklyn Heights. / Minard Lafever Archt.*

1845

Image 17 1/16 × 11⅞" sheet 21 9/16 × 14 7/16"

On stone by F. & S. Palmer Lithrs. 55 Ludlow St. New York. Entered . . . 1845 by S. Palmer.

Holding institution: American Antiquarian Society

Illustrated, gallery plate 2

2-11 *Junction of Fulton & Court Sts.*

Undated, ca. 1845

Sheet 9 2/5 × 8"

Drawn & Printed by F. & S. Palmer 55 Ludlow St. N.Y. Designed by R. Butt. Archt. & Lithogh.

Holding institution: Museum of the City of New York

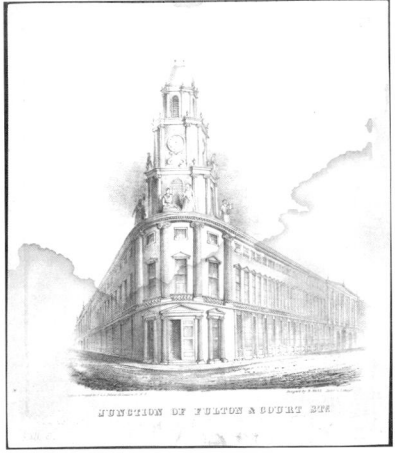

In *Old Brooklyn Heights: New York's First Suburb*, Clay Lancaster notes that in 1845 "a gentleman styling himself, 'R. Butt, architect and lithographer,' issued a booklet proposing an unusual scheme, a hollow triangular edifice encircling the whole block, having shops on the ground floor and the city offices above" for the site of the new city hall in Brooklyn Heights at Joralemon, Fulton, and Court Streets.[4]

Courtesy of the Museum of the City of New York, 29.100.3547.

2-12 *My Mountain Home / A favorite Song. / The Poetry by / Samuel Lover, Esqr. / The Music Composed & Dedicated / to / Dr. Geo. O. Jarvis. / By William J. Wetmore*

1844 [ca. 1846–47?]

Image 8½ × 7¼" sheet 13 × 10"

Entered . . . 1844 by William E. Millet . . . Lith of F & S Palmer 43 Ann St. N.Y. New-York. Published at Millet's Music Saloon. 329 Broadway.

Holding institution: Lester S. Levy Sheet Music Collection, Johns Hopkins University

Illustrated, p. 34

There does not seem to be a signature by F. F. Palmer on the image. The Palmers' address, "43 Ann St.," suggests that although the music was copyrighted in 1844, the cover was issued later. Another sheet-music cover for *My Mountain Home*, signed with "Fleetwood" as the artist and lithographer, is a poorly drawn, crude version of the Palmers' cover, with slight differences in the figures, trees, and rocks.

2-13 *Battle of Palo-Alto. / Charge of Capt. May's Dragoons, / in which Genl. La Vega was taken prisoner*

1846

11⅓ × 15 2/5"

F.P. (initials on stone, lower part of image). Entered . . . 1846 by F. & S. Palmer . . . Lith of F. & S. Palmer, 43 Ann St.

Holding institution: Library of Congress

Illustrated, p. 39

2-14 *The Mexican Rulers, / migrating from Matamoras [sic] with their Treasures*

1846

Image 9¼ × 13¼, sheet 11 4/5 × 16 1/10"

Entered . . . 1846, by Thomas Odham . . . Lith. & Pub. by F. & S. Palmer, 43 Ann St., N. Y.

Holding institution: Library of Congress

The copy held by the Library of Congress includes the additional line "T. B. Peterson Agent 98 Chesnut St. Philadelphia" below the publisher's imprint.

Illustrated, p. 38

2-15 *No. 1! and Northin Else*

Undated [1846]

Image 11¼ × 15⅝"

Lith of F & S Palmer 43 Ann St. NY.

Holding institution: New-York Historical Society

The copy held by the Huntington Library includes the additional line "T. B. Peterson Agent 98 Chesnut St. Philadelphia" below the publisher's imprint.

Illustrated, p. 35

2-16 *Take Ca-are What ar-ye 'bout. / No. 2*

Undated [1846]

Image 10⅝ × 15⅝"

Lith. & Pub. by F & S Palmer, 43 Ann St. N.Y.

Holding institution: New-York Historical Society

The version of this print held by the Huntington Library has the imprint "Lith of F. & S. Palmer. 128 Fulton St. N.Y."

Courtesy of the Old Print Shop.

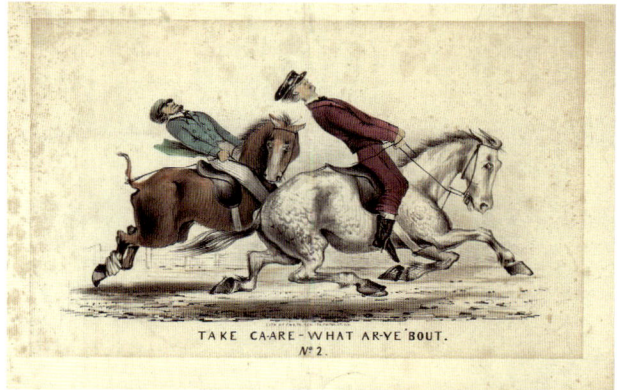

2-17 *One of the B'Hoys. / No 3 Striking the Pavements*

Undated [1846]

Image 11½ × 17"

Lith & Pub by F & S Palmer 43, Ann St. N.Y.

Holding institution: New-York Historical Society

Courtesy of the New-York Historical Society.

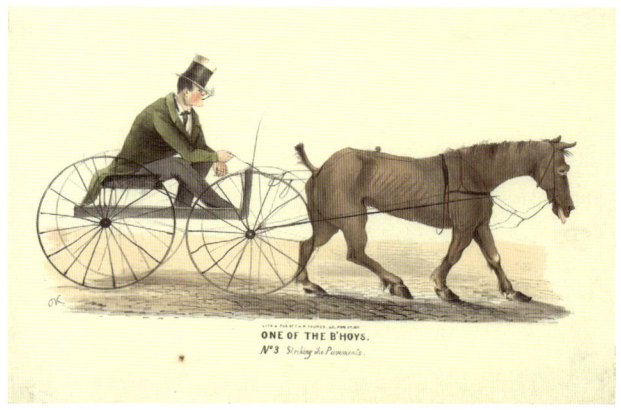

2-18 *Two of The B'Hoys. / No. 4 Breaking*

Undated [1846]

Sheet 11 × 16⅛"

Lith & Pub by F & S Palmer 43 Ann St. N.Y.

Holding institution: New-York Historical Society

The version of this print held by the Old Print Shop has the imprint "Lith of F. & S. Palmer. 128 Fulton St. N.Y."

Illustrated, p. 35

2-19 *Heigh___gh! Wake up there, what are ye at? / No. 5*

1846

Image 10¼ × 15¼" sheet 11½ × 17"

Entered . . . 1846, by Thomas Odham . . . Lith. & Publ. by F. & S. Palmer, 43 Ann St. N.Y.

Holding institution: New-York Historical Society

The copy held by the Huntington Library includes the additional line "T. B. Peterson Agent 98 Chesnut St. Philadelphia" below the publisher's imprint.

Courtesy of the New-York Historical Society.

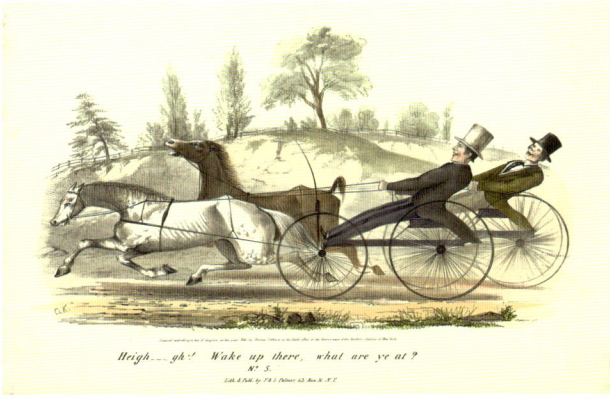

2-20 *Ho–Ho–Ho–Sambo—get along there what ar' you at? / No. 6*

1846

Sheet 11½ × 17"

Entered . . . 1846, by Thomas Odham . . . Lith. & Publ. by F. & S. Palmer, 43 Ann St. N.Y.

Holding institution: New-York Historical Society

Illustrated, p. 200

2-21 *Volunteers for Texas / As You Were*

1846

Image 12⅓ × 12 1/10"

Entered . . . 1846 by Thomas Odham. Lith. F. & S. Palmer 43 Ann Street, N.Y.

Holding institution: Library of Congress

The drawing does not seem to be in Palmer's style; perhaps it was lithographed from Odham's cartoon. The copy of this print held by the Huntington Library has a different title, *One of the B'Hoys, & his Company. As you were*, and lacks the Odham copyright statement.

Illustrated, p. 38

2-22 *War! Or No War*

1846

Image 11½ × 16 3/5"

F.P. (initials on stone on wall at back center of image). Entered . . . 1846 by Thomas Odham. Lith. F. & S. Palmer—43 Ann Street N. York.

Holding institution: Library of Congress

Illustrated, p. 37

2-23 *Yankee Doodle* Illustrated, p. 36

1846

Image 10 × 7½" sheet 11¼ × 8½"

P (initial on stone at lower left of image). Published at William H. Graham's 160 Nassau Street. Tribune Building.

Holding institution: American Antiquarian Society

This is the cover for the first issue of the new comic magazine *Yankee Doodle* and several subsequent issues. Palmer also did the first full-page caricature (*The Naughty Boy Who Didn't Do His Errand*), for the October 17, 1846, issue.

The Architect: A Series of Original Designs, for Domestic Cottages and Villas, Connected with Landscape Gardening, Adapted to the United States. Illustrated by Drawings of Ground Plots, Plans, Perspective Views, Elevations, Sections, and Details, by William H. Ranlett. 2 vols.

1847–49

Both William Ranlett, the architect and author of this two-volume work, and Fanny Palmer worked on the illustrations for this series. The Palmers involvement in the plates varied: in the introduction to volume 1, Ranlett noted that "the most difficult" plates were "executed on the stones by Mrs. F. Palmer," while F. Meyer executed the ground plans and details, and that all of the lithographic plates were "from the well-known lithographic press-room of Messrs. Palmer" (unpaginated, around p. 1). The Palmers' imprint, with various addresses, appears on most of the plates. Notably, though, the "33 Ann Street" address listed for the Palmers on the copyright page appears to be a typo for 34 Ann Street. An edition of the series published in 1851, along with images by the Palmers, also includes plates with the imprint "Mayer & Korff, Lith. 93 Nassau St., N.Y."

The Architect: A Series of Original Designs, for Domestic Cottages and Villas, Connected with Landscape Gardening, Adapted to the United States. Illustrated by Drawings of Ground Plots, Plans, Perspective Views, Elevations, Sections, and Details. Vol. I. By William H. Ranlett, Architect. New York: William H. Graham, Tribune Buildings, 1847. Snowden & Prall, Printers, Ann Street, cor. Nassau. F. & S. Palmer, Lithographers, 33 Ann Street.

14¼ × 11¼"

Holding institution: Huntington Library

2-24 *Cottage & Villa /Architecture / By W. H. Ranlett. / Residence of the author—Staten Island* (frontispiece)
F.P. (initials on stone at bottom left of image). F & S. Palmer's Lith. 34 Ann St.

2-25 *Plate 1. Design 1st. Perspective View*
On Stone by F. Palmer (on stone at bottom right). Designed & del. by Wm. H. Ranlett.
    Lith of F. & S. Palmer. 43 Ann St. N.Y.

2-26 *Plate 2nd. Design 1st. Ground Plot*
[no imprint]

2-27 *Plate 3rd. Design 1st*
Lith of F. & S. Palmer. 43 Ann St. N.Y.

2-28 *Plate 4th. Design 1st. Front Elevation; Side Elevation* (two images on one page)

2-29 *Plate 5th. Design 1st*
Lith of F. & S. Palmer 43 Ann St. N.Y.

2-30 *Plate 6th. Design 1st*
Lith of F. & S. Palmer, 43 Ann St. N.Y.

2-31 [Plate 7.] *Design II. Perspective View*
P (initial on stone at bottom left of image). On Stone by F. Palmer. Designed & del. by
    Wm. H. Ranlett. Lith of F & S Palmer. 43 Ann St.

2-32 *Plate 8. Design II. Ground Plot*
Lith. F. & S. Palmer 43 Ann St.

2-33 *Plate 9. Design II*
Lith. F. & S. Palmer 43 Ann St.

2-34 *Plate 10. Design II. Garden Front; Entrance Front* (two images on one page)
Lith. F. & S. Palmer 43 Ann St.

2-35 *Plate 11. Design II*
Lith. F. & S. Palmer 43 Ann St.

2-36 *Plate 12. Design II*
Lith. F. & S. Palmer 43 Ann St.
2-37 *Plate 13. Design III. Garden Front; Entrance Front* (two images on one page)
Designed & del. by Wm. H. Ranlett. Lith of F. & S. Palmer. 43 Ann St. N.Y.

2-38 *Plate 14. Design III*
Lith F & S Palmer 43 Ann St.

2-39 *Plate 15. Design IV. Front Elevation; Side Elevation*
P (initial on stone at lower right of bottom image). Designed & del. by Wm. H. Ran-
    lett. Lith of F. & S. Palmer. 43 Ann St. N.Y.

2-40 *Plate 16. Design IV*
Lith F & S Palmer 43 Ann St.

Courtesy of the Huntington Library, San Marino, CA, RB 388205 v. 1.

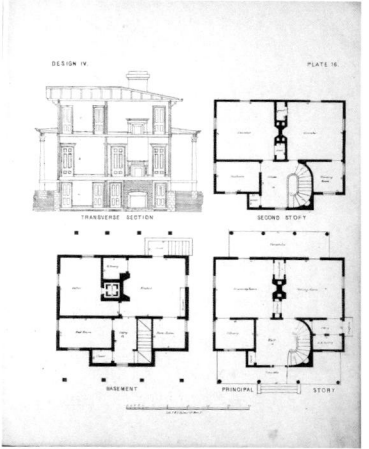

2-41 *Plate 17. Design IV*
Lith F & S Palmer 43 Ann St.

2-42 *Plate 18. Design III & IV. Ground Plot*
Lith F & S Palmer 43 Ann St.

2-43 *Plate 19. Design V*
(Imprint not visible in Huntington Library copy.)

2-44 *Plate 20. Design V. Lawn front; Entrance front*
Designed & del. by Wm. H. Ranlett. Lith of F. & S. Palmer, 34 Ann St. N.Y.

2-45 *Plate 21. Design V*
(Imprint not visible in Huntington Library copy.)

2-46 *Plate 22. Design V*
(Imprint not visible in Huntington Library copy.)

2-47 *Plate 23. Design V. Ground Plot*
(Imprint not visible in Huntington Library copy.)

2-48 *Plate 24. Design V. Perspective View*
F. Palmer. Lith. (on stone at bottom right of image). Designed & del. by Wm. H.
    Ranlett. Lith of F. & S. Palmer, 34 Ann St.

2-49 *Plate 25. Design VI. Perspective View / in the English Style; Perspective View /
    in the Grecian Style*
Designed by Wm. H. Ranlett. Lith F & S Palmer 43 Ann St.

2-50 *Plate 26. Designs VI & VII*
Lith F. & S. Palmer 43 Ann St.

2-51 *Plate 27. Design VIII. English Cottage Style; English Cottage Style* (two images on one page)
Designed & del by Wm. H. Ranlett (text below both images at right). Lith. F & S. Palmer 43 Ann St. (text below bottom image).

2-52 *Plate 28. Design VIII & IX*
Lith. F & S Palmer 43 Ann St. N.Y.

2-53 *Plate 29. Design VIII*
Lith F. & S. Palmer 43 Ann St.

2-54 *Plate 30. Design IX*
Lith F. & S. Palmer 43 Ann St.

2-55 *Plate 31. Design X. Anglo Grecian Villa*
P (initial on stone at bottom right of image). Designed & del. by Wm. H. Ranlett. Lith of F. & S. Palmer 43 Ann St. N.Y.

2-56 *Plate 32. Design X*
Lith. F. & S. Palmer 43 Ann St. N.Y.

2-57 *Plate 33. Design X*
Lith. of F. & S. Palmer 43 Ann St. N.Y.

2-58 *Plate 34. Design X*
Lith. of F. & S. Palmer 43 Ann St. N.Y.

2-59 *Plate 35. Design X*
Lith. F. & S. Palmer 43 Ann St. N.Y.

2-60 *Plate 36. Design XI. Scenic View*   Illustrated, p. 47
P (initial on stone at bottom right of image). Drawn by Wm. H. Ranlett. Lith. of F. & S. Palmer 43 Ann St. N.Y.

2-61 *Plate 37. Design XII*
W. H. Ranlett. F. & S. Palmer's Lith. 34 Ann St.

2-62 *Plate 38. Design XII. A Villa in the Swiss Style. / Lawn Front; Entrance Front* (two images on one page)
Del. & desnd. by Wm. H. Ranlett. Lith. F. & S. Palmer 34 Ann St. N.Y.

2-63 *Plate 39. Design XII. Exterior Details*
W. H. Ranlett. F. & S. Palmer's Lith. 34, Ann St. N.Y.

2-64 *Plate 40. Details*
Lith. F. & S. Palmer 34 Ann St.

2-65 *Plate 41. Design XIII. A Cottage in the Swiss Style. / Entrance Front;*
Garden Elevation
Del. & desnd. by Wm. H. Ranlett. Lith. F. & S. Palmer 34 Ann St. N.Y.

2-66 *Plate 42. Design XI & XII*
Lith. F. & S. Palmer 34 Ann St. N.Y.

2-67 *Plate 43. Design XIV. Ornamental Cottage / in the Elizabethan Style; A Small*
Villa / in the Indian Style (two images on one page)
Des. & del by Wm. H. Ranlett (text below both images at left). F. & S. Palmer's Lith.
34 Ann St. (text below bottom image at right).

2-68 *Plate 44. Design XVI. Design XIV. Design XV & XVII*
W. H. Ranlett. F. & S. Palmer's Lith. 43 Ann St. N.Y.

2-69 *Plate 45. Design XVI. Ornamental Cottage. / in the early English Style; Design*
XVII. Parsonage, / in the Tudor Style (two images on one page)
F. Palmer, Lith. (on stone at lower right of bottom image). Des. & del. by Wm.
H. Ranlett (text below both images at left). F. & S. Palmer's Lith. 34 Ann. St.

2-70 *Plate 46. Design XV. Indian Details*
Wm. H. Ranlett. F. & S. Palmer's Lith. 34 Ann St.

2-71 *Plate 47. Design XVI. Details*
Wm. H. Ranlett. F. & S. Palmer's Lith. 34 Ann St.

2-72 *Plate 48*
Des. & del. by Wm. H. Ranlett. F. & S. Palmer's Lith. 34 Ann St.

2-73 *Plate 49. Design XVII. Side Entrance Elevation. / Romanesque Style; Front*
Entrance Elevation (two images on one page)
F.P. (initials on stone at bottom left of top image). Designed & drawn by W. H.
Ranlett. F. & S. Palmer's Lith. 34 Ann St. N.Y.

2-74 *Plate 50. Design XVIII*
W. H. Ranlett. F. & S. Palmer's Lith. 34 Ann St.

2-75 *Plate 51. Design XIX*
Designed & drawn by W. H. Ranlett. Lith. of F. & S. Palmer, 34 Ann St. N.Y.

2-76 *Plate 52. Design XVIII*
W. H. Ranlett. F. & S. Palmer's Lith. 34 Ann St.

2-77 *Plate 53. Design XVIII. Details*
W. H. Ranlett. F. & S. Palmer's Lith. 34 Ann St.

2-78 *Plate 54*
W. H. Ranlett. F. & S. Palmer's Lith. 34 Ann St.

2-79 *Plate 55. Design XX. A Villa in the French Style, / Side Elevation; Front*
Elevation (two images on one page)
F. Palmer (signature on stone at lower right of bottom image). Des. & Drawn by W. H.
Ranlett. Lith. of F. & S. Palmer 34 Ann St. N.Y.

2-80 *Plate 56. Design XX*
Wm. H. Ranlett. F. & S. Palmer's Lith. 34 Ann St. N.Y.

2-81 *Plate 57. Design XX. Exterior Details*
Wm. H. Ranlett. F. & S. Palmer's Lith. 34 Ann St. N.Y.

2-82 *Plate 58. Design XX. Interior Details*
W. H. Ranlett. Lith. of F. & S. Palmer, 34 Ann St. N.Y.

2-83 *Plate 59. Design XXI. Cottage in the French Style, / Side Elevation;*
Entrance Elevation (two images on one page)
F. Palmer (signature on stone at lower left of bottom image). Des. & Drawn by W. H.
Ranlett. Lith. of F. & S. Palmer 34 Ann St. N.Y.

Courtesy of the Huntington Library, San Marino, CA, RB 388205 v. 1.

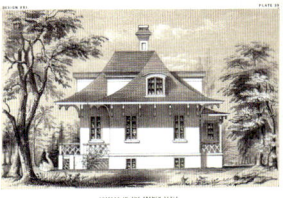

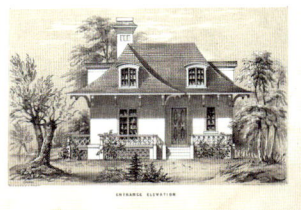

2-84 *Plate 60. Design XXI*
Wm. H. Ranlett. F. & S. Palmer's Lith. 34 Ann St. N.Y.

The Architect: A Series of Original Designs, for Domestic Cottages and Villas, Connected
with Landscape Gardening, Adapted to the United States. Illustrated by Drawings of
Ground Plots, Plans, Perspective Views, Elevations, Sections, and Details. Vol. II. By
William H. Ranlett, Architect. New York: Published by Dewitt & Davenport, Tribune
Buildings, 1849. J. P. Prall, Printer, No. 9 Spruce street, N.Y. F. & S. Palmer, Lithographers, 33 Ann Street.

14¼ × 11¼"

Holding institution: Huntington Library

Only one plate in the book includes F. Palmer's initials on stone (plate 3), but almost all of
the plates include various imprints and addresses for the Palmers, including: F. Palmer &
Co. 98 Nassau St.; F. & S. Palmer's Lith. 27 Ann St. N.Y.; F. & S. Palmer's Lith. 43 Ann St.;
Palmer & Co. 43 Ann.; Palmer & Co. 98 Nassau St.; and F. Palmer Co. 98 Nassau St. N.Y.

2-85 *Plate 1. Design XXIII. Cottage Villa. / In the Italian Style; Design XXII. Cottage Villa / in the Rustic Style* (two images on one page)
Des. & Del. by W. H. Ranlett. Lith. of F. Palmer & Co. 98 Nassau St. (text below bottom image)

2-86 *Plate 2. Design XXIII; Design XXII*
W. H. Ranlett. Lith of F. & S. Palmer, 34 Ann St.

2-87 *Plate 3. Design XXIV. A Plain Cottage / English Style; Design XXV. A Plain Cottage / English Tudor Style* (two images on one page)
F.P. (initials in stone, lower right of image). Des. & Drawn by W. H. Ranlett. F. & S. Palmer's Lith. 34 Ann St.

2-88 *Plate 4. Design XXIV; Design XXV*
W. H. Ranlett. F. & S. Palmer's Lith. 34 Ann St.

2-89 *Plate 5*
W. H. Ranlett. F. & S. Palmer's Lith. 34 Ann St.

2-90 *Plate 6*
W. H. Ranlett. F. & S. Palmer's Lith. 34 Ann St.

2-91 *Plate 7. Design XXVI. Italian Bracketed Villa, / Perspective View*   Illustrated, p. 48
F.P. (initials in stone, lower left of image). Des. & Drawn by W. H. Ranlett. F. & S. Palmer's Lith. 34 Ann St.

2-92 *Plate 8. Design 26*
W. H. Ranlett. F. & S. Palmer's Lith. 34 Ann St. N.Y.

2-93 *Plate 9. Design XXVI. Principal Elevation; South Front Elevation* (two images on one page)
Des. & del. by Wm. H. Ranlett. F. & S. Palmer's Lith. 34 Ann St. (text below bottom image).

2-94 *Plate 10. Design 26*
W. H. Ranlett. F. & S. Palmer's Lith. 34 Ann St. N.Y.

2-95 *Plate 11. Design 26*
W. H. Ranlett. F. & S. Palmer's Lith. 34 Ann St. N.Y.

2-96 *Plate 12*
W. H. Ranlett. F. & S. Palmer's Lith. 34 Ann St. N.Y.

2-97 *Plate 13. Design XXVII. & XXVIII*
W. H. Ranlett. F. & S. Palmer's Lith. 34 Ann St. N.Y.

2-98 *Plate 14. Design XXVII. Principal Front. / Villa in the Persian Style; Lawn Front* (two images on one page)
Des. & Del. by W. H. Ranlett. F. & S. Palmer's Lith. 27 Ann St. (text below bottom image).

2-99 *Plate 15. Design XXVIII*
W. H. Ranlett. F. & S. Palmer's Lith. 27 Ann St.

2-100 *Plate 16. Design XXIX. Cottage in Rustic Style; Design XXX. Bracketted Cottage / Englisch [sic] Style* (two images on one page)
Des. & Del. by W. H. Ranlett. F. & S. Palmer's Lith. 27 Ann St. (text below bottom image).

2-101 *Plate 17. Details*
W. H. Ranlett. F. & S. Palmer's Lith. 27 Ann St. N. York.

2-102 *Plate 18. Details for Design XXVII*
W. H. Ranlett. F. & S. Palmer's Lith. 27 Ann St. N. York.

2-103 *Plate 19. Design XXXI. Italian Villa. / Lawn Front; Entrance Front* (two images on one page)
W. H. Ranlett. F. & S. Palmer's Lith. 43 Ann St.

2-104 *Plate 20. Design XXXI*
W. H. Ranlett. F. & S. Palmer's Lith. 43 Ann St. N.Y.

2-105 *Plate 21. Design XXXII; Design XXXIII*
W. H. Ranlett. F. & S. Palmer's Lith. 43 Ann St.

2-106 *Plate 22. Design XXXII. Italian Villa; Design XXXIII. Italian Villa* (two images on one page)
W. H. Ranlett. F. & S. Palmer's Lith. 43 Ann St.

2-107 *Plate 23. Design XXXI. Exterior Details*
W. H. Ranlett. F. & S. Palmer's Lith. 43 Ann St. N.Y.

2-108 *Plate 24. Details for Design XXXII & XXXIII*
W. H. Ranlett. Lith of F. & S. Palmer's 43 Ann St.

2-109 *Plate 25. Design XXIV; Design XXXV*
W. H. Ranlett. F. & S. Palmer's Lith. 43 Ann St. N.Y.

2-110 *Plate 26. Design XXXIV. Cottage / English Style; Design XXXV. Cottage / English Style*
W. H. Ranlett. F. & S. Palmer's Lith. 43 Ann St. N. York.

2-111 *Plate 27. Design XXXVI*
W. H. Ranlett. F. & S. Palmer's Lith. 43 Ann St. N.Y.

2-112 *Plate 28. Design XXVI. End Elevation; Cottage. / Front Elevation* (two images
    on one page)
Design by W. H. Ranlett for G.R. Ward Esq. New Brighton. F. & S. Palmer's Lith. 43
    Ann St. N.Y.

2-113 *Plate 29. Ground Plot*
W. H. Ranlett. F. & S. Palmer's Lith. 43 Ann St. N.Y.

2-114 *Plate 30.*
W. H. Ranlett. F. & S. Palmer's Lith. 43 Ann St. New York.

2-115 *Plate 31. Design XXXVII. Anglo Norman Villa. / Lawn Front; Entrance Front*
Designed & del by W. H. Ranlett. F. & S. Palmer's Lith. 43 Ann St. N.Y.

2-116 *Plate 32. Design XXXVII*
W. H. Ranlett. Lith. of F. & S. Palmers. 43 Ann St. N. York.

2-117 *Plate 33. Design XXXVII. Exterior Details. / Norman Style*
W. H. Ranlett. F. & S. Palmer's Lith. 43 Ann St. N.Y.

2-118 *Plate 34. Design XXXVII*
W. H. Ranlett. F. & S. Palmer's Lith. 43 Ann St. N. York.

2-119 *Plate 35. Design XXXVIII. Cottage Villa / in the Anglo Norman Style;*
    Entrance Elevation. Garden Elevation (two images on one page)
Des. & Del. by W. H. Ranlett. F. & S. Palmer's Lith. 43 Ann St. N.Y. (text below
    bottom image).

2-120 *Plate 36. Design XXXVIII*
W. H. Ranlett. F. & S. Palmer's Lith. 43 Ann St. N. York.

2-121 *Plate 37. Design XXXIX*
W. H. Ranlett. Lith of Palmer & Co. 43 Ann.

2-122 *Plate 38. Design XLI & XLII. Two Plain Cottages; The Same Ornamented*
    (two images on one page)
Des. & Del. by W. H. Ranlett. Palmer & Co. Lith. 98, Nassau St.

2-123 *Plate 39. Designs XLI, XLII & XLIII*
W. H. Ranlett. Palmer & Co. Lith. 98, Nassau St.

2-124 *Plate 40. Design XLIII. Front Elevation; Entrance Elevation* (two images on
    one page)
W. H. Ranlett. Lith of Palmer & Co. 98 Nassau St. N.Y.

2-125 *Plate 41. Design XLIII*
W. H. Ranlett, Architect. Lith. of Palmer & Co. 98 Nassau St. N.Y.

2-126 *Plate 42. Details*
Ranlett del. Palmer & Co. Lith. 98 Nassau St.

2-127 *Plate 43. Design for a Vinery & Green House*
W. H. Ranlett. Lith of F. Palmer & Co. 98 Nassau St. N.Y.

2-128 *Plate 44. Design XLIV*
W. H. Ranlett. Lith of F. Palmer & Co. 98 Nassau St.

2-129 *Plate 45. Design XLIV & XLV. English Cottage / Ornamented in the Swiss
     style; Cottage Villa. / Indian Style* (two images on one page)
Des. & del. by W. H. Ranlett. Lith. of F. Palmer & Co. 98 Nassau St. N. York (text
     below bottom image).

2-130 *Plate 46. Designs XLVI & XLVII. Cottage Villa / Italian Style; English
     Cottage / Rural Style*
Des. & Del. by W. H. Ranlett. Lith. of F. Palmer & Co. 98 Nassau St. N. York (text
     below bottom image).

2-131 *Plate 47. Design XLV*
W. H. Ranlett, Architect. Lith. of F. Palmer & Co. 98 Nassau St. N.Y.

2-132 *Plate 48. Designs for Grapery*
W. H. Ranlett, Architect. Lith. of F. Palmer & Co. 98 Nassau St. N.Y.

2-133 *Plate 49. Design XLVIII*
W. H. Ranlett, Architect. Lith. of F. Palmer & Co. 98 Nassau St. N.Y.

2-134 *Plate 50. Design XLVIII. Villa in the American Style / Side Elevation; Front
     Elevation* (two images on one page)
Des. & del. by W. H. Ranlett. Lith. of F. Palmer & Co. 98 Nassau St. N.Y. (text below
     bottom image).

2-135 *Plate 51. Design XLVIII*
W. H. Ranlett, Architect. Lith. of F. Palmer & Co. 98 Nassau St. N. York.

2-136 *Plate 52. Designs XLIX & L*
W. H. Ranlett, Architect. Lith. of F. Palmer & Co. 98 Nassau St. N.Y.

2-137 *Plate 53. Design XLIX. Villa / in the Tudor Style; Design L. Villa / in the Greco
     Italian Style* (two images on one page)
W. H. Ranlett, Architect. Lith. of F. Palmer & Co. 98 Nassau St. N.Y.

2-138 *Plate 54. Design XLIX & L. Details*
W. H. Ranlett, Architect. Lith. of F. Palmer & Co. 98 Nassau St. New York.

2-139 *Plate 55. Design LI*
W. H. Ranlett, Architect. Lith. of F. Palmer & Co. 98 Nassau St. N.Y.

2-140 *Plate 56. Design LI. Stone Villa / in the Italian and Composition Style / River Front; Entrance Elevation* (two images on one page)
Des. & del. by W. H. Ranlett. Lith. of F. Palmer & Co. 98 Nassau St. New York (text below bottom image).

2-141 *Plate 57. Design LI*
W. H. Ranlett, Architect. Lith. of F. Palmer & Co. 98 Nassau St. N.Y.

2-142 *Plate 58. Design LI. Details*
W. H. Ranlett. Lith. of F. Palmer & Co. 98 Nassau St.

2-143 *Plate 59. Designs LII & LIII. Details*
W. H. Ranlett, Architect. Lith. of F. Palmer & Co. 98 Nassau St. N. York.

2-144 *Plate 60. Design LII. Cottage Villa / in the Anglo Swiss Style; Design LIII. Cottage Villa / in the earliest English Style* (two images on one page)
Des. & Del. by W. H. Ranlett. Lith. of F. Palmer & Co. 98 Nassau St. N.Y. (text below bottom image).

2-145 *Battle of Buena Vista. / View of the Battle-Ground and Battle of "the Angostura" fought near Buena Vista, Mexico February 23rd, 1847. (Looking S. West.)*   Illustrated, p. 40

1847

Image 18½ × 28¾" sheet 22 × 30⅜"

F. Palmer (signature on stone, lower left of image). From a sketch taken on the spot by Major Eaton, Aid de Camp to Genl. Taylor. Published and printed in colors by H. R. Robinson, 142 Nassau St. N. York.

Holding institution: Library of Congress

The New York Drawing Book, Containing a Series of Original Designs and Sketches of American Scenery, No. 1, by F. Palmer. New York: Published by W. H. Graham, Tribune Buildings.—Price 25 cents. 1847. Entered . . . 1847, by S. Palmer.

8½ × 11¾"

Holding institution: American Antiquarian Society

This drawing book contains four pages of sample drawings, with advertising for the Palmers on the back cover. *The New York Drawing Book*, No. 2 (p. 266), in the same style, was also published in 1847.

2-146 *Old Entrance to Greenwood Cemetery* (page 1)   Illustrated, p. 41
P. (initial on stone, lower right of image). Lith F. & S. Palmer. 43 [Ann St.].

2-147 Page 2 contains two picturesque rustic vignettes. On the top half is a log cabin and mill with waterwheel and trees. On the bottom half is a vignette showing a quaint log bridge curving backward dramatically across a stream, leading to a rustic log farmhouse on the opposite cliff. Both drawings are signed at the bottom of the images with a capital P. At the bottom of the page, below the images, is the inscription "Designed & Lith. by F & S. Palmer 43 Ann St. N.Y."

Courtesy of the American Antiquarian Society.

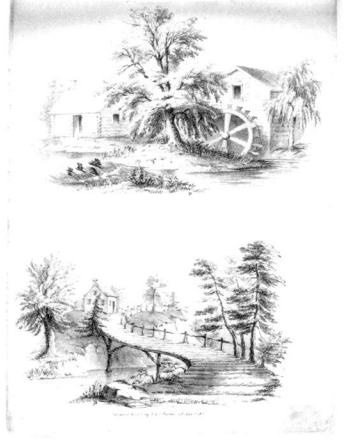

2-148 Page 3 contains two studies: at the top are two resting cattle shaded by a tree, with a farmhouse in the left distance. Below the two studies is the inscription "Designed & Lith. by F & S. Palmer 43 Ann St. N.Y." Both drawings are signed with a squarish capital P on the image at bottom left.

Courtesy of the American Antiquarian Society.

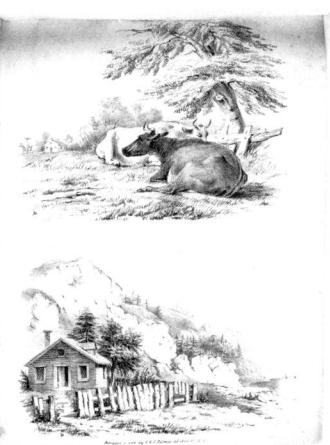

2-149 *Sketch on the Gowanus Road, L.I. / Washington's Head Quarters* (page 4)   Illustrated, p. 42
P (initial on stone, lower right of image). Lith of F. & S. Palmer 43 Ann St.
A drawing of this subject from a different point of view is at the New-York Historical Society (p. 343). N. Currier issued a print of this subject, *The Old Stone House, L.I., 1699* (undated), that may be derived from Palmer's study. The lithograph is very close to Palmer's sketch, which seems to be drawn from life. According to the inscription, Nathaniel Currier lithographed it, although Palmer seems to have made the original drawing.

The New York Drawing Book, Containing a Series of Original Designs and Sketches of American Scenery, No. 2, by F. Palmer. New York: Published by W. H. Graham, Tribune Buildings.—Price 25 cents. 1847. Entered . . . 1847, by S. Palmer.

8⅜ × 12 15/16"

Holding institution: Metropolitan Museum of Art

2-150 *Fort Lee Landing* (page 1)
P (initial on stone, lower left of image). Lith. of F. & S. Palmer 43 Aun [*sic*] St. N.Y.

Courtesy of the Metropolitan Museum of Art, Harris Brisbane Dick Fund, 1954.

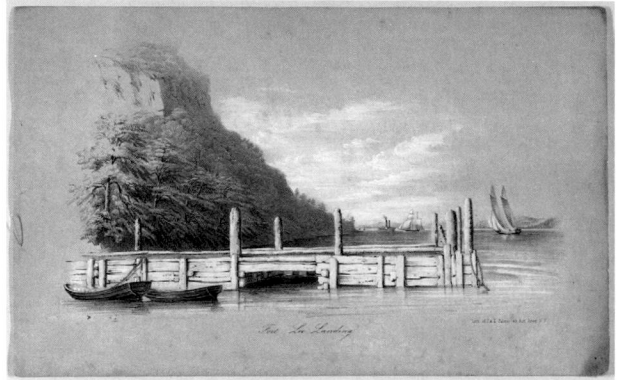

2-151 Page 2 contains three vignettes: at top there are two sheep; at lower left there are two cows standing in a pond with a tree and farmhouse in the background; and at lower right there is a man bending down to wrap a bale of sticks next to a tree with a house in the background. The bottom-right image has the initials F.P. at lower right.

Courtesy of the Metropolitan Museum of Art, Harris Brisbane Dick Fund, 1954.

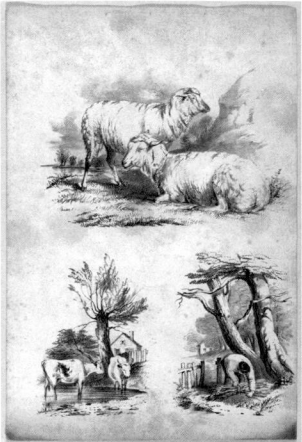

2-152 Page 3 contains a half-length portrait of a young woman holding flowers. The image is signed with a capital P at lower right and the inscription "Lith. of F. &. S. Palmer 43 Aun [*sic*] Street N.Y."

Illustrated, p. 43

2-153 *Sylvan Lake. Greenwood Cemetery* (page 4)
F.P. (initials on stone, lower left of image). Lith. of F. & S. Palmer, 43 Ann St. N.Y.

Illustrated, p. 42

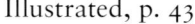

2-154 *St. John's Church, Buffalo*

1847

Sheet 35 13/20 × 24½"

C. N. Otis, Archt. Entered . . . 1847, by Derby & Hewson . . . Lith. of F. & S. Palmer, 34 Ann. St. N.Y. Published by Derby & Hewson, Bookseller, Buffalo.

Holding institution: Library of Congress

Courtesy of the Prints and Photographs Division, Library of Congress, LC-DIG-pga-02338.

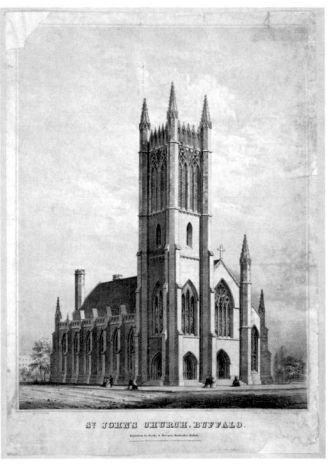

2-155 *Walker's / Patent Improved Hot Air / Furnace, / for / heating churches / and other / public buildings, / dwellings, / stores / &c. / Sold by / Geo. Walker / 296 Broadway, / N.Y.*

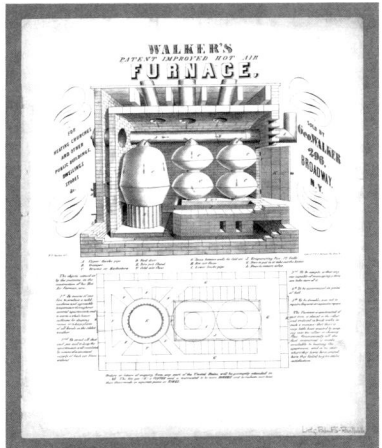

Undated, ca. 1847

12 × 10"

W. H. Ranlett, del. Lith. of F & S Palmer, 34 Ann St.

Holding institution: American Antiquarian Society

This undated advertisement is on the last page of both volumes of Ranlett, *The Architect* (1847).

Courtesy of the American Antiquarian Society.

Flower Tokens. Published by J. C. Riker, 129 Fulton St., N.Y., undated, ca. 1847.

7¾ × 6¼"

Holding institution: American Antiquarian Society

Autograph album in color, with six colored illustrations. The copy held by the Huntington Library bears an inscription on the flyleaf dated 1847.

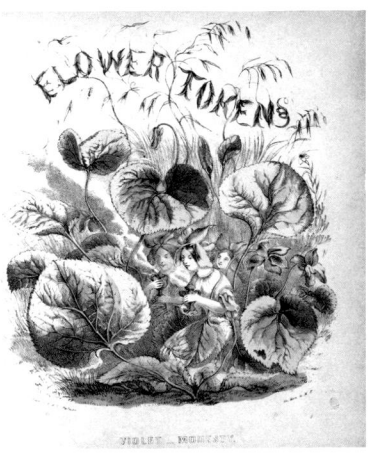

2-156 *Violet—Modesty* (title page)
F.P. (initials on stone, lower right of image) Lith. of F. & S. Palmer, 34 Ann St., N.Y.

Courtesy of the American Antiquarian Society.

2-157 *Forget Me Not*
Lith. of F. & S. Palmer, 34 Ann St., N.Y.

2-158 *Flax—Industry*
Lith. of F. & S. Palmer, 34 Ann St., N.Y.

2-159 *Snowdrop—Youthful Hope*
Lith. of F. & S. Palmer, 34 Ann St., N.Y.

2-160 *Orange Flower—Purity*
Lith. of F. & S. Palmer, 34 Ann St., N.Y.

2-161 *Convolvolus—Repose*
F.P. (initials on stone, lower right of image) Lith. of F. & S. Palmer, 34 Ann St., N.Y.

Flowers in Frolic. Published by J. C. Riker, 129 Fulton St. N.Y., undated, ca. 1847–48?.

7½ × 6"

Holding institution: American Antiquarian Society

Autograph album. Images in this album were copied or adapted from the steel engravings of J. J. Grandville's illustrations in *Flowers Personified*, a translation by Nehemiah Cleaveland of *Les fleurs animeés* (New York: R. Martin, 1847).

2-162 (Untitled group of personified flowers dancing) (title page)
F. & S. Palmer's Lith. 34 Ann St.

2-163 *Pomegranate—Foolishness*
F. & S. Palmer's Lith. 34 Ann St.

Courtesy of the American Antiquarian Society.

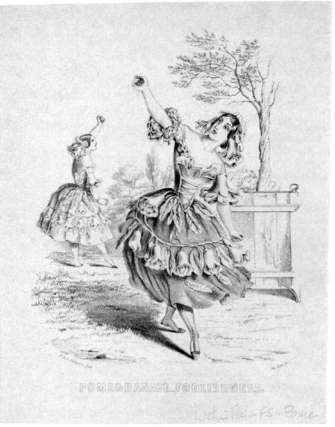

2-164 *Poppy—Forgetfulness*
F. & S. Palmer's Lith. 34 Ann St.

2-165 *Mallow—Mild or Sweet Disposition*
F. & S. Palmer's Lith. 34 Ann St.

2-166 *Sensitive Plant*
F. & S. Palmer's Lith. 34 Ann St.

2-167 *Thistle—Austerity*
F. & S. Palmer's Lith. 34 Ann St.

Flowers of Loveliness. Published by J. C. Riker, 129 Fulton St. N.Y., undated, ca. 1847–48?.

7⅝ × 6¼"

Holding institution: American Antiquarian Society

Autograph album with six illustrations.

2-168 *Rose—Beauty* (title page)
F & S. Palmer's Lith. 34 Ann St. N.Y.

Courtesy of the American Antiquarian Society.

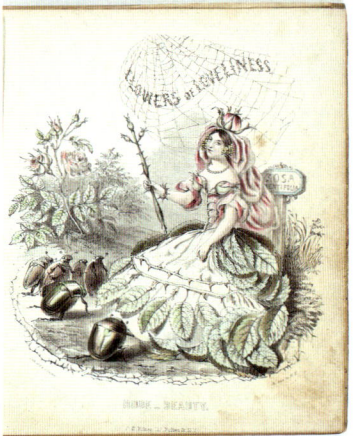

2-169 *Pansy—Pleasant Thoughts*
F & S. Palmer's Lith. 34 Ann St. N.Y.

2-170 *White Lily—Modesty*
F & S. Palmer's Lith. 34 Ann St. N.Y.

2-171 *Water Lily—Purity of Heart*
F & S. Palmer's Lith. 34 Ann St. N.Y.

2-172 *Eglantine—Poetry*
F & S. Palmer's Lith. 34 Ann St. N.Y.

2-173 *Carnation—Pride*
F & S. Palmer's Lith. 34 Ann St. N.Y.

Love and the Flowers. Published by J. C. Riker, 128 Fulton St., N.Y. [spelled Ricker on the title page], undated, ca. 1847–48?.

Holding institution: Huntington Library

Autograph album with six illustrations.

2-174 *Love* (title page)
Lith of F. & S. Palmer, 34 Ann St., N.Y.

2-175 *Lilac—First Emotion of Love*
Lith of F. & S. Palmer, 34 Ann St., N.Y.

2-176 *Tulip—Declaration of Affection*   Illustrated, p. 45
Lith of F. & S. Palmer, 34 Ann St., N.Y.

2-177 *Scabius—Marygold—Unfortunate Attachment—Grief*
Lith of F. & S. Palmer, 34 Ann St., N.Y.

2-178 *Camellia—My Heart Bleeds for You*
Lith of F. & S. Palmer, 34 Ann St., N.Y.

2-179 *Narcissus—Delusive Hope*
Lith of F. & S. Palmer, 34 Ann St., N.Y.

2-180 *Richmond Seminary, Staten Island, N.Y.*   Illustrated, p. 32

Undated, ca. 1847–48?

Image 8⅝ × 13½" sheet 13 × 15⅝"

From Nature & on Stone by F. Palmer. Lith. of F. & S. Palmer, 34 Ann St., N.Y.

Holding institution: Metropolitan Museum of Art

Around 1852, when the Richmond Seminary was converted into the Richmond Hill Hotel, Palmer's image was converted into a wood engraving by T. Horton & Co. for an advertisement for the hotel, with the credit line "Mrs. Palmer Del." The Staten Island Historical Society has a copy of this item.

2-181 *Baptist Mariners Chapel. / New York. / Rev. Ira R. Steward, Pastor. / Residence /*
177 Cherry Street   Illustrated, p. 30

Undated, ca. 1848

Image 18¾ × 15¼" sheet 23¼ × 18⅜"

F.P. (initials on stone, lower left corner of the image). F. & S. Palmers Lith. 43 Ann St. N.Y.

Holding institution: Metropolitan Museum of Art

Text around the title states, "First Baptist Mariners' Church New York organized A.D. 1843. Chapel erected 234, Cherry Street, between Rutger & Pike Sts. A.D. 1848."

2-182 *Mobile & New Orleans. / U.S. Daily Mail Line. Consisting of Steamers, Creole,*
James L. Day, Oregon & California

Undated, ca. 1848

20 × 34¼"

F. Palmer (on stone, lower-right corner of image). From a painting by James Bard. Lithd & Printed in colors by H. R. Robinson, 142 Nassau St. N.Y.

Holding institution: Mariners' Museum

The *California* was built in 1847 and started running from New Orleans the following year.

Courtesy of the Mariners' Museum, Newport News, VA.

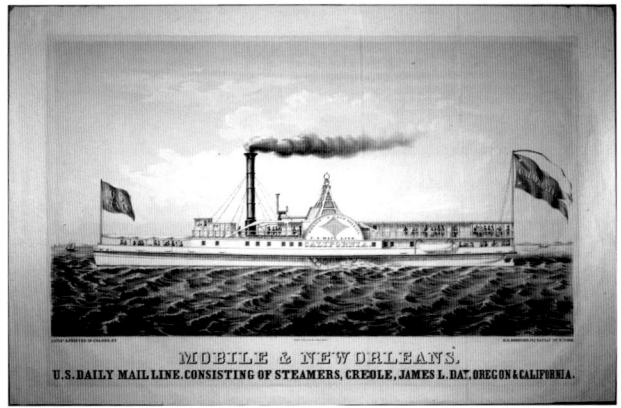

The American Flora or History of Plants and Wildflowers

1848

This publication by Dr. A. B. Strong appeared in a number of variants from around 1846 through 1851. They were first issued separately in parts with paper covers and then bound in volumes and printed by several different publishers (including Strong and Bidwell; J. C. Burdick; and Green and Spencer). The books included lithographed illustrations printed on separate plates that were copied from Strong's drawings by several different lithographers, including W. M. Moody, E. Whitefield, F. Michelin, and the Palmers. The illustrations by F. & S. Palmer appear in volumes 2 and 3, where the company is credited variously at 34 Ann St., 43 Ann St., and 27 Ann St.

The American Flora or History of Plants and Wildflowers; Containing Their Scientific and General Description, Natural History, Chemical and Medical Properties, Mode of Culture, Propagation, &c. Designed as a Book of Reference for Botanists, Physicians, Florists, Gardeners, Students, Etc. By A. B. Strong, M.D. Vol. II. New York: Published by Green & Spencer, 140 Nassau-street, 1848.

Holding institution: Huntington Library

2-183 *The American Flora. From a Friend. Vol. II* (frontispiece)   Illustrated, p. 43
Lith. of F. & S. Palmer, 34 Ann St. N. York

2-184 *Cinchona Oblongifolia* (between pages 26 and 27)
Lith. of F. & S. Palmer, N.Y.

2-185 *Arum Ariphylum* (between pages 34 and 35)
Lith. of F. & S. Palmer, 43 Ann St., N.Y.

2-186 *Pinus balsamea* (between pages 38 and 39)
Lith. of F. & S. Palmer, N.Y.

2-187 *Poinciana pulcherrima* (between pages 42 and 43)
Lith. of F. & S. Palmer, 34 Ann St. N.Y.

2-188 *Vitis vinefera* (between pages 48 and 49)
Lith. of F. & [S.] Palmer, N.Y.

2-189 *Dendrobium Fimbriatum* (between pages 64 and 65)
Lith. of F. & S. Palmer, 43 Ann St. N.Y.

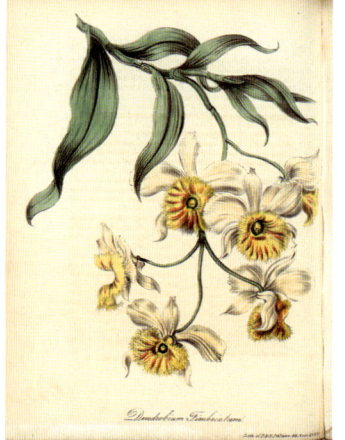

2-190 *Convolvulus Scammonia* (between pages 66 and 67)
Lith. of F. & S. Palmer, 34 Ann. St. N.Y.

2-191 *Daphne Mezereum* (between pages 94 and 95)
F. & S. Palmer, Lith. 34 Ann St.

2-192 *Magnolia Yulans* (between pages 112 and 113)
F. & S. Palmer, Lith. 34 Ann St.

2-193 *Nicotiana Tabacum* (between pages 124 and 125)
F. & S. Palmer, Lith. 34 Ann St, N.Y.

2-194 *Artocarpus incise* (between pages 142 and 143)
F. & S. Palmer, Lith. 34 Ann St., N.Y.

2-195 *Capparis spinosa* (between pages 164 and 165)
F. & S. Palmer, Lith. 34 Ann St. N.Y.

The American Flora, or History of Plants and Wildflowers: Containing Their Scientific and General Description, Natural History, Chemical and Medical Properties, Mode of Culture, Propagation, &c. Designed as a Book of Reference for Botanists, Physicians, Florists, Gardeners, Students, Etc. By A. B. Strong, M.D. Vol. III. New York: Published by Green & Spencer, 140 Nassau-street, 1849.

Holding institution: Huntington Library

2-196 *Linnaeus* (frontispiece)

F. & S. Palmer, Lith. 34 Ann St.

A three-quarter-length portrait of Linnaeus, the father of modern botanical taxonomy,
derived from a full-length portrait (or an engraved adaptation of the painting)
painted by Martin Hoffman in 1737.

Courtesy of the Huntington Library, San Marino, CA, RB 315449 v. 3.

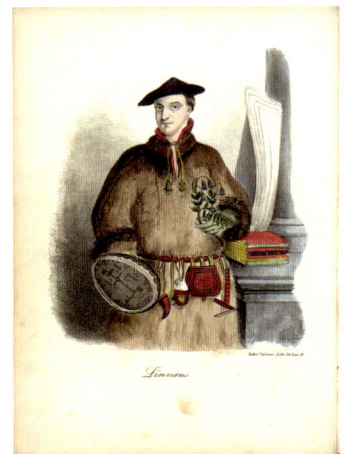

2-197 *Teucrium marum. Hypericum monogynum* (between pages 30 and 31)
F. & S. Palmer, Lith. 34 Ann St.

2-198 *Mimulus aurantiacus* (between pages 40 and 41)
F. & S. Palmer, Lith. 34 Ann St.

2-199 *Geranium Sanguineum* (between pages 78 and 79)
F. & S. Palmer, Lith. 27 Ann St. N.Y.

2-200 *Paeonia edulis Reevesiana* (between pages 86 and 87)   Illustrated, p. 44
F. F. & S. Palmer, Lith. 27 Ann St.

2-201 *Wolves Attacking a Sleigh*

April 1848

Holding institution: American Antiquarian Society

A magazine illustration in *The Rural Gem and Fireside Companion Devoted to Moral and Religious, Useful and Entertaining Literature* 3, no. 4 (1848) (published by S. A. Whitney and J. Bean, Worcester, MA). Attributed to F. & S. Palmer in the "Lithographs in Books" card file at the American Antiquarian Society.

Courtesy of the American Antiquarian Society.

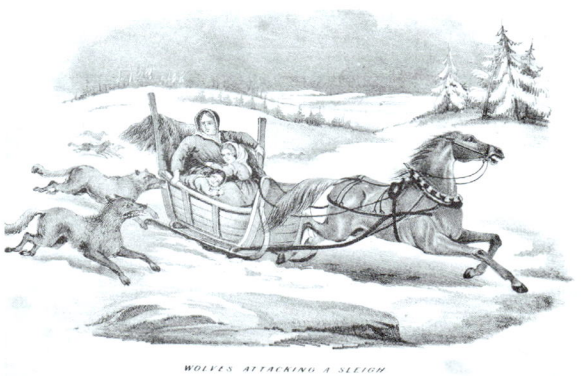

2-202 *The Hunting Leopard*

May 1848

Lith of F. & S. Palmer, 34 Ann St.

Holding institution: American Antiquarian Society

A magazine illustration in *The Rural Gem and Fireside Companion Devoted to Moral and Religious, Useful and Entertaining Literature* 3, no. 5 (1848) (published by S. A. Whitney and J. Bean, Worcester, MA).

Courtesy of the American Antiquarian Society.

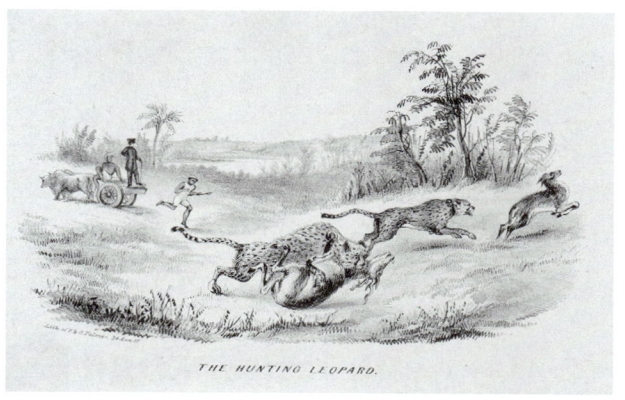

2-203 *Music of the Great Southern / Original Sable Harmonists, The Best Band of / Singers in the United States. / Arranged & Sung by them at all their concerts*

1848

13¼ × 10¼"

Lith of F. & S. Palmer, 43 Ann St. New York. Published at Millets Music Saloon 329 Broadway.

Holding institution: Lester S. Levy Sheet Music Collection, Johns Hopkins University

An elaborate sheet-music cover. The music has an 1848 copyright statement.

Illustrated, p. 45

2-204 *New England Hotel. / P. Wight Prop. . [sic] / 111 Broadwy. Adjoining Trinity Church Yard New-York*

Undated, ca. 1848

Image 10⅜ × 14 7/16" sheet 12 15/16 × 16 15/16"

F. & S. Palmer's Lith. 43 Ann St. NY.

Holding institution: Metropolitan Museum of Art

P. Wight changed the name of his hotel from "New England House" to "New England Hotel" around 1848.[5]

Courtesy of the Metropolitan Museum of Art, Gift of Mrs. Edmund R. Burry, 1948.

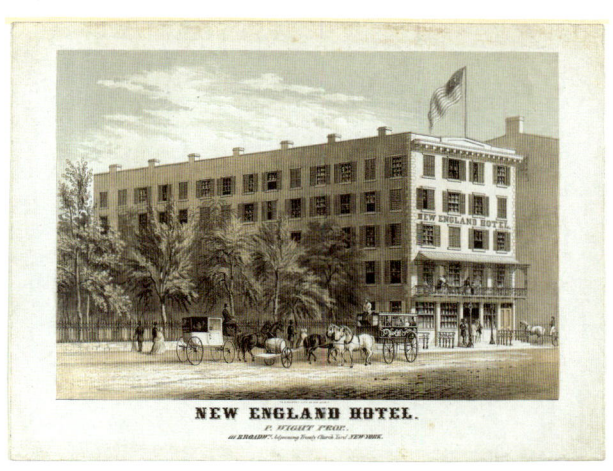

2-205 *New Line between Boston & New York—Via New Port & Fall River. / Composed of the New Steamers / Bay State & Empire State, / Each of 1600 Tons Burthen*

Undated, ca. 1848?

36½ × 21⅛"

Painted by W. Marsh Esqre N.Y, Lith by F & S Palmer, 34, Ann St, N.Y.

Holding institution: Mariners' Museum

Courtesy of the Mariners' Museum, Newport News, VA.

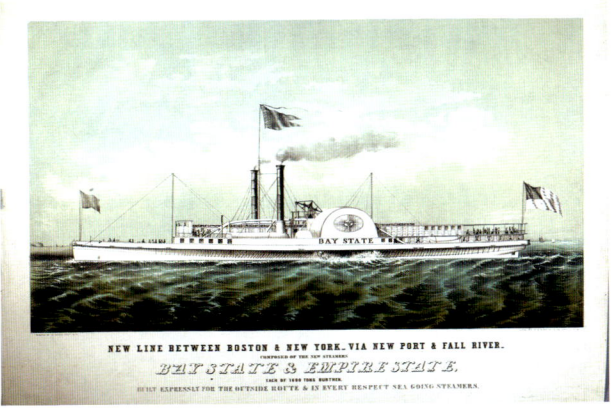

2-206 *Crescent City, / New-York, Havana and New-Orleans*

Undated, ca. 1848?

16¾ × 32½"

Painted by William Marsh, Esq. N.Y., Lith. by F. & S. Palmer, 43 Ann St. N.Y.

Holding institution: Mariners' Museum

The version of this print held by the Huntington Library contains the text "Charles Stoddard, Commander" below the words "Crescent City." The Palmers also reissued this print with the imprint "Lith. by F. & S. Palmer, 98 Nassau St. N.Y."

Courtesy of the Mariners' Museum, Newport News, VA.

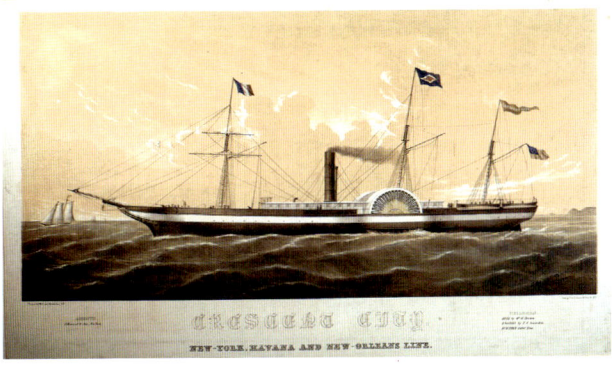

2-207 *St. Paul's Chapel, St. Ann's Parish, Morrisania, Westchester Co., N.Y. / Published in Aid of the funds of the Chapel.*

Undated, ca. 1849–50

14.4 × 18.9"

James P. Fitch, Builder, West Farms. T. R. Jackson, Architect, New York. F. Palmer & Co. Lith. 89 [i.e., 98] Nassau Street.

Holding institution: Museum of the City of New York

Courtesy of the Museum of the City of New York, 29.100.2716.

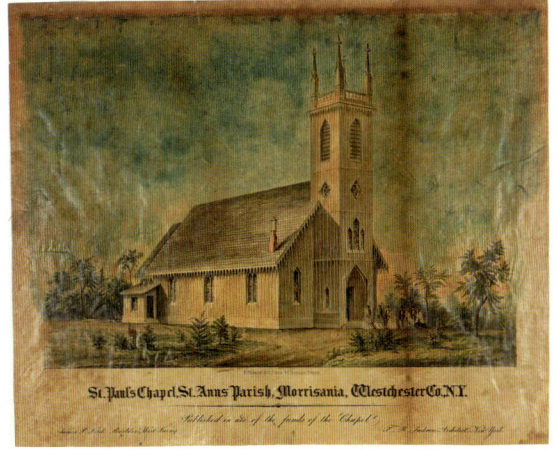

2-208 *Berkshire House—Great Barrington, Massachusetts. Built in 1839,— / of Blue Granite Three Stories high—50 feet front & 110 feet deep.— / W.A. Forbes, Proprietor*

Undated, [1849]

Image 8¼ × 13" sheet 10 × 13"

Minard La-Fever of New-York Architect. F. Palmer & Co. lith. 98 Nassau street New-York.

Holding institution: American Antiquarian Society

2-209 *Empire City Line*

Undated, ca. 1849–50

18 × 32⅝"

Painted by William Marsh, Esq. N.Y. Lith. of F. Palmer & Co. 98 Nassau St. N.Y. J. Howard & Son Agents, 54 Broadway, New York.

Holding institution: Huntington Library

The version in the Mariners' Museum includes text for the "New York and Chagress Line," whereas the version held in the Huntington Library advertises the "Pacific Steam Ship Northerner."

Courtesy of the Huntington Library, San Marino, CA, priJLC_MAR_001444.

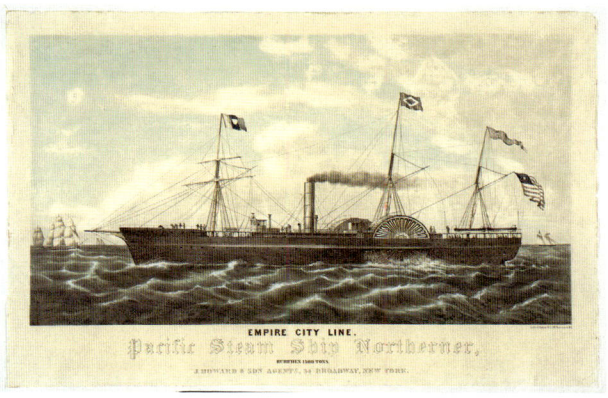

2-210 *The Broadway Tabernacle*

Illustrated, p. 49

Undated, ca. 1849–50

Image 5½ × 7 5/16" sheet 9⅝ × 11½"

Lith. of F. Palmer & Co., 98 Nassau Street, N.Y.

Holding institution: New York Public Library

The rather primitive drawing in this print seems unlike Palmer's work. The print may have been adapted with changes in the figures and aisles from a much more polished lithograph issued in 1848 by Sarony & Major, entitled *Distribution of the American Art-Union Prizes at the Tabernacle-Broadway, New York; 24th Dec. 1847.* A very similar print to Palmer's, *The Broadway Tabernacle, in Anniversary Week*, was published by Snyder, Black & Sturn in 1856.

2-211 *Faustin Soulouque. / Président d'Haiti. / 1re Mars 1847*

Illustrated, p. 46

Undated, ca. 1849–50

5⅓ × 4 1/5"

Lith. of F. Palmer & Co., 98 Nassau St. N.Y.

Holding institution: American Antiquarian Society

2-212 *Reindeer, / Capt. Albert Degroot*

Undated, ca. 1850–51

17½ × 32⅝"

Painted by James Bard, N.Y., F. Palmer & Co. Lith. 100 Nassau St., N.Y.

Holding institution: Mariners' Museum

From an oil painting by James Bard (1850).

Courtesy of the Mariners' Museum, Newport News, VA.

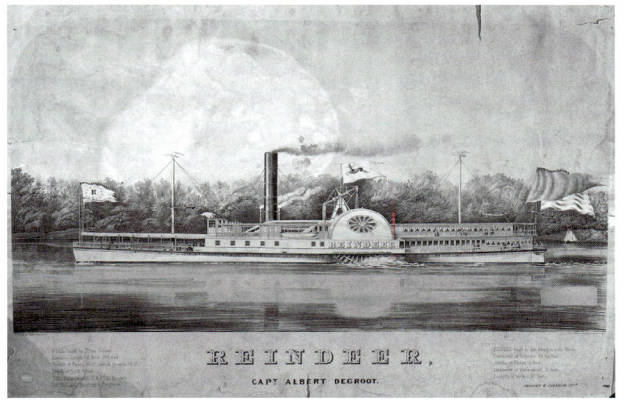

2-213 *East View of St. Paul's Church, Buffalo. / Revd. William Shelton. D.D. Rector. / Richd. Upjohn, Arct.*

Illustrated, p. 29

Undated, ca. 1851?

Image and text 17¾ × 11" sheet

20½ × 15¾"

F. Palmer & Co. Lith. 100 Nassau St. N.Y.

Holding institution: American Antiquarian Society

2-214 *West View of St. Paul's Church, Buffalo. / Revd. William Shelton. D.D. Rector. / Richd. Upjohn, Arct.*

Illustrated, p. 29

Undated, ca. 1851?

Image and text 17¾ × 11" sheet 20½ × 15¾"

F. Palmer & Co. Lith. 100 Nassau St. N.Y.

Holding institution: American Antiquarian Society

This lithograph was taken almost exactly from an original drawing by Richard Upjohn, though there are some structural differences between the two images, including different steeple designs and entrance.

2-215 *Neptune House / New Rochelle, West Chester County, New York*

Undated, ca. 1851?

Sheet 20⅞ × 26 15/16"

Lith of F. Palmer & Co. 100 Nassau St. N.Y.

Holding institution: Yale University Art Gallery

Courtesy of the Yale University Art Gallery.

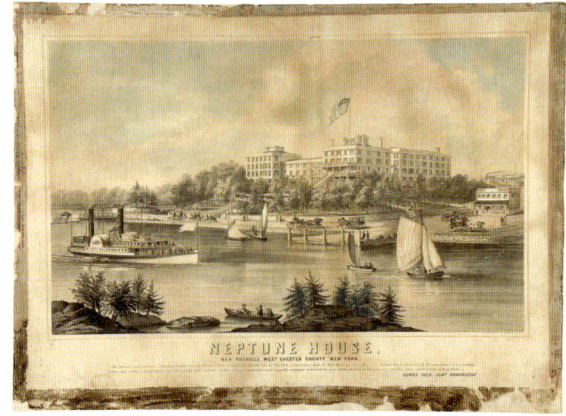

2-216 *Spanish Gipsies / composed & dedicated to / his friend & pupil / Miss Berry of Mount Vernon / by H. Craven Griffiths R.S.W. / No. 1 Song, No. 2 Polka, price 38 cents*

Undated, ca. 1852?

Image 9¾ × 8¼" sheet 13¼ × 10½"

F. F. Palmer Lith. Printed by F Michelin 225 Fulton St. N.Y. Published by Gould & Berry 297 Broadway, N.Y.

Holding institution: New York Public Library

The music is copyrighted 1852.

2-217 *View of Richmond Va.*

Undated, ca. 1852–53?

Sheet 21 3/16 × 38 5/16"

J.W. Hill, del. On Stone by F. Palmer. Lith. & Published by Smith Brothers & Co.

Holding institution: New York Public Library

This very large and ambitious print is enriched with at least two tint stones (salmon pink and blue).

Illustrated, p. 125

2-218 *St. James Church and Rectory. / Chicago, Illinois*

1856

Image 26 × 16 1/5" sheet 29 7/10 × 21 4/5"

F. F. Palmer, Lith. William Backus, Architect, 1856. Sarony, Major & Knapp, New York.

Holding institution: Winterthur Museum

2-219 *St. John's P.E. Church, Mt. Morris. / Livingston Co. N.Y. Cleaveland & Backus Brothers Architects, New York 1856*

1856

Illustrated, p. 124

Image and text 12 7/10 × 14½"

F. Palmer Lith. Sarony & Co. Imp. New York

Holding institution: American Antiquarian Society

This print was a freelance assignment completed for Sarony & Co. while Palmer was working for Nathaniel Currier. The strokes and technique are characteristic of her work, but the absence of a signature on the image indicates it was likely lithographed from the architect's drawing.

Prints Incorrectly Attributed to Edmund S. Palmer

Rev. Sylvanus Palmer

1844

7½ × 6"

From life on stone, by S. Palmer jr. March 1844.

Holding institution: American Antiquarian Society

This crudely drawn and printed portrait, sometimes attributed to Frances Palmer, is almost certainly not her work or her husband's. It doesn't bear a legend crediting F. & S. Palmer as the printers. The primitively drawn trees, the peculiar technique of shading the figure, and the amateurish cursive lettering of the inscriptions may be the work of Rev. Sylvanus Palmer's son, Sylvanus Ward Palmer Jr.[6] No print issued by F. & S. Palmer was as poorly drawn or printed as this one. In addition, F. & S. Palmer inscriptions are much more professionally lettered and carry the name of the company, "F. & S. Palmer." Mrs. Palmer's signature differs from this handwriting.

Rev. Albert Amerman / Pastor of "True Reformed Dutch Churches" of Hackensack and Patterson, N. Jersey

1844

10 × 7 3/10"

Drawn from life on stone by S. Palmer jr., Jan. 1844.

Holding institution: American Antiquarian Society

This work, like the previous one, is crudely drawn and signed in a primitive handwriting and may also be the work of the son of Reverend Sylvanus Palmer, an amateur artist. It does not appear to be the work of Fanny or Edmund Seymour Palmer and does not bear the F. & S. Palmer identification or give an address. The strokes of the pencil and the very amateurishly drawn figure and hands are set in an oval with crudely executed decoration framing the oval image.

Prints for Currier & Ives

This list contains Palmer's work for Currier & Ives and includes C and G numbers referring to the print's corresponding entry numbers in Frederic A. Conningham, *Currier & Ives Prints: An Illustrated Checklist* (New York: Crown, 1983), and Gale Research Group, *Currier & Ives: A Catalogue Raisonné* (Detroit: Gale Research, 1984).

The Currier & Ives prints that do not have copyright dates are listed as "undated." Although some circa dates have been included for these undated prints based on additional information known about the print or depicted event, most circa dates are based solely on the company name and address visible in the imprint:

1850–56	N. Currier, 152 Nassau St.
1857–72	Currier & Ives, 152 Nassau St.
1872–74	Currier & Ives, 125 Nassau St.

The entries note the prints that were selected as part of the original "best fifty" large-folio Currier & Ives prints and published on consecutive days in the *New York Sun* beginning on January 21, 1933, as well as the "new best fifty" chosen in 1990 by the American Historical Print Collectors Society.

3-1 *Across The Continent. / "Westward the Course of Empire takes its way."* Illustrated, gallery plate 8

1868

17½ × 27"

C-33, G-0039

Drawn by F. F. Palmer. J. M. Ives, Del. Entered . . . 1868 by Currier & Ives . . . New York Published by Currier & Ives 125 Nassau St.

Number 19 on the original best-fifty large-folio prints; number 4 of the new best-fifty large-folio prints.

3-2 *American Autumn Fruits* Illustrated, p. 153

1865

19 15/16 × 27⅞"

C-106, G-0117

F. F. Palmer, Del. Entered . . . 1865 by Currier & Ives . . . Lith of Currier & Ives, N.Y. New York, Published by Currier & Ives, 152 Nassau Street.

3-3 *American Country Life. / May Morning*

1855

16¾ × 23⅞"

C-121, G-0134

F. F. Palmer, Del. Entered . . . 1855 by N. Currier . . . Lith. by N. Currier. New York, Published by N. Currier, 152 Nassau Street.

Illustrated, p. 207

3-4 *American Country Life. / October Afternoon*

1855

16⅝ × 23 13/16"

C-122, G-0135

F. F. Palmer, Del. Entered . . . 1855 by N. Currier . . . Lith. by N. Currier. New York, Published by N. Currier, 152 Nassau Street.

Illustrated, p. 181

3-5 *American Country Life. / Pleasures of Winter*

1855

16⅞ × 23⅞"

C-123, G-0136

F. F. Palmer, Del. Entered . . . 1855 by N. Currier . . . Lith. by N. Currier. New York, Published by N. Currier, 152 Nassau Street.

Illustrated, p. 202

3-6 *American Country Life. / Summers [sic] Evening*

1855

16⅝ × 23⅞"

C-124, G-0137

F. F. Palmer, Del. Entered . . . 1855 by N. Currier . . . Lith. by N. Currier. New York, Published by N. Currier, 152 Nassau Street.

Illustrated, gallery plate 19

3-7 *American Dead Game*

1866

19 11/16 × 27 11/16"

C-125, G-0138

F. F. Palmer, Del. Entered . . . 1866 by Currier & Ives . . . Currier and Ives, Lith, N.Y. New York, Pub'd by Currier & Ives, 152 Nassau St.

American Game (p. 284) has the same composition.

Illustrated, p. 188

3-8 *American Express Train*

1864

17⅝ × 27¾"

C-130, G-0143

F. F. Palmer, Del. Entered . . . 1864 by Currier & Ives . . . Lith of Currier & Ives, N.Y. New York, Published by Currier & Ives, 152 Nassau St.

Number 14 of the Currier & Ives new best-fifty large-folio prints. The same image was published later with a new title, *Atlantic, Mississippi and Ohio Railroad* (p. 286).

Illustrated, gallery plate 9

3-9 *American Farm Scenes. / No. 1*

1853

16¾ × 24"

C-134, G-0146

F. F. Palmer, Del. Entered . . . 1853 by N. Currier . . . Lith. and Pub. by N. Currier, 152 Nassau St. N.Y.

Illustrated, p. 208

3-10 *American Farm Scenes. / No. 2*

1853

16⅝ × 24"

C-135, G-0147

F. F. Palmer, Del. Entered . . . 1853 by N. Currier . . . Lith & Pub. by N. Currier, 152 Nassau St. N.Y.

Illustrated, p. 114

3-11 *American Farm Scenes. / No. 3*

1853

17 × 24"

C-133, G-0148

F. F. Palmer, Del. Entered . . . 1853 by N. Currier . . . Lith. & Pub. by N. Currier, 152 Nassau St. N.Y.

Illustrated, p. 151

3-12 *American Farm Scenes. / No. 4*

1853

16 13/16 × 23 15/16"

C-136, G-0149

F. F. Palmer, Del. Entered . . . 1853 by N. Currier . . . Lith. & Pub. By N. Currier, 152 Nassau St. N.Y.

Number 13 of the original best-fifty large-folio prints; number 8 of the new best-fifty large-folio prints.

Illustrated, gallery plate 4

3-13 *American Farm Yard—Evening*   Illustrated, p. 119

1857

16⅞ × 23⅞"

C-138, G-0152

F. E. [*sic*] Palmer, Del. Entered . . . 1857 by Currier & Ives . . . Lith of Currier & Ives, N.Y.
New York, Published by Currier & Ives, 152 Nassau St.

3-14 *American Farm Yard—Morning*   Illustrated, p. 118

1857

16 11/16 × 23⅞"

C-139, G-0151

F. E. [*sic*] Palmer, Del. Entered . . . 1857 by Currier & Ives . . . Lith of Currier & Ives, N.Y.
New York, Published by Currier & Ives 152 Nassau St.

3-15 *American Forest Game*   Illustrated, p. 155

1866

19¾ × 27¾"

C-156, G-0169

F. F. Palmer, Del. Entered . . . 1866 by Currier & Ives . . . Currier & Ives, Lith. N.Y. New
York, Pub'd by Currier & Ives, 152 Nassau St.

3-16 *American Game*

1866

19¾ × 27 9/16"

C-163, G-0176

F. F. Palmer, Del. Entered . . . 1866 by Currier & Ives . . . Currier & Ives, Lith. N.Y. New
York, Pub'd by Currier & Ives, 152 Nassau St.

This is the same composition as *American Dead Game* (p. 282).

Courtesy of the Old Print Shop.

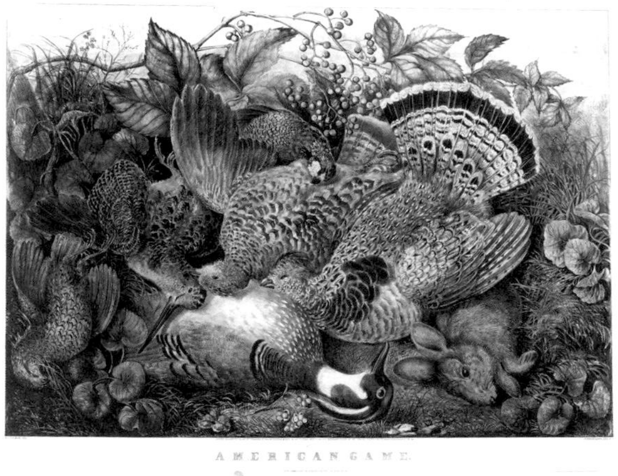

3-17 *American Game Fish*   Illustrated, p. 155

1866

19¾ × 27 11/16"

C-164, G-0177

F. F. Palmer, Del. Entered . . . 1866 by Currier & Ives . . . Currier & Ives, Lith. N.Y. New
York Pub'd by Currier & Ives, 152 Nassau St.

3-18 *American Prize Fruit*

1862

19⅝ × 27¾"

C-183, G-0197

F. F. Palmer, Del. Entered . . . 1862 by Currier & Ives . . . Lith. of Currier & Ives N.Y. New York, Published by Currier & Ives, 152 Nassau St.

Illustrated, p. 152

3-19 *American Winter Scenes. / Evening*

1854

16 14/16 × 24⅛"

C-207, G-0221,

F. F. Palmer, Del. Entered . . . 1854 by N. Currier . . . Lith & Pub by N. Currier, 152 Nassau St.

Number 19 of the new best-fifty large-folio prints.

Illustrated, gallery plate 3

3-19A *American Winter Scenes. Evening*

1854

16 14/16 × 24⅛"

C-unlisted, G-unlisted

F. F. Palmer, Del. Entered . . . 1854 by N. Currier . . . Lith & Pub by N. Currier, 152 Nassau St.

Alternate state of the preceding print and likely the first state of the two. The horses are drawn on a larger scale, and the lead sleigh has only one rider.

Courtesy of the Old Print Shop.

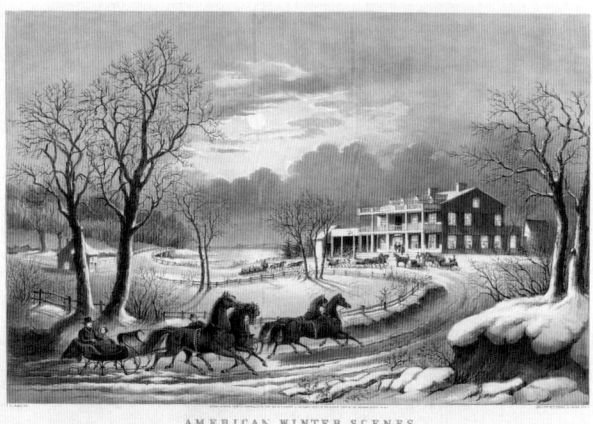

AMERICAN WINTER SCENES.

3-20 *American Winter Scenes. / Morning*

1854

16 5/16 × 24"

C-208, G-0222

F. F. Palmer, Del. Entered . . . 1854 by N. Currier . . . Lith & Pub by N. Currier, 152 Nassau St.

Number 30 of the original best-fifty large-folio prints; number 25 of the new best-fifty large-folio prints.

Illustrated, p. 112

3-21 *Atlantic, Mississippi and Ohio Railroad*

1864 [after 1869]

17¾ × 27¾"

C-298, G-0319

F. F. Palmer, Del. Entered . . . 1864 by Currier & Ives . . . Lith. of Currier & Ives, N.Y.

Same image as *American Express Train* (p. 283). When the Atlantic, Mississippi and Ohio Railroad was formed in 1870, Currier & Ives recycled the earlier image, changing the title but leaving the original copyright date, although the new print was actually published several years later.

Courtesy of the Old Print Shop.

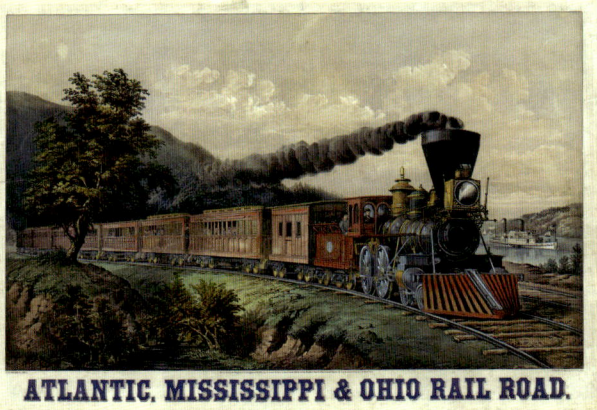

3-22 *The Banks of Doon. / Burns Monument*

Undated, ca. 1857–72

14 15/16 × 20¼"

C-356, G-0390

F. F. Palmer Del. Currier & Ives Lith N.Y. New York, Published by Currier & Ives, 152 Nassau St.

This print may have been adapted, with changes, from a painting by Patrick C. Auld from 1839.

Illustrated, p. 157

3-23 *Bass Fishing. / At Macomb's Dam Harlem River, N.Y.*

1852

12½ × 20⅛"

C-375, G-0417

From nature and on stone by F. F. Palmer. Entered . . . 1852, by N. Currier . . . Lith. and Published by N. Currier, 152 Nassau St. New York.

Sometime after 1856, Currier & Ives published a slightly larger state of the same image, retitled *View on the Harlem River, N.Y. The Highbridge in the Distance* (p. 323). The original Nathaniel Currier copyright date was left on the print, but the publisher was changed to Currier & Ives.

Illustrated, gallery plate 18

3-24 *Blackwells Island, East River. / From Eighty Sixth Street, New York*

1862

11 × 15½"

C-562, G-0627

F. F. Palmer, Del. Entered . . . 1862, by Currier & Ives . . . Lith Currier & Ives, N.Y. New York, Published by Currier & Ives 152 Nassau St.

Illustrated, p. 100

3-25 *The Cattskill Mountains, / From the Eastern Shore of the Hudson*

Illustrated, p. 129

1860

14 13/16 × 20⅜"

C-860, G-0949

F. Palmer, Del. Entered . . . 1860, by Currier & Ives . . . Lith. of Currier & Ives, N.Y. New York, Published by Currier & Ives, 152 Nassau St.

The misspelling "Cattskill" is corrected as "Catskill" in Conningham, *Currier & Ives Prints.*

3-26 *Centre Harbor. / Lake Winnipiseogee, N.H.*

Undated, ca. 1857–72

11 11/16 × 20 7/16"

C-955, G-1048

F. Palmer, Del. Lith. of Currier & Ives, N.Y. New York, Published by Currier & Ives, 152 Nassau St. NY.

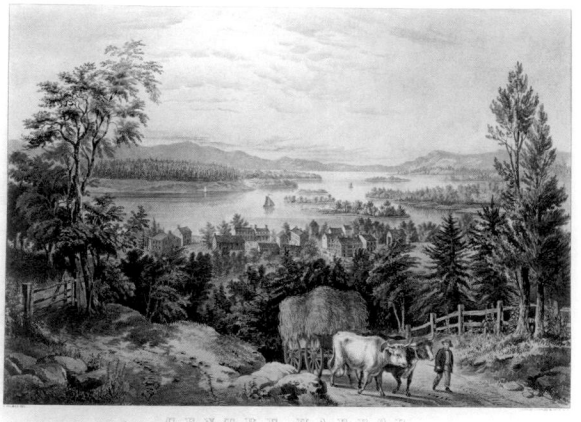

This same image appears as *Lake Winnipiseogee, From Centre Harbor, N.H.* (p. 297). Probably influenced by W. H. Bartlett's illustration in Nathaniel P. Willis, *American Scenery* (London: G. Virtue, 1840).

Courtesy of the Old Print Shop.

3-27 *The Champions of the Mississippi. / "A Race for the Buckhorns"*

Illustrated, gallery plate 6

1866

18¼ × 27⅞"

C-992, G-1076

F. F. Palmer Del. Entered . . . 1866, by Currier & Ives . . . Lith of Currier & Ives, N.Y. New York. Published by Currier & Ives, 152 Nassau St.

Number 11 of the new best-fifty large-folio prints. The identical image was also issued as *A Race for the Buckhorns / On the Mississippi* (C-unlisted, G-unlisted), with the same 1866 copyright statement but lacking Palmer's name.

3-28 *Cherry-Time*

Illustrated, p. 154

1866

9 15/16 × 13 15/16"

C-1023, G-1121

F. F. Palmer, Del. Entered . . . 1866, by Currier & Ives . . . Currier & Ives, Lith. N.Y. New York, Pub'd by Currier & Ives 152 Nassau St. N.Y.

3-29 Clipper Ship "Contest"

1853

16 × 23⅛"

C-1141, G-1258

F. F. Palmer, Lith. Entered . . . 1853 by N. Currier . . . Lith. by N. Currier. New York Published by N. Currier, 152 Nassau Street.

With the following text around the title: "To Danl. D. Westervelt Esq. builder of the New York [clipper ship *Contest*] / This print is respectfully dedicated by the Publisher."

Courtesy of the Michele and Donald D'Amour Museum of Fine Arts, Springfield, MA. Gift of Lenore B. and Sidney A. Alpert, supplemented with Museum Acquisition Funds. Photography by David Stansbury. 2004. D03.526.

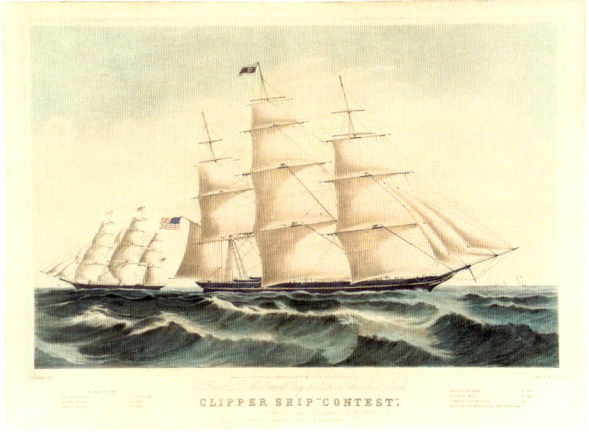

3-30 Clipper Ship "Hurricane" / of New York

1852

14½ × 21¾"

C-1153, G-1270

F. F. Palmer, Del. Entered . . . 1852 by N. Currier . . . Lith. by N. Currier. New York Published by N. Currier, 152 Nassau Street.

Illustrated, gallery plate 14

3-31 Clipper Ship "Sweepstakes"

1853

16 5/16 × 23⅝"

C-1168, G-1286

J. E. Butterworth (signature on stone at bottom left of image). F. F. Palmer, Lith. Entered . . . 1853 by N. Currier . . . Lith. by N. Currier. New York Published by N. Currier 152 Nassau Street.

With the following text around the title: "To Aaron J. Westervelt Esq. builder of the New York, [clipper ship *Sweepstakes*] / This print is respectfully dedicated by the Publishers. / W. A. Macgill, Comdr."

Illustrated, p. 103

3-32 *Clipper Ship "Young America"*

1853

16 × 23¼"

C-1171, G-1289

J. E. Butterworth (signature on stone at bottom left of image). F. F. Palmer, Lith. Entered . . . 1853 by N. Currier . . . Lith. by N. Currier. New York, Published by N. Currier 152 Nassau Street.

With the following text around the title: "To George Daniels Esq. owner, of the New York [clipper ship *Young America*] / This print is respectfully dedicated by the Publishers."

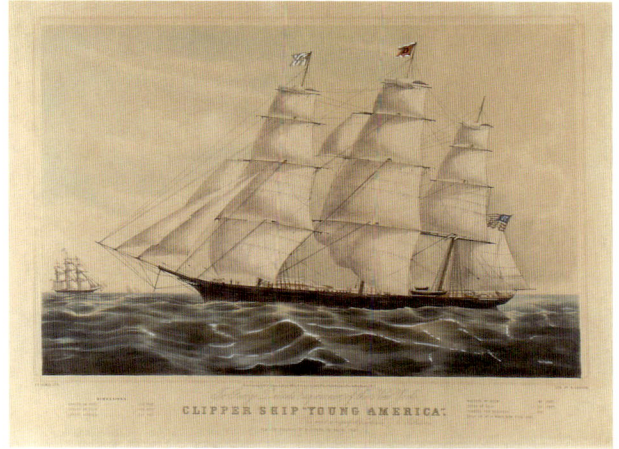

3-33 *The Clipper Yacht "America"*

Undated, ca. 1851–52

12 × 17⅞"

C-1173, G-1290 (listed without Palmer's name)

F. F. Palmer, Lith. Lith. by N. Currier. Published by N. Currier 152 Nassau St. New York.

With the following text below the title: "Built by Mr. George Steers of New York for John C. Stevens Esq. and Associates of the New York Yacht Club."

Illustrated, p. 102

3-34 *Close Quarters*

1866

25 × 19¾"

C-1181, G-1298

F. F. Palmer, Del. Entered . . . 1866, by Currier & Ives . . . Currier & Ives, Lith. N.Y. Publis'd by Currier & Ives, 152 Nassau St.

Companion print to *Pointing a Bevy* (p. 308).

Illustrated, gallery plate 16

3-35 *The Cottage Door-Yard.—Evening*

1855

10 5/16 × 14 13/16"

C-1265, G-1388

F. Palmer, Del. Entered . . . 1855, by N. Currier . . . N. Currier, Lith.

Illustrated, p. 209

3-36 *Cozzen's Dock, West Point. / Hudson River*

Undated, ca. 1857–72

10 13/16 × 15¼"

C-1277, G-1399

F. F. Palmer, Del. Currier & Ives Lith. N.Y. New York Published by Currier & Ives, 152 Nassau St.

Illustrated, p. 134

3-37 *Cumberland Valley. / From Bridgeport Heights Opposite Harrisburg, Pa.*

1865

14¾ × 20 7/16"

C-1327, G-1451

F. F. Palmer, Del. Entered . . . 1865, by Currier & Ives . . . Currier & Ives, Lith. N.Y. New York, Published by Currier & Ives, 152 Nassau Street.

Courtesy of the Old Print Shop.

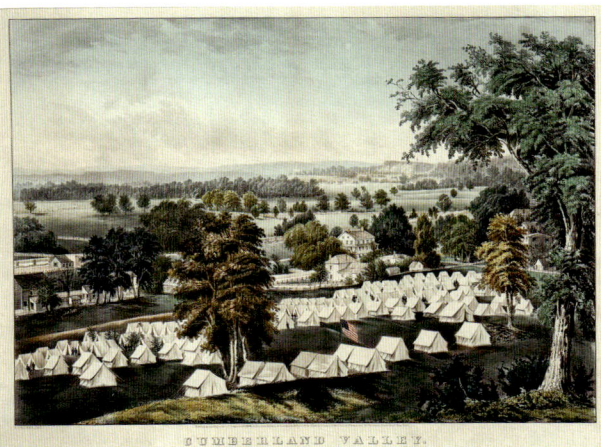

3-38 *Cutter Yacht "Maria" / Modelled by R. E. Stevens, Esq. / Owned By The Messrs. Stevens In New York*

1852

16¾ × 24"

C-1342, G-1466

J. E. Butterworth (signature on stone at bottom right of image). F. F. Palmer Del. Entered . . . 1852 by N. Currier . . . Lith. by N. Currier. New York, Published by N. Currier, 152 Nassau Street.

With the following text below the title: "To John C Stevens, Esq. Commodore of the New York Yacht Club / this Print is with permission, respectfully dedicated by / the Publisher."

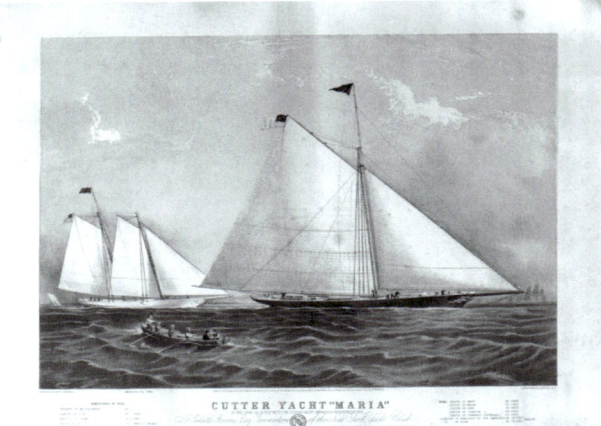

3-39 *The Drive through the Highlands*

Undated, ca. 1857–72

10 5/16 × 14¾"

C-1627, G-1765

F. F. Palmer, Del. Lith by Currier & Ives, N.Y. New York, Published by Currier & Ives 152 Nassau Street.

Illustrated, p. 130

3-40 *Fairmount Water Works. / Philadelphia*

Undated, ca. 1865

10 15/16 × 15½"

C-1813, G-1964

F. F. Palmer, Del. Currier & Ives, N.Y. Pubd. By Currier & Ives, 152 Nassau St. N.Y.

In *Currier & Ives Prints*, Conningham provides a different subtitle for this print: *From the Canal, showing Wire Bridge.*

Illustrated, p. 98

3-41 *The Farmers [sic] Home—Autumn*

1864

15 15/16 × 23¼"

C-1889, G-2045

F. F. Palmer, Del. Entered . . . 1864 by Currier & Ives . . . Lith. of Currier & Ives, N.Y. New York Published by Currier & Ives, 152 Nassau Street.

Illustrated, p. 161

3-42 *The Farmers [sic] Home—Harvest*

1864

16 3/16 × 23½"

C-1890, G-2046

F. F. Palmer, Del. Entered . . . 1864 by Currier & Ives . . . Lith. of Currier & Ives, N.Y. New York. Published by Currier & Ives, 125 Nassau Street.

Number 35 on the new best-fifty large-folio prints.

Illustrated, gallery plate 20

3-43 *The Farmers [sic] Home—Summer*

1864

16 3/16 × 23⅜"

C-1891, G-2047

F. F. Palmer, Del. Entered . . . 1864 by Currier & Ives . . . Lith. Currier & Ives, N.Y. New York Published by Currier & Ives, 152 Nassau Street.

The penciled notations on the fine preparatory drawing for this print (Museum of the Fine Arts, Boston [p. 339]) show how Palmer's employers modified her compositions.

Illustrated, p. 191

3-44 *The Ferry Boat*

Undated, ca. 1850–56

14⅞ × 10¼"

C-1942, G-2109

F. Palmer Del. N. Currier, Lith. N.Y. New York, Published by N. Currier 152 Nassau St.

Illustrated, p. 116

3-45 *Fording the River*

Undated, ca. 1850–56

10⅜ × 14 15/16"

C-2081, G-2259

F. Palmer, Del. N. Currier, Lith.

Courtesy of the Old Print Shop.

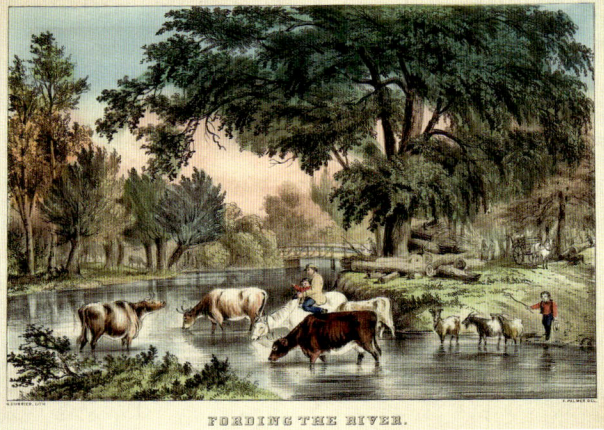

3-46 *Forest Scene on the Lehigh*

Undated, ca. 1857–72

14 15/16 × 20 3/16"

C-2084, G-2262

F. Palmer, Del. Lith. by Currier & Ives, N.Y. New York, Pubd. by Currier & Ives, No. 152 Nassau Street.

Palmer's lithograph was adapted from Swiss artist Karl Bodmer's illustration in Maximilian, Prince of Wied, *Travels in the Interior of North America*, 2 vols. (London: Ackerman, 1843), 2:plate 1.

Courtesy of the Yale University Art Gallery.

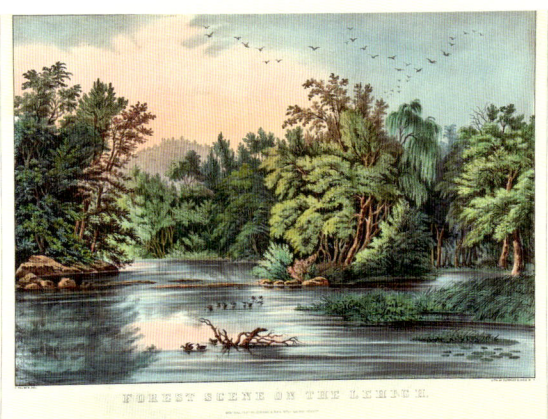

3-47 *The Four Seasons of Life: Childhood. / "The Season of Joy"*

1868

15 13/16 × 23¾"

C-2096, G-2274

Drawn by F. F. Palmer and J. Cameron. J. M. Ives, Del. Entered . . . 1868, . . . by Currier & Ives . . . New York Published by Currier & Ives 152 Nassau Street.

Illustrated, p. 147

3-48 *The Four Seasons of Life: Middle Age. / "The Season of Strength"*

1868

15⅞ × 23⅞"

C-2097, G-2276

Drawn by F. F. Palmer and J. Cameron. J. M. Ives, Del. Entered . . . 1868, by Currier & Ives . . . New York, Published by Currier & Ives, 152 Nassau Street.

The lithograph stone of Palmer's composition reportedly broke during the printing process; the subject was subsequently reassigned to Parsons and Atwater, who produced a more consumer-oriented composition, showing the father entering the well-furnished interior of the family's prosperous home. Parsons and Atwater also completed the print *The Four Seasons of Life: Old Age (Winter).*[7]

Illustrated, p. 149

3-49 *The Four Seasons of Life: Youth. / "The Season of Love"*

1868

15 13/16 × 23⅞"

C-2100, G-2278

Drawn by F. F. Palmer and J. Cameron. J. M. Ives, Del. Entered . . . 1868, by Currier & Ives . . . New York Published by Currier and Ives 152 Nassau Street.

Illustrated, p. 148

3-50 *Fruit and Flower Piece*

1863

10¾ × 15 1/16"

C-2160, G-2340

F. F. Palmer, Del. Entered . . . 1863 by Currier & Ives . . . Currier & Ives, Lith. N.Y. Published by Currier & Ives, 152 Nassau St.

Courtesy of the Old Print Shop.

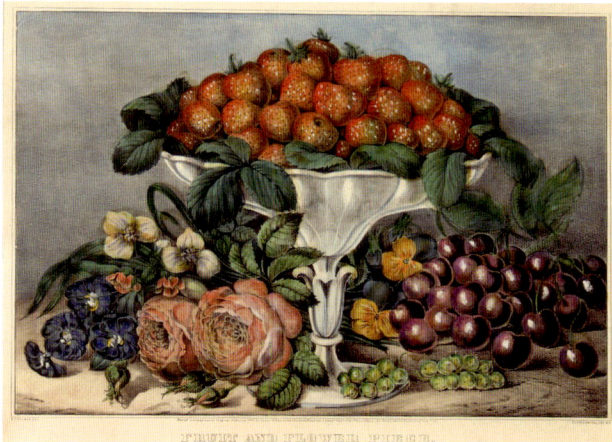

3-51 *Garden Orchard and Vine*

1867

14 11/16 × 20⅜"

C-2221, G-2406

F. F. Palmer, Del. Entered . . . 1867, by Currier & Ives . . . Lith. of Currier & Ives, N.Y. New York Published by Currier & Ives, 152 Nassau St.

Illustrated, p. 154

3-52 *A Glimpse of the Homestead*

1865

11¼ × 16"

C-2386, G-2592

F. F. Palmer Del. Entered . . . 1865 by Currier & Ives . . . Currier & Ives Lithog. N.Y. Published Currier & Ives 152 Nassau St. N.Y.

A second version of this print, identical except for an earlier copyright date of 1863, is commonly listed (C-2385, G-2591). However, examination of a number of impressions of this print shows that the numeral 5 in the year is somewhat indistinct and could easily be mistaken for a 3. In fact, all versions are from 1865, and the date 1863 is a mistake.

This print is a good example of how Palmer copied elements from an earlier company lithograph (*A Glimpse of the Homestead*, anonymous, 1859) but changed the design into a much stronger composition. In her version, the horse, chickens, and ducks have been reversed, a barn added behind them, a wagon placed in front of a more modest home on the right, and the trees massed gracefully in the background.

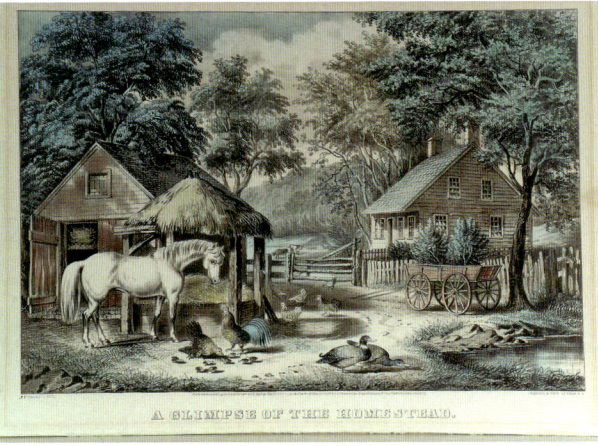

3-53 *Gray's Elegy. / In a Country Church Yard*

1864

16 × 23⅛"

C-2562, G-2780

F. F. Palmer, Del. Entered . . . 1864 by Currier & Ives . . . Lith by Currier & Ives. New York. Published by Currier & Ives, 152 Nassau Street.

Illustrated, p. 157

3-54 *The Happy Family. / Ruffed Grouse and Young*

1866

19 13/16 × 27 13/16"

C-2712, G-2940

F. F. Palmer, Del. Entered . . . 1866, by Currier & Ives . . . Currier & Ives, Lithog. N.Y.

Illustrated, gallery plate 21

3-55 *Happy Little Chicks*

1866

9⅞ × 13 15/16"

C-2716, G-2944

From nature by F F Palmer. Entered . . . 1866, by Currier & Ives . . . Currier & Ives Lith N.Y. Pub'd. by Currier & Ives, 152 Nassau St. N.Y.

Courtesy of the Old Print Shop.

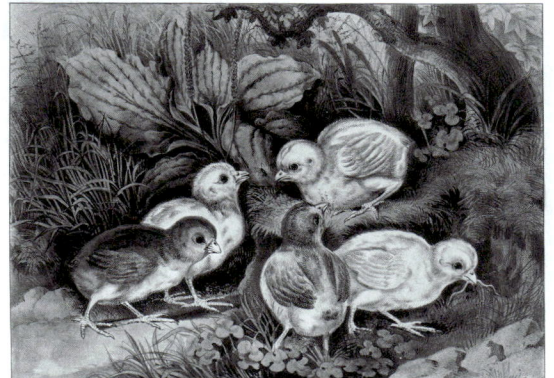

3-73 *Life In the Country. / Morning*

1862

11 3/16 × 15 7/16"

C-3509, G-3777

F. F. Palmer, Del. Entered . . . 1862 by Currier & Ives . . . Currier & Ives, Lith. N.Y. New York, Published by Currier & Ives, 152 Nassau St.

Courtesy of the Old Print Shop.

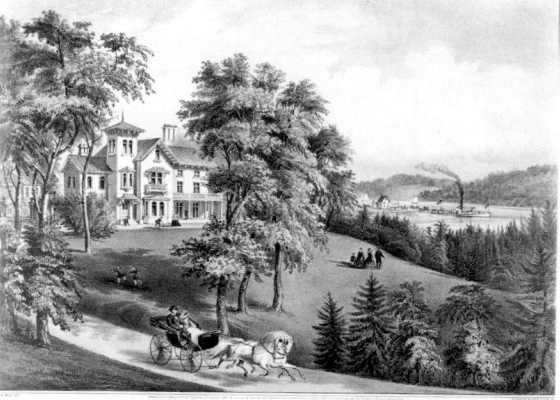

3-74 *The "Lightning Express" Trains. / "Leaving the Junction"*

1863

17¾ × 27⅝"

C-3535, G-3803

Del. by F. F. Palmer. Entered . . . 1863 by Currier & Ives . . . Lith by Currier & Ives. New York. Published by Currier & Ives, 152 Nassau Street.

Number 7 of the original best-fifty large-folio prints; number 13 of the new best-fifty large-folio prints.

Illustrated, gallery plate 10

3-75 *The Little Wanderer*

1867

13⅞ × 9 15/16"

C-3730, G-4040

F. F. Palmer, Del. Entered . . . 1867 by Currier & Ives . . . Currier & Ives Lith, N.Y. Pub'd by Currier & Ives, 152 Nassau St. N.Y.

Illustrated, p. 150

3-76 *Lookout Mountain, Tennessee. / And the Chattanooga Rail Road*

1866

14 11/16 × 20½"

C-3771, G-4088

F. F. Palmer, Del. Entered . . . 1866 by Currier & Ives . . . Currier & Ives, Lith. N.Y. New York, Pub'd by Currier & Ives, 152 Nassau St.

Illustrated, p. 138

3-77 *Low Water in the Mississippi*

1867

17 15/16 × 27 15/16"

C-unlisted, G-4149

J. M. I. Del. (signature on stone, lower left of image). F. E. [*sic*] Palmer. Entered . . . 1867, by Currier & Ives . . . Lith. of Currier & Ives, N.Y. New York, Published by Currier & Ives, 152 Nassau St.

Companion print to *"High Water" in the Mississippi* (p. 295). This print exists in a few states, beginning with the black-and-white version submitted to the Library of Congress with an 1867 copyright date (though a handwritten 8 has been added lightly over the seven). Gale Research created two entries for this print: one with the 1867 copyright date and a second entry for the 1868 version with quotation marks added around "Low Water." Conningham created only one entry for the 1868 copyright date, without adding quotation marks.

3-77A *Low Water in the Mississippi*

1868

17 15/16 × 27 15/16"

C-3824, G-4150

J. M. I. Del. (signature on stone, lower left of image). F. E. [*sic*] Palmer. Entered . . . 1868, by Currier & Ives . . . Lith. of Currier & Ives, N.Y. New York, Published by Currier & Ives, 152 Nassau St.

Same image as the preceding entry but with a slightly later copyright date. Gale Research's entry for this image includes quotation marks around "Low Water." Communication with the Museum of the City of New York and the Missouri Historical Society, the two institutions identified by Gale as having this print, has indicated that neither copy includes quotation marks in the title. The Museum of the City of New York also has this same print with the imprint "New York, Published by Currier & Ives, 115 Nassau St.," indicating that Currier & Ives reissued the print sometime between 1877 and 1894.

3-78 *The Lucky Escape*

Undated, ca. 1850–56

10¼ × 14 13/16"

C-3829, G-4153

F. Palmer, Del. N. Currier, Lith.

Courtesy of the Old Print Shop.

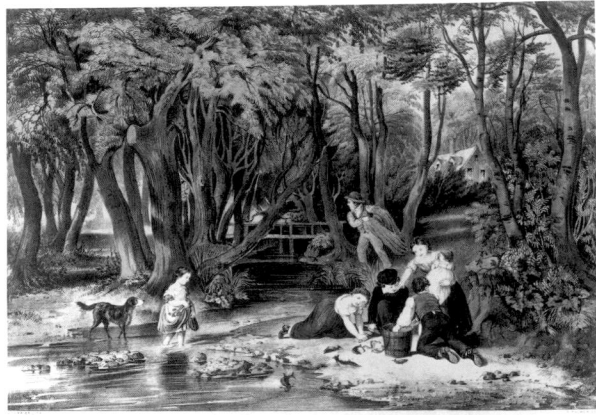

THE LUCKY ESCAPE.

3-79 *Melrose Abbey*

1862

11¼ × 15⅝"

C-4105, G-4462

F. F. Palmer, Del. Entered . . . 1862 by Currier & Ives . . . Lith. Currier & Ives N.Y.
Published by Currier & Ives, 152 Nassau St. N.Y.

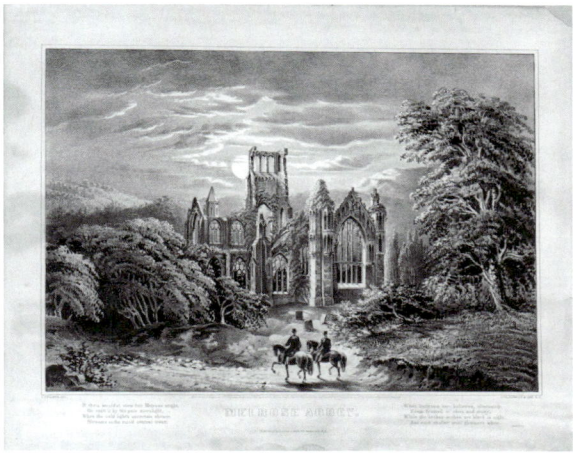

3-80 *A Midnight Race on the Mississippi*

1860

18 × 27 13/16"

C-4116, G-4476

F. F. Palmer Del. from a sketch by H. D. Manning of the Natchez. Entered . . . 1860, by Currier & Ives . . . Lith. of Currier & Ives, N.Y. New York, Published by Currier & Ives 152 Nassau St.

Number 21 of the original best-fifty large-folio prints; number 2 of the new best-fifty large-folio prints.

Illustrated, p. 136

3-81 *Mill River Scenery*

Undated, ca. 1857–72

17¾ × 14⅜"

C-4126, G-4494

F. F. Palmer, Del. Lith by Currier & Ives, N.Y. New York, Published by Currier & Ives, 152 Nassau St.

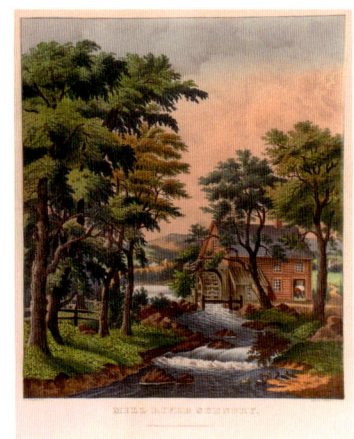

3-82 *The Mill-Stream*

Undated, ca. 1857–72

11 1/16 × 15⅝"

C-4127, G-4495

F. F. Palmer, Del. Lith. Currier & Ives, N.Y. New York, Published by Currier & Ives, 152 Nassau St.

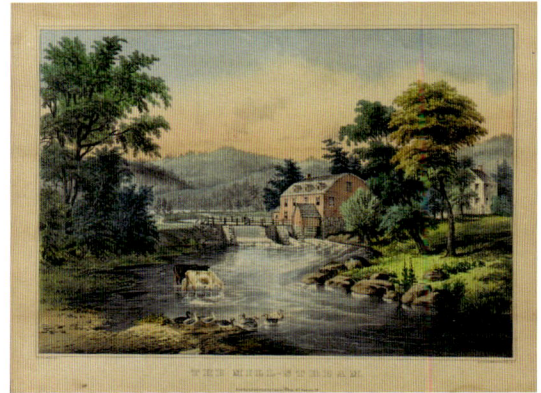

3-83 *The Mississippi in Time of Peace*

1865

18⅜ × 27 13/16"

C-4160, G-4519

F. F. Palmer, Del. Entered . . . 1865, by Currier & Ives . . . Lith of Currier & Ives NY. New York, published by Currier & Ives, 152 Nassau Street.

Number 33 of the new best-fifty large-folio prints. Companion print to *The Mississippi in Time of War.*

Illustrated, gallery plate 11

3-84 *The Mississippi in Time of War*

1865

18¼ × 27¾"

C-4161, G-4520

F. F. Palmer, Del. Entered . . . 1865, by Currier & Ives . . . Currier & Ives, lith. N.Y. New York, Published by Currier & Ives, 152 Nassau Street.

Companion to *The Mississippi in Time of Peace.*

Illustrated, gallery plate 12

3-85 *Morning in the Woods*

1852, ca. 1857–72

14 13/16 × 20⅛"

C-4196, G-4562

From nature and on stone by F. F. Palmer . . . Entered . . . 1852 by N. Currier . . . Lith of Currier & Ives, N.Y. New York, Pubd by Currier & Ives, 152 Nassau St.

The composition is the same as Palmer's print *Partridge Shooting* (1852) (p. 307) but does not include that print's group of dead game birds in the foreground, implying a later time of day, after the hunt. This is typical of Currier & Ives's practice of changing a composition slightly in order to create more prints from the same design. This print retains the same 1852 copyright date as *Partridge Shooting* but has the Currier & Ives imprint.

Courtesy of the Museum of the City of New York, 56.300.66.

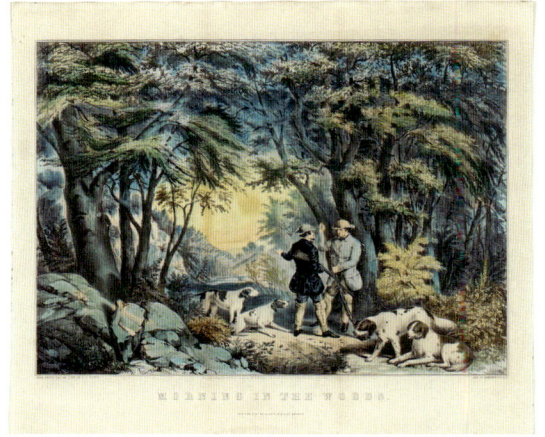

3-86 *Morning in the Woods*

Illustrated, p. 110

1865

14¾ × 20½"

C-4197, G-4563

F. F. Palmer Del. Entered . . . 1865 by Currier & Ives . . . Lith. of Currier & Ives, N.Y. New York, Published by Currier & Ives, 152 Nassau St.

In 1865, Palmer created a different composition with the same title as the 1852 version of this subject, notably with two dogs instead of four. Palmer drew this composition, but someone else lithographed it from her drawing. A different artist (probably John Cameron) seems to have worked on the figures.

3-87 *Mothers [sic] Wing*

1866

9 15/16 × 11¾"

C-4239, G-4606

F. F. Palmer, Del. Entered . . . 1866, by Currier & Ives . . . Currier & Ives, Lith. N.Y. Pub'd by Currier & Ives, 152 Nassau St. N.Y.

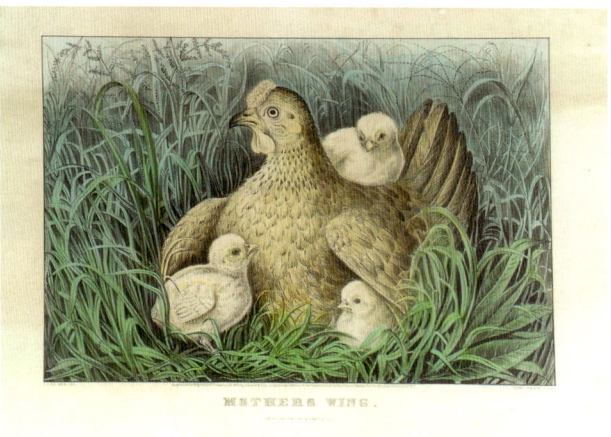

3-88 *Mount Washington and the White Mountains, / From the Valley of Conway*

Illustrated, p. 179

1860

14 15/16 × 20⅜"

C-4242, G-4614

F. Palmer, Del. Entered . . . 1860, by Currier & Ives . . . Lith. by Currier & Ives, N.Y. New York, Published by Currier Ives, 152 Nassau St.

Adapted, with considerable changes, from James Smillie's Art-Union engraving (1851) of John F. Kensett's painting *Mount Washington from the Valley of Conway* (1851).

3-89 *The Mountain Pass. / Sierra Nevada*

Illustrated, p. 217

1867

17½ × 25¾"

C-4243, G-4609

F. F. Palmer, Del. Entered . . . 1867, by Currier & Ives . . . Lith. of Currier & Ives, N.Y. New York, Published by Currier & Ives, 152 Nassau Street.

3-90 *The Mountain Spring. / Near Cozzen's Dock, West Point*   Illustrated, p. 134

1862

11 × 15 9/16"

C-4245, G-46115

F. F. Palmer, Del. Entered . . . 1862, by Currier & Ives . . . Lith. Currier & Ives, N.Y. New York, Published by Currier & Ives, 152 Nassau Street.

3-91 *My Cottage Home*   Illustrated, p. 213

1866

16 1/16 × 23 7/16"

C-4283, G-4655

F. F. Palmer, Del. Entered . . . 1866, by Currier & Ives . . . Currier & Ives, Lith. N.Y. New York, Published by Currier & Ives, 152 Nassau St.

3-92 *New England Scenery*   Illustrated, p. 160

1866

23 7/16 × 16⅜"

C-4419, G-4800

F. F. Palmer Del. Entered . . . 1866 by Currier & Ives . . . Lith. of Currier & Ives, N.Y. New York, Published by Currier & Ives, 152 Nassau St.

3-93 *New York Bay. / From Bay Ridge, L.I.*   Illustrated, p. 99

1860

14⅞ × 20"

C-4435, G-4821

F. F. Palmer, Del. Entered . . . 1860, by Currier & Ives . . . Lith of Currier & Ives, N.Y. New York, Published by Currier & Ives 152 Nassau St.

3-94 *New York Crystal Palace. / For the Exhibition of the Industry of all Nations*   Illustrated, p. 96

1853

17⅛ × 25¼"

C-4440, G-4827

F. F. Palmer, Del. Entered . . . 1853, by N. Currier . . . Lith. & Pub. by N. Currier. 152 Nassau St. N.Y.

One version of this print keys the identification "Latting Observatory" directly under the image; another omits it.

3-95 *A Night on the Hudson. / "Through at Daylight"*

1864

17⅞ × 27 13/16"

C-4474, G-4860

F. E. [*sic*] Palmer, Del. Entered . . . 1864 by Currier & Ives . . . Lith. by Currier & Ives. New York. Published by Currier & Ives, 152 Nassau Street.

Number 47 of the new best-fifty large-folio prints.

Illustrated, gallery plate 13

3-96 *Old Blandford Church. / Petersburg Virginia*

Undated, ca. 1857–72

8 × 12½"

C-4549, G-4937

F.F.P. (initials on stone on gravestone, lower-right corner of the image). Published by Currier & Ives 152 Nassau St. New York.

Illustrated, p. 198

3-97 *The Old Farm Gate*

1864

16 1/16 × 23⅜"

C-4555, G-4943

F. F. Palmer, Del. Entered . . . 1864, by Currier & Ives . . . Currier & Ives, N.Y. New York, Published by Currier & Ives, 152 Nassau St.

Palmer's preparatory watercolor sketch of this image is at the Museum of the City of New York.

Illustrated, p. 215

3-98 *The Old Homestead*

1855

9 11/16 × 14⅞"

C-4561, G-4948

F. Palmer Del. N. Currier Lith. Entered . . . 1855 by N. Currier . . .

The earliest of three versions with the same title and with similar but not identical compositions. The third version lacks the Palmer imprint.

Courtesy of the Old Print Shop.

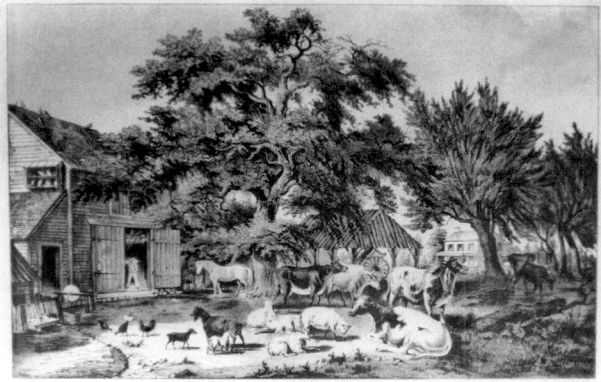

3-99 *The Old Homestead*

Undated, ca. 1857–72

11⅛ × 16"

C-4562, G-4949

F. F. Palmer, Del. Lith of Currier & Ives, N.Y. New York, Published by Currier & Ives, 152 Nassau St., N.Y.

A later version of *The Old Homestead* issued after Ives became Currier's partner. Similar to the previous print of 1855, but the composition is less cluttered: the farmer and animals in the front yard remain, but the shed, cart, and cows drinking from a stream in the middle distance have been eliminated, and the stream has been moved forward to the right-front corner of the print, making room for a larger, closer view of a home with side wing and front lawn in the background, separated from the barnyard by a white picket fence. Two large trees have been modified to frame the house.

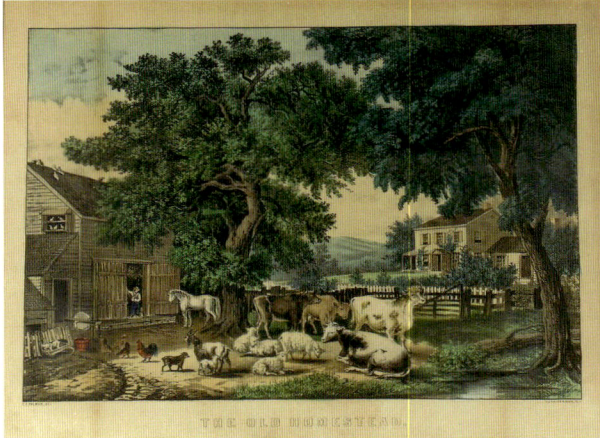

3-100 *The Old Norman Castle*

Undated, ca. 1850–56

15 × 20¼"

C-4575, G-4959

F. Palmer, Del. Lith. by N. Currier, N.Y. New York, Published by N. Currier, 152 Nassau St.

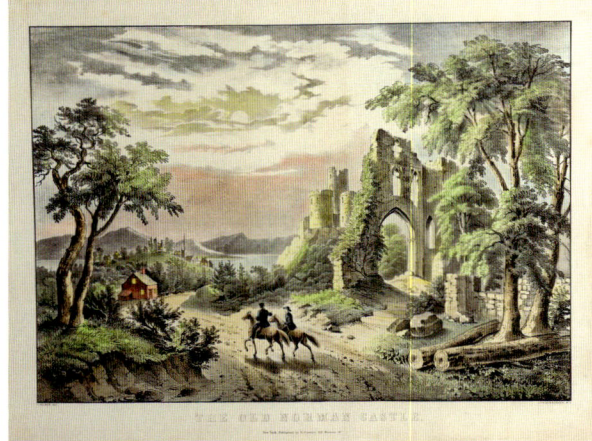

3-101 *The Old Norman Castle*

Undated, ca. 1857–72

15 × 20¼"

C-unlisted, G-unlisted

F. F. Palmer, Del. Currier & Ives, N.Y. New York, Published by Currier & Ives, 152 Nassau St.

A later version of *The Old Norman Castle* (previous entry) showing the same basic composition as the earlier version, with some changes: rocks have replaced two logs in the foreground, and there are changes in the castle architecture and trees.

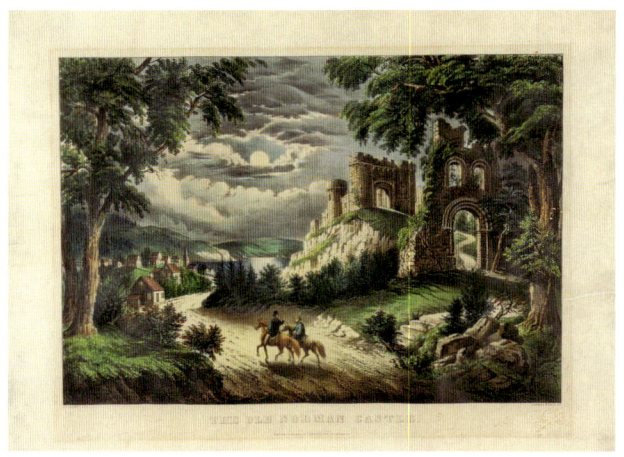

3-102 *The Old Oaken Bucket*

1864

15¼ × 22½"

C-4576, G-4961

F. F. Palmer, Del. Entered . . . 1864, by Currier & Ives . . . Currier & Ives, N.Y. New York, Published by Currier & Ives, 152 Nassau Street.

Illustrated, p. 163

3-103 *The Old Windmill*

Undated, ca. 1857–72

10⅜ × 14 13/16"

C-4591, G-4976

F. F. Palmer, Del. Lith. of Currier & Ives, N.Y. New York Published by Currier & Ives 152 Nassau St.

Courtesy of the Old Print Shop.

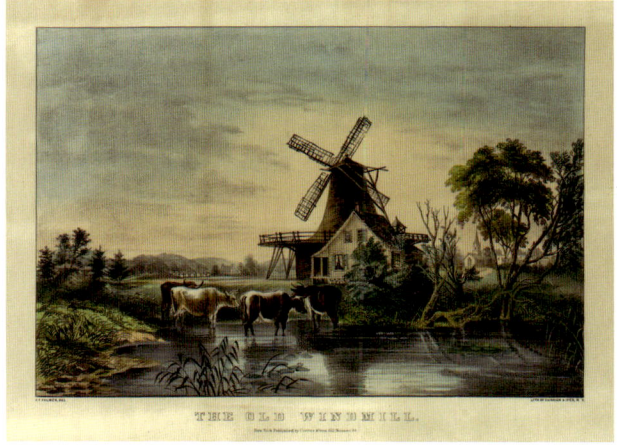

3-104 *On a Point*

1855

9 13/16 × 14 13/16"

C-4592, G-4979

F. Palmer Del. N. Currier Lith. Entered . . . 1855 by N. Currier . . .

Illustrated, p. 106

3-105 *Partridge Shooting*

1852

12⅝ × 20 3/16"

C-4714, G-5112

From nature and on stone by F. F. Palmer. Entered . . . 1852 by N. Currier. Lith. of N. Currier, N.Y. Published by N. Currier, 152 Nassau St. New York.

One of the Long Island Series of sporting prints published in 1852. This image has two hunters and four dogs. In the same year, this print was altered by removing the dead game, increasing the height slightly, and publishing it as *Morning in the Woods* (p. 302)—a typical example of how the company created more than one print out of a single composition by changing minor elements of the image.

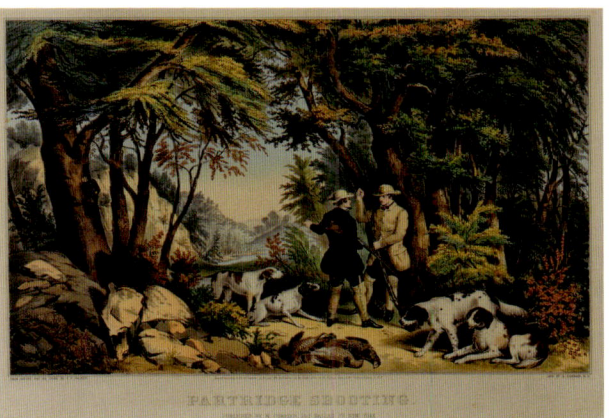

3-106 *Partridge Shooting*

1865

12 13/16 × 20⅜"

C-4717, G-5114

F. F. Palmer, Del. Entered . . . 1865, by Currier & Ives . . . Currier & Ives, Lith. N.Y. New York Published by Currier & Ives 152 Nassau St.

In 1865, Palmer drew a different version of this ever-popular subject, depicting two dogs and two hunters, with the same title as her print published in 1852. The figures, which are shorter and stockier than her early ones, seem to be drawn by a different hand, possibly John Cameron, who often collaborated with Palmer. In 1855, Currier issued another print with this same title, but it lacks Palmer's name (p. 336).

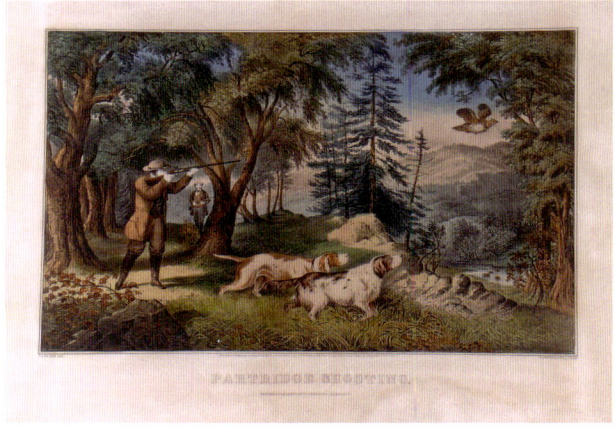

3-107 *The Pioneer's Home. / On the Western Frontier*

1867

18¾ × 26⅞"

C-4786, G-5189

F. F. Palmer, Del. Entered . . . 1867, by Currier & Ives . . . Currier & Ives, Lith. NY. New York. Published by Currier & Ives, 152 Nassau St.

Illustrated, p. 166

3-108 *Pointing a Bevy*

1866

24 13/16 × 12⅞"

C-4817, G-5224

F. F. Palmer, Del. Entered . . . 1866, by Currier & Ives . . . Currier & Ives, Lith. N.Y. New York Published by Currier & Ives, 152 Nassau St.

Companion print to *Close Quarters* (p. 289).

Illustrated, gallery plate 15

3-109 *Quail Shooting. / Setters the Property of S. Palmer Esq., Brooklyn, L.I.*

1852

13 × 20⅜"

C-4989, G-5414

From nature and on stone by F. F. Palmer. Entered . . . 1852 by N. Currier . . . Lith and published by N. Currier, 152 Nassau St. New York.

One of Palmer's Long Island Series of sporting prints.

Illustrated, p. 105

3-110 *Rail Shooting. / On The Delaware*

1852

12⅞ × 20⅛"

C-5054, G-5481

From nature and on stone by F. F. Palmer. Entered . . . 1852 by N. Currier . . . Lith. and published by N. Currier, 152 Nassau St. New York.

One of Palmer's Long Island Series of sporting prints (though this particular print is not a Long Island scene). Number 37 of the original best-fifty large-folio prints.

Courtesy of the Michele and Donald D'Amour Museum of Fine Arts, Springfield, MA. Gift of Lenore B. and Sidney A. Alpert, supplemented with Museum Acquisition Funds. Photography by David Stansbury. 2004. D03.457

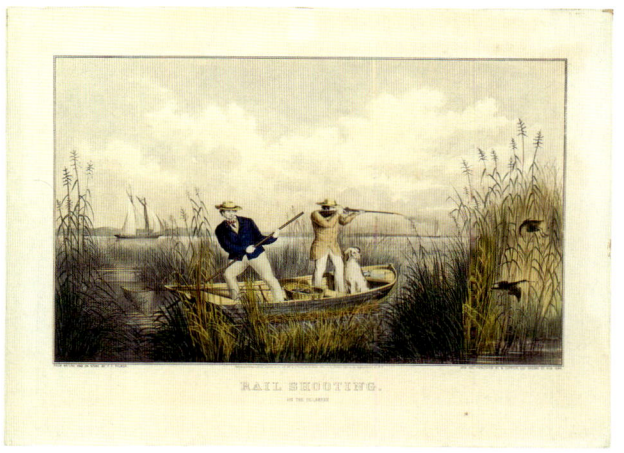

3-111 *The Return from the Pasture*

Undated, ca. 1857–72

18 9/16 × 27⅞"

C-5130, G-5565

F. F. Palmer, Del. Lith. by Currier & Ives, N.Y. New York, Pubd. by Currier & Ives, 152 Nassau St.

Palmer created at least three variations of this print, all of which show a man, accompanied by his dog, leading seven cattle home across a shallow stream in the foreground, with minor variations in the house and landscape on the shore behind them. In this version, on the bank behind the stream a woman looks out of the top half of a Dutch door in the entryway of a stone cottage with a slate (or shingled) roof. In front of the house, a man sits on a log. A rustic wooden bridge over the left side of the stream connects with a path to the front door.

3-112 *The Return from the Pasture*

Undated, ca. 1857–72

18 15/16 × 27⅞"

C-5128, G-5566

F. F. Palmer, Del. Lith. by Currier & Ives, N.Y. New York, Pubd. by Currier & Ives, 152 Nassau St.

Same composition as the previous print but without the man seated on a log to the right of the doorway.

Courtesy of the Old Print Shop.

Illustrated, p. 123

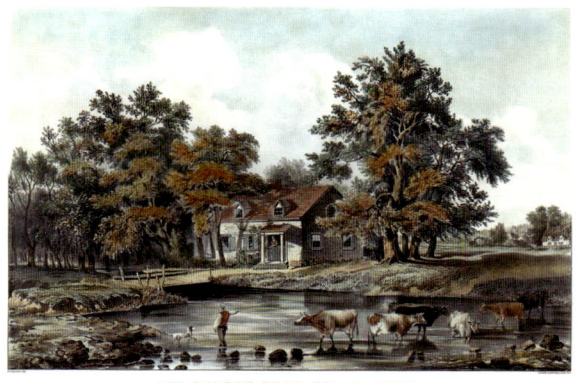

3-113 *The Return from the Pasture*

Undated, ca. 1857–72

19¾ × 27 13/16"

C-5129, G-5567 (listed without Palmer's name)

F. F. Palmer, Del. Lith. by Currier & Ives, N.Y. New York, Pubd. by Currier & Ives, 152 Nassau St.

In a third variation of this title, a man and dog lead cattle home across a stream, but on the bank behind him a woman and child stand on the front lawn of a thatched-roof cottage. The door is open, and there is no portico over the entrance. The man seated on a log has been eliminated. The plank bridge across the stream on the left is partially obscured by a bush, and an additional dirt road leads directly from the stream to the welcoming open front door of the house.

Courtesy of the Old Print Shop.

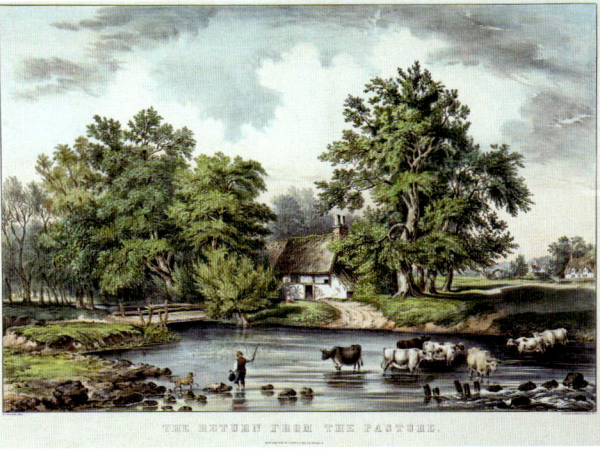

3-114 *The Return from the Woods*

Undated, ca. 1857–72

11 × 15 5/16"

C-5131, G-5568

F. F. Palmer, Del. Currier & Ives Lith. N.Y. New York, Published by Currier & Ives, 152 Nassau St.

Illustrated, p. 111

3-115 *The Riverroad*

Undated, ca. 1857–72

11 1/16 × 15½"

C-5158, G-5593 (listed without Palmer's name)

F. F. Palmer, Del. Published by Currier & Ives.

From the same stone as *View Near Highbridge. Harlem River, N.Y.* (p. 320).

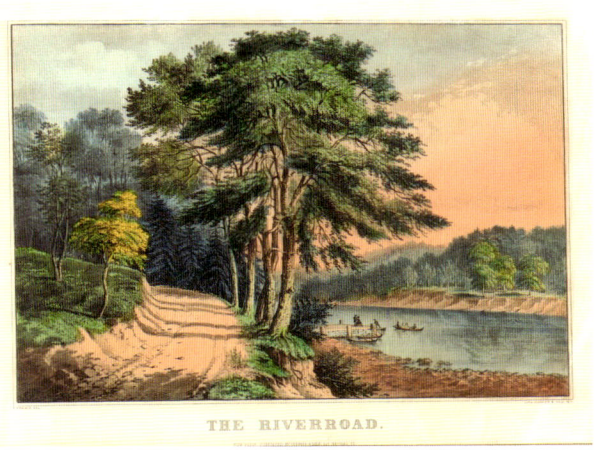

3-116 *The Riverside*

Undated, ca. 1857–72

11 × 15¼"

C-5164, G-5596

F. F. Palmer, Del. Lith. Currier & Ives, N.Y. New York, Published by Currier & Ives, 152 Nassau St.

Currier & Ives issued multiple prints with the title *The River Side* that were not by Palmer. Palmer's print centers on men fishing.

Courtesy of the Old Print Shop.

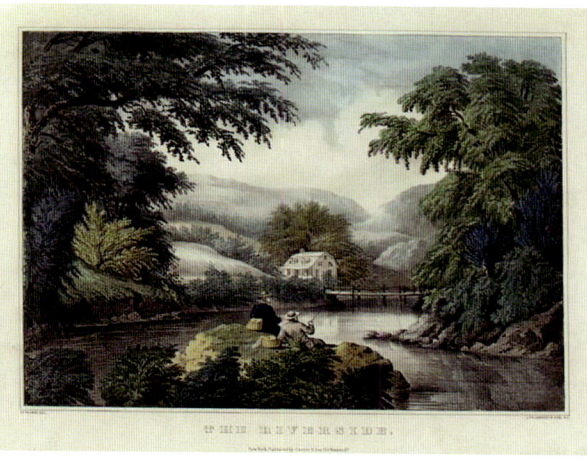

3-117 *The Rocky Mountains. / Emigrants Crossing the Plains*

1866

17¼ × 25⅝"

C-5196, G-5633

F. F. Palmer, Del. Entered . . . 1866, by Currier & Ives . . . Currier & Ives, Lith. N.Y. New York, Published by Currier & Ives, 152 Nassau St.

Number 9 of the original best-fifty large-folio prints; number 12 of the new best-fifty large-folio prints.

Illustrated, gallery plate 7

3-118 *"Rounding a Bend" on the Mississippi. / The parting Salute*

1866

18¼ × 27¾"

C-5223, G-5662

F. F. Palmer Del. Entered . . . 1866, by Currier & Ives . . . Currier & Ives, Lith. N.Y. New York, Published by Currier & Ives, 152 Nassau St.

This print was reissued later with the imprint "New York, Published by Currier & Ives, 115 Nassau St."

Illustrated, p. 185

3-119 *Royal Mail Steam Ship. / Arabia*

1853

13½ × 21½"

C-5235 (listed without Palmer's name), G-5671 (listed without Palmer's name)

F. F. Palmer, Del. Entered . . . 1853 by N. Currier . . . Lith. & Pub. By N. Currier 152 Nassau St. cor. Of Spruce N.Y.

Palmer is not listed as the artist in Conningham and Gale, but her name is clearly marked on the print held by the Mariners' Museum.

Illustrated, p. 104

3-120 *Royal Mail Steam Ship, / Asia*

1851

13⅞ × 22⅛"

C-5236, G-5672

Palmer, Del. & Lith. Entered . . . 1851 by N. Currier . . . Lith & Pub. By N. Currier, 152 Nassau St. cor. Of Spruce N.Y.

Courtesy of the Prints and Photographs Division, Library of Congress, LC-DIG-pga-03634.

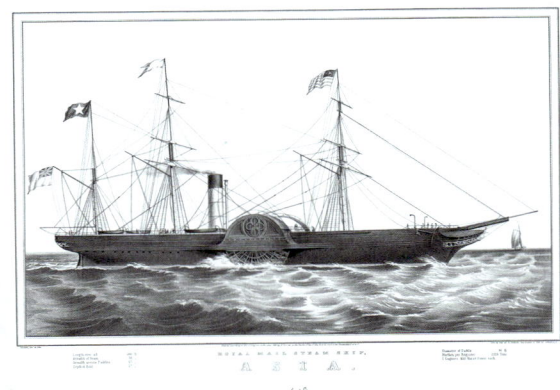

3-121 *The Ruins of the Abbey*

1856

15⅛ × 20¾"

C-5251, G-5691

F. Palmer, Del. Entered . . . 1856, by N. Currier . . . Lith. by N. Currier. N.Y. New York, Published by N. Currier, 152 Nassau St.

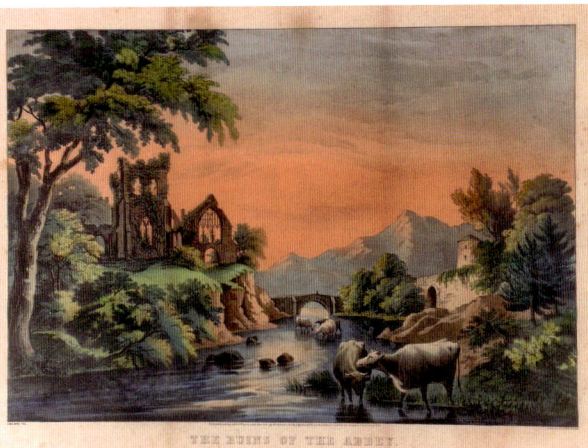

3-122 *The Rural Lake*

Undated, ca. 1857–72

10⅜ × 14 13/16"

C-5261, G-5701

F. Palmer Del. Currier & Ives, Lith. N.Y. New York, Pubd. by Currier & Ives, 152 Nassau St.

Courtesy of the Old Print Shop.

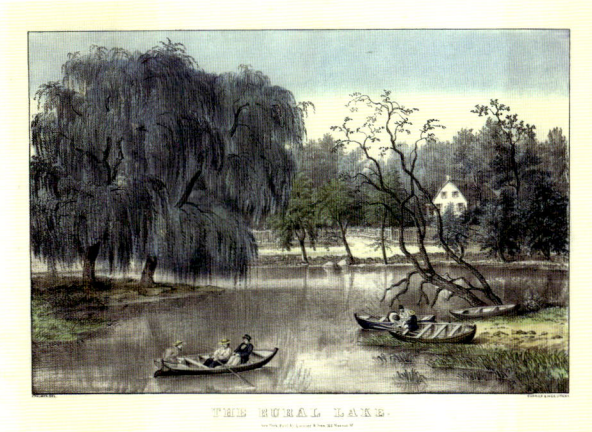

3-123 *The Scenery of the Hudson. / View, Near "Anthony's Nose"*

Undated, ca. 1857–72

15 × 20¼"

C-5421, G-5817

F. Palmer, Del. Lith. by Currier & Ives, N.Y. New York Published by Currier & Ives. 152, Nassau St.

This composition was probably adapted, with minor changes, from W. H. Bartlett's illustration *View Near Anthony's Nose, Hudson Highlands* in Willis, *American Scenery* (1840).

Illustrated, p. 128

3-124 *The Season of Blossoms*

1865

15 13/16 × 23 5/16"

C-5449, G-5844

F. F. Palmer, Del. Entered . . . 1865, by Currier & Ives . . . Currier & Ives, Lith. N.Y. New York, Published by Currier & Ives, 152 Nassau St.

Courtesy of the Yale University Art Gallery.

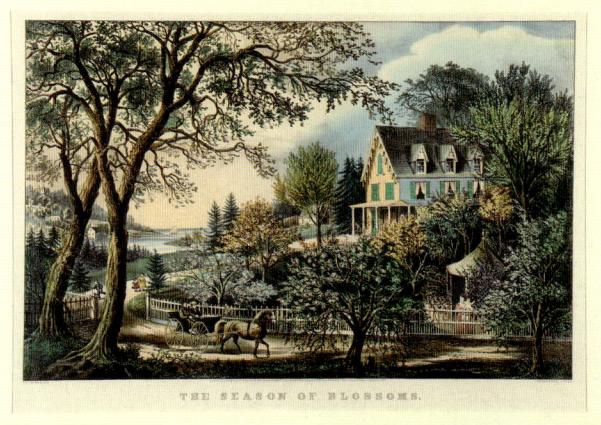

3-125 *"Sleepy Hollow" Church, / Near Tarrytown, N.Y.*

1867

11½ × 16¼"

C-5551, G-5844

F. F. Palmer, Del. Entered . . . 1867, by Currier & Ives . . . Pub'd. by Currier & Ives, 152 Nassau St. N.Y.

Illustrated, p. 130

3-126 *Snipe Shooting*

1852

12¾ × 20"

C-5577, G-5974

From nature and on stone by F. F. Palmer. Entered . . . 1852 by N. Currier . . . Lith of N. Currier N.Y. Published by N. Currier, 152 Nassau St. New York.

One of Palmer's Long Island Series of sporting prints published in 1852.

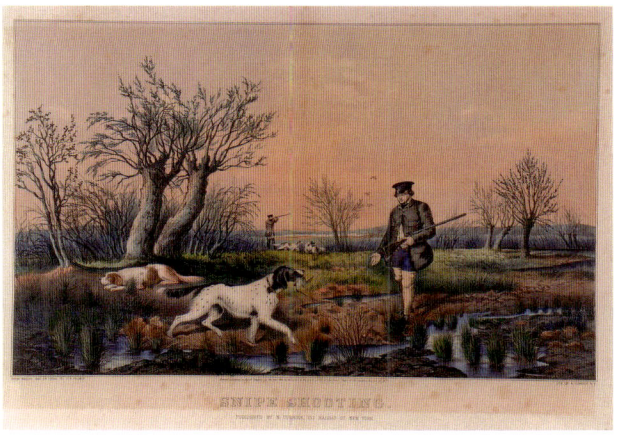

3-127 *A Snowy Morning*

1864

11 9/16 × 16⅜"

C-5582, G-5979

F. F. Palmer, Del. Entered . . . 1864, by Currier & Ives . . . New York, Published by Currier & Ives, 152 Nassau St.

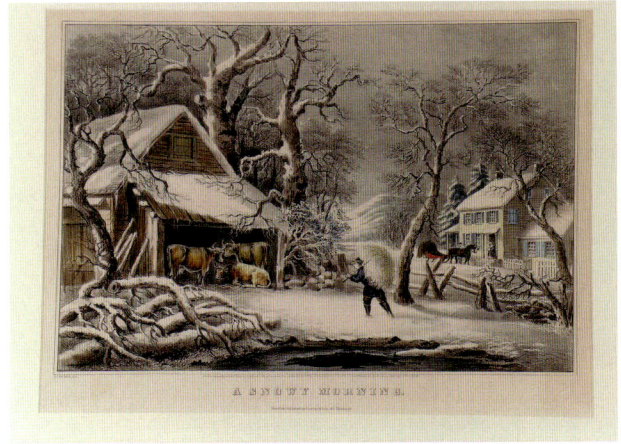

3-128 *Staten Island and the Narrows. / From Fort Hamilton*

1861

14⅞ × 20⅛"

C-5715, G-6123

F. F. Palmer, Del. Entered . . . 1861, by Currier & Ives . . . Lith Currier & Ives, N.Y. New York, Published by Currier & Ives, 152 Nassau St.

Comparing this print with William Bartlett's illustration in Willis's book *American Scenery* (1840) and Palmer's watercolor study (New-York Historical Society [p. 342]) shows how Palmer strengthened and refined the composition.

Illustrated, p. 183

3-129 *The Suburban Gothic Villa, Murray Hill / Residence of W. C. Waddell*

1846

Image unlocated, small folio, dimensions unknown

C-5846, G-6313

Drawn by A. J. Davis. On stone by F. Palmer.

This print originally lithographed by E. Jones & E. Palmer around 1844 was purportedly reissued by Currier in 1846. According to Mary Cowdrey, Currier added "on stone by F. Palmer" to Palmer's rendering of the Waddell Villa and published it under his own label,[8] but I have thus far not found a copy of this print with the Currier imprint.

3-130 *Summer in the Country*

1866

16⅛ × 23 7/16"

C-5864, G-6327

F. F. Palmer, Del. Entered . . . 1865, by Currier & Ives . . . Lith. of Currier & Ives, N.Y. New York, Published by Currier & Ives, 152 Nassau St.

Illustrated, p. 211

3-131 *Summer Morning*

Undated, ca. 1857–72

14¾ × 10¼"

C-5870, G-6335

F. F. Palmer, Del. Lith. by Currier & Ives, N.Y. New York, Published by Currier & Ives, 152 Nassau Street.

Illustrated, p. 220

3-132 *Summer Time*

Undated, ca. 1857–72

17 11/16 × 14 7/16"

C-5878, G-6345

F. F. Palmer, Del. Lith. of Currier & Ives, N.Y. New York, Published by Currier & Ives, 152 Nassau St.

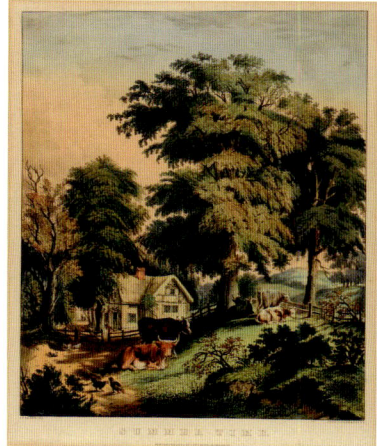

3-133 *A Summer's Afternoon*

Undated, ca. 1857–72

19⅝ × 27⅞"

C-5880, G-6342

F. F. Palmer, Del. Lith. by Currier & Ives, N.Y. New York, Pubd. by Currier & Ives. No. 152 Nassau St.

Palmer is not listed as the artist in Conningham, but she is in Gale, and her name appears on known examples of this print.

Courtesy of the Museum of the City of New York, 56.300.62.

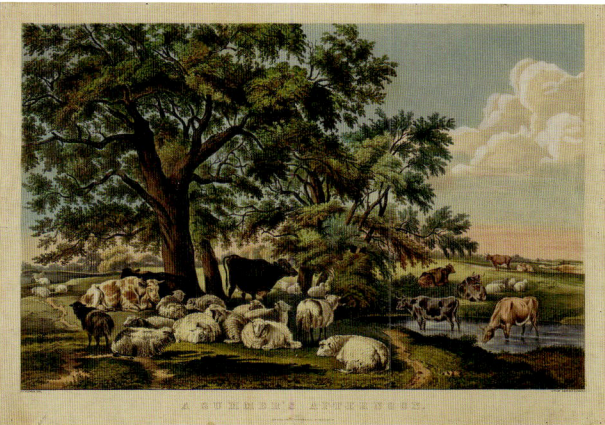

3-134 *The Sunset Tree*

Undated, ca. 1857–72

11⅜ × 16 1/16"

C-5896, G-6362

F. F. Palmer Del. Currier & Ives, N.Y. Published by Currier & Ives 152 Nassau St. NY.

Illustrated, p. 211

3-135 *Taking Comfort*

1866

9⅞ × 14"

C-5958, G-6424

F. F. Palmer, Del. Entered . . . 1866, by Currier & Ives . . . Currier & Ives, Lith. N.Y. Pub'd by Currier & Ives 152 Nassau St. N.Y.

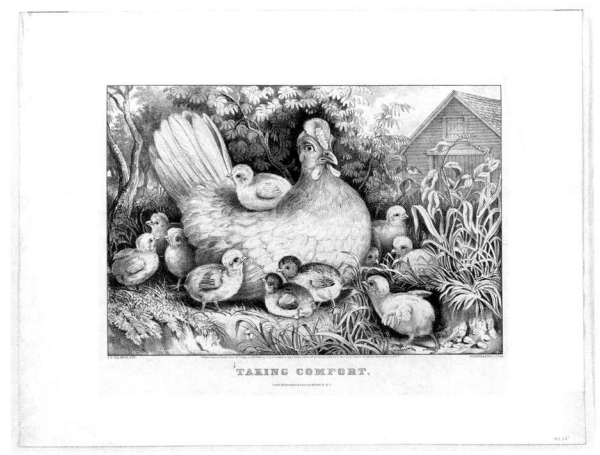

Courtesy of the Prints and Photographs Division, Library of Congress, LC-DIG-pga-05040.

3-136 *Terrific Engagement between the "Monitor" 2 Guns, and "Merrimac" 10 Guns, In Hampton Roads, March 9th, 1862. / The First Fight between Iron Ships of War. / In which the Merrimac was crippled, and the whole Rebel-Fleet driven back to Norfolk*

Illustrated, p. 140

1862

15 11/16 × 22 5/16"

C-5998, G-6465

F. F. Palmer, Del. Entered . . . 1862, by Currier & Ives . . . Currier & Ives, Lith. N.Y. Pubd by Currier & Ives, 152 Nassau St., New York.

Palmer's lively preparatory watercolor of this print (p. 343) is at the New-York Historical Society.

3-137 *The Trappers Camp-Fire*

Illustrated, p. 165

1866

17 × 25½"

C-6123, G-6604

F. F. Palmer, Del. Entered . . . 1866 by Currier & Ives . . . Currier & Ives, Lith, N.Y. New York, Published by Currier & Ives, 152 Nassau St.

Companion print to *The Trappers Camp-Fire. A Friendly Visitor.*

3-138 *The Trappers Camp-Fire. / A Friendly Visitor*

Illustrated, p. 205

1866

17 × 25⅞"

C-6124, G-6605

F. F. Palmer, Del. Entered . . . 1866 by Currier & Ives . . . Currier & Ives, Lith. N.Y. New York, Published by Currier & Ives, 152 Nassau St.

In this companion print to *The Trappers Camp-fire*, Palmer has added a Native American sitting around the campfire. Also, there is no moon in this image.

3-139 *Trolling for Blue Fish*

1866

18½ × 27⅞"

C-6158, G-6641

F. F. Palmer, Del. Entered . . . 1866, by Currier & Ives . . . Currier & Ives, Lith. N.Y. New York, Published by Currier & Ives, 152 Nassau Street.

Number 10 of the original best-fifty large-folio prints; number 17 of the new best-fifty large-folio prints. Comic illustrator Thomas Worth claimed that he provided Palmer with a drawing of the boat and perhaps of the figures.[9]

3-140 *The Trout Brook*

1862

11 × 15¼"

C-6227, G-6711

F. F. Palmer, Del. Entered . . . 1862, by Currier & Ives . . . Lith. Currier & Ives, N.Y. New York, Published by Currier & Ives, 152 Nassau St.

Courtesy of the Old Print Shop.

Illustrated, gallery plate 17

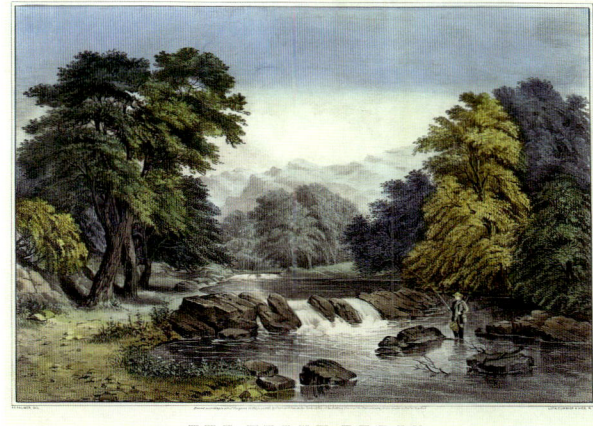

3-141 *Trout Fishing*

1852

12½ × 20 3/16"

C-6228, G-6712

From nature and on stone by F. F. Palmer. Entered . . . 1852, by N. Currier . . . Lith. and Published by N. Currier, 152 Nassau St. New York. Published by N. Currier, 152 Nassau St. New York.

One of Palmer's Long Island Series. Currier & Ives reissued this print with slight changes as *The Trout Stream* after 1856. Princeton University holds this print in its Graphic Arts collection.

3-142 *The Trout Stream*

1852 [ca. 1857–72]

14 11/16 × 20⅛"

C-6230, G-6715

From nature and on stone by F. F. Palmer. Entered . . . 1852, by N. Currier . . . Lith by Currier & Ives N.Y. New York, Pub. by Currier & Ives 152 Nassau Street.

A second state of *Trout Fishing* (1852). The original copyright date by N. Currier remains on the print, but the publisher is now Currier & Ives, indicating that this popular subject was republished after 1856 with a different title and an almost identical composition, except for a two-inch increase in height, slightly narrower width, and no fish on the ground near the seated lad holding a net.

Illustrated, p. 109

3-143 *Union Place Hotel. / Union Square, New-York. / J.C. Wheeler, John Wheeler, Proprietors. / Most Fashionable and Elegant Quarter of the City, and is Unsurpassed in all its Departments for Convenience, Quietness and Luxury.*

Undated, ca. 1850–56

8 11/16 × 11⅞"

C-6286, G-6773

F. F. Palmer, del. N. Currier Lith. N.Y.

Courtesy of the Museum of the City of New York, 57.100.44.

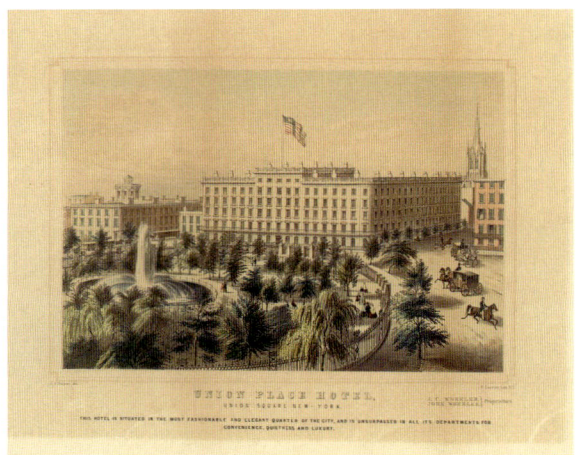

3-144 *U.S. Military Academy, West Point. / From the opposite Shore*

1862

10⅞ × 15 5/16"

C-6325, G-6839

F. F. Palmer, Del. Entered . . . 1862, by Currier & Ives . . . Currier & Ives, Lith. N.Y. New York, Published by Currier & Ives, 152 Nassau St.

Palmer's signed pencil drawing of the landscape and buildings, *West Point Academy* (undated, Museum of Fine Arts, Boston [p. 344]), suggests that she was actually in the region, making on-site sketches around 1862. The figures were added later.

Illustrated, p. 132

3-145 *The Valley of the Shenandoah*

1864

14⅞ × 19 15/16"

C-6357, G-6866

F. F. Palmer, Del. Entered . . . 1864, by Currier & Ives . . . Lith. of Currier & Ives, N.Y.
New York, Published by Currier & Ives, 152 Nassau St.

Courtesy of the Old Print Shop.

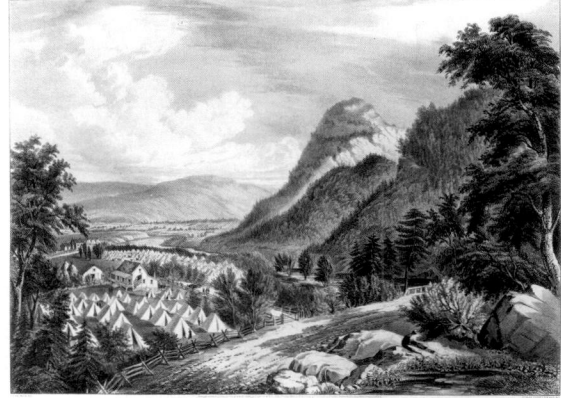

3-146 *The Victorious Attack on Fort Fisher, N.C. Jan. 15th 1865. / By the U.S. Fleet
under Rear Admiral D.D. Porter, and Troops under Major Genl. A.H. Terry*

1865

15¾ × 22⅞"

C-6372, G-6882

F. F. Palmer, Del. Entered . . . 1865, by Currier & Ives . . . Lithogrd. By Currier & Ives.

Illustrated, p. 141

3-147 *View From Peekskill. / Hudson River, N.Y.*

1862

11 3/16 × 15⅝"

C-6381, G-6892

F. F. Palmer, Del. Entered . . . 1862, by Currier & Ives . . . Lith. Currier & Ives, N.Y. New
York, Published by Currier & Ives, 152 Nassau St.

Courtesy of the Old Print Shop.

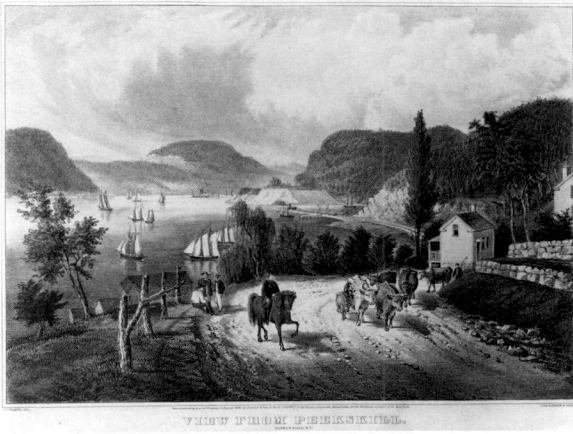

3-148 *View in Dutchess County, N.Y.*

Undated, ca. 1857–72

15 × 20¼"

C-6385, G-6896

F. F. Palmer, Del. Lith Currier & Ives, Lith. N.Y. Published by Currier & Ives, 152 Nassau
St. N.Y.

Illustrated, p. 180

3-149 *View Near Highbridge. / Harlem River, N.Y.*

Undated, ca. 1857–72

10⅞ × 15½"

C-6387, G-6898

F. F. Palmer [*sic*], Del. Lith. Currier & Ives, N.Y. Pubd. By Currier & Ives, 152 Nassau St. N.Y.

An early state of this print is marked "F. F. Pamer," as in the copy held by the Metropolitan Museum of Art. This print was also issued with the title *The Riverroad* (p. 310).

Courtesy of the Yale University Art Gallery.

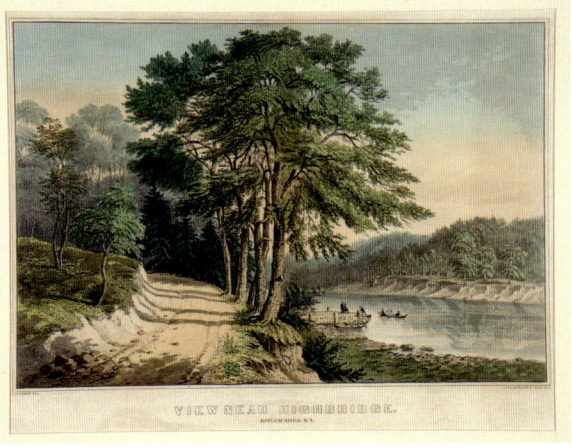

3-150 *View of Astoria, L.I. / From the New York Side.*

1862

11 × 15⅝"

C-6388, G-6901

F. F. Palmer, Del. Entered . . . 1862, by Currier & Ives . . . Lith Currier & Ives N.Y. New York, Published by Currier & Ives, 152 Nassau St.

Palmer's lively preparatory study *View of Astoria, Long Island* (New-York Historical Society [p. 344]) was probably painted on site.

Illustrated, p. 101

3-151 *View of New York. / From Brooklyn Heights*

1849

12 9/16 × 17⅛"

C-6403, G-6915

Palmer Del. Entered . . . 1849 by N. Currier . . . N. Currier, Lith. N.Y. Pub. By N. Currier, 152 Nassau St. cor. of Spruce N.Y.

First state of the next print but with only sixteen landmarks keyed below the title (lacking "Delmonico's Broadway" and the "Brick Church").

Courtesy of the Old Print Shop.

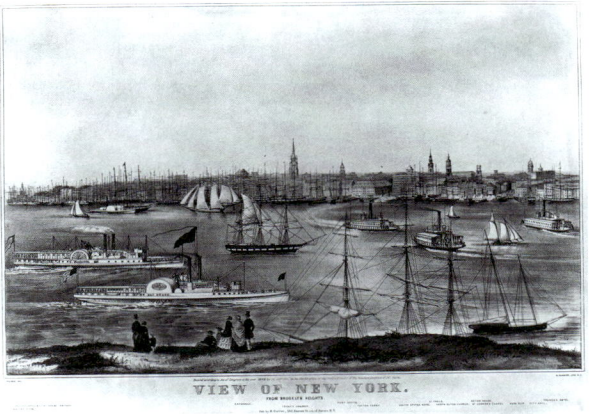

3-152 *View of New York. / From Brooklyn Heights*

Illustrated, p. 94

1849

11 5/16 × 16 13/16"

C-6402, G-6914

Palmer Del. Entered . . . 1849 by N. Currier . . . N. Currier, Lith. N.Y. Pub. By N. Currier, 152 Nassau St. cor. of Spruce N.Y.

Second state of the preceding print with slightly larger dimensions and showing the spire of the Brick Church and eighteen keyed landmarks. The copy with copyright deposit note held by the Library of Congress is vignetted.

3-153 *View of New York. / From Weehawken*

1849

12 11/16 × 21⅜"

C-unlisted, G-6917

Palmer, Del. Entered . . . 1849 by N. Currier . . . N. Currier, Lith. N.Y. Pub. by N. Currier, 152 Nassau St. cor. of Spruce N.Y.

Twenty-three keyed landmarks are listed below the image; same image as *View of New York. From Weehawken–North River* (next entry).

Courtesy of the Prints and Photographs Division, Library of Congress, LC-DIG-pga-05061.

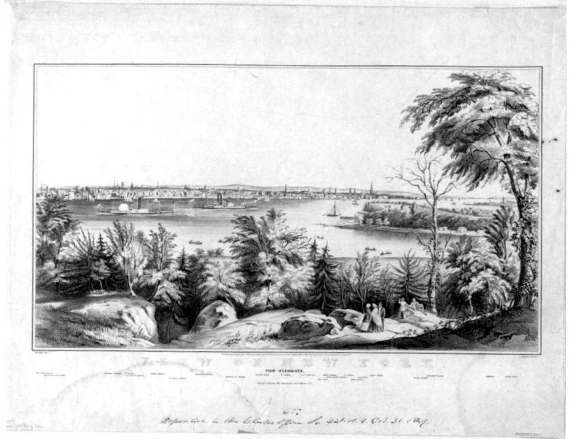

3-154 *View of New York. / From Weehawken–North River*

Illustrated, p. 95

1849

12 11/16 × 21⅜"

C-6405, G-6918

Palmer, Del. Entered . . . 1849 by N. Currier . . . N. Currier, Lith. N.Y. Pub. by N. Currier, 152 Nassau St. cor. of Spruce, N.Y.

Same image as *View of New York. From Weehawken* (previous entry) but listing "Havermeyers Sugar House" instead of just "Sugar House," and some copies of the print also have a twenty-fourth keyed landmark, "R.L. & A. Stuarts, New Sugar Refinery."

3-155 *View of San Francisco, California. / Taken from Telegraph Hill, April 1850, By Wm. B. McMurtrie, Draughtsman Of The U.S. Surveying Expedition*

1851

14⅞ × 29⅞"

C-unlisted, G-6922

On stone by F. Palmer, Entered . . . 1851 by N. Currier . . . Lith & Pub. by N. Currier, 152 Nassau St. cor. Spruce, N.Y. Published by N. Currier, N.Y. ___ and for Sale by Wm. B. McMurtrie, San Francisco.

Unlike the final colored print listed in the next entry, the original black-and-white print submitted to the US Copyright Office on March 7, 1851, and now held by the Library of Congress has square upper corners and no keyed landmarks, and it includes the text "and for Sale" before McMurtrie's name in the publisher's line.

Courtesy of the Prints and Photographs Division, Library of Congress, LC-DIG-pga-00957.

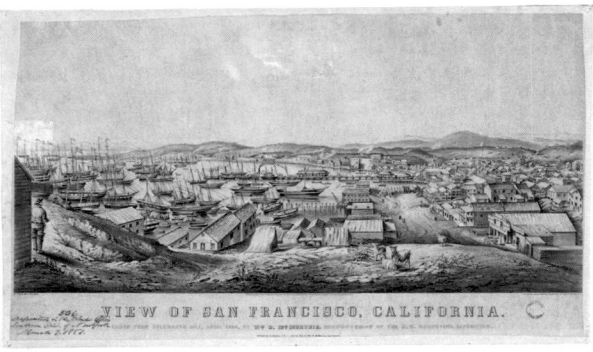

3-156 *View of San Francisco, California. / Taken from Telegraph Hill, April 1850, By Wm. B. McMurtrie, Draughtsman Of The U.S. Surveying Expedition*

1851

14⅞ × 29⅞"

C-6409, G-6923

On stone by F. Palmer, Entered . . . 1851 by N. Currier . . . Lith & Pub. by N. Currier, 152 Nassau St. cor. Spruce, N.Y. Published by N. Currier, N.Y. ___ Wm. B. McMurtrie, San Francisco.

Number 25 of the original best-fifty large-folio prints. Same print as the previous entry but with rounded corners and nine keyed landmarks below the image; also, the publisher's line omits the text "and for Sale" before McMurtrie's name.

Illustrated, gallery plate 26

3-157 *View on Lake George, N.Y.*

1866

15 × 20⅜"

C-6435, G-6952

F. F. Palmer, Del. Entered . . . 1866, by Currier & Ives . . . Lith. of Currier & Ives, N.Y. New York, Published by Currier & Ives, 152 Nassau Street.

A different image from the next entry: a deer's antlers are visible in the lake, but otherwise the lake is still and lacking boats.

Courtesy of the Prints and Photographs Division, Library of Congress, LC-DIG-pga-05062.

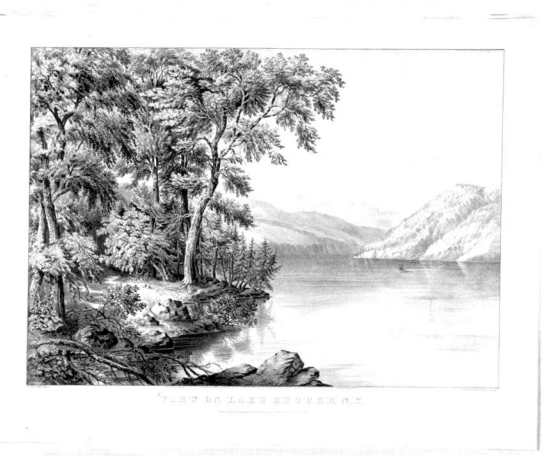

3-158 *View on Lake George, N.Y.*

Undated, ca. 1857–72

15 × 20⅜"

C-6436, G-6953

F. Palmer, Del. Lith. by Currier & Ives, N.Y. New York, Published by Currier & Ives, 152 Nassau St.

A different image from the previous entry, showing men in rowboats and a sailboat and lacking a copyright entry. This print was probably adapted, with a different title and slight changes, from W. Bartlett's illustration *The Narrows, Lake George*, engraved in Willis's travel book *American Scenery* (1840).

Courtesy of the Yale University Art Gallery.

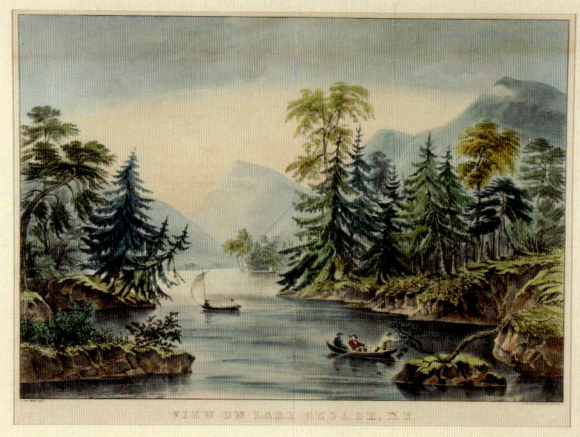

3-159 *View on Long Island. N.Y.*

1857

14 15/16 × 20⅜"

C-6437, G-6954

F. Palmer, Del. Entered . . . 1857, by Currier & Ives . . . Lith. by Currier & Ives, N.Y. New York, Pubd. by Currier & Ives, 152 Nassau Street.

Illustrated, p. 117

3-160 *View on the Harlem River, N.Y. / The Highbridge in the Distance*

1852 [ca. 1857–72]

14½ × 19 15/16"

C-6441, G-6958

From nature and on stone by F. F. Palmer. Entered . . . 1852 by N. Currier . . . Lith. by Currier & Ives, N.Y. New York, Pubd. by Currier & Ives 152 Nassau St.

Originally published in 1852 by N. Currier as *Bass Fishing. At Macomb's Dam Harlem River, N.Y.* (p. 286), this print was reissued with a new title sometime after 1857 when Ives became Currier's partner. Although the name "N. Currier" is retained on the print with the 1852 copyright date and Palmer as the artist, the publisher is now listed as Currier & Ives. The revised print is slightly higher and has somewhat thicker tree foliage on the left but is basically unchanged.

Illustrated, p. 52

3-161 *View on the Hudson*

Undated, ca. 1857–72

15 × 20 11/16"

C-6444, G-6961

F. F. Palmer, Del. Lith. of Currier & Ives, N.Y. New York, Published by Currier & Ives, 152 Nassau St.

One of two Palmer lithographs (see the next entry) with the same title and similar but not identical compositions. This version includes two steamboats and five sailboats in the foreground as well as other tiny sailboats in the distance. Palmer's composition resembles the general design of W. H. Bartlett's illustration *Hudson Highlands (From Bull Hill)* in Willis's travel book *American Scenery* (1840). Bartlett included a figure viewing the scene from an outcropping in the left foreground and does not include a steamboat.

Courtesy of the Old Print Shop.

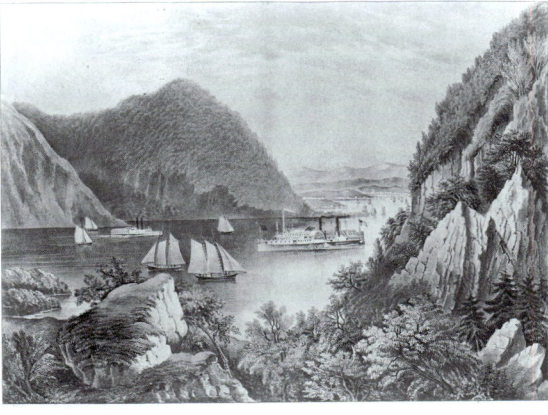

3-162 *View on the Hudson*

Undated, ca. 1857–72

14¾ × 19¾"

C-6445, G-6962

F. Palmer, Del. Lith. by Currier & Ives, N.Y. New York, Published by Currier & Ives, 152 Nassau St.

One of two Palmer lithographs with the same title (see the previous entry) and similar but not identical compositions. This version shows one steamboat and nine sailboats in the foreground as well as more tiny sailboats in the distance. There is also slight variation in the foliage and the shape of hills in the two prints.

Courtesy of the Yale University Art Gallery.

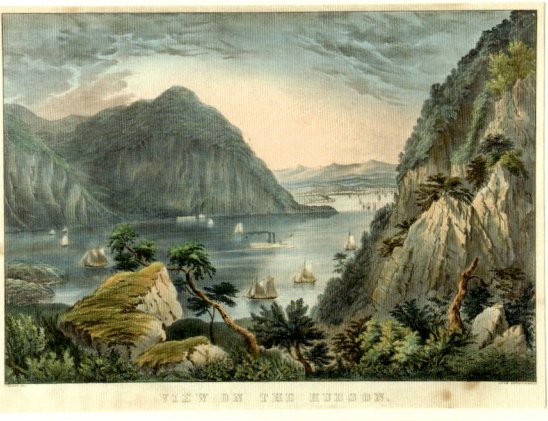

3-163 *View on the Potomac. / Near Harper's Ferry*

1866

15 × 20 3/16"

C-6449, G-6966

F. F. Palmer, Del. Entered . . . 1866 by Currier & Ives . . . Currier & Ives, Lith. N.Y. New York Pub'd by Currier & Ives, 152 Nassau St.

Courtesy of the Yale University Art Gallery.

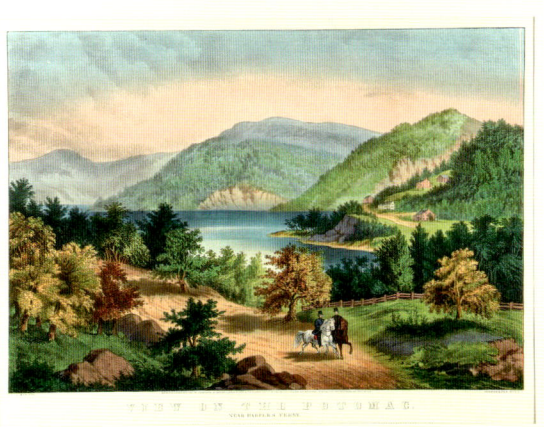

3-164 *View on the Rondout*

Undated, ca. 1857–72

10⅛ × 15¼"

C-6451, G-6968

F. F. Palmer, Del. Lith. Currier & Ives N.Y. New York, Published by Currier & Ives, 152 Nassau St.

Courtesy of the Old Print Shop.

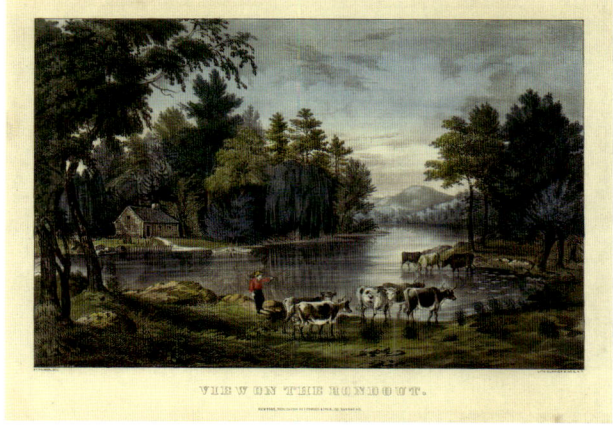

3-165 *The Village Blacksmith*

Undated, ca. 1850–56

9⅞ × 14⅞"

C-6460, G-6977 (listed without Palmer's name)

F. Palmer Del. N. Currier Lith. Lith. & Pub. by N. Currier 152 Nassau Street N.Y.

The earlier of two different Palmer versions of this subject (see the next entry), this one is published by N. Currier. This peaceful country print does not include any of the lines of Longfellow's poem or follow its narrative.

Courtesy of the Old Print Shop.

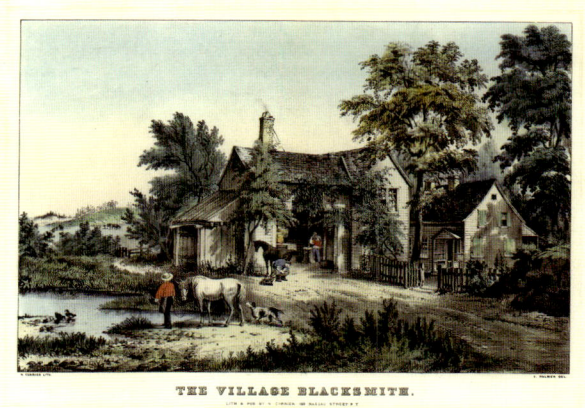

3-166 *The Village Blacksmith*

1864

15 15/16 × 23 5/16"

C-6462, G-6976

F. F. Palmer, Del. Entered . . . 1864 by Currier & Ives . . . Lith. by Currier & Ives. New York. Published by Currier & Ives 152 Nassau Street.

Palmer's second version of this print (see the previous entry) closely follows the opening lines of Longfellow's poem, which is printed on both sides of the title.

Illustrated, gallery plate 24

3-167 *The Village Street*

1855

10⅜ × 14⅞"

C-6464, G-6980

F. Palmer, Del. N. Currier, Lith. Entered . . . in 1855 by N. Currier.

Illustrated, p. 221

3-168 *Warwick Castle. / On the Avon*

Undated, ca. 1857–72

11¾ × 15 9/16"

C-6500, G-7024

F. F. Palmer, Del. Lith. Currier & Ives, N.Y. New York, Published by Currier & Ives, 152 Nassau St.

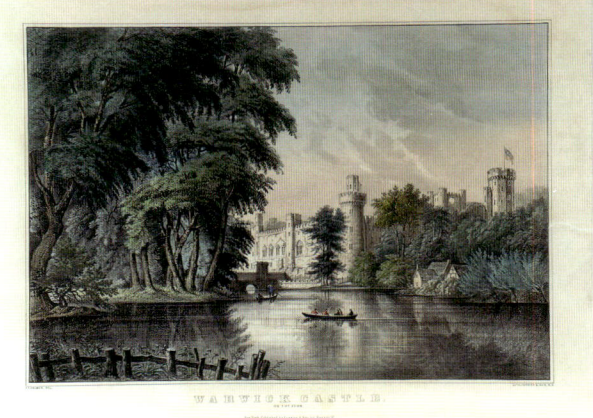

3-169 *The Wayside Inn*

1864

15⅞ × 23⅜"

C-6587, G-7103

F. F. Palmer, Del. Entered . . . 1864, by Currier & Ives . . . Currier & Ives, N.Y. New York, Published by Currier & Ives 152 Nassau St.

Courtesy of the Yale University Art Gallery.

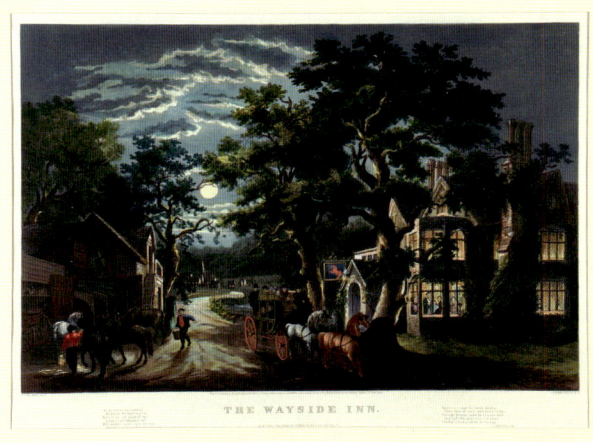

3-170 *West Point Foundry, Cold Spring. / Hudson River N.Y.*

1862

10¾ × 15⅜"

C-6617, G-7152

F. F. Palmer, Del. Entered . . . 1862 by Currier & Ives, Lith. New York, Published by Currier & Ives, 152 Nassau St.

Illustrated, p. 133

3-171 *Wild Duck Shooting*

1852

12¾ × 20⅛"

C-6669, G-7208

From nature and on stone by F. F. Palmer. Entered . . . 1852 by N. Currier . . . Lith. of N. Currier, N.Y. Published by N. Currier, 152 Nassau St. New York.

One of the Long Island Series of sporting prints.

Illustrated, gallery plate 22

3-172 *Winter Moonlight*

1866

14 7/16 × 17¾"

C-6739, G-7276

F. F. Palmer, Del. Entered . . . 1866, by Currier & Ives . . . Currier & Ives, Lith. N.Y. New York, Pub'd by Currier & Ives, 152 Nassau St.

Courtesy of the Prints and Photographs Division, Library of Congress, LC-DIG-pga-05081.

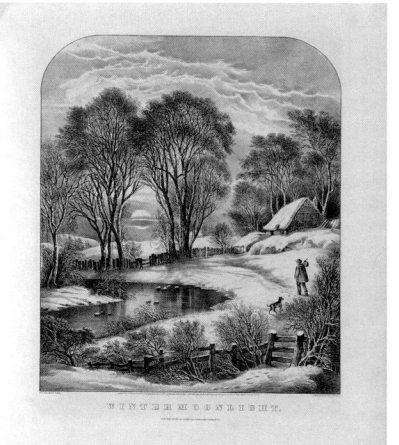

3-173 *Winter Morning*   Illustrated, p. 186

1861

11 5/16 × 15 5/16"

C-6740, G-7277

F. F. Palmer, Del. Entered . . . 1861, by Currier & Ives . . . Currier & Ives Lith. N.Y. New York, Published by Currier & Ives, 152 Nassau St.

Number 29 of the new best-fifty small-folio prints.

3-174 *Winter Pastime*   Illustrated, gallery plate 25

1855

10 7/16 × 14 15/16"

C-6743, G-7281

F. Palmer, Del. Entered . . . 1855, by N. Currier . . . N. Currier, Lith.

The US Postal Service reproduced this ever-popular print on a thirteen-cent Christmas stamp in 1976.

3-175 *Woodcock Shooting*   Illustrated, p. 107

1852

13 1/16 × 20 5/16"

C-6774, G-7320

From nature and on stone by F. F. Palmer. Entered . . . 1852 by N. Currier . . . Lith. of N. Currier N.Y. Published by N. Currier, 152 Nassau St. New York.

One of Palmer's Long Island Series of sporting prints. This print was later reissued with a Currier & Ives publication line. Gale assigned that version a different number (G-7321), but Conningham did not list it separately.

3-176 *"Wooding Up" on the Mississippi*   Illustrated, gallery plate 5

1863

18 × 27¾"

C-6776, G-7326

F. F. Palmer, Del. Entered . . . 1863 by Currier & Ives . . . Currier & Ives, Lith. N.Y. New York, Published by Currier & Ives, 152 Nassau St.

Number 23 of the new best-fifty large-folio prints.

3-177 *Yosemite Valley—California. / "The Bridal Veil" Fall*   Illustrated, p. 169

1866

18 × 27¾"

C-6830, G-7385

F. F. Palmer, Del. Entered . . . 1866 by Currier & Ives . . . Currier & Ives, Lith NY. New York, Published by Currier & Ives, 152 Nassau St.

Currier & Ives Prints
Attributed to Fanny Palmer

3A-1 *American Landscape. / Early Morning*

1866

15¾ × 23¼"

C-176, G-0190

Entered . . . 1866 by Currier & Ives . . . Pub'd by Currier & Ives, 152 Nassau St., N.Y.

Conningham lists Palmer as the artist, although no artist is credited on the known copies of the print.

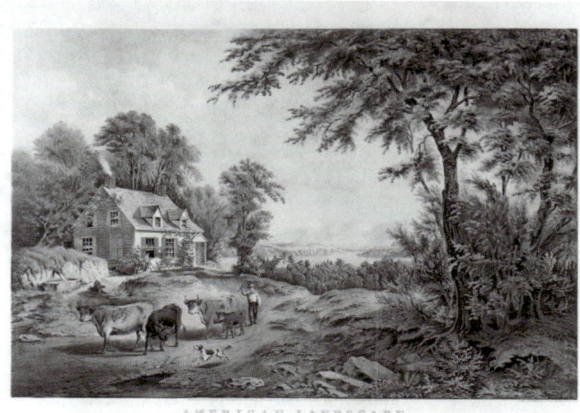

3A-2 *American Mountain Scenery*

1868

9 9/16 × 16¾"

C-179, G-0193

Entered . . . 1868 by Currier & Ives . . . New York, Published by Currier & Ives, 152 Nassau St.

The American Antiquarian Society has a proof of this print, lacking title and imprint, with a hand-written pencil inscription on it that reads, "American Mountain Scenery. Drawn by F. F. Palmer, Proof," and the Museum of the City of New York has a proof with the pencil inscription "Drawn by F. F. Palmer Proof No 2318."

Courtesy of the American Antiquarian Society.

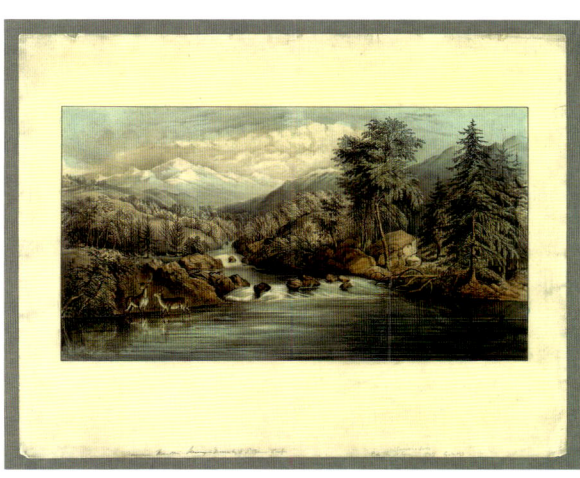

3A-3 *American River Scenery. / View on the Androscoggin, Me.*

Undated, ca. 1857–72

9¾ × 16½"

C-190, G-0204

New York Published by Currier & Ives, 152 Nassau St.

An American Art Galleries sales catalog from 1919 describes a copy of this print as "Drawn by F. F. Palmer . . . Proof, with artist's name in pencil."[10]

Courtesy of the Yale University Art Gallery.

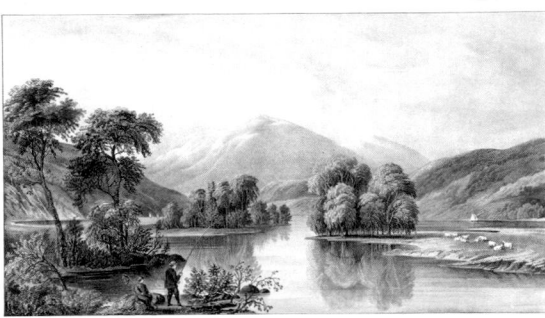

3A-4 *American Winter Sports. / Deer Shooting "On The Shattagee" (Northern New York)*

1855

17⅞ × 25⅞"

C-209, G-0223

L. Maurer 55 (signature on stone, lower right of image). L. Maurer, Del . . . Entered . . . 1855 by N. Currier . . . Lith. by N. Currier, N.Y. . . . New York, Published by N. Currier, 152 Nassau Street.

Louis Maurer is the only one credited as the artist on this print, but he reported to author Harry Peters that Palmer drew the landscape background for it.[11] The lithograph was adapted, with many changes, from a painting by A. F. Tait (*Still Hunting on the First Snow: A Second Shot*, 1855, Adirondack Museum), though Tait is not credited as the source.

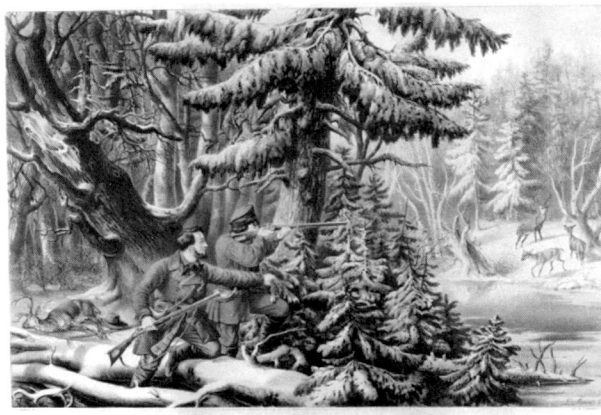

3A-5 *The Barefoot Boy*

1872

11⅞ × 8⅜"

C-368, G-0409

(Initials on stone, lower left of image). Entered . . . 1872, by Currier & Ives . . . Published by Currier & Ives 125 Nassau St New York.

Attributed to Palmer by Conningham based on initials on the lower left of the image that Conningham identifies as "FFP." A small, late print, somewhat crudely rendered compared to Palmer's usual technique. The initials actually appear to read "SGP" or "SHP." The initials appear very similar to those found on *The Little Alms-Giver* (p. 334) and *More Free Than Welcome* (p. 334).

Courtesy of the Prints and Photographs Division, Library of Congress, LC-USZC2-576.

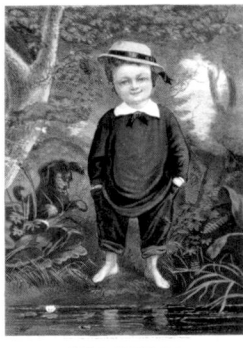

3A-6 *Black Bass Spearing, / on the Restigouche. New Brunswick*

Undated, ca. 1857–72

11½ × 15¾"

C-543, G-0610

New York, Published by Currier & Ives, 152 Nassau St.

An American Art Galleries sales catalog from 1919 describes this print with a pencil note as "Drawn by F. F. Palmer. Proof."[12]

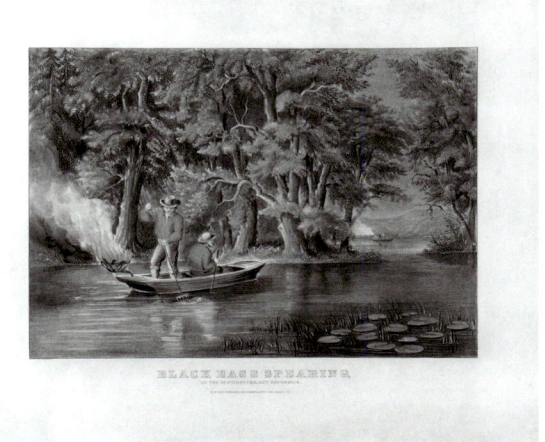

3A-7 *Bothwell Bridge, / on the Clyde*

Undated, ca. 1857–72

11 9/16 × 17"

C-624, G-698

New York, Published by Currier & Ives, 152 Nassau St.

A proof of this print held by the Old Print Shop was included in an undated typescript list by Mary Bartlett Cowdrey of proofs containing "pencilled notation on bottom margin 'Drawn by F. F. Palmer.'"[13]

Courtesy of the Prints and Photographs Division, Library of Congress, LC-DIG-pga-04733.

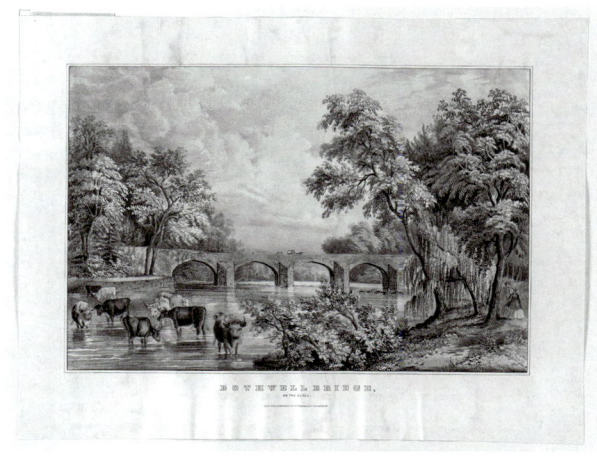

3A-8 *The Champions of the Field. / Steady on a Point*

Undated, ca. 1877–94

Sheet 11¾ × 15⅞"

C-991, G-1075

(Initials on stone, lower left of image.) Published by Currier & Ives. 115 Nassau St. New York.

This profile portrait of two dogs in a grassy field has been attributed to Fanny Palmer because of the initials identified by Conningham as "FP" on the lower left of the image. However, the initials actually appear to read "F3." Her full name is not printed anywhere, and the address, "115 Nassau St.," indicates that the lithograph was published between 1877 and 1894. The firm moved to 115 Nassau in 1877, a year after Palmer's death.

Courtesy of the Museum of the City of New York, 57.300.471.

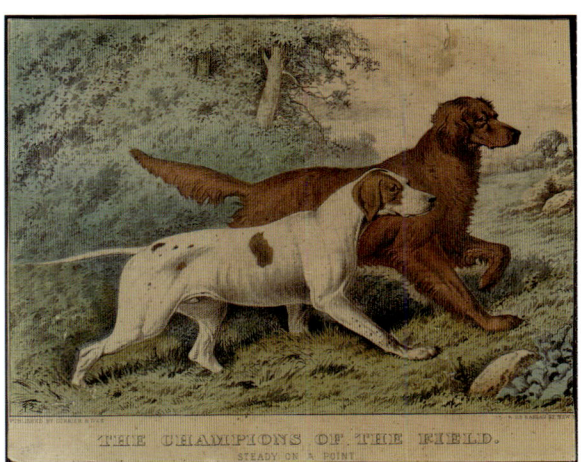

3A-9 *Chatham Square, New York*

Undated, ca. 1847?

8 1/16 × 12⅝"

C-1020, G-1118

(Initials on stone, lower left of image.) Lith. & Pub. by N. Currier, 152 Nassau St. Cor. of Spruce N.Y. (Some prints include the stock number 609 below the title.)

Attributed to Palmer by Conningham based on initials on the lower left of the image that Conningham identifies as "FP" but that actually appear to read "ER."

Courtesy of the Old Print Shop.

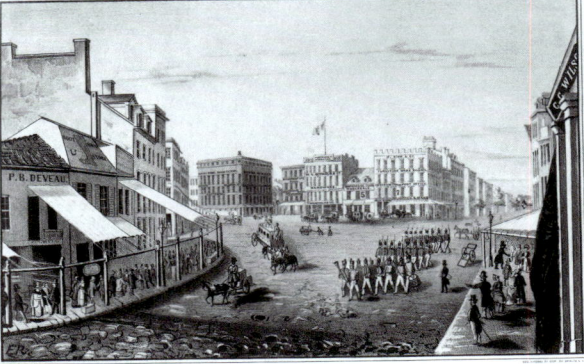

3A-10 *Early Autumn in the Catskills*

Undated, ca. 1857–72

Sheet 14 × 17 15/16"

C-1648, G-1787

New York, Published by Currier & Ives, 152 Nassau St.

The Museum of the City of New York has a proof of this print with the handwritten pencil inscription "Drawn by F. F. Palmer Proof No. 4112."

Courtesy of the Yale University Art Gallery.

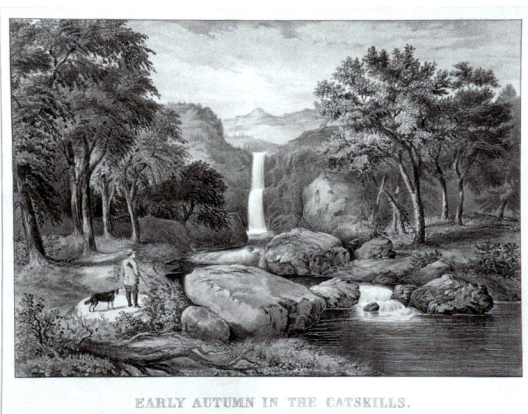

3A-11 *The Harvest Moon*

Undated, ca. 1857–72

11 11/16 × 16 3/16"

C-2746, G-2977

Published by Currier & Ives, 152 Nassau St. New York.

A proof of this print held by the Old Print Shop was included in an undated typescript list by Mary Bartlett Cowdrey of proofs containing "pencilled notation on bottom margin 'Drawn by F. F. Palmer.'"[14]

Courtesy of the Prints and Photographs Division, Library of Congress, LC-DIG-pga-04872.

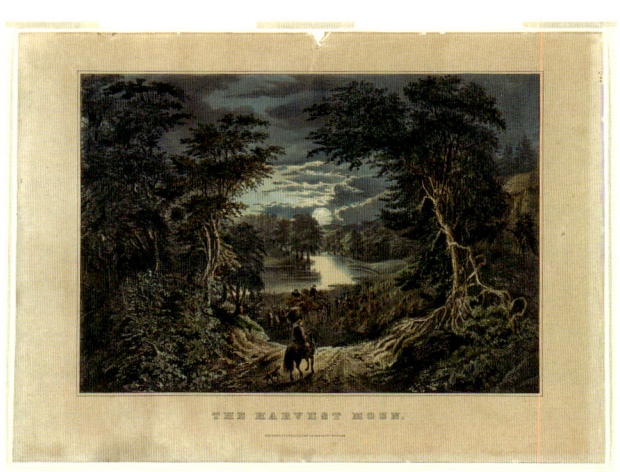

3A-12 *The Heart of the Wilderness*

Undated, ca. 1857–72

11 7/16 × 16½"

C-2772, G-2997

Published by Currier & Ives 152 Nassau St. New York.

A proof of this print held by the Old Print Shop was included in an undated typescript list by Mary Bartlett Cowdrey of proofs containing "pencilled notation on bottom margin 'Drawn by F. F. Palmer.'"[15]

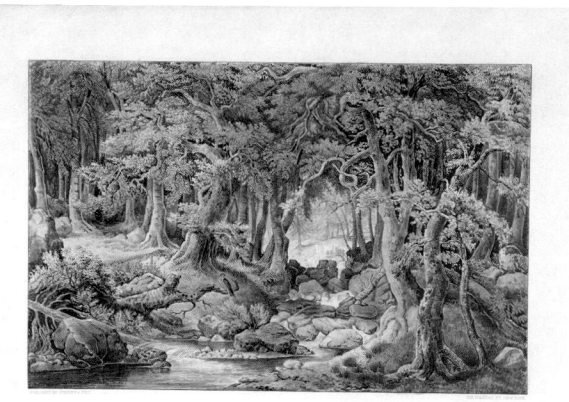

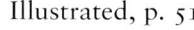

3A-13 *The High Bridge at Harlem, N.Y.*

1849

7⅞ × 12½"

C-2810, G-3039

Lith. & Pub. by N. Currier. Entered . . . 1849 by N. Currier . . . 152 Nassau St. Cor. of Spruce N.Y.

Palmer's name does not appear on this print, but the print seems to have been adapted from her watercolor *High Bridge New York* (signed "F.F.P, 1849," New York Public Library [p. 340]) and thus was one of her earliest contributions to Currier's company before being hired as a staff artist.

Illustrated, p. 51

3A-14 *The Home of the Deer*

Undated, ca. 1857–72

9 15/16 × 15 7/16

C-2866, G-3098

New York, Published by Currier & Ives, 152 Nassau St.

The Museum of the City of New York has a proof of this print with the handwritten pencil inscription "Drawn by F. F. Palmer Proof."

Courtesy of the Museum of the City of New York, 58.300.110.

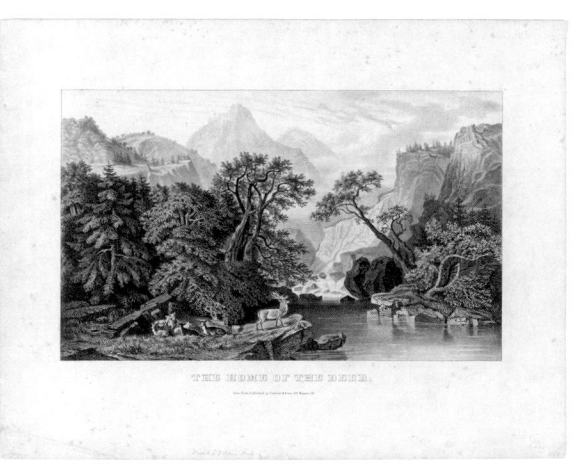

3A-15 *The Little Alms-Giver. "The Lord Loveth a Cheerful Giver"*

Undated, ca. 1872–74

12 1/16 × 8 9/16"

C-3560, G-3832

(Initials on stone, lower right of image.) Published by Currier & Ives 125, Nassau St. New York.

Attributed to Palmer by Conningham based on initials on the lower left of the image that Conningham identifies as "FP." The initials appear very similar to those found on *The Barefoot Boy* (p. 330) and *More Free Than Welcome* (p. 334).

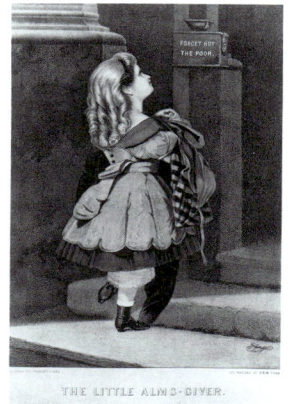

3A-16 *Mill in the Highlands*

Undated

9½ × 16¾"

C-4125, G-4493

Lith. of Currier & Ives. New York Published by Currier & Ives [?] Nassau St.

An American Art Galleries sales catalog from 1919 describes this print as "Drawn by F. F. Palmer. Proof before letters."[16]

Courtesy of the Old Print Shop.

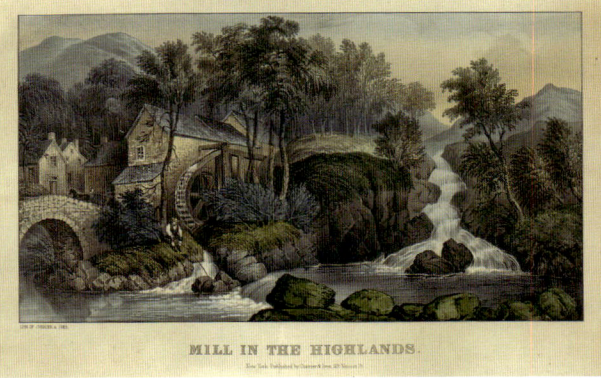

3A-17 *More Free Than Welcome*

Undated, ca. 1872–74

12½ × 8"

C-4187, G-4552

(Initials on stone, lower left of image.) Published by Currier & Ives, 125 Nassau Street, New York.

Conningham does not attribute this print to Palmer but does read the initials on stone as "FP." Gale, though, does identify the artist as Palmer based on the signature.[17] The initials appear very similar to those found on *The Barefoot Boy* (p. 330) and *The Little Alms-Giver* (p. 334).

Courtesy of the Graphic Arts Collection, National Museum of American History, Smithsonian Institution, GA*21437.

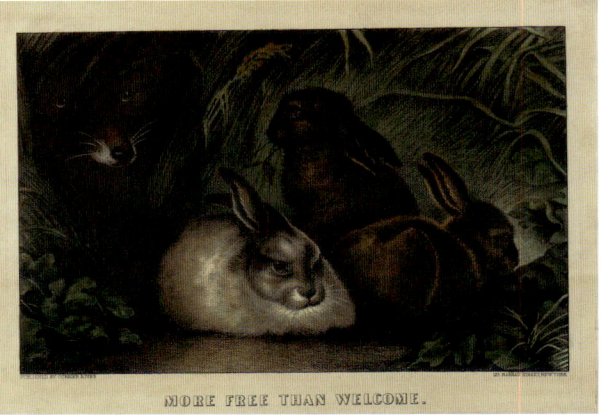

3A-18 *The Mountain Stream*

Undated, ca. 1857–72

9 11/16 × 16¾"

C-4246, G-4612

New York, Published by Currier & Ives, 152 Nassau St.

An American Art Galleries sales catalog from 1919 describes this print as "After the painting by F. F. Palmer. Proof."[18]

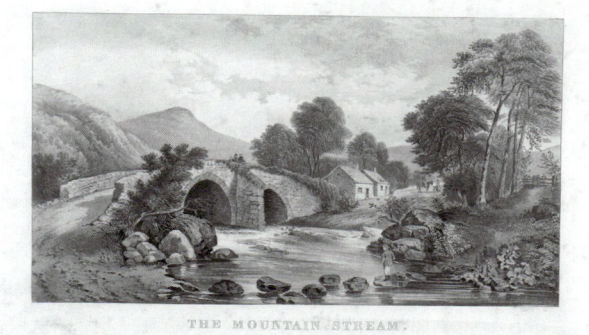

3A-19 *Night by the Camp-Fire*

1861

10¼ × 14 15/16"

C-4472, G-4855

Entered . . . 1861, by Currier & Ives . . . Lith. Currier & Ives, N.Y. New York, Published by Currier & Ives, 152 Nassau St.

The Museum of the City of New York has a proof of this print with the handwritten pencil inscription "Drawn by F. F. Palmer Proof."

Courtesy of the Michele and Donald D'Amour Museum of Fine Arts, Springfield, MA. Gift of Lenore B. and Sidney A. Alpert, supplemented with Museum Acquisition Funds. Photography by David Stansbury. 2004.D03.346

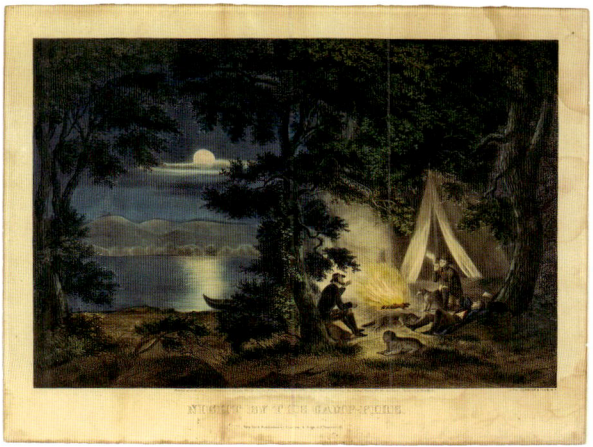

3A-20 *October Landscape*

Undated, ca. 1857–72

11⅝ × 16¼"

C-4529, G-4915

Published by Currier & Ives 152 Nassau St. New York.

A proof of this print held by the Old Print Shop was included in an undated typescript list by Mary Bartlett Cowdrey of proofs containing "pencilled notation on bottom margin 'Drawn by F. F. Palmer.'"[19]

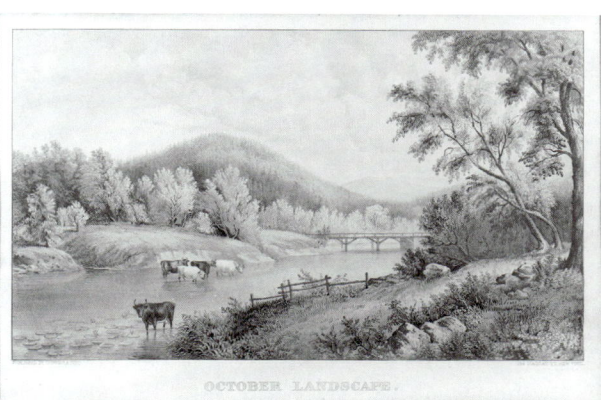

3A-21 *The Old Homestead*

Undated, ca. 1872–74

10⅞ × 15½"

C-unlisted, G-unlisted

Published by Currier & Ives 125 Nassau St. New York.

A smaller, anonymous third version of this title (see the two prints with the same title on pp. 305–6), not listed in Conningham or Gale, has been attributed to Palmer. The address indicates that it would have been one of her latest prints, completed shortly before her death. Although similar to the earlier versions, this print shows the barn door open wide, revealing a ladder leaning against the hayloft behind the farmer. The sheep and goats have been pushed to the left front, providing space for two horses eating hay from a square wooden bin in the center of the composition. Two ducks have been included on the pond at lower right. The home looks more rustic, like a Dutch farmhouse with dormer windows. The white picket fence has been removed, leaving only the barnyard fence separating the animals from the house.

Courtesy of the Michele and Donald D'Amour Museum of Fine Arts, Springfield, MA. Gift of Lenore B. and Sidney A. Alpert, supplemented with Museum Acquisition Funds. Photography by David Stansbury. 2004. D03.256

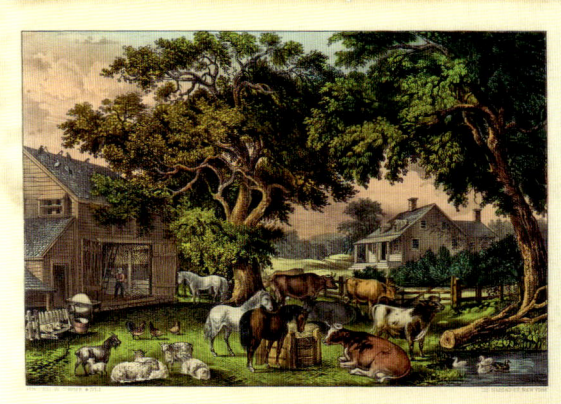

3A-22 *Partridge Shooting*

1855

8 1/16 × 12⅝"

C-4715, G-5113

Entered . . . 1855 by N. Currier . . . Lith. & Pub. By N. Currier, 152 Nassau Street N.Y.

Conningham describes this small stock print with two dogs and one hunter as "unquestionably by Palmer but unsigned."[20]

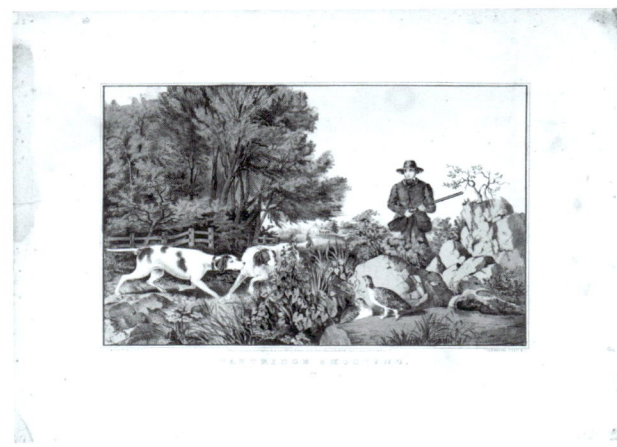

3A-23 *Pleasures of the Country. / Sweet Home*

1869

9⅞ × 16⅞"

C-4808, G-5216

Entered . . . 1869, by Currier & Ives . . . Lith. Currier & Ives, N.Y. New York, Published by Currier & Ives, 152 Nassau St.

A proof of this print held by the Old Print Shop was included in an undated typescript list by Mary Bartlett Cowdrey of proofs containing "pencilled notation on bottom margin 'Drawn by F. F. Palmer.'"[21]

Courtesy of the Prints and Photographs Division, Library of Congress, LC-DIG-pga-04973.

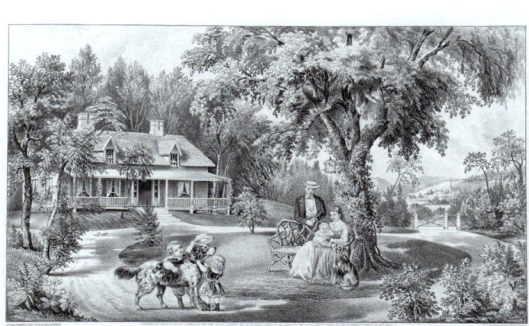

3A-24 Pointers

1846

8 7/16 × 12⅞"

C-4816, G-5223

P (initial on stone, lower left of image). Entered . . . 1846 by N. Currier . . . Lith. & Pub. By N. Currier, 33 Spruce St. N.Y.

The letter P in the lower-left corner of the image suggests that this print may be an early Palmer print for N. Currier before she became a permanent member of Currier's staff. According to Conningham, the image was taken from a sporting print published by Ackerman & Son.[22]

Courtesy of the Prints and Photographs Division, Library of Congress, LC-USZC2-2920.

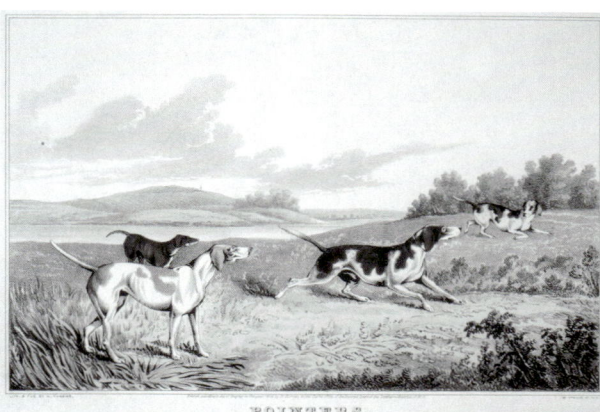

3A-25 Snowed Up. / Ruffed Grouse in Winter

1867

14¾ × 20½"

C-5581, G-5979

Published by Currier & Ives 152 Nassau St. N.Y. Entered . . . 1867, by Currier & Ives . . .

Number 38 of the original best-fifty large-folio prints; number 39 of the new best-fifty large-folio prints. Anonymous but usually attributed to Fanny Palmer by scholars on stylistic grounds.[23]

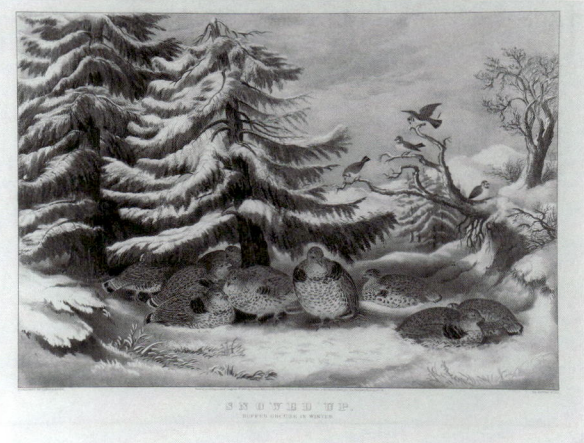

3A-26 Summer in the Woods

Undated, ca. 1857–72

9⅞ × 15⅜"

C-5866, G-6332

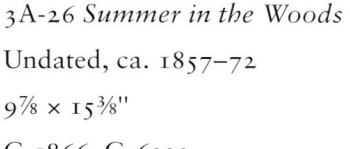

New York, Published by Currier & Ives, 152 Nassau St.

A proof of this print held by the Old Print Shop was included in an undated typescript list by Mary Bartlett Cowdrey of proofs containing "pencilled notation on bottom margin 'Drawn by F. F. Palmer.'"[24]

Courtesy of the Michele and Donald D'Amour Museum of Fine Arts, Springfield, MA. Gift of Lenore B. and Sidney A. Alpert, supplemented with Museum Acquisition Funds. Photography by David Stansbury. 2004. D03.268

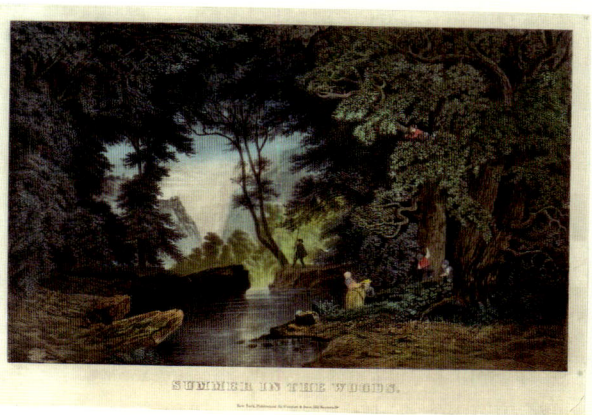

3A-27 *Tropical and Summer Fruits*

Illustrated, p. 156

1867

14¾ × 20 5/16"

C-6159, G-6642

Entered . . . 1867 by Currier & Ives . . . Lith. of Currier & Ives 152 Nassau St. New York Published by Currier & Ives, 152 Nassau St.

It is generally believed that Palmer had a hand in a number of lithographs for which she was not credited by name on the print. This anonymous print may be derived, with changes, from Palmer's pencil drawing now at the New-York Historical Society (on the verso of the watercolor study for *Terrific Engagement between the "Monitor" 2 Guns, and "Merrimac" 10 Guns* [p. 343]). The cat has been eliminated but the rest of the print is very close; the composition appears to have been traced or copied and then reversed in printing.

3A-28 *Windsor Castle and Park*

Undated, ca. 1857–72

11⅛ × 15¼"

C-6720, G-7257

Published by Currier & Ives 152, Nassau St. New York.

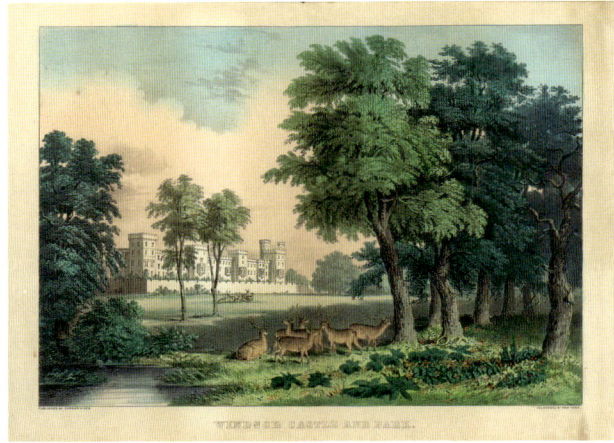

A proof of this print held by the Old Print Shop was included in an undated typescript list by Mary Bartlett Cowdrey of proofs containing "pencilled notation on bottom margin 'Drawn by F. F. Palmer.'"[25]

Courtesy of the Houghton Library, Harvard University.

Drawings by Fanny Palmer

Fanny Palmer claimed that she began to draw at the age of eight and no doubt produced many drawings and paintings in her youth, but none of them has turned up thus far. Her first documented works are three pencil drawings, *Railway Bridge over the Trent*, *Ullesthorpe Station*, and *The Viaduct at Sileby Line*, which became illustrations in *The Midland Counties' Railway Companion* in 1840, when she was already twenty-eight years old and had been conducting drawing classes in Leicester for some time. An additional twenty-four drawings, created after the Palmers immigrated to the United States, have been located. These drawings are arranged alphabetically by title here.

4-1 Across the Continent (First Sketch)

1862

Pencil drawing on paper, 24 × 31½"

Sketched by F. Palmer 1862 (handwritten note, lower left of image).

Holding institution: Museum of the City of New York

4-2 *Across the Continent (Second Sketch)*   Illustrated, p. 170

Undated, ca. 1868

Pencil drawing on paper, 19¾ × 27¾"

Holding institution: Museum of the City of New York

This more finished sketch is on the verso of the first sketch and does not include Palmer's signature.

4-3 *Farmers [sic] Home—Summer*   Illustrated, p. 191

Undated, ca. 1864?

Pencil drawing on paper, image 16⅝ × 23 15/16" sheet 19 × 25⅞"

F. Palmer (signature in pencil, lower-left margin).

Holding institution: Museum of Fine Arts, Boston

A preliminary contour study for the print *Farmers Home—Summer* (1864) (p. 291). The Museum of Fine Arts had previously listed this drawing with the titles *A Suburban Home* and *The Artist's Home*. The verso contains a pencil study of a house.

4-4 *High Bridge New York*

1849

Watercolor on paper, 8 1/5 × 12⅓"

F.F.P. 1849 (signature at lower left of image).

New York Public Library

"Fanny F. Palmer" is signed in pencil on a scrap of paper accompanying the watercolor.

Illustrated, p. 50

4-5 *Horses grazing and drinking from a pond*

Undated

Pen-and-wash drawing on paper, 17¾ × 24 × ¾"

F. Palmer (signature in pencil, lower-left margin).

Holding institution: Museum of the City of New York

With sketch on the verso of cows grazing with horses.

Courtesy of the Museum of the City of New York, X2012.5.38.

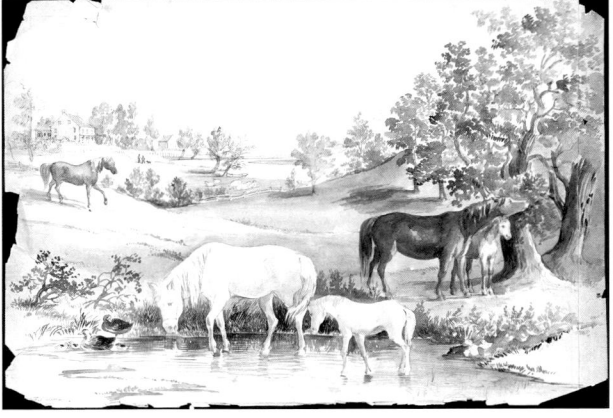

4-6 *Hudson from West Point, N.Y.*

Undated, ca. 1862

Watercolor on paper, 10 × 14⅞"

Holding institution: New-York Historical Society

Attributed to Palmer, this work may be a preliminary watercolor for the print *The Hudson, From West Point. Grounds of the U.S. Military Academy* (1862) (p. 296). The verso has pencil sketches of a cannon and visitors examining the historic chains from the American Revolution.

Illustrated, p. 193

4-7 *Landing at Fort Fisher*

1865

Pencil with watercolor wash on paper, 12 × 27½"

Holding institution: US Marine Corps Museums Art Collection, Washington, DC

Preliminary watercolor for the print *The Victorious Attack on Fort Fisher, N.C. Jan. 15th 1865* (1865) (p. 319).

4-8 *Lookout Mountain, Tennessee*

Undated, ca. 1866?

Drawing, large folio (dimensions unknown)

F. Palmer (signature on drawing).

Unlocated

Described in the *Old Print Shop Portfolio* for November 1942 as "an original drawing signed *F. Palmer* . . . an original of the large folio of that title, published in 1866, and varies from the print only in minute details."[26]

4-9 *Love, Marriage, and Separation*   Illustrated, p. 212

Undated

Pen-and-ink drawing on paper, 12 × 29¾"

Holding institution: Museum of the City of New York

4-10 *Low Water in the Mississippi 1859*   Illustrated, p. 145

1862

Pencil drawing on paper, 24 × 31¾"

Holding institution: Museum of the City of New York

"Sketched by F. Palmer 1862" is written in pencil in the bottom left margin. The verso has a pencil drawing of a country scene with oxen pulling a load of hay and standing in a stream.

4-11 *The Mississippi in Time of Peace*   Illustrated, p. 194

1865

Watercolor and pencil on paper, 18 5/16 × 28¼"

Holding institution: Museum of Fine Arts, Boston

4-12 *The Mississippi in Time of War*   Illustrated, p. 195

1862

Watercolor, colored crayons, and pencil on paper, 18 1/16 × 28⅛"

F F P 1862 (signature in ink at lower left of image).

Holding institution: Museum of Fine Arts, Boston

4-13 *The Old Farm Gate*

Undated

Watercolor on paper, dimensions unknown

Holding institution: Museum of the City of New York

Attributed to Palmer though unsigned; the mat has the note "Printed by Currier & Ives 1847."

4-14 *Railway Bridge over the Trent*

Undated, ca. 1840

Pencil drawing on paper, 8 2/5 × 11 3/5"

Holding institution: Leicestershire Museums and Art Galleries

"F. F. Palmer, Leicester" and the title "Railway Bridge over the Trent" are handwritten in pencil below the image.

Courtesy of Leicestershire County Council Museums Service.

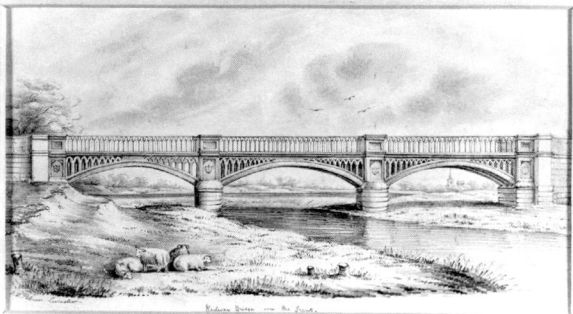

4-15 *Samuel Fleet Homestead*

Undated, ca. 1850s

Watercolor over pencil on paper, 18⅜ × 27¼"

F. F. Palmer (signature at lower left)

Holding institution: Brooklyn Museum

4-16 *Staten Island and the Narrows. From Fort Hamilton*

Undated

Watercolor on paper, 16¾ × 27¾"

Holding institution: New-York Historical Society

Attributed to Fanny Palmer, this watercolor may also be a copy of the print published by Currier & Ives in 1861 (p. 314).

Courtesy of the New-York Historical Society.

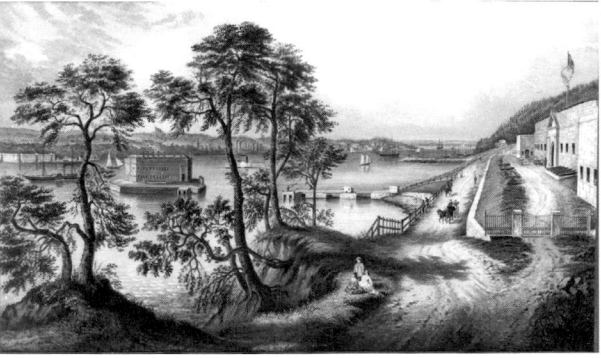

4-17 *Steamboats on the Mississippi*

Undated

Pencil drawing on paper, dimensions unknown

Unlocated; photograph on file, Frick Art Library

Art dealer Victor D. Spark confirmed that he sold this drawing in the 1940s or 1950s and gave a photograph of the drawing to the Frick Art Library.[27]

4-18 *The Studio of Richard Upjohn in Trinity Churchyard, New York*

Undated

Watercolor on paper, 8¼ × 11 15/16"

Holding institution: Metropolitan Museum of Art

This watercolor was originally identified as the work of Mrs. A. W. Palmer but is now attributed to Frances Palmer. The watercolor shows Richard Upjohn's Studio, located behind Trinity Church during the period, in the early 1840s, when he was working on Trinity. Palmer could have easily visited the site and sketched the subject.

4-19 *Terrific Engagement between the "Monitor" 2 Guns, and "Merrimac" 10 Guns*   Illustrated, p. 140

Undated, ca. 1862

Watercolor on paper, 18½ × 26¼"

Fanny Palmer (signed in pencil, bottom center).

Holding institution: New-York Historical Society

Study for the Currier and Ives print (1862) (p. 316). The verso contains a pencil study of a still life of fruit with a cat stalking a bird (15 × 20¾"; p. 156), which appears to be a study for *Tropical and Summer Fruits* (1867) (p. 338).

4-20 *Ullesthorpe Station*   Illustrated, p. 9

Undated, ca. 1840

Pencil drawing on paper, 8¼ × 10"

Holding institution: Leicestershire Museums and Art Galleries

"F. F. Palmer" and "Ullesthorpe Station" are written in pencil below the image.

4-21 *Vechte-Cortelyou House, Gowanus, Brooklyn, N.Y.*   Illustrated, p. 190

Undated

Pencil drawing on paper, 6⅛ × 9¾"

Holding institution: New-York Historical Society

With the note "original drawing of the Cortelyou House by Fanny Palmer" in pencil along bottom left edge. The drawing depicts a different point of view of the scene shown in *Sketch on the Gowanus Road, L.I.* (p. 266), lithographed by F. & S. Palmer for *The New York Drawing Book*, no. 1 (1847). N. Currier's print *The Old Stone House, L.I., 1699* (undated) may be derived from Palmer's study.

4-22 *The Viaduct at Sileby Line*

Undated, ca. 1840

Pencil on paper, 8 3/10 × 10 3/5"

Holding institution: Leicestershire Museums and Art Galleries

4-23 *View of Astoria, Long Island / From the New York Side*   Illustrated, p. 193

Undated, ca. 1862

Watercolor and pencil on paper, 10½ × 15¼"

Holding institution: New-York Historical Society

4-24 *View of New York: From Brooklyn Heights: Study for a Lithograph; below a
separate view of Castle Garden, New York City*   Illustrated, p. 24

1845

Pencil drawing on paper, 10½ × 16⅛"

Holding institution: New-York Historical Society

A quick notation of the lower New York skyline and a small sketch of Castle Garden
below it on the same sheet. The verso contains the note "Drawn by Fanny Palmer."

4-25 *West Point Academy*   Illustrated, p. 132

Undated

Pencil drawing on paper, sheet 10⅜ × 13 7/16"

Fr Pal (fragment of signature in pencil, lower right).

Holding institution: Museum of Fine Arts, Boston

The drawing appears to have been used to form the background of the print *U.S. Military
Academy, West Point. From the opposite Shore* (1862) (p. 318).

Notes

Preface

1. Virginia Penny, *The Employments of Women: A Cyclopedia of Woman's Work* (Boston: Walker, Wise, 1863), 69.

2. Charles Hart, "Lithography, Its Theory and Practice. Including a Series of Short Sketches of the Earliest Lithographic Artists, Engravers and Printers of New York," unpublished manuscript, 1902, 196, photocopy in the collection of the American Antiquarian Society from the original held by the New York Public Library.

3. Charlotte Rubinstein, *American Women Artists: From Early Indian Times to the Present* (Boston: G. K. Hall, 1982).

4. "A Supplement to the Research Data on Currier & Ives" (Nov. 1957), microfilm reel 681, frame 0008, Harriet Endicott Waite Papers, Archives of American Art, Smithsonian Institution, Washington, DC.

5. "Time spent by Miss Waite in compiling data on Currier & Ives, Their Artists and Publications," microfilm reel 681, frame 0030, Waite Papers.

6. Harry T. Peters, *Currier & Ives: Printmakers to the American People*, 2 vols. (Garden City, NY: Doubleday, Doran, 1929–31).

7. Mary Bartlett Cowdrey to Carl Zigrosser, June 27, 1961, MSS 556, Mary Bartlett Cowdrey Papers, Special Collections, University of Delaware Library, Newark.

8. Charlotte Rubinstein, "The Early Career of Frances Flora Bond Palmer," *American Art Journal* 17 (Autumn 1985): 71.

9. Georgia B. Barnhill, "Business Practices of Commercial Nineteenth-Century American Lithographers," *Winterthur Portfolio* 48, nos. 2–3 (Summer–Autumn 2014): 213.

10. Hart, "Lithography," 196. Joseph F. Knapp (1832–91) later joined the lithographic firm that became Sarony, Major, & Knapp before founding Metropolitan Life Insurance.

Introduction

1. Patricia Hills, "Picturing Progress in the Era of Westward Expansion," in *The West as America: Reinterpreting Images of the Frontier*, ed. William H. Truettner (Washington, DC: Smithsonian Institution Press, 1991), 121.

2. Harry T. Peters, *Currier & Ives: Printmakers to the American People*, abridged (Garden City, NY: Doubleday Doran, 1942), 29; this is a mass-market, abridged edition of Peters's two-volume work published in 1929–31.

3. Russel Crouse, *Mr. Currier and Mr. Ives: A Note on Their Lives and Times* (Garden City, NY: Garden City Publishing, 1937), 9.

4. "Del." stands for *delineavit*, or "he or she drew it," which was used on prints to designate the artist.

5. Harry T. Peters, *America on Stone: The Other Printmakers to the American People, a Chronicle of American Lithography, Other Than That of Currier & Ives* (Garden City, NY: Doubleday, Doran, 1931), 305–7.

6. Mary Bartlett Cowdrey, "Fanny Palmer, an American Lithographer," in *Prints: Thirteen Essays on the Art of the Print*, ed. Carl Zigrosser (London: Peter Owen, 1962), 217–34.

1. A Childhood in Leicester

1. St. Margaret's Church, records, Leicester, UK.

2. Palmer's name appears as "Fanny" in the Letters of Administration of her father's estate (Aug. 1839, PROB 6/215, Public Record Office, London).

3. Penny, *Employments of Women*, 69.

4. A. Temple Patterson, *Radical Leicester: A History of Leicester, 1780–1850* (Leicester, UK: Leicester Univ. Press, 1954), 328.

5. Mrs. Charles Baker, interview, microfilm reel 681, frame 0104, Waite Papers. Mrs. Baker was a longtime friend of Palmer's sister Maria Bond.

6. Robert Chambers, *The Book of Days: A Miscellany of Popular Antiquities in Connection with the Calendar*, 2 vols. (London: W. & R. Chambers, 1864), 1:348.

7. *London Morning Post*, Apr. 24, 1787, quoted in William Andrews, "Miss Mary Linwood—an Artist with the Needle," in *Bygone Leicestershire*, ed. William Andrews (Leicester, UK: Frank Murray, 1892), 237.

8. *London Morning Post*, May 12, 1787, quoted in Andrews, "Miss Mary Linwood," 238.

9. [Elizabeth Stone], *The Art of Needle-work, from the Earliest Ages*, ed. Countess of Wilton (London: Henry Colburn, 1840), 395–96.

10. Quoted in Norma R. Whitcomb, *Mary Linwood* (Leicester, UK: City of Leicester Museums and Art Gallery Department of Antiquities, n.d.), unpaginated.

11. Mary Kirby, *"Leaflets from My Life": A Narrative Autobiography* (London: Simpkin, Marshall, 1887), 38.

12. Both West and Farington quoted in Susan Lasdun, "A Taste for Crewels and Yarns: Mary Linwood's Needlework Pictures," *Country Life*, Apr. 15, 1976.

13. John Constable to John Dunthorne, Jan. 8, 1802, in John Constable, *John Constable's Correspondence II: Early Friends and Maria Bicknell (Mrs. Constable)*, ed. R. B. Beckett (Suffolk, UK: Suffolk Records Society, 1964), 27.

14. J. D. Bennett, "John Flower 1793–1861," *Transactions of the Leicestershire Archaeological and Historical Society* 42 (1966–67): 76, at https://www.le.ac.uk/lahs/downloads/FlowerPagesfromvolumeXLII-6.pdf.

15. Mary Linwood to unknown recipient, 1822, Archives Department, Leicestershire Museum and Art Gallery, Leicester, UK.

16. Kirby, *"Leaflets from My Life,"* 39.

17. School bill, Mar. 25, 1792, Mary Linwood Correspondence File, Leicestershire Record Office, Leicester, UK.

18. List of student expenses, Linwood Correspondence File.

19. See Ann Sutherland Harris and Linda Nochlin, "The Nineteenth Century: England, France, and the United States" in *Women Artists: 1550–1950* (New York: Knopf, 1976), 50–53. A few daring women managed to defy these restrictions. See Margaret A. Oppenheimer, "'The Charming Spectacle of a Cadaver': Anatomical and Life Study by Women Artists in Paris, 1775–1815," *Nineteenth Century Art Worldwide*, Spring 2007, at http://www.19thc-art worldwide.org/spring07/142-qthe-charming-spectacle-of-a-cadaverq-anqthe -charming-spectacle-of-a-cadaverqanatomical-and-life-study-by-women-artists -in-paris-17751815atomical-and-life-study-by-women-artistsin-paris-17751815.

20. I am indebted to Michael Twyman for informing me that Jones was referred to as "Miss Jones" in a review of the *Landscape Alphabet* in the October 22, 1831, issue of *The Spectator*, 21. In Jones's fanciful work, each letter is integrated into the form of a picturesque landscape (see Ruth Mortimer, *The Landscape Alphabet* [Northampton, MA: Friends of the Smith College Library, 1981]). Elizabeth Gould's illustrations are included in John Gould, *A Century of Birds from the Himalaya Mountains* (London: n.p., 1831) and *The Birds of Australia* (London: John Gould, 1840–48). The travel books by Maria Graham (Lady Maria Callcott, 1785–1842) are also illustrated with Gould's lithographs.

21. "Remarks by Miss L. Shaw," microfilm reel 681, frame 0103, Waite Papers.

2. F. & E. S. Palmer: Lithographers of Leicester

1. Register of Marriages, Saint Mary's Church, Newington, Surrey, P92/MRY, Item 70 (99, no. 295), London Metropolitan Archives.

2. Will of Thomas Clare, of Chelsea, Middlesex, vicar of St. Bride's, Fleet Street, London, proved in the Prerogative Court of Canterbury, Apr. 10, 1829. Rev. Clare, a widower whose wife had been related to the extended Palmer family, had no heirs and therefore left trust funds to a number of her relatives in his will.

3. In the US census data for Brooklyn, New York, in 1850, Edmund Jr.'s birthplace is listed as Wales (census data for Brooklyn Ward 4, Kings, New York, in US Census Bureau, *Seventh Census of the United States, 1850*, Microfilm Publication M432, p. 379B, image 219, Records of the Bureau of the Census, Record Group 29, National Archives, Washington, DC, made available at Ancestry.com).

4. August 1839, PROB 6/215, Public Record Office, London.

5. Advertisement, *Leicester Journal*, July 12, 1839, emphasis added. All Leicester newspapers were accessed by microfilm at the Leicester Central Library.

6. Patterson, *Radical Leicester*, 328.

7. Will of Edward Seymour Palmer, signed and dated March 4, 1840, proved in London, March 7, 1860, National Archives, London.

8. *The Midland Counties' Railway Companion, with Topographical Descriptions of the Country through Which the Line Passes; and Time, Fare, and Distance Tables* (Nottingham, UK: R. Allen; Leicester, UK: E. Allen, 1840). Edward Allen was a local stationer, bookbinder, and publisher.

9. Quoted in Stephen Daniels, *Fields of Vision: Landscape Imagery and National Identity in England and the United States* (Princeton, NJ: Princeton Univ. Press, 1993), 129. Wordsworth had at first hailed the coming of the trains, until they began to encroach on the Lake District.

10. Census data for Leicester, St. Mary's Parish, District 2, Leicestershire County, England, in *Census Returns of England and Wales, 1841*, Public Record Office, 1841, Folio 26, p. 18, National Archives of the United Kingdom, Kew, made available at Ancestry.com.

11. Will of Thomas Clare.

12. Penny, *Employments of Women*, 69. The approximate date of Palmer's training is deduced from Penny's statement based on direct communication with the artist around 1862 that "she had spent twenty-two years in lithographing."

13. It has taken a considerable amount of detective work to discover who this seven-fingered artist might be, but Michael Twyman, a leading scholar of nineteenth-century lithography, was fortunately able to furnish the answer. I am grateful to Professor Twyman for identifying Haghe and for generously sending me advance proofs of his short biography of the artist, "Haghe, Louis (1806–1885)," which subsequently appeared in *Oxford Dictionary of National Biography* (Oxford: Oxford Univ. Press, 2004), 24:447–48.

14. Ibid., 447.

15. William Simpson, *The Autobiography of William Simpson, R. I.*, ed. George Eyre-Todd (London: T. Fisher Unwin, 1903), 15–17. After retiring from lithography, Haghe became the president of the New Society of Painters in Water Colours.

16. Such an application was unusual but not unprecedented. The poet and lithographer Edward Lear taught Elizabeth Gould, who lithographed many of the fine bird prints for the ornithological books by her husband, John Gould.

17. Simpson, *Autobiography*, 16.

18. "Remarks by Miss L. Shaw," microfilm reel 681, frames 0103–0104, Waite Papers.

19. Simpson, *Autobiography*, 16.

20. Ibid.

21. Drawings could also be made on a special transfer paper and transferred to the stone, but that was also a tricky process.

22. Twyman, "Haghe, Louis (1806–1885)," 448. On Hullmandel, see Michael Twyman, "Charles Joseph Hullmandel: Lithographic Printer Extraordinary," in *Lasting Impressions: Lithography as Art*, ed. Pat Gilmour (London: Alexandria Press, 1988), 42–90.

23. Advertisement for "E. S. Palmer, Lithographic Printer, Princes-street, Leicester," in Thomas Cook, *The Leicestershire Almanack, Directory, and*

Advertiser for the Year 1842 (Leicester, UK: T. Cook, 1842), unpaginated (around page 139).

24. Thomas Cook, *A Guide to Leicester, Containing a List to Streets, Lanes, Yards &c.: A Directory of the Principal Inhabitants, Classification of Trades, and Professions* (Leicester, UK: T. Cook, 1843), 81.

25. Advertisement, *Leicester Journal*, July 22, 1842.

26. Twyman, "Haghe, Louis (1806–1885)," 448.

27. T. R. Potter, *The History and Antiquities of Charnwood Forest* (London: Hamilton, Adams; Nottingham, UK: R. Allen; Leicester, UK: E. Allen, 1842), v.

28. The lithograph was probably from a drawing by the architect.

29. The "Barnard" referred to here was probably George Barnard, a well-known London lithographer.

30. "Leicester General News Room and Library," *Leicester Journal*, May 13, 1842.

31. Advertisement, *Leicester Journal*, June 24, 1842.

32. Architect William Parsons had trained and taken Abraham Gill, the husband of Palmer's sister Felicia, as a partner.

33. "Sketches in Leicestershire," *Leicester Journal*, July 1, 1842.

34. See Rubinstein, *American Women Artists*, 271, 307.

35. "Sketches in Leicestershire—Part 2nd," *Leicester Journal*, Aug. 12, 1842.

36. "Palmer's Sketches in Leicestershire. No. 2," *Leicester Chronicle*, Aug. 13, 1842.

37. *Midland Counties' Railway Companion*, 60. The manufacturer was driven out by workers who feared that the machines would eliminate their jobs.

38. Advertisement, *Leicester Chronicle*, Sept. 3, 1842. The advertisement was presumably alluding to the usual practice of grinding the image off the stone after sufficient prints had been made in order to leave a smooth new surface for new drawings.

39. "Sketches in Leicestershire," *Leicester Journal*, Sept. 9, 1842.

40. "Art and Literature. *Palmer's Sketches in Leicestershire. No. 3,*" *Leicester Chronicle*, Sept. 10, 1842.

41. "Sketches in Leicestershire," *Leicester Journal*, Oct. 28, 1842.

42. "Under the Patronage of Her Gracious Majesty the Queen Adelaide," advertisement, *Leicester Chronicle*, Dec. 31, 1842. For example, Bradgate Park was the ancestral home of Lady Jane Gray, the ill-fated nine-day queen of Henry VIII, and Ashby-de-la-Zouch was the setting for a duel in Sir Walter Scott's medieval novel *Ivanhoe*.

43. Patterson, *Radical Leicester*, 329, paraphrasing Kirby, "*Leaflets from My Life.*" Cooper was leading a march in support of the Chartist movement for universal (male) suffrage. At that time, there were still property qualifications for voting.

44. "Palmer's Sketches in Leicestershire," *Leicester Journal*, Dec. 17, 1842, emphasis added.

45. This is a reference to two much earlier illustrated histories of Leicestershire: John Throsby's *Select Views in Leicestershire* (1789) and John Nichols's *History and Antiquities of the County of Leicester* (1795–1811). John Flower's lithographs of Leicester are not mentioned, perhaps because the Palmers were reluctant to attack an admired contemporary.

46. "Now Ready, Parts VII. & VIII., of Sketches in Leicestershire," advertisement, *Leicestershire Journal*, June 16, 1843.

47. J. F. Hollings, *Sketches in Leicestershire: From Original Drawings with Historical and Descriptive Notices* (Leicester, UK: John Sydney Crossley, 1846), unpaginated (around p. ii). Thanks to John Bennett, Leicester historian, for this information.

3. BRAVE NEW WORLD

1. The Palmers and Robert Bond Jr. have not been located on any passenger list. The last reference to them in Leicester is June 1843, and the first dated prints in New York are in January 1844. They were probably already in New York by October 1843 because Maria Bond, who came separately that month, most likely followed them after they were settled.

2. A view of New York from Brooklyn Heights below a separate view of Castle Garden, New York City, pencil drawing, 1845, drawing collection, New-York Historical Society.

3. Index to Passenger Lists of Vessels Arriving at New York, New York, 1820–1846, microfilm reel 261, National Archives, Washington, DC.

4. *The New-York City Directory for 1844 & 1845* (New York: John Doggett, 1844), 267.

5. In a few years, the neighborhood would be known as "Little Germany" when a wave of "forty-eighters," fleeing from the failed German democratic revolution of 1848, settled there (Stanley Nadel, *Little Germany: Ethnicity, Religion, and Class in New York City, 1845–80* [Urbana: Univ. of Illinois Press, 1990], 29–35).

6. *New-York City Directory for 1844 & 1845*, 171.

7. *New-York City Directory for 1846 & 1847* (New York: John Doggett, 1846), 302. Typesetters and lithographic letterers unwittingly changed "Frances" to "Francis" on several occasions, assuming that a lithographer would have to be a man.

8. Walt Whitman, "Sun-Down Poem," in *Leaves of Grass* (Brooklyn, NY: Walt Whitman, 1856), 219; the observer is quoted in Edward K. Spann, *The New Metropolis: N.Y.C. 1840–57* (New York: Columbia Univ. Press, 1981), 95.

9. Spann, *New Metropolis*, 96.

10. *Brooklyn Eagle*, May 5, 1843. Cleaveland advertised that he was director of a "School for Young Ladies" at 42 Pierrepont Street. See also the autobiographical entry in Nehemiah Cleaveland, *History of Bowdoin College* (Boston: James Ripley Osgood, 1882), 171–73.

11. Mary Bartlett Cowdrey, *National Academy of Design Exhibition Record: 1826–1860*, 2 vols. (New York: New-York Historical Society, 1943), 2:63.

12. Mahlon Dickerson, "Opening Address of the 20th Annual Fair, on the 5th day of October, 1847," in *Sixth Annual Report of the American Institute of the City of New-York* (Albany, NY: Charles Van Benthuysen, 1848), 488.

13. *Catalogue Containing a Correct List of Every Article Exhibiting at the 19th Annual Fair of the American Institute of the City of New York, 1846* and *Catalogue Containing a Correct List of Every Article Exhibiting at the 20th Annual Fair of the American Institute of the City of New York, 1847.*

List of Premiums Awarded by the Managers of the Twentieth Annual Fair of the American Institute, October, 1847, 10, New-York Historical Society, New York. Also see Pre-1877 Exhibition Catalogue Index, Smithsonian American Art Museum, Washington, DC.

14. For some of the unusual women who were able to survive as professional painters at this time, see Rubinstein, *American Women Artists*, chap. 3.

15. See Helena E. Wright, *With Pen & Graver: Women Graphic Artists before 1900* (Washington, DC: National Museum of American History and Smithsonian Institution, 1995).

16. Spann, *New Metropolis*, 24.

17. Philip Hone, *The Diary of Philip Hone, 1828–1851*, 2 vols., ed. Bayard Tuckerman (New York: Dodd, Mead, 1889), entry for Apr. 7, 1845, 2:246.

18. "Portrait of President Polk," *Brooklyn Daily Eagle*, June 4, 1844.

19. See praise of Basham, "an artist of fine taste and practiced skill," and his work in "Editor's Table," *The Knickerbocker or New-York Monthly Magazine*, July 1844.

20. Federal Writers' Project, *The WPA Guide to New York City: The Federal Writers' Project Guide to 1930s New York* (1939; reprint, New York: Pantheon Books, 1982), 447. This congregation later merged with the Plymouth Congregational Church made famous by the abolitionist preacher Henry Ward Beecher.

21. The spire in the drawing, added in 1860, would be taken down again in the early twentieth century because it was deemed a hazard (Jacob Landy, *The Architecture of Minard Lafever* [New York: Columbia Univ. Press, 1970], 105–12).

22. "Lithograph of the New Church," *Brooklyn Daily Eagle*, Apr. 20, 1847.

23. E. Palmer to Richard Upjohn, Mar. 13, 1846, Box 12, Richard Upjohn and Richard Michell Upjohn Papers, Manuscripts and Archives Division, New York Public Library.

24. Ann S. Stephens, *Fashion and Famine* (1854), quoted in Roger Hale Newton, *Town & Davis: Architects, Pioneers in American Revivalist Architecture, 1812–1870, Including a Glimpse of Their Times and Their Contemporaries* (New York: Columbia Univ. Press, 1942), 224–25.

25. Newton, *Town & Davis*, 228.

26. Among Elliottsville's residents were Sydney Howard Gay, an editor of the *National Anti-Slavery Standard*, as well as the liberal Shaw family, whose son Robert Gould Shaw grew up there and led the first black regiment in the Civil War (Thomas Matteo, "Staten Island's Role in the Civil War," *Staten Island Advance*, Sept. 25, 2011).

27. Barbaralee Diamonstein-Spielvogel, *The Landmarks of New York: An Illustrated Record of the City's Historic Buildings* (Albany: State Univ. of New York Press, 2011), 165.

28. The school was demolished, but the hill is known as "Kellett's Hill" after J. P. Kellett, who owned the property and ran the school. He converted it to a hotel and finally sold the property (Charles W. Leng and William T. Davis, *Staten Island and Its People: A History 1609–1929*, 5 vols. [New York: Lewis Historical Publishing, 1930], 1:515).

29. Hone, *Diary of Philip Hone*, entry for Sept. 16, 1843, 2:193–94.

30. A sulky is a light, two-wheeled, horse-drawn vehicle with only one seat, for the driver.

31. The New-York Historical Society has hand-colored copies of the prints that are signed in pencil "O.K." or "O.K. Clarke," suggesting they may be the final "bon à tirer" proofs made before printing.

32. "Sambo" was a slang expression for a black man. It does not refer to the children's book *Little Black Sambo*, first published in 1899.

33. The late Wendy Shadwell, longtime print curator at the New-York Historical Society, informed me that the hot-pink coloring on the girl's dress in the example in the society's collection was a hue often used to indicate a prostitute.

34. Editor of the *Literary World* and a promoter of emerging American authors, Evert A. Duyckinck hosted a famous salon at his Greenwich Village home.

35. Evert A. Duyckinck to his brother, Sept. 15, 1846, Duyckinck Family Papers, Manuscript and Archives Division, New York Public Library. I am grateful to Richard Samuel West, author and expert on early American periodicals, for sharing with me his discovery of Palmer's cover and the reference to Palmer in the Duyckinck Papers.

36. Duyckinck to his brother, Oct. 8, 1846, Duyckinck Family Papers.

37. *Yankee Doodle*, Oct. 10, 1846.

38. See Elizabeth Johns, *American Genre Painting: The Politics of Everyday Life* (New Haven, CT: Yale Univ. Press, 1991), 137–75.

39. Hone, *Diary of Philip Hone*, entry for Mar. 31, 1847, 2:303–4.

40. See David Tatham, "David Claypoole Johnston's Militia Muster," *American Art Journal*, Spring 1987, 4–15.

41. Bernard F. Reilly Jr., *American Political Prints, 1766–1876: A Catalog of the Collections in the Library of Congress* (Boston: G. K. Hall, 1991), 255–56.

42. Ronnie C. Tyler, *The Mexican War: A Lithographic Record* (Austin: Texas State Historical Association, 1973), 23.

43. William Graham, the book dealer and publisher in the nearby Tribune Building who published Palmer's cover on the magazine *Yankee Doodle*, also published F. Palmer, *The New York Drawing Book, Containing a Series of Original Designs and Sketches of American Scenery*, nos. 1 and 2 (New York: W. H. Graham, 1847).

44. See Peter C. Marzio, *The Art Crusade: An Analysis of American Drawing Manuals, 1820–1860* (Washington, DC: Smithsonian Institution Press, 1976). Rembrandt Peale and other prominent artists were publishing drawing books with the aim of raising average Americans' level of taste and skill. One of their goals was to improve the design quality of American products so that they could compete with European products. Drawing was considered a utilitarian art, useful to everyone, in the era before the dominance of photography.

45. "Local Intelligence. The Homes of the Dead," *New York Times*, Mar. 30, 1866. Green-Wood Cemetery continues to be the burial place of many great New Yorkers from De Witt Clinton to Leonard Bernstein. On this cemetery, see Jeffrey I. Richman, *Brooklyn's Green-Wood Cemetery: New York's Buried Treasure* (Brooklyn, NY: The Cemetery, 1998).

46. *American Flora or History of Plants and Wildflowers* was reprinted by several New York publishers, including Strong and Bidwell (1846–50), Green and Spencer (1848–53), and Hull & Spencer (1855).

47. The original portrait is in the Linnémuseet at Uppsala University, Sweden.

48. J. J. Grandville, illus., *Les fleurs animées*, introduction by Alphonse Karr and text by Taxile Delord (Paris: Gabriel de Gonet, 1847). I am indebted to Professor Daniel Tatham and Ruth Ann Appelhof, executive director of Guild Hall, for generously sharing this discovery with me.

49. "The language of the flowers" was very popular in Victorian times, often used by lovers as a form of hidden or symbolic communication. See Beverly Seaton, *The Language of Flowers: A History* (Charlottesville: Univ. of Virginia, 1995).

50. Nehemiah Cleaveland, trans., *The Flowers Personified; Being a Translation of Grandville's "Les fleurs animées"* (New York: R. Martin, 1847).

51. Nehemiah Cleaveland, *Green-Wood Illustrated*, with illustrations by James Smillie (New York: R. Martin, 1847).

52. William H. Ranlett, *The Architect: A Series of Original Designs, for Domestic and Ornamental Cottages and Villas, Connected with Landscape Gardening, Adapted to the United States*, vol. 1 (New York: W. H. Graham, 1847), unnumbered page following plate 60, emphasis added.

53. Peters, *Currier & Ives*, 1:114. The true origins of Peters's claims regarding Palmer's lithographic abilities are somewhat unclear. In a letter dated February 14, 1936, Milton L. Bernstein wrote to Peters: "I believe you said during the lecture that Louis Maurer did very few of the actual lithographs on the stone. That surprised me very much because Mr. Maurer told me on two occasions when I visited him that he and Fannie Palmer were practically the only two on Currier's staff who could sit down at the stone and draw on it without a copy." To which Peters replied on February 17, 1936, that he had heard directly from Maurer "that Fanny Palmer, so far as he ever knew, never worked on the stone itself" (Harry T. Peters Papers, 1790–1988, Museum of the City of New York).

54. Peters, *America on Stone*, 305.

55. *Seventh Annual Report of the American Institute of the City of New-York* (Albany: Weed, Parsons, 1849), 91.

56. William H. Ranlett, *The Architect: A Series of Original Designs, for Domestic and Ornamental Cottages and Villas, Connected with Landscape Gardening, Adapted to the United States*, vol. 2 (New York: Dewitt & Davenport, 1849).

57. H. R. Hearne and W. J. Hearne, *Brooklyn Directory and Yearly Advertiser, for 1848–9* (Brooklyn, NY: Lee & Foulkes, 1848), 235.

58. Brian C. R. Zugay describes the stormy history of the Broadway Tabernacle in his essay "In What Manner Shall We Build? The Broadway Tabernacle, New York," in *Sacred Spaces: Building and Remembering Sites of Worship in the Nineteenth Century*, curated by Virginia Chieffo Raguin and Mary Ann Powers (Worcester, MA: College of the Holy Cross and the American Antiquarian Society, 2002), 78–79. Finney was reluctantly forced to segregate black and white members of his congregation.

59. Hone, *Diary of Philip Hone*, entry for Apr. 25, 1844, 2:214.

60. Printed by Sarony & Major and published by John P. Ridner. See Maybelle Mann, *The American Art-Union* (Otisville, NY: ALM Associates, 1977), and Mary Bartlett Cowdrey, *American Academy of Fine Arts and American Art-Union: Introduction 1816–1852* (New York: New-York Historical Society, 1953), 218. Thanks to Georgia B. Barnhill, director of the Center for Historic American Visual Culture, American Antiquarian Society, for her invaluable help in locating much of this and other information.

61. On the back of the Metropolitan Museum of Art's version of Palmer's print, someone has written "In Anniversary Week." Christian organizations celebrated Anniversary Week each year in early May, and the American Institute also celebrated its anniversary at the Tabernacle for several years.

62. Cowdrey's essay "Fanny Palmer" states that the publisher reissued Palmer's rendering of the Waddell Villa under his own label (219), but I did not find a copy of this print with the Currier imprint. *Pointers* (1846), a lithograph of hunting dogs, carries the same square initial P found on early Palmer prints.

63. This is mentioned by Duyckinck to his brother, Sept. 15, 1846, Duyckinck Family Papers.

64. Hone, *Diary of Philip Hone*, entry for Oct. 8, 1842, 2:150–51.

65. For a discussion of the bridge and the many artists who painted it, see William H. Gerdts, *Impressionist New York* (New York: Abbeville Press, 1994), 174–79.

66. Census data for Brooklyn Ward 4, Kings, New York, in US Census Bureau, *Seventh Census of the United States, 1850*, Microfilm Publication M432, p. 379B, image 219. The hotel name is from "City News and Gossip," *Brooklyn Daily Eagle*, Mar. 7, 1859.

67. "Queries," *New York Times Saturday Review of Books*, May 25, 1907.

4. The Palmers in Transition

1. Quoted in Spann, *New Metropolis*, 253.

2. Clay Lancaster, *Old Brooklyn Heights: New York's First Suburb* (New York: Dover, 1979), 13.

3. William H. Smith, *Smith's Brooklyn Directory for the Year Ending May 1st, 1855* (Brooklyn, NY: William H. Smith. 1854), 249.

4. US Census Bureau, *Seventh Census of the United States, 1850*, Microfilm Publication M432, p. 379B, image 219.

5. Cowdrey, "Fanny Palmer," 231.

6. Peters, *Currier & Ives* (1942), 27.

7. "Mr. Maurer's Remarks on Mrs. Palmer," n.d., microfilm reel 681, frame 0244, Waite Papers.

8. "Remarks by Mrs. D. W. Logan," microfilm reel 681, frame 0105, Waite Papers. Waite interviewed the wife of Daniel W. Logan, the man who assumed the job of head salesman and shipping manager of Currier & Ives from his father and eventually took over the business in its last years.

9. "Remarks by Mrs. Chas. R. Baker," microfilm reel 681, frame 0104, Waite Papers, emphasis in original.

10. "Remarks by His Nephew, Mr. Joseph W. Currier," microfilm reel 681, frame 0085, Waite Papers.

11. Ibid.

12. According to Louis Maurer, Palmer "did all her work at home" ("Mr. Maurer's Remarks on Mrs. Palmer," frame 0244).

13. Maurer nevertheless enjoyed the relationship with Currier so much that he continued to take on freelance assignments for him ("Louis Maurer," microfilm reel 681, frame 0098, Waite Papers).

14. Penny, *Employments of Women*, 68.

15. Ibid., 68–69.

16. A shadowy figure sometimes referred to as "Dubois" (Sally Pierce and Catharina Slautterback, *Boston Lithography: 1825–1880* [Boston: Boston Athenaeum, 1991], 3).

17. "Remarks by Mrs. Chas. R. Baker," frame 0104.

18. Mrs. Baker stated that Maria taught music and art at the Misses Day's Private School ("Remarks by Mrs. Chas. R. Baker," frame 0104). In New York City directories, she is listed as a music teacher, and Mary Day is listed as running a school at 77 S. Third St. in the late 1860s. See Geo T. Lain, *The Brooklyn City and Business Directory for the Year Ending May 1st, 1869* (Brooklyn, NY: Lain, 1868), 51, 147.

19. "Remarks by Miss L. Shaw," n.d., microfilm reel 681, frame 0104, Waite Papers.

20. Robert Bond first appears in the New York City directory in 1851 as an "artist" at 118 E. Twenty-First Street; in the 1852 and 1853 directories as an artist at 263 Ninth Street; and in 1854 as an artist with a business address at 208 Broadway and a home at 186 E. Twenty-First Street. See *The New-York City Directory for 1851 & 1852* (New York: Doggett & Rode, 1851), 64; *The New-York City Directory for 1852 & 1853* (New York: Doggett & Rode, 1852), 63; and H. Wilson, *Trow's New-York City Directory for 1854–1855* (New York: John F. Trow, 1854), 79.

21. "Remarks by Miss L. Shaw," frame 0104. *Broadway at Grand Street* (1852) is at the New-York Historical Society. A watercolor of the Old Van Vorst Homestead by Robert Bond appeared at auction in 2003, and the periodical *The Old Print Shop Portfolio* attributed some Connecticut watercolor scenes to him in its February 1945 issue.

22. "Remarks by Miss L. Shaw," frame 0104.

23. Peters, *Currier & Ives* (1942), 28.

24. Penny, *Employments of Women*, 69.

25. "Mr. Maurer's Remarks on Mrs. Palmer," frame 0102. Edmund is listed (as Seymour Palmer) as working at a "tavern" and "hotel" at 293 Adams between 1851 and 1853. While he was working at the Abbey tavern, it was renamed the Woodcock, perhaps in honor of his favorite avocation. See *Hearne's Brooklyn City Directory for 1850–1851* (Brooklyn, NY: Henry R. & William J. Hearne, 1850), 284; *Hearne's Brooklyn City Directory for 1851–1852* (Brooklyn, NY: Henry R. & William J. Hearne, 1851), 335; and *Hearne's Brooklyn City Directory for 1853–1854* (Brooklyn, NY: Henry R. & William J. Hearne, 1853), 419. His work address disappears after 1854–55.

26. "Remarks by Mrs. Chas. R. Baker," frame 0104.

27. Ibid.

28. Penny, *Employments of Women*, 69.

29. "Remarks by Miss L. Shaw," frame 0103. Miss Shaw recalled that "Mrs. Palmer applied herself very closely to lithography. And even refused to execute orders."

5. Life at N. Currier & Co.

1. Peters, *Currier & Ives* (1929–31), 1:57.

2. There had been earlier attempts, but this was the first ongoing, successful commercial operation.

3. Pierce and Slautterback, *Boston Lithography*, 3.

4. David Tatham, "The Lithographic Workshop, 1825–50," *Proceedings of the American Antiquarian Society* 105, pt. 1 (Apr. 1995): 71–78.

5. Pierce and Slautterback, *Boston Lithography*, 8.

6. The primary sources for information about the businesses and employees of N. Currier and later Currier & Ives in this and subsequent chapters are chiefly from the research done by Harriet Endicott Waite, represented in the Harriet Endicott Waite Papers, and by Harry Peters for *Currier & Ives* (1929–31), 1:19–128.

7. Robert L. Searjeant, "Foreword to the 1983 Edition," in Frederic A. Conningham, *Currier & Ives Prints: An Illustrated Checklist* (New York: Crown, 1983), x.

8. See, for example, *The Great Mississippi Steamboat Race*, in Gale Research Group, *Currier & Ives: A Catalogue Raisonné* (Detroit: Gale Research, 1984), nos. 2849 and 2850.

9. "Uncolored Prints Published by Currier & Ives, No. 152 Nassau Street, N.Y.: Adapted to Grecian Oil and Oriental Painting, Italian or Diaphanic Pictures on Glass, and Any Other of the Popular Methods of Painting or Coloring," undated catalog (ca. 1860), Museum of the City of New York.

10. Currier & Ives, *Descriptive Catalogue of Prints, Published and for Sale by Currier & Ives, 152 Nassau Street, New York* (New York: French & Wheat, ca. 1858), 13, copy in the collection of the Museum of the City of New York.

11. Advertisement for N. Currier, *The Spirit of the Times: A Chronicle of the Turf, Agriculture, Field Sports, Literature, and the Stage*, Apr. 5, 1851, 83. This advertisement was repeated on May 17 and in several subsequent issues.

12. "Ned" Currier to his father and mother, Sept. 25, 1881, microfilm reel 2323, frame 0809, Nathaniel Currier Papers, Archives of American Art, Smithsonian Institution, Washington, DC.

13. Ibid. Nathaniel's son Ned had taken over as partner after his father's retirement in 1880. His letters to his father would soon change to sad reports that business was gradually dropping off.

14. "Employees," microfilm reel 681, frame 0068, Waite Papers.

15. "Remarks by Miss L. Shaw," microfilm reel 681, frame 0103, Waite Papers. Shaw knew Palmer after coming to America in 1865, when the artist was fifty-three years old. Scholars have frequently attributed Palmer's spinal curvature to her long, hard labor over the stones, but it might have been caused by osteoporosis or some other factor.

16. "Remarks by [Charles Currier's] Son Mr. Joseph W. Currier," microfilm roll 681, frame 0081, Waite Papers.

17. "Remarks of [Charles Currier's] Son F. E. Currier," microfilm reel 681, frame 0080, Waite Papers.

18. "Remarks by [Charles Currier's] Son Mr. Joseph W. Currier," frame 0081. Joseph claimed that his father was especially good at transferring drawings from one stone to another, and, according to Louis Maurer, Charles was a superb printer who was at one point in charge of printing at the company ("Remarks by Mr. Louis Maurer," microfilm roll 681, frame 0077, Waite Papers).

19. "The Oldest Artist in America," *Literary Digest*, Feb. 21, 1931.

20. Warder H. Cadbury, *Arthur Fitzwilliam Tait: Artist in the Adirondacks* (Newark: Univ. of Delaware Press, 1986), 16–21, 59.

21. Ibid., 68. In a letter to Louis Prang dated April 13, 1867, Tait claimed that he had cut off his connection with Currier & Ives more than a year earlier (ibid., 68).

22. Martha Young Hutson, *George Henry Durrie (1820–1863): American Winter Landscapist, Renowned through Currier and Ives* (Santa Barbara, CA: Santa Barbara Museum of Art and American Art Review Press, 1977), 170–71, 174.

23. Palmer's prints for Currier that are labeled "from nature and on stone" include *Bass Fishing. At Macomb's Dam Harlem River, N.Y.* (1852); *A Home in the Country* (undated, ca. 1857–72); *Morning in the Woods* (1852, ca. 1857–72); *Partridge Shooting* (1852); *Quail Shooting. Setters the Property of S. Palmer Esq., Brooklyn, L.I.* (1852); *Rail Shooting. On The Delaware* (1852); *Snipe Shooting* (1852); *Trout Fishing* (1852); *The Trout Stream* (undated, ca. 1857–72); *View on the Harlem River, N.Y. The Highbridge in the Distance* (1852, ca. 1857–72); *Wild Duck Shooting* (1852); and *Woodcock Shooting* (1852).

24. Quoted in Harriet Waite to Harry Peters, undated, microfilm roll 681, frame 0023, Waite Papers.

25. James Brust has corrected the oft-repeated error that Ives first joined the company in 1852, a mistake taken from Harry Peters's books on Currier & Ives. Ives was working for Currier at least as early as 1845, perhaps even earlier, and remained with the business for more than fifty years until his death in 1895 ("Notes on the Life of James Merritt Ives with a Reappraisal of When He Joined Nathaniel Currier," *Imprint* 33, no. 1 [Autumn 2008]: 36–45).

26. These are typical pencil notations by James Ives, found on Palmer's pencil drawing for *Across the Continent* (Museum of the City of New York).

27. Penny, *Employments of Women*, 68–69.

28. Ibid., 70. Chestnut Street is Philadelphia's main shopping street.

6. Prints for the People

1. In 1866, Palmer's most productive year, her name appeared on twenty-six Currier & Ives prints (Cowdrey, "Fanny Palmer," 224).

2. Lilly Martin Spencer (1822–1902), whose unusually progressive parents made it possible for her to get training unavailable to most women of the era, was one of very few women who became prominent genre painters. Her work would make an interesting comparison with Palmer's.

3. Author and historian J. T. Headley, address in "Proceedings at the Annual Meeting, December 19, 1845," in *Transactions of the American Art Union, for the Year 1845* (New York: American Art Union, 1845), 12.

4. The American Art-Union copied the lottery idea from the British art unions. See Joy Sperling, "'Art, Cheap and Good': The Art Union in England and the United States, 1840–60," *Nineteenth-Century Art Worldwide* 1, no. 1 (Spring 2002), at http://www.19thc-artworldwide.org/spring02/85-spring02/spring02article/196.

5. James Smillie engraved Kensett's painting, and Thomas Doney engraved George Caleb Bingham's.

6. Quoted in Bryan Le Beau, *Currier & Ives: America Imagined* (Washington, DC: Smithsonian Institution Press, 2001), 1.

7. Martha R. Wyatt, "Endicott & Co. Lithographs at the Mariners' Museum," *Imprint* 27, no. 2 (Autumn 2002): 17. In *The House of Harper:*

A Century of Publishing in Franklin Square (New York: Harper & Brothers, 1912), J. Henry Harper describes Charles Parsons as "a fine water-color painter" (204) but makes no mention of his long career as a lithographer.

8. "The Oldest Artist in America," *Literary Digest*, Feb. 21, 1931.

9. Bryan Le Beau develops this theme at length in his book *Currier & Ives*.

10. Walt Whitman, "Sun-Down Poem," in *Leaves of Grass* (1856), 218–21; the two spellings "Manhatta" and "Manahatta" are given in the poem. The poem was later published as "Crossing Brooklyn Ferry."

11. Fitz-Greene Halleck, *Fanny* (New York: Wiley, 1819), 37–38, quoted in Albert Boime, *The Magisterial Gaze: Manifest Destiny and American Landscape Painting, c. 1830–1865* (Washington, DC: Smithsonian Institution Press, 1991), 17.

12. John Hill engraved Wall's paintings *New York from the Heights Near Brooklyn* (ca. 1820–23) and *New York from Weehawk* (ca. 1820–23) for the *Hudson River Port-folio* (ca. 1821–25). British artist William H. Bartlett provided *View of New York, from Weehawken* (date unknown), which was engraved for Nathaniel P. Willis's travel book *American Scenery* (London: G. Virtue, 1840).

13. See Robert D. Monroe, "William Birch McMurtrie: A Painter Partially Restored," *Oregon Historical Quarterly* 60, no. 3 (Sept. 1959): 371.

14. Local businessmen used the advance information about incoming cargoes to predict prices and plan their purchases.

15. This thesis is developed in Boime, *The Magisterial Gaze*.

16. Bayard Taylor, *At Home and Abroad: A Sketch-book of Life, Scenery, and Men* (New York: G. P. Putnam, 1862), 59, quoted in Boime, *The Magisterial Gaze*, 108. The reference to "race" reflects Taylor's intense Anglo-centric and often racist viewpoint.

17. Dell Upton, "Inventing the Metropolis: Civilization and Urbanity in Antebellum New York," in *Art and the Empire City: New York, 1825–1861*, ed. Catherine Hoover Voorsanger and John K. Howat (New York: Metropolitan Museum of Art, 2000), 40–41.

18. Walt Whitman, "The Song of the Exposition," in *Leaves of Grass* (Boston: James R. Osgood, 1881–82), 160. The poem was commissioned for the opening of the American Institute Fair in 1871 at a time when its leaders had drawn up plans, never fulfilled, to create a museum of industry and art. Whitman drew on memories of the earlier New York Crystal Palace. See also Ed Cutler, "Passage to Modernity: *Leaves of Grass* and the 1853 Crystal Palace Exhibition in New York," *Walt Whitman Quarterly Review* 16, no. 2 (Fall 1998): 65–89.

19. A source for this print may be the Nagel & Weingärtner lithograph *New York Crystal Palace for the Exhibition of the Industry of All Nations*, issued a year earlier (1852), before the Latting Observatory was built. In that print, two Chinese men and a turbaned Arab are in the crowd.

20. Among others, Thomas Birch and Thomas Doughty painted and drew the scene, and Bartlett produced an illustration for Willis's travel book *American Scenery*.

21. Charles Dickens, *American Notes for General Circulation*, 2 vols. (London: Chapman and Hall, 1842) 1:221–22. Later, the muckraking journalist Nellie Bly had herself incarcerated at the asylum on Blackwell's Island

and wrote an exposé that led to the asylum's closure. In the late twentieth century, the city began redeveloping the island, renamed Roosevelt Island, into an attractive modern suburb reached by an aerial tram and a subway line tunneled under the river, with ruins of some of the old civic buildings restored.

22. Glenn A. Knoblock, *The American Clipper Ship, 1845–1920* (Jefferson, NC: McFarland, 2014), 26.

23. "The New-York Yacht Club. Dinner to Commodore Stevens," *New York Daily Times*, Oct. 3, 1851.

24. "Clipper Yacht 'America,'" advertisement, *Spirit of the Times*, May 15, 1852.

25. James E. Buttersworth's last name was misspelled so often that he finally began signing his paintings "Butterworth" (Peters, *Currier & Ives* [1929–31], 1:134), as seen in his signatures on the works Palmer adapted for Currier & Ives.

26. Jan Seidler Ramirez, ed., *Painting the Town: Cityscapes of New York. Paintings from the Museum of the City of New York* (New York: Museum of the City of New York; New Haven, CT: Yale Univ. Press, 2000), 124.

27. Currier stated that the steamship pictures were taken from daguerreotypes. See "The Trotting Horses of America," advertisement, *Spirit of the Times*, Feb. 22, 1851.

28. "Sportsmen, Attention," advertisement, *Spirit of the Times*, May 15, 1852.

29. Relatives, friends, and colleagues suggested that both the senior Edmund Seymour and his son wasted inordinate amounts of time and money on these hobbies instead of helping to support the family (see microfilm reel 681, frames 0103–0104, Waite Papers). Several prints in this sporting series show an older man with a youth about Edmund Jr.'s age.

30. Although drawn from life, the print *Wild Duck Shooting* (1852) may have been influenced by William Tylee Ranney's painting *On the Wing* (1850), engraved by the American Art-Union. Palmer's sportsmen wear nattier hunting attire, emphasizing the middle-class aspect of the scene.

31. "Sportsman, Attention," advertisement, *Spirit of the Times*, May 15, 1852.

32. "Elegantly Colored Prints," advertisement, *Spirit of the Times*, Dec. 4, 1852.

33. Roy King and Burke Davis, *The World of Currier & Ives* (New York: Random House, 1968), 100.

34. "Remarks by Mrs. Chas. R. Baker," microfilm roll 681, frame 0104, Waite Papers.

35. Peters, *Currier & Ives* (1929–31), 1:72.

36. These lighthouses were the first American lighthouses equipped with Fresnel lenses and were rebuilt in 1862. The two beacons, one flashing and the other fixed, were easy to recognize from the water at night.

37. Marshall B. Davidson, *Life in America*, 2 vols. (Boston: Houghton Mifflin, 1951), 1:403.

38. "Remarks by Mrs. Chas. R. Baker," frame 0104.

39. Sarah Burns, *Pastoral Inventions: Rural Life in Nineteenth-Century American Art and Culture* (Philadelphia: Temple Univ. Press, 1989), 18–19.

40. Ibid., 52–57.

41. "By avarice and selfishness, and a grovelling habit, from which none of us is free, of regarding the soil as property, or the means of acquiring property . . . husbandry is degraded with us, and the farmer leads the meanest of lives. He knows Nature but as a robber" (Henry David Thoreau, *Walden; or Life in the Woods* [Boston: Ticknor and Fields, 1854], 179).

42. Burns, *Pastoral Inventions*, 78.

43. A. J. Downing, *The Architecture of Country Houses* (New York: D. Appleton. 1850), vi.

44. Currier & Ives, *Descriptive Catalogue of Prints* (ca. 1858), 1.

45. Ibid.

46. Ibid., emphasis added.

47. Ibid., 4.

48. Description of *American Farm Scene: Summer*, in ibid., 1.

49. "City News and Gossip," *Brooklyn Daily Eagle*, Mar. 7, 1859; see Peters, *Currier & Ives* (1929–31), 1:115, and "Mr. Maurer's Remarks on Mrs. Palmer," microfilm reel 681, frames 0102–0103, Waite Papers.

50. Genealogical burial listing information for Lot 4659, Section 58, records, Green-Wood Cemetery.

51. Palmer's granddaughter was named after two of her sisters, Felicia and Maria.

52. J. Lain, *The Brooklyn City Directory for the Year Ending May 1st, 1860* (New York: Lain, 1859), 310.

53. Census data for Brooklyn Ward 4, Kings, New York, in US Census Bureau, *1860 United States Federal Census*, Microfilm Publication M653_764, p. 753, Records of the Bureau of the Census, National Archives, Washington, DC, made available at Ancestry.com.

54. Ibid.

7. CREATING AN AMERICAN EPIC

1. Harriet Endicott Waite to Harry Peters, Jan. 7, 1926, microfilm reel 681, frame 0023, Waite Papers.

2. Ives's name appears on *Across The Continent.* "*Westward the Course of Empire takes its way*" (1868); *The Four Seasons of Life: Childhood.* "*The Season of Joy*" (1868); *The Four Seasons of Life: Middle Age.* "*The Season of Strength*" (1868); *The Four Seasons of Life: Youth.* "*The Season of Love*" (1868); *Haying-Time. The First Load* (1868); *Haying-Time. The Last Load* (1868); "*High Water*" *in the Mississippi* (1868); and *Low Water in the Mississippi* (1867).

3. Quoted in Sherwin Cody, *Four Famous American Writers: Washington Irving, Edgar Allan Poe, James Russell Lowell, Bayard Taylor* (New York: Werner School, 1899), 17.

4. Frances Trollope, *Domestic Manners of the Americans*, 2 vols. (London: Whittaker, Treacher, 1832), 2:236–37. The pinnacles described were carved out by a deep fiord in the region. See also the diaries of Fanny Kemble and George Templeton Strong.

5. David Reel, curator of Fine Art & Decorative Art of the West Point Museum from 1998 to 2005, wrote of this print that it was "a fairly accurate representation of the academy as seen from the East shore. The figures themselves are standing in what is now called Garrison, New York. The buildings

visible are the two riding halls [long, narrow structures closest to the waterline]. The Gothic looking building with the observatory top was the library. The two other buildings were a barracks (left) and the clock tower was the academic building" (David Reel to Charlotte Streifer Rubinstein, email, date unavailable as of Sept. 2017).

6. Betsy Fahlman, "John Ferguson Weir: Painter of Romantic and Industrial Icons," *Archives of American Art Journal* 20, no. 2 (1980): 2–9.

7. Tuckerman quoted in Harold Holzer and Mark E. Neely Jr., *Mine Eyes Have Seen the Glory: The Civil War in Art* (New York: Orion Books, 1993), 230.

8. Benson J. Lossing, *The Hudson, from the Wilderness to the Sea* (New York: Virtue and Yorston, 1866), 252, 254.

9. Fanny Kemble, *Fanny Kemble: Journal of a Young Actress*, ed. Monica Gough (New York: Columbia Univ. Press, 1990), 78.

10. King and Davis, *World of Currier & Ives*, 29.

11. Quoted in ibid., 34.

12. Quoted in ibid.

13. Mark Twain, *Life on the Mississippi* (New York: Harper & Brothers, 1901), 127–29.

14. Ibid., 130.

15. Ibid., 169.

16. Leo Marx, "The Railroad-in-the-Landscape: An Iconological Reading of a Theme in American Art," in *The Railroad in American Art: Representations of Technological Change*, ed. Susan Danly and Leo Marx (Cambridge, MA: MIT Press, 1988), 186.

17. Dickens, *American Notes*, 1:145–46.

18. Robert Louis Stevenson, *Across the Plains with Other Memories and Essays* (London: Chatto & Windus, 1892), 26–68; Stephen E. Ambrose, *Nothing Like It in the World: The Men Who Built the Transcontinental Railroad 1863–1869* (New York: Simon and Schuster, 2000), 241.

19. See *U.S. Military Academy, West Point* (1862); *West Point Foundry, Cold Spring* (1862); *The "Lightning Express" Trains. Leaving the Junction* (1863); *Lookout Mountain, Tennessee* (1866), and other Palmer prints. The Blandford Church, depicted in *The Old Blandford Church* (undated, ca. 1857–72), was used as a Confederate hospital during the Civil War.

20. Mark E. Neely Jr. and Harold Holzer, *The Union Image: Popular Prints of the Civil War North* (Chapel Hill: Univ. of North Carolina Press, 2000), 112.

21. Ibid., 111.

22. Currier & Ives issued several small anonymous prints of the subject, not to be confused with Palmer's. The *Merrimac* was actually called the *Virginia* by this time. It had been reconstructed from the original *Merrimac*.

23. Neely and Holzer, *Union Image*, 118.

24. Neely and Holzer point out that the Confederate ironclad should be rounded on both ends and lacks details of seams and bolts, but in the absence of available documentation the artist did her best to envision the scene (ibid., 117, 246). Overall, Palmer was greatly respected for the accuracy of her images of technical subjects: steamboats, trains, architecture.

25. Ibid., 110.

26. The more famous ocean-going Monitors with revolving gun turrets came a little later.

27. Neely and Holzer, *Union Image*, 110.

28. Michael Hatt, "'Making a Man of Him': Masculinity and the Black Body in Mid-Nineteenth-Century American Sculpture," *Oxford Art Journal* 15, no. 1 (1992): 23–24.

29. In 1868, Congress passed the Reconstruction Act, pushed through the Fourteenth Amendment, and tried to impeach President Johnson.

30. After his victorious March to the Sea, General William Tecumseh Sherman issued Special Field Orders No. 15 on January 16, 1865, setting aside the Sea Islands and a tract along the southeastern coast for the exclusive settlement of freed slave families and promised a loan of army mules. Soon after Lincoln's assassination, President Johnson unilaterally revoked the order while Congress was not in session, throwing thousands of black people off the land. The phrase "40 acres and a mule" became a rallying cry for many African Americans.

31. Peter C. Marzio, *The Democratic Art: Pictures for a 19th-Century America* (Fort Worth, TX: Amon Carter Museum of Western Art, 1979), 116–26.

32. Le Beau, *Currier & Ives*, 191–92.

33. Barbara Welter, "The Cult of True Womanhood, 1820–1860," *American Quarterly* 18, no. 2, pt. 1 (Summer 1966): 151–74.

34. Phrenology was a widely followed pseudoscience based on the premise that the shape of the head reveals character traits. For example, women supposedly have slanting brows, which according to this science indicates less intellect.

35. Catherine E. Beecher and Harriet Beecher Stowe, *The American Woman's Home* (New York: J. B. Ford, 1869), 94.

36. Ibid., 90.

37. Such sentimental portrayal of innocent childhood was a major theme in the postbellum period. See Sarah Burns, "Barefoot Boys and Other Country Children: Sentiment and Ideology in Nineteenth-Century American Art," *American Art Journal* 20, no. 1 (1988): 25–50.

38. Charles Parsons's son, Charles R. Parsons (1844–1920), and lithographer Lyman Atwater (1835–91).

39. On Currier & Ives's self-promotion, see E. McSherry Fowble, "Currier & Ives and the American Parlor," *Imprint* 15, no. 2 (Autumn 1990): 14–19.

40. Currier & Ives, *Descriptive Catalogue* (ca. 1858), 1.

41. Wolfgang Born, *Still-Life Painting in America* (New York: Oxford Univ. Press, 1947), 39.

42. William Bartlett, *Centre Harbor: Lake Winnepesaukee* (1838), in Willis, *American Scenery. Mount Washington and the White Mountains* (1860) is probably adapted from James Smillie's engraving for the American Art-Union of John Kensett's painting from 1851.

43. See William H. Truettner and Roger B. Stein, eds., *Picturing Old New England: Image and Memory* (New Haven, CT: Yale Univ. Press, 1999), a fine collection of essays accompanying a Smithsonian National Museum of American Art exhibition.

44. Dona Brown and Stephen Nissenbaum, "Changing New England: 1865–1945," in *Picturing Old New England*, ed. Truettner and Stein, 1–5.

45. Some of the motifs in *The Farmers Home—Autumn* may be inspired by Jerome Thompson's popular painting *Apple Gathering* (Brooklyn Museum,

1856). Thompson shows the flirting between boys and girls that was an integral part of such occasions, but Palmer, a respectable lady, mutes this aspect.

46. Henry Wadsworth Longfellow, "The Village Blacksmith," in *The Poetical Works of Henry Wadsworth Longfellow* (London: George Routledge, 1858), 81.

47. Hills, "Picturing Progress," 98. Albert Bierstadt's equally glamorized painting, *Emigrants Crossing the Plains*, completed a year later, in 1867, shows the wagon train traveling toward the western setting sun. He included the bones of dead animals on the path, reminders of the hardships encountered on the journey by those who went before.

48. See Dawn Glanz, *How the West Was Drawn: American Art and the Settling of the West* (Ann Arbor: UMI Research Press, 1978, 1982), 72–75. Old master painters in earlier centuries had used the motif of returning with examples of the bounty of a new land.

49. Ibid., 73–74.

50. For Cole's environmentalism, see Alan Wallach, "Thomas Cole's *River in the Catskills* as Antipastoral," *Art Bulletin*, June 2002, 334–50. In a pair of before-and-after paintings, Cole expressed his bitter disappointment at a railroad's devastation of the landscape in his Hudson Valley neighborhood.

51. Sanitary fairs were mammoth philanthropic events to raise funds for medical supplies and to care for wounded army troops during the Civil War.

52. "Letter from 'Mark Twain.' [No. 24.]," *Daily Alta* (San Francisco), Aug. 4, 1867, quoted in Nancy K. Anderson and Linda S. Ferber, *Albert Bierstadt: Art & Enterprise* (New York: Brooklyn Museum in association with Hudson Hills Press, 1990), 91.

53. For a discussion of how artists romanticized scenes of the West, see Nancy K. Anderson, "'The Kiss of Enterprise': The Western Landscape as Symbol and Resource," in *The West as America*, ed. Truettner, 237–83.

54. James F. Rusling, *Across America: Or the Great West and the Pacific Coast* (New York: Sheldon, 1874), 428, quoted in Wesley S. Griswold, *A Work of Giants: Building the First Transcontinental Railroad* (New York: McGraw-Hill, 1962), 195; see also Ambrose, *Nothing Like It in the World*, 240. General Rusling made the trip to the Sierra Nevada in May 1867.

55. Asa Whitney, a trader with China, exhorted Congress to transform the United States into the chief conduit of trade between Europe and Asia, and engineer Theodore Judah surveyed and developed the first plans.

56. Quoted in James Neal Primm, *Lion of the Valley: St. Louis, Missouri, 1764–1980* (St. Louis: Missouri Historical Society Press, 1998), 205.

57. The feat of laying ten miles of track in a single day took place a year after Palmer's print *Across The Continent* (1868) appeared. See David Haward Bain, *Empire Express: Building the First Transcontinental Railroad* (New York: Viking, 1999), 638–39.

58. Curator Susan Danly Walther suggests that Palmer was influenced by British artist Thomas Talbot Bury's painting *View of the Railway across Chat Moss* (1831), which shows "a similar flattened plain bisected diagonally by railroad tracks" (*The Railroad in the American Landscape, 1850–1950. The Wellesley College Museum, Wellesley, Massachusetts, 15 April–8 June 1981* [Wellesley, MA: Wellesley College Museum, 1981], 91).

59. Hills, "Picturing Progress," 100–102.

60. Wolfgang Born, *American Landscape Painting: An Interpretation* (New Haven, CT: Yale Univ. Press, 1948), 88.

61. The phrase Leutze used for the title of his mural became a rallying cry for the westward movement. It comes from Bishop George Berkeley's poem "Verses on the Prospect of Planting Arts and Learning in America," written in 1726 and first published in 1752. Ironically, Berkeley had written it to describe his vision of creating a missionary school for Native Americans, whom he regarded as ideal candidates for conversion to Christianity.

62. Truettner, *The West as America*.

63. It became government policy to destroy the Plains Indians' principal source of food and shelter, the buffalo herds. The railroad companies even organized sporting parties to shoot buffalos from the windows of trains.

64. Described in Ambrose, *Nothing Like It in the World*, 217–20.

65. Glanz, *How the West Was Drawn*, 84.

66. The Credit Mobilier scandal revealed that Union Pacific director Thomas Durant had set up a dummy company to capture all the profits from construction payments. Others bribed congressmen with shares of stock to gain their support. The West Coast "Big Four" got off unscathed because records of the Central Pacific were conveniently destroyed on the eve of the government investigation.

67. Walt Whitman, "Nay Tell Me Not To-day the Publish'd Shame," in *Leaves of Grass: A Comprehensive Reader's Edition*, ed. Harold Blodgett and Sculley Bradley (New York: New York Univ. Press, 1965), 578.

68. James Campbell, farewell speech, printed in the *Chicago Tribune*, May 12, 1869, quoted in Bain, *Empire Express*, 671.

69. Ambrose, *Nothing Like It in the World*, 17–18.

70. Patricia Hills compares these two prints in *American Frontier: Images and Myths* (New York: Whitney Museum of American Art, 1973), 13.

71. Hills makes this point (ibid.).

8. The Last Years

1. "Remarks by Miss L. Shaw," microfilm reel 681, frame 0104, Waite Papers; "Edmund S. Palmer," microfilm reel 681, frame 0103, Waite Papers.

2. Three small prints—*The Barefoot Boy* (1872), *The Little Alms-Giver* (undated, ca. 1872–74), and *More Free Than Welcome* (undated, ca. 1872–74)—have been attributed to Palmer based on the initials on stone but do not appear to be her work (Conningham, *Currier & Ives Prints*, 23, 162; Gale Research Group, *Currier & Ives*, 463).

3. "Remarks by Miss L. Shaw," frame 0103.

4. The Hamilton Street house was destroyed with construction of the Verrazano Bridge. The address 92 Hall is listed in J. Lain, *The Brooklyn City Directory for the Year Ending May 1st, 1868* (Brooklyn: Lain, 1867), 479, and G. Lain, *The Brooklyn City and Business Directory for the Year Ending May 1st, 1869* (Brooklyn: Lain, 1868), 482; 122 Ryerson is listed in Geo T. Lain, *The Brooklyn City and Business Directory for the Year Ending May 1st, 1870* (Brooklyn, NY: Lain, 1869), 511; 111 Hamilton is listed in Geo T. Lain, *The Brooklyn City and Business Directory for the Year Ending May 1st, 1871* (Brooklyn, NY: Lain, 1870), 557; for 123 Hamilton, see Geo T. Lain, *The Brooklyn City and Business Directory for the Year Ending May 1st, 1872* (Brooklyn, NY: Lain,

1871), 577, and Geo T. Lain, *The Brooklyn City and Business Directory for the Year Ending May 1st, 1876* (Brooklyn, NY: Lain, 1875), 695.

5. Census data for Brooklyn Ward 20, Kings, New York, is given in US Census Bureau, *1870 United States Federal Census*, Microfilm Publication M593_960, p. 73B, National Archives, Washington, DC, made available at Ancestry.com.

6. Ibid. Fanny's daughter, Frances Edgecombe, was listed as a widow in the Brooklyn directory for 1876–77 (Geo T. Lain, *The Brooklyn City and Business Directory for the Year Ending May 1st, 1877* [Brooklyn, NY: Lain, 1876], 260).

7. "Frances Flora Palmer: Brooklyn Board of Health," microfilm reel 681, frame 0103, Waite Papers.

8. "Died," *Brooklyn Daily Eagle*, Aug. 22, 1876. The notice also appeared in the *New York Herald*, Aug. 22, 1876.

9. "Remarks by Mrs. D. W. Logan," microfilm reel 681, frame 0105, Waite Papers.

10. "Remarks by Miss L. Shaw," frame 0103.

11. G. Lain, *The Brooklyn City and Business Directory for the Year Ending May 1st, 1877*, 260; Geo T. Lain, *The Brooklyn City Directory for the Year Ending May 1st, 1878* (Brooklyn, NY: Lain, 1877), 262.

12. "Remarks by Mrs. Chas. R. Baker," microfilm reel 681, frame 0104, Waite Papers.

13. Maria Bond died at home at 17 Greene Avenue in Brooklyn ("Died," *Brooklyn Daily Eagle*, Feb. 12, 1896).

14. Genealogical burial listing information for Lot 4659, Section 58, Green-Wood Cemetery Records.

15. Peters, *Currier & Ives* (1929–31), 1:27.

16. John and Barbara Rudisill, longtime members of the American Historical Print Collectors Society, estimate the total number of titles at 8,500 (introduction to *A Gallery of Currier & Ives Lithographs*, maintained by Vanessa Rudisill Stern, n.d., at http://freepages.rootsweb.ancestry.com/~vstern/introduction.htm, accessed Mar. 2, 2015).

9. The Vicissitudes of Taste

1. Quoted Currier & Ives tagline from the undated catalog *New Catalogue of Cheap and Popular Pictures*, reproduced in Gale, *Currier & Ives*, xli.

2. The story of Waite's efforts forms a dramatic subplot all by itself. She complained bitterly that Peters had taken all the credit, paid her very little, and reaped the reward of her years of labor. See Harriet Endicott Waite, document dated Nov. 1957, microfilm reel 681, frame 0002–0012, Waite Papers. Waite also challenged Peters's mistaken assertion that Palmer never lithographed on the stones (Harriet Endicott Waite to Harry Peters, Dec. 4, 1929, microfilm reel 681, frame 0781, Waite Papers).

3. Palmer's prints included in this original "best-fifty" large-folio list, in ranking order, are: 7. *The "Lightning Express" Trains. "Leaving the Junction"* (1863); 9. *The Rocky Mountains. Emigrants Crossing the Plains* (1866); 10. *Trolling for Blue Fish* (1866); 13. *American Farm Scenes. No. 4* (1853); 19. *Across The Continent. "Westward the Course of Empire takes its way"* (1868); 21. *A Midnight Race on the Mississippi* (1860); 25. *View of*

San Francisco, California. Taken from Telegraph Hill, April 1850* (1851); 30. *American Winter Scenes. Morning* (1854); 37. *Rail Shooting. On The Delaware* (1852); 38. *Snowed Up. Ruffed Grouse in Winter* (1867), attributed to Palmer; and 48. *Landscape, Fruit and Flowers* (1862).

4. See "Ten Collectors Jointly Name Best Fifty Currier Prints," *New York Sun*, Jan. 21, 1933.

5. Peters, *Currier & Ives* (1942), 29; Crouse, *Mr. Currier and Mr. Ives*, 9.

6. Cowdrey, "Fanny Palmer," 217–34.

7. Marshall R. Berkoff, ed., *Currier & Ives: The New Best 50* (Farmingdale, NY: American Historical Print Collectors Society, 1991), catalog for an exhibition at the Milwaukee Art Museum. Palmer's prints included in the "new best fifty," in ranking order, are: 2. *A Midnight Race on the Mississippi* (1860); 4. *Across The Continent. "Westward the Course of Empire takes its way"* (1868); 8. *American Farm Scenes. No. 4* (1853); 11. *The Champions of the Mississippi. "A Race for the Buckhorns"* (1866); 12. *The Rocky Mountains. Emigrants Crossing the Plains* (1866); 13. *The "Lightning Express" Trains. "Leaving the Junction"* (1863); 14. *American Express Train* (1864); 17. *Trolling for Blue Fish* (1866); 19. *American Winter Scenes. Evening* (1854); 23. *"Wooding Up" on the Mississippi* (1863); 25. *American Winter Scenes. Morning* (1854); 33. *The Mississippi in Time of Peace* (1865); 35. *The Farmers Home—Harvest* (1864); 39. *Snowed Up. Ruffed Grouse in Winter* (1867), attributed to Palmer; 45. *Landscape, Fruit and Flowers* (1862); and 47. *A Night on the Hudson. "Through at Daylight"* (1864).

10. The Art of F. F. Palmer

1. Barbara Novak, *Nature and Culture: American Landscape and Painting, 1825–1875* (New York: Oxford Univ. Press, 1980), 25, 228–30.

2. Smillie's engraving of Kensett's painting was distributed to thirteen thousand people by the American Art-Union and was probably the source of Palmer's adaptation. See *American Paradise: The World of the Hudson River School* (New York: Metropolitan Museum of Art, 1987), 150.

3. Quoted in Cadbury, *Arthur Fitzwilliam Tait*, 41–42.

4. See the descriptions of *American Farm Scenes. No. 1* (1853) and *American Farm Scenes. No. 3* (1853), in Currier & Ives, *Descriptive Catalogue of Prints* (ca. 1858), 1.

5. "Uncolored Prints Published by Currier & Ives," undated catalog (ca. 1860).

6. Palmer's collaboration with Charles Currier in developing the crayons is noted in "Remarks by Mr. Louis Maurer," microfilm reel 681, frame 0077, Waite Papers; "Charles Currier: Remarks by His Son F. E. Currier," microfilm reel 681, frame 0080, Waite Papers; "Charles Currier: Remarks by His Son Mr. Joseph W. Currier," microfilm reel 681, frame 0081, Waite Papers.

7. Sue Welsh Reed and Carol Troyen, *Awash in Color* (Boston: Museum of Fine Arts in association with Bullfinch Press, Little Brown, 1993), 14–15.

8. Linda S. Ferber and Annette Blaugrund, "American Watercolors and Pastels at the Brooklyn Museum," *Magazine Antiques*, Aug. 1984.

9. "The Trotting Horses of America," advertisement, *Spirit of the Times*, Feb. 22, 1851.

1. Daniels, *Fields of Vision*, 179.

2. Carolyn Oldenbusch, "Suitable for Framing," in Carolyn Oldenbusch and Charlotte Streifer Rubinstein, *Fanny Palmer: A Long Island Woman Who Portrayed America* (Cold Spring Harbor, NY: Society for the Preservation of Long Island Antiquities, 1997), 3–4.

3. Headley, address in "Proceedings at the Annual Meeting, December 19, 1845," 14.

4. This widely held concept of the history of civilization was promoted by such leaders as William Gilpin and Senator Thomas Hart Benton and echoed by Walt Whitman in his poem "Passage to India."

5. Currier & Ives, *Descriptive Catalogue of Prints* (ca. 1858), 9.

6. Ibid.

7. Trollope, *Domestic Manners of the Americans*, 1:316.

8. Robert Louis Stevenson, *From Scotland to Silverado*, ed. James D. Hart (Cambridge, MA: Belknap Press of Harvard Univ. Press, 1966), 139. Stevenson's work first appeared as *Across the Plains* in *Longman's Magazine* in August 1883. The chapter entitled "Despised Races" gives a picture of some of the virulent prejudices of the time.

9. Peters, *Currier & Ives* (1929–31), 2:75–76.

10. Le Beau, *Currier & Ives*, 244–56.

11. Cyrus Mason, *Oration on the Thirteenth Anniversary of the American Institute, Delivered by Cyrus Mason at the Broadway Tabernacle, October 15th, 1840* (New York: Hopkins & Jennings, 1840), 8, 10.

12. Peters, *Currier & Ives* (1929–31), 1:111.

13. Le Beau, *Currier & Ives*, 216–18.

14. *Wake Up There! What'r Ye 'Bout* was published by Edward Jones and George W. Newman. Jones was Edmund Seymour Palmer's partner for a brief period.

15. Robert C. Toll, *Blacking Up: The Minstrel Show in Nineteenth-Century America* (New York: Oxford Univ. Press, 1974), 38–39.

16. As opposed, for example, to the black man chopping firewood in the background of Louis Maurer's print *Preparing for Market* (1856).

17. Johns, *American Genre Painting*, 229.

18. Currier & Ives, *Descriptive Catalogue of Prints* (ca. 1858), 1.

19. See Adrian Desmond and James Moore, *Darwin's Sacred Cause: How a Hatred of Slavery Shaped Darwin's Views on Human Evolution* (Boston: Houghton Mifflin Harcourt, 2009).

20. Northern publishers were producing most of the prints for the South at this time. See Mark E. Neely Jr., Harold Holzer, and Gabor S. Boritt, *The Confederate Image: Prints of the Lost Cause* (Chapel Hill: Univ. of North Carolina Press, 1987), 99–103.

21. Ibid., 101.

22. As late as 1884, Currier & Ives issued prints designed by William Walker (noted for such subjects) showing black men and women contentedly picking cotton on a huge plantation as if nothing had changed in the South. For a discussion of this complex period, see Eric Foner, *Reconstruction: America's Unfinished Revolution, 1863–1877* (New York: Harper and Row, 1988), and Eric Foner and Joshua Brown, *Forever Free: The Story of Emancipation and Reconstruction* (New York: Vintage Books, 2006). James McPherson discusses literature on this subject in "The Great Betrayal," *New York Review of Books*, Nov. 30, 2006.

23. Peters, *Currier & Ives* (1929–31), 1:80.

24. Ibid., 1:80–82.

25. Peters makes his own crude references to African Americans in his pioneering two-volume work *Currier & Ives* (1929–31). Describing a *Darktown* cartoon of a black woman who hopes to emulate upper-class white people by embarking on a yachting trip, he chuckles, "*Miss Tiny, a three-hundred-pound chocolate drop*, is stepping aboard the boat, which is capsized" (1:83, emphasis added). On page 171, as an analogy to fluctuating tastes and consequently to auction prices, the author tells a joke about an "old colored lady who went to the judge to obtain a divorce. 'Aunty, just why do you want a divorce from Elijah?' asked his honor. 'Well, jedge,' she replied, 'Ah jus nachully los ma taste fo dat nigger.'" Sixty-four years after the end of the Civil War, Peters was still echoing the dialect of the minstrel show.

26. George F. Ruxton, *Adventures in Mexico and the Rocky Mountains* (New York: Harper & Brothers, 1848), 235.

27. Boime, *The Magisterial Gaze*, 79.

28. The history and ongoing contributions of the Yosemite, a vibrant community today, are featured in a museum in the park. For a firsthand account of the bloody skirmishes and the amazement of white intruders on first seeing the beauty of the Yosemite region, read Lafayette Houghton Bunnell, *Discovery of the Yosemite, and the Indian War of 1851, Which Led to That Event*, 3rd ed. (New York: Fleming H. Revell, 1892).

29. Ambrose, *Nothing Like It in the World*, 150.

30. The famous photograph of the joining of the two train lines in Utah does not include the Chinese laborers who laid those lines. A few photographers and magazine illustrators documented their presence, but most omitted them. In the following decades, the Chinese who built those tracks traveled in segregated coaches; hatred of the so-called Yellow Peril swept through the country; and extreme laws prohibiting Chinese immigration, citizenship, and intermarriage remained in effect until 1943. Finally, in 1999, the Chinese railroad laborers were given full recognition when Congressman John T. Doolittle rose in the House of Representatives to express America's gratitude as he announced the unveiling of a memorial plaque dedicated to them on Highway 174 near Colfax, California.

31. Palmer did show workmen stringing telegraph wires and laying rails in *Across The Continent* and African American longshoremen loading steamboats in "*Wooding Up*" on the Mississippi.

32. For example, *Harper's Weekly* featured a Winslow Homer wood engraving of men, women, and children factory workers leaving work at the end of the day ("New England Factory Life—'Bell-Time,'" *Harper's Weekly*, July 25, 1868). On this topic, see also Joshua Brown, *Beyond the Lines: Pictorial Reporting, Everyday Life, and the Crisis of Gilded Age America* (Berkeley: Univ. of California Press, 2002).

33. The youth helping the farmer with plowing in *American Farm Scenes. No. 1* has holes in the knees of his pants.

34. Elizabeth Johns discusses this phenomenon in *American Genre Painting*, 170–74. See also Patricia Hills, *The Painters' America: Rural and Urban*

Life, 1810–1910 (New York: Praeger in association with the Whitney Museum of Art, 1974), 75–76.

35. Catherine E. Beecher, *A Treatise on Domestic Economy, for the Use of Young Ladies at Home and at School* (Boston: Thomas H. Webb, 1843), 27.

36. See, for example, *Arguing the Point*, published by Currier & Ives in 1855 (Hills, *Painters' America*, 12–16).

37. Burns, *Pastoral Inventions*, 101–2, 217. In actuality, of course, American farm wives had very hard lives.

38. Trollope, *Domestic Manners of the Americans*, 1:97.

39. Welter, "The Cult of True Womanhood," 152.

40. Census data for Brooklyn, in US Census Bureau, *Seventh Census of the United States, 1850*, p. 379B, image 219.

41. Contrast Palmer's work with artworks by Lilly Martin Spencer, the leading woman genre painter of the era, whose pictures of women in domestic scenes were very popular (Johns, *American Genre Painting*, 160–75).

42. King and Davis, *World of Currier & Ives*, 100. King and Davis note, without source, that Palmer "was herself an ardent fisherwoman. . . . She sailed and trolled . . . often with her family."

43. An exception to this general rule is Currier's early print *The Star of the Road* (1849, not by Palmer). A pretty young woman in a bright-red dress, holding a whip and driving a spirited pair of horses, may be related to a series of images of courtesans published that year. Thomas Worth showed matrons driving carriages in Central Park, but in a postwar print.

44. Currier & Ives, *Descriptive Catalogue of Prints* (ca. 1858), 12.

45. Art historian Bonnie Yochelson suggests that Palmer may have created the cartoon as an in-house joke that was never intended for publication. Her colleagues were well aware that there were difficulties in her family situation ("The Happy Family," in *Currier & Ives, Printmakers to the American People: Highlights from the Collections of the Museum of the City of New York, April 10, 1996–August 4, 1996*, n.d., at http://www.mcny.org/currierives /happy.htm, accessed Jan. 20, 2001).

46. Hone, *Diary of Philip Hone*, entry for May 1, 1847, 2:305.

47. But several publishers felt free to publish the misogynistic print *The Seven Stages of Matrimony* (undated, not by Palmer), an attack on the destructive role of a woman who charms her suitor into marriage but ends up ruining him with a huge separation settlement. In the final image, she holds their infant and thumbs her nose at her husband while she waves a sheet labeled "annuity" in his face. This image is particularly unjust when we remember that divorce was still very difficult for women of that era: they had few property rights, suffered a great loss of income and social status, and frequently lost custody of their children. On this subject, see James Brust, "Prints of Questionable Taste That Nathaniel Currier Would Not Sign," *Imprint* 20, no. 1 (Spring 1995): 11, and "Prints of Questionable Taste That Nathaniel Currier Would Not Sign: An Update," *Imprint* 23, no. 2 (Autumn 1998): 26.

48. Currier & Ives, *Descriptive Catalogue of Prints* (ca. 1858), 13.

49. Ibid., 1, emphasis added.

50. Investigation of the verses on the print reveals that the original theme mutated. "The Old Farm Gate" was, in fact, a poem by the British nineteenth-century radical feminist Eliza Cook, set to music by Henry Russell in 1840. Cook's original verses describe two urchins playing with the gate:

'Twas here where *the urchins* would gather to play
In the shadows of twilight or sunny mid-day;
For the stream running nigh, and the hillocks of sand
Where temptations no *dirt loving rogue* could withstand . . .

In Russell's lyrics and later versions of Cook's poem, "the urchins" was changed to "my sisters" and "dirt loving rogue" to "child":

'Twas there where *my sisters* would gather to play,
In the shadows of twilight, or sunny mid-day.
How we'd laugh and run wild mid those hillocks of sand
Where temptations existed *no child* could withstand.

Eliza Cook, "The Old Farm-Gate" in *Melaia, and Other Poems* (London: Charles Tilt, 1840), 84, italics added, compared to Eliza Cook, lyricist, *The Old Farm Gate, a Ballad*, composed by Henry Russell (Boston: Wm. H. Oakes, 1840), italics added.

51. For a picture of postwar political corruption and greed, see Mark Twain and Charles Dudley Warner, *The Gilded Age: A Tale of Today* (Hartford, CT: American Publishing, 1873).

52. George Templeton Strong, *The Diary of George Templeton Strong: The Turbulent Fifties, 1850–1859*, ed. Allan Nevins and Milton Halsey Thomas (New York: Macmillan, 1952), entry for July 7, 1851, 2:57. Strong was a Manhattan attorney who recorded his impressions of daily life from 1835 to 1875.

53. See Boime, *The Magisterial Gaze*.

54. See Nicolai Cikovsky Jr., "'The Ravages of the Axe': The Meaning of the Tree Stump in Nineteenth-Century American Art," *Art Bulletin* 61, no. 4 (Dec. 1979): 611–26, and Novak, *Nature and Culture*, 157–200.

55. Walt Whitman, "Song of the Broad-Axe," in *Leaves of Grass* (1881–82), 155–57.

56. Walt Whitman, "Song of the Redwood-Tree," in *Leaves of Grass* (1881–82), 167–69.

57. See Wallach, "Thomas Cole's *River in the Catskills* as Antipastoral," 344, 350 n. 70.

58. Leo Marx, *The Machine in the Garden: Technology and the Pastoral Ideal in America* (New York: Oxford Univ. Press, 1964).

59. Thomas Cole, "Lecture on American Scenery: Originally Delivered before the Catskill Lyceum, April 1, 1841," quoted in Wallach, "Thomas Cole's *River in the Catskills* as Antipastoral," 341.

60. Hills, "Picturing Progress," 100.

12. F. F. PALMER'S CONTRIBUTIONS TO AMERICAN ART

1. Among the sites are the Blandford Church in Petersburg, Virginia; the Fairmount Water Works in Philadelphia; Lookout Mountain in Tennessee; the Sleepy Hollow Church in Westchester, New York; the Woodworth House in Scituate, Massachusetts (*The Old Oaken Bucket* [1864]); the Wayside Inn in Sudbury, Massachusetts; the US Military Academy at West Point; Fort Fisher in Wilmington, North Carolina; Shenandoah Valley; Lake George in New

York; West Point Foundry; Yosemite Valley; St. Paul's Church in Buffalo, New York; and the Church of the Holy Trinity in New York City.

2. Poe wrote, "In some thirty years every noble cliff will be a pier, and the whole island will be densely desecrated by buildings of brick, with portentous facades of brown-stone" (quoted in Spann, *The New Metropolis*, 104).

3. Thomas Cole, "Essay on American Scenery," *American Monthly Magazine*, Jan. 1836.

CHECKLISTS OF THE WORK OF F. F. PALMER

1. The use of tint stones often helps differentiate between proofs and later states of a print, but Robert Newman of the Old Print Shop has found that although Currier & Ives often saved and reused the black-ink stone for later printings, it did not typically save the print's corresponding tint stone. As an example, Newman notes having four different tint-stone variations for Palmer's print *A Midnight Race on the Mississippi* (1860). For Currier & Ives prints, Palmer also likely drew only the black-ink stone (Robert Newman to Diann Benti, email, May 31, 2016).

2. Cowdrey, "Fanny Palmer," 219.

3. "New Music," *The Anglo American* 4, no. 14 (Jan. 25, 1845): 334.

4. Lancaster, *Old Brooklyn Heights*, 31.

5. See *Oneida Morning Herald*, Aug. 8, 1848.

6. Thanks to Helena Wright of the Smithsonian Institution for this suggestion.

7. Peters, *Currier & Ives* (1929–31), 1:138.

8. Cowdrey, "Fanny Palmer," 219.

9. Peters, *Currier & Ives* (1929–31), 1:72.

10. *Catalogue of Colored Fishing Prints, Mezzotints, and Line-Engravings from a Notable Private Collection and a Portion of Those Gathered by the Late Charles Roberts of Philadelphia* (New York: American Art Association, Jan. 1919), Lot 47.

11. Peters, *Currier & Ives* (1929–31), 1:176.

12. *Catalogue of Colored Fishing Prints*, Lot 48.

13. Mary Bartlett Cowdrey, "Proofs, F. F. Palmer," undated typescript index card, MSS 556, Cowdrey Papers.

14. Ibid.

15. Ibid.

16. *Catalogue of Colored Fishing Prints*, Lot 68.

17. Conningham, *Currier & Ives Prints*, 23, 162; Gale Research, *Currier & Ives*, 463.

18. *Catalogue of Colored Fishing Prints*, Lot 214.

19. Cowdrey, "Proofs, F. F. Palmer."

20. Conningham, *Currier & Ives Prints*, 205.

21. Cowdrey, "Proofs, F. F. Palmer."

22. Conningham, *Currier & Ives Prints*, 210.

23. See Cowdrey, "Fanny Palmer," 225. Cowdrey rejects Harry T. Peters's attribution of *Snowed Up* to A. F. Tait in favor of Palmer.

24. Cowdrey, "Proofs, F. F. Palmer."

25. Ibid.

26. "*Lookout Mountain, Tennessee,*" undated, ca. 1866?, *Old Print Shop Portfolio*, Nov. 1942, 61–62.

27. Victor D. Spark to Charlotte Streifer Rubinstein, Mar. 23, 1985.

Bibliography

ARCHIVAL SOURCES

Catalogue Containing a Correct List of Every Article Exhibiting at the 19th Annual Fair of the American Institute of the City of New York, 1846. New-York Historical Society, New York.

Catalogue Containing a Correct List of Every Article Exhibiting at the 20th Annual Fair of the American Institute of the City of New York, 1847. List of Premiums Awarded by the Managers of the Twentieth Annual Fair of the American Institute, 1847. New-York Historical Society, New York.

Census Returns of England and Wales, 1841. Public Record Office, 1841. National Archives of the United Kingdom, Kew.

Cowdrey, Mary Bartlett, Papers. Special Collections, Univ. of Delaware Library, Newark.

Currier, Nathaniel, Papers. Microfilm. Archives of American Art, Smithsonian Institution, Washington, DC.

Duyckinck Family Papers. Manuscripts and Archives Division, New York Public Library.

Green-Wood Cemetery. Records. Brooklyn, NY.

Hart, Charles. "Lithography, Its Theory and Practice. Including a Series of Short Sketches of the Earliest Lithographic Artists, Engravers and Printers of New York." Unpublished manuscript, 1902. Manuscript Division, New York Public Library.

Index to Passenger Lists of Vessels Arriving at New York, New York, 1820–1846. National Archives, Washington, DC.

Leicestershire Museum and Art Gallery. Archives Department. Leicester, UK.

Linwood, Mary, Correspondence File. Leicestershire Record Office, Leicester, England.

Peters, Harry T., Papers, 1790–1988. Museum of the City of New York.

Pre-1877 Exhibition Catalogue Index. Smithsonian American Art Museum, Washington, DC.

Public Record Office, London.

St. Margaret's Church. Records. Leicester, UK.

Saint Mary's Church. Register of Marriages. Newington, Surrey. London Metropolitan Archives.

"Uncolored Prints Published by Currier & Ives, No. 152 Nassau Street, N.Y.: Adapted to Grecian Oil and Oriental Painting, Italian or Diaphanic Pictures on Glass, and any other of the Popular Methods of Painting or Coloring." Undated catalog (ca. 1860). Museum of the City of New York.

Upjohn, Richard and Richard Michell, Papers. Manuscripts and Archives Division, New York Public Library.

US Census Bureau. *1860 United States Federal Census.* Microfilm Publication M653_764. Records of the Bureau of the Census. National Archives, Washington, DC.

———. *1870 United States Federal Census.* Microfilm Publication M593_960. National Archives, Washington, DC.

———. *Seventh Census of the United States, 1850.* Microfilm Publication M432. Records of the Bureau of the Census, Record Group 29. National Archives, Washington, DC.

Waite, Harried Endicott, Papers. Microfilm. Archives of American Art, Smithsonian Institution, Washington, DC.

BOOKS AND ARTICLES

Ambrose, Stephen E. *Nothing Like It in the World: The Men Who Built the Transcontinental Railroad 1863–1869.* New York: Simon and Schuster, 2000.

The American Flora or History of Plants and Wildflowers. Vol. 2. New York: Green & Spencer, 1848.

American Paradise: The World of the Hudson River School. New York: Metropolitan Museum of Art, 1987.

Anderson, Nancy K. "'The Kiss of Enterprise': The Western Landscape as Symbol and Resource." In *The West as America: Reinterpreting Images of the Frontier*, edited by William H. Truettner, 237–83. Washington, DC: Smithsonian Institution Press, 1991.

Anderson, Nancy K., and Linda S. Ferber. *Albert Bierstadt: Art & Enterprise.* New York: Brooklyn Museum in association with Hudson Hills Press, 1990.

Andrews, William. "Miss Mary Linwood—an Artist with the Needle." In *Bygone Leicestershire*, edited by William Andrews, 236–43. Leicester, UK: Frank Murray, 1892.

Bain, David Haward. *Empire Express: Building the First Transcontinental Railroad*. New York: Viking, 1999.

Barnhill, Georgia B. "Business Practices of Commercial Nineteenth-Century American Lithographers." *Winterthur Portfolio* 48, nos. 2–3 (Summer–Autumn 2014): 213–32.

Beecher, Catherine E. *A Treatise on Domestic Economy, for the Use of Young Ladies at Home and at School*. Boston: Thomas H. Webb, 1843.

Beecher, Catherine E., and Harriet Beecher Stowe. *The American Woman's Home*. New York: J. B. Ford, 1869.

Bennett, J. D. "John Flower 1793–1861." *Transactions of the Leicestershire Archaeological and Historical Society* 42 (1966–67): 76–81. At https://www.le.ac.uk/lahs/downloads/FlowerPagesfromvolume XLII-6.pdf.

Berkoff, Marshall R., ed. *Currier & Ives: The New Best 50*. Farmingdale, NY: American Historical Print Collectors Society, 1991.

Boime, Albert. *The Magisterial Gaze: Manifest Destiny and American Landscape Painting, c. 1830–1865*. Washington, DC: Smithsonian Institution Press, 1991.

Born, Wolfgang. *American Landscape Painting: An Interpretation*. New Haven, CT: Yale Univ. Press, 1948.

———. *Still-Life Painting in America*. New York: Oxford Univ. Press, 1947.

The Brooklyn City Directory, for the Year Ending May 1st, 1860. New York: Lain, 1859.

Brown, Dona, and Stephen Nissenbaum. "Changing New England: 1865–1945." In *Picturing Old New England: Image and Memory*, edited by William H. Truettner and Roger B. Stein, 1–13. New Haven, CT: Yale Univ. Press, 1999.

Brown, Joshua. *Beyond the Lines: Pictorial Reporting, Everyday Life, and the Crisis of Gilded Age America*. Berkeley: Univ. of California Press, 2002.

Brust, James. "Notes on the Life of James Merritt Ives with a Reappraisal of When He Joined Nathaniel Currier." *Imprint* 33, no. 1 (Autumn 2008): 36–45.

———. "Prints of Questionable Taste That Nathaniel Currier Would Not Sign." *Imprint* 20, no. 1 (Spring 1995): 7–12.

———. "Prints of Questionable Taste That Nathaniel Currier Would Not Sign: An Update." *Imprint* 23, no. 2 (Autumn 1998): 25–26.

Bunnell, Lafayette Houghton. *Discovery of the Yosemite, and the Indian War of 1851, Which Led to That Event*. 3rd ed. New York: Fleming H. Revell, 1892.

Burns, Sarah. "Barefoot Boys and Other Country Children: Sentiment and Ideology in Nineteenth-Century American Art." *American Art Journal* 20, no. 1 (1988): 25–50.

———. *Pastoral Inventions: Rural Life in Nineteenth-Century American Art and Culture*. Philadelphia: Temple Univ. Press, 1989.

Cadbury, Warder H. *Arthur Fitzwilliam Tait: Artist in the Adirondacks*. Newark: Univ. of Delaware Press, 1986.

Catalogue of Colored Fishing Prints, Mezzotints, and Line-Engravings from a Notable Private Collection and a Portion of Those Gathered by the Late Charles Roberts of Philadelphia. New York City: American Art Association, Jan. 1919.

Chambers, Robert. *The Book of Days: A Miscellany of Popular Antiquities in Connection with the Calendar*. 2 vols. London: W. & R. Chambers, 1864.

Cikovsky, Nicolai, Jr. "'The Ravages of the Axe': The Meaning of the Tree Stump in Nineteenth-Century American Art." *Art Bulletin* 61, no. 4 (Dec. 1979): 611–26.

Cleaveland, Nehemiah, trans. *The Flowers Personified; Being a Translation of Grandville's "Les fleurs animées."* New York: R. Martin, 1847.

———. *Green-Wood Illustrated*. With illustrations by James Smillie. New York: R. Martin, 1847.

———. *History of Bowdoin College*. Boston: James Ripley Osgood, 1882.

Cody, Sherwin. *Four Famous American Writers: Washington Irving, Edgar Allan Poe, James Russell Lowell, Bayard Taylor*. New York: Werner School, 1899.

Cole, Thomas. "Essay on American Scenery." *American Monthly Magazine*, Jan. 1836.

Conningham, Frederic A. *Currier & Ives Prints: An Illustrated Checklist*. New York: Crown, 1983.

Constable, John. *John Constable's Correspondence II: Early Friends and Maria Bicknell (Mrs. Constable)*. Edited by R. B. Beckett. Suffolk, UK: Suffolk Records Society, 1964.

Cook, Eliza. *Melaia, and Other Poems*. London: Charles Tilt, 1840.

Cook, Thomas. *A Guide to Leicester, Containing a List to Streets, Lanes, Yards &c.: A Directory of the Principal Inhabitants, Classification of Trades, and Professions*. Leicester, UK: T. Cook, 1843.

———. *The Leicestershire Almanack, Directory, and Advertiser for the Year 1842*. Leicester, UK: T. Cook, 1842.

Cowdrey, Mary Bartlett. *American Academy of Fine Arts and American Art-Union: Introduction 1816–1852*. New York: New-York Historical Society, 1953.

———. "Fanny Palmer, an American Lithographer." In *Prints: Thirteen Essays on the Art of the Print*, edited by Carl Zigrosser, 217–34. London: Peter Owen, 1962.

————. *National Academy of Design Exhibition Record: 1826–1860.* 2 vols. New York: New-York Historical Society, 1943.

Crouse, Russel. *Mr. Currier and Mr. Ives: A Note on Their Lives and Times.* Garden City, NY: Garden City Publishing, 1937.

Currier & Ives. *Descriptive Catalogue of Prints, Published and for Sale by Currier & Ives, 152 Nassau Street, New York.* New York: French & Wheat, ca. 1858.

Cutler, Ed. "Passage to Modernity: *Leaves of Grass* and the 1853 Crystal Palace Exhibition in New York." *Walt Whitman Quarterly Review* 16, no. 2 (Fall 1998): 65–89.

Daniels, Stephen. *Fields of Vision: Landscape Imagery and National Identity in England and the United States.* Princeton, NJ: Princeton Univ. Press, 1993.

Davidson, Marshall B. *Life in America.* 2 vols. Boston: Houghton Mifflin, 1951.

Desmond, Adrian, and James Moore. *Darwin's Sacred Cause: How a Hatred of Slavery Shaped Darwin's Views on Human Evolution.* Boston: Houghton Mifflin Harcourt, 2009.

Diamonstein-Spielvogel, Barbaralee. *The Landmarks of New York: An Illustrated Record of the City's Historic Buildings.* Albany: State Univ. of New York Press, 2011.

Dickens, Charles. *American Notes for General Circulation.* 2 vols. London: Chapman and Hall, 1842.

Dickerson, Mahlon. "Opening Address of the 20th Annual Fair, on the 5th Day of October, 1847." In *Sixth Annual Report of the American Institute of the City of New-York,* 488–98. Albany, NY: Charles Van Benthuysen, 1848.

Downing, A. J. *The Architecture of Country Houses.* New York: D. Appleton, 1850.

Eight Views of Charnwood. Loughborough: R. Griffin & Son, ca. 1840.

Fahlman, Betsy. "John Ferguson Weir: Painter of Romantic and Industrial Icons." *Archives of American Art Journal* 20, no. 2 (1980): 2–9.

Federal Writers' Project. *The WPA Guide to New York City: The Federal Writers' Project Guide to 1930s New York.* 1939. Reprint. New York: Pantheon Books, 1982.

Ferber, Linda S., and Annette Blaugrund. "American Watercolors and Pastels at the Brooklyn Museum." *Magazine Antiques,* Aug. 1984.

Foner, Eric. *Reconstruction: America's Unfinished Revolution, 1863–1877.* New York: Harper and Row, 1988.

Foner, Eric, and Joshua Brown. *Forever Free: The Story of Emancipation and Reconstruction.* New York: Vintage Books, 2006.

Fowble, E. McSherry. "Currier & Ives and the American Parlor." *Imprint* 15, no. 2 (Autumn 1990): 14–19.

Gale Research Group. *Currier & Ives: A Catalogue Raisonné.* Detroit: Gale Research, 1984.

Gerdts, William H. *Impressionist New York.* New York: Abbeville Press, 1994.

Glanz, Dawn. *How the West Was Drawn: American Art and the Settling of the West.* 1978. Reprint. Ann Arbor: UMI Research Press, 1982.

Gould, John. *The Birds of Australia.* London: John Gould, 1840–48.

————. *A Century of Birds from the Himalaya Mountains.* London: n.p., 1831.

Grandville, J. J., illus. *Les fleurs animées.* Introduction by Alphonse Karr and text by Taxile Delord. Paris: Gabriel de Gonet, 1847.

Griswold, Wesley S. *A Work of Giants: Building the First Transcontinental Railroad.* New York: McGraw-Hill, 1962.

Halleck, Fitz-Greene. *Fanny.* New York: Wiley, 1819.

Harper, J. Henry. *The House of Harper: A Century of Publishing in Franklin Square.* New York: Harper & Brothers, 1912.

Harris, Ann Sutherland, and Linda Nochlin. *Women Artists: 1550–1950.* New York: Knopf, 1976.

Hatt, Michael. "'Making a Man of Him': Masculinity and the Black Body in Mid-Nineteenth-Century American Sculpture." *Oxford Art Journal* 15, no. 1 (1992): 21–35.

Headley, J. T. Address in "Proceedings at the Annual Meeting, December 19, 1845." In *Transactions of the American Art Union, for the Year 1845,* 12–17. New York: American Art Union, 1845.

Hearne, H. R., and W. J. Hearne. *Brooklyn Directory and Yearly Advertiser, for 1848–9.* Brooklyn, NY: Lee & Foulkes, 1848.

Hearne's Brooklyn City Directory for 1850–1851. Brooklyn: Henry R. & William J. Hearne, 1850.

Hearne's Brooklyn City Directory for 1851–1852. Brooklyn: Henry R. & William J. Hearne, 1851.

Hearne's Brooklyn City Directory for 1853–1854. Brooklyn: Henry R. & William J. Hearne, 1853.

Hills, Patricia. *American Frontier: Images and Myths.* New York: Whitney Museum of American Art, 1973.

————. *The Painters' America: Rural and Urban Life, 1810–1910.* New York: Praeger in association with the Whitney Museum of Art, 1974.

————. "Picturing Progress in the Era of Westward Expansion." In *The West as America: Reinterpreting Images of the Frontier,* edited by William H. Truettner, 97–147. Washington, DC: Smithsonian Institution Press, 1991.

Hollings, J. F. *Sketches in Leicestershire: From Original Drawings with Historical and Descriptive Notices.* Leicester, UK: John Sydney Crossley, 1846.

Holzer, Harold, and Mark E. Neely Jr. *Mine Eyes Have Seen the Glory: The Civil War in Art.* New York: Orion Books, 1993.

Hone, Philip. *The Diary of Philip Hone, 1828–1851.* 2 vols. Edited by Bayard Tuckerman. New York: Dodd, Mead, 1889.

Hutson, Martha Young. *George Henry Durrie (1820–1863): American Winter Landscapist, Renowned through Currier and Ives.* Santa Barbara, CA: Santa Barbara Museum of Art and American Art Review Press, 1977.

Johns, Elizabeth. *American Genre Painting: The Politics of Everyday Life.* New Haven, CT: Yale Univ. Press, 1991.

Kemble, Fanny. *Fanny Kemble: Journal of a Young Actress.* Edited by Monica Gough. New York: Columbia Univ. Press, 1990.

King, Roy, and Burke Davis. *The World of Currier & Ives.* New York: Random House, 1968.

Kirby, Mary. *"Leaflets from My Life": A Narrative Autobiography.* London: Simpkin, Marshall, 1887.

Knoblock, Glenn A. *The American Clipper Ship, 1845–1920.* Jefferson, NC: McFarland, 2014.

Lain, Geo. T. *The Brooklyn City and Business Directory for the Year Ending May 1st, 1869.* Brooklyn, NY: Lain, 1868.

———. *The Brooklyn City and Business Directory for the Year Ending May 1st, 1870.* Brooklyn, NY: Lain, 1869.

———. *The Brooklyn City and Business Directory for the Year Ending May 1st, 1871.* Brooklyn, NY: Lain, 1870.

———. *The Brooklyn City and Business Directory for the Year Ending May 1st, 1872.* Brooklyn, NY: Lain, 1871.

———. *The Brooklyn City and Business Directory for the Year Ending May 1st, 1876.* Brooklyn, NY: Lain, 1875.

———. *The Brooklyn City and Business Directory for the Year Ending May 1st, 1877.* Brooklyn, NY: Lain, 1876.

———. *The Brooklyn City Directory for the Year Ending May 1st, 1878.* Brooklyn, NY: Lain, 1877.

Lain, J. *The Brooklyn City Directory for the Year Ending May 1st, 1860.* New York: Lain, 1859.

———. *The Brooklyn City Directory for the Year Ending May 1st, 1868.* Brooklyn, NY: Lain, 1867.

Lancaster, Clay. *Old Brooklyn Heights: New York's First Suburb.* New York: Dover, 1979.

Landy, Jacob. *The Architecture of Minard Lafever.* New York: Columbia Univ. Press, 1970.

Lasdun, Susan. "A Taste for Crewels and Yarns: Mary Linwood's Needlework Pictures." *Country Life,* Apr. 15, 1976.

Le Beau, Bryan. *Currier & Ives: America Imagined.* Washington, DC: Smithsonian Institution Press, 2001.

Leng, Charles W., and William T. Davis. *Staten Island and Its People: A History 1609–1929.* 5 vols. New York: Lewis Historical Publishing, 1930.

Longfellow, Henry Wadsworth. *The Poetical Works of Henry Wadsworth Longfellow.* London: George Routledge, 1858.

Lossing, Benson J. *The Hudson, from the Wilderness to the Sea.* New York: Virtue and Yorston, 1866.

Love and the Flowers. New York: J. C. Riker, n.d. [ca. 1847–48?].

Mann, Maybelle. *The American Art-Union.* Otisville, NY: ALM Associates, 1977.

Marx, Leo. *The Machine in the Garden: Technology and the Pastoral Ideal in America.* New York: Oxford Univ. Press, 1964.

———. "The Railroad-in-the-Landscape: An Iconological Reading of a Theme in American Art." In *The Railroad in American Art: Representations of Technological Change,* edited by Susan Danly and Leo Marx, 183–208. Cambridge, MA: MIT Press, 1988.

Marzio, Peter C. *The Art Crusade: An Analysis of American Drawing Manuals, 1820–1860.* Washington, DC: Smithsonian Institution Press, 1976.

———. *The Democratic Art: Pictures for a 19th-Century America.* Fort Worth, TX: Amon Carter Museum of Western Art, 1979.

Mason, Cyrus. *Oration on the Thirteenth Anniversary of the American Institute, Delivered by Cyrus Mason at the Broadway Tabernacle, October 15th, 1840.* New York: Hopkins & Jennings, 1840.

Matteo, Thomas. "Staten Island's Role in the Civil War." *Staten Island Advance,* Sept. 25, 2011.

Maximilian, Prince of Wied. *Travels in the Interior of North America.* 2 vols. London: Ackermann, 1843.

McPherson, James. "The Great Betrayal." *New York Review of Books,* Nov. 30, 2006.

The Midland Counties' Railway Companion, with Topographical Descriptions of the Country through Which the Line Passes; and Time, Fare, and Distance Tables. Nottingham, UK: R. Allen; Leicester, UK: E. Allen, 1840.

Monroe, Robert D. "William Birch McMurtrie: A Painter Partially Restored." *Oregon Historical Quarterly* 60, no. 3 (Sept. 1959): 352–74.

Mortimer, Ruth. *The Landscape Alphabet.* Northampton, MA: Friends of the Smith College Library, 1981.

Nadel, Stanley. *Little Germany: Ethnicity, Religion, and Class in New York City, 1845–80.* Urbana: Univ. of Illinois Press, 1990.

Neely, Mark, Jr., and Harold Holzer. *The Union Image: Popular Prints of the Civil War North.* Chapel Hill: Univ. of North Carolina Press, 2000.

Neely, Mark, Jr., Harold Holzer, and Gabor S. Boritt. *The Confederate Image: Prints of the Lost Cause.* Chapel Hill: Univ. of North Carolina Press, 1987.

Newman, Ewell L. "The History and Romance of Currier & Ives Prints." Revised by Ladd MacMillan. In *Currier & Ives: 19th Century Printmakers to the American People. A Special Loan Exhibition at Heritage Plantation of Sandwich, Sandwich, Massachusetts,* 7–12. Sandwich, MA: Heritage Plantation of Sandwich, 1973.

"New Music." *The Anglo American* 4, no. 14 (Jan. 25, 1845): 334.

Newton, Roger Hale. *Town & Davis: Architects, Pioneers in American Revivalist Architecture, 1812–1870, Including a Glimpse of Their Times and Their Contemporaries.* New York: Columbia Univ. Press, 1942.

The New-York City Directory for 1844 & 1845. New York: John Doggett, 1844.

The New-York City Directory for 1846 & 1847. New York: John Doggett, 1846.

The New-York City Directory for 1851 & 1852. New York: Doggett & Rode, 1851.

The New-York City Directory for 1852 & 1853. New York: Doggett & Rode, 1852.

Novak, Barbara. *Nature and Culture: American Landscape and Painting, 1825–1875.* New York: Oxford Univ. Press, 1980.

Oldenbusch, Carolyn. "Suitable for Framing." In Carolyn Oldenbusch and Charlotte Streifer Rubinstein, *Fanny Palmer: A Long Island Woman Who Portrayed America*, 3–15. Cold Spring Harbor, NY: Society for the Preservation of Long Island Antiquities, 1997.

Oppenheimer, Margaret A. "'The Charming Spectacle of a Cadaver': Anatomical and Life Study by Women Artists in Paris, 1775–1815." *Nineteenth Century Art Worldwide*, Spring 2007. At http://www.19thc-artworldwide.org/spring07/142-qthe-charming-spectacle-of-a-cadaverq-anqthe-charming-spectacle-of-a-cadaverqanatomical-and-life-study-by-women-artists-in-paris-17751815atomical-and-life-study-by-women-artistsin-paris-17751815.

Palmer, F. *The New York Drawing Book, Containing a Series of Original Designs and Sketches of American Scenery.* Nos. 1 and 2. New York: W. H. Graham, 1847.

Patterson, A. Temple. *Radical Leicester: A History of Leicester, 1780–1850.* Leicester, UK: Leicester Univ. Press, 1954.

Penny, Virginia. *The Employments of Women: A Cyclopedia of Woman's Work.* Boston: Walker, Wise, 1863.

Peters, Harry T. *America on Stone: The Other Printmakers to the American People, a Chronicle of American Lithography, Other Than That of Currier & Ives.* Garden City, NY: Doubleday, Doran, 1931.

———. *Currier & Ives: Printmakers to the American People.* 2 vols. Garden City, NY: Doubleday, Doran, 1929–31.

———. *Currier & Ives: Printmakers to the American People.* Abridged. Garden City, NY: Doubleday Doran, 1942.

Pierce, Sally, and Catharina Slautterback. *Boston Lithography: 1825–1880.* Boston: Boston Athenaeum, 1991.

Potter, T. R. *The History and Antiquities of Charnwood Forest.* London: Hamilton, Adams; Nottingham, UK: R. Allen; Leicester, UK: E. Allen, 1842.

Primm, James Neal. *Lion of the Valley: St. Louis, Missouri, 1764–1980.* St. Louis: Missouri Historical Society Press, 1998.

Ramirez, Jan Seidler, ed. *Painting the Town: Cityscapes of New York. Paintings from the Museum of the City of New York.* New York: Museum of the City of New York; New Haven, CT: Yale Univ. Press, 2000.

Ranlett, William H. *The Architect: A Series of Original Designs, for Domestic and Ornamental Cottages and Villas, Connected with Landscape Gardening, Adapted to the United States. Illustrated by Drawings of Ground Plots, Plans, Perspective Views, Elevations, Sections, and Details.* Vol. 1. New York: W. H. Graham, 1847.

———. *The Architect: A Series of Original Designs, for Domestic and Ornamental Cottages and Villas, Connected with Landscape Gardening, Adapted to the United States. Illustrated by Drawings of Ground Plots, Plans, Perspective Views, Elevations, Sections, and Details.* Vol. 2. New York: Dewitt & Davenport, 1849.

Reed, Sue Welsh, and Carol Troyen. *Awash in Color.* Boston: Museum of Fine Arts in association with Bullfinch Press, Little, Brown, 1993.

Reilly, Bernard F., Jr. *American Political Prints, 1766–1876: A Catalog of the Collections in the Library of Congress.* Boston: G. K. Hall, 1991.

Richman, Jeffrey I. *Brooklyn's Green-Wood Cemetery: New York's Buried Treasure.* Brooklyn, NY: The Cemetery, 1998.

Rubinstein, Charlotte Streifer. *American Women Artists from Early Indian Times to the Present.* Boston: G. K. Hall, 1982.

———. "The Early Career of Frances Flora Bond Palmer." *American Art Journal* 17 (Autumn 1985): 71–88.

Rusling, James F. *Across America: Or the Great West and the Pacific Coast.* New York: Sheldon, 1874.

Ruxton, George F. *Adventures in Mexico and the Rocky Mountains.* New York: Harper & Brothers, 1848.

Searjeant, Robert L. "Foreword to the 1983 Edition." In Frederic A. Conningham, *Currier & Ives Prints: An Illustrated Checklist*, x–xi. New York: Crown, 1983.

Seaton, Beverly. *The Language of Flowers: A History.* Charlottesville: Univ. of Virginia, 1995.

Seventh Annual Report of the American Institute of the City of New-York. Albany, NY: Weed, Parsons, 1849.

Simpson, William. *The Autobiography of William Simpson, R. I.* Edited by George Eyre-Todd. London: T. Fisher Unwin, 1903.

Smith, William H. *Smith's Brooklyn Directory for the Year Ending May 1st, 1855.* Brooklyn: William H. Smith, 1854.

Spann, Edward K. *The New Metropolis: N.Y.C. 1840–57.* New York: Columbia Univ. Press, 1981.

Sperling, Joy. "'Art, Cheap and Good': The Art Union in England and the United States, 1840–60." *Nineteenth-Century Art Worldwide* 1, no. 1 (Spring 2002). At http://www.19thc-artworldwide.org/spring02/85-spring02/spring02article/196.

Stevenson, Robert Louis. *Across the Plains with Other Memories and Essays*. London: Chatto & Windus, 1892.

———. *From Scotland to Silverado*. Edited by James D. Hart. Cambridge, MA: Belknap Press of Harvard Univ. Press, 1966.

[Stone, Elizabeth.] *The Art of Needle-work, from the Earliest Ages*. Edited by the Countess of Wilton. London: Henry Colburn, 1840.

Strong, George Templeton. *The Diary of George Templeton Strong: The Turbulent Fifties, 1850–1859*. Edited by Alan Nevins and Milton Halsey Thomas. New York: Macmillan, 1952.

Tatham, David. "David Claypoole Johnston's Militia Muster." *American Art Journal*, Spring 1987, 4–15.

———. "The Lithographic Workshop, 1825–50." *Proceedings of the American Antiquarian Society* 105, pt. 1 (Apr. 1995): 71–78.

Taylor, Bayard. *At Home and Abroad: A Sketch-book of Life, Scenery, and Men*. New York: G. P. Putnam, 1862.

Thoreau, Henry David. *Walden; or Life in the Woods*. Boston: Ticknor and Fields, 1854.

Toll, Robert C. *Blacking Up: The Minstrel Show in Nineteenth-Century America*. New York: Oxford Univ. Press, 1974.

Trollope, Frances. *Domestic Manners of the Americans*. 2 vols. London: Whittaker, Treacher, 1832.

Truettner, William H., ed. *The West as America: Reinterpreting Images of the Frontier*. Washington, DC: Smithsonian Institution Press, 1991.

Truettner, William H., and Roger B. Stein, eds. *Picturing Old New England: Image and Memory*. New Haven, CT: Yale Univ. Press, 1999.

Twain, Mark. *Life on the Mississippi*. New York: Harper & Brothers, 1901.

Twain, Mark, and Charles Dudley Warner. *The Gilded Age: A Tale of Today*. Hartford, CT: American Publishing, 1873.

Twyman, Michael. "Charles Joseph Hullmandel: Lithographic Printer Extraordinary." In *Lasting Impressions: Lithography as Art*, edited by Pat Gilmour, 42–90. London: Alexandria Press, 1988.

———. "Haghe, Louis (1806–1885)." In *Oxford Dictionary of National Biography*, 24:447–48. Oxford: Oxford Univ. Press, 2004.

Tyler, Ronnie C. *The Mexican War: A Lithographic Record*. Austin: Texas State Historical Association, 1973.

Upton, Dell. "Inventing the Metropolis: Civilization and Urbanity in Antebellum New York." In *Art and the Empire City: New York, 1825–1861*, edited by Catherine Hoover Voorsanger and John K. Howat, 3–45. New York: Metropolitan Museum of Art, 2000.

Wallach, Alan. "Thomas Cole's *River in the Catskills* as Antipastoral." *Art Bulletin*, June 2002, 334–50.

Walther, Susan Danly, curator. *The Railroad in the American Landscape, 1850–1950*. The Wellesley College Museum, Wellesley, Massachusetts, 15 April–8 June 1981. Wellesley, MA: Wellesley College Museum, 1981.

Welter, Barbara. "The Cult of True Womanhood, 1820–1860." *American Quarterly* 18, no. 2, pt. 1 (Summer 1966): 151–74.

Whitcomb, Norma R. *Mary Linwood*. Leicester, UK: City of Leicester Museums and Art Gallery Department of Antiquities, n.d.

Whitman, Walt. *Leaves of Grass*. Brooklyn, NY: Walt Whitman, 1856.

———. *Leaves of Grass*. Boston: James R. Osgood, 1881–82.

———. *Leaves of Grass: A Comprehensive Reader's Edition*. Edited by Harold Blodgett and Sculley Bradley. New York: New York Univ. Press, 1965.

Willis, Nathaniel P. *American Scenery*. London: G. Virtue, 1840.

Wilson, H. *Trow's New-York City Directory for 1854–1855*. New York: John F. Trow, 1854.

Wright, Helena E. *With Pen & Graver: Women Graphic Artists before 1900*. Washington, DC: National Museum of American History and Smithsonian Institution, 1995.

Wyatt, Martha R. "Endicott & Co. Lithographs at the Mariners' Museum." *Imprint* 27, no. 2 (Autumn 2002): 16–26.

Yochelson, Bonnie. "The Happy Family." In *Currier & Ives, Printmakers to the American People: Highlights from the Collections of the Museum of the City of New York, April 10, 1996–August 4, 1996*. n.d. Formerly at http://www.mcny.org/currierives/happy.htm. Accessed Jan. 20, 2001.

Zugay, Brian C. R. "In What Manner Shall We Build? The Broadway Tabernacle, New York." In *Sacred Spaces: Building and Remembering Sites of Worship in the Nineteenth Century*, curated by Virginia Chieffo Raguin and Mary Ann Powers, 78–81. Worcester, MA: College of the Holy Cross and the American Antiquarian Society, 2002.

Illustration Credits

American Antiquarian Society, Worcester, MA
2-10; 2-23; 2-146; 2-147; 2-148; 2-149; 2-155; 2-156; 2-163; 2-168; 2-201; 2-202; 2-211; 2-213; 2-214; 2-219; 3A-2; cover of *The New York Drawing Book*, no. 1; *Wake Up There! What'r Ye 'Bout?* (E. Jones & G. W. Newman); package of No. 2 Lithographic Crayons manufactured by Charles Currier

Archives of American Art, Smithsonian Institution
Photograph of Frances ("Fanny") Flora Bond Palmer; photograph of Maria P. Bond with grandniece Maria F. Mary Edgecombe

William L. Clements Library, University of Michigan
2-4

Houghton Library, Harvard University
3A-28 Dickinson Room *Windsor Castle and Park* [print recto] (2011M-138), 1 pf folder

Huntington Library, San Marino, CA
1-6; 1-8; 1-10; 1-11; 1-13; 1-14; 1-15; 1-16; 1-17; 1-18; 1-19; 1-20; 1-21; 1-22; 1-23; 1-26; 1-27; 2-40; 2-60; 2-83; 2-91; 2-176; 2-183; 2-189; 2-196; 2-200; 2-209; *Tulip* (illustration from *The Flowers Personified*)

Leicester Arts and Museums Service
Mary Linwood's House, Belgrave Gate, Leicester (Lithograph by A. B. Pillans)

Leicestershire County Council Museums Service, Leicester, UK
1-50; 4-14; 4-20

Library of Congress
2-1; 2-13; 2-14; 2-21; 2-22; 2-145; 2-154; 3-7; 3-66; 3-77; 3-120; 3-135; 3-138; 3-153; 3-155; 3-157; 3-172; 3A-5; 3A-7; 3A-11; 3A-23; 3A-24; *Through to the Pacific* (Currier & Ives); *Mount Washington. From the Valley of the Conway* (painting by John F. Kensett); *The Cares of a Family* (N. Currier)

The Mariners' Museum, Newport News, VA
2-8; 2-182; 2-205; 2-206; 2-212; 3-119

The Metropolitan Museum of Art, http://www.metmuseum.org/
2-5; 2-150; 2-151; 2-152; 2-153; 2-204; 2-180; 2-181; *Winter Morning in the Country* (Currier & Ives); *Still Life: Flowers and Fruit* (painting by Severin Roesen); *The Rocky Mountains, Lander's Peak* (painting by Albert Bierstadt)

Michele and Donald D'Amour Museum of Fine Arts, Springfield, MA
3-29; 3-86; 3-110; 3A-19; 3A-21; 3A-26

Museum of Fine Arts, Boston
4-3; 4-11; 4-12; 4-25

Museum of the City of New York
2-11; 2-207; 3-30; 3-85; 3-133; 3-143; 3A-8; 3A-14; 4-2; 4-5; 4-9; 4-10

National Gallery of Art, Washington, DC
The Jolly Flatboatmen (painting by George Caleb Bingham)

New York Public Library, the Miriam and Ira D. Wallach Division of Art, Prints, and Photographs: Print Collection, New York Public Library Digital Collections
2-2; 2-210; 2-217; 3-152; 3-154; 3A-13; 4-4

New-York Historical Society
2-15 (Cartoon and Caricature File, PR010, flat file, 1846, image #91849d); 2-17 (Cartoon and Caricature File, PR010, flat file, 1846, image #91850d); 2-19 (Cartoon and Caricature File, PR010, flat file, 1846, image #91851d); 2-20 (Cartoon and Caricature File, PR010, flat file, 1846, image #63895); 3-65 (Maritime History File, PR100, flat file, Large---Steamships "S", image #91878d); 4-6 (object #1899.2); 4-16 (object #1925.147); 4-19 recto and verso (object #1900.10); 4-21 (object #1899.5); 4-23 (object #1899.3); 4-24 (object #1899.4)

Old Print Shop, New York

2-16; 2-18; 3-2; 3-4; 3-5; 3-8; 3-15; 3-16; 3-18; 3-19A; 3-21; 3-26; 3-33; 3-35; 3-36; 3-37; 3-39; 3-40; 3-44; 3-45; 3-47; 3-48; 3-50; 3-51; 3-55; 3-57; 3-63; 3-69; 3-70; 3-71; 3-72; 3-73; 3-76; 3-78; 3-80; 3-83; 3-88; 3-90; 3-93; 3-96; 3-98; 3-103; 3-104; 3-109; 3-112; 3-113; 3-114; 3-116; 3-118; 3-122; 3-125; 3-131; 3-134; 3-136; 3-139; 3-139; 3-140; 3-142; 3-144; 3-145; 3-147; 3-148; 3-151; 3-161; 3-164; 3-165; 3-167; 3-170; 3-171; 3-175; 3A-9; 3A-16; 3A-27; *The Narrows. (From Fort Hamilton.)* (Currier & Ives)

Palmer Museum of Art, Pennsylvania State University

3-56

Sheridan Libraries, Lester S. Levy Collection of Sheet Music, Johns Hopkins University

2-7; 2-9; 2-12; 2-203

National Museum of American History, Graphic Arts Collection, Smithsonian Institution

3A-17

University of Leicester, specialcollections.le.ac.uk

Views in Leicestershire (Leicester, E.S. Palmer, 184-) [SCD 00053]: 1-36; 1-37; 1-38; 1-39; 1-40; 1-41; 1-42

J. F. Hollings, *Sketches in Leicestershire: From Original Drawings with Historical and Descriptive Notices* (Leicester, UK: John Sydney Crossley, 1846), [SCH 00029]: 1-44; 1-45; 1-46; 1-47; 1-48; 1-51; 1-52; 1-53; 1-54; 1-55; 1-56; 1-57; 1-58; 1-59; 1-60; 1-61; 1-62; 1-63; 1-64; 1-65; 1-66; 1-67; 1-68; 1-69; 1-70

University of Pittsburgh

http://dx.doi.org/10.5962/bhl.title.34776

1-24; 1-25

Yale Center for British Art

1-28; 1-29; 1-30; 1-31; 1-32; 1-33; 1-34; 1-35; *Newstead Abbey, The Seat of the Late Lord Byron* (Lithograph by Louis Haghe)

Yale University Art Gallery

2-215; 3-1; 3-3; 3-6; 3-9; 3-11; 3-12; 3-13; 3-14; 3-20; 3-24; 3-25; 3-27; 3-41; 3-42; 3-43; 3-46; 3-49; 3-58; 3-59; 3-61; 3-62; 3-68; 3-74; 3-84; 3-89; 3-91; 3-94; 3-95; 3-102; 3-107; 3-111; 3-117; 3-123; 3-124; 3-128; 3-137; 3-146; 3-149; 3-158; 3-159; 3-162; 3-163; 3-166; 3-169; 3-176; 3-177; 3A-3; 3A-10

Private Collectors

1-49; 2-3; 2-6; 3-10; 3-17; 3-19; 3-22; 3-23; 3-28; 3-31; 3-32; 3-34; 3-38; 3-52; 3-53; 3-54; 3-60; 3-64; 3-67; 3-75; 3-79; 3-81; 3-82; 3-87; 3-92; 3-97; 3-99; 3-100; 3-101; 3-105; 3-106; 3-108; 3-115; 3-121; 3-126; 3-127; 3-130; 3-132; 3-150; 3-156; 3-160; 3-168; 3-173; 3-174; 3A-1; 3A-4; 3A-6; 3A-12; 3A-15; 3A-18; 3A-20; 3A-22; 3A-25; *The Four Seasons of Life: Middle Age. "The Season of Strength"* (Parsons & Atwater version)

Index

Italic page numbers denote illustrations.

Charlotte Streifer Rubinstein (1921–2013) was an artist, scholar, and art teacher. She received degrees from Brooklyn College, Otis-Parsons Art Institute, and Columbia University. Rubinstein's publications include *American Women Artists: From Early Indian Times to the Present* (1982) and *American Women Sculptors: A History of Women Working in Three Dimensions* (1990). She lived in Laguna Beach, California.

Diann Benti is a supervising librarian at the Huntington Library in San Marino, California. She has degrees from Kenyon College and the University of Maryland and previously worked at the American Antiquarian Society and the Harvard University Archives.